THE RISE AND FALL OF
Jewish Nationalism

THE RISE AND FALL OF
Jewish Nationalism

Doron Mendels

WILLIAM B. EERDMANS PUBLISHING COMPANY
GRAND RAPIDS, MICHIGAN / CAMBRIDGE, U.K.

First published 1992 by Doubleday,
a division of Bantam Doubleday Dell Publishing Group, Inc.,
666 Fifth Avenue, New York, NY 10103,
as part of the Anchor Bible Reference Library

This edition published 1997 by
Wm. B. Eerdmans Publishing Company
255 Jefferson Ave. S.E., Grand Rapids, Michigan 49503 /
P.O. Box 163, Cambridge CB3 9PU U.K.

Printed in the United States of America

02 01 00 99 98 97   5 4 3 2 1

Library of Congress Cataloging-in-Publication Data

Mendels, Doron.
The rise and fall of Jewish nationalism / Doron Mendels.
p.   cm.
Includes bibliographical references and index.
ISBN 0-8028-4329-8 (pbk.)
1. Judaism — History — Post-exilic period, 586 B.C.–210 A.D.
2. Jewish nationalism. 3. Judaism and state. 4. Jews — History —
168 B.C.–135 A.D. 5. Church history — Primitive and early church, ca. 30–600.
6. Ethnicity — Religious aspects — Christianity.
I. Title.
BM176.M384   1997
933 — dc21   97-13245
CIP

For my Parents

Contents

Preface to the Second Edition

Since the publication of the first edition in November 1992, I have had many reactions, some oral, some through reviews and some through scholarly work. I was happy to realize that the book's thesis was on the whole favorably received by many scholars, and that its ideas generated discussion in the field. I should like to clarify some points as a consequence of the reactions to this book.

First and foremost, it should be emphasized that the book contributes a great deal to the question (so popular in recent years in the U.S.) of the historical Jesus. Being an ancient historian I view Jesus and the Christian movement as playing a completely natural and integral role in the historical flow of the first century. It is my view in this book that Jesus cannot be understood as a historical figure unless he is seen within the context of Jewish nationalism, and the various political currents and streams of thought of this century. Jesus cannot be seen as fictional against the authentic background that this book grants his acts and ideas. The evangelists write very clearly about an authentic figure whose person was embellished by his disciples.

Second, some of my readers were uncomfortable with the term "nationalism", which I still believe can be applied in many of its aspects to the world of antiquity. Renan's description of nationalism in the ancient world is still valid today (see chapter 1). The term "nationalism" (and ethnicity) can be used in particular with reference to the Jewish nation. The term "schizophrenia" should likewise not bother people since it is used here in its very down-to-earth literary meaning, namely "the maintenance of two apparently conflicting attitudes, opinions, etc." *(The New Shorter Oxford English Dictionary)*. Readers who for some reason or another dislike the term can always use the term "dualism" instead, which I use alternately throughout the book.

Thirdly, in recent years the Jewish Diaspora has received a great deal of attention. In this book I refer extensively to the Jewish Diaspora where it bears on my theme of Jewish nationalism. I did not think that Jewish Diaspora views should be given a special chapter, but that they should rather be compared to Palestinian Judaism within the chapters dealing with Jewish nationalism in Palestine.

I have taken this opportunity to add to the notes relevant material which has been published since 1992.

I should like to thank my reviewers and all those who took the time to read and comment on the book.

Doron Mendels   Jerusalem, November 1996

Preface to the First Edition

This book was written with the intention of approaching a wide audience of students and readers who have an interest in Christianity, Judaism, and ancient history. Although it is not always possible, I have tried to avoid very detailed scholarly debates and to bring the reader very close to the original texts. Most of the bibliography mentioned is selected from among works that have been published since 1980 and is particularly aimed at an English-speaking public. The dossier was effectively closed in the winter of 1990–1991.

I wish to thank friends and colleagues who read portions of this work in earlier drafts and made invaluable suggestions and criticisms. D. M. Smith read the parts dealing with the New Testament. H. W. Attridge read chapters 4 and 9, and D. E. Aune, chapters 5 and 10. S. J. D. Cohen commented on chapters 2 and 12, while B. D. Shaw made suggestions on chapters 1 and 7. My colleague from Jerusalem I. Shatzman improved chapters 6 and 11, and D. R. Schwartz reviewed chapters 3 and 8. H. Lichtenberger was kind enough to read the whole work. All of them helped me to improve the manuscript considerably. I am grateful for their efforts.

I would also like to thank Carolyn Kornblith and D. Freedholm for helping me edit the English. I am indebted in particular to D. N. Freedman, who read the manuscript and made important suggestions. From his insightful critique I profited very much.

Finally, I should like to express my gratitude to J. H.

Charlesworth, who some years ago encouraged me to undertake this difficult task. R. M. Frye and D. W. Hardy enabled me to stay for three wonderful semesters at the Center of Theological Inquiry in Princeton. They and the staff of the Center, as well as its stimulating members, made my stay not only very pleasant, but also very productive. Also I would like to thank M. L. Iannazzi and the staff of Doubleday for their contribution in bringing this book to press.

My wife Michal managed, among her other duties, to read the manuscript and made many useful suggestions.

Doron Mendels   The Hebrew University of Jerusalem
                                 Center of Theological Inquiry, Princeton
                                 February 1991

THE RISE AND FALL OF
JEWISH NATIONALISM

The Problem

The issue of Jewish nationalism during the Second Temple period has received an enormous amount of attention from scholars all over the world. It has usually been examined within the context of the three major Jewish uprisings: the Maccabean revolt (169/8–160 B.C.E.), the Great War against Rome (66–70 C.E.), and the revolt of Bar Kokhba against Rome (132–135 C.E.).[1] In fact, every historical survey of the Jewish people during the Second Temple period made in modern times is a history of the Jewish nation. Most of these surveys reveal a point of view that is the result of the particular standpoint of the writer, as well as of the time at which it was written. It is therefore fascinating to compare the various approaches that emerge from the great histories of J. G. Klausner, B. Dinur, S. Dubnow, and H. Graetz, as well as the ones of E. Schürer ("the old and the new"), M. Hengel, M. Stern, and many others.[2]

This book is not intended to be yet another comprehensive history of the Jews in the Second Temple period; instead it is an attempt to understand Jewish nationalism within the context of the nationalism of the Hellenistic world.

The nations of the ancient Near East that were the neighbors of the Jews had specific and well-defined symbols of political nationalism, namely, the temple, territory, kingship, and the army. The intention of this book is to stress the political aspects of these symbols within Palestinian Judaism during the period 200 B.C.E.–135 C.E. Furthermore, only those nationalistic symbols which can be traced throughout the historical process will be examined. It is not as easy to trace the development of the law and the language, because of the fragmentary nature of the available evidence. Thus the more general facets of nationalism, such as the calendar, the law, and the language, will only be mentioned when they have a direct bearing on the political aspects of nationalism.

The method to be used in this book is new, inasmuch as an attempt will be made to separate the various symbols of political nationalism, and to examine them one by one within their changing historical context. In other words, this book hopes to present a comprehensive historical evaluation of the main symbols of political nationalism, not only during times of crisis, but also throughout the whole of the period under discussion. The focus here will be on the question of how Jews and Christians viewed the symbols of nationalism, and not on the attitude of the "four sects" in Judaism toward the issue of statehood. In his *Antiquities* Josephus, our main source for the period, proposes his famous division of the four "schools" or "philosophies" in Israel (18.11–25). He speaks about the Essenes, the Sadducees, the Pharisees, and the Fourth Philosophy. His details vary from description to description, but essentially this division has become accepted in scholarly works.[3] Scholars, however, were divided among other things on the issue of the nature of the political involvement as well as on the degree of influence one group had on another, particularly in the case of the Pharisees. This emphasis is quite natural because only the Pharisees seem to have survived after 70 C.E. as a group, and it was they who created what was to become mainstream Judaism in the subsequent centuries.[4] This is not the place to examine how much the Pharisees influenced politics and how extensive their influence on the masses was prior to 70 C.E. Scholars are divided in answering this question, in particular because of the nature of Josephus's evidence. In the *Jewish War,* when he relates the events before the sixties of the first century C.E., there is no emphasis on the role of the Pharisees, whereas in the *Antiquities* when dealing with the same period he ascribes to them a much greater role. Scholars have usually "blamed" Josephus's personal biases for this discrepancy.[5] Josephus's categorization will be tackled in passing in the following chapters; it suffices to say here that although Josephus made this famous categorization of the various

Jewish sects in a few passages in his historical works, he did not necessarily use these definitions when he related the history of the period. In addition, political figures who appear in his historical works are not usually assigned to one of these groups.[6] A careful reader of Josephus can observe that much of the historical role is played by the "Jews" (*Iudaioi*), the "masses" or crowds (*ho plethos, hoi polloi, ho demos*), the "priests," the "robbers" (*lestai*), and, in the time of the Great War, the "zealots" and "Sicarii." The Pharisees, the Sadducees, the Essenes, and the Fourth Philosophy are also mentioned, but to a much lesser extent.[7] The Pharisees appear as a political force mainly in Josephus's description of the times of Hyrcanus I through Salome (135–67 B.C.E.), but then seem to recede from the political scene (from 63 B.C.E. through the Great War). Some scholars put the blame for this change on Josephus's sources, his biases, or on both, while others, more correctly, have accepted as a fact that the Pharisees were more active politically during the Hasmonean period than they were later.[8]

When nationalism is mentioned—and much of Josephus's histories is about the national existence of the Jews in the ancient Near East—it is the "Jews," the people, not just the Pharisees or just the Sadducees or just the Essenes, who bear responsibility for the rise of nationalism. According to Josephus, the "Jews" were the ones who thought, with varying degrees of emphasis, of a national state in Palestine. Every religious Jew who believed in the scriptures had nationalistic ideas. The Bible contains many examples of Jewish statehood, as does the related literature. The question is therefore not one of whether one group was more nationalistic than the other, but of how much emphasis each group put on political nationalism. One should also ask about the kinds of nationalistic visions that were circulating among the various groups within Judaism. Were they ideal, utopian, or practical? And in what circumstances and to what degree did each group want to use violence to achieve its nationalistic goals?

During most of the time covered in this book, the majority of the Jews had a "passive" kind of nationalism. At certain junctures during the period 200 B.C.E.–135 C.E., however, this nationalism became more active, for instance during the Maccabean revolt and at the beginning of the Great War against Rome. The absence of some kind of nationalistic activity at a particular time does not mean that the

Jews of that time were not nationalistic. It should be noted that in Josephus's description of the four "philosophies" he never says that they disagreed about the need for a Jewish state. He only mentions in his description of the Fourth Philosophy that they differed on the question of how nationalistic goals were to be achieved.[9]

Every chapter in this book that deals with a nationalistic symbol includes two basic parts: a historical part and a literary part. The sources for the historical part of the study are mainly those which were written with the intention of relating events, such as the *First and Second Books of Maccabees*, Josephus's *Jewish War* and his *Antiquities*, as well as the works of various non-Jewish historians. The historiography is at times heavily biased and was in many instances written a long time after the events took place. Nevertheless, scholars who have been trained to read Hellenistic historiography have the tools to attempt (not always successfully) at distinguishing between bias and fact.[10] Hellenistic historiography, under whose influence Josephus wrote his historical books, reflects its bias in many ways, but this bias did not necessarily result in distortion and falsification of the facts. Thus, in spite of the shortcomings of the available historical sources, a fairly good picture can be drawn of how each of the symbols of nationalism listed above appeared throughout this long span of time.

It is true that the historical surveys in 1 and 2 Maccabees and Josephus's *Jewish War* and *Antiquities* should not be considered "sacred texts" that reveal exactly what happened.[11] One should bear in mind, however, that every historical evaluation of any given period in history is an evaluation of what others have transmitted. When writing history we are in fact relating the history as it was preserved in the historical consciousness of certain authors with certain biases. In our case it should be emphasized that Josephus and the authors of 1 and 2 Maccabees were much closer to the events they relate and understood the spirit of the times much better than we can in modern times. Hence, we do not pretend to relate a history as it really happened, but as the historians of the time (and one or two generations later) perceived it. Their perception of Jewish nationalism is what this book is about. Additionally, whereas for the years 175 B.C.E. through 70 C.E. we have a more or less continuous survey of historical events, for the years 70 C.E. through 132 C.E. we have none.

Each nationalistic symbol will be examined against the background of the Hellenistic world. The various symbols of nationalism in Judaism such as temple, territory, kingship, and army will be seen to have some traits in common with the symbols of other nations in the Hellenistic period. The Jews, however, were unique and can be distinguished from neighboring nations, just as the Babylonians can be distinguished from the Egyptians, and the latter in turn distinguished from the Cappadocians and Arabs. This uniqueness already comes to the fore simply by the definition of the nations in the sources. The title of "Judaioi" (Jews) and "Israelitai" (as well as "Hebraioi")[12] underlines the fact that they are generically different from the Hellenes (Greeks) or the Babylonians.

I shall also discuss what the Jews and early Christians thought of nationalism and examine their reflections on the various nationalistic symbols that are found in the so-called apocrypha and pseudepigrapha, as well as in the New Testament and related sources. But these sources have their own shortcomings, as they were usually written for religious purposes. In the ancient Near East, however, one cannot entirely distinguish between religion and politics. Such a distinction would be artificial. For instance, it will be seen that the early Christians, who wanted to dissociate themselves from politics, nevertheless thought in political terms. Jesus used the term *basileia* (kingdom), which was a current term in the political vocabulary of the day (that is the Greek word recorded in the Gospels, whereas Jesus himself would have used the Aramaic *malkuta*). Hence, thoughts of a nationalistic nature, which were basic to life in Palestine, could not be concealed very easily, especially from the eyes of a careful historian who reads religious documents.

Whereas many parts of the New Testament can be used for evaluating pre-70 C.E. Palestine,[13] as can many compositions that belong to the apocrypha and pseudepigrapha, rabbinic literature poses something of a problem. Rabbinic traditions were composed and put into writing centuries after the events took place, and therefore cannot be used as evidence for the period under discussion.[14] Rabbinic sources will therefore only be used in certain instances as illustrations.

The outcome of this study should interest scholars of both Judaism and Christianity. It will show that before the Hasmonean national uprising (200–168 B.C.E.), a man like Ben Sira, while possibly being content with the religious autonomy the Jews enjoyed at the time, nevertheless dreamed that the Jewish nation would regain the political grandeur it had enjoyed in the past. Political nationalism—that is to say, the wish for a Jewish state in Palestine—was imbued with an awareness of how the Jewish state appeared in the biblical literature. During the uprising (168–160 B.C.E.) and the Hasmonean state itself (143–67 B.C.E.), the national symbols of temple, territory, army, and kingship (or rulership) emerge very clearly as political entities, and the literature of the time shows that a new nationalistic phase in Judaism was dawning. There are many references to the Temple as a political institution, and there are discussions about the nature of Jewish kingship and how it should be related to the high priesthood. The problems of non-Jews in Palestine and how they should be settled within the territorial boundaries of the emerging Jewish state are also vigorously debated.

When the Hasmonean state finally fell with the Roman conquest of Palestine in 63 B.C.E., the national symbols underwent a kind of metamorphosis. As the situation of the institutions changed, the nature of the symbols altered, and they became "false" symbols of political nationalism for the majority of the Jewish population in Palestine (and the Diaspora). Some Jews could live with the symbols as they were at the time, while others rejected them as false and deeply resented their current status. Herod the Great and his successors were seen by many Jews as alien rulers, while in the eyes of others they were the symbols of a Jewish state of some sort. Certain Jews could cope with a "paganized" Palestine, while others could not. Some Jews could accept that Jerusalem and the Temple were divested of some of their political importance by the foundation of a competitive "capital," Caesarea, while others could not. Even those who learned to live with the new meaning of the symbols after the Roman conquest did not necessarily think that it was an ideal situation. But for them something was better than nothing. We shall see in the following discussions that the religiopolitical tensions of the times were not just caused by a "dualism" existing between the gentiles and the Jews of Palestine,[15] but arose from a much more complex set of circumstances. The changing nature of Jewish nationalism within the awareness of the different strata of Palestinian society brought about a great deal of religiopolitical turmoil, instability, and change.

This phase in the history of the Jews (after 63 B.C.E.), part of which took place under pseudo-Jewish rulers (clients of the Roman Empire) and part under direct Roman rule (63 B.C.E.–66 C.E.), encompassed four different kinds of reaction to political nationalism.

During much of this time, most of the Jews did very little about their desire to be free from Roman rule and to create a Jewish state in Palestine. This passivity does not mean that they had no hopes for a Jewish state. Thus, when a real opportunity arose in 66 C.E. and a Roman legion was defeated by the Jews, the masses (instigated by a violent, revolutionary nationalistic group) launched a war for freedom. For a short while they believed that God was supporting them in their war with the Romans and in their attempt to reestablish a Jewish state.[16]

Some groups in Judaism, including the so-called early Christian group, started to view nationalistic symbols as spiritual entities rather than political ones. According to this view, which was a reaction to the distortion of the nationalistic symbols by the events after 63 B.C.E., the territory was no longer a political idea, the Temple became more and more a spiritual institution, and kingship was no longer that of the historical David, but a spiritual and transcendental one. Many Jews, including Jesus, Peter, and Paul, became tired of Jewish nationalism in its real and physical aspects and created a spiritual alternative of the *basileia tou theou* or *malchut shamaim* (kingdom of God).

The violent, revolutionary nationalistic group seems to have been marginal in Judaism at the time under survey. Although this movement was in existence during a great deal of the period, it remained under the surface and waited for the right opportunity to fight for freedom from Roman rule. It may be that this group, along with the larger passive groups mentioned above, was responsible for the messianic concept of the son of David, which had very close political associations with the biblical kingdoms of David and Solomon. It is interesting that this ideology never looks back to the Hasmonean dynasty, but always to the Davidic one.[17]

Finally, there were Jews who accepted Roman rule and were quite content with it. That is, they actively supported the Romans because they believed either that God had justly deprived them of their state or that the Jews did not need an independent state.

The consciousness of political nationalism in its pure nature (i.e., independent and sovereign) remained latent and submerged as long as some sort of Jewish sovereignty was apparent (i.e., Herod the Great and his successors). When even this remnant of political nationalism was taken away by the Romans in 44 C.E. after the death of Agrippa I, it was only a matter of time until the mounting frustration led to a violent outburst against Rome. It was, among other factors, the diversity of views on nationalism among the Jews in Palestine (and the Diaspora) and the internal dissatisfaction and dissension among the different groups and factions that brought about the Great War against Rome. The historical sources relate the events leading up to the Great War. At its start one can see very clearly that the four symbols of Jewish nationalism figured prominently in Jewish political awareness. The leaders of the rebellion, who were widely supported at its outbreak, revived these nationalistic symbols. They convened in the Temple to make the political decisions that they were to carry out; they founded a Jewish army, conquered parts of the Land, and some even initiated the foundation of a new Jewish kingdom. They even seem to have created a new calendar. It would be naïve to think that all of this happened by coincidence. For the majority of the Jews, Jewish nationalism had existed under the surface for many years. After 70 C.E., the literature of this stormy period shows that, alongside the mourning for the lost Land, the Jews did not completely give up on the idea of a Jewish state, even after the destruction of the Temple. They believed this state should be shaped in a very specific way, as can be deduced from Josephus's interpretations of Jewish history written after 70 C.E. (*Antiquities*). They believed that the present was not the right time for such a state to emerge, but that in the near future it surely would. Jewish political nationalism did not die out after 70 C.E.[18]

Although the book focuses on Palestinian Judaism, some views held by Diaspora Jews concerning political nationalism will occasionally be mentioned. The Jews in the Diaspora were first and foremost citizens of their respective countries outside Palestine. They served as soldiers (and even as generals) in foreign armies (Egyptian, Syrian, and Roman) and spoke the local languages. They showed their obedience to Hellenistic kings and later to the Roman emperor wherever they were settled. The Temple was seen by some as a religious center for all Jews in the world (Philo Alexandrinus), and the

Land became an amorphous idealistic concept for others (Aristeas). The Jews in the Diaspora, however, did not have one opinion on the issue of political nationalism. They were very much divided on this issue, just as they were on many other issues, a matter to be discussed further in the following chapters.[19]

Notes

1 For a good general survey on the years 175 B.C.E.–135 C.E., see E. Schürer, *The History of the Jewish People in the Age of Jesus Christ,* rev. G. Vermes et al. (Edinburgh, 1973–1987), vol. 1.

2 For a useful, but partial, survey of modern scholarly trends, see S. J. D. Cohen, in *Early Judaism and Its Modern Interpreters,* ed. R. A. Kraft and G. W. E. Nickelsburg (Atlanta, 1986) pp. 33–56; also M. Hengel, "Der alte und der neue 'Schürer,' " *Journal of Semitic Studies* 35.1 (1990): 19–72.

3 See also his description in *Jewish War* 2.119–166, and cf. A. I. Baumgarten, "Josephus and Hippolytus on the Pharisees," *Hebrew Union College Annual* 55 (1984): 1–25.

4 Cf., for instance, J. Neusner, "The Formation of Rabbinic Judaism: Yavneh (Jamnia) from A.D. 70 to 100," *Aufstieg und Niedergang der römischen Welt* 2.19.2 (1979): 3–42. For a different view see S. J. D. Cohen, "The Significance of Yavneh: Pharisees, Rabbis, and the End of Jewish Sectarianism," *Hebrew Union College Annual* 55 (1984): 27–53. (He admits, however, that "in all likelihood most of the rabbis were Pharisees.") For the 'Gründungslegende' of Javneh after the catastrophe of 70 C.E., see P. Schäfer, "Die Flucht Johanan b. Zakkais aus Jerusalem und die Gründung des 'Lehrhauses' in Jabne," *Aufstieg und Niedergang der römischen Welt* 2.19.2 (1979): 44–101.

5 See in particular D. R. Schwartz, "Josephus and Nicolaus on the Pharisees," *Journal for the Study of Judaism in the Persian, Hellenistic and Roman Period* 14 (1983): 157–171; and A. J. Saldarini, *Pharisees, Scribes, and Sadducees in Palestinian Society* (Wilmington, Del., 1988), pp. 128–133 and passim. For a good recent survey concerning this problem in modern scholarship, see D. Goodblatt, "The Place of the Pharisees in First-Century Judaism: The State of the Debate," *Journal for the Study of Judaism in the Persian, Hellenistic and Roman Period* 20 (1989): 12–30. Recently an entire book was devoted to this problem; see S. Mason, *Flavius Josephus on the Pharisees* (Leiden and Cologne, 1991). See, for the Sadducees in Josephus, G. Baumbach, "The Sadducees in Josephus," in *Josephus, the Bible, and History,* ed. L. H. Feldman and G. Hata (Detroit, 1989), pp. 173–195.

6 And cf. M. Stern, "Aspects of Jewish Society: The Priesthood and Other Classes," in *Compendia rerum iudaicarum ad Novum Testamentum,* ed. S. Safrai et al. (Assen, 1974–1976), 2.610–611.

7 The Gospels always make the distinction between Jesus' group and the Pharisees, Sadducees, and Scribes. The stature of these groups varies from gospel to gospel and Acts; see recently Saldarini, *Pharisees,* pp. 144–198. See also K. Berger, "Jesus als Pharisäer und frühe Christen als Pharisäer," *Novum Testamentum* 30 (1988): 231–262; and R. L. Mowery, "Pharisees and Scribes, Galilee and Jerusalem," *Zeitschrift für die neutestamentliche Wissenschaft* 80 (1989): 266–268. J. Neusner (*From Politics to Piety* [Englewood Cliffs, N.J., 1973], chap. 4) argues that

the description of the Pharisees in the New Testament (e.g., their polemics on purity issues, the sabbath observance, and the tithe) shows that in the first century C.E. they abandoned politics altogether and became a purely religious sect. One objection to this claim might be that the issues that were at stake between the early Christians and the Jews were only nonpolitical ones. The early Christians were completely uninterested in political issues (as defined in my study), hence the Pharisees did not find it necessary to argue about politics with them, though they themselves may have been politically oriented. Another objection might be that all groups agreed on political matters, so they did not come up in the discussions.

[8] L. I. Levine, "The Political Struggle Between Pharisees and Sadducees in the Hasmonean Period," in *Jerusalem in the Second Temple Period: Abraham Schalit Memorial Volume,* ed. A. Oppenheimer et al. (Jerusalem, 1980), pp. 61–83 (Hebrew), and idem, "On the Political Involvement of the Pharisees under Herod and the Procurators," *Kathedra* 8 (1978): 12–28 (Hebrew).

[9] Cf. *Antiquities* 18.23–24, and see M. Stern, "The Suicide of Eleazar ben Jair and His Men at Masada, and the 'Fourth Philosophy,'" in his *Studies in Jewish History* (Jerusalem, 1991), pp. 313–343 (Hebrew).

[10] Literature on Hellenistic historiography and its mode of writing abounds: see, for instance, some of the literature quoted in the next chapter.

[11] Cohen, *Early Judaism,* pp. 37–41.

[12] I cannot go into a discussion of the terms "Ioudaios," "Israelites," "Hebraios," and related terms. Cf. for instance S. Zeitlin's attempts: "The Jews: Race, Nation or Religion—Which?" in his *Studies in the Early History of Judaism* (New York, 1973–1978), 2.435–469; idem, "Who Is a Jew?—A Halachic-Historic Study," ibid., 2.470–499; and idem, "Judaism as a Religion—An Historical Study," ibid., 3.1–245 passim. Cf. also the attempts of Y. Amir, "The Term 'Joudaismos': A Study in Jewish Hellenistic Self-Identification," *Immanuel* 14 (1982): 34–41; P. J. Tomson, "The Names Israel and Jews in Ancient Judaism and in the New Testament," *Tijdschrift voor filosophie en theologie* 47 (1986): 120–140; R. S. Kraemer, "On the Meaning of the Term 'Jew' in Greco-Roman Inscriptions," *Harvard Theological Review* 82.1 (1989): 35–53; S. J. D. Cohen, "Crossing the Boundary and Becoming a Jew," *Harvard Theological Review* 82.1 (1989): 13–33; and Carl R. Holladay, *Fragments from Hellenistic Jewish Authors* (Atlanta, 1989), 2.176. Much more research should be done on this issue.

[13] We can view the New Testament as reflecting opinions and events going back to pre–70 C.E. Palestine, in the very same manner as we use the First and Second Books of Maccabees. These two books were written with a heavily theological bias many years after the events they describe took place. Yet they are used by historians as evidence for the "facts." It is not necessary to go into the question of the datings of the various books of the New Testament along the lines of works such as J. A. T. Robinson's *Redating the New Testament* (Philadelphia, 1976), or J. Carmignac's *Birth of the Synoptics* (Chicago, 1987). Instead my purpose is to show that some of its probable early layers correspond to material of other sources of pre–70 C.E.

Judaism. Unlike rabbinic sources, many of the books of the New Testament were written before 70 C.E. (Paul's Epistles), and some about 70 C.E. For early local traditions in the synoptics, see G. Theissen, *Lokalkolorit und Zeitgeschichte in den Evangelien* (Göttingen, 1989).

14 For the problem in particular see J. Neusner, *The Mishnah Before 70* (Atlanta, 1987).

15 As M. Hengel presents it in *The "Hellenization" of Judaea in the First Century after Christ* (Philadelphia, 1989); and see also B. Otzen, *Judaism in Antiquity* (orig. 1984), trans. F. H. Cryer (Sheffield, 1990), pp. 59–60 and passim. See also A. Kasher, *Jews and Hellenistic Cities in Eretz Israel* (Tübingen, 1990).

16 Cf. the view of S. J. D. Cohen, *From the Maccabees to the Mishnah* (Philadelphia, 1987), pp. 27–34, about the adherence to passivity according to the prophet Jeremiah: "the basic political stance of the Jews of both the land of Israel and the diaspora was not rebellion but accommodation" (p. 34).

17 It is of interest that the Hasmonean dynasty was suppressed in the later rabbinic sources; for this problem see G. Alon, "Did the Jewish People and Its Sages Cause the Hasmoneans to be Forgotten?" in his *Jews, Judaism and the Classical World* (Jerusalem, 1977), pp. 1–17.

18 For the various scholarly opinions about 70 C.E. as a turning point in the history of the Jewish nation, see M. D. Herr, "From the Destruction of the Temple to the Revolt of Bar Kokhba," *The History of Eretz Israel,* ed. M. Stern (Jerusalem, 1984), 4.286–287 (Hebrew). For Jewish political thought after 70 C.E., see an interesting approach of S. A. Cohen, *The Three Crowns: Structure of Communal Politics in Early Rabbinic Jewry* (Cambridge and Sydney, 1990).

19 For a useful survey of the literature from Diaspora Judaism see recently J. M. G. Barclay, *Jews in the Mediterranean Diaspora from Alexander to Trajan (323* B.C.E.-117C.E.) (Edinburgh, 1996).

CHAPTER 1

Nationalism in the Hellenistic World in the Third Through First Centuries B.C.E.

Can one speak of nationalism in the ancient world? Yes, but not in the sense it has in modern times. The aim in this chapter is not to venture a definition of nationalism in antiquity, or to compare modern nationalism with that of the ancient world, or to apply modern ideas of nationalism to the Hellenistic age. By and large, there is a major question whether one can use the modern models and descriptions of nationalism proposed by distinguished historians and sociologists such as E. Kedouri, E. Gellner, and A. D. Smith in any discussion about antiquity.[1] Thus I would not even risk entering the arena of definitions of nationalism in the Hellenistic age. Instead this chapter will merely attempt to describe how the Hellenistic world coped with the issue of ethnicity, which will for convenience be called here "nationalism." In order to explain the use of the word "nationalism" it should be remembered that scholars of antiquity use terms that have been used to describe other later phenomena. The term "imperialism" is an example. Although the word derives from Rome (*imperium*), today we speak of the existence of empires before the Roman epoch.[2] The same applies to the term "utopia." The word is used today to denote a very particular literary genre in antiquity, although the term was probably created by Sir Thomas More in the sixteenth century.[3]

In the Hellenistic period, nationalistic traits (or, to use Gellner's term for the nationalistic trait of language, "potential nationalism") can be discerned in many *ethne* (peoples) of the Hellenistic world, traits that distinguish them from one another. Perhaps the most important factor is that the various peoples of the ancient world were aware of how they differed in terms of language, territory, history, culture, and religion.[4] At times peoples accented only one or two of these aspects of their particular tradition, and yet were not willing to fight for them. At the same time, it is true that sociologists point to the very obvious similar patterns of behavior and institutions to be found in many societies that are also very different in their ethnic definitions.[5] Nevertheless, particularism, local-patriotism, and individualism of peoples did persevere for centuries. For instance, temples in Mesopotamia, Egypt, Israel, and Phoenicia had many things in common, but when the details of each temple are examined, in terms of architecture, liturgy, and status of priests, many unique characteristics and variations are found. Moreover, even universalistic ideas created by empires as well as by philosophical speculation did not abolish nationalistic feelings. On the contrary, in many instances these feelings increased. This is a paradox of history. Alexander the Great and his successors were imbued with the notion of the unity of mankind, or at least the unification of parts of the inhabited world, but they never succeeded in abolishing the existence of nations. Neither did Napoleon, who, as one of the greatest "universalistic" rulers of Europe, caused the emergence of strong nationalistic feelings among some of his subjects. Both in antiquity and in modern history various national groups have emphasized the individual characteristics that separate them from their neighbors, at times even while being under the same imperial roof. Let us see how this paradox worked in the Hellenistic period.

Most of the Near Eastern world before Alexander's conquest at the end of the fourth century B.C.E. was in the hands of the Persian Empire. From the time of Alexander's conquest of the East (334–324 B.C.E.) until the final Roman conquest of the Mideast (the conquest of Egypt in 30 B.C.) the region was under the so-called Macedonian rule of Alexander and his successors. Then came the Roman domination. Fortunately, we are relatively well-informed about the peoples (*ethne*) who were part of these successive empires. Thus one could make a comparative study of existing descriptions of the peoples in Persian times (sixth and fifth centuries B.C.E.) and those of the first and second centuries C.E. under Roman domination. In spite of the fact that various empires dominated the ancient Near East for centuries, peoples in this portion of the world (hereafter called the "East," for convenience) remained different from one another and emphasized their particularistic and individualistic traits such as language, historical awareness, borders, and calendar. This does not mean that they necessarily had their own state, in other words, that there was an identity between the *ethnos* (people, nation) and a political state. Many peoples could cope with the idea of being a nation through the preservation of their religion and culture without being within the framework of an independent state of their own. Evidence for this position comes both from Greek historians and geographers and from archaeological and epigraphic material deriving from the peoples, or nations, themselves. The Scythians, Egyptians, Phoenicians, Libyans, Iranians, and others are examples.[6]

The descriptions of the peoples of the ancient Near East by Herodotus (fifth century B.C.E.) should be compared with those of Arrian of Nicomedia (partly based on accounts from the time of Alexander's conquests in the fourth century B.C.E.), Hieronymus of Cardia (fourth–early third centuries B.C.E., whose descriptions appear in the writings of Diodorus Siculus of the first century B.C.E.), Strabo in the first century C.E., and Arrian in the second. These accounts cover a wide span of time and should be critically examined, because some of them give a wealth of valuable information, while others just copy their predecessors or invent facts. Although these descriptions come from Greek sources,[7] we learn from them, as well as from archaeological evidence, that the Scythians, for example, remained a self-contained nation throughout the Hellenistic era in terms of elements such as language and material culture, as did the indigenous Egyptians and other peoples as well. In other words, far into the Roman period nations kept their ethnic consciousness of what one would call today self-definition and self-identity, even though most of the time they were under the rule of one kingdom or another. Today one would say that they were "subdued" by another power, but these peoples did not necessarily think so. Many of the indigenous tribes and *ethne* of both the Hellenistic and the Roman Near East projected their thoughts of statehood (i.e., political nationalism) onto the power that dominated them at the time, without giving up their own cultural and religious identities. Many of the Hellenistic rulers helped them to do so by posing as indigenous national figures. The Ptolemies and Seleucids, as well as the Roman emperors after them, are a good example of this practice. Thus national feelings were not necessarily suppressed; on the contrary, they played a very important role in the Hellenistic period. At the same time, the Hellenistic monarchs also knew how to act as the leaders of the Greek populations that settled in the ancient Near East in great numbers after Alexander the Great, that is, by behaving like Macedonians (i.e., Greeks). So despite the universalism that was in the air after Alexander the Great, the indigenous populations not only distinguished among one another but also between themselves and the Greeks who had settled among them.

Did nationalistic feelings become passive during the Hellenistic period? There are many examples of both active and passive nationalism. There are some extreme cases of resistance to the foreign rulers, but they were uncommon in the Hellenistic kingdoms.[8] Most indigenous populations remained passive because in most instances they either identified themselves with the new rulers or just ignored them. But resistance to or cooperation with the Greek and Roman rulers was also dependent on how far away from the center of the empire the nation was located and how harsh these rulers were. It also depended on how effective the foreign rule was in one region or another and how much it tolerated the indigenous culture, language, and cult. In addition, it depended on the extent of the nationalistic traits in the indigenous population and the degree to which the indigenous population wished to be distinguished from other ethnic groups. The extent of the spread of Hellenism after Alexander the Great in the ancient Near East provides an answer to such questions.[9] The intensity of the penetration of Greek culture in the ancient Near East decided to what degree certain strata of society emphasized either their indigenous and traditional or their more universal traits. Arabia was less inhabited by Greeks than was, for instance, the coastal plain of Palestine,[10] a factor that had its effect on the "national" organization in these two regions.

Alexander the Great's conquest changed a great deal in the East.[11] What was the impact of his conquest on the nationalistic scene? While J. G. Droysen and his followers have argued that after Alexander large sections of the Near East became a melting pot of Greek and eastern cultures,[12] it is now clear that a somewhat different picture should be drawn. After Alexander there was indeed a different Near East from the one that existed before his conquest.

Schematically, three main strata of society can be discerned in the Hellenistic era: (1) the indigenous population; (2) the Greek rulers and settlers; and (3) the "Hellenists," the stratum of society in which people from the other social groups were able to mingle. This schematic division can be seen in the societies of most places in the Hellenistic Near East and applies also to the situation in the first two centuries of Roman domination over the East. One should remember, however, that this characteristic division differed in emphasis from place to place and from time to time during the period under survey. This division is fundamental to the understanding of the nuances of nationalism.[13]

The indigenous populations (1) kept their original (indigenous) cultures for centuries—in certain regions more effectively than in others. The Egyptians, Syrians, Iranians, Libyans, Edomites, Babylonians, and others adhered with great perseverance to their ancient traditions without interference from the dominating kingdoms. Culture in the Hellenistic Near East was not just a religious matter, but had heavily political overtones (cf. the next chapter). Many examples over a very long time-span (i.e., from Alexander's conquest to the second century C.E. and even later) could be adduced. It should be emphasized that the degree of Hellenization differed from place to place and from century to century, but the indigenous populations basically remained nationalistic and in many cases wanted to stress this aspect. For instance, the Egyptians carried on writing hieroglyphs and using hieratic and demotic scripts, and they adhered to their mythology long into the Roman period (second and third centuries C.E.).[14] The same holds true for the Babylonians, Libyans, and others.[15] Although not all of the indigenous peoples could still read their ancient scripts, the stubborn preservation of these scripts and mythologies in the temples is of great importance. Even Coptic, which has considerable Greek lexical influence in it, remained an Egyptian nationalistic language. The Jews, for example, used paleo-Hebrew (the ancient Hebrew script) on coinage and some other artifacts. The commoners spoke Aramaic (the lingua franca of the time) and Hebrew, and most of the literary heritage from the Hasmonean period was in Hebrew, written in the Jewish script. All of this evidence points to the indigenous use of the language.[16]

It also should be noted that many local (i.e., national) gods were worshiped without interruption all over the ancient Near East.[17]

Hence during the Hellenistic period the indigenous populations found more than ever that their leaders were the priesthoods centered around the temples of the ancient Near East, such as Babylon, Memphis, and Tyre. Calendars also became a nationalistic issue during this period. There are some examples of the adherence to traditional national calendars (such as the Egyptian and Babylonian calendars) by indigenous populations and the creation of new national calendars by the Hellenistic kingdoms (e.g., the Seleucid calendar versus the traditional Babylonian one).[18]

The different indigenous nations did not necessarily oppose foreign rulers. As already stated, in many cases they cooperated because these foreign rulers often posed as nationalistic rulers. Some sporadic references to opposition does not mean that the native populations were anti-Macedonian or anti-Roman. In fact, very little opposition of a nationalistic nature to these empires can be traced in the sources of the Hellenistic period. In the few cases of which we do know, the opposition may have been economically motivated.[19]

Shortly after Alexander's conquests a vast Greek stratum (2) emerged in many regions of the Near East, usually called by scholars the "ruling class." The Greeks, who differentiated themselves very clearly from the local population by calling themselves "Hellenes,"[20] created from the beginning a dichotomy between their culture and the native one. It is a known fact that these Greeks, who were mainly located in the Greek cities and settlements that had been founded after Alexander's rule in the East (and some even before that), kept on speaking Greek, thought in Greek, and wrote in Greek. They yearned for a past and for heroes that they had inherited from their Greek homeland. They worshiped the traditional Greek gods in the many Greek temples that were built all over the East.[21] Still, even in the Greek world, which was in many respects universal, one can find "national" nuances resulting from differences in territorial location, historical awareness, and mythological lore. Thus in spite of the fact that the Greeks shared a common history and cultural, religious, and linguistic heritage, a Greek from Athens differed from a Greek from Thebes or Sparta, Ephesus or Messene; and he usually cared to emphasize this fact. When Alexander went on his eastern enterprise in 334 B.C.E., the historians described his Greek army according to its ethnic makeup.[22] These differences among Greeks of the various regions of the Greek homeland were partially transferred to the East. There is even evidence of a tribal division in a citizen body imported from Greek cities in Greece to an eastern one (Memphis and Alexandria).[23] By virtue of the common circumstances of constituting the ruling class among a foreign population (some of whom had remained unknown to Greeks for centuries), however, these Greeks had more in common with one another than with their respective indigenous populations. This fact can be observed deep into the Roman era. So a Greek from Alexandria had much more in common with a Greek from Antiochia or Acco-Ptolemais than with his indigenous Egyptian compatriot—but only within limits. The limits were created by the formation of new kingdoms in the East by the successors of Alexander the Great. During a bloody and terrible war, the war of the Diadochi, which lasted for about forty years (323–284 B.C.E.), four kingdoms emerged: Thrace, Macedonia, the Seleucid Empire, and the Ptolemaic Empire. The only one that was a continuation of an earlier polity was Macedonia, while Thrace disappeared soon after its formation. The remaining three kingdoms very quickly became new, well-defined national superstructures. Later in the Hellenistic era other kingdoms were added, such as Pergamon, Judea, and Cyrenaica. This proliferation of political entities created "national" distinctions also among the Greeks of the Hellenistic Near East. Thus, besides their common ties as Greeks (in terms of language, the *koine*—common heritage— etc.), they developed a local patriotism, which was expressed in their literature and art.[24] Essentially, they had a new identity alongside their traditional one.

One can find the creation of this new world expressed in the Jewish documents. The Book of Daniel, chapters 1–6 of which were written after the four principal kingdoms were created (presumably at some point during the third century B.C.E.), is aware of world history as a background for Jewish history. The passage concerning Alexander and the Diadochi and their role in world history is Dan 8:3–8, written during the sixties of the second century B.C.E.:

As I looked about, I saw a ram standing before the gate. It had two long horns; one was longer than the other and appeared after it. I noticed that the ram was butting toward the west, the north, and the south; and no beast could withstand it or be rescued from its power. It did as it pleased and became mighty. As I was looking on, I saw a he-goat come from the west, and cross the whole earth without touching the ground; and a conspicuous horn was on its forehead. The he-goat came up to the two-horned ram that I saw standing before the gate, and rushed at it with savage force. I noticed that, when it reached the ram, it was enraged against it, and gave it such a blow that it broke off its two horns; for the ram had not the power to withstand it. The he-goat knocked the ram to the ground and trampled it down; and there was no one to rescue the ram from its power. The he-goat then grew exceedingly. But at the height of its power, its big horn broke off, and in its place four conspicuous ones came up toward the four winds of the heavens.

The author of Daniel 7–12 viewed these events as figuring the beginning of a new era. He describes Alexander's crushing of the Persian (and Median) empire as being symbolized by the double-horned ram. Alexander himself is symbolized by the he-goat. The four winds mentioned are the four empires.[25] It is an important description because the entire apocalyptic structure in Judaism is built upon world history and Israel's place within it.[26] Here we have a typical example of a native writing vis-à-vis the Greek conquerors of the East.

Alexander's generals and successors crowned themselves kings about twenty years after Alexander's death, so their territories became monarchies. Antigonus was the first to do so,[27] then Ptolemy and Seleucus followed suit. It took them twenty years to overcome the trauma of Alexander's death, as Hieronymus of Cardia's famous story about Alexander's empty throne demonstrates. In 318 B.C.E. (five years after his death) Eumenes, one of Alexander's generals, recounted that "in his sleep he had seemed to see Alexander the king, alive and clad in his kingly garb, presiding over a council, giving orders to the commanders, and actively administering all the affairs of the monarchy." Alexander's generals then decided to "make ready a golden throne from the royal treasure, and that after the diadem, the sceptre, the crown, and the rest of the insignia have been placed on it, all the commanders must at daybreak offer incense to Alexander before it, hold the meetings of the council in its presence, and receive their orders in the name of the king just as if he were alive and at the head of his own kingdom." This idea was indeed carried out later.[28]

The new rulers, who were all from Macedonian (i.e., Greek) stock, founded dynasties and created new national identities alongside them. What does this mean? On the one hand, they did not just continue Alexander's universalistic and syncretistic ideas; he was dead and so was his short-lived world empire. In some respects, however, they did continue Alexander's tradition.

One was the legitimacy of their own rule. The new kings quickly understood that in order to appease the native populations they had first of all to let them keep most of their traditional national features such as culture, language, and cult. Some autonomy was even granted through the recognition by the new kings of the local priests as the leaders of the indigenous populations. Moreover, the new kings did all they could to pose as the successors of the traditional indigenous dynasties. Thus the Ptolemies wanted to be seen as pharaohs and hence as the legitimate rulers of Egypt. There is scarcely any evidence that the Hellenistic rulers hindered the continuity of the national life of the native populations. In other words, a superstructure with a national identity was created in the new Hellenistic kingdoms, which in many of its aspects was identified with the native populations as expressing their own nationalistic heritages. This situation is more apparent in Egypt than in the Seleucid Empire, which was multinational. For the majority of the Greek population these Hellenistic rulers were, and remained throughout the Hellenistic period, Macedonian kings, and thereby constituted their own expression of a new national existence in the East. These Greeks could no longer identify themselves with the political atmosphere of Greece, namely, of the city-state and its traditional political structures such as oligarchy and democracy. They now identified themselves politically as Greeks living in a new national organization, such as the empire of the Ptolemies, that of the Seleucids, or that of Commagene.[29]

The Hellenist stratum (3) can be described as the mixture of the two cultures, Greek and indigenous. This group consisted of intellectuals and officials who were bilingual, knew the heritage of both cultures, created religious syncretisms, and, most importantly, invented a new national identity. This point must be clarified.

Not every native who spoke or wrote in Greek was hellenized. But a person willing to live a new cultural and religious life, containing both cultures, can be called a Hellenist. All over the Near East (and beyond it) there were groups who, in varying degrees, lived a life that straddled these two cultures and in many ways constituted the bridge between them. How did their position influence their national identity? Whereas the native populations in the Near East identified themselves mainly with their traditional heritages (hence Ptolemy was regarded as a pharaoh), and the Greek stratum identified mostly with the Greek tradition (viewing Ptolemy as a Macedonian, or a Greek god such as Dionysus), the Hellenists created something between these two worlds. Their ideas of the state were thus a mixture of eastern and western concepts of statehood and nationality. For them, the new kings of the eastern kingdoms indeed represented new institutions. For them the Hellenistic king was neither a Greek institution nor an eastern one. They lived in a world of religious syncretism (which in certain instances may have been only theoretical) and attempted to find the equivalents for Greek gods in the various pantheons available in the ancient Near East. Thus Toth became Hermes, Osiris became Dionysus, and Melkart, Heracles. In Egypt this group was even associated with the worship of a completely new Hellenistic deity called Serapis. (I shall elaborate on this aspect of Hellenism later.) Thus the sociocultural divisions in the societies of the ancient Near East, and their attitude to Hellenism, were important factors in the question of nationalism.

How did the Jews fit into this setup? German and French scholars of the seventeenth through nineteenth centuries always used the Jews as the example par excellence of nationalism in ancient times. That the Jews were the only specimen of a "modern" nation to be found in antiquity is certainly not true, as can be deduced from what has already been said. The Jews are indeed an outstanding example, inasmuch as for a certain period they (being an indigenous population) actualized their political nationalism, that is, they created a Jewish state. It will be shown later that the Jewish nation, like other nations in the same environment, kept its cultural as well as its religious national traits. But it will also be seen that the Jews emphasized their distinctive traits even more than their neighbors did. One can observe that the nations of the ancient Near East emphasized their nationalistic traits to varying degrees. For instance, some of the *ethne* disappeared or were assimilated by their environment (Ammonites, Moabites, etc.); some peoples had a very tenuous relationship with their national tradition (Phoenicians in certain places); while others showed a strong sense of nationalism (Jews, Samaritans, some of the Edomite nation, Arabs, and Egyptians).[30]

It should be emphasized that, while in terms of culture and religion most of the nations of the Hellenistic Near East retained some sort of distinguishing identity, in most instances they could easily project their feelings of political nationalism (i.e., statehood) onto the Hellenistic kingdoms and later onto the Roman Empire. It was impossible for the majority of the Jews to do so, because the symbols of these new rulers were statues placed in temples and public places as well as images engraved on coins, something absolutely forbidden by Jewish law. It is primarily for this reason that the Jews were the only nation in the ancient Near East that could not adjust to foreign rulers and had to create their own state. When it was impossible for them to do so, they were frustrated. Still, the degrees of emphasis put on nationalism in Palestinian society differed from group to group (groups 1, 2, and 3) and from time to time. As long as the foreign rulers did not insist on imposing forbidden political symbols on the Jews, most of them could live peacefully, holding the concept of a Jewish state as an ideal instead of agitating for its immediate creation.

For a general background, the historical development of nationalism from the Maccabean upheaval to 67 B.C.E. will now be described.[31] As the national symbols will be elaborated on later in the book, it will suffice here to give a short survey.

When Alexander the Great arrived in Judea in 332 B.C.E., according to a famous apocryphal story he was welcomed by the Jewish priests, who came to meet him outside Jerusalem. Whether this story is factual or not, its core, namely, that Alexander wanted to receive the legitimation of the "local" God in Jerusalem, may be true.[32] Alexander did the same in many other places he passed. The refusal of the people of Tyre to let him enter the temple of Melkart (called by the Greeks Heracles) resulted in a terrible war.[33] As a consequence of Alexander's death and the partition of the empire among the Diadochi, Palestine became Ptolemaic for more than a century, after some harsh wars were fought for it between the Ptolemies and Seleucids. About 200 B.C.E. the country became Seleucid[34] and remained so, at least de jure, until 143/2 B.C.E. Both kingdoms treated the Jews as they did indigenous populations elsewhere. They let them practice much of their traditional and national life but did not grant them independence. So the Jews were essentially autonomous, which was a familiar mechanism used by the Hellenistic kingdoms all over their empires. In other words, both Ptolemaic and Seleucid rulers, as well as various usurpers, usually treated the Jews as they treated other nationalities within their spheres of influence, but with greater tolerance, for the Jews were exempted from putting a royal cult in their Temple and public places. During the eighties and seventies of the second century B.C.E., however, the social stratum of the Hellenists (group 3 mentioned above) became more and more powerful culturally, as well as socially and politically. Among the leading figures of this stratum were priests who were attracted to Greek culture in varying degrees (from group 2, who were settled in many cities of Palestine). It is very difficult for us to know exactly what happened during this stormy period because both 1 and 2 Maccabees, books that tell us about hellenization among the upper strata of Jewish society, were not very objective in this respect; they denigrate the process of hellenization altogether. The terrible intrigues of the leading figures of this stratum brought about the massive military and political intervention of the Seleucids, who wished to gain politically from the mounting tensions between the Hellenists (group 3) and the Jews (group 1) who resisted them. The terrible clash with the Seleucids started as a religious upheaval in which the Jews fought for religious independence, and ended up being a more nationalistic upheaval led by the Maccabean brothers, a priestly house from Modiʿin, a small village near Lod.[35]

The main goal of this movement was the purification of the Temple, which was achieved in 164 B.C.E. Led by Judas Maccabeus, the Maccabees then proceeded to free Jerusalem, the political and religious capital of the Jews. They only partly succeeded in this aim, and Jerusalem was not liberated completely until 143 B.C.E. when the last gentiles left the Akra, the fortress overlooking the Temple Mount. During the fifties and forties of the second century B.C.E. the successors of Judas Maccabeus, his brothers and their sons, followed in his path. Through cunning policies and service under the various claimants to the Seleucid throne, they brought about the establishment of a Jewish state, though one ill-defined in character. The end of the forties signified the consolidation of the achievements of the previous decades. We read, "In the 170th year (143/2 B.C.E.), the yoke of the heathen was lifted from Israel" (1 Macc 13:41; *Jewish War* 1.53). Simeon, by approval of the Jews and priests, became leader and high priest and also a military leader, as well as high judge. We will return to these matters later; it suffices to mention here that after 143/2 B.C.E. it was not long before a Jewish kingship was established. In addition, from the end of the forties a tremendous effort was made to regain the Land, wresting it from the foreigners settled on it. John Hyrcanus's reign signified the materialization of the policies launched by Simeon, which included broadening borders, building an army, and judaizing the Edomites. He might even have become the first Jewish king, but that distinction was reserved for Aristobulus I, who put a diadem on his head in 104/3 B.C.E. A Jewish kingdom became a reality and survived as an independent entity until 63 B.C.E.

Thus about the middle of the second century the Jews, exploiting the global political situation (the weakness of Seleucids and Ptolemies, the rise of Rome, and the fall of Macedonia), suddenly got rid of their former Greek rulers. They became free to decide their own affairs and future. This political situation, in which an indigenous nation was freed and released from the upper stratum, the foreign Greek ruling class, can be seen as unique in the Hellenistic context. Historical roles were changed. The Greeks (and other gentiles) who lived in Palestine, and who were socially and politically associated with the ruling class in the region, were ruled by the indigenous population, the pious Jews. The latter, unlike those in other places in the ancient Near East at the time, had a double problem: they were stuck between non-Greek gentiles on the one hand and Greeks on the other. We shall return to this problem later; at any rate, they took over authority, and the so-called Hellenists, who had become powerful for a while (people such as Menelaus, Jason, and Alcimus) were gradually weakened in their political and social position (as were the other non-Greek gentiles in the land). The nationalistic symbols, which had been suppressed since the return to Zion after Cyrus's declaration (538 B.C.E.) or even since the destruction of the First Temple in 587/6 B.C.E., were suddenly brought out into the open. Rome supported the Jews while other powers in the region showed signs of decay. The Jews underwent a national revival, which was expressed in the purification of their Temple in Jerusalem; in the foundation of a Jewish rulership, which by the end of the century had become a kingship; in the conquest of territory in the Holy Land; and in a life in line with their laws, which included the special laws concerning a Jewish sovereign state. All of this occurred within a short period (164–67 B.C.E.).

The Jews, and in some ways the Nabataeans (i.e., Arabs), were the only examples of an indigenous population successfully creating a national state. Their short-lived kingdom, which only came into existence because of the unique international circumstances, was not able to survive when Rome reached the region in 67 B.C.E. This short-lived independent Jewish state sowed the seeds for a stronger nationalistic awareness, which was to come to the fore after 63 B.C.E. But at the same time it led to the catastrophes of the two subsequent centuries, when certain groups of Jews persistently sought to reestablish this independent state. After 63 B.C.E. (the Roman conquest of Jerusalem and Palestine), many Jews did not understand that the Hasmonean state belonged to the past and could only be transient because of the international politics of the time. Once Rome had penetrated the region, the creation of an independent nation-state was no longer possible.

Notes

[1] H. Kohn, *The Idea of Nationalism: A Study in Its Origins and Background* (New York, 1946); idem, *The Age of Nationalism: The First Era of Global History* (New York, 1962); E. Kedourie, *Nationalism* (London, 1960); E. Gellner, *Nations and Nationalism* (Ithaca, N.Y. and London, 1983); see also A. D. Smith, *The Ethnic Revival* (Cambridge, 1981). There is no need to enter into the complicated issue of the concept of nation in antiquity. For a good presentation of the problem concerning Ptolemaic Egypt, see K. Goudriaan, *Ethnicity in Ptolemaic Egypt* (Amsterdam, 1988), pp. 1–13 and passim.

[2] See, for instance, the collection of papers in P. D. A. Garnsey and C. R. Whittaker, *Imperialism in the Ancient World* (Cambridge, 1978), which deals with empires much older than the Roman.

[3] Cf. M. I. Finley, "Utopianism Ancient and Modern," in his *Use and Abuse of History* (London, 1975), pp. 178–192.

[4] This aspect of nationalism was pointed out by the great nineteenth-century scholar E. Renan in his famous lecture "Qu'est-ce qu'une Nation?" (Paris, 1882). In fact, until the very late nineteenth century and the early twentieth, almost no one drew clear distinctions among "nation," "race," and "ethnic."

[5] As for instance R. Bendix did on kingship, without, however, ignoring the historical point of view: *Kings or People: Power and the Mandate to Rule* (Berkeley, 1978).

[6] For the special culture of the Scythians, see *Abriss der Geschichte antiker Randkulturen*, ed. W. D. v. Barloewen (Munich, 1961), pp. 133–138; and R. Rolle, *The World of the Scythians* (Berkeley, Los Angeles, and Oxford, 1989) (she also mentions the Scythians of the Hellenistic and Roman periods). For the special world of the Egyptians in Hellenistic and Roman times, see A. K. Bowman, *Egypt after the Pharaohs, 332 B.C.–A.D. 642* (London, 1986). For the Phoenicians, see J. C. L. Gibson, *Textbook of Syrian Semitic Inscriptions* (Oxford, 1982) vol. 3 (Phoenician Inscriptions), esp. pp. 101–159; and F. Millar, "The Phoenician Cities: A Case Study in Hellenization," *Proceedings of the Cambridge Philological Association* 209 (1983): 55–71. For Iran's cultural background in those days see R. Ghirshman, *Persian Art 249 B.C.–A.D. 651: The Parthian and Sassanian Dynasties* (New York, 1962), esp. pp. 15–28. For Jewish ethnicity, see M. Hengel, *Jews, Greeks, and Barbarians* (Philadelphia, 1980).

[7] Cf. for instance F. Hartog, *The Mirror of Herodotus: The Representation of the Other in the Writing of History* (Berkeley, Los Angeles, and Oxford, 1988); *Hérodote et les peuples non Grecs*, Entretiens sur l'antiquité classique 35 (Geneva, 1988); and cf. the following chapter.

[8] Because of the nature of the evidence, it is not always possible to decide what the motives behind an insurrection are. For instance, there is a debate over the motives of the insurrectionists in Ptolemaic Egypt at certain junctures: see W. Per-

emans, "Les Révolutions égyptiennes sous les Lagides," in *Das ptolemaische Ägypten*, ed. H. Maehler and V. M. Strocka (Berlin, 1976), pp. 39–50; and *The Cambridge Ancient History* (hereafter *CAH*), 2d ed. (Cambridge, 1984–1989), 7.1.157–159 (Turner).

[9] For Hellenism in the East, see in particular C. Preaux, *La Civilization Hellénistique*, 2d ed. (Paris, 1965), and eadem, *Le Monde hellénistique*, 2 vols. (Paris, 1978); A. Kuhrt and S. Sherwin-White, eds., *Hellenism in the East* (Berkeley, Los Angeles, and London, 1987); F. E. Peters, *The Harvest of Hellenism* (London, 1972); C. Schneider, *Kulturgeschichte des Hellenismus*, 2 vols. (Munich, 1967–1969); R. Bichler, *Hellenismus* (Darmstadt, 1983); H. Bengtson, *Die Hellenistische Weltkultur* (Stuttgart, 1988); and M. Hengel, *Judaism and Hellenism*, 2 vols. (London and Philadelphia, 1974). Some useful information with the older bibliography may also be found in P. Green, *Alexander to Actium* (Berkeley, Los Angeles, and Oxford, 1990). For aspects of Hellenism in the Gulf, see D. T. Potts, *The Arabian Gulf in Antiquity* (Oxford, 1990), vol. 2, chaps. 1, 2, and 4.

[10] For the coastal plain of Palestine there are only partial scholarly works, such as E. Schürer, *The History of the Jewish People in the Age of Jesus Christ*, rev. G. Vermes et al. (Edinburgh, 1973–1987), 2.85–183; and Y. Meshorer, *City Coins of Eretz Israel and the Decapolis in the Roman Period* (Jerusalem, 1985). Now see also A. Kasher, *Jews and Hellenistic Cities in Eretz Israel* (Tübingen, 1990). For Hellenistic and Roman Arabia, cf. G. W. Bowersock, *Roman Arabia* (Cambridge, Mass., and London, 1983); and D. F. Graf, "The Nabataeans and the Decapolis," in *The Defence of the Roman and Byzantine East*, ed. P. Freeman and D. Kennedy (Oxford, 1986), 2.785–796. Interestingly, Josephus, in book 1 of his *Antiquities* (retelling Genesis), says (221): "These [the Arab tribes] occupied the whole country extending from the Euphrates to the Red Sea and called it Nabatene; and it is these who conferred their names on the Arabian *nation* and its tribes."

[11] For a useful survey on Alexander the Great see J. R. Hamilton, *Alexander the Great* (London, 1973); also A. B. Bosworth, *Conquest and Empire: The Reign of Alexander the Great* (Cambridge, 1988).

[12] J. G. Droysen, *Geschichte des Hellenismus*, 2d ed. (Basel, 1952), vols. 1–3.

[13] We get this impression not only from the literary evidence, but in particular from the archaeological and numismatic evidence. The same holds true of some regions in Asia Minor, where the evidence points to an isolation of the Greeks in the cities from the natives. From a recently published Greek inscription from Cilicia we learn that a separation existed between Greeks and "barbarians" there: see C. P. Jones and C. Habicht, "A Hellenistic Inscription from Arsinoe in Cilicia," *Phoenix* 43 (1989): 317–346. Paul in the first century C.E. makes a distinction between Greeks and barbarians, in Romans 1:14.

[14] Cf. in particular H. Sternberg, *Mythische Motive und Mythenbildung in den Ägyptischen Tempeln und Papyri de griechisch-römischen Zeit* (Wiesbaden, 1985), and in general the survey of Bowman, *Egypt after the Pharaohs*. We can find at the time also two different legal systems, one Greek and the other Egyptian; see for this

problem N. Lewis, *Greeks in Ptolemaic Egypt* (Oxford, 1986); also Goudriaan, *Ethnicity.*

[15] Kuhrt and Sherwin-White, *Hellenism.* And cf. G. J. P. McEwan, *Priest and Temple in Hellenistic Babylonia* (Wiesbaden, 1981), passim, who shows not only that cuneiform writing continued on a grand scale in Babylonian Uruk and other places, but also that the cult in the various temples continued unhindered under the Seleucids. Cf. chapter 5, below. D. J. Thompson also shows this for Memphis, in *Memphis under the Ptolemies* (Princeton, 1988), pp. 113–114, stressing that "in spite of such marginal integration, however, in major respects the temples remained what they had always been in Egypt—strongly independent, native communities which were also important centers both of economic activity (see chapter 2) and of learning. The sacred books contained in temple libraries formed a repository of religious learning." For the case of the Phoenicians in Palestine in the Persian and early Hellenistic periods, cf. J. Naveh, "Unpublished Phoenician Inscriptions from Palestine," *Israel Exploration Journal* 37 (1987): 25–30, and M. Stern, "Judaism and Hellenism in Palestine in the 3rd and 2nd Centuries B.C.," in *Acculturation and Assimilation: Continuity and Change in the Cultures of Israel and the Nations,* ed. Y. Kaplan and M. Stern (Jerusalem, 1989), pp. 41–60 (Hebrew). For the languages of the indigenous people in the East during the period under survey, see Strabo 11.16. The different peoples of the ancient Near East, though they all spoke dialects of the same language (as for instance Aramaic), nevertheless developed scripts that were distinctive and representative of the various indigenous cultures. Just as the dialects tended to vary so did the scripts, and both reflected the separate cultures of the different groups, expressing in another way their nationalism. For instance, the Nabataeans developed in the Hellenistic period individual traits to the Aramaic script, which eventually became their "national" script (cf. J. Naveh, *Early History of the Alphabet* [Jerusalem and Leiden, 1982], pp. 153–162).

[16] Y. Meshorer, *Ancient Jewish Coinage* (New York, 1982), 1.50–51; C. Rabin, "Hebrew and Aramaic in the First Century," *Compendia rerum iudaicarum ad Novum Testamentum,* ed. S. Safrai et al. (Assen, 1974–1976), 2.1007–1039; and Naveh, *Early History,* pp. 112–124, 162–174. The unique coinage found in different places in the Hellenistic Near East serves as an argument against the thesis of T. R. Martin, *Sovereignty and Coinage in Classical Greece* (Princeton, 1985), who argues in his conclusion that coinage was not associated with claims of sovereignty. There may be some universal traits in Hellenistic coinage, but coins provide perfect evidence for distinguishing one nation from another. Cities and indigenous nations who received permission to mint their own coins in the Hellenistic and Roman periods emphasized their indigenous characteristics (cf. in Palestine the cities in the coastal plain as well as in other places, Meshorer, *City Coins,* and J. Geiger, "Local Patriotism in the Hellenistic Cities of Palestine," in *Greece and Rome in Eretz Israel,* ed. A. Kasher et al. [Jerusalem, 1990], pp. 141–150).

[17] R. MacMullen, *Paganism in the Roman Empire* (New Haven and London, 1981), pp. 1–48. Many local gods were associated with nationalism, such as the Edomite god Cos, the Tyrian Melkarth, and the Egyptian Osiris. Local gods were

associated already before the Hellenistic period with territory, kingship, and many other nationalistic aspects. See in particular D. I. Block, *The Gods of the Nations* (Jackson, Miss., 1988).

[18] The calendar had many political overtones in antiquity. We know of the indigenous calendars of the neo-Babylonians (McEwan, *Priest and Temple*, pp. 159–182), and the Egyptians (A. E. Samuel, *Greek and Roman Chronology: Calendars and Years in Classical Antiquity* [Munich, 1972], pp. 145–151). The change of a calendar signified at times the beginning of a new era (e.g., the Seleucid calendar starting in 311 B.C.E. and the Julian one starting under Julius Caesar in 46 B.C.E.; see in general Samuel, *Greek and Roman Chronology*, pp. 139–145, 155–158). The Jews adopted the Seleucid one, but when the Essenes wanted to dissociate themselves religiously and politically from the mainstream, they changed their calendar. The literature on this issue abounds: see the calendrical importance of the MMT (which is a letter from a leader at Qumran to the Wicked Priest), E. Qimron and J. Strugnell, "An Unpublished Halakhic Letter from Qumran," *The Israel Museum Journal* 4 (1985): 9–12; and the secondary literature on the Jewish calendar: S. Talmon, "The Calendar Reckoning of the Sect from the Judaean Desert," *Scripta Hierosolymitana* 4 (1958): 164-199; J. C. VanderKam, "2 Maccabees 6, 7A and Calendrical Change in Jerusalem," *Journal for the Study of Judaism* 12 (1981): 52–74; P. R. Davies, "Calendrical Change and Qumran Origins: An Assessment of VanderKam's Theory," *Catholic Biblical Quarterly* 45 (1983): 80–89; B. Z. Wacholder, "The Calendar of Sabbath Years During the Second Temple Era: A Response," *Hebrew Union College Annual* 54 (1983): 123–133; and C. Milikowsky, "*Seder ʿOlam* and Jewish Chronography in the Hellenistic and Roman Periods," *Proceedings of the American Academy of Jewish Research* 52 (1985): 115–139.

[19] The opposition against the Hellenistic monarchs was exaggerated by both H. Fuchs (*Der geistige Widerstand gegen Rom in der Antiken Welt* [Berlin, 1938]) and S. K. Eddy (*The King is Dead: Studies in the Near Eastern Resistance to Hellenism, 334–31 B.C.E.* [Lincoln, Neb., 1961]). One of the famous cases of opposition can be found in a document from Egypt called "The Oracle of the Potter," in which a native Egyptian expresses hostility against the Hellenistic rulers of Egypt (see S. M. Burstein, *The Hellenistic Age from the Battle of Ipsos to the Death of Kleopatra VII* [Cambridge, 1985], pp. 136–139); see also J. Johnson, "Is the Demotic Chronicle an Anti-Greek Tract?" in *Grammata Demotika*, ed. H. J. Thissen and K. T. Zauzich (Würzburg, 1984), pp. 107–124. Some sporadic references associated with opposition in three hundred years of Greek rule in the East, however, are not sufficient for portraying an overall picture of opposition to the Hellenistic monarchs.

[20] Cf. in general Preaux, *Le Monde hellénistique;* and now also some aspects in Green, *Alexander to Actium*, pp. 312–335.

[21] It is important to note that the "class" of the *philoi* (friends) around the Ptolemies and the Seleucids remained basically Greek: see C. Habicht, "Die herrschende Gesellschaft in den hellenistischen Monarchien," *Vierteljahrsschrift für Sozial- und Wirtschaftsgeschichte* 45 (1958): 1–16; L. Mooren, "Macht und Nationalität," in *Das ptolemaische Ägypten*, ed. H. Maehler and V. M. Strocka (Ber-

lin, 1976), pp. 51–57; and G. Herman, "The 'Friends' of the Early Hellenistic Rulers: Servants or Officials?" *Talanta* 12–13 (1980–1981): 103–127. Therefore, during the Hellenistic period a broad class existed from which the kings could recruit their high officials.

22 J. R. Hamilton, *Alexander the Great* (London, 1973), passim.

23 Cf. E. Bevan, *A History of Egypt under the Ptolemaic Dynasty* (London, 1927), pp. 90–109; P. M. Fraser, *Ptolemaic Alexandria* (Oxford, 1972), 1.38–54. See also the Greek tribal names found at Neapolis (Shechem) (to be published soon).

24 See Theocritus (Greek poet in Egypt) versus Dius (Greek writer of Phoenicia), and Menander of Ephesus (Greek writer of Phoenicia) versus Hecataeus of Abdera (Egypt; see the next chapter). In art, though scholars at times argue for the existence of a *koine* (common tradition) in Hellenistic art, one can detect many differences in Greek art in several regions of the East. For instance, in Pergamon we discover already in the third century B.C.E. a Pergamene interpretation of Greek art as a result of a new "national" description of Greek mythology after the war with the Galatians: see H.-J. Schalles, *Untersuchungen Zur Kultupolitik der Pergamenischen Herrscher im dritten Jahrhundert vor Christus* (Tübingen, 1985). For Greek art in Commagene see F. K. Doerner, *Der Thron der Götter auf dem Nemrud Dag: Kommagene, das grosse archäologische Abenteuer in der östlischen Turkei* (Lubbe, 1987). Concerning Hellenistic art, I benefited much from my conversations with Hugo Meyer, professor at Princeton University.

25 For a commentary on this passage, see L. F. Hartman and A. A. Di Lella, *Daniel,** ad loc. (Commentaries marked by an asterisk [*] are in the Anchor Bible series; those marked by a dagger [†] are in the Hermeneia series.) For the empires see D. Mendels, "The Five Empires: A Note on a Propagandistic Topos," *American Journal of Philology* 102 (1981): 330–337 (with addendum of H. Tadmor), and recently also J. M. Alonso Núñez, "The Emergence of Universal Historiography from the 4th to the 2nd Centuries B.C.," in *Purposes of History,* ed. H. Verdin et al. (Louvain, 1990), pp. 173–192.

26 Cf. in general J. J. Collins, *The Apocalyptic Imagination: An Introduction to the Jewish Matrix of Christianity* (New York, 1987).

27 For Antigonus see R. A. Billows, *Antigonos the One-Eyed and the Creation of the Hellenistic State* (Berkeley, Los Angeles, and Oxford, 1990).

28 Diodorus Siculus 18.60.4–6. For the importance of the throne in the imagery of kingship see chapter 3 below; L. Y. Rahmani also discusses some interesting aspects of the throne in "Stone Synagogue Chairs: Their Identification, Use and Significance," *Israel Exploration Journal* 40 (1990): 192–214.

29 The whole political-ideological world of the Greeks in the East underwent a change, as is pointed out by W. W. Tarn and G. T. Griffith, *Hellenistic Civilisation,* 3d ed. (London, 1966). For various aspects of this change, see now also Green, *Alexander to Actium.*

30 A newly discovered hoard of Samaritan coins was recently published by Y. Meshorer and S. Qedar (*The Coinage of Samaria in the Fourth Century B.C.E.* [Jerusalem, 1991]), evidence of their strong national awareness in the Persian period. Still other evidence points to this fact: the Edomites showed a strong national awareness during the first century B.C.E., and even in the first century C.E. (a long time after their judaization by John Hyrcanus I). For the political history of Arabs and Edomites, see A. Kasher, *Jews, Idumaeans, and Ancient Arabs* (Tübingen, 1988). For the Phoenicians in Palestine during the Hellenistic period, see B. Isaac, "A Seleucid Inscription from Jamnia-on-the-Sea: Antiochus V Eupator and the Sidonians," *Israel Exploration Journal* 41 (1991): 132–144.

31 There are many good surveys: Schürer, *History*, 1.137–242.

32 In general, for his visit to Jerusalem, see A. Momigliano, "Flavius Josephus and Alexander's Visit to Jerusalem," *Athenaeum* 57 (1979): 442–448; G. Delling, "Alexander der Grosse als Bekenner des Jüdischen Gottesglaubens," *Journal for the Study of Judaism in the Persian, Hellenistic and Roman Period* 12 (1981): 1–51; D. Pacella, "Alessandro e gli ebrei nella Testimonianza dello Ps. Callistene," *Annali della Scuola Normale Superiore di Pisa* 12.4 (1982): 1255–1269; S. J. D. Cohen, "Alexander the Great and Jaddus the High Priest According to Josephus," *Association for Jewish Studies Review* 7–8 (1982–1983): 41–68; and E. J. Bickerman, *The Jews in the Greek Age* (Cambridge, Mass. and London, 1988), pp. 3–7.

33 Cf. Arrian, *Anabasis* 2.16–24, with A. B. Bosworth, *A Historical Commentary on Arrian's History of Alexander* (Oxford, 1980), vol. 1 ad loc.

34 For this transition period see also the Hefzibah inscription, and J. M. Bertrand, "Sur l'Inscription d'Hefzibah," *Zeitschrift für Papyrologie und Epigraphik* 46 (1982): 167–174. For Ptolemaic rule in Palestine there is relatively little evidence. We have the Zenon Papyri (and see R. S. Bagnall, *The Administration of the Ptolemaic Possessions Outside Egypt* [Leiden, 1976], pp. 11–24, 176–251), and some literary evidence that is attributed to the third century B.C.E. (such as some of the Enochic material and Aramaic Daniel; see M. E. Stone, *Scriptures, Sects, and Visions* [Oxford, 1980], esp. chaps. 4–5), as well as the edition of 1–2 Chronicles: S. Japhet, *The Ideology of the Book of Chronicles and Its Place in Biblical Thought* (Frankfurt am Main and Paris, 1989). The stories about the house of the Tobiads found in Josephus's *Antiquities* may go back to the third century B.C.E. See in general M. Stern, "Notes on the Story of Joseph the Tobiad," in his *Studies in Jewish History* (Jerusalem, 1991), pp. 22–34 (Hebrew). For the eventual propagandistic uses of these stories see D. Gera, "On the Credibility of the History of the Sons of Tobiads," in *Greece and Rome in Eretz Israel,* ed. A. Kasher et al. (Jerusalem, 1990), pp. 21–38.

35 On which see my subsequent chapters. For the process of hellenization in Judea for the years 200 B.C.E. to the end of the first century C.E. (e.g., group 3) see M. Hengel, *Judaism and Hellenism;* and idem, *The "Hellenization" of Judaea in the First Century after Christ* (Philadelphia, 1989). Hengel has the most extensive survey on this subject. Still, a decision on the extent and the rigor of hellenization in

Palestine in the different periods under discussion depends on the emergence of further evidence. See also Schürer, *History,* 2.29–80, and O. Kaiser, "Judentum und Hellenismus," *Verkündigung und Forschung* 27 (1982): 68–88; E. Will and C. Orrieux, *Ioudaismos-hellenismos* (Nancy, 1986); and G. Delling, "Die Begegnung zwischen Hellenismus und Judentum," in *Aufstieg und Niedergang der römischen Welt* 2.20.1 (1987): 21–39.

CHAPTER 2

Nationalism and the Concept of History in the Ancient Near East

Because this survey of nationalism depends mainly on the literary sources, it would be helpful to discuss the nature of these sources in a concise manner.

In the literature of the Greek homeland of the third through the first centuries B.C.E., one can notice a historiographical trend that goes back to Thucydides and is mainly preoccupied with rationalistic (or scientific) historical writing (to be called here "type A"). Its main representative is Polybius of Megalopolis, who lived during the years 200 to 120 B.C.E. In the Greek West many historians followed in the footsteps of Polybius, whereas in the Greek Near East, during the third and second centuries B.C.E., rationalistic historiography was not part of the mainstream of historical writing. Although we can find a linear history of "facts" in the first book of Maccabees, written in Hebrew probably during Hyrcanus I's reign, it is still very far from the high standard of the historical writing of Polybius, and is more in line with biblical historiography (such as the First and Second Books of Kings).[1]

In the Near East in this period we find more of a "creative" historiography (to be called here "type B"). It is creative in the sense that it refers back to "canonical" nationalistic histories, which are changed and embellished in accordance with the real circumstances surrounding the Hellenistic writer. For a man like Polybius such a procedure was the worst way a historian could treat his sources. His views on the writing of history are to be found mainly in his twelfth book, where he elaborately lays out his views on causation (*aitia, prophasis, arche*).[2] Polybius denigrates historians who are uncritical of their sources and emphasizes the necessity for a historian to possess the *gnome* and *episteme* (knowledge) of the material to be related. He mentions synchronic (simultaneous events) and diachronic (the linear movement of history) historical accounts. He argues for the writing of the "whole" (*ta katholou*) instead of monographs (*kata meros*). For this reason he himself wrote a "universal" history of the ecumene of his own day. In his opinion the historian should take care to present his reader with a *symploke* (intertwining, combination) after having made the *cheirourgia* (analysis) of his sources. Only after doing so will he be able to handle the *pharmakon* (remedy). In 12.25d–e, he says, "as there are three parts of medicine, first the theory of disease, next dietetics, and thirdly surgery and pharmaceutics. . . . In the same fashion systematic history too consists of three parts, the first being the industrious study of memoirs and other documents and a comparison of their contents, the second, the survey of cities, places, rivers, lakes, and in general all the peculiar features of land and sea, and the distance of one place from another, and the third being the review of political events." Here in a concise form is the analysis of Polybius's working method as a writer of *pragmatike historia*.[3] History has roles to play in the instruction of peoples—a political, a moral, and a military one—so the historian has a responsibility to recount an accurate portrayal of events. If the Greek Near East could have had a Polybius to tell its history from the third century onward, our knowledge of it would have been much greater.

In the Greek Near East during Hellenistic times, we find a continuation of the historiographical line of Herodotus and perhaps Ctesias, instead of the rationalistic one of Ephorus and Polybius. But in contradistinction to Herodotus, we find much more of the linear approach to history in Hellenistic historical accounts. It is beyond the scope of this chapter to go into detail about why a fundamental gap in historiographic method existed between the Greek homeland and the Near East. One should emphasize, however, that various forms of "creative" history (i.e., type B) can also be found in the Greek West and in particular in Rome, especially when we make a distinction between the reproduction of ancient history by historians in antiquity and the history they write of their own times (in fact, the distinction between the work of a Dionysius of Halicarnassus in the first books of the *Roman Antiquities*—mainly type B history—and that of a Tacitus—mainly type A history). Henceforward I will not refer to the latter (the so-called "rationalistic" or "scientific" history, type A) because it was nonexistent in the East in the third and second centuries B.C.E. Nevertheless, it will be useful to state at the outset that every historian is creative in one way or another. Thucydides, Polybius, Josephus, and Tacitus were inventive (particularly in their accounts of speeches), but they still had the real intent of writing a truthful account of the events of their own times. Regardless of their biases, historians for centuries have recognized that much of Polybius's *Histories* was intended to reflect "what really happened," and that his information is corroborated by much external evidence. Thus the extent of any historian's "creativity" should always be examined, that is to say, where on the continuum between type A and type B the narrative can be placed: the intensity of creativity changes dramatically when one goes from Aristotle's *Athenaion Politeia* and Josephus's *Antiquities* books 1–11 (largely type B) to Thucydides' *Peloponnesian War* and Josephus's later books of the *Antiquities* (mostly type A).

Be that as it may, the Hellenistic historians in the Near East created much of their past anew. Unfortunately for the scholar interested in this period, they dealt for the most part with their own ancient histories instead of writing contemporary ones. Even the mythological past was considered to be part of history by some ancient historians, as we can learn from the concept of history inherent in the works of Diodorus Siculus and Dionysius of Halicarnassus. Polybius in *Histories* 9.2 states that he would not touch "genealogical" history (about which see the next paragraph) because he cannot apply his strict historiographical methods to this kind of history; but he no doubt thought that mythology was part of history. Strabo thought differently, stating that "a peculiar thing has happened in the case of the account of the Amazons. For our account of other peoples keeps a distinction between the mythical and the historical elements; for the things that are ancient and false and monstrous are called myths, but history wishes for the truth (*aletheia*), whether ancient or recent, and contains no monstrous element, or else only rarely. But as regards the Amazons, the same stories are told now as in early times, though they are marvellous and beyond belief" (11[3]C504, and cf. C507[2]–508[3]).

It is quite clear that the "creative" historical writing emerging in this period in the Near East (type B) was connected with the creation of new "national" identities in the rising Hellenistic kingdoms.[4] (It should be emphasized that the motifs and issues found in the creative historiography of the Hellenistic era are different from the ones we find in the literature antedating Alexander the Great, or from the ones we can detect in the Hellenistic epos found in the West.) The term "national" identities refers to the great "national" powers, such as Ptolemaic Egypt and the Seleucid Empire on the one hand, and the various nations within these superstructures on the other, such as the Arabs, Libyans, Syrians, or Babylonians, who preserved their own national identities. As I have already said, Judea was in many respects a Hellenistic kingdom like those which surrounded her at that time, but it appeared on the international scene almost two centuries after the neighboring kingdoms were formed. Coming to the Near East in large numbers in the wake of Alexander the Great, the Greeks needed a historical background with which to identify themselves. Yet it was not only the immigrants who needed such a framework, but also the indigenous peoples, some of whom became hellenized and had to search for a new identity. Thus we find more and more intellectuals who, having liberated themselves from the bonds of canonical histories, created their own national history anew. Polybius, who was aware of a similar kind of historical writing in Greece, argues against it, calling it "genealogical history."[5]

Let us now consider some of the views that the Hellenistic writers held concerning their past, taking as an example a man like Hecataeus of Abdera, a Greek who came to Egypt at the end of the fourth century B.C.E. and then wrote his *Aegyptiaca*.[6] Hecataeus, like many other Greek immigrants who came to the Near East, arrived in Egypt with an awareness of having left behind a rich history, which could not necessarily be replaced by the history of his new abode. Like many others, he landed in an unfamiliar territory, knowing neither the language nor the sites nor the indigenous people. Unlike Herodotus he most probably did not come merely as a visitor, but as one of the Greek conquerors, who had come to settle (group 2, as discussed in the last chapter). As is known from analogous instances, when arriving in their new homelands, immigrants immediately look for a new identity (at times also keeping their original one). What could one have expected from a person like Hecataeus? Would he have continued to recount the battles of Marathon and Salamis for his children? Or, instead, would it have had any relevance to his new life (except, of course, for his general intellectual interests) to identify himself with the battle of Kedesh on the Orontes River (the campaign of Rameses II against the Hittites in 1288 B.C.E.)? Would it have been relevant for him to identify himself repeatedly with the Homeric "history" and its magnificent figures? This would surely have become irrelevant in the face of his new circumstances. Thus he became part of group 3 mentioned above. One should, however, emphasize that there was a circle of intellectuals in Alexandria who continued to live in a more or less isolated Greek cultural environment (group 2); they had been encouraged to do so by the first Ptolemies. But even Theocritus, a member of this circle who was not a historian, was not blind to the developments of the time, and he sometimes allowed himself to view the past through his own subjective perception.[7] The same trend of adhering to Greek mythology, but with a special nationalistic approach, can be traced in Pergamene art from the Hellenistic period, and elsewhere.[8]

Hecataeus and his circle were looking for a history that would provide ties to their new homeland. That is why Hecataeus, in contrast to Herodotus, wrote a new "linear" history with which his generation could identify, and thereby find a place again within the linear dynamics of that history. Hecataeus reworked the data that he received from his sources and from his own investigations in Egypt, and blended them with his Greek knowledge. The outcome was a mixture of Egyptian and Greek concepts, which were given a unified, linear, chronological framework. This new history represented the melting pot of Hellenism, but was far from being "real" history. At the same time, Hecataeus (like Manetho) gave the "cyclic" Egyptian historiography a new linear shape.[9] For its greater part, Hecataeus's *Aegyptiaca* is a fabricated history with many sentimental overtones, political and social. Without going into the difficult question of the relationship between Diodorus Siculus 1 (in which we find Hecataeus's *Aegyptiaca*) and Hecataeus, I will offer an example.

Sesostris (who was a mixture of kings of the twelfth dynasty) was depicted as a forerunner of Alexander the Great, but from an Egyptian, Ptolemaic, universalistic point of view. Egyptian history was recreated anew as a concoction of Greek and Egyptian traditions, and the chapters "On kingship" that describe the Egyptian pharaohs were presented in line with Hellenistic documents of that kind (Diodorus Siculus 1.69–72). This example and many others show that Egyptian ancient history was completely changed and given a new shape as a consequence of the new circumstances.

Hecataeus wrote his history from the conqueror's (i.e., Greek) point of view, but we also know of Egyptians who wished to identify themselves with the Greek oppressor and who also created their own history. Manetho, an Egyptian priest of the third century B.C.E., is a typical example: He, or his epitomator, interpreted Egyptian history in accordance with the "alter ego" of the Ptolemaic court, which encouraged the preservation of the indigenous population's culture. Nevertheless, the Ptolemaic perspective of his *Aegyptiaca* is obvious. For instance, by describing in detail the expulsion of the Hyksos from Egypt to Judea (one should remember that they formed a legitimate dynasty in pharaonic Egypt, Fifteenth and Sixteenth Dynasties), Manetho most probably attempted to justify Ptolemaic Egypt's claims to Palestine.[10] In Hecataeus the Jews are sent as an Egyptian colony to Palestine (Diodorus Siculus 1.28), an *apoikia*. Both versions are obvious Hellenistic creations.

Manetho also declared himself opposed to his Jewish neighbors, who had at that time started to use the Septuagint version of the Pentateuch. The story of the Exodus no doubt offended Manetho's circle, and he retaliated by telling fabricated stories—partly using an Egyptian literary formula—about the contamination of the Jews and their shameful expulsion from Egypt into Palestine.[11] Thus both Hecataeus (a Greek) and Manetho (an Egyptian) presented a strong Egyptian patriotism in their "creative" histories written in Greek.

Let us now consider some other examples. Recently A. Kuhrt has argued correctly that Berossus's *Babyloniaca* is historically incorrect in many of its details. Berossus probably created these incorrect details in order to justify Seleucid activities.[12] For instance, Berossus presented Nabopolassar and his son Nebuchadnezzar II "as wielding control over Phoenicia, Coele-Syria, and Egypt itself (F8)—the last being historically quite incorrect. It seems as though the activities of these two famous rulers may have been expanded to function as a counterbalance to Sesostris III in Hecataeus' history."[13] It should be added that Sesostris III's conquests of the ecumene were praised by historians in Ptolemaic Egypt in order to provide a precedent for universalistic visions circulating in the court at the time.[14] The Cyrenean (i.e., Libyan) intellectuals may also have retrojected their views of universal rule in the ecumene onto Myrina, the heroic queen of the Amazons. She, according to Dionysius Scytobrachion, launched her world conquests from Libya, her "national" base, and,

> passing over into Egypt she struck a treaty of friendship with Horus, the son of Isis, who was king of Egypt at that time, and then, after making war to the end upon the Arabians and slaying many of them, she subdued Syria; but when the Cilicians came out with presents to meet her and agreed to obey her commands, she left those free who yielded to her . . . she also conquered in war the races in the region of the Taurus, peoples of outstanding courage, and descended through Greater Phrygia to the sea; then she won over the land lying along the coast and fixed the bounds of her campaign at the Caicus River . . . she seized also some of the islands, and Lesbos in particular.

From there she continued to other islands as well, but was later defeated by Mopsus of Thrace.[15]

Nationalistic impulses of this kind are also behind compositions like the *Indica* of Megasthenes, the *Parthica* of Apollodorus,[16] and the Phoenician histories of Laetus and Dius to be mentioned later. One can find them also in the Roman Near East (in compositions like Philo Byblos's *Phoenician History* and Arrian's *Indica*). In spite of the fact that the local epos in Greece itself during the Hellenistic period (*Messeniaca* [Rhianus], *Thessaliaca*, and *Aetoliaca*) had "nationalistic" aspects (as K. J. F. Ziegler showed many years ago), the creative sort of history was different in the East as a result of the changing sociocultural and religious situation there after Alexander the Great.[17]

At the same time Jewish intellectuals, both in the Diaspora and in Palestine, had begun to take part in the emerging polemical trend concerning the antiquity and historicity of nations. In the Diaspora, Jewish intellectuals differed among themselves in the degree of emphasis they put on Hellenism. On the one hand we find a writer like Ezekiel the Tragedian, who adhered to Judaism and at the same time showed that he was not unaware of his non-Jewish environment.[18] On the other we find intellectuals like Artapanus who were typical Hellenists (they reveal an amalgamation of Egyptian, Greek, and Jewish cultures) but adhered wholeheartedly to monotheism.[19] This observation is important for my case: it really does not matter whether Jewish compositions show a strong Hellenistic influence. Independently, they followed the same pattern of creating their history anew. If we can trust the preserved fragments of the Jewish Hellenistic writers at all—and this question remains problematic[20]— we can assume that their fabricated histories were shaped in ways that would help them identify themselves with their homeland, Egypt. We should remember that both Ezekiel and Artapanus were first of all Jews, and only secondarily Egyptians (as well as Hellenists). Thus they refer back to a period of Israel's history that is connected to Egypt, and, as with Hecataeus and the intellectuals of his group, the result is an amalgamation of Egyptian, Greek, and Jewish histories. Egypt was their new physical homeland; for this reason there is in Artapanus's composition an identification of Moses (and Joseph) with the mythical Egyptian Sesostris, who was a popular figure in Hellenistic Egypt. Moreover, some of the Jewish writers in the Diaspora in the third and second centuries B.C.E. ignored the Land of Israel and its history in their original writings; others described it in a utopian manner (in line with the euhemeristic literature), as did for instance Aristeas. The Jews of Egypt adhered to a new historical perspective in which the heroes of the past took on new meanings. They were mainly interested in figures like Moses, who never entered Palestine, and Joseph, who was the underdog in Palestine and became a prominent figure in their new land, Egypt.[21] In doing so, however, they drastically changed the biblical portrayals of these figures.

A creative approach to history can be traced in the newly emerging Jewish state of the Hellenistic period. Many of the Jewish writings of the second century B.C.E. (and earlier, as for instance the Books of Chronicles) should be viewed as reinterpretations of Israel's canonical history for pragmatic purposes.[22] The Jewish writings from Palestine constitute part of a *Zeitgeist* in the use and reshaping of the past to address present concerns. Although it is not always apparent, Jewish literature abounds in polemical material aimed at the outside world. Jewish literature of the Hasmonean period that retells the past reveals many national, territorial, cultural, and religious concerns that were current all over the Hellenistic world.[23] Taking, for instance, a historian like Eupolemus the son of John, who was probably the ambassador of Judas Maccabeus to Rome in 160 B.C.E., we can detect in his book *The Kings of Judah* (written in Greek) the same type of historical interpretation that we find in Hecataeus of Abdera's *Aegyptiaca,* Berossus's *Babyloniaca,* the Hellenist behind Philo Byblos's *Phoenician History,* and Dionysius Scytobrachion's *Fabulae Libyacae.*[24] Dionysius Scytobrachion, for example, invented a great quantity of data in order to enhance Libya's "national" stature. For instance, he transferred the origins of gods to Libya in order "to connect Dionysus as firmly with Ammon as Alexander had been."[25] As mentioned before, Scytobrachion made Libya a universal empire as a result of the conquests of the Amazons, who were "indigenous" citizens of Libya. The queen of Libya, Myrina, formed an alliance with Egypt in the mythological past. This detail should be read against the background of the complex relations between Egypt and Cyrene during the Hellenistic period. Even if these stories were not invented during the Hellenistic period, they no doubt became popular at that time as a result of the changing circumstances. But let us now return to Eupolemus.

Eupolemus, it should be emphasized, was not faced with the problem that confronted Hecataeus a century earlier. Eupolemus was not an immigrant; he was living in his own land. Nevertheless, he had very similar problems in terms of his identity. He lived during an exciting period of Jewish history, when a new state was on the horizon. Eupolemus and his circle had to define anew their national loyalties, the borders of their new sovereign territory, the character of rulership, and their relations with the foreigners in the Land and outside it. Eupolemus referred back to his canonical history—in the same manner that Manetho and Berossus turned to theirs—to find the answers for current, burning issues; but this canonical history was no longer relevant. Eupolemus therefore changed the biblical tradition to suit the new circumstances. For instance, Eupolemus elaborated on the building of the Solomonic Temple in a very original way, with the purpose of showing it to be more important than the competing temple of Onias IV in Leontopolis in Egypt, which was already built at the time of his writing. Eupolemus wished to show that the Solomonic Temple was authorized by an older pharaoh than the one who granted permission to build the temple of Onias (Ptolemy VI). Therefore he invented an uncanonical letter (from Vaphres the king of Egypt), which resembled the one Ptolemy VI had sent to Onias IV granting him permission to build the temple at Leontopolis. It is also likely that Eupolemus was polemicizing against the Hellenistic non-Jewish writers who showed a strong Phoenician bias in their interpretation of the relationship of Hiram and Solomon, such as Dius, Menander of Ephesus, and Laetus.[26]

I believe that one can interpret the Book of Jubilees along similar lines. Contrary to the opinion of most scholars regarding the date of composition of Jubilees (the beginning of the Maccabean revolt), I suggest that it was composed about 125 B.C.E. when Hyrcanus I conquered Edom and judaized its inhabitants.[27] For the present purpose the exact date does not really matter. The book was written by an indigenous Jew, who rewrote Genesis through Exodus 12 (the canon was recognized as history among the Jews, much the way that the Egyptian king-lists were in Egypt, and the mythological past among some Greek historians). But the author embellished and changed canonical history in accordance with the rising nationalism of his own day. Even if one does not always get an answer, the historian should ask: Cui bono? Why did the author of Jubilees change this part rather than another one? (The same question should be asked when reading Hecataeus or Manetho.)

The answer has to do with the picture of the new Jewish state that emerges in the Book of Jubilees. For example, the Book of Jubilees is preoccupied with the issue of dual rulership. This issue had become a point of contention by the end of John Hyrcanus I's reign (who was, like his predecessors, both secular ruler and high priest). The author of Jubilees had a very clear opinion on this problem, namely, that there should be a separation between secular and religious authority. He therefore created new historical roles for both Levi and Judah, granting Judah the secular authority and Levi the religious one. In doing so, he drastically changed their original roles as found in the Book of Genesis, just as Hecataeus changed the role of Menas (Diodorus Siculus 1.45) and Manetho, the role of

Heracles, whom he identifies as a king of the Twenty-third Dynasty (probably because he had a special status among the Ptolemies).[28] These are all examples of the transformation of the biblical and mythological characters.

Another exciting example in Jubilees is the embellishment of the Esau-Jacob relationship. The extensive elaborations on this theme show that there was concern about the relations between these two nations. This is a good example of the dichotomy between so-called rationalistic historiography and creative historiography. Many years after Edom was conquered, Josephus says in a short, dry sentence that "Hyrcanus also captured the Idumaean cities of Adora and Marisa and, after subduing all the Idumaeans, permitted them to remain in their country as long as they had themselves circumcised and were willing to observe the laws of the Jews" (*Antiquities* 13.254–258).[29] The author of Jubilees felt himself free to reveal the sentiments that were hidden behind such a neutral account as the one quoted from Josephus. In a masterful way he showed that Edom was a brother of Israel, and that despite the enmity of years it remained a brother. Many ideas and emotions concerning the national clash with the Edomites (and Arabs) of his own time were transferred by the author of Jubilees into the past, thereby changing the canonical history completely.

In conclusion, there are three main points to bear in mind when examining the historical accounts. First, to judge from the available evidence, "creative" history was the mainstream of historiography in the Hellenistic Near East during the third and second centuries B.C.E. Second, during that time the past was constantly pressed into the service of the present and reinterpreted for a great variety of reasons in order to justify present nationalistic activities. And finally, many of the Jewish compositions of the third and second centuries B.C.E. that are concerned with the past should be reexamined against the background of contemporary historical nationalistic writing in the Hellenistic Near East. The Jewish writers could not resist the generic influence of so many writers who were manipulating the past, using it to serve their own immediate needs.

When we enter the first century B.C.E. and the first century C.E. the picture changes somewhat, but not dramatically. In fact, even the sparse historical writing of contemporary events (e.g., 1 and 2 Maccabees) that we find from the first period (200–63 B.C.E.) cannot be found from the second (63 B.C.E.–70 C.E.). There has survived no contemporary history of the Jewish nation written by a Jewish historian from the time 2 Maccabees was written until Josephus started his *Jewish War* (written after the Great War). This dearth is not accidental: the religious Jews, who in the past had been responsible for writing Israel's history, probably thought at the time that there was nothing worth recording from their point of view during the years 63 B.C.E.–70 C.E. Whatever the reason might be, it is remarkable that there are no histories available for this period like those of 1–2 Kings, 1–2 Chronicles, and 1–2 Maccabees, because in Greece and Rome during this time the great histories of Poseidonius, Dionysius of Halicarnassus, and Diodorus Siculus appeared. The only one in Palestine who tried to write a universal history was none other than the non-Jew Nicolaus of Damascus, who was Herod the Great's "friend" (*philos*). The work itself is lost, but some of it is preserved in Josephus's works, for he used it extensively.[30]

But the Jews apparently continued to create their biblical history anew (type B), as they had done during the first period, and produced as well many summaries of Israel's history. The "epitome" (summary) of Israel's history was a familiar genre at the time; thus we can find such summaries in the New Testament as well as in Jewish compositions (the Testament of Moses, Josephus, and 2 Baruch as well as 4 Ezra).[31] These epitomes are reminiscent of summaries found in the Hebrew Bible, though the genre of historical summaries can also be found in non-Jewish literature of the period in the West.[32] There is apparently no influence of the latter on the Jewish summaries found in Palestinian and Diaspora literature; they usually imitate Old Testament summaries of the kind.

Only after 70 C.E. do we find again a comprehensive history of Israel written by a Jew, Josephus. But even after 70 his work was unique: no other history was created by Jews between 70 and 135 C.E. In the seventies Josephus wrote his *Jewish War*, in a Polybian style (type A), and in the nineties he wrote in Rome his comprehensive history of the Jewish people from the Creation to his own time, the *Antiquities* (a combination of types A and B).[33] The latter work, written in imitation of Dionysius of Halicarnassus's nationalistic

Roman Antiquities, may be divided into two parts, books 1–11 and books 12–20. In the first part, Josephus uses the Bible (Septuagint version of the Old Testament as well as the Hebrew one) and additional external sources. Although he mentions several times that his goal is to relate the "truth," he nevertheless embellishes, but not in an extreme manner, as the creative historians of the biblical past (type B) had done during the Hellenistic period. The extent of his creativity in certain cases is a result of his biases, his aims, and the nature of his sources. For instance, he omits details that are offensive to his non-Jewish readers, such as the affair of the Golden Calf. Polemics of a nationalistic nature are very strong in Josephus's interpretations of biblical history.

Books 12–20 present an account of the more recent history, and much of it contains the history of Josephus's own days (until the sixties of the first century c.e.). In this part he tries to become much more of a Polybius (type A), drawing heavily on the universal history of Nicolaus of Damascus (though he sometimes criticizes him heavily, e.g., *Antiquities* 16.183–187), as well as on other sources. His polemical views also come to the fore in his *Contra Apionem* and his autobiography, the *Vita.* Be that as it may, Josephus has one most important feature in common with the literature mentioned above that is of interest to us here: he wrote a nationalistic history, that is to say, a history of the Jewish people. It is more comprehensive than any of the Jewish histories already mentioned and equates the Jews with all other important nations of the era, such as the Greeks and Romans. Unfortunately, however, Josephus does not continue his history far beyond 70 c.e., and for the years 70 c.e. through Bar Kokhba's revolt (132–135 c.e.), there exists no history of the Jewish people. It is perhaps not accidental that all sources that include historical or quasi-historical data which were written after 70 c.e. always refer to the history of pre-70 c.e. Judaism. The same is true of the narrative parts of the New Testament, which limit their accounts to the period before 70 c.e.

Against this background, the attitude of the New Testament to Israel's nationalistic history takes on a new dimension. It is impossible to discuss this issue elaborately in this introductory chapter, but some points of clarification should be made.

The narrative portions of the New Testament vary greatly. We have the three synoptic Gospels, John, and Acts, each with its own tendencies and special style. Still, each of them tells a story of Jesus and his disciples and successors. Whether this "history" (or rather "histories") is creative (type B), rationalistic (type A), or both is much discussed among scholars. What can be said is that the different authors of the narrative parts of the New Testament had no intention of either writing or rewriting the history of the Jewish nation in the first century C.E.—and in this regard they were in line with what happened in Judaism during the second period (63 B.C.E.– 70 C.E.)—or during any other time. The authors of the Gospels believed that they were reporting a true story, and Luke even says so very clearly in his introduction: "to write an orderly account for you, most excellent Theophilus, that you may know the truth concerning the things of which you have been informed" (1:2–3). In making this statement he shows his awareness of the convention of Hellenistic writers, namely, to say that they relate the truth (introduction to the Letter of Aristeas; also Josephus in the early sections of his *Antiquities,* who claims repeatedly that he is going to relate the truth, e.g., 8.56). In terms of historiography, most New Testament scholars would agree that various techniques found in Hellenistic historiography have influenced the writings of Luke and the other Gospels.[34] At the same time, biblical techniques were definitely used by the authors of the Gospels and Luke-Acts. I will briefly bring forward some points concerning these techniques, which have a direct bearing on the issue of historiography and nationalism.

A.   The three synoptic Gospels as well as John and Acts have much in common with biographies of the time (Nepos, Plutarch, Suetonius). Nevertheless, one cannot ignore the fact that the Hebrew Bible and related literature contain biographical elements as well: for example, "biographies" of the Judges, and the books of Esther, Judith, and Susanna.[35]

B.   The second part of Acts (chapter 13 onward) is reminiscent of the memoirs literature of the Hellenistic era (Aratus and the *hypomnemata*).[36] The Hebrew Bible contains examples of this genre as well (Ezra and Nehemiah).

C.   Both in the biblical tradition and in Hellenistic historiography, many speeches are freely invented, but are intertwined in the narrative as if they were authentic.[37]

D.   Genealogies for purposes of justification are found both in the Hebrew Bible and in Hellenistic literature.[38]

E.   A synoptic handling of historical material can be found both in the Bible (the Chronicler as a parallel to 1 and 2 Kings) and in Josephus (*Jewish War* books 1–2 as a parallel to part of the *Antiquities*). Polybius analyzes this concept in his twelfth book.

F.   An independent interpretation of history by a group or a school was a well-known phenomenon in Israel during the Hellenistic period; for instance the Ezra, Baruch, and Enoch "schools." This may be compared to the different "schools" of Mark, Matthew, Luke, and John.[39]

G.   The transfiguration of heroes of the past (i.e., that they receive a different role than they have in canonical writings) was common in Hellenistic literature and in the Hebrew Bible (and its related literature).

Therefore, in the narrative parts of the New Testament literary elements from both biblical and Greek Hellenistic historiography of both type A and type B can be discerned. It is hardly possible to distinguish between the Greek literary devices and the biblical ones in the narrative parts of the New Testament. In spite of the fact that the narrative parts of the New Testament have literary elements in common with some of the nationalistic histories discussed above, they nevertheless differ significantly in terms of content.

All four Gospels show no interest in the rewriting of Israel's history or any other history, as was seen in Hecataeus of Abdera, Eupolemus, Jubilees, and Josephus. They are not concerned with the question of a new reshaped national identity in its *political* form. They also show no interest in defining themselves as a new nation in contrast to other nations in the region (as Jubilees and Josephus did). Although the biblical figures at times receive new roles, it is quite surprising that the Gospels take Jewish canonical history as given.[40] In the few instances that indicate an interest in Jewish history as a linear phenomenon, it appears outside the Gospels, and in the form of a summary (epitome), a genre that, as we have already discovered, was very common in Jewish literature (cf. Acts 7, 13; Romans 9–11 with Josephus in many places, and the Testament of Moses). In these summaries the various authors are extremely traditional in their outlook and try to present a historical continuity between Judaism and Christianity.[41] They leave out data and describe Jewish history as it fits their own purposes. But they keep very strictly to the biblical framework, and neither embellish nor invent in the manner of the creative historians. We shall see later what implications this approach has for our theme.

Notes

[1] Biblical historiography shares many elements with type B, discussed in the following. For 1 Maccabees, see M. Stern, "Maccabim," *Encyclopaedia Biblica* (1968), 5.287–292 (Hebrew); J. A. Goldstein, *I Maccabees.**

[2] For Polybius see F. W. Walbank, *Polybius* (Berkeley, Los Angeles, and London, 1972); and K. S. Sacks, *Polybius on the Writing of History* (Berkeley, Los Angeles, and London, 1981).

[3] Cf. F. W. Walbank, *A Historical Commentary on Polybius* (Oxford, 1967), vol. 2 ad loc. for Polybius's passage. See also G. Schepens, "Polemic and Methodology in Polybius' Book XII," in *Purposes of History,* ed. H. Verdin et al. (Louvain, 1990), pp. 39–61. In general on issues of ancient historiography see A. Momigliano, *Essays in Ancient and Modern Historiography* (Middletown, Conn., 1977); E. Gabba, "True History and False History in Classical Antiquity," *Journal of Roman Studies* 71 (1981): 50–62; and C. W. Fornara, *The Nature of History in Ancient Greece and Rome* (Berkeley, Los Angeles, and London, 1983).

[4] For the formation of the Hellenistic kingdoms, see E. Will, *Histoire politique du monde hellénistique (323–30 av JC)*, 2d ed. (Nancy, 1979), 1.19–131.

[5] Polybius, *Histories* 9.1–2, and Walbank, *Historical Commentary,* ad loc.

[6] In general for Hecataeus of Abdera, see P. M. Fraser, *Ptolemaic Alexandria* (Oxford, 1972), 1.496–505; A. Burton, *Diodorus Siculus Book I: A Commentary* (Leiden, 1972).

[7] For instance, Theocritus, *Idyll* 17; cf. A. S. F. Gow, *Theocritus,* 2d ed. (Cambridge, 1952), 2.325–347; and F. T. Griffith, *Theocritus at Court* (Leiden, 1979).

[8] K. P. Staehler, *Das unklassische im Telephosfries* (Münster, 1966), esp. pp. 76–210, and H.-J. Schalles, *Untersuchungen zur Kulturpolitik der Pergamenischen Herrscher im dritten Jahrhundert vor Christus* (Tübingen, 1985). For Hellenistic art in general, see M. Robertson, *A History of Greek Art* (Cambridge, 1975), 1.504–590; Cornelius Vermeule, *Greek Art: Socrates to Sulla* (Boston, 1980), 2.55–112 (for the very wide public).

[9] For the Egyptian cyclical concept of history see W. K. Simpson, *The Ancient Near East: A History* (New York, Chicago, San Francisco, and Atlanta, 1971), pp. 195–196.

[10] For Manetho's approach, see D. Mendels, "The Polemical Character of Manetho's *Aegyptiaca*," in *Purposes of History,* ed. H. Verdin et al. (Louvain, 1990), pp. 92–110.

[11] For text and commentary, see M. Stern, *Greek and Latin Authors on Jews and Judaism* (Jerusalem, 1974–1984), 1.62–86.

[12] Cf. A. Kuhrt and S. Sherwin-White, eds., *Hellenism in the East* (Berkeley, Los Angeles, and London, 1987), pp. 32–56.

[13] Ibid., p. 56.

[14] Mendels, "Polemical Character."

[15] Diodorus Siculus 3.55.4–11. For Dionysius Scytobrachion's "Libyan Stories" see J. S. Rusten, *Dionysius Scytobrachion* (Cologne, 1980), pp. 102–112.

[16] In general see J. Wolski, "Untersuchungen zur frühen parthischen Geschichte," *Klio* 58 (1976): 439–457.

[17] For the local epos in the Hellenistic era, see K. J. F. Ziegler, *Das hellenistische Epos; ein vergessenes Kapitel griechischer Dichtung*, 2d ed. (Leipzig, 1966).

[18] Cf. H. Jacobson, *The Exagoge of Ezekiel* (Cambridge, 1983); also R. G. Robertson, "Ezekiel the Tragedian," in *The Old Testament Pseudepigrapha*, ed. J. H. Charlesworth (New York, 1983–1985), 2.803–819.

[19] For Artapanus, see H. W. Attridge, "Artapanus," in *Jewish Writings of the Second Temple Period*, ed. M. Stone (Assen and Philadelphia, 1984), pp. 166–168. See also E. Schürer, *The History of the Jewish People in the Age of Jesus Christ*, rev. G. Vermes et al. (Edinburgh, 1973–1987), 3.1.521–525.

[20] Cf. Schürer, *History*, 3.1.505–513.

[21] Cf. D. Mendels, *The Land of Israel as a Political Concept in Hasmonean Literature* (Tübingen, 1987), pp. 125–129.

[22] For the Books of Chronicles, see S. Japhet, *The Ideology of the Book of Chronicles and Its Place in Biblical Thought* (Frankfurt am Main and Paris, 1989).

[23] Cf. Mendels, *The Land*.

[24] For the *Aegyptiaca*, see note 6 above; for the *Babyloniaca* see P. Schnabel, *Berossos und die babylonisch-hellenistische Literatur* (Leipzig, 1923). For a general survey of this "genre" of historical writing see Fornara, *Nature of History*, pp. 12–16; and K. Meister, *Die griechische Geschichtsschreibung* (Stuttgart and Cologne, 1990), pp. 137–142.

[25] Rusten, *Dionysius Scytobrachion*, p. 110.

[26] Cf. Mendels, *The Land*, pp. 29–46, 131–143. Even if some traditions that appear in the apocrypha and pseudepigrapha are from the time antedating Alexander the Great, they were reshaped in the Hellenistic period.

[27] Cf. ibid., pp. 57–88.

[28] Mendels, "Polemical Character."

[29] For the historical circumstances, see Schürer, *History*, 1.200–215.

[30] B. Z. Wacholder, *Nicolaus of Damascus* (Berkeley, 1962); and M. Stern, "Nicolaus of Damascus as a Source of Jewish History in the Herodian and Hasmonean Age," in *Studies in Bible and Jewish History Dedicated to the Memory of*

J. Liver (Jerusalem, 1971), pp. 375ff. (Hebrew) (in M. Stern, *Studies in Jewish History* [Jerusalem, 1991], pp. 445–464 [Hebrew]).

[31] See for these summaries G. Reese, "Die Geschichte Israels in der Auffassung des frühen Judentums . . . ," diss., Heidelberg, 1967.

[32] For instance Tacitus, *Annals* 1.1–4, 3.26–28.

[33] For Josephus's *Antiquities* in general see H. W. Attridge, *The Interpretations of Biblical History in the Antiquitates Judaicae of Flavius Josephus* (Missoula, Mont., 1976); P. Villalba i Varneda, *The Historical Method of Flavius Josephus* (Leiden, 1986).

[34] See an excellent survey, with the older literature, in D. E. Aune, *The New Testament in Its Literary Environment* (Philadelphia, 1987); and *Greco-Roman Literature and the New Testament,* ed. D. E. Aune (Atlanta, 1988). For the claim made by classical authors that they write the truth see now T. J. Luce, "Ancient Views on the Causes of Bias in Historical Writing," *Classical Philology* 84.1 (1989): 16–31.

[35] For the Gospels as Greco-Roman/biblical biography, see Aune, *New Testament,* pp. 27–76 (with bibliography).

[36] K. Meister, "Autobiographische Literatur und Memoiren (Hypomnemata) (F Gr Hist 227–238)," in *Purposes of History,* ed. H. Verdin et al. (Louvain, 1990), pp. 83–89. See also Aune on the "we" passages, *New Testament,* pp. 122–124.

[37] For speeches in Hellenistic historiography, see Fornara, *Nature of History,* pp. 142–168. See also Aune, *New Testament,* pp. 124–128. For speeches in the Hebrew Bible, see M. Weinfeld, *From Joshua to Josiah* (Jerusalem, forthcoming), chaps. 12–13 (Hebrew).

[38] For genealogies in Greek historiography see Fornara, *Nature of History,* pp. 4–12; Aune, *New Testament,* pp. 84–85, 121–122; and in the Hebrew Bible, cf. J. Liver, "Yaḥas," *Encyclopaedia Biblica* (1965), 3.663–671.

[39] Unpublished public lecture by J. Strugnell in the École Biblique (Jerusalem, 1986).

[40] There are no doubt theological reasons for this acceptance, which should be viewed together with the issue of the canonical exegesis. The latter aspect is beyond the scope of this book; see in particular D. M. Smith, "The Use of the Old Testament in the New," in *The Use of the Old Testament in the New and Other Essays: Studies in Honor of W. F. Stinespring* (Durham, N.C., 1972), pp. 3–65; B. S. Childs, *The New Testament as Canon: An Introduction* (Philadelphia, 1984), and the reaction of D. M. Smith, "John, the Synoptics, and the Canonical Approach to Exegesis," in *Festschrift F. E. Ellis* (Grand Rapids, Mich., 1987), pp. 166–180.

[41] Namely, do not invent new data. One might have expected Paul, when he left Palestine and went into the ecumene, to have tried to connect Palestinian history

with that of the world. He does not do that at all (Romans 9–11), but on the contrary keeps a very traditional view of Israel's history. Both the Jesus group and Peter, as well as Paul, viewed themselves as being part of Jewish history, with which they were familiar from the Hebrew Bible. Only much later do Africanus and Christian chronographers attempt to combine the history of the Jews with world history.

CHAPTER 3

Jewish Kingship in the Hasmonean Period

The better to understand Hasmonean kingship and its expression in the literature of the Hasmonean period, it is necessary to examine some aspects of kingship in the non-Jewish Hellenistic environment of the time.

When Alexander the Great arrived in the East, he traveled with his Macedonian *philoi* (friends), some of whom became kings of the monarchies of the ancient Near East in the Hellenistic period. In Egypt he declared himself the son of Amon, if we may believe the stories concerning his visit to Siwa. He also tried to associate his kingship with that of the pharaohs. When later he declared himself "King of Asia," married Persian princesses, and asked his soldiers and "friends" to perform *proskynesis* (obeisance), his Macedonian kingship had become mingled with Persian (i.e., eastern) aspects.[1] Alexander thus created the concept of Hellenistic kingship. His successors adhered to this concept and made it the basis of their dynasties.[2] On the one hand they were and remained Greek kings; on the other they became eastern kings as well (Egyptian, Babylonian, Persian, etc.).

For example, the Ptolemaic kings seem to have been "schizophrenic," or, to put it more mildly, dualistic kings. Although they were the kings of Egypt, a great part of their lives was dominated by their position as Greek kings for the Greek strata of their people. They thus spoke Greek, dressed as Macedonians, and in many instances defined themselves as Macedonians. At court they employed

Greek *philoi* (advisers), and even the royal library was largely Greek, as were the scholars they brought into this library (called the *Mouseion*).[3] Ptolemaic foreign policy in particular turned toward the Greek world during the first two centuries of its existence (after Ptolemy IV's reign Egypt was forced to adopt a more passive foreign policy in the Greek world).[4] Their coins bear their images, wearing Greek mythological garb.[5] The Greek characteristics of the Ptolemaic kings persisted with varying degrees of emphasis until their final fall as a consequence of the Roman conquest of Egypt in 30 B.C.E. Likewise, the Seleucid kings had eastern characteristics alongside their Greek ones. In the temples of Babylon, texts were found that mention the rites of kingship as well as the royal cult ("ritual of Seleucus and his offspring"), which reflect the dualism mentioned above. In other words, in spite of his Greek traits, the king was viewed by the natives who adhered to their Babylonian culture as one of their legitimate gods.[6] The evidence, however, is not as abundant here as it is in the Ptolemaic case.

The alter ego of the Hellenistic king—namely, his eastern side—can again be illustrated by examining the Ptolemies. The Ptolemaic kings made great efforts to pose as pharaohs before the native Egyptian population.[7] In fact, they were motivated by the belief that they were the natural successors of the pharaonic dynasties. They felt that they ought to receive the approval of the natives who continued to adhere to the traditional religion, culture, and language as if nothing had changed in Egypt after Alexander's conquest. It is therefore not surprising that the Ptolemaic kings were depicted as Horus and Amon in some reliefs just as the pharaohs before them were, and that they were depicted as Osiris after their deaths. Even so, this identification with indigenous tradition did not deter them from appearing as Dionysus and Heracles on royal portraits, and as Dionysus (who was equated with Osiris) in their yearly procession (*pompe*).[8] The Seleucids, as well as some local rulers, also adopted this dualistic way of ruling their realms.

On the one hand, the dualism of Greek and eastern features in Hellenistic kingship underlined the sociocultural and religious tensions that existed between the natives and the Greek classes. On the other, it was a unifying symbol because one person was king of the whole state. It was the Hellenists (group 3, as described above), spread out all over the ancient Near East, who could most easily cope with this kind of kingship, which was after all a perfect expression of the Hellenism they were striving for.

The different attitudes to kingship in the Hellenistic Near East influenced the concept of nationalism. There is some limited evidence from Egypt that when the indigenous populations did not identify with their king as a national symbol they followed Seth (brother and mortal enemy of Osiris), the villain god in the eyes of the priests of Memphis at the time.[9] It will be seen later on that a great deal of the unrest among the native Jews during Herod's reign was much like the unrest in other areas of the Near East, when at certain junctures they refused to recognize their ruler as their "national" king.

The throne, the diadem, the purple color, and the scepter were the kings' main insignia, and they were always associated with the gods by the native population, something that was inherited in the main from eastern kingship.[10] Royal portraits from all over the Hellenistic world show that this practice was also applied to the "Greek side" of kings, in that they usually associated themselves with Greek gods and heroes of the past. A dynastic concept was well established in Hellenistic royal houses, and a great deal of intermarriage can be found among the different Diadochi.[11] In this respect the Hellenistic era resembles the era of absolutism in Europe. There was fierce territorial competition among the dynasties of the Hellenistic world, in which the sign of being a powerful king was to rule over as much territory as possible. As will be shown later, the legitimacy of a territory's boundaries was often associated with the concept of god and kingship. There always existed the possibility of reverting to Alexander's visions of a world empire or to more traditional local views about borders and boundaries.[12] But kings did not always need a justifiable reason, for they often used the right of might.

Most of the Hellenistic Diadochi had more than one wife, some of whom had great influence in the realm (e.g., Arsinoe II during the time of Ptolemy II). Some were killed during court intrigues. Hellenistic kings were dependent on mercenaries, and this practice even depleted the population in Greece during the second century B.C.E.[13] The kings at times recruited natives for their army (a famous example is Ptolemy IV at the battle of Raphia, and Antiochus III in Magnesia is another).[14] The kings themselves were the chief military commanders in the most important wars, whereas at other times they would send their generals. Usually a Hellenistic king had several palaces scattered over his kingdom, but his most important ("official") one would be located in the capital, which was also the political center of the kingdom (such as Alexandria for the Ptolemies and Seleucia on the Tigris for the Seleucids). He would usually also have a dwelling place in the traditional religious centers, mainly for the indigenous population, who continued the traditional cults in their traditional cities (such as Memphis for the Ptolemies and Babylonia for the Seleucids).

The Hellenistic kings minted their own coins, which bear, other than their images, Greek inscriptions as well as Greek deities such as Dionysus and Heracles. Their family ties with remote mythological figures, both eastern and Greek, or with Alexander the Great, were illustrated on coins, inscriptions, reliefs, and in contemporary literary works.[15] It should be emphasized that even those kings who were not originally among the Greek conquerors of the East, such as some rulers of Hellenistic monarchies in Asia Minor, had some of the characteristics typical of these "dualistic" Hellenistic kings. For instance, the kings of Bithynia, who had varying attitudes regarding the Greek population, cared very much to keep their own national Bithynian identity separate from their Hellenic one.[16] There were, however, cases in Asia Minor in which kings merely accented their Greek identity (Pergamon).[17]

This brief look at Hellenistic kings shows that they usually took great care to be the central national figure for all strata of society, for the Greeks, Hellenists, and natives alike. This care can be seen in the ruler cult of the king, something that will be addressed in chapter 5. Still, the various strata of society were not always convinced that their king was indeed their national leader, which led to sporadic conflicts—though not many—during the Hellenistic period.[18]

Did the Jewish kings from Aristobulus I to Aristobulus II (104–63 B.C.E.) have any traits in common with the Hellenistic kings? How was Jewish kingship viewed as a nationalistic symbol? A brief historical survey may help to answer these questions.

Aristobulus I, the son of Hyrcanus I, declared himself king of Judea in 104/3 B.C.E. It had taken the Hasmonean state about sixty years to become a monarchy (160–104/3). After Judas Maccabeus's death in 160 B.C.E., his brothers had followed in his steps and gradually paved the way for an independent Jewish rulership. This was an inevitable process, because from as early as the fifties of the second century B.C.E. the emerging Jewish state played political games that were much like the games played by its neighboring nations, and it was therefore politically very much influenced by them. The Maccabean brothers became generals by their own merit and in many cases served the local Diadochi who taught them what Hellenistic kings were like, though sometimes in a harsh manner. Jonathan paid with his life for playing the political and military games of a Hellenistic Diadoch. Hence when Jonathan's brothers, John and Simeon, operated as commanders in the service of Hellenistic rulers in the region, being at the same time leaders of the Jewish emerging national political cause (that is, they led a Jewish army), they affected the concept of Jewish authority that developed later in the century.[19]

The actions of Simeon in 143/2 B.C.E. marked a turning point for Jewish authority. He declared Judea's complete independence from the non-Jews, and by approval of the "Jews and the priests" became "leader (*hegemon*) and high priest forever, until a true prophet should arise" (1 Macc 14:41). He also became the military leader (1 Macc 14:27–47) and received the authority to nominate judges and heads of courts.[20] Viewing these functions against the background of those of Hellenistic kings, Simeon in 140 B.C.E. formalized some of the aspects of kingship—not necessarily Hellenistic—that the Hasmoneans had gradually been acquiring during the past twenty years. Yet he still did not have the official title of king.

It is significant that at the moment that independence was officially declared by Simeon, the ruling authority and its precise functions were defined by, and gained the approval of, the people (that is, the assembly of the people).[21] Political authority, *independent and sovereign,* was perhaps the most important aspect of the nationalistic concept in antiquity (Herod's rule in Judea at a later time was different, because he was a client king of the Romans). The question remains why Simeon, when he declared Judea independent, did not assume the kingship as Aristobulus did forty years later. The sources do not answer this question, and one can only guess that independence was in itself a firm and revolutionary step taken at this juncture by the Jews. The Hasmoneans were, throughout the years 160–104 B.C.E., gradually assimilated into their environment in terms of their *political* behavior. But it seems that in 142 B.C.E. they were not yet ready to establish a real kingship. They were probably reluctant to be seen by the Jews as having anything in common with the Hellenistic kingship from which they were trying to dissociate themselves. This reluctance is evident in their coins, because they refrained from using images. Thus they remained satisfied with their high priesthood. Moreover, kingship was, in the perception of many traditional Jews, an institution that had to gain God's approval, and the first Hasmonean brothers were very careful not to appear pretentious, and thus to avoid an increase in the opposition coming already from among certain circles over their high priesthood. This position also becomes understandable in light of the concept of kingship in Judaism. It has always been a disputed institution in Jewish thought, as can be seen in the Hebrew Bible.[22] Also, most passages in the Hebrew Bible that have a bearing on the issue of the king behaving as a priest resent this link between the two offices. The first Hasmoneans were thus very careful not to offend those who may have felt uncomfortable with kingship.

This explanation receives support from what is known about the behavior of Simeon's son and successor, John Hyrcanus I (135–104 B.C.E.). He acted like a real king, but still did not adopt the title.[23] His coins bear the inscription "John the high priest and the congregation of the Jews." His kingly behavior was perhaps the reason why a later tradition claims that Hyrcanus rather than Aristobulus I was the first Hasmonean king. Hyrcanus perhaps had some prophetic traits (the famous *bat qol,* i.e., heavenly voice that spoke to him, *Jewish War* 1.69), which—along with the saying in 1 Maccabees "until a true prophet should arise"—made a certain late author think that he was a king.[24] He acted like a king not only because he had a native army (comprised of Jews) at his disposal but because he recruited mercenaries, like other Hellenistic kings of the time. John Hyrcanus I, from the little information there is about his rule, emerges as a strong personality who did not want to abandon his function of high priest. His time marked the beginning (or perhaps the increase) of the controversy over the dual authority of the Hasmonean rulers. Jonathan, in 152 B.C.E., was the first of the Hasmonean brothers known to have taken the high priesthood along with the secular leadership. Subsequent secular rulers were also the high priests. This combination was offensive to many Jews, as will be discussed in chapter 5.

It is this reason that Josephus gives for Hyrcanus's break with the Pharisees, who were against this dualistic authority. One of the Pharisees, Eleazar by name, said to him, "If you wish to be righteous, give up the high priesthood and be content with governing the people." Hyrcanus then left the Pharisees and joined the "party" of the Sadducees (*Antiquities* 13.288–298).

This episode may be explained merely as an etiological story concerning a controversy that is also found in other literature of the period.[25] But, just as has been seen with other traits of kingship, the holding of both priesthood and kingship by one person in the Hasmonean family can perhaps be understood as a part of their gradual adoption of—or, rather, response to—certain characteristics of Hellenistic kingship. In the long history of the Jewish people up to 152 B.C.E. there is no precedent for a successive line of king-priests (probably it only exists in the schismatic Israelite kingdom during its first years).[26] As we have already seen, however, the Hellenistic kings received much of their authority and real power among the native population as a result of their strong association with the gods. The Hasmoneans obviously could not imitate Hellenistic kings in this regard, so they had to be content with the high priesthood, which gave them the holiness and the religious authority to be the mediators between men and God.[27] Moreover, if they were alert to what happened in neighboring countries, they knew perfectly well that the priesthoods were usually the champions of native indigenous nationalism. Thus, for the Hasmoneans, functioning as high priest and king eliminated eventual opposition from the priesthood. By holding the high priesthood they became the symbol of Jewish nationalism in the Jewish state (a matter that was strongly resented by the Essenes). Apparently for this reason, therefore, the Hasmoneans did not want to give up this dual role under any circumstances. Also, their sanctity granted them a higher position among the gentile rulers and kings.

A substantial part of the concept of Hellenistic kingship was that the king was to reign over as much territory as possible and was to subjugate other peoples. Whereas Judas Maccabeus and his successor, Jonathan, ruled over the small region of Judea and its vicinity,

Simeon and in particular John Hyrcanus I launched attacks to make territorial acquisitions in Palestine, following a pattern similar to that of other Hellenistic rulers. The Hasmoneans were in fact following in the footsteps of their old traditions concerning the territory, and they used them to justify their conquests, the most important tradition being God's promise of the Land.[28] It is also interesting to note that the Hasmoneans operated in conjunction with a *gerousia* (council of elders), which can be easily compared to the institution of *philoi* that was common at the courts of Hellenistic rulers.[29] We do not know much about their wives, but the Hasmoneans, unlike Hellenistic kings in the region, probably had only one wife at a time. When Judea officially became a kingdom in 104/3 B.C.E. the name of its first king, Aristobulus, was Greek, and some of the insignia of kingship (throne, scepter, diadem, and purple) may have resembled those of Hellenistic kings, though we do not possess any evidence to this effect. Aristobulus is called by Josephus "Philhellen" (*Antiquities* 13.318).

The four monarchs who ruled independent Judea in succession until the Roman conquest of Palestine in 63 B.C.E. were Aristobulus I (104–103), Alexander Jannaeus (103–76), Salome (76–67), and Hyrcanus II (and his brother Aristobulus II (67–63). They merely consolidated and intensified what their predecessors had started in terms of Jewish authority, and in some respects they became more and more like neighboring kings. Nevertheless, conclusions about the extent of their hellenization as kings should be made with caution. Greek names, along with the adoption of some Hellenistic traits of kingship, do not necessarily point to an overall hellenization of Jewish kingship. A famous rabbi of the third century B.C.E. was called Antigonus. Also note that even Nicomedes I, the second king of Bithynia, who came from an indigenous family and was not a great friend of Hellenism, had a Greek name. His image on his coins shows similarity to Greek gods, and his foundation of the city of Nicomedeia can be seen as part of his Hellenistic side.[30] Moreover, it is important to remember that, except for the coinage and some archaeological remains, Josephus is the main source for Jewish kingship at this time. He writes in Greek, using at times non-Jewish Greek sources (aiming at a Greek-speaking Jewish audience as well as a non-Jewish one); thus his Greek nomenclature of kingship at times may give misleading impressions. He does not tell much about the nature of Hasmonean kingship, but scholars assume that Alexander Jannaeus had more Hellenistic traits than his predecessors or his wife, the later queen.

If this assumption is true, then the more Jannaeus showed his Hellenistic side,[31] the more he was resented as a national leader by the majority of native Jews, in particular the Pharisees.[32] An intense civil war ensued, which can be compared to the one Ptolemy IV had to fight with the Egyptian natives after the battle of Raphia (217 B.C.E.). Like Ptolemy V, who had to make concessions to his native population (reflected in the famous Rosetta stone), so Alexander Jannaeus made a concession to his "natives" by minting coins that are the only Hasmonean coins to use Aramaic instead of paleo-Hebrew. J. Naveh may be right in claiming that Alexander wanted to reach the commoners who could not read paleo-Hebrew and Greek. The coins were issued after the end of his rift with the Pharisees in 78 B.C.E.[33]

Evidence is limited, but nevertheless some idea of how Hasmonean kings behaved can be seen, particularly on their coinage, and in a more limited way in archaeology. Their coinage reflects their wish to hark back to the First Temple period by using paleo-Hebrew. Also, other objects of this time use paleo-Hebrew. Their coins never portray a human figure or an animal, which indicates their strict adherence to Jewish law. In some of the coins, however, we find a Greek inscription using *basileus* and the king's name (Alexander Jannaeus, John Hyrcanus II, and later also Mattathias Antigonus). But these Greek inscriptions are alongside paleo-Hebrew ones (and Aramaic inscriptions, in the case of one series from the reign of Alexander Jannaeus), which in itself is different from the foreign coinage at the time (including the coinage of foreigners used by the Jews themselves in Palestine, as for instance the Tyrian one). Foreign coins usually had human figures depicted on them, either mythological characters or portraits of the actual kings. Thus the Jewish coinage of the Hasmonean period was an important element that distinguished the Jews from all others in the region. Moreover, some symbols found on Hasmonean coins were non-Jewish, such as the helmet, the anchor, the lily, the ivy wreath, and the double cornucopias. The Jews, who never during the Hasmonean period adopted human images on their coinage, cared in many instances to reshape the above-mentioned symbols in order to give them a special "Jewish" appearance. All of this evidence can be considered to be in line with their wish on the one hand to be a state similar to other states within the Hellenistic political arena, and on the other, to be unique and Jewish.[34] It is important to add here that after the Roman occupation of Palestine in 63 B.C.E., it was the remnants of the Hasmonean dynasty who led the vigorous nationalistic upheavals against Rome.[35]

This concise summary shows that Jewish kingship had some of the characteristics of Hellenistic kingship, perhaps rather fewer than scholars sometimes want to see. The possession of a mercenary force, or having Greek military advisers, or building in the Greek Hellenistic style, does not necessarily mean that a monarch was entirely Hellenistic. Aristobulus I and Jannaeus may have been more Hellenistic than Hyrcanus I (who was not a king) or Salome. Like some Hellenistic rulers in Asia Minor, the Jewish kings came from the native population, and thus in most of the period they had nothing in common with the "schizophrenic" attitude of the Ptolemies and Seleucids. The Hasmoneans had one capital, religious as well as political; they had one Temple; they even judaized some of the non-Jews in Palestine in order to eliminate, as much as the circumstances allowed, the existence of a divided population in the Land of Israel. Still, as can be learned from Jannaeus's rift with the Pharisees and the Essenes (which was mainly a result of his holding the high priesthood and kingship simultaneously), even the small effect Hellenistic kingship had on Jannaeus may have been vigorously opposed by the native population. This opposition became even worse at the time of Herod the Great. Herod, who was half Edomite and an ardent Hellenist, was a "schizophrenic" ruler, which separated him even more than his predecessor Jannaeus from most of the native elements in Palestine and prevented his kingship from becoming a complete national symbol. This issue will be dealt with further in chapter 8.

So far, kingship has been studied within its historical framework. Now we shall examine kingship, both gentile and Jewish, as it is expressed in the literature of the period. In the literary evidence of the non-Jews during the Hellenistic period there is a blend of the concept of the king as found in Greek literature before Alexander (i.e., the concept of kingship the Greeks brought with them to the East with Alexander and his successors) with the one found in eastern literature. My aim is to examine how the national symbol of kingship appears in Jewish literature and whether the Hellenistic picture of kingship influenced the Jews in any way.

The Greek views concerning kingship before Alexander the Great can be summed up as follows:[36] From the sixth century B.C.E. onward Greek thinkers speculated about the best political constitution (*politeia*) because, in contrast to eastern thought at the time, the Greeks were rational thinkers, and the well-being of the individual (*anthropos*) was central to their political thought. The Greeks based many of their views on their practical experience. The city-states of Greece underwent a process of *metabole* (change) of regimes, usually within short periods—for example, a change from kingship to aristocracy and from aristocracy to democracy can be seen. It should be emphasized that monarchy was among the regimes viewed by the Greeks as being a possible option for the city-state; it was part of the *metabole* process. In the fifth century B.C.E., when the Greek city-state was more or less stable politically and socially, there is little in the literature about monarchy: it was not fashionable at the time. As early as the beginning of the fourth century B.C.E., however, Greek political thinkers viewed the ideal monarch as a sound alternative for the decaying polis. There was no agreement about how the ideal monarch should be educated or how he should rule. But most political thinkers agreed that a good monarch should have an excellent education, which would make his *arete* (virtue) exceed that of his subjects. They thought that a good monarch should combine the special character of one who has the ability to rule with the knowledge to do so. Some thought that he should also have the consent of his subjects to rule them. Some believed that he should also rule according to the laws—an unlawful king, who ruled without his subjects' consent, was a tyrant, according to most political thinkers of the period. Tyranny became the disruptive evil side of monarchy (as oligarchy was of aristocracy: Josephus even describes aristocracy as "divine" [*Antiquities* 6.36], concerning Samuel). In the political thought of the fourth century one finds the belief that a *basileia* (kingship), like other regimes, was liable to change and decay. It was never seen as a holy and enduring kind of regime. It is ironic that Greek thinkers of the fourth century B.C.E. took their examples of kingship not merely from the city-state of Sparta, which was unique in certain respects, but mainly from kingships outside the Greek motherland, such as Cyprus, Syracuse, and Persia. The reason is that for almost two centuries before the rise of Alexander the Great, the Greeks themselves had no monarchies in the city-states.

Thus the Greek views regarding both monarchy and other regimes were of a universal nature and did not necessarily come from one particular nation. The ideas concerning kingship remained theoretical and, as they appeared in the political thought of the fourth century B.C.E., had very little to do with the gods and other transcendental ideas. Even Xenophon's *Cyropaedeia,* which refers to the kingship of the Persian king Cyrus, is in its greater part imbued with Greek concepts of kingship.[37]

In the East before the conquest of Alexander the Great, the institution of kingship was taken for granted, unlike in Greece. Few philosophical speculations can be found about political science in general or kingship in particular. It was a matter of theology: the king was either a god, or the son of a god, or strongly associated with the gods. In many instances he was deified after his death. The reason for the dichotomy in political thought between the ancient Near East and the Greek West was that in the Greek West the individual was the main concern of every political and social speculation (in other words, it was an anthropocentric society), whereas in eastern societies there was a theocentric concept of the state. In the ancient Near East, where the king was strongly associated with the gods, there could not be any institutional alternative to kingship. When a king was murdered, and this happened frequently in eastern monarchies, it was explained by his having lost the approval of the gods (the biblical stories about Saul and David clearly demonstrate this view).[38] As *individuals* kings could lose the approval of their protecting gods, but the institution as such never did. The Egyptian treatment of the deceased king shows how essential this concept was for Egyptian political thought: every deceased king became an Osiris.[39] Scattered in the literature of the ancient Near East are instructions or advice for a good king. But never, as far as I know, is there any discussion in eastern literature comparable to the one in Greek literature, where as early as the sixth century B.C.E. the merits of aristocracy, tyranny, democracy, and monarchy were discussed by the *magoi* of Herodotus (3.80–83).[40] In the Hebrew Bible, as we have seen, pros and cons of kingship can be found, but there is not

really any serious debate over the merits of kingship over other
kinds of regimes. The Bible reflects much of what was happening in
the East until the sixth century. An example of eastern literature that
discusses the position of a king is the Instruction of King Amen-em-
het I of the Twelfth Dynasty to his son. At one point he writes,

> Thou that hast appeared as a god, hearken to what I have to say
> to thee, that thou mayest be king of the land and ruler of the
> regions, that thou mayest achieve an overabundance of good.
> Hold thyself apart from those subordinate to (thee), lest that
> should happen to whose terrors no attention has been given.
> Approach them not in thy loneliness. Fill not thy heart with a
> brother, nor know a friend. . . . Even when thou sleepest guard
> thy heart thyself because no man has adherents on the day of
> distress.[41]

Another document that anticipates the Hellenistic approach to
kingship is the Victory Stele of Sennacherib (690 B.C.E.), where the
king described himself as the "desired king, protector of truth, lover
of justice, the one who performs favors, companion of the crippled,
he who searches goodness, the perfect young man, the warlike male
foremost of all kings."[42]

When Alexander arrived in the East, Greek and eastern concepts
of kingship were combined in one person. He himself did not live
long enough to see the changes he brought about, but his successors
did. As we have seen, the Hellenistic king began to take on a kind of
duality, a tension between his Greek characteristics and his eastern
ones. This changing role was reflected in the literature of the time,
which on the subject of kingship falls into two generic groups.

The first includes the so-called *peri basileias* documents, emanating in particular from the East, which contain detailed discussions of
what constituted a "good" king.[43] Some features of the ideal king
are based on actual praise to the king (found in papyri and inscriptions), and others on the wishful thinking of their writers. For an
example of the way that the image of the Hellenistic king, with his
mixture of Greek and eastern characteristics, is seen, we will examine Diodorus Siculus 1.70–72, which derived its view of Egyptian
kingship probably from Hecataeus of Abdera's *Aegyptiaca*. At one
point he says,

The life which the kings of the Egyptians lived was not like that of other men who enjoy autocratic power and do in all matters exactly as they please without being held to account, but all their acts were regulated by prescriptions set forth in laws. . . . For instance, in the morning, as soon as he was awake, he first of all had to receive the letters which had been sent from all sides . . . then after he had bathed and bedecked his body with rich garments and the insignia of his office, he had to sacrifice to the gods, etc.[44]

The *peri basileias* documents present systematic theoretical descriptions of kingship and have only a limited contact with the reality of the kingship at the time. Nevertheless, their notions can be found also in documents that refer back to history. Hecataeus of Abdera's *Aegyptiaca,* in which the history of ancient Egypt is viewed through the behavior of good and bad kings, is a good example. His history of Egypt is not merely a re-creation of Herodotus's history of that country (2.99ff.); it describes Hellenistic concepts of kingship that reflect an amazing mixture of Egyptian and Greek characteristics.[45] Also in Josephus's *Antiquities* we can occasionally find ideas reminiscent of the *peri basileias* concepts, which are intervoven in his history of ancient Israel.[46]

The second group consists of those writings which refer to the king as a hero who had been transformed into a god. This school of thought is classified by scholars as euhemerism, in which many gods were heroes who had become gods after performing heroic acts (Dionysus, Heracles, and even Zeus).[47] Some documents do, however, refer directly to Hellenistic kings as gods (e.g., Osiris and Dionysus). In contrast to the universalistic and theoretical views of Greek political thought, a great deal of the Hellenistic literature of this group referring to kingship was nationalistic in nature. Although this literature was influenced by Greek ideas of kingship as well as eastern ones, much of it refers particularly to pharaonic, Babylonian, Cyrenian, and Jewish kingship.

Did this body of writing in any way influence Jewish political thought during the formation of the Jewish state? Ben Sira about 190 B.C.E. had already emphasized the "good" kings of Israel's history, but he seems to have been independent of the Hellenistic concepts found in the *peri basileias* documents. When the Hasmonean

state emerged in the middle of the second century B.C.E., the Jews
had their own traditional biblical model of kingship in mind. The
period of David and Solomon was idealized, as is shown in *On the
Kings of Judah* by Eupolemus the son of John.[48]

During the era of the Hasmonean kingdom both kinds of literature concerning kingship can be found in the Jewish world. On the
one hand there are *peri basileias* documents both from Palestine and
from the Diaspora. For instance, the famous Temple Scroll, which
includes a section on kingship, probably from Alexander Jannaeus's
time, comes from Palestine.[49] This section contains a treatise on
what makes a "good" king. It shows a knowledge of both Hellenistic and Jewish kingship, but is solely Jewish in its content. From the
Temple Scroll one can learn that the Jews viewed their kingship as a
nationalistic symbol derived from Jewish tradition. The relevant section in this interesting document is based on Deuteronomy 17,
which has a positive view of kingship. For example,

> When you come to the land which I give you, and you possess it
> and dwell in it, and then say, "I will set a king over me, like all
> the nations that are around me" you may set there as king over
> you him whom I shall choose. One from among your brethren
> you shall set as king over you . . . Only he must not multiply
> horses for himself, or cause the people to return to Egypt for war
> . . . And he shall not take a wife from all the daughters of the
> nations, but from his father's house he shall take unto himself a
> wife. . . . (col. 56.12–59.21)

From the Diaspora there is the famous Letter of Aristeas containing a chapter "On Kingship," which presents kingship in a more
universal manner.[50] Here there is a mixture of biblical and Hellenistic ideas. Kingship is less nationalistic here than in the Temple Scroll
because Diaspora Jews wished to universalize their national symbols. There are many examples from this section in which Jewish
sages coming from Jerusalem teach Ptolemy (ostensibly Philadelphus
II) a lesson in ruling his people:

> (the king) asked the occupant of the first couch (they were seated
> according to age), "How can one keep his kingdom without of-
> fense to the end?" After a short pause he replied, "You would

administer it best by imitating the eternal goodness of God. By using long-suffering and treatment of those who merit (punishment) more leniently than they deserve, you will convert them from evil and bring them to repentance." The king commended the answer and asked the next guest, "How should one act in each case?" The reply was, "If he practiced just dealing toward all, he will perform each task well for himself, believing that every thought is manifest to God. Take the fear of God as your guiding principle, and you will not fail in anything." (187–189)

Yet there is also evidence that the contemporary problems of Jewish kingship were transposed into the historical past, just as they were in Hellenistic literature of the time. Eupolemus in his book *On the Kings of Judah* transferred much of his own spiritual present into the past and re-created the history of the Davidic dynasty in the shape of his own present experience, as did Hecataeus in Egypt and Berossus in Babylonia. He gave David and Solomon a higher status than their neighbor kings in terms of their power and political standing. Moreover, the authors of the Hasmonean period show that their real concern was the separation of kingship from the high priesthood.[51] In the literature there are interesting stories on this theme, usually interspersed in a scriptural framework in order to present a historical justification for opinions on acute contemporary problems. In the Temple Scroll the issue of separation was solved within the systematic speculation of the document, which claimed that the high priest should be a different person from the king, and above him in authority.[52] The Book of Jubilees and the Testament of the Twelve Patriarchs solved the problem by changing the historical biblical tradition. Judah, Jacob's son, became a king, whereas Levi functioned as high priest. In some instances Levi was superior to Judah, in others he was equal to him.[53]

Interestingly, just as it is in the Hellenistic literature, kingship is associated in Jewish literary sources with "mythology." The Jews did not worship their kings because it was against their religion and ethos, but they could associate their kings—as the Egyptians did with Dionysus, Horus, and Osiris—with "demythologized" figures such as the first ancestors of Israel. Thus in the two major documents from Palestine mentioned above, kingship was associated with Judah, and not with Levi the priest. Judah, like Osiris in the

Ptolemaic court, was given precedence over his brothers, and he was given a nonscriptural historical role that really fits a Jewish king of the Hellenistic period.

From the Egyptian Diaspora we have another example. According to Ezekiel's *Exagoge* (probably third century B.C.E.), Moses had a dream that was later interpreted by his father-in-law, Reguel:

> I dreamed there was on the summit of Mount Sinai
> A certain great throne extending up to heaven's cleft,
> On which there sat a certain noble man
> Wearing a crown and holding a great scepter
> In his left hand. With his right hand
> He beckoned to me, and I stood before the throne.
> He gave me the scepter and told me to sit
> On the great throne. He gave me the royal crown
> And he himself left the throne.
> I beheld the entire circled earth
> Both beneath the earth and above the heaven,
> And a host of stars fell on its knees before me;
> I numbered them all,
> They passed before me like a squadron of soldiers.
> Then, seized with fear, I rose from my sleep.

His father-in-law interprets the dream thus:

> O friend, that which God has signified to you as good;
> Might I live until the time that these things happen to you.
> Then you will raise up a great throne
> And it is you who will judge and lead humankind;
> As you beheld the whole inhabited earth,
> The things beneath and the things above God's heaven,
> So will you see things present, past, and future.

In this scene Moses receives his kingship from God, and there is no doubt that he becomes a universal kind of king. There are scholars who wish to see in it a replica of Alexander the Great's visit to the temple of Amon, where he received the world kingship from Amon.[54] There exists also the possibility of viewing Moses' kingship against the political background of Ptolemaic Egypt.

Ptolemaic kingship had a very strong universalistic flavor. Ptolemy was equated with Dionysus and with Osiris, the deceased king, both of whom were universal king-gods. The Jews living under Ptolemaic kings (either in Egypt or in its possessions outside Egypt, namely, Palestine, Cyrene, Cyprus, and other places), could not identify themselves with kings who were seen as gods (as we know for instance from 3 Maccabees). The indigenous population in Egypt viewed the Greek kings as pharaohs, that is, as Egyptian gods like Amon or Horus; and the deceased kings were seen to be like Osiris. The Greeks in Egypt viewed the Ptolemies as Greek gods, such as Dionysus, Zeus, and others. What could pious Jews (and Ezekiel was a pious Jew) who were Egyptians do in this situation? They could not identify with the pagan gods, yet they had to identify with some king associated with Egypt (because they wanted to be considered part of the Egyptian "nation"). They thus turned to their own past, and within this framework "invented" their own king, an Egyptian Hebrew, who received his kingship from the king of kings, God, just as the Ptolemies had received their kingship from their own gods. A precedent was thereby created in which the pious non-syncretistic Jew shows his own "national" god as being a universalistic God (which thus includes also Egypt). Unlike Artapanus, who transforms Joseph and Moses into the Egyptian Sesostris, Ezekiel is not syncretistic and makes Moses the universal king who received his kingship from God. By this strategy the Jews might be able to feel more at home in Egypt.

Be that as it may, the Jews always viewed their earthly kings as human beings. In their literature, however, they always revealed the tension, or rather the dualism, in their tradition between kingship as an earthly institution and God who is the "king of kings." In some texts God appears as a nationalistic God, in others as a more universal one.[55] Yet the "king of kings" was described at times with terminology used of the earthly kings. The best example from the period under survey, which drew heavily on biblical material, is the *Songs of the Sabbath Sacrifice,* apparently from before the first century B.C.E.[56] Here God appears—in many ways like the eastern concept of a god—as a king (*melek*) who dwells in the heavenly Temple and rules (*molek*) everything from his throne (*mosab, kisse*) in heaven. His angels and his priests are sometimes viewed in terms of the advisers of earthly kings. There does not appear to be any Hellenistic influence in the presentation of God as a king in this document, but God is portrayed in a universalistic manner as being the king of justice, truth, and might.[57] The more nationalistic "king of kings" comes to the fore in 1 and 2 Maccabees, Jubilees, and the War Scroll from Qumran, where we read that the "king of Israel will have the kingship" (1QM 6.4–6) and that he will be the high military commander in the war of the end of the days (1QM 12.1–5).[58]

In conclusion: the ideas of kingship from the Hasmonean period seem to have been created against the background of the Hellenistic views on kingship, but remained purely Jewish in their content. The views from the Diaspora, by contrast, show much more of a mixture of Hellenistic ideas of kingship with Jewish ones. This picture indeed corresponds to the conclusions reached in the historical survey of Jewish kingship earlier in this chapter. When Herod the Great became king in 37 B.C.E., much changed. Herod was recognized by many as the "king of the Jews," but he was in fact an Idumaean and in many respects became more of a Hellenistic (Greek) king than his predecessors had been, that is, a dualistic or "schizophrenic" king with a tension between his Hellenistic and Judaic sides. His ascent to the throne and the creation of a new dynasty under Roman aegis also brought about some different nuances concerning kingship in the literature of the period, which will be considered in chapter 8.[59]

Notes

¹ For the *proskynesis* of Alexander, see J. R. Hamilton, *Alexander the Great* (London, 1973), pp. 105–106. This mixture is still evident in the surviving ancestor reliefs from Nemrud Dagh. Concerning the kings of Commagene, see R. R. R. Smith, *Hellenistic Royal Portraits* (Oxford, 1988), pp. 102–104, 121.

² This dual identity is reflected in the art of the Hellenistic era; see J. J. Pollitt, *Art in the Hellenistic Age* (Cambridge, 1986), passim; Smith, *Portraits;* B. S. Ridgway, *Hellenistic Sculpture* (Madison, Wisc., 1990), vol. 1, esp. pp. 108–148.

³ For the *philoi* see in particular L. Mooren, "Macht und Nationalität," in *Das ptolemaische Ägypten,* ed. H. Maehler and V. M. Strocka (Berlin, 1976), pp. 51–57. The Greek nature of the *philoi* (also in the Seleucid court) is shown very nicely by Mooren. See also idem, "The Governors General of the Thebaid in the Second Century B.C. (II)," *Ancient Society* 5 (1974): 147–152. For the nature of Ptolemaic kingship, see Bowman, *Egypt after the Pharaohs, 332 B.C.–A.D. 642* (London, 1986), pp. 21–37; A. E. Samuel, *The Shifting Sands of History: Interpretations of Ptolemaic Egypt* (Lanham, Md., and London, 1989), pp. 67–81.

⁴ For the foreign policy of the Ptolemies, see E. Bevan, *A History of Egypt under the Ptolemaic Dynasty* (London, 1927), passim; R. S. Bagnall, *The Administration of the Ptolemaic Possessions Outside Egypt* (Leiden, 1976), passim; P. Green, *Alexander to Actium* (Berkeley, Los Angeles, and Oxford, 1990), passim.

⁵ For the coins of the Ptolemies see Smith, *Portraits,* chap. 9 and passim, with the older literature. For Seleucid coins, see A. Houghton, *Coins of the Seleucid Empire from the Collection of Arthur Houghton* (New York, 1983).

⁶ G. J. P. McEwan, *Priest and Temple in Hellenistic Babylonia* (Wiesbaden, 1981), esp. pp. 159–182; A. Kuhrt and S. Sherwin-White, "Aspects of Seleucid Royal Ideology: the Cylinder of Antiochus I from Borsippa," *Journal of Hellenic Studies* 111 (1991): 71–86.

⁷ Bowman, *Egypt after the Pharaohs.*

⁸ Smith, *Portraits,* pp. 44, 48, and passim; for the Ptolemaic procession see E. E. Rice, *The Grand Procession of Ptolemy Philadelphus* (Oxford, 1983).

⁹ Cf. in general D. J. Thompson, *Memphis under the Ptolemies* (Princeton, 1988), pp. 118–120. But these seem to be isolated examples; for the "Oracle of the Potter" see S. M. Burstein, *The Hellenistic Age from the Battle of Ipsos to the Death of Kleopatra VII* (Cambridge, 1985), pp. 136–139. And for the unrest under Ptolemy IV see W. Peremans, "Les Révolutions égyptiennes sous les Lagides," in *Das ptolemaische Ägypten,* ed. H. Maehler and V. M. Strocka (Berlin, 1976), pp. 39–50. (See also the story of Antiochus and the priests of Nanaea, which reflects a tension between the king and the national priesthood, in 2 Macc 1:13–17; and J. A. Goldstein, *II Maccabees,** ad loc.)

[10] For the insignia of kingship cf. Smith, *Portraits,* pp. 34–38, with *CAH,* 2d ed., 7.1.62–100 (Walbank).

[11] Cf. for instance the famous example of the monument of Antiochus I of Commagene (70–30 B.C.E.) with Smith, *Portraits,* pp. 25–26. See in general for the dynasty of Commagene R. D. Sullivan, *Near Eastern Royalty and Rome, 100–30 B.C.* (Toronto and London, 1990), pp. 59–62, 193–198. For the ruler cult of the Attalids of Pergamon, see E. V. Hansen, *The Attalids of Pergamon,* 2d ed. (Ithaca, N.Y. and London, 1971), pp. 453–470. For Parthian kingship in the Hellenistic era, see R. N. Frye, *The History of Ancient Iran* (Munich, 1984), pp. 216–218. For the dynastic marriages among the various Hellenistic royal houses, see J. Seibert, *Historische Beiträge zu den dynastischen Verbindungen in hellenistischer Zeit* (Wiesbaden, 1967).

[12] Antiochus IV's invasions of Egypt in 169–168 B.C.E. provide a good indication that Alexander's vision of a big eastern empire was not dead. Some of *Antiochus'* coins bear the inscription "king of Asia."

[13] See the still useful books of G. T. Griffith, *The Mercenaries of the Hellenistic World* (repr. Groningen, 1968) and of M. Launey, *Recherches sur les armées hellénistiques,* 2 vols. (Paris, 1949–1950).

[14] See below, chapter 6.

[15] Cf. Smith, *Portraits,* passim. For Seleucid coinage, see Houghton, *Coins of the Seleucid Empire.*

[16] Of a king like Prusias, who reigned there for forty-five years, it is said by D. Magie that "with all his efforts to appear in the light of a Hellenic prince, he was no true friend of Hellenism" (*Roman Rule in Asia Minor* [Princeton, 1950], 1.314–315). For the later kings of Arabia, who in many aspects remained indigenous, see G. W. Bowersock, *Roman Arabia* (Cambridge, Mass. and London, 1983), pp. 45–75. For Cappadocia, see Sullivan, *Near Eastern Royalty,* pp. 51–58, 174–185.

[17] For Pergamon, see Hansen, *Attalids of Pergamon,* and R. E. Allen, *The Attalid Kingdom: A Constitutional History* (Oxford, 1983). For some of the other dynasties see Sullivan, *Near Eastern Royalty,* passim.

[18] Cf. above, chapter 1.

[19] For a historical survey see Schürer, *History,* 1.174–228.

[20] Cf. E. E. Urbach, *The Halakhah* (Jerusalem, 1986), pp. 55–57.

[21] For the role of the *demos* at the time, see J. Sievers, *The Hasmoneans and Their Supporters* (Atlanta, 1990), passim.

[22] See for instance Deut 17:14–20 as opposed to 1 Samuel 8; and for kingship in the Old Testament in general, cf. F. M. Cross, *Canaanite Myth and Hebrew Epic* (Cambridge, Mass., 1973), pp. 145–289, and J. J. M. Roberts, "In Defence of the Monarchy: The Contribution of Israelite Kingship to Biblical Theology," in *Ancient Israelite Religion,* ed. P. D. Miller et al. (Philadelphia, 1987), pp. 377–396, with the

older literature. For the opposition to the hold of the priesthood by Israelite kings, see note 26 below.

23 His coins bear the inscription "Yehoḥanan the high priest and the congregation of the Jews." It is likely that he was the first to mint coins. This view is, however, opposed by Y. Meshorer (*Ancient Jewish Coinage* [New York, 1982], 1.35–39), who claims that these coins are to be ascribed to Hyrcanus II, and the first to mint coins was Jannaeus. He has, however, changed his mind recently, and claims that the first coins should be attributed to Hyrcanus I (see *Masada,* vol. 1: *The Coins of Masada* [Jerusalem, 1989], p. 71).

24 Probably Nicolaus of Damascus (Josephus, *Antiquities* 13.288).

25 M. Stern, "Aspects of Jewish Society," in *Compendia rerum iudaicarum ad Novum Testamentum,* ed. S. Safrai et al. (Assen, 1974–1976), 2.568–569; and Mendels, *The Land,* pp. 57–108. Cf. also Schürer, *History,* 1.214.

26 It seems that Jeroboam, according to 1 Kings 13, took upon himself priestly functions alongside his kingly ones. The Hebrew Bible reflects a great deal of this tension between priest and king. Just to mention some examples: Gen 14:18–20 describes a non-Israelite king, Melchizedek, as both a priest and a king. Psalm 110 says of the new king (a psalm probably used at the accession of a new king to the throne): "the lord has sworn and will not change his mind, You are a priest forever after the order of Melchizedek." 2 Sam 6:12–15 portrays King David bringing the Ark to Jerusalem. He offers sacrifices and wears a priestly garment, a linen ephod, as he leads a liturgical procession. 2 Sam 8:18 names David's sons as priests. 1 Kgs 8:55 suggests that Solomon blessed the people assembled for worship, which is a priestly function. 1 Kgs 8:62–66 indicates that Solomon offered sacrifices at the dedication of the Temple in Jerusalem. It seems that by the postexilic period the functions of offering sacrifices and blessing for the worshiping community are reserved only for the priest and not the king. For instance, Num 6:22–27, a text from the Priestly tradition, reserves to the high priest Aaron and his sons the special privilege of blessing the community (this blessing is now known from two silver amulets excavated in Jerusalem, which are dated to the late seventh century B.C.E.: see G. Barkay, *Ketef Hinnom: A Treasure Facing Jerusalem's Walls* [Jerusalem, 1986], pp. 29–31). The exilic text of Ezekiel 44 restricts the offering of sacrifices to the priests alone and even excludes the Levites from this function. 2 Chr 26:16–21, a postexilic text, sees the cause of King Uzziah's leprosy to be his sacrilege in offering incense. In the later Chronicles parallel to the text of 2 Sam 8:18, David's sons are not priests, as in the Samuel text. The Chronicler changes their role from priests to "the chief officials in the service to the king" (1 Chr 27:32). I am grateful to Dennis Olson for his advice and discussion on matters of biblical kingship.

27 In the ancient Near East in the Hellenistic period, we have some examples of "high" priests who are secondary to the local kings, but have a great deal of political and economic power (cf. Strabo, books 11–12, and Magie, *Roman Rule,* passim). At times the Roman emperors also thought that the high priesthood (*pontifex maximus*) could bring them a great deal of additional holiness and political author-

ity (for this problem see G. W. Bowersock, "The Pontificate of Augustus," in *Between Republic and Empire,* ed. K. A. Raaflaub and M. Toher [Berkeley, Los Angeles, and Oxford, 1990], pp. 380–394). In general, for priesthoods in the pagan world at the time, see M. Beard and J. North, *Pagan Priests: Religion and Power in the Ancient World* (Ithaca, N.Y., 1990).

28 Cf. chapter 4 below.

29 The first to mint coins, John Hyrcanus I, may have referred to this *gerousia* on his coins: "congregation of the Jews."

30 Magie, *Roman Rule,* 1.311–312. For Greek names of the Hasmonean family, see T. Ilan, "The Greek Names of the Hasmoneans," *Jewish Quarterly Review* 78 (1987): 1–20. Greek names, however, do not necessarily point to hellenization.

31 There is, however, no decisive evidence for this characterization, because a Greek inscription on a coin could be aimed at the outer Greek world and the Greek cities of Palestine instead of having any significance for the issue of hellenization. For Jannaeus's supposed hellenization see M. Hengel, *The "Hellenization" of Judaea in the First Century after Christ* (Philadelphia, 1989), passim; cf. also T. Fischer, "Another Hellenizing Coin of Alexander Jannaeus?" *Israel Exploration Journal* 34 (1984): 47–48.

32 Cf. in general L. I. Levine, "The Political Struggle Between Pharisees and Sadducees in the Hasmonean Period," in *Jerusalem in the Second Temple Period: Abraham Schalit Memorial Volume,* ed. A. Oppenheimer et al. (Jerusalem, 1980), pp. 61–83 (Hebrew).

33 J. Naveh, "Dated Coins of Alexander Janneus," *Israel Exploration Journal* 18 (1968): 20–26; and Meshorer, *Ancient Jewish Coinage,* 1.79–81.

34 A drastic turn toward the use of typical Jewish symbols (menorah and table) was made by Mattathias Antigonus during the period 40–37 B.C.E. This shift is quite understandable as a result of the menace to his throne by a rival not of Hasmonean descent, supported by the Romans, namely, Herod. For this whole problem, see Meshorer, *Ancient Jewish Coinage,* 1.60–68, 87–97; Schürer, *History,* 1.602–605.

35 Other *ethne* (peoples) such as the Egyptians and Babylonians could live a cultural and religious national life while projecting their political nationalism (i.e., statehood) onto the Hellenistic kings and later onto the Roman Caesars, who served as nationalistic symbols for most of the indigenous populations. The Jews, however, were not allowed by their religious law to worship their kings as non-Jews could. Thus they were restless at various junctures regarding their political nationalism, when rulers such as Antiochus IV and Caligula did not want to tolerate their special status in this respect. In this regard they were exceptional in the ancient Near East, in their revolt against Rome.

36 The literature abounds. See for instance T. A. Sinclair, *A History of Greek Political Thought* (London, 1951), and *CAH,* 2d ed., 7.1.62–100 (Walbank). There are some useful remarks in Smith, *Portraits,* pp. 46–53, along with the older literature. It is impossible to enter here into the issue of kingship in preclassical Greek

mythology. It would be sufficient to say that heavenly kingship found in Hesiod (eighth century B.C.E.) was very much influenced by eastern ideas from the ancient Near East: see in particular M. L. West, *Hesiod Theogony* (Oxford, 1966); idem, *Hesiod Works and Days* (Oxford, 1978); and in general W. Burkert, *Greek Religion* (Oxford, 1985).

[37] For this peculiar composition see J. Tatum, *Xenophon's Imperial Fiction: On the Education of Cyrus* (Princeton, 1989).

[38] See in general Cross, *Canaanite Myth*, pp. 219–273. On kingship in Sumer, see S. N. Kramer, *The Sumerians* (Chicago, 1963), pp. 33–72, and on kingship in Babylon, see H. W. F. Saggs, *The Greatness that Was Babylon*, 2d ed. (London, 1988), pp. 311–338.

[39] Cf. H. Frankfort, *Kingship and the Gods* (Chicago, 1948).

[40] Cf. Sinclair, *Political Thought*, pp. 33–42.

[41] *Ancient Near Eastern Texts*, ed. J. B. Pritchard, 3d ed. (Princeton, 1969), pp. 418–419.

[42] Stele now in the Walters Art Gallery, Baltimore. Cf. A. K. Grayson, "The Walters Art Gallery Sennacherib Inscription (with 4 plates)," *Archiv für Orientforschung* 20 (1963): 83–96.

[43] Cf. D. Mendels, " 'On Kingship' in the 'Temple Scroll' and the Ideological *Vorlage* of the Seven Banquets in the 'Letter of Aristeas to Philocrates,' " *Aegyptus* 59 (1979): 127–136; and Schürer, *History*, 3.1.677–687.

[44] Cf. A. Burton, *Diodorus Siculus, Book I: A Commentary* (Leiden, 1972), ad loc.

[45] Cf. O. Murray, "Hecataeus of Abdera and Pharaonic Kingship," *Journal of Egyptian Archaeology* 56 (1970): 141–171.

[46] Cf. for instance *Antiquities* 5.233–234, 6.35–37, and elsewhere.

[47] For euhemerism see J. Ferguson, *Utopias of the Classical World* (London, 1975), pp. 102–110; Green, *Alexander to Actium*, pp. 108–109 and passim.

[48] See above, chapter 2.

[49] Mendels, " 'On Kingship' "; M. Hengel, J. H. Charlesworth, and D. Mendels, "The Polemical Character of the 'On Kingship' in the Temple Scroll: An Attempt at Dating 11Q Temple," *Journal of Jewish Studies* 37 (1986): 28–38.

[50] For Aristeas, see Schürer, *History*, 3.1.677–687.

[51] For more detailed discussions and the older literature, see D. Mendels, *The Land of Israel as a Political Concept in Hasmonean Literature* (Tübingen, 1987), passim.

[52] Although the author (or authors) of the Temple Scroll did not say clearly that the Jewish king would live in Jerusalem, there is no reason to imagine that he

thought otherwise. It is quite clear that the Temple was given political overtones, if only from the fact that the king was in many respects subordinate to the high priest of the Temple (57:1–59:21).

[53] Cf. for instance Mendels, *The Land,* pp. 105–107 and passim.

[54] See in general for Ezekiel H. Jacobson, *The Exagoge of Ezekiel* (Cambridge, 1983), and for this particular scene P. W. Van der Horst, "Moses' Throne Vision in Ezekiel the Dramatist," *Journal of Jewish Studies* 34 (1983): 21–29. Cf. also C. R. Holladay, *Fragments from Hellenistic Jewish Authors* (Atlanta, 1989), vol. 2 ad loc.

[55] For a collection of examples for a God as king in texts of the Second Temple period, see O. Camponovo, *Königtum, Königsherrschaft und Reich Gottes in den Frühjüdischen Schriften* (Göttingen, 1984).

[56] Cf. C. Newsom, *Songs of the Sabbath Sacrifice: A Critical Edition* (Atlanta, 1985).

[57] Newsom, *Songs* (concordance). Cf. also in the Thanksgiving Scroll, where he is called "the prince of the gods and the king of the glorious ones" (10.1.8).

[58] See the examples in Camponovo, *Königtum.*

[59] See now for a prayer for the welfare of King Jonathan (probably Alexander Jannaeus) and his kingdom: E. Eshel, H. Eshel, and Ada Yardeni, "A Qumran Compostion Containing Part of Ps. 154 and a Prayer for the Welfare of King Jonathan and his Kingdom," *IEJ* 42 (1992): 199-229. Inter alia we read there in columns B-C: ". . . Holy over king Jonathan and all the congregation of your people Israel who are in the four winds of heaven peace be (for) all and upon your kingdom your name be blessed because you love Isr[ael (?) in the day and until evening, etc."

For other interpretations on kingship at the time see now D. Goodblatt, *The Monarchic Principle: Studies in Jewish Self-Government in Antiquity* (Tübingen, 1994), pp. 6-76.

CHAPTER 4

The Concept of Territory:
Borders and Boundaries (200-63 B.C.E.)

Can we speak of political borders in the Hellenistic world during this period? From the non-Jewish Hellenistic sources, literary as well as epigraphic, we learn that four kinds of borders were recognized in the Hellenistic world: (1) natural borders, which corresponded to mountains, rivers, deserts and oceans (Strabo 11.1 [C490]); (2) ethnic borders, which relied on the identity of the nation, the *ethnos*, and its territory (in many instances the ethnic border received its justification from tradition); (3) political borders, which were usually created in an artificial manner by the Hellenistic states; and (4) a perimeter that embraced many countries, and at times great parts of the eastern known world; this was a border of what we would call an empire.

At times a congruity existed between the natural and the political borders, and sometimes between the ethnic and political ones as well. From what is known about the occurrences after the death of Alexander the Great, political borders did not necessarily take into consideration the various nations that were within those borders. The name of the game was power politics, or rather the right of might. In the years after Alexander the Diadochi conquered whatever territory they could and formed kingdoms with arbitrary borders. Borders were flexible, and only toward the end of the wars of the Diadochi (ca. 280 B.C.E.) did three dominant blocks emerge: the Seleucid kingdom, the Ptolemaic kingdom, and Macedonia. By the beginning of the third century B.C.E. Thrace had already disappeared

from the political map, and shortly afterward the "fourth" kingdom
was replaced by Pergamon in Asia Minor. During the later Hellenistic period some smaller kingdoms emerged as a result of the weaken-
ing of the Seleucid Empire, such as Bithynia, Pontus, Cappadocia,
and Commagene. The Jewish Hasmonean kingdom was established
in the second century B.C.E. as a consequence of the same set of
events.

The Hellenistic kingdoms almost uninterruptedly fought with
their neighbors over territorial disputes. These disputes occurred as
a result of two factors: because the political boundaries between the
kingdoms were not always defined, and because some monarchs had
expansionist aims and did not care at all about borders. Even so,
within the vast territories that the Ptolemaic and Seleucid kingdoms
in particular possessed, a great variety of nations (*ethne*) continued
to hold—usually with no hindrance from the great power—their
traditional "borders"; in some instances they were even granted autonomy within these borders.[1]

How did the Jews fit into this picture? During the third century
B.C.E. Judea enjoyed religious autonomy under Ptolemaic rule. We
know very little about Jewish life at the time; the little we know
about Palestine is through the Zenon Papyri, which are concerned
with economic matters, and from the chapters of Josephus describing the house of Tobias in Transjordan (as well as the Wadi Daliyeh
Papyri). There is also a whole section of 1 Enoch that is attributed to
the third century B.C.E., and there exists some archaeological evidence as well.[2] We can get a clearer glimpse of Jewish political life
after the year 200 B.C.E., when the Jews were granted religious autonomy by the Seleucids who had conquered Palestine.[3] This grant
of autonomy may have been the seed that grew into the nationalistic
religious upheaval thirty years later. One might apply to this situation A. de Tocqueville's famous insight concerning the French before
the French revolution[4]: when the Jews tasted freedom their appetites
grew as time went on. Very little is known about Jewish culture
during this period. The conquest of Palestine by the Seleucids turned
out to be crucial for the Jews.

In the nineties of the second century B.C.E., besides being in Jerusalem and its vicinity, which served as their religious center, the Jews
were scattered among the non-Jews all over Palestine. The sovereigns of Palestine in those days were the Seleucids.[5] Ben Sira, who

lived at that time,[6] reflects the academic atmosphere in Jerusalem and refers nostalgically to the Land of Israel in its better days. He viewed the Land of Israel as it had once been in remote biblical times; he had not yet been confronted with a situation in which, because of changing politics, there would be a Jewish state with defined borders. He did not drastically alter the scriptures to correspond to new conditions; he just referred to the Land using some of the terms he found in the canon, which at the time was still in the process of crystallization. Ben Sira's views will be dealt with in detail later on.

The seventies of the second century B.C.E. brought about strife between Hellenists and traditional Jews; this was the time of the Seleucid interference and the Maccabean revolt.[7] We have already shown that during the years of upheaval (168–160 B.C.E.) the Jews were not yet interested in the conquest of the whole Land. If we may trust the sources, only the City (Jerusalem), the Temple, and the Torah were the first goals of the Maccabean upheaval. After 160 B.C.E. territorial considerations also influenced the policies of the Maccabean brothers, but their hands were tied by the various foreign princes they were serving.[8] When the independence of the Jewish state was proclaimed in 143/2 B.C.E. (twenty years after the revolt!), Simeon declared that he wanted to acquire the territory of his fathers, saying, "We have neither taken any other man's land, nor do we hold dominion over other people's territory, but only over the inheritance of our fathers. On the contrary, for a certain time it was unjustly held by our enemies; but we, seizing the opportunity, hold fast the inheritance of our fathers" (1 Macc 15:33–34). Simeon did not draw any exact border, which is significant because the biblical concepts of the Promised Land also show variations.[9] Simeon quite obviously did not want to commit himself while only Judea and some adjacent territories were under Jewish rule. Whether Simeon's declaration is historical or not, it remains a fact that he himself set out to conquer additional territory. He conquered Gezer, purified it, and settled there (1 Macc 13:43–48, 53).[10] He also conquered Joppa and, as in the case of Gezer, settled Jews there (13:11; 14:5, 34; 15:28, 35). It is not by accident that the author of 1 Maccabees linked the conquest of Joppa with Simeon's general policies, saying in a biblical tone, "He broadened the borders of his nation, and ruled over the land" (14:6). John Hyrcanus I, his successor, conquered Idumaea after 130 B.C.E. and judaized its inhabitants. He conquered Shechem, as well as parts of Transjordan, and subdued the Samaritans (*Antiquities* 13.254–258). In 104/3 B.C.E. Aristobulus I judaized the Itureans in the upper Galilee and apparently annexed their territory, but his short-lived reign brought to the throne Alexander Jannaeus, who was the greatest Jewish conqueror after King David. With a great deal of bloodshed, civil strife, and agony, he succeeded in getting hold of almost the whole of Palestine, that is, the territory east and west of the Jordan (except Ascalon). His empire was short-lived, however, and his wife, Salome, lost some of the recently conquered land. After her death, Palestine was torn to pieces and conquered by the Romans, to be discussed later, in chapter 9.[11]

Let us examine this period further. During the Hasmonean era certain Jewish circles, as we shall see later, had visions of their Promised Land reminiscent of Scripture because they were well acquainted with their Bible. But during the various stages of conquest they were pragmatic and adapted to the idea of being sovereigns of only parts of this Promised Land. This view, which was in line with pragmatic political ideas of borders at that time, had to take into consideration many factors such as relations with the non-Jews outside and inside Palestine, the military power of the Hasmonean state, internal opposition to the policies of the Hasmoneans, and the like.

What were the Jewish views concerning the territory during this period? Did they correspond to their neighbors' ideological approach to the issue of borders? In order to answer these questions we need to survey the concept of borders in the non-Jewish Hellenistic environment.

It is extraordinary to see how many Near Eastern peoples' awareness of traditional nationalistic borders did not undergo major change from the times antedating Alexander's conquests to the times afterward. This continuity may be seen when we compare some of Herodotus's descriptions of the Near East from the fifth century B.C.E. (as well as those of the historians of Alexander the Great) with those of Diodorus Siculus and Strabo (first century B.C.E. and C.E., respectively), many of which reflect Hellenistic times and the beginning of the Roman era.[12] Unfortunately we do not have much evidence in the Hellenistic period deriving from the nations themselves on their boundaries. Yet in many instances, the descriptions of national borders that we find in Hellenistic compositions were based on what the local inhabitants themselves told the historians, some of whom traveled in the Near East. We should also take into account that the Greek authors described the *barbaroi* in a tendentious manner. Still, we may say that the natural as well as the historical borders of many nations (Egypt, India, Libya, etc.) were preserved in Greek writings dealing with the ancient Near East.

Berossus, a writer of the third century B.C.E. who in many ways still represented the national views of the Babylonians in the Hellenistic period,[13] defines the perimeter of Babylon. His depiction reflects the older views about what the perimeter of Babylon should be. Berossus was preoccupied with the question of borders in his *Babyloniaca* (of which we possess only second-rate fragments), saying that "the land of the Babylonians lies between the Tigris and Euphrates rivers. . . . In the first year a beast named Oannes appeared from the Erythraean Sea, in a place adjacent to Babylonia."[14] In the light of the literature of his time, we may assume that in the original composition much more space was given to the description of the natural borders of Babylon. Later he mentions the "land of the Assyrians as opposed to the one of the Babylonians."[15] For him, as for most Hellenistic writers, political and natural borders were identical. Another historian, Dionysius Scytobrachion, describes in his *Fabulae Libyacae* (which was composed at some point during the third or second century B.C.E.) the perimeter of Libya according to the mythological point of view,[16] the awareness of which was very strong in the third and second centuries B.C.E. Mythology was nourished by wishful thinking. This interesting historian refers to borders in a utopian manner (Diodorus Siculus 3.52.4–53.6).

The Jewish Hellenistic writer Ezekiel the Tragedian, who wrote a tragedy in Greek about the Exodus of the Jews from Egypt, depicts Libya as a political entity with "clear" borders.[17] Reading between the lines of his work, we can discern some current Hellenistic notions that were transferred into Libya's past.[18] The Indian border, where apparently the "political" corresponded with the natural, emerges through Diodorus Siculus's description, probably deriving from Megasthenes' *Indica,* written at the end of the fourth and the beginning of the third centuries B.C.E. He says (Diodorus Siculus 2.35), "India is four-sided in shape and the side which faces east. . . . The countries which surround India, they say, such as Scythia,

Bactria, and Ariana, are higher than India."[19] Egypt in Diodorus Siculus 1 and Strabo is also defined by both its natural and its traditional borders, as are the territories of many other peoples of the Hellenistic period. This brings us nearer to Palestine.[20]

The question of a Phoenician border arises from the work of Philo Byblos. Although Philo wrote his *Phoenician History* during the Roman era, he nevertheless shows that until late into Roman times the idea of the traditional historical borders of Byblos was still alive (Phoenicia = Byblos, Tyre, Sidon, etc.).[21] The same holds true of the Samaritans and their borders. The Samaritans, according to Josephus, claimed to be the heirs of Ephraim and Manasseh (Joseph's sons), which means that they based the legitimacy of their territorial position on a tradition going back to the remote past.[22] According to Genesis 48 their territory was given to the two sons of Joseph by Jacob in the region of the Samarian hills. Here we find a striking example of the identity between "ethnic" (e.g., nationalist) and "territorial" borders as preserved (probably) in the awareness of the Samaritans themselves. They did not strive for the occupation of the whole of Palestine, but were satisfied—at least during the Hellenistic period—with their little territory in the midst of Palestine, the territory granted to Ephraim and Manasseh.[23] We hear about the perimeter of the major city of the Samaritans, Shechem, from the Samaritan Hellenist Theodotus, who presented it in a utopian manner. Pseudo-Eupolemus, also a Samaritan writer, mentions the perimeter of the city of Shechem in connection with the temple on Mount Gerizim. These two authors are preserved in a very fragmentary state,[24] but even from the few fragments we can learn about their awareness of the territorial dimension.

The Book of Jubilees, written in the second century B.C.E., gives us an idea of a "fluctuating" Edomite border, both before and after the territorial expansion of the Edomites.[25] This notion may have been invented by the author of Jubilees, yet it reveals an awareness of a political border for that nation in the second century B.C.E. Although it emanates from an adversary to the Idumaean cause, it still represents a notion of a national border. Many more examples could be given, but these will suffice for the moment.

The evidence shows that Hellenistic authors writing about the nations of the ancient Near East usually emphasized either the natural, or the traditional and ethnic borders of the nations they surveyed. In many cases the perimeter was legitimized by some god's "ownership" of it.[26] Naturally, historians of the Hellenistic era were the ones to refer more to the artificial political borders. But even in the harsh political games of the era, ethnic boundaries were not altogether forgotten—for instance, in the famous partition of Alexander's conquests in Babylon and Triparadeisus after his death. At the conference that took place at Triparadeisus in July 320 B.C.E., the territories of Alexander were distributed by Antipater. He assigned Egypt to Ptolemy and "gave Syria to Laomedon of Mitylene and Cilicia to Philoxenus. Of the upper satrapies Mesopotamia and Arbelitis were given to Amphimachus, Babylonia to Seleucus, Susiane to Antigenes . . . Persia to Peucestes, Carmania to Tlepolemus, Media to Pithon, Parthia to Philip. . . . Of the satrapies that face the north, Cappadocia was assigned to Nicanor, Great Phrygia and Lycia to Antigonus as before, Caria to Asander, Lydia to Cleitus, and Hellespontine Phrygia to Arrhidaeus" (Diodorus Siculus 18.39.5–7).[27] These were not just geographical divisions; some of them represented deeply rooted ethnogeographical notions going back to much earlier times, of which people were still fully aware in the Hellenistic era.

The concept of an exact perimeter is only part of the picture. Universalistic views of the world were circulating before Alexander the Great's conquests, both in the ancient Near East and the Greek West. They were usually associated with mythology and did not necessarily aim at depicting any exact perimeter of a particular border. They were in most instances exempt from the more imperialistic overtones that will be discussed later in this chapter. Many of the universalistic views merely described famous mythological figures or heroes who wandered through the then-known world or parts of it. Sometimes they walked through an imaginary world. Homer's Odysseus is a familiar example, but what world he moved in is not altogether clear (Vergil's Aeneas travels in a much more realistic world).[28] The search for the Golden Fleece led the heroes from Greece to the eastern shores of the Black Sea (perhaps in the footsteps of Greek colonies that were founded at the time),[29] an indication that Greek mythology of the classical era already knew many parts of the world outside the Greek motherland.

Many universalistic ideas of that kind can also be found in the ancient Near East—for instance, the third-millennium Mesopotamian view concerning the four corners of the world[30] and the Egyptian ones (incorporated in Amun-Re and the Aten disk).[31] More general and abstract ideas can be found in the Old Testament.[32] Some of these views reflect current political overtones, but usually they only express the theocentric thought found in the East, namely, that God and his representatives on earth rule the universe and the world. But more imperialistic universal views were also circulating in the ancient Near East, which had much more of a defined perimeter (e.g., the Egyptian god-king who conquered specific territories outside Egypt).[33] But let us return to the Greek Hellenistic world.

When the great Hellenistic historian Polybius wrote his universal history of the ecumene (the inhabited world known to western writers) in the second century B.C.E., he showed astonishment that Rome was in the process of conquering great parts of the Mediterranean basin.[34] He was not in the least concerned with the probability that Rome would conquer the eastern ecumene (i.e., east to Asia Minor and Palestine). It just did not occur to him that Rome would follow in the wake of Alexander the Great's conquests. Thus a clear-cut distinction can be seen in the thought of the early Hellenistic period in Greece and in Rome between the eastern ecumene and the western ecumene. The East was known to have been ruled by empires in the remote past, unlike the West in Polybius's time. For the first time the West was being gradually conquered by an empire (Carthage was not an empire in the regular sense of the word; it had many commercial strongholds in the Mediterranean basin before the Romans embarked on their imperial enterprises).[35] Until the Romans penetrated the eastern Mediterranean in the seventies of the first century B.C.E., this part of the world only knew the eastern empires: Assyria, Babylon, Media, and Persia.[36]

It is therefore not surprising that a variety of imperialistic views, which were associated with local gods as well as with heroes of the past, were to be found in the East well before Alexander the Great. Therefore, when he reached the East in 333 B.C.E., both Greek and eastern universal concepts had been circulating for many years. W. W. Tarn, following classical authors such as Strabo (15.3–7 [C686–C687]), thought that Alexander wanted to compete with Dionysus's famous journey to India, already known in Greece in the fifth century B.C.E., and with that of Semiramis, the Assyro-Persian goddess.[37] But whether Alexander was influenced by these journeys remains questionable until it can be ascertained that the later Alexander historians such as Arrian did not retroject later views into Alexander's motivations for conquering the world.[38] A universal empire embracing the whole of the eastern world was not a new phenomenon in praxis when Alexander appeared in the East: the great empires of Assyria, Babylon, Media, and Persia were already matters of the past. After Alexander's conquest, universal ideas of a common boundary for the eastern ecumene flourished in the various regions of the ancient Near East, some associated with gods, others with historical figures. These ideas were usually adapted to fit the new era. We can see this tendency in, for example, the presentation of Amun-Re, who was associated with many past imperialistic enterprises in Egyptian history. It can also be seen in the mythological Myrina, the queen of the Amazons, who conquered a Hellenistical empire of her own in the eastern Mediterranean; and in Osiris, the Egyptian god who drew a perimeter resembling that of Alexander the Great, but starting from Egypt rather than from Macedonia.[39] But more historical figures were also associated with imperialism, such as Nebuchadnezzar II the Babylonian king (Megasthenes, *Indica*) and the quasi-historical Sesostris, the Egyptian king.[40] It should be emphasized that conquests were attributed to these two figures that they did not necessarily make. Even Cambyses and Darius, the Persian kings who conquered Egypt, were viewed there as universal leaders—the Egyptians called the Persian king "Asia's ruler."[41] Hence it is not surprising that some of the Seleucid kings put the same title on their coins.[42]

Thus, in the literature of the Hellenistic period there is frequently found a coexistence of local, particularistic, and ethnic views with universal and imperialistic ones. Chapter 9 will show that in the course of time the imperialistic expansion of Rome was given its mythological "precedent" in Heracles the wanderer. The wandering god Heracles drew a perimeter that was juxtaposed to the eastern versions found in the Egyptian Osiris myth, the Libyan Myrina conquests, Megasthenes' Dionysus, and the Assyro-Persian Semiramis legend.

Alexander's great achievement was the actual conquest of the eastern ecumene (this time by a Macedonian king).[43] For the first time (except for a minor incident when Darius conquered part of Thrace at the end of the sixth century B.C.E.) Greece and Macedonia became an integral part of the eastern ecumene, which included Asia Minor, Egypt, Palestine, Babylonia, Iran, and many regions eastward to India. Alexander attempted to make this new ecumene one unified world; as already mentioned elsewhere, he only partially succeeded.

What is meant when a "border" is mentioned? Is it only a well-defined perimeter, a line drawn between points that signifies the division between different territories? Is there any ideological reference at all to the contents of a territory? What is the meaning of territory within certain borders? The territory itself was a significant factor in the perception of the territorial dimension, as Strabo's detailed descriptions show. A good example comes from the "western" historian Polybius, who described the Cynaethans. According to Polybius the people of Arcadia in Greece differed from their neighbors because of their special location and special climatological and topographical circumstances (4.20–21).[44] In other words, location, the quality of territory, and climatological conditions within the perimeter were decisive factors for the creation of the differences among the nations and peoples of the inhabited world. Rousseau and Montesquieu did not invent this idea; it can be found in Plato, Polybius, and Strabo.

Two different approaches to a territory can be found in Hellenistic literature. First, some of the literature abounds with utopian motifs that refer to the general conditions of a land in its national context. On examining writers such as Iambulus and Euhemerus, as well as Dionysius Scytobrachion, it can be seen that within the borders much was described in a utopian or idealistic manner.[45] Many antithetical aspects (i.e., antithetical to the real world) are apparent in such descriptions. Whereas Iambulus's island is an invention, Aristeas's description of Palestine (made by a Jew from the Diaspora) constitutes an example of the use of utopian motifs in a nationalistic context. The territorial dimension of the land thus was ideal in all its aspects: it was climatologically perfect and self-contained (*autarkeia*), the crops were *automatoi* (growing naturally without any human intervention) and minerals were exported (or preserved; cf. also Eupolemus). When these qualities were used to describe a particular nation or tribe, they were used in order to enhance the stature of the nation involved. The utopian description naturally ignored the difficulties apparent in the territory, such as hostile foreign nations occupying it, bad climatological conditions, wars, and the like.[46] But there is a second approach to the idea of territory: in certain instances the literature revealed some of the more ugly features of reality, which in one way or another influenced the national identity of the population. Wars, bad climate, illnesses, bad geopolitical conditions, insufficiency of crops—all of these factors, according to classical authors, had their impact on the existence of the nation in antiquity. Like the utopian elements, these features infiltrated the literature under discussion. The sources provide ample information about the variety of methods by which territory was acquired, whether by missionary, cultural, military, or economic means.[47]

Against this background, so typical of Hellenistic culture, the territorial views of the Jews at the time of their movement toward statehood will be examined. The reader may already have received the impression from the previous chapters that the Jews were like their non-Jewish neighbors in many respects, though not necessarily directly influenced by them. The Jews were part of the ancient Near East, as can be seen in their territorial considerations both in the practical dimension and in the ideological sphere. The Jewish state did not act within a vacuum—it maintained diplomatic relations with other states, it played a powerful role in the region throughout the time of its existence, it conquered a lot of territory, and it had to justify its actions. Relations with political entities surrounding the Jewish state were active and at the same time of a complicated nature. For these reasons, in the Hasmonean literature one finds many of the same issues that were current in the non-Jewish literature of the Hellenistic world. A great deal of what has been said about the territorial political awareness of the surrounding world may sound familiar. Nevertheless, we will see that the Jews remained very traditional in terms of the answers (i.e., contents) they gave to the questions of their time.

The Jews, like other nations of the region, were aware of the historical heritage of their borders. In contradistinction to most other nations of this period, we happen to know through the Jewish literature what the idea of border and its related concepts were in

Israel. A synchronic description of territorial acquisitions and their reflection in the literature of the era has been given elsewhere.[48] The difficulties are enormous, in particular because of the lack of substantial information about the Hasmonean conquests. Also, the available documents of the pseudepigrapha and apocrypha cannot be dated exactly. Thus a more thematic method will be used to describe the attitudes that emerge from the pseudepigrapha and apocrypha concerning the territorial dimension of the period 168–63 B.C.E.

Many documents from the period under survey reveal the variations of the territorial dimension. These documents emanated from various ideological strata of society, which cannot always be differentiated from one another, such as the Pharisees, Essenes, and Sadducees (as well as Jews from the Diaspora). They all shared a great passion for the Land, as well as the technique of recourse to the past to justify their holding of the Land.

The Jews of the Hellenistic period referred frequently to God's promise of the Land, which in many of its nuances goes back to the natural borders of Palestine. According to this promise the borders were to be identical with the political national one.[49] According to one version, the Jews would be situated in a vast region of the Mideast and then would eliminate all other nations from their national territory (the War Scroll). The natural physical borders were the basis for God's promise of the Land, which the Jews in their long history never abandoned. For instance, it is repeated more than once in the Book of Jubilees (13:19–21; 14:18; 15:10; 17:3; 32:19), where the author also emphasizes that the country was a "good country" (12:30; 13:2–7; 25:17; etc.). Most literate Jews knew their scriptures very well. Thus associations with their past constituted a significant facet of their life. When they mentioned for example the Israelite kingdom, they made immediate associations with kingship, territory, and other aspects of the national existence.

Ben Sira, even before the recreation of the Jewish state was on the agenda, viewed the Land in a romantic, traditional manner.[50] For him Abraham constituted a symbol of the divine promise of the Land (44:21): "to cause them to inherit from sea to sea and from the River to the ends of the earth." Jacob stood among other things for the unity of the whole nation settled on its Land: ". . . and gave him the inheritance and he set him in tribes as to be divided into twelve" (44:23). Ben Sira viewed the conquest of the Land from its indigenous peoples through the historical figures of Joshua and Caleb (46:1–10):

> Joshua, the son of Nun, was mighty in war,
> . . . To take vengeance on the enemies that rose up against
>   them,
> So that he might give Israel their possessions. . . .
> This champion was followed by one
> Who in the days of Moses did an act of piety,
> None other than Caleb, . . .
> These two alone were preserved
> Out of six hundred thousand people on foot
>
> To bring them into their possessions,
> To a land running with milk and honey.

At one point, however, Ben Sira alludes to his own day and the peoples of the Land, saying, "When he [David] had put on the diadem he fought and subdued the enemies on all sides and plundered the Philistine cities and broke their horn unto this day" (47:6–7). This claim was but wishful thinking on his part. In 50:25–26 he mentions that "For two nations doth my soul feel abhorrence, yea, and [for] a third, which is not a people; the inhabitants of Seir and Philistia, and the foolish nation that dwelleth in Shechem." In general Ben Sira was very interested in the historical biblical figures who had crushed the enemies of the Land. He associated Wisdom with the Land. When it searched for a place to settle, Wisdom was commanded by God to tie up its future with the people settled in Palestine, namely, the Jews (24:6–14). Ben Sira used the sites of Palestine for his imagery: "I was exalted like a cedar in the Lebanon, Or a cypress in the mountain of Hermon." He wished that God would "gather all the tribes of Jacob, that they may receive their inheritance as in the days of old." Others, apart from Ben Sira, were also thinking of God's promise of the Land, but propounded different ideas.

When Eupolemus in later years mentioned David and Solomon, he paid much attention to the political borders they acquired for the nation through conquest and subjugation of foreign nations.[51] Although he was mostly interested in Jerusalem and its Temple, Eupolemus projected onto the history of these two kings all of his wishful thinking concerning the borders of the nation in his own time. In line with the embellishments of biblical history that had become more and more fashionable, he said that David "subdued the Syrians who live on the shores of the Euphrates and in the region of Commagene and the Assyrians of Galadene, and the Phoenicians. He also led an army against the Idumeans," and many others "whom he compelled to pay tribute to the Jews" (in Eusebius, *Praeparatio evangelica* 9.30.3–5). This border is broader than the one we get from the biblical picture of David's realm, and shows clearly what Eupolemus's dreams were. Within this border he wished to see the nations subjugated to Israel (including the ones that were in his day friends of Israel, such as the Nabataeans). Eupolemus's description of the political borders of King David's realm closely corresponded to the borders promised to Israel by God in the Bible. Yet when he referred to Solomon's realm, the foreign nations such as the Ammonites and Edomites had "disappeared" and a regional division of Palestine was described instead. The perimeter of the Land during Solomon's reign was according to Eupolemus smaller than the one of David's time, but did not contain foreigners (*Praeparatio evangelica* 9.33). What matters here is that the border of the Israelite United Kingdom was drawn like the political borders of the nations mentioned above in this chapter.

The Book of Jubilees (which retells Genesis through Exodus 12) takes us back to the first fathers of the nation, Abraham, Isaac, and Jacob, who had wandered in the "virginal" Land that had no definite political borders.[52] Thus the Land, in place of the Temple and Jerusalem, is the focal point in this composition. According to Jubilees 10 the people of Israel were given a place within the ecumene together with many other nations of the world.[53] The conflict in the time of Jubilees with the nations of Palestine is transferred to this newly created history of the patriarchs. Jubilees states that when the people of Israel received their territory, Canaan (who symbolizes the foreigners on the Land) hindered them in the process of settlement (10:28–30). But his father, Ham, and his brothers, Cush and Mizraim, said to him, "You have dwelt in a land which is not yours nor did it come forth for us by lot. Do not do this . . . but he would not listen to them and he dwelt in the land of Lebanon from

Hamath to the entrance of Egypt, he and his sons, until this day. And, therefore, that land is called Canaan" (10:30–34).

The universalism that can be found in Jewish literature corresponds very well to what has been traced in Hellenistic literature. There is a "mythological" universalism in the Genesis Apocryphon and other related literature, which may have its sources in the second century B.C.E. and may be somehow related to the Book of Jubilees (perhaps they share a common source). Abraham is portrayed as walking in the world that was promised to him by God (21:5–9): "So I, Abram, set out to go around and look at the land. I started going about from the Gihon River, moving along the sea, until I reached the Mount of the Ox. I journeyed from [the coast] of this Great Salt Sea and moved along the Mount of the Ox toward the east through the breadth of the land, until I reached the Euphrates River. I traveled along the Euphrates, until I came to the Reed Sea in the east. (Then) I moved along the Reed Sea, until I reached the tongue of the Reed Sea, which goes from the Red Sea. (From there) I journeyed to the south, until I reached the Gihon River. Then I returned, came home safely, and found all my household safe and sound." (According to an unpublished document from Qumran, Noah moves about in the eastern ecumene.) The drawing of a perimeter of the world and the placement of the Jews in it which are found in Jubilees 10 and the Genesis Apocryphon are reminiscent of the maps drawn by Osiris and Sesostris in which Egypt was given a central place in the ecumene among the other nations.[54] Palestine and the Jews of the Land remained central to the Jews of the Hellenistic period settled in Palestine.

The Testament of the Twelve Patriarchs may be a reflection of the polemical debates on the territory between the Jews and the Samaritans in the second century B.C.E. The Samaritans claimed that they had a legitimate right to be settled on the territory that was given by Jacob to Ephraim and Manasseh, according to Genesis 48:17–22. If the boundaries of the emerging Jewish state are reflected in this document (i.e., the southern part of Palestine symbolized by the southern tribes), then there clearly was a claim made by the Jews to the whole of Palestine, which is symbolized in this document by the twelve tribes of Israel. In the Testament we can discern a tension between the presentation of the twelve tribes on the one hand, and a partial domination of the Jews over the Land on the other (before Alexander Jannaeus's time).[55] The concept of twelve tribes recurs again and again in the documents of the Hasmonean period, and can also be found in the Jewish literature of the Roman period. The number twelve, signifying the completeness of the Jewish nation, is also associated with the settlement of the nation on the most extensive territory the Jews were believed to have possessed in their past. Other documents of the period, such as Judith, 1 and 2 Maccabees, and perhaps 1 Enoch 85–90, give the same impression as that received from John Hyrcanus's territorial statement mentioned above. There was no fixed idea about the perimeter of the borders of the Hasmonean state—the literature exactly reflected the political situation (which was true also of the Hellenistic environment). Borders could be broadened or shrunk, and many events from the past could be brought forward to justify them. It should then be emphasized that during the Hasmonean period the Jews had achieved no consensus on the perimeter of their emerging state. To judge from their literature, they seem to have been pluralistic in this respect. Their dreams and speculations were based on the Hebrew Bible, which also was not consistent in describing the dimensions of the Land. The literature could refer to the Promised Land, the borders of David and Solomon, and those of other Israelite kings as well. They could embellish on other territorial variations and refer to the borders described in the Books of Chronicles, which were significantly different from parallel descriptions in Samuel and Kings.[56]

Jewish literature of the Hellenistic period, just like the literature of the non-Jews, reveals a great deal about wars with intruders and foreign nations that jeopardized the rule of the nation on its land (Manetho, Scytobrachion, Megasthenes, Euhemerus). One of the major problems with which the Jews were confronted during the period of their independence in the Land was the presence in certain regions of it of foreign nations (they were there also later, but then the clashes would have different overtones, as perhaps reflected in Josephus, the New Testament, and Pseudo-Philo). From Persian times onward clashes between the Jews and the Samaritans, Arabs, Ammonites, Edomites, and others are well known. These struggles had their roots, among other factors, in national differences. 1 Enoch 85–90 surveyed this bloody struggle throughout the long history of the Jews. According to the author's extreme view, the Land in the past was never a guarantee of the safety of the Jewish people. In his own time, however, a new era started as a result of the Maccabean leadership.[57]

When the Land came under Jewish sovereignty in the second century B.C.E., the Jews suddenly had become the new masters of some of those unfriendly nations within the Land, namely, the Edomites, Itureans, Arabs, Phoenicians, and Greeks in the coastal cities. The problematic relations with these nations are reflected in the literature of the period. While in the literature from the Diaspora these clashes are not evident at all (though the people settled around Palestine are mentioned), the Palestinian writers explain the presence of foreign nations in the Land through etiological tales.

Jewish nationalism gained its strength from the examples it drew on from its past.[58] Here one can trace some interestingly nuanced Jewish attitudes to non-Jews settled on their land, such as aggression, which probably emanates from the Essenes (but was probably shared by other groups as well). In their so-called War Scroll, they propounded the idea that at the end of the days the elect Jews, directed by God and the heavenly angels, would eliminate all other nations in the Land and rule over almost the whole of the ancient Near East (i.e., a region that is greater than the Promised Land in its widest extent). This document may have been a radical reaction to the actual conquest of the Land by the Hasmoneans and their peaceful relations with some of the people settled on it (2 Macc 12:10–12, 29–31). Other attitudes about this problem were more practical: some wished to crush and subjugate the foreign nations settled on the Land (see for instance Judith and Eupolemus), while others wished to judaize them (see [Ruth], Judith, Prayer of Nabonidus, and in a way also Jubilees). Dreams of the conquest and subjugation of other peoples were very popular in Hellenistic literature, as were those of assimilating the enemy.[59] In many instances the current attitude of Israel to the nations was retrojected into the past, where a rapport and even a kinship between Jews and the ancestors of these same nations was presented. The Book of Jubilees made up various historical situations, which were rewritten into the past history of Israel. For example, the ancestors of Edom and the Arabs were presented as having family ties with the ancestors of the Jewish people in early times, and were shown even to have adhered to Judaism. This link would have made them potentially eligible to become Jews and to be part of the Jewish nation. This is no longer the individual judaizing that is found in the books of Ruth, Judith (Achior), Daniel, and the Prayer of Nabonidus. Jubilees may have been written against the background of the attempts to justify the judaizing of Idumaeans in Hyrcanus I's reign (125 B.C.E.). It is not accidental that such a variety of attitudes appeared in the literature at the time that the Land was actually conquered by the Jews during the Hasmonean period.

Is there any opposing literature from that period, maintaining that the conquest of territory was a negative thing? Perhaps some of the *Pesharim* (commentaries) from Qumran, which have a very critical opinion of the Hasmoneans, allude to such an attitude.[60] The reason may be that some Essenes wanted a pure land, with no other nations on it, a land in which the Jewish *ethnos* and its land would be congruent. It is interesting to note that in the historiography dealing with the Hasmonean period (1–2 Maccabees and Josephus's *Antiquities* and *Jewish War*) no attempt was made to discuss the ideological aspects of the dimensions of the territory. Both the expansion of the Jewish state and its loss of territory in terms of political borders (which were each achieved through power politics) were described according to the conventions of Hellenistic historiography.

The Jews were interested in the constituitive elements of the territory, that is to say, how the characteristics of their nation were presented, just as Hellenistic writers were. In the literature from Palestine as well as in that of the Diaspora, utopian conceptions of the dimensions of the territory similar to those found in Hellenistic literature can be seen, such as in the Letter of Aristeas and the Book of Jubilees. The depiction of the Land that emanates from the Diaspora found in the Letter of Aristeas is interesting in that it shows how a Diaspora Jew described his national land in utopian terms (107–120): "The zeal of the farmers [in Palestine] is indeed remarkable. In fact their land is thickly covered with large numbers of olive trees and corn crops and pulse, and moreover with vines and abundant honey. . . . They have many flocks and herds of various kinds, with ample pasture for them. . . . The land is agricultural and well fitted also for commerce; the city is the home of many crafts, and there is no lack of goods imported from overseas, because of its convenient harbors that supply them, such as Ascalon,

Joppa, and Gaza, and also Ptolemais (Acco). . . . The district is well watered everywhere, has everything in abundance, and is very secure" (112–115). Aristeas presented his national territory as an ideal place, as Euhemerus probably did with Egypt, Megasthenes with India, and Scytobrachion with Libya.

In Hellenistic literature we have come across certain "territorial" heroes who became prominent during the time of nationalistic conquests, such as Osiris, Semiramis, Sesostris, Nebuchadnezzar, and Myrina. The national interest in territorial boundaries is likewise reflected in the description of the heroes of Israel's past and their exploits. The promise of the Land to Abraham is usually made clear, as are the wanderings of his descendants through the Land. The twelve eponyms of the nation are mentioned again and again, whereas David and Solomon appear in their "territorial" roles rather than in their other roles, the latter being David's messianic role and Solomon's wisdom (which became apparent after the Roman occupation of Palestine). Much of the emphasis on these and other figures changes in the period after 63 B.C.E.

In sum, the Jews were well familiar with the passages in their holy scriptures that contain opinions concerning the dimensions of the territory. When they gradually started to create a Jewish state on their Land in the second century B.C.E., they, like their neighbors in the Hellenistic world, expressed a great interest in their Land. They did not just refer back to the biblical concepts about the Land, but embellished on them in order to adjust them to their new circumstances. Also, they were fully aware of the territorial and national issues that concerned their neighbors, but still used their *own* traditional material to justify their actions during the process of the conquest of Palestine. In most of the literature from this period the territorial idea is very much alive, and it becomes one of the main symbols of Jewish nationalism of the time. This situation will change altogether during the period 63 B.C.E.–70 C.E.

Notes

¹ For the history of the period see W. W. Tarn and G. T. Griffith, *Hellenistic Civilisation*, 3d ed. (London, 1952); *CAH,* 2d ed., 7.1.2, 8 (with the older bibliography). See in particular C. Habicht, "The Seleucids and Their Rivals," *CAH* 8.324–387. For the states of Asia Minor, see H. Heinen, "The Syrian-Egyptian Wars and the New Kingdoms of Asia Minor," *CAH* 7.1.412–433.

² Cf. V. Tcherikover, *Hellenistic Civilization and the Jews* (Philadelphia, 1959), pp. 39–116; H. Bengtson, *Die Strategie in der hellenistischen Zeit* (Munich, 1937–1952), 3. 166–171; M. T. Lenger, *Corpus des ordonnances des Ptolémées* (Brussels, 1964); B. Lifshitz, "Der Kult des Ptolemaios IV Philopator in Jafa," *Zeitschrift des deutschen Palästina-Vereins* 78 (1962): 82–84; R. S. Bagnall, *The Administration of the Ptolemaic Possessions Outside Egypt* (Leiden, 1976), pp. 11–24 and passim; M. Stern, "Notes on the Story of Joseph the Tobiad," in his *Studies in Jewish History* (Jerusalem, 1991), pp. 22–34 (Hebrew); F. M. Cross, "The Discovery of the Samaria Papyri," *Biblical Archaeologist* 26 (1963): 110–121; M. E. Stone, *Scriptures, Sects and Visions* (Oxford, 1980), in particular chaps. 4 and 5. See also F. M. Abel, "La Syrie et la Palestine au temps de Ptolémée Ier Soter," *Revue biblique* 44 (1935): 559–581.

³ Cf. chapter 5 below.

⁴ A. de Tocqueville, *L'Ancien Régime et la Révolution* (1856), esp. book 2, chap. 1.

⁵ For the Jews being scattered all over Palestine see 1 Maccabees passim. For the Seleucids at this period see *CAH* 7.1.175–220 (Musti), and Habicht, cited in note 1 above. For Seleucid rule in Palestine, see Bengtson, *Strategie,* 2.159–188; A. Mittwoch, "Tribute and Land-Tax in Seleucid Judaea," *Biblica* 36 (1955): 352–361; Y. H. Landau, "A Greek Inscription Found near Heftzibah," *Israel Exploration Journal* 16 (1966): 54–70; T. Fischer, "Zur Seleukideninschrift von Hefzibah," *Zeitschrift für Papyrologie und Epigraphik* 33 (1979): 131–138.

⁶ See in general P. W. Skehan and A. A. Di Lella, *The Wisdom of Ben Sira,** pp. 8–127.

⁷ Cf. for the different approaches M. Hengel, *Judaism and Hellenism* (London and Philadelphia, 1974), vol. 1, chap. 4, and F. Millar's reaction in *Journal of Jewish Studies* 29.1 (1978): 1–21.

⁸ Cf. W. D. Davies, *The Territorial Dimension of Judaism* (Berkeley, Los Angeles, and London, 1982), pp. 62–63 and D. Mendels, *The Land of Israel as a Political Concept in Hasmonean Literature* (Tübingen, 1987), passim.

⁹ Cf. M. Buber, *Israel and Palestine: The History of an Idea* (London, 1952); *Das Land Israel in biblischer Zeit,* ed. G. Strecker (Göttingen, 1983), pp. 7–153; H. M. Orlinsky, "The Biblical Concept of the Land of Israel: Cornerstone of the Covenant Between God and Israel," *Eretz Israel* 18 (1985): 43–55; Davies, *Territo-*

rial Dimension, pp. 6–28; and M. Weinfeld, "Inheritance of the Land—Privilege Versus Obligation," *Zion* 49 (1984): 115–137 (Hebrew).

[10] R. Reich, "The Boundary of Gezer—On the Jewish Settlement at Gezer in Hasmonean Times," *Eretz Israel* 18 (1985): 167–179 (Hebrew), and his article "The 'Boundary of Gezer' Inscriptions Again," *Israel Exploration Journal* 40 (1990): 44–46.

[11] For the history of the Hasmonean conquests, see H. Jagersma, *A History of Israel from Alexander the Great to Bar Kochba* (Philadelphia, 1985), pp. 79–94; E. Schürer, *The History of the Jewish People in the Age of Jesus Christ,* rev. G. Vermes et al. (Edinburgh, 1973–1987), 1.164–242; and U. Rappaport, *The History of Eretz Israel* (Jerusalem, 1981), pp. 193–232 (Hebrew). For Jannaeus's foreign relations, see M. Stern, "Judaea and Her Neighbors in the Days of Alexander Jannaeus," *The Jerusalem Cathedra* 1 (1981): 22–46.

[12] For geographical descriptions in general see P. Pédech, *La Géographie des Grecs* (Paris, 1976).

[13] For Berossus see S. M. Burstein, *The Babyloniaca of Berossus* (Malibu, Calif., 1978) (with the older bibliography); and especially A. Kuhrt, "Berossus' *Babyloniaka* and Seleucid Rule in Babylonia," in *Hellenism in the East,* ed. A. Kuhrt and S. Sherwin-White (Berkeley, Los Angeles, and London, 1987), pp. 32–56. For a concept of a border among the Babylonians and Assyrians, see A. K. Grayson, *Assyrian and Babylonian Chronicles* (New York, 1975), pp. 51–55, 157–170.

[14] Burstein, *Babyloniaca,* p. 13.

[15] Ibid., p. 24.

[16] For Dionysius, see J. S. Rusten, *Dionysius Scytobrachion* (Cologne, 1980). Cf. chapter 2 above.

[17] Ezekiel, *Exagoge* lines 59–65; and R. G. Robertson, "Ezekiel the Tragedian," in *Old Testament Pseudepigrapha,* ed. J. H. Charlesworth (New York, 1983–1985), 2.810–811. In general for Ezekiel, see H. Jacobson, *The Exagoge of Ezekiel* (Cambridge, 1983).

[18] Sepphora describes Libya: "Stranger, this land is called Libya. It is inhabited by tribes of various peoples, Ethiopians, black men. One man is the ruler of the land: he is both king and general. He rules the state, judges the people, and is a priest" (Ezekiel, *Exagoge* 60–65).

[19] For Megasthenes' *Indica* see T. S. Brown, "The Reliability of Megasthenes," *American Journal of Philology* 76 (1955): 18–33; idem, "The Merits and Weaknesses of Megasthenes," *Phoenix* 11 (1957): 12–24; A. Zambrini, "Gli *Indikā* di Megastene," *Annali della Scuola Normale Superiore di Pisa* 12.1 (1982): 71–149; idem, "Gli Indikā di Megastene. II," *Annali . . . di Pisa* 15.3 (1985): 781–853. Cf. in general for such accounts R. Drews, *The Greek Accounts of Eastern History* (Cambridge, Mass., 1973).

[20] Diodorus Siculus 1.31.6 and passim; and cf. Strabo, 17.1–2 passim, and D. Mendels, "The Polemical Character of Manetho's *Aegyptiaca*," in *Purposes of History*, ed. H. Verdin et al. (Louvain, 1990), pp. 92–110. Cf. Theocritus, *Idyll* 17.85–91, who describes Egypt's present border within a mythological context: "And of all Lord Ptolemy is king. Aye, and of Phoenicia he takes himself part, and of Arabia, and Syria and Libya and of the swart Ethiopians. In all Pamphylia his word is law, and with the spearmen of Cilicia, the Lycians and the warlike Carians; in the Isles of the Cyclades also, for the best ships that sail the seas are his"; see A. S. F. Gow, *Theocritus* (Cambridge, 1952), vol. 2 ad loc.

[21] Chapter 15, "and a woman called Berouth, who settled the area called Byblos." Cf. H. W. Attridge and R. A. Oden, *Philo of Byblos: The Phoenician History* (Washington, D.C., 1981), b, 10, c20 and especially p. 81, n. 47. In general for Philo Byblos see A. I. Baumgarten, *The Phoenician History of Philo of Byblos* (Leiden, 1983). Coins from Beirut of Antiochus IV bear an inscription in the Phoenician language: "of Laodicea which is in Canaan" (A. Houghton, *Coins of the Seleucid Empire from the Collection of Arthur Houghton* [New York, 1983], pp. 69–70). For the issue of Phoenician patriotism in Roman times see F. Millar, "The Phoenician Cities," *Proceedings of the Cambridge Philological Association* 209 (1983): 55–71; and G. Brizzi, "Il nazionalismo Fenicio di Filone di Byblos e la politica ecumenica di Adriano," *Oriens antiquus* 19 (1980): 117–131.

[22] In general for Josephus and the Samaritans see R. Egger, *Josephus Flavius und die Samaritaner* (Fribourg and Göttingen, 1986). This comes also to the fore in a recently published text from Qumran. Cf. E. Schuller, "4Q372:1: A Text about Joseph," *Revue de Qumran* 14(55) (1990): 349–376.

[23] Mendels, *The Land*, pp. 89–108.

[24] C. R. Holladay, *Fragments from Hellenistic Jewish Authors* (Chico, Calif., and Atlanta, Georg., 1983–1989), 1.157–187 and 2.51–204; and Mendels, *The Land*, pp. 109–119.

[25] Cf. Mendels, *The Land*, pp. 57–88.

[26] For this concept in the ancient Near East before Alexander the Great see D. I. Block, *The Gods of the Nations* (Jackson, Miss., 1988), with the previous literature cited there.

[27] For these partitions see D. Mendels, "Aetolia 331–301: Frustration, Political Power, and Survival," *Historia* 33 (1984): 129–180, with the older bibliography cited there. See also P. Green, *Alexander to Actium* (Berkeley, Los Angeles, and Oxford, 1990), pp. 8–9, 14–15.

[28] Cf. M. I. Finley, *The World of Odysseus*, 2d ed. (London, 1977); J. H. Finley, Jr., *Homer's Odyssey* (Cambridge, Mass., 1978), pp. 55–73 and passim; cf. Vergil, *Aeneid*, vols. 1 and 2 in the Loeb Classical Library edition.

[29] See already J. B. Bury's comment in *The History of Greece*, 3d ed. (London, 1951): "The voyage of the Argonauts in quest of the golden fleece commemorates in

a delightful legend the memorable day on which Greek sailors for the first time burst into the waters of the Euxine Sea" (p. 89).

[30] See for Mesopotamia C. J. Gadd, "The Dynasty of Agade and the Gutian Invasion," *CAH*, 3d ed., 1.2.448; 736–738 (H. Lewy); for instance a late inscription, the Victory Stele of Sennacherib (690 B.C.): "Sennacherib, the great king, the mighty king, king of the universe, king of Assyria, king of the four quarters" (inscription in Baltimore, the Walters Art Gallery, translated by Grayson).

[31] Cf. *CAH,* 3d ed., 1.2, 2.1, and 2d ed., 3.1 passim.

[32] Cf. Isa 2:1–4; Pss 2; 47:7–10. H. W. F. Saggs, *Civilization before Greece and Rome* (New Haven and London, 1989), pp. 176–194.

[33] Cf. Mendels, "Polemical Character."

[34] P. S. Derow, "Polybius, Rome and the East," *Journal of Roman Studies* 69 (1979): 1–15.

[35] On Carthage see in general S. Moscati, *Carthage: Art and Civilization* (Milan, 1982); W. Huss, *Geschichte der Karthager* (Munich, 1985); G. Charles-Picard, *Carthage: A Survey of Punic History and Culture from Its Birth to Final Tragedy* (London, 1987).

[36] Cf. D. Mendels, "The Five Empires: A Note on a Propagandistic *Topos,*" *American Journal of Philology* 102 (1981): 330–337; also A. Momigliano, "The Origins of Universal History," in his *On Pagans, Jews, and Christians* (Middletown, Conn., 1987), pp. 31–57.

[37] W. W. Tarn, *Alexander the Great* (Cambridge, 1948), 2.49–50 (and elsewhere). See also, for these matters, P. Goukowsky, *Essai sur les origines du mythe d'Alexandre,* 2 vols. (Nancy, 1978–1981).

[38] A. B. Bosworth, *A Historical Commentary on Arrian's History of Alexander,* vol. 1 (Oxford, 1980), ad loc.

[39] Cf. Mendels, "Polemical Character." See chapter 2 above.

[40] Kuhrt, "Berossus"; and for Sesostris, see A. B. Lloyd, "Nationalist Propaganda in Ptolemaic Egypt," *Historia* 31 (1982): 33–56. (And see also his article on Herodotus's description of Pharaonic history, "Herodotus' Account of Pharaonic History," *Historia* 37 [1988]: 22–53.)

[41] M. Lichtheim, *Ancient Egyptian Literature* (Berkeley, Los Angeles, and London, 1973–1980), 3.36–40, 42, 108.

[42] In a dedication to Antiochus IV, he is called "savior of Asia" (S. M. Burstein, *The Hellenistic Age from the Battle of Ipsos to the Death of Kleopatra VII* [Cambridge, 1985], p. 55).

[43] See in general A. B. Bosworth, *Conquest and Empire: The Reign of Alexander the Great* (Cambridge and New York, 1988).

⁴⁴ F. W. Walbank, *A Historical Commentary on Polybius* (Oxford, 1957), vol. 1 ad loc.

⁴⁵ For utopias of the ancient world in general see J. Ferguson, *Utopias of the Classical World* (London, 1975).

⁴⁶ M. I. Finley, "Utopianism Ancient and Modern," in his *The Use and Abuse of History* (London, 1986), pp. 178–192.

⁴⁷ For example: Diodorus Siculus 1.17.3–20.6, and books 1–5 passim.

⁴⁸ Cf. Mendels, *The Land,* passim.

⁴⁹ For the concept before the time of Alexander see Block, *Gods of the Nations;* and for the biblical concept in Israel in postbiblical times, see Weinfeld, "Inheritance," and some aspects in E. Schweid, *The Land of Israel* (Rutherford, N. J., 1985); *Das Land Israel,* ed. Strecker; and Orlinsky, "Biblical Concept."

⁵⁰ For more details, see Mendels, *The Land,* pp. 9–17 and Di Lella, *Ben Sira,* * ad loc.

⁵¹ Mendels, *The Land,* pp. 29–46.

⁵² For more details see ibid., pp. 57–88.

⁵³ Cf. P. S. Alexander, "The Imago Mundi of Jubilees," *Journal of Jewish Studies* 33 (1982): 197–213; and Mendels, *The Land.* See also F. Schmidt, "Jewish Representations of the Inhabited Earth During the Hellenistic and Roman Periods," in *Greece and Rome in Eretz-Israel,* ed. A. Kasher et al. (Jerusalem, 1990), pp. 119–134.

⁵⁴ For the text cf. N. Avigad and Y. Yadin, *A Genesis Apocryphon* (Jerusalem, 1956), and J. A. Fitzmyer, *The Genesis Apocryphon of Qumran Cave I,* 2d ed. (Rome, 1971); Mendels, *The Land,* pp. 63–64.

⁵⁵ Mendels, *The Land,* pp. 89–108.

⁵⁶ S. Japhet, *The Ideology of the Book of Chronicles and Its Place in Biblical Thought* (Frankfurt am Main, 1989).

⁵⁷ Mendels, *The Land,* pp. 19–28.

⁵⁸ Ibid., passim.

⁵⁹ Diodorus, Strabo, and Appian, as well as many others, abound in descriptions of that sort concerning the pagan world.

⁶⁰ The *Pesharim* are critical of every aspect of the Hasmonean rule (cf. in particular *Pesher Nahum* and *Pesher Habakkuk*). The Essenes were of the opinion that Israel itself (with the help of God's angels) would take the Land of Israel by force

from all foreigners settled on it. Hence, they no doubt were opposed to the fact that the impurified Hasmoneans made only partial conquests of the Land (instead of conquering the whole of it), and also left many foreigners on it, which made it impure. For the *Pesharim* in general, see P. M. Horgan, *Pesharim: Qumran Interpretation of Biblical Books* (Washington, D.C., 1979).

CHAPTER 5

Jerusalem: Capital, Temple, and Cult (200-63 B.C.E.)

How did other nations in the Hellenistic era view their temples? Was there necessarily a link between a religious center and a political capital? How did the Jews view their Temple, and what was their relationship with their priests? Did they ignore all their other traditional religious centers such as Hebron, Bethel, and Shechem? Can we say that the attitude of the Jews to the Temple and their understanding of its relation to the state was like that of their neighbors during the period under survey?

In the ancient Near East, after its conquest by Alexander the Great, we can see that the temples of the indigenous populations took on great political significance. Why did temples become so important politically, and why did they become symbols of nationalism in the Hellenistic era? In the first place, temples in the East had been associated with king and state long before Alexander the Great appeared on the scene, an association that continued after his death. Usually, kings were considered to be gods, or sons of the gods of the state, and temples were built in obedience to the wish of a god.[1] Second, the institution of priesthood in the ancient Near East was of major political significance. The priesthood became very powerful in various kingdoms and temple states because of its religious power and economic strength. It remained thus during the Hellenistic age.[2] Third, during the Persian occupation of the Near East, the indigenous secular leadership in many places was gradually being eliminated, and members of the priesthood were often the natural replacements for these secular leaders. Fourth, the priesthood gradually became the symbol of tradition and stood for the continued existence of the indigenous population. Priests became the leaders in the preservation of the autochthonous culture, language, and special ethnic customs. Thus, after Alexander the Great, the priesthood was almost the only institution in the various countries recognized by the indigenous populations as the champion of their national interests— as can be seen in Judea in the sixties of the second century B.C.E., when a minor priestly house started a national upheaval. In fact, we can see that in the Near East during the Hellenistic period, the priesthood in many places dominated much of the daily life and the "politics" of the indigenous populations who did not mingle with the Greek classes.

The continuity of ethnic traditions and their preservation by the local priesthoods emphasized not only the differences between the Greek strata of society and the native ones, but also the differences among the various nations of the Near East. The vast differences between the temples of Egypt and those of Asia Minor and the Seleucid Empire in terms of architecture, mythology, liturgy, and the social structure of their local priesthoods actually emphasized the uniqueness of the various nations in the ancient Near East. Ptolemaic Egypt has left us with much archaeological and epigraphic evidence of the strength, political, economic, and religious, in the native priesthood during the Hellenistic period.[3] Hellenistic Babylon and Uruk reveal the same.[4] The literary evidence coming from the East shows as well the political and religious strength of the local priesthoods (Manetho, Hecataeus, Berossus, Philo Byblos, etc.). In the light of these data from Babylon and Uruk as well as from other places in Mesopotamia, it seems that relations between the priesthoods and the royal Seleucid family were much more relaxed there than in Egypt.[5] In short, the temple and priesthood of the native populations played an important role in the preservation of a nationalistic awareness in the autochthonous populations in the ancient Near East, a role that continued well into the Roman period.[6]

On the Greek mainland and islands during the period under discussion, temples were also part of the political and social life of the *poleis* and federal states. But they did not necessarily accentuate the differences among "nations" in Greece (i.e., between Boeotians and Athenians) to the same degree as did the temples of various nations in the East. Also, in the East temples had a higher religiopolitical status than they did in classical Greece, where they declined in status after the fourth century B.C.E. Many of the former retained a high status throughout the Hellenistic period, the reasons for which are obvious. Whereas the Greeks adhered to the concept of an anthropocentric society (where the *anthropos,* the individual, was central), the society in the Near East was theocentric. God was the center of the world and was the one who directed it; the human being was considered insignificant.[7] God's dwelling place, the temple, thus played a major role. If we remember that the king in the East was thought to be closely associated with the gods (at times being the god or his son), then we see that the temple was equivalent to a political center.[8] The economic and political strength of the temples in the East brought about in many places the so-called temple-states, which had an autonomous *locus standi* and which at times even exercised independence in conducting foreign policy, as we learn from the geographer Strabo.[9]

Thus, in the ancient Near East from the third millennium B.C.E. temples had great political significance, and many examples can be given to illustrate this relation between politics and religion. Even so, not all temples achieved the same political status. There were some religious centers that acquired a very special political status, such as Memphis, Thebes, Jerusalem, and Babylon. The issue of religious center versus the political capital was highlighted in times of major political changes. For instance, the Hyksos dynasty made Avaris their capital, and when Akhenaten, the famous king of the Eighteenth Dynasty, carried out his religious reforms he founded a new religiopolitical capital at Tell el-Amarna. The Ramesides wished to highlight their dynasty and ancestry, and founded Pi-Ramessu.[10] When the Parthians advanced westward to enlarge their empire in 239 B.C.E., they at first built a capital at Nisa, in the province of Parthia. About 217 B.C.E. they made Hecatompylus the religiopolitical capital, and Ctesiphon became its heir about 50 B.C.E.[11] It is not accidental that Ctesiphon was founded as a capital just facing the old Seleucid capital of Seleucia on the Tigris. The old Israelite monarchy points to the same trend.

When the Israelite United Kingdom split into northern and southern monarchies in the late tenth century B.C.E., Jeroboam, the first king of the Northern Kingdom, founded "new" religiopolitical centers in Bethel and Dan to signify the drastic change in the political arena. Jerusalem, however, continued to serve as a religiopolitical center for all Israelites.[12] Omri, the North Israelite king, established a new capital for the Northern Kingdom in the ninth century B.C.E., in Samaria.[13] Ahab, his son, built a temple there for Baal. Interestingly, after Cyrus's declaration in 538 B.C.E., the returnees who were from the southern tribes (but who represented in their ideology the whole of Israel, i.e., the twelve tribes) returned to Jerusalem and not to Dan, Bethel, Tirzah, or Samaria.[14]

From the Hellenistic era comes an interesting case of the foundation of a new religiopolitical capital, the great Hellenistic city of Alexandria. Upon his arrival in Egypt, Alexander went first to Memphis by way of Heliopolis, then founded Alexandria. Next he went to the temple of Amon in Siwa to receive the approval of the god (interpreted as Zeus by the Greeks), and then traveled back to Memphis. He wished Memphis to be seen by the indigenous population as the religious and political center (he was crowned there as the king of Egypt, and made a sacrifice to the Apis bull).[15] But he founded Alexandria for the already existing Greek population in Egypt. He did so, I believe, in line with those pharaohs who, wishing to emphasize a break from former times, founded new political capitals such as Avaris, Pi-Ramessu, and Tell el-Amarna. In this way Alexander anticipated the "schizophrenic" or dualistic policy of the future Hellenistic kings. Ptolemy I Soter actually moved from Memphis to Alexandria, probably by 320/19 B.C.E.,[16] but the Egyptians hoped for many years that Memphis would be restored as the capital city.[17] Similarly, there is the case of Seleucus I, who founded Seleucia on the Tigris as a new capital for his kingdom only sixty miles away from the traditional religiopolitical center of Babylon (Strabo 16 [C738–C743(16)]; Pausanias 1.16.3; Pliny, 6.30.121). Note also the foundation of Caesarea Maritima by Herod the Great in the first century B.C.E.: apparently he wanted a new religiopolitical capital for the non-Jewish Hellenistic stratum of Judea's society. (This subject will be discussed in chapter 10.)

The examples just cited suffice to show the separation made at certain points in history between new religiopolitical capitals and the old traditional ones. The new Greek capitals such as Alexandria, Ptolemais in upper Egypt, and Seleucia, along with Caesarea Maritima, became the political and religious centers of the Greek strata of society in the various states of the ancient Near East, who did not feel any devotion to the old traditional centers. Naturally some tension existed between the old capital cities and the new ones. As has already been mentioned, the traditional religiopolitical centers were a dominant factor in the nationalism of the Hellenistic age because, along with language and traditional cultural heritage, they created distinctions among the different nations of the ancient Near East. Even the small city-states of the Palestinian coast, which consisted of a mixture of natives, Phoenicians, and Greeks, seemed to have some sort of national consciousness based on their autochthonous traditional temples, such as Ashdod and Dor.[18]

What was the attitude of the Hellenistic rulers regarding such temples and priesthoods? They seem to have pursued a sort of "dualistic" policy toward these institutions. On the one hand Hellenistic rulers imported Greek gods and supported the building of Greek temples all over the ancient Near East, as archaeological excavations have shown very clearly.[19] The ruler cult in the temples (and in other places as well) was initiated by the cities and their inhabitants, usually in the form of cult statues and sacred precincts. Conversely, in their capital cities the kings themselves founded royal cults as well as dynastic ones, as we can find in Alexandria, Seleucia, and Pergamon.[20] At the same time, these same rulers supported—and in certain cases even built—temples for the traditional gods who had been worshiped by the native populations for many centuries.[21] The kings incorporated their royal cult into these local temples, and they became part of the traditional religious customs of these places (Babylon, Uruk, and Memphis). The Ptolemies, who wanted to create a unifying nationalistic symbol for both Greeks and natives, created a new god called Serapis,[22] but apparently they were not imitated in this regard by the Seleucids.

If a Greek from the West had traveled through the ancient Near East during the third and second centuries B.C.E., he would have discovered native populations worshiping in their own temples, with the priesthoods acting as their cultural, spiritual, and ethnic leadership. Intertwined in the various regions of the Near East were the Greek cities with their Greek temples and gods. The inhabitants of these cities behaved as if they had merely transplanted their traditional religious life from mainland Greece to the ancient Near East.[23] There was a vast Greek population in these cities, but the indigenous population managed to settle in them as well. It is quite clear that not everyone in the Greek cities could trace their origins back to Greece and the Aegean islands. Yet people who wanted to live a Greek life identified themselves as "Hellenes" regardless of their true origin. In the *chora,* that is, in the countryside, as well as in the old traditional cities, we find the indigenous populations: Phoenicians and Arabs in Palestine; Babylonians, Arabs, and Iranians in Syria; native Egyptians, Jews, Arabs, and others in Egypt; and so on. Although the kings made efforts to be seen as national figures in the religious sphere (at times putting the royal cult of the dynasty into both the Greek temples and the native ones), the native populations remained in many places very divided over their religious-national values. As various kings in the Hellenistic Near East were seen as Heracles, Zeus, Apollo, Dionysus, and Alexander, this identification became a common religiocultural denominator between the Greeks of Alexandria and their counterparts in Seleucia and Pergamon. It seems that the Greeks had much less in common with the natives in terms of religion, common history, culture, and language. Those who wished to mingle the cultures used the existing Greek and native cults but, except in the case of Serapis, neither invented new gods nor created special temples. For example, the Phoenician Melkart became Heracles in the eyes of the Hellenistic syncretists, but he remained unchanged in appearance in his temple in Tyre and elsewhere.[24] Here we meet one of the limits of syncretism.

Against this background we will examine the issue of capital, temple, and priesthood in Judea. Three phases can be discerned during the Seleucid domination of Judea (200–143 B.C.E.). The first is from 200 to about 175, when the Seleucid kings viewed the Jerusalem Temple as just another native temple and were very tolerant of it, even agreeing not to place their royal cult within the Temple. This degree of tolerance was usually not found in Hellenistic monarchs. The second (175–152 B.C.E.) was a troublesome period for the Temple, partly because of the intrigues of the priests at that time in Jerusalem, but also because the Seleucid kings needed more and more money, which they wished to extract from the Jerusalem Temple, and thus became impatient and intolerant. During the early Hasmonean period (152–143 B.C.E.) the concept of one "native" Temple, which was to be identical with the political capital, prevailed in the emerging Jewish state. Other native traditional places in the Land, such as Bethel and Hebron, were suppressed by the Hasmonean authorities, as the First and Second Books of Maccabees as well as Josephus's account show. We shall see that during the seventies, the sixties, and the beginning of the fifties of the second century B.C.E., attempts were made by certain priestly circles to imitate their neighbors and transform the Jerusalem Temple into a Hellenistic temple. From the end of the fifties onward these Hellenistic priests disappeared from the scene, and the Temple returned to being a unifying national symbol, with its priesthood becoming more than ever the national symbol of native leadership. Nevertheless, the awareness of other traditional holy places in Palestine remained very strong among the writers of the time, as some of the pseudepigraphic and apocryphal literature shows. After 152 B.C.E. the high priests became also the secular leaders of the emerging Jewish state, and from 104/3 B.C.E. they also were the kings of this state. When Herod the Great was crowned king of Judea by the Romans in 40 B.C.E., the whole situation changed. Then, as we shall see later, the Temple again became "native" in the sense that all other native temples in the East were under Hellenistic monarchs. The Temple was divested of its dominant political role in the Jewish client state of Herod; the high priesthood became of secondary importance because the king was no longer the high priest. The political capital was removed, in the eyes of at least part of the population (the Greeks and Hellenists), to Caesarea, while Jerusalem remained the capital in the eyes of the native Jews. (I shall come back to this in a later chapter.) Let us now survey the political role of capital, Temple, and priesthood from 200 to 63 B.C.E.[25]

In 200 B.C.E. Palestine changed masters. Antiochus III, the Seleucid king, fought a decisive battle with Ptolemy V Epiphanes, king of Egypt, and as a result annexed Palestine to his own kingdom (Josephus, *Antiquities* 12.131–133). The Jews of Jerusalem, who cared for their religious and spiritual center, "of their own will went over to him [Antiochus III] and admitted him to their city and made abundant provisions for his entire army and his elephants" (12.133). These Jews did not at that time reveal any political and nationalistic aspirations for freedom in association with the Temple. Antiochus III, in line with the tolerant attitude of Hellenistic kings to native temples, granted the Jews a handful of concessions that were recorded by Josephus (12.138–144):[26] "We have seen fit on our part to requite them for these acts and to restore their city which has been destroyed by the hazards of war. . . . In the first place we have decided, on account of their piety, to furnish them for their sacrifices an allowance of sacrificial animals, wine, oil, and frankincense to the value of twenty thousand pieces of silver, and sacred artabae of fine flour. . . . And it is my will that these things be made over to them as I have ordered, and that the work on the temple be completed, including the porticoes and any other part that it may be necessary to build. . . . The like shall be done with the other materials needed for making the restoration of the temple more splendid. And all the members of the nation shall have a form of government in accordance with the laws of the country . . . and the priests, the scribes of the temple, and the temple singers shall be relieved from the poll-tax."

Later Josephus tells of another edict, which stated that "It is unlawful for any foreigner to enter the enclosure of the temple which is forbidden to the Jews, except to those of them who are accustomed to enter after purifying themselves . . . nor shall anyone bring into the city the flesh of horses or of mules . . . of any animals forbidden by the Jews. . . . But only the sacrificial animals known to their ancestors . . . shall they be permitted to use. And the person who violates these statutes shall pay to the priests a fine" (145–146). Ben Sira gives us an example of how Jerusalem was viewed at that time. For him Jerusalem was an autonomous religious and spiritual place, and, though in bad physical condition, the city was the dwelling place of Wisdom. (I shall refer to this point later.) Unfortunately, within two decades the relatively peaceful conditions the Jews enjoyed within Jerusalem and the Temple changed. The first to trespass against the Temple were the high priests themselves, as we will soon learn.

The considerable autonomy given to the priesthood of the Jerusalem Temple brought about on the one hand the rise of nationalistic feelings among the native Jews that came to the surface when the Maccabees started the war against the Seleucids. On the other hand there was a struggle for power among the ruling priests, which brought about internal intrigues and conflicts that culminated in Seleucid military intervention. Fortunately, there is more historical evidence for these matters than for other matters dealt with in this book.

At some time after the Seleucid takeover in 200 B.C.E., quarrels started between the high priest, Onias III, who inherited his high priesthood from his father, Simeon the Just, and the hellenized priests from the order of Bilga. These quarrels intensified during Seleucus IV's reign (187–175 B.C.E.). We hear about them in 2 Macc 3:1–6: there were times "when the holy city was governed in a perfectly peaceable manner and the laws were preserved as well as could be, because of the piety of Onias the high priest [Onias III] and his hatred of wickedness. Even kings came to honor the sacred place. They showed their high esteem for the temple with the finest gifts. So true was this that even Seleucus (IV), king of Asia, paid out of his own revenues all the expenses required for the service of the sacrifices. But a certain Simeon (who was head of the Bilga order) . . . who had been appointed provost (*prostates*) of the temple, came into disagreement with the high priest over the regulation of the city market (*agoranomia*). Unable to prevail over Onias, he went to Apollonius of Tarsus, who was at that time governor of Coele Syria and Phoenicia. He told him that the treasury in Jerusalem was teeming with untold wealth."[27]

Seleucus IV sent Heliodorus to expropriate the Temple's treasures. He was received cordially by the high priest, who was recognized by the Seleucid kings and by the Jews themselves as the highest political representative of the Jews. He told Heliodorus that the treasury was composed of deposits entrusted to his care, but that they belonged among others to widows and orphans. "He went on to say that to inflict injury upon those who put their reliance in the holiness of the sacred Place and in the dignity and inviolability of a sanctuary honored throughout the entire world was utterly unthinkable" (2 Macc 3:9–12). We are told in great detail how the people of Jerusalem reacted to Heliodorus's insistence on taking the treasury of the Temple, a reaction that is reminiscent of later opposition by pious Jews who appealed to Roman governors when they thought that their religious (and economic) autonomy had been offended[28]: "The priests in their priestly robes prostrated themselves before the altar, calling to heaven to Him who gave the law regarding deposits, begging Him to keep them safe for depositors. If anyone had looked upon the mien of the high priest, his heart would have been deeply touched to see his countenance change color, thus showing his anguish of soul. Fear and trembling had seized the man. . . . People came teeming out of houses in crowds to join in communal supplication because the Place was in danger of being defiled" (2 Macc 3:13–18). The author of 2 Maccabees depicted the scene in a very dramatic manner, which shows that many years after the event these priests were still highly regarded. But this situation was to change very quickly. It is quite clear that neither Seleucus IV nor Heliodorus had any intention of offending the Jews and their Temple. Their attempt should be explained as part of the efforts of the Seleucids (Antiochus III and Seleucus IV) to solve the financial problems of the monarchy. They also tried elsewhere to extract money from native temples.

Let us now complete the story of Heliodorus. 2 Macc 3:22–26 very dramatically expresses the situation at the time:

> Here then we have them invoking the Almighty God to keep the deposits entrusted to Him safe and secure for the depositors, and here was Heliodorus, ready to carry out his orders,—he and his guard already in front of the Treasury. Then it was that the Lord of spirits and of all authority caused a great apparition to appear so that all who had been bold enough to accompany him were struck with panic at the power of God and were faint with wretched fear. For a horse appeared to them with a fearful rider caparisoned with magnificent harness. Charging at full speed ahead, it plunged wildly at Heliodorus with its forefeet. The rider appeared to have a golden suit of armor. Two other youths . . . flogged him unceasingly.

After this attack Onias offered a sacrifice for Heliodorus's recovery; he did indeed recover. Later it is reported to the king that the Temple was haunted by some divine power. It is clear that Heliodorus did not succeed in his mission, and at some time later Onias III went to Seleucus to assure him of his loyalty after he was slanderously accused by Simeon, the provost of the Temple. He did not, however, achieve much because Seleucus died while he was at Antiochia in 175 B.C.E. (2 Macc 4:1–7).

Antiochus IV, the new king, was persuaded by Onias III's brother Jason to appoint him instead of his brother as high priest in Jerusalem. Jason offered him large sums of money and also promised to found a gymnasium and an ephebeum in Jerusalem and turn the city into a Greek polis (2 Macc 4:7–11).[29] The king was more than happy with this proposal because he needed great sums of money for his enterprises, and Jason's offers were in accord with his policy of spreading Hellenism in his realm. 1 Maccabees describes the situation in a statement typical of Hellenistic historiography: "At that time there came forth from Israel certain lawless men who persuaded many, saying, Let us go and make a treaty with the heathen around us, because ever since we separated from them, many evils have come upon us" (1:11–15). Apparently the plan was attractive, and a delegation went "eagerly" to the king, who gave them permission to perform rites of the gentiles. Coming back to Jerusalem, they built a gymnasium there "in accordance with the customs of the heathen" and subjected themselves to uncircumcision. It should be emphasized that Jason, despite his apparent faults, descended from the legitimate high priestly house. This was the first time in the history of the Second Temple period that a high priest was appointed while his predecessor (Onias III) was still alive.[30]

It is intriguing to observe the metamorphosis the high priesthood underwent within a short time. Why did it happen? An easy answer, which is sometimes given, is that some members of the priestly houses were hellenized and decadent. But the fact remains that up to the mid seventies (when Onias III was dismissed and Jason was nominated by Antiochus IV, about 175/4 B.C.E.), the high priests were well regarded by most of the population and were both religious and spiritual leaders. Hellenism did not penetrate into priestly circles in one day, but was rather a gradual process. Thus the answer is very complex. I should only underline the fact that during the seventies of the second century, the opportunity arose for the high priests to become political figures in the ordinary hellenistic style, because they were the ones to initiate and handle all political relations with the kings (and pretenders) of the neighboring nations. This opportunity encouraged them to use more power than was previously entrusted to them as high priests. In the near future, as we shall see, this marriage of priests and politics on the national level, as well as on the international one, became unhappy.

Second Maccabees tells us in a dramatic—and probably exaggerated—manner about the profanation of the Temple by the priests at that time. In fact, after permission was granted by the king to register the Jerusalemites as Antiocheans and to build the Greek institu-

tions in Jerusalem "as a result of the wickedness of Jason," many
priests abandoned the service in the Temple, "despising the temple
and neglecting the sacrifices, they would hasten to participate in the
unlawful exercises of the palaestra as soon as the summons came for
the discus throwing" (4:14). It should be noted that the gymnasium,
which was perhaps the most important social institution in the
Greek city of the Hellenistic Near East, was built on the Temple
Mount itself. For the hellenizers it became a spiritual and social
substitute for the Temple.

Another example that shows the degree of hellenization of the
high priest can be seen in the episode related in 2 Macc 4:18–20.
Jason, the high priest, sent ambassadors with three hundred silver
drachmas to Tyre for the sacrifice to Heracles during the festival held
there. The ambassadors themselves felt that this was not the right
thing to do and asked the Tyrians to use the money for another
purpose, a request that was granted. Jason's ambassadors turned out
to be more righteous than he was. Yet this story reveals also how the
"native" national leaders of Judea at that time wished to cross the
line between the indigenous population and the Greek ruling classes,
just as other "native" leaders had in other nations of the ancient
Near East. They wished to become part of the Near Eastern Hellenic
upper classes, but a few years later the Maccabees were to put a stop
to this trend altogether.

Jason was high priest for three years (174–171 B.C.E.), and in his
time "Antiochia in Jerusalem" was established.[31] This event is interesting in relation to what we have just observed about the issue of a
religious capital versus a political one. The foundation of this Greek
polis within Jerusalem was not just a change of name, as the name of
the city Acco-Ptolemais had been changed to Antiochia or as Gaza
had been changed in name to Antiochia. In the case of Jerusalem, the
establishment of a Greek *polis* can be seen as the founding of a new
center for the sake of a certain defined stratum of the population,
namely, the Hellenists. It marks the beginning of the so-called
"schizophrenia," which remained latent in Judea as a political and
social phenomenon during the Hasmonean period but reemerged in
a vigorous manner during Herod the Great's time. Jason and his
followers could not (and probably did not intend to) do what Seleucus once did in his kingdom—establish a new capital outside the
traditional religious one. Neither did they conceive of what Herod

the Great would do for the gentile population a century later, that is, found Caesarea Maritima. On the one hand they did not have the power to do so, and on the other, they still wished to be associated with the old religious capital of Jerusalem, in that they were priests in the Temple and saw themselves as leaders of the whole population of Palestine. But the *patrios politeia* (ancestral constitution), which was traditionally Jewish—in other words, the Torah—and was granted legitimacy by the Seleucids in 200 B.C.E., was now partly abolished by the Hellenistic priests. Jerusalem received a new constitution, that of a Hellenistic *polis,* which was granted the approval of the Seleucid royal court. Yet the old institutions continued to exist; Jason remained high priest, and the Jewish *Gerousia* stayed intact. The foundation of this new Hellenistic "capital" within the framework of the old one created (just as in other societies in the ancient Near East) two strata in the population of Jerusalem and Judea—the elite group, who were citizens of this new *polis* (perhaps three thousand, which was a large number for a city at the time), and those who remained "natives" and had to accommodate themselves to the fact that they were residents of just the "older" Jerusalem and the adjacent territory of Judea, which became the *chora* of the new city. Jason, the high priest, was also the "secular head" of this new ministate. Then about 171 B.C.E. he was deposed by the king, and Menelaus from the Bilga order (the brother of Simeon, the provost of the Temple), was installed as high priest in his place. It was the first time in the history of the Second Temple period that a priest who was not from the traditional high priestly house was appointed high priest in Jerusalem. How did it happen?

Jason sent Menelaus to the king to hand over money and settle various affairs, and the latter was able to persuade the king to depose Jason and appoint him instead, offering the king three hundred talents of silver more than Jason did. 2 Macc 4:23–26 vividly comments, "After receiving the royal orders, he [Menelaus] returned, possessing no qualifications worthy of the high priesthood, endowed as he was only with the passion of a savage tyrant and the natural impulses of a wild beast. Thus Jason, who had supplanted his own brother by corruption, was supplanted in turn by another, and driven as a fugitive into the country of the Ammonites." It was this promise by Menelaus—somewhat differently presented by Josephus, in *Antiquities* 12.237[32]—that brought about a deterioration in the condition of Jerusalem, because he could not provide the money he promised. This was too much for Antiochus: both Menelaus, the new high priest, and the Seleucid governor of the citadel (Akra, overlooking the Temple Mount) were summoned to appear before the king. Menelaus left his brother Lysimachus as high priest and went to meet Andronicus, whom the king had left in charge while he himself left for the south of Asia Minor. Menelaus presented to Andronicus some golden vessels that he had stolen from the Temple (he had already sold others at Tyre and adjacent cities). "When Onias discovered the theft, he sharply rebuked him and retired to a place of asylum at Daphne, near Antioch." Menelaus, who wanted once and for all to get rid of Onias, convinced Andronicus to kill Onias, which he ruthlessly did in 170 B.C.E. (2 Macc 4:32–34). Later the king killed Andronicus too.

While Menelaus was thus preoccupied, many acts of sacrilegious plunder had been committed in the city by Lysimachus, with the approval of Menelaus. These offenses were too much for those Jews who had opposed hellenization. They joined forces in order to save the remainder of the golden vessels and probably other artifacts stolen from the Temple. In the struggle that ensued between Menelaus's faction (three thousand in number), led by Lysimachus, and those Jews opposing hellenization, the latter got the upper hand, and Lysimachus was killed (4:39–42). But the aftermath was tragic. The three delegates from the *Gerousia* (council) who went to the king in Tyre to accuse Menelaus were put to death. The king needed Menelaus in Jerusalem while his war against Ptolemaic Egypt was imminent. Menelaus hence "remained in office, continually growing in evil, ever considered a great betrayer of his fellow citizens" (4:50).

In connection with these events, four points suggest themselves. For one thing, the more the high priests were involved in international intrigues and politics, the more they tended to forget their role as the religious and spiritual leaders of the Jewish nation. For another, the request for Seleucid intervention, initiated by the high priests and their friends, alienated them more and more from those Jews who were against hellenization. Furthermore, the almost unique situation in which there were "native" priests who had great political power, but who did not receive the support of the indigenous population, was one of the reasons for the inevitable clash between the Jews and the Seleucids some years later. The willingness of the hellenized priests to compromise with the Seleucids, as in fact the priesthood of Egypt was doing at the time with the Ptolemies, did not receive the consent of the majority of the Jewish people. And finally, as a consequence of the priests' actions the Temple of Jerusalem, which was associated with the wicked priesthood, became defiled in the eyes of many pious Jews.

Menelaus remained in office for some time, supported by the royal court. But events in the ancient Near East were again to change the course of history for the Jews. On his way back from his first campaign in Egypt in the autumn of 169 B.C.E., Antiochus IV came to Jerusalem with a great army. He entered the Temple "in his arrogance" and stole among other artifacts the menorah and its equipment, the golden altar, the table of the show-bread, the cups, the curtain, the crowns, the precious vessels, and the hidden treasures he managed to find. He also killed many people and "spoke most arrogantly" (1 Macc 1:20–24; *Antiquities* 12.247). This information is further corroborated by Josephus (*Contra Apionem* 2.83, a tradition that probably goes back to the famous Greek historian Polybius). Antiochus's offensive behavior (which was in keeping with his pattern of robbing temples in Egypt beforehand, if this tradition can be believed) contributed to the anger the Jews felt already against the Seleucids.

It should be emphasized that the author of 1 Maccabees, writing during the second part of the second century B.C.E., intertwined throughout the narrative laments on the City and its Temple. Similar laments appeared again and again in the literature of the period until the final destruction of the Temple in 70 C.E., and they intensified even more after that event. Prophecies of the destruction of the Temple were nourished by the experience of continuous lamentation over the City and its Temple, and are reminiscent of the Book of Lamentations, which uses the same figures and expresses the same sentiments. (I mention this here for the reader who is interested in 4Q179, the so-called little Apocalypse of Mark 13, and other literature of the same kind). A typical lamentation can be found in 1 Macc 1:25–28, which laments the robbing of the Temple by the Seleucid monarch: "Great was the sadness in Israel, everywhere; both rulers and elders groaned; maidens and young men languished, the beauty of women was altered, every bridegroom took up lamentation, and she that sat in a bridal chamber mourned. Shaken was the earth over those who dwelt therein, and the whole house of Jacob was clothed with shame."

During the second campaign of Antiochus IV in Egypt in 168 B.C.E. rumors were spread that the king was dead.[33] Rumors in the ancient Near East were usually taken as facts. Thus Jason, the dismissed high priest who had been driven into the land of the Ammonites, gathered soldiers and drove Menelaus and his supporters out of Jerusalem. This action was in fact a revolt against the royal court, which supported Menelaus. Yet even 2 Maccabees, which should have praised such an act, condemns it altogether (2 Macc 5:1–10). In fact, the king was not really dead; he was frustrated by his failure in Egypt, caused by a resolute Roman ultimatum ordering him to leave Egypt immediately. He attacked Judea with great anger to quell the revolt. Jason escaped before his arrival, and Antiochus caused a great deal of damage in the city and its Temple: "Within three days eighty thousand were destroyed, forty thousand in hand-to-hand fighting. An equal number to those slaughtered were sold into slavery. Not satisfied with this, he (Antiochus) dared to enter the most holy Temple of the whole earth with Menelaus, who had become a traitor both to the Jews and to his country, as his guide. He took the sacred vessels with polluted hands, and the votive offerings presented by other kings to increase the glory and honor of the sacred place, he impiously swept away" (2 Macc 5:14–16). Whether the account describes a factual episode or is just a literary duplicate of the first attack mentioned above, the reaction of the author of 2 Maccabees is what matters. He adds that "In his overweening spirit, Antiochus failed to recognize that it was due to the transgressions of the citizens themselves that the Lord was moved to temporary anger. For that reason alone there had been lack of protective regard for the place" (2 Macc 5:17). These somewhat imaginative thoughts of an author in the second or first century B.C.E. anticipate the views of Josephus and Jesus later concerning the coming destruction of the Temple. Both Josephus and other Jews could have had such views a long time before 70 C.E.; it was not the destruction of the Temple that created them.

Antiochus IV left Philip the Phrygian as commander in chief of Judea; but at the end of 168 (or early 167) B.C.E. the king sent an officer, Apollonius, to Jerusalem. Apollonius misled the Jews, who thought he was coming on a mission of peace, and then suddenly attacked the city on the Sabbath, dealing it a great blow. Along with deeds such as despoiling the city, burning parts of it, and taking the women and children captive while stealing their cattle, he built the notorious Akra, a fortress in the midst of Jerusalem overlooking the Temple Mount in which "sinful people" and "transgressors against the law" were imprisoned (1 Macc 1:29–36).[34] Here again is a lament on the City and Temple:

They shed innocent blood around the altar
and polluted the sanctuary,
because of them the inhabitants of Jerusalem
fled, she became a dwelling place of
foreigners, And foreign she became to her own
brood, and her children forsook her.
Her sanctuary was laid waste like a wilderness
her feasts were turned into sadness,
her sabbaths into a reproach,
her honor into contempt.
As great as had been her glory,
by so much was her dishonor increased,
and her high renown was turned into sadness.

It is doubtful whether this lament reflects historical reality, because it is very much in keeping with Jewish lamentations in general (Lamentations, 1 Baruch). It can be assumed, however, that while many foreigners settled in Jerusalem at the time, the Temple still remained the center for the Jewish population, and if one can judge from the silence of our sources no pagan temple was erected there.[35]

This was not the end of the troubles the Jews had over their Temple and City, but it is the end of a significant phase of this study. For a decade the priesthood of Israel and its Temple had in the opinion of traditional Jews been abused. Their so-called national leaders were in fact murderers, thieves, merchants of artifacts stolen from the Temple, and the like. These religious leaders who became politicians made these years unhappy, for a "secular," charismatic leader of a unified nation had not yet arisen. In both books of Maccabees the priesthood of those days is heavily denigrated, and in fact

it is directly blamed for the events leading to the Seleucid intervention. Even if these accusations of wrongdoing are the result of the
bias of the pro-Hasmonean sources, writing after the Maccabean
revolt, they probably have a core of truth. Josephus, who used the
books of Maccabees for his history in book 12, reflects more or less
the same picture but smooths over most of the more dreadful portrayals of the priesthood.

In 167 B.C.E. the Seleucid king sent orders to his kingdom, of
which 1 Maccabees tells us in a concise manner (1:41–50). Among
other places in his realm Antiochus IV sent letters to Jerusalem and
the cities of Judea, ordering them to "follow customs foreign to the
land, to withhold burnt offerings and sacrifices, and drink offerings
from the sanctuary, to profane the sabbaths and festivals, to pollute
the sanctuary and the holy ones, to build high places, and sacred
groves and idols," and "on the twenty-fifth day of Kislev in the one
hundred and forty-sixth year [167 B.C.E.], he erected an abomination
of desolation upon the altar, and in the surrounding cities of Judah
they erected altars." (1:54). 2 Maccabees adds some details concerning these stormy days. 2 Macc 6:2–5 underlines the terrible act of
pollution of the Temple in Jerusalem, "that was to be called thence-
forth after the name of Olympian Zeus," and adds: "This onset of
evil came to be harsh and odious for everyone. For the heathen filled
the Temple with riotous revelry. They dallied with prostitutes and
consorted with women in the sacred enclosures; moreover, they
brought in sacrifices that were forbidden. The altar was filled with
abominable sacrifices which the law prohibited." This was, according to 2 Maccabees, the starting point of the Maccabean uprising.

Although 1 Maccabees wants us to believe that Antiochus IV
established this new policy for all his realm (in order to show that
the Jews were the only ones who courageously fought back), it
seems that his act was against the Jews only.[36] The Hellenistic rulers,
as well as the Romans later, were usually tolerant of other religions,
as polytheistic religions usually were, unless some religion threatened its very existence or constituted a menace to the civil order. We
know of some examples of these exceptions.[37] In the case of Antiochus IV and the Jews, however, it is obvious that the king associated the Jewish religion with Jewish political nationalism, which had
expressed itself before he issued his orders in riots and tumults, par-

ticularly in Jerusalem against the royal court. He associated the religious leadership with national unrest, and understood that the split in the Jewish nation at that time was the cause of these troubles. For him the Jerusalem Temple was just another native temple, like the ones of Tyre, Gerizim, Uruk, and Babylon, but it was a temple that caused significant political troubles. Thus he initiated his policy of hellenizing the Jews for purely political reasons. He attempted to eliminate the native religious element altogether. It is in fact interesting to note in this context that we have no evidence that the king oppressed the Jews of the Diaspora. Antiochus was of the opinion that the Jewish aristocracy in Palestine, which in the past had reacted favorably in various degrees to Hellenism, would cooperate with Menelaus, who was still high priest in Jerusalem. This assumption was completely mistaken. Josephus's account that Lysias accused Menelaus of being "the cause of the mischief by persuading the king's father to compel the Jews to abandon their father's religion" goes too far (*Antiquities* 12.384; cf. 2 Macc 13:4–5, which only makes him a scapegoat).

The Maccabean revolt started at Modi'in. It should be noted that Jews had been massacred by the Seleucids even before the incident there, especially on the sabbaths when they could not fight back. But an "official" leadership was created in Modi'in by Mattathias and his sons, who claimed their descent from the priestly division of Yehoyarib.[38] The incident in Modi'in is seen by 1 Maccabees as the beginning of the Maccabean upheaval against the Seleucids. When Mattathias saw the terrible, blasphemous statue to which the Jews were forced to sacrifice, he said (1 Macc 2:7–13),

Wretched am I, why was I born to behold,
the dissolution of my people and the
destruction of the holy city,
to sit idly by while it is given into the hand
of its enemies,
the sanctuary into the hand of foreigners?
. . .
Instead of a free woman, she has become a
slave. Yea, behold, our sanctuary and our
beauty, and our glory have been laid
waste.

In this lament we see how Jerusalem and the Temple were central to the Jews as religious places, and although they were "only" profaned, the Jews viewed them as destroyed.

It is not accidental that the Maccabean upheaval started in the outskirts of Judea, led by a minor *native* priest, and not in the city itself under some leading priestly figure. When one of the "liberal" Jews at Modi'in went to sacrifice to an idol, Mattathias, filled with zeal, killed him "as Phineas had done toward Zimri." His slogan at the time was "let everyone who is zealous for the Law, and would maintain the covenant, follow me" (1 Macc 2:27). He and his followers fled to the mountains to launch the so-called Maccabean revolt. 1 Maccabees emphasizes the slogan of the Hasidim, the pious Jews, and the Maccabees, saying that they were fighting for the Law (2:42). This slogan was revealed by Mattathias in his deathbed speech (2:49–68). The fight for the Torah was limited at that time to the aim of abolishing the offensive edicts of Antiochus IV, and to a return to the religious autonomy (centering around their Torah, City, and Temple) that the Jews had entertained under Antiochus III.

Three years passed from the king's disastrous edicts until the purification of the Temple by Judas Maccabeus (167–164 B.C.E.). During these years Judas's main goals were to survive, to purify the Temple, and to free Jerusalem from the Seleucid garrison stationed in the Akra as well as from Menelaus and his party. During these years of revolt, there were at least two attempts by the Seleucids to reach a settlement with the rebels (2 Macc 11:14–21, 27–33), both in the years 165 and 164 B.C.E.: but these settlements could not really have been accepted in the long run by Judas and his party because his goals had not yet been achieved. The books of Maccabees emphasize several times that during the revolt of Judas in 167–164 B.C.E., the City and the Temple were uppermost in the minds of the Jews. This emphasis should not be seen as an invention of Hasmonean historiography, but as merely reflecting the actual concerns of the Jews at the time.[39]

The majority of Jews did not sit still, and along with their laments on their capital and Temple (for instance, 1 Macc 3:44–45) they attempted to conquer Jerusalem. They succeeded in 164 B.C.E., and after the battle of Beth-zur, according to 1 Macc 4:36, Judas purified the Temple. For the present purpose it is important to note the following passage:

Judas and his brothers said: "Now that our enemies are crushed, let us go up to purify and dedicate the sanctuary," which they immediately did. "The entire army gathered together and went up to Mount Zion. They saw the sanctuary desolated and the altar profaned, the gates burned up, and weeds growing in the courts as in a forest or as on one of the mountains, and the priests' chambers turned down. They tore their garments and made great lamentation, and put ashes on their heads, and fell on their faces on the ground. . . . Judas appointed certain men to fight against the garrison in the citadel, until he could cleanse the sanctuary. He selected priests without blemish, whose delight was in the Law, and they purified the sanctuary. . . . They took counsel as to what they should do about the altar of burnt offering, which had been defiled. A good plan occurred to them, namely, to tear it down, lest it become a reproach to them, because the heathen had defiled it. So they pulled down the altar, and put away the stones in the Temple Mount, in a suitable place, until a prophet should come to decide what to do with them. They took whole stones, according to the Law, and constructed a new altar like the former one. They built the sanctuary and the interior of the temple . . . the altar of incense and the table into the temple. . . .

"They burned incense. . . . On the twenty-fifth day of the ninth month, that is, the month of Kislev . . . they arose early and offered sacrifice according to the Law upon the new altar. . . . All the people fell on their faces and prostrated themselves, and uttered praises to Heaven who had caused them to prosper. They celebrated the dedication of the altar for eight days. . . . They also adorned the front of the Temple with golden crowns and small shields, and rededicated the gates and the priests' chambers, and fitted them with doors. . . . At that time they built high walls and strong towers around Mount Zion, so that the heathen could never again come and destroy them." (1 Macc 4:36–61; 2 Macc 10:1–8)

Although the Temple was purified at that time, Jerusalem was not yet free from Seleucid rule.

The First Book of Maccabees attributes the death of Antiochus IV to the Jewish insurrection, an account that is, of course, apocryphal. It is said that, while he was in Persia, the Jews had pulled down the abomination that he had constructed on the altar in Jerusalem and then surrounded the sanctuary with high walls. Antiochus then is said to have recalled the evils that he did in Jerusalem, when he took all of the silver and gold vessels that were in it, and attributed his punishment to this sin. He died there in 165/4 B.C.E.[40] From then on preemptive wars were waged by Judas to rescue Jews all over Palestine. Interestingly, the First Book of Maccabees associates the rebuilding of the sanctuary in Jerusalem with the attacks of the heathen all over Palestine against the Jews (5:1). The war between non-Jews and Jews in Palestine went on intensively from the spring of 163 B.C.E. to the spring of 162 B.C.E. One of Judas's major enterprises was the bringing of the Jewish inhabitants of the Gilead to Judea. When these people arrived at Jerusalem, they first went up to "Mount Zion with gladness and joy and offered burnt offerings, because not even one of them had fallen before they returned in peace" (5:54).

Then Judas decided to conquer the Akra, which was "hemming Israel around the sanctuary." Hence, a war ensued first in Beth-Zecharia and later in the city of Jerusalem itself. It is important to note that all of the Maccabean wars with the Seleucids at that time took place in the regions encircling Jerusalem, which shows that for the Jews, the main goal of this war was to capture Jerusalem and its Temple, and for the Seleucids, it was to maintain control over the religiopolitical capital of the Jews. Lysias, accompanied by the young king, Antiochus V, was again the general who at a certain point, because of internal problems in the Seleucid monarchy, wished to make peace with the Jews so that they could "follow their own laws, as heretofore, for because of their laws which we abolished they became angry and did all these things" (1 Macc 6:55–59; *Antiquities* 12.379–381). He executed Menelaus, probably as a precondition set by Judas and his party for making peace, and appointed Alcimus as high priest in his stead (2 Macc 13:1–8; *Antiquities* 12.383–385). Before leaving Palestine he gave orders to tear down the wall encircling Mount Zion (6:62). Antiochus V ordered Lysias to be more lenient with the Jews and to let them perform their cult in the Temple without hindrance (2 Macc 11:22–26).

In the autumn of 162 B.C.E., Antiochus V and Lysias were killed by Demetrius, the son of Seleucus IV, who had escaped to the Near

East after the Roman authorities had refused to give him permission to leave Rome, where he was an exile. Demetrius became king, an event that changed the fragile status quo in Judea, where Judas and his followers had reluctantly abstained from attacking Alcimus and the hellenizers. When Demetrius became king "all the lawless and irreligious men of Israel came to him, with Alcimus, wishing to serve as High Priest," and blamed Judas for deposing Alcimus de facto from his position as high priest (1 Macc 7:1–7; 2 Macc 14:1–10).

In one of the most notorious episodes of that time (again involving a high priest), Demetrius, who wanted to follow the hard line of Antiochus Epiphanes on Judea, sent Bacchides and Nicanor in the winter of 162 B.C.E. as generals with the assignment of installing Alcimus as high priest in Jerusalem (1 Macc 7:9; 2 Macc 14:3–4). A large Seleucid army came to Judea with Alcimus in its camp. When they arrived in Judea, Bacchides sent messengers to deceive Judas and his brothers "with peaceful words" (7:10). The Maccabees, however, disregarded this mission. But "a company of scribes" approached Alcimus and Bacchides to seek justice.[41] The Hasidim took the lead among the Israelites who sought peace from them, for they said, "One who is a priest of the tribe of Aaron has come with the soldiers, and he will do us no harm" (1 Macc 7:10–14). This piece of information is interesting because it seems that the Hasidim wanted peace even if they had to acknowledge a Hellenistic high priest—he was after all a legitimate priest. This group of peace seekers was to appear again in the future. Bacchides then killed sixty of the Hasidim, and 1 Macc 7:17 adds, "The flesh of Thy saints and their blood They did shed around Jerusalem, and there was no one to bury them." After another massacre in Beth-Zayit of Jews who had deserted from Judas's camp to Alcimus's, Bacchides left Judea and handed the country over to Alcimus, who was supported by a Seleucid military force (1 Macc 7:19–20).

Still Judas did not keep quiet, and fought Alcimus "in all the frontiers around Judea" (7:21–25). Alcimus sent to the Seleucid king for help. The king sent Nicanor, who came to Jerusalem with a great army. First he met Judas, who discovered that he had been misled. When Judas managed to escape, Nicanor went up to Mount Zion, where some of the priests came out of the sanctuary along with some of the elders. They were peaceful and wanted to show the Seleucid general "the whole burnt offering that was being offered in honor of

the king" (7:34). Nicanor was not impressed, for he wanted to capture Judas alive. The Seleucid general, following the orders of King
Demetrius, solely supported Alcimus's party. The priests then "entered and stood before the altar and the sanctuary, and wept and
said, Thou hast chosen this house to be called by Thy name, to be a
house of prayer and supplication for Thy people. Take revenge on
this man and on his army; let them fall by the sword; be mindful of
their blasphemies, and give them no peace" (1 Macc 7:36–38).
These priests, who apparently were altogether opposed to Hellenism, wanted the Temple to be a place of prayer and supplication
rather than an institution embroiled in politics. This attitude about
the Temple anticipates one found later in many circles in Judaism.

Later, when the two armies were ready for war at Adassa, Judas
said, "In the same manner shatter this army before us today, that
those who remain may know that he spoke wickedly of Thy sanctuary" (1 Macc 7:42). Judas wished to stop Nicanor from getting to
Jerusalem (in 161 B.C.E.), which shows again that the war, even after
the official cleansing of the Temple in 164 B.C.E., remained essentially
a battle over Jerusalem and its Temple. For some Jews, such as the
Hasidim and many priests, once the Temple had been cleansed, the
war was over. Judas and his men wanted more than that—they
wanted political as well as religious autonomy, which for them
meant the elimination of the disturbing Akra. The Hellenists with
Alcimus at their head wished to rule the Jews from the position of
high priest with the support of the Seleucids. They had a clear political interest in the Temple and the priesthood.

The centrality of Jerusalem and the Temple in both books of
Maccabees is not just the result of the *Tendenz* of the authors of
these two apocryphal works.[42] They may have oversharpened the
picture, but there is no doubt that the documents reflect much of the
reality of the time. The main goal for most Jews in the sixties and
fifties was not a free Jewish state, but freedom to worship in Jerusalem, independent of the hellenizers and their supporters, the
Seleucids. The two books were written after the Hasmonean state
had become a reality, which is why their description of Jewish motives during the sixties seems so authentic. There may have been
dreams in the sixties and fifties of an independent Jewish state, but it
was clearly not the main goal of the war at the time. In the forties
and thirties this limited goal of freeing Jerusalem and Temple was to

be expanded into the goal of the conquest of all of Palestine and the establishment of an independent state there.

The battle of Adassa ended with a Seleucid defeat and with the killing of the Seleucid general, Nicanor (March 161 B.C.E.). Judas then made a treaty with Rome, and the tablet upon which the treaty was engraved was sent to Jerusalem (1 Macc 8:22; 2 Macc 4:11). By this act, the Romans "acknowledged" Jerusalem as the capital of the native Jews. For King Demetrius this agreement was crucial, and he again sent Bacchides with an army (Alcimus the high priest was in his camp again). This time Judas himself found his death in the battle (Elassa, 160 B.C.E.; 1 Macc 9:1–22). The Seleucids conquered Jerusalem and, according to 1 Macc 9:23, "After the death of Judas, it came about that the law breakers [i.e., the Hellenists] began to show their heads in all the borders of Israel." Bacchides chose some of the Hellenistic party and made them rulers of the country, and before leaving for Syria he put the sons of the leaders of the country into the Akra as hostages (1 Macc 9:53). Meanwhile Jonathan, Judas's brother, became leader of the Maccabean party (1 Macc 9:31), and a new phase of the war started.

The Hellenists, with Alcimus as their leader, now had the opportunity to show their firmness. In the spring of 159 B.C.E. Alcimus ordered the wall of the inner court of the Temple torn down, "thus destroying the works of the prophets." As a result, according to 1 Maccabees, Alcimus was struck down. He became paralyzed and "was no longer able to say a word or to give orders concerning his household." He died shortly thereafter (1 Macc 9:54–56; *Berešit Rabbah* 65). The high priesthood remained vacant for seven years, during which time Jonathan was granted permission from the Seleucids to "judge" the people in Michmash, about seven miles north of Jerusalem.[43] But when he was approached by King Demetrius, about 154/3 B.C.E., who asked him to equip troops and to be his ally, Jonathan went to Jerusalem and read the letter in the presence of the men who were in the Akra. (We shall see again later that important national announcements were preferably made in Jerusalem, though not always.) Jonathan began to build and restore the city, and in order to guard parts of Jerusalem effectively he gave orders to encircle Mount Zion with walls. From then on he himself resided in the city (1 Macc 10:6–11). Most of Jerusalem, it should be emphasized, was still in the hands of the Seleucids and the Hellenists. Nevertheless, from 160 B.C.E. onward the wars with the various Seleucid generals were no longer centered on Jerusalem and the Temple, though the Akra was still a menace to the Jews in Jerusalem until 143/2 B.C.E., when Simeon conquered it.

Now we come to a crucial juncture in the history of the period, which has an important bearing on the present theme. In 152 B.C.E. a war was started by a claimant to the Seleucid throne named Alexander Balas. The two warring parties approached Jonathan and offered a few concessions. Although King Demetrius I offered much more than Balas, the latter, unlike the former, offered Jonathan the high priesthood. Jonathan, flattered by the offer, accepted it. In order to better understand this choice, let us compare the proposals. Alexander Balas wrote a letter that opened as follows: "King Alexander to his brother Jonathan, greetings! We have heard about you, as a mighty man of valor worthy to be our Friend. We have appointed you today as High Priest of your nation (*ethnos*), and to be called Friend of the King" (1 Macc 10:18-20).[44]

When Demetrius heard that "Jonathan put on the sacred vestments," he wrote a letter that is too long to quote in full; but its main points are the following: "For the present, I free you and release all Jews from the poll taxes, from the custom on salt, and from the crown tax. Instead of one-third of the seed and of half of the fruit of the trees which I receive as my share, from this day on I release for all time the right to take from the land of Judah and from the three districts which are added to it from Samaria and Galilee. Let Jerusalem and her borders, her tithes and taxes, be holy and exempt. I give up, also, my authority over the citadel in Jerusalem" (1 Macc 10:25-45). In the letter there is a lot more concerning the autonomy of religion, the enrollment of Jews as mercenaries to the royal army, and more.[45]

Three questions should be asked. First, why did Demetrius not offer the high priesthood to Jonathan? He apparently knew of Balas's offer (according to 1 Macc 10:22), but did not respond in kind. Even if he did not know of it, he was surely aware that this was a crucial matter to the Jews. Second, why did Jonathan prefer Balas to Demetrius, and why did he accept the offer of high priesthood from a foreign pretender to the Seleucid throne? Finally, why was the position of high priesthood vacant for seven years? The last question may be easier to answer. From Alcimus's death in 159 B.C.E. until 152 B.C.E. the Hellenists were in a strong position in Jerusalem, profiting from the protection provided by the Seleucid citadel of the Akra. At the same time, Jonathan and the Hasmonean forces, with their center in Michmash and later in Jerusalem, also had the approval of the Seleucids. Thus a modus vivendi may have been created in order not to nominate a new high priest, who would have shattered the status quo.

The first and second questions are connected. Demetrius I, the official king for more than eight years, knew that the appointment of Jonathan as high priest, a secular leader of good priestly stock who had an army and may have had political aspirations as well, might throw open the way for Judea to become independent of the Seleucid kingdom. He also knew that it was a dangerous precedent for the royal court to give an indigenous, nationalistic leader the legitimacy inherent in this religious office. Balas, conversely, had nothing to lose. He was a pretender to the throne and therefore granted Jonathan the most precious concession of all, the high priesthood. Jonathan, because of the reasons mentioned above, accepted Balas's offer. True, Balas was supported by Pergamon, Cappadocia, and Egypt, as well as by Rome, but Demetrius had already proved himself to be a strong king. This decision clearly illustrates the importance of the priesthood as a nationalistic symbol in the ancient Near East.

Jonathan accepted the high priesthood and, according to 1 Macc 10:21, "donned the holy robe in the seventh month at the Feast of Tabernacles." By accepting the high priesthood Jonathan brought about an important change. He, like the Hellenistic high priests Jason, Menelaus, and Alcimus, received the post from a foreign king (in fact, a pretender to the throne). Although Jonathan was from a priestly house, he was not from the legitimate high priestly house of Zadok. First Maccabees does not disparage Jonathan's appointment as high priest, as it does with regard to his predecessors. The Essenic literature may have done so, though scholars differ as to the identity of the *kohen harasha*, the wicked priest, mentioned in their literature.[46] Be that as it may, for the first time after three decades a consensus on the high priesthood seems to have been reached. The opposition to the Maccabees by the Hellenistic groups had gradually disappeared as a meaningful force in Palestine. The Jews accepted this grant of high priesthood, and for the first time a political leader with a nationalistic ethos became the high priest. Former high priests such as Jason and Menelaus, as has already been mentioned, were of a more universalistic persuasion; that is to say, they wanted to integrate Judaism into the Hellenistic environment. Thus, the year 152 B.C.E. was a crucial juncture on the road to political independence.

Balas gained the victory, and Jonathan, the high priest of the Jews, was accepted with great pomp in Acco-Ptolemais during the wedding of Balas into the Ptolemaic royal house. Along with being a *philos* (friend) of the king, he was officially made both the civil and the military governor of Judea (1 Macc 10:59–66), which is important because a Jewish high priest gained international recognition by the two major forces of the Mideast, the Seleucids and the Ptolemies. Balas's reign did not last very long, but the status of the Hasmoneans as high priests and secular leaders was to remain unchanged for many years to come.

From then until 142 B.C.E., when the Jews declared their independence, there were many efforts to conquer the troublesome Akra that overlooked the Temple Mount, but all were in vain. The Hasmonean high priests increasingly became political figures and were acknowledged as such by many powers, both in the region and outside it. They were the heads of state in every respect. In the forties their concern became the conquest of the whole Land, in that Jerusalem, except the Akra, was basically under their sway. When Simeon took over in 142 B.C.E., he began his reign in Jerusalem. There he gathered the people and encouraged them by saying, "You yourself know how much I and my brothers and my father's house have done for the laws and the sanctuary. . . . I will take revenge for my nation, for the sanctuary, for your wives and children" (1 Macc 13:1–6). The people asked him to be their leader; he then "mustered all the fighting men, hastened to complete the walls of Jerusalem, and surrounded it with fortifications" (13:8–10). Simeon was also confirmed in Jerusalem as high priest, as well as general and ruler of the Jews (1 Macc 13:41–42). Josephus says (*Antiquities* 13.213) that "Simeon, after being chosen high priest by the populace, in the first year of his high priesthood liberated the people from servitude to the Macedonians [i.e., Seleucids], so that they no longer had to pay tribute to them." If Josephus is correct, Simeon's election by the populace was unusual for the post of high priest in Israel. In 141

B.C.E. the Akra was conquered by Simeon, who thought that by this act the Temple "might be higher than" the Akra (*Antiquities* 13.215). Jerusalem was freed, "and thereafter the Temple stood high above everything else, once the citadel and the hill on which it stood had been demolished" (*Antiquities* 13.215–217). The way was opened for the conquest of the entire Land (1 Macc 13:41–54). The First Book of Maccabees mentions among the great deeds of Simeon that he "glorified the sanctuary and multiplied the vessels of the temple" (14:15).[47]

From the sources we learn that from then on the capital and the Temple were the heart of the Jewish nation, and the high priesthood was its highest political office. When Simeon died in 135 B.C.E., John Hyrcanus, his son and successor, having assumed the high-priestly office of his father, "first propitiated God with sacrifices, and then marched out against Ptolemy" (*Antiquities* 13.230). The high priesthood became transferable from father to son without the intervention or permission of a higher ruler, and was the most important office in Judea because it was directly connected to the military leadership. The Temple appears again in the story of Antiochus Sidetes' siege on Jerusalem in 132 B.C.E. (*Antiquities* 13.236–248). Josephus relates that at a certain juncture of the war the festival of Tabernacles came and Antiochus, on the request of John Hyrcanus, granted the Jews, who were besieged within the walls of Jerusalem, a truce of seven days and even sent a sacrifice to the Temple. He was thus called *Eusebes,* "God-fearing" (*Antiquities* 13.242–244). As part of the treaty with Antiochus Sidetes that was concluded later, Hyrcanus pulled down the walls encircling the city (*Antiquities* 13.247). John Hyrcanus, as high priest, on many occasions had to act not just as a religious leader but also as a politician and statesman (*Antiquities* 13.259; cf. 267, 269). But opposition to his acting as both secular and religious leader emerged during his reign and, according to Josephus, Eleazar of the Pharisees asked Hyrcanus to give up the high priesthood "and be content with governing the people" (*Antiquities* 13.288–292).

The Hasmoneans, however, did not want to give up the high priesthood because this office gave them greater authority than would a purely secular position. They did not want to share their authority over the nation with anyone else. During those days, the Temple and the high priesthood were probably the most important national symbols of the unified nation. Yet this situation was to change during Herod the Great's time, as we shall see later. Herod made the Temple and high priesthood secondary to the secular authority, namely, to his kingship. Also, as high priests, the Hasmoneans had higher stature in the eyes of the foreign rulers such as the Seleucids, Ptolemies, Spartans, and Romans. When the opposition against John Hyrcanus became fiercer, he forsook the Pharisees for the Sadducees, who apparently did not mind his being the secular as well as the religious ruler. Nevertheless, Josephus had only praises for Hyrcanus (*Antiquities* 13.299–300): "Now he was accounted by God worthy of three of the greatest privileges, the rule of the nation, the office of high priest, and the gift of prophecy; for the Deity was with him and enabled him to foresee and foretell the future" (and *Jewish War* 1.68–69). We can find an echo of this view in the rabbinic tradition. The favorable description of Hyrcanus is also a result of his successful conquest of the Samaritans and the destruction of their temple on Mount Gerizim, about which more will be said later.

The opposition against the Hasmoneans on the issue of their holding both the secular and the religious leadership continued and even increased during the time of Alexander Jannaeus. Josephus gives us the reason for the rift between Alexander Jannaeus and the Pharisees, saying, "As for Alexander, his own people revolted against him—for the nation was aroused against him—at the celebration of the festival and as he stood beside the altar and was about to sacrifice, they pelted him with citrons" (*Antiquities* 13.372).[48] As a consequence, the king later killed six thousand of them (no doubt an exaggerated number). He also placed a wooden barrier around the altar and the Temple, "and by this means blocked the people's way to him" (*Antiquities* 13.373). Jerusalem and its Temple were the religiopolitical heart of the Hasmonean kingdom, which, of course, Jannaeus knew all too well. Thus he, like his predecessors, did not give up the high priesthood. Jannaeus, like the Roman generals who returned to Rome after victories, took care to return to Jerusalem after his battles (*Antiquities* 13.375). Yet Jerusalem was his only political and religious center, unlike Herod the Great, who later had two such capitals. The issue of the dual function of the high priesthood was finally solved when Salome, Jannaeus's wife, became queen in 76 B.C.E. As a woman, she could not become high priest, so she entrusted the high priesthood to one of her sons, which kept that post firmly in the grip of the Hasmonean family.

Although the historiography of this period does not elaborate on the spiritual and religious centrality of the Temple, these characteristics, along with the nationalistic political ones, created the raison d'être of its very existence. We can see a continuity of the service and other religiospiritual functions in the Temple from the foundation of the Second Temple in 515 B.C.E. through 70 C.E. Josephus, in passing, hints at these "other" aspects, saying that Judas the Essene, "when he saw Antigonus passing by the temple, cried out to his companions and disciples, who were together with him for the purpose of receiving instruction in foretelling the future, that it would be well for him to die as one who had spoken falsely" (*Antiquities* 13.311). Also, the story about Semaia and Pollion (Shemaia and Abtalion) supporting Herod the Great's entry into Jerusalem in 37 B.C.E. points to the fact that during the Hasmonean era Jerusalem was a very important religious and spiritual center for many Jewish groups.

The preceding survey of the history of Jerusalem, the Temple, and the priesthood in their political dimensions has shown that for a short time the Hellenistic approach of universalizing the religious institutions, the capital, and the priesthood got the upper hand. In the long run, however, the "native," more traditional views prevailed. The Temple remained a symbol of traditional nationalism, as was typical of temples during this period. As an institution, it remained free of Hellenistic influence from about 152 B.C.E. onward, unlike some other indigenous temples in the ancient Near East.[49] The Jews were the only ones in the ancient Near East at that time who, with their indigenous priestly leadership, managed to use their religiocultural symbols to accomplish their practical nationalistic goal: statehood.

Five stages can be discerned in this time span. (1) In the first period, the Temple became autonomous in a religious sense, and some of the high priests were both the religious and the spiritual leaders of the people, as in fact they were beforehand (200–ca. 180 B.C.E.). (2) In the second, the Temple and the priesthood were abused for the purpose of hellenization (ca. 180–164 B.C.E.). The main goal of the Maccabean revolt was to purify the Temple. This goal was achieved in 164 B.C.E. (3) During the third period, the Temple, though purified, remained under the threat of the Akra. The high priesthood remained for part of the time in the hands of the Hellenists, who remained powerful even when the high priesthood remained vacant (164–152 B.C.E.). In this period, the office of the high priest was gradually politicized. (4) In the fourth period, Jerusalem and Temple were gradually freed from Hellenistic influence (152–142 B.C.E.), but were still threatened by the Akra. (5) In the fifth period, the Jewish state became independent, and the Akra was overthrown (142–76 B.C.E.). The Temple became the most important symbol of national political independence. The high priests were the secular rulers of the nation, without any dependence on foreign rulers.

It is evident that the Temple and the priesthood of the Jewish state were major components of the political national awareness of the Jewish people during the Hasmonean period. As a national symbol the Temple was much like other indigenous temples in the region: it was a center for the preservation of the traditional culture and religion. The Temple symbolized the continuity of the Jewish people since the reign of King Solomon. It should again be emphasized that the temples of the indigenous populations were institutions that embodied the uniqueness of those populations. Thus Memphis, Thebes, and Siwa symbolized the indigenous Egyptians; Tyre, the Phoenicians; Uruk and Babylon, the Babylonians; Jerusalem, the Jews; and Mount Gerizim, the Samaritans.[50] Nevertheless, the Jerusalem Temple was the only temple in the region that became a real, independent political center for almost a whole century.

But how are the Temple and the priesthood treated in the literature of the time? Was Jewish literature influenced by the literature of its neighbors in its treatment of these institutions? Let us examine the political aspects of the Temple and the priesthood against the background of the descriptions of non-Jewish temples found in Hellenistic literature. We shall discover that the Jerusalem Temple and its priesthood were central to Jewish national awareness. Also we will see that the notions of priesthood and Temple in Judaism remained exceptional.

Temples are described in various ways in the literature of the

Hellenistic period. Viewed schematically, the many descriptions of temples have much in common with Greek literature and with the Hellenistic literature from the East after Alexander the Great. The reason for this similarity is that there is some degree of continuity to be found between classical Greek concepts of the temple and Hellenistic ones. Thus, against the background of Hellenistic descriptions of temples in Greek that were common at the beginning of Alexander's empire, it seems that Jewish literature was not exceptional in its description of the Jerusalem Temple. It is clear that while the Jews used their own traditional (biblical) descriptions of the Temple, they were also aware of typical Hellenistic descriptions of temples. The Jews seem to have participated in the "academic" comparisons and speculations surrounding temples in the ancient Near East during the Hellenistic era. After all, some Jewish literature was written in Greek for non-Jews to read. They embellished on their own traditional material when they were writing in Greek. Also, in many instances, these compositions had generic similarities to Hellenistic ones. But here we run into a problem when attempting to measure the impact of Hellenism on Jewish literature. A work written in Greek may give the misleading impression—because of the use of Greek terminology—that the original composition is heavily influenced by Hellenism.

During the years 168–143/2 B.C.E. the Temple and Jerusalem constituted the main goal of the Jewish struggle, whereas the territorial acquisitions in Palestine became the main concern after that date until deep into Jannaeus's reign. Thus, from 143/2 B.C.E. through Salome's rule (76–67 B.C.E.) the liberated Temple was taken for granted, unlike the territory, which was still high on the agenda of the Hasmonean state. Also, whereas the problem of the separation of priesthood from secular rule was not of great concern in the beginning of the Hasmonean period, say between 168 and 135 B.C.E., it became more and more acute from the reign of John Hyrcanus I to that of Jannaeus. These shifts are reflected in the literature of the period. Let us then examine, against the background of available Hellenistic descriptions of temples in Greek as well as against the biblical descriptions, how the Jews treated the priesthood and Temple in their own literature, and how they were viewed by the Jews as unique nationalistic symbols. It should be emphasized that it is unlikely that Jewish literature of the Hellenistic period drew directly on eastern descriptions from the time antedating Alexander the Great.

First, there are realistic descriptions of temples—or certain elements of the temple—in Greek literature in the classical age. In some Greek compositions there is an attempt to describe temples as they looked in reality, and to describe their priesthood, as well as their history, in an informative manner. In antiquity, attempts at realism never excluded the use of some imagination to enhance the descriptions.[51] We can find such descriptions in Herodotus, Ctesias, and Hecataeus of Abdera in the fifth through third centuries B.C.E. Yet the Hebrew Bible also uses this kind of description, probably in line with similar descriptions known from Near Eastern literature.[52] For example, there is an attempt to describe the Temple of Solomon in a realistic manner (1 Kings 6–7). The Jerusalem Temple was described in real terms also in some Jewish compositions of the Hellenistic period. Ben Sira describes the Jerusalem Temple as it appeared before the troubled era of the Hellenization of the high priests. He says, while emphasizing the uniqueness of Jerusalem and its Temple, "I ministered before him in the holy tent, and so I was established in Zion" (24:10–11)[53] and then in 36:12–13, "have mercy, Lord, on the people that has borne your name, / And on Israel, whom you compared to your first born. / Have pity on the city of your sanctuary, Jerusalem, the place where you rest, / Fill Zion with the celebration of your goodness." Ben Sira may have felt, like the Jews who had returned from the exile many years before, according to Nehemiah, that the present Temple was poor in comparison to the former Solomonic one; hence he did not linger on its physical dimensions. He did, however, highlight the priesthood of his time, saying,

He [Moses] exalted Aaron, a holy man like him, who was his brother, from the tribe of Levi. He made him an everlasting ordinance, and gave him the priesthood of the people. He blessed him with stateliness, and put on him a splendid robe; he clothed him with glorious perfection, and strengthened him with garments of authority, the drawers, the robe, and the apron, and he surrounded him with pomegranates, with very many gold bells all around to ring out as he walked, to make their sound heard in the temple, to remind the sons of his people. (45:6–9)

Ben Sira emphasized the legitimacy of the high priesthood, which was to become a real problem some decades later when the Hasmoneans were both the high priests and the secular leaders. His description of the attire of the high priest is reminiscent of descriptions of the high priest found in the Bible. Note that Ben Sira, when describing the high priest, refers to Phinehas, a biblical figure, claiming that "Phinehas, the son of Eleazar who is the third in glory, for he was zealous for the fear of the Lord, and stood fast, when the people turned away, in the goodness and eagerness of his soul, atoned for Israel. Therefore an agreement of peace was established with him, that he should be the leader of the saints and of his people, that he and his posterity should possess the dignity of the priesthood forever" (45:23–24). Ben Sira accurately reflects the period during which the leadership and high authority in Jerusalem was in the hands of the legitimate Zadokite priestly order when he portrays the high priest not as a political, but as a religious and spiritual figure. At the time he was writing, the political authority was indeed in the hands of a Seleucid king, probably Antiochus III, who was tolerant to the Jews.

It is important to note that the holy scriptures were authoritative for Ben Sira and the people of his generation. His heroes, unlike the biblical heroes appearing in the literature later in the century, are not embellished upon; that is, their biblical roles remain unchanged. The same is true of his description of the Temple: nostalgia led Ben Sira's thoughts to the Solomonic Temple as it appeared in the biblical account (unlike Eupolemus later in the century, who created it anew). In 47:13 we read that "Solomon reigned in days of peace, and God gave him rest on every side, so that he might erect a house in his name, and provide a sanctuary forever." Ben Sira gave some details on Jerusalem's tragic past (48:17–18): "Hezekiah fortified his city, and brought water into the midst of it; he dug the sheer rock with iron, and built wells for water. In his days Sennacherib came up, and sent the commander, and departed, and he raised his hand against Zion, and uttered great boasts in arrogance." And in 49:4–6 it is said that "Except David and Hezekiah and Josiah, they all sinned greatly . . . they [the Kings of Judah] set fire to the city chosen for the sanctuary, and made her streets desolate." Then 49:11–13: "How shall we magnify Zerubbabel, for he was like a signet on the right hand, so was Jeshua, the son of Jozadak, . . .

for they in their days rebuilt the house, and raised a temple holy to the Lord, prepared for everlasting glory. The memory of Nehemiah also is lasting, for he raised up for us the walls that had fallen, and set up barred gates, and rebuilt our houses."

In 50:1–21 comes the crucial passage, where Ben Sira describes his own generation and again concentrates on the high priest and the Temple. He says:

> It was Simeon, the son of Onias, the great priest, who in his lifetime repaired the house, and in his days strengthened the sanctuary. He laid the foundation for the height of the double wall, the lofty substructure for the temple enclosure. In his days a water cistern was hewed out, a reservoir in circumference like the sea. He took thought for his people to protect them from calamity, and fortified the city against siege. How glorious he was, surrounded by the people, as he came out of the sanctuary . . . and when he went up to the holy altar He made the court of the sanctuary glorious.

Ben Sira reflects in this chapter in particular the centrality of the priesthood of Jerusalem, and the religious autonomy the Jews enjoyed in his time. The Jewish kingdom belonged to the past, and the national awareness of the present was concentrated on the Temple and the priesthood as religious entities. Ben Sira expressed a nostalgia for the past grandeur of Jewish existence but seemed to be satisfied with the present religious autonomy, which allowed the high priest to be the "secular" leader of the nation. The Temple and its history are described by Ben Sira in a traditional manner, which shows that he was not influenced by Greek descriptions of temples and priesthoods. It is even questionable whether he knew any Greek at all. His composition was translated into Greek by his grandson at the end of the second century B.C.E.[54] When reading the translation one may get the impression that the document is heavily influenced by Greek culture; but the Hebrew version, which was found at Masada, shows clearly that the original was not. Ben Sira reveals that the Temple and priesthood were very deeply rooted in the consciousness of the people at the time, which in fact provided the seeds for the unrest that later occurred when the Jews began to feel religiously oppressed. As shown above, the liberation of their Temple came to be their main goal in the time of religious upheaval. A priestly house from Modiʿin was to become the champion of this upheaval.

Second, some of the Hellenistic eastern authors who wrote in Greek seem to have been participating in arguments over the priority of cultures, religions, and nations. Such polemics can be discerned in the repetition of the topics and issues in compositions from different regions in the Hellenistic period. Temples are given a major role in these international polemics. It seems that intellectuals all over the ancient Near East were debating which nations of the East had the more beautiful, more ancient, and more holy temples. Berossus's description of Babylon probably included a description of one or more temples, as can be deduced when it is read against the background of descriptions of temples found in Hecataeus of Abdera and Dionysius Scytobrachion, who described magnificent temples in Egypt and Libya. Also, temples became, more than in classical Greek descriptions, part of the notion of constitution and state (*politeia*). Temples were a matter of competition because they were seen as an important facet of the vitality, centrality, and power of a nation within the family of nations. Thus Menander of Ephesus, a writer of the second century B.C.E., claimed that the magnificent temples in Tyre were already there before the Temple of Jerusalem was built. The Samaritans claimed in a composition written in Greek (Greek was used to reach a wider audience among non-Jews) that their temple on Mount Gerizim already existed at the time of the patriarch Abraham. This assertion was mere propaganda designed to show that the Gerizim temple was founded earlier than the Jewish one in Jerusalem and that it was even visited by Abraham, which, of course, goes against the evidence of the Hebrew Bible.[55] An even more striking example is the one found in Jewish literature of the second century B.C.E., the description of the Temple of Solomon by Eupolemus.[56] Eupolemus, who wrote a composition in Greek called *The Kings of Judah,* was no doubt aware of the typical Hellenistic presentation of temples as major nationalistic symbols. By writing in Greek he participated in the polemics current in the Hellenistic world—as may be seen in the issues he raised in his work. That he wrote in Greek does not mean that he was a Hellenist imbued with Greek culture, a syncretist. On the contrary, he used the Jewish canonical material to make his case against competitive claims, but also created much material himself.

Historians today wish to detect influences, Greek as well as eastern, in every Jewish document from this period. But at times they tend to forget that the authors of these documents were original thinkers. Thus we should not always ask whether we find a Greek influence here or an eastern one there, but rather we should ask what material the author used, how he cleverly reworked it, and how original he was. Eupolemus is a good case in point. In his work the Solomonic Temple is presented in a way that goes against the canonical descriptions of this Temple, yet is biblical in its perception. There is nothing in his description that points to any particular Greek influence on the architecture of the Temple or on any other aspects of it. Eupolemus's description is an original one based on the biblical material. Whereas Ben Sira describes the Temple as it actually looked in his own day (a religious place), Eupolemus embellishes and fabricates its place in history as well as its architecture in a very original manner. He does not describe a utopian temple; instead he emphasizes its political, nationalistic role, showing that the Jerusalem Temple was an internationally acknowledged temple from the start. In Eupolemus's description, the building of the Temple was a major enterprise in the ancient Near East and received its religio-political legitimation from the two great powers of the time, Hiram the king of Tyre, and the king of Egypt. These powers can be viewed as the predecessors of the Seleucids and Ptolemies of Eupolemus's own time. This presentation is understandable when it is seen to come from within a society that thinks in terms of historical precedents.

Also, according to Eupolemus and against the biblical description, Solomon's Temple was no less ancient than many other temples of the neighboring countries, which had existed for hundreds and even thousands of years. The issue of antiquity and authenticity became very important in the Hellenistic East. Whether Eupolemus's description was also launched as a polemic against Onias IV's Jewish temple in Leontopolis is a matter of conjecture. But there is no doubt that his description was designed to show the political significance the Solomonic Temple enjoyed on the international scene. Here we see the connection in Jewish writings between the king and the Temple, and between the state as a political entity and the Temple as one of its major symbols. Eupolemus's description was possibly written at the beginning of the national revival, in the sixties and the beginning of the fifties of the second century B.C.E., when the liberation of the Temple and Jerusalem was still the main goal of the Maccabees.

Third, there are utopian and idealized descriptions of temples. We find this literary genre already in classical literature before Alexander's time, and the most famous example is the *Atlantis* of Plato (in the *Timaeus* and *Critias* 116 C–D). Here in the midst of the kingly palace is a temple, described in a utopian manner, as is the whole of this extraordinary city. Hellenistic utopias are divided between those which deny the existence of a temple in the political community (*politeia*), and those which make it the center of political life. Euhemerus represents the Hellenistic utopia at its best. The temple is described by Euhemerus in a very idealistic way and is probably partly invented and only partly based on some concrete example; · the priests in this temple have a major role in the politics of the utopian state (Diodorus Siculus 5.43.6–44.5). It should be emphasized that utopian descriptions in antiquity and later are very clear and concrete in terms of the architectural features. In this case we can again see that the Jews showed awareness of their surrounding cultures, but tended to stay within the Judaism of the day concerning matters of substance. Hence it can be shown that utopian descriptions of temples in Jewish literature were new in terms of their literary framework, but stayed within the biblical tradition. The prophet Ezekiel's utopian description perhaps nourished the notion of a Jewish utopia (40–42), as did perhaps descriptions of the tabernacle in the Wilderness and Isaiah 6. The author (or authors) of the famous Temple Scroll (second century B.C.E.) shows that he was aware of the issues on the agenda in the regions surrounding Judea, as we have seen in the case of his treatise *On Kingship*. He elaborately depicts an idealistic, even utopian, Jewish Temple. This description shows that the author of this document, who is probably representative of the circles from which this document emanated (the Essenes), was not absolutely against a Temple in Jerusalem, but only opposed the existing unpurified one. The Essenes, like some of the Greek utopian descriptions, were motivated by the wish to see *another* temple, with another physical structure. Yet they were of the opinion that the institution should constitute a part of the future

Jewish state. The physical shape of temples played a crucial role in non-Jews' appreciation of them as religious centers, and the same was true among the Jews, as we can learn from Ezra 3 and in particular from Ezekiel 40–44. It is not accidental that Eupolemus, along with the Temple Scroll and the Letter to Aristeas, elaborately described a Temple different in form from Solomon's Temple, as depicted in the Hebrew Bible. Why is this so?

All of these documents wished to create a different image of the Temple as a result of the changing circumstances. They needed to justify a new situation, a new national setup. For this reason they did not just copy Ezekiel's description of the ideal Temple, but created original ones on the basis of the biblical material. Against the background of the not very impressive present Temple, a need was felt in the second century B.C.E. to emphasize the centrality of the ideal Temple, which was beautiful and important. The Temple Scroll, for example, does not concentrate on the Land of Israel and all its traditional "national" and religious centers of the past, such as Bethel, Shechem, and Hebron. Instead it emphasizes the twelve tribes as the necessary framework of the setup of the Temple in Jerusalem, but the Land remains almost an amorphous entity.[57] Both Eupolemus and the Temple Scroll stress the centrality of the Temple and its magnificent new shape. Both authors were aware of their world, in which the competition among temples played an important role within the larger competition among nations. The physical shapes and forms of temples were part of this contest, in which the Jews participated. But in doing so they adhered to their own traditional descriptions.

The same holds true of the Temple as depicted in the Letter of Aristeas. Although in this case a Diaspora Jew wished to show his non-Jewish neighbors that the Jews had a Temple in Jerusalem that was similar to theirs, it was nevertheless represented in a very Jewish manner. Yet many elements that are in keeping with the Euhemerian portrayals can be discerned in this description from the Diaspora, as V. Tcherikover showed many years ago. The poet Philo the Elder may have written a similar description, but few fragments of his composition have survived. The Letter carefully shows that the Jerusalem Temple is the highest and most magnificent of the ("Greek") temples to be found.[58] The Temple has been central to Jews in the Diaspora, and their tie with it during the time being surveyed speaks for itself. It is interesting to note that the Land of Israel seems secondary to the Temple in the Letter, though depicted in a utopian manner. As we can also learn from 3 Maccabees, the Temple remained very important to the Jews in the Diaspora. Here we should also mention a fragment from Qumran with a description of Jerusalem in Aramaic (*New Jerusalem*). Some scholars wish to see Greek architectural influences in it, but whether there was any direct influence from Greek descriptions remains entirely speculative.

Fourth, there are negative attitudes about temples within the political framework, found for instance in Aristophanes' *Birds,* Plato's *Politeia,* and more clearly in the Early Stoa and some of the Hellenistic utopias. The temple was played down by Plato, who wrote against the vicissitudes of the *polis,* the Greek city-state of his own time. The Stoa (Zeno of Citium) and Hellenistic utopias were opposed to temples, because they disliked other political institutions in the state as well. Many utopian ideas of this kind infiltrated into the works of other writers of the Hellenistic period (e.g., Megasthenes). The negative attitude about the temples in the utopias is usually interpreted as a reaction against the actual role temples played in the politics of the ancient Near East. Iambulus replaced all institutions with the rule of the elderly, whereas the Stoa probably replaced all institutions with the rule of the wise.[59]

Are there negative attitudes to the Temple in Judaism of the Hellenistic period? This is a crucial question because it bears on the whole problem of early Christianity and its attitude to the Temple.

In the biblical prophetic literature we find condemnation of various people for doing bad things in the Temple, or outside it for that matter. But the prophets do not attack the Temple itself as an institution. On the contrary, we frequently hear about the uniqueness of the Jerusalem Temple, not only in the deuteronomistic literature but also elsewhere. In the Persian period the Temple was central to the Jews who returned from the Exile. It has been claimed by many that the Essenes opposed the Temple, but I have already mentioned that they only opposed the present Temple of Jerusalem, and wished to have another one in its stead. Even if the Qumran community was influenced in their mode of living by Hellenistic utopias, some utopias placed temples in the center of their political edifices. We shall see later that opposition to the Temple was usually directed against the impurity of its priests, as well as against its poor dimensions, complaints that never ceased and can be found frequently in rabbinic literature after 70 C.E.[60] But there was no opposition to the institution as such in Judaism of the Hellenistic period. It was, and remained, the main national symbol for all Jews.[61] Also Jesus (and even Paul), as we shall see later, did not simply eliminate the Temple from their theology—in actuality, their views were very much in line with Jewish thought. All of this evidence shows again that the Jewish attitudes about their Temple were hardly influenced by Greek thought.

Fifth, we find the idea of an apocalyptic temple, which is absent from the descriptions in Greek literature of the time, but appears in eastern thought, in the Bible (perhaps Ezekiel, if it is an apocalyptic temple) and the early Enochic material.[62] 1 Enoch 90:28-36, probably from the early Maccabean period, is a good example.[63] According to Enoch, the present Temple would be destroyed and another built above its ruins. The new one is an apocalyptic temple, which emerges as an amorphous entity, unlike the one that appears in 1 Enoch 14, which may derive from an earlier period. It is not described in clear architectural terms like the one of Ezekiel, but some vague outline can still be discerned. In this eschatological Temple, God will appear in due course.[64] Another striking example of a so-called heavenly Temple, which draws heavily on the biblical material, can be found among the writings of Qumran in a composition called the *Songs of the Sabbath Sacrifice*. The question arises whether the document reflects Essene views or the views of other circles (one fragment was found outside Qumran), and its exact date of composition is unclear.[65] It is important for us to note that unlike the Temple of Eupolemus or even the one of the Temple Scroll, the heavenly Temple of the *Songs of the Sabbath Sacrifice* is clearly dissociated from the actual political sphere. The description of the heavenly Temple in the *Songs* alludes to the possibility that its author sees it as a heavenly apolitical *duplicate* (not an alternative!) of the present real Temple, which is so politically oriented. But three points should be made clear: (a) Unlike the Temple Scroll, the so-called heavenly Temple of the *Songs* is described in vague terms. As far as we can deduce from the fragments, it is not a clear and detailed architectural edifice, as we find in the Temple Scroll. (b) It is the home, or place of the heavenly King (God), which shows that the author could not dissociate himself completely from the earthly political imagery surrounding the Temple.[66] (c) The priests are God's servants; their cultic and religious functions are emphasized.

Sixth, the tension that can be traced between the religious and the political capitals in the monarchies and lesser states of the Hellenistic ancient Near East is reflected in the contemporary literature. The natives of Memphis in Hellenistic Egypt never accepted the idea that the capital had moved to Alexandria. Thebes, the old capital, even broke away from Alexandria during the second century B.C.E. The tension between these two old capitals is still expressed in the Hellenistic era. In Diodorus Siculus 1, probably from Hecataeus's *Aegyptiaca,* we hear that Thebes started to wane when Memphis was founded, and that the latter increased "until the time of Alexander the king; for after he had founded the city on the sea that bears his name, all the kings of Egypt after him concentrated their interest on the development of it" (Diodorus Siculus 1.50.6). The truth is, however, that the *floruit* of Thebes occurred in the Eighteenth Dynasty, many centuries after the founding of Memphis. It is unlikely that this was just a mistake made by Greek authors; it was perhaps a tradition that enhanced Memphis and at the expense of Thebes. According to this distorted version, Alexandria was the direct heir of Memphis.

Berossus's lingering on the description of Babylon in his *Babyloniaca* may reflect a polemic on the priority of the old capital over the new one, erected by the Seleucids in Seleucia on the Tigris. In Jewish literature one can see a similar tension, which seems to have taken the shape of a theoretical speculation. The Jews, until perhaps the foundation of Caesarea Maritima by Herod, were not confronted with such a national problem in their political life (as the Babylonians or Egyptians of the Hellenistic era had been). No Greek ruler, neither the Ptolemies nor the Seleucids, pressed the Jews to remove their natural religious and political center away from Jerusalem. For a short while the Jews were annoyed by the hellenized Jews who founded a Greek *politeuma* in Jerusalem, but this was a short-lived episode. Nevertheless, the Jews had the memory of some traumatic experiences involving Jerusalem which they carried with them far into the Second Temple period, just as the Egyptians of the Hellenistic period carried similar memories involving their old religious centers. In the First Temple period, the Jews had been confronted both with the split in their nation and with the foundation of competitive religious and political centers such as Dan, Bethel, Samaria (Shomron), and Tirzah. Moreover, according to their holy scriptures they possessed several traditional religious centers in Palestine.

How did the Jews cope with this issue in the Hellenistic period? They continued to remember Bethel and Shechem, which became a major problem in the Hellenistic age because of the Samaritans who claimed it to be their own center, both religious and political, as well as Hebron, Beersheba, and Shiloh. Thus when, according to the Book of Jubilees (chap. 32), Jacob wished to erect a temple in Bethel and even held a service there, he was deterred from doing so and was commanded by God not to dwell in it "because this is not the place" (32:23). Perhaps as in the Ptolemaic case, wherein one religious center received political preference over another and its theology was raised in stature, so also in the era under survey Jerusalem was made the undoubted political and religious center of the Judaic world. Hence it attained a preferred position in the literature of the period over all other competitive religious centers.

The wish for only one religiopolitical center is a dominant motif in much of the literature of the period. At that juncture of their history the Jews well knew that in the past, competitive religiopolitical centers had brought about their own national destruction; and, indeed, ten tribes were lost (cf. Ezekiel 23). From the Persian period onward, they knew that the uniqueness of Jerusalem and its Temple, along with its role as a unifying symbol for world Jewry, was crucial for Jewish existence, not only in the world but in particular (during Hasmonean times) on the Land. For this reason they felt uncomfortable with other Jewish religious centers such as Leontopolis, Shechem, and Araq el-Emir. The Samaritan temple on Mount Gerizim was, of course, the main problem. The Samaritans, who claimed to be the descendants of Ephraim and Manasseh, said that the real Jewish religiopolitical capital was Shechem. We can sense the tension between Jews and Samaritans in the literature of both sides, in particular through their interpretation of biblical history. It is thus not accidental that the story about the rape of Dinah by Shechem is brought to the fore, and that the kingdom of Melchizedek, the priest-king of Genesis 14, was set by the Samaritans at biblical Shechem, whereas it was put in Jerusalem by the Jews. Be that as it may, the attempts to show that the Jews worshiped in other centers, such as Bethel and Dan, during this period are unconvincing.[67]

In Jewish literature, Jerusalem and the Temple were treated as crucial parts of the political, national existence of the Jewish people. When describing these places they did not just copy biblical descriptions, but changed them and used them loosely in order to meet the new circumstances that confronted them. They showed a great deal of self-confidence in their use of their own tradition on the one hand. On the other, they showed an awareness of what was happening outside their tradition and culture without necessarily adopting foreign elements. The Jews emphasized the continuity of their traditional Temple, just as the Babylonians and Egyptians did for their temples. It is not accidental therefore that non-Jewish literature of the Hellenistic period frequently emphasizes, among other "strange" habits of the Jews, the uniqueness of their Temple, which appeared to be so different from other temples in the region.[68]

Throughout Jewish literature of the period under survey both the Temple and Jerusalem were seen as central to the Jewish people, focal to their religiopolitical existence. The Temple was never criticized as an institution; alternative architectonic temples were suggested, but the Temple as such was never eliminated. In some documents the Temple emerges as the principal national symbol of the Jewish state, as it acquired a political dimension. No alternative to the Temple was propounded until after 63 B.C.E. The priestly order of the legitimate Zadokite house was institutionally praised, but denigrated on the personal level (i.e., the various Hellenistic high priests).[69] The Hasmoneans as high priests were only criticized by some Jews over the question of separation of secular and religious authority. The high priesthood emerges from some documents as it really was—a symbol of political authority of the independent Jewish state. Others only emphasized its religious and spiritual functions. This picture, however, was to change somewhat in the second period.

Notes

1 Temples were built often in obedience to the wish of the gods. An example can be found in Gudea's words (Lagash, 2150 B.C.): "Lord whose word is supreme . . . Son of Enlil, the Hero, you have given me orders. I have truly fulfilled them for you. O Ningirsu, I have built your house for you. May you enter therein in Joy" (now at the Oriental Institute, Chicago). There is a vast literature concerning the temple in the ancient Near East. See for instance, for Egypt, H. Frankfort, *Kingship and the Gods* (Chicago, 1948); E. Hornung, *Conceptions of God in Ancient Egypt* (Ithaca, N.Y., 1982); P. Spencer, *The Egyptian Temple* (London, 1984); and W. Helck, ed., *Tempel und Kult* (Wiesbaden, 1987); for Sumer, Mesopotamia, and Babylon, T. Jacobsen, "The Temple in Sumerian Literature," in *Biblical Archaeology Today: Proceedings of the International Congress of Biblical Archaeology* (Jerusalem, 1985), pp. 284–285; S. N. Kramer, "The Temple in Sumerian Literature," in *Temple in Society*, ed. M. V. Fox (Winona Lake, 1988), pp. 1–16; A. L. Oppenheim, "The Mesopotamian Temple," *Biblical Archaeologist* 7 (1944): 54–63; E. Heinrich, *Die Tempel und Heiligtümer im alten Mesopotamien: Typologie, Morphologie und Geschichte* (Berlin, 1982); K. H. Golzio, *Der Tempel im alten Mesopotamien und seine Parallelen in Indien* (Leiden, 1983); Y. Calvet, "Le Temple babylonien de Larsa," in *Temples et Sanctuaires* (Paris, 1984); pp. 9–22; and E. Sollberger, "The Temple in Babylonia," in *Le Temple et le culte, 20me rencontre* (Leiden, 1975), pp. 31–34; for the Hittites, H. G. Güterbock, "The Hittite Temple According to Written Sources," in *Le Temple et le culte, 20me rencontre* (Leiden, 1975), pp. 125–132; for Israel, G. E. Wright, "The Temple in Palestine-Syria," *Biblical Archaeologist* 7 (1944): 65–77; M. Haran, *Temple and Temple-Service in Ancient Israel* (Oxford, 1978); and S. Talmon, *King, Cult and Calendar in Ancient Israel* (Jerusalem, 1986). In general, see J. M. Lundquist, *Studies on the Temple in the Ancient Near East* (Ann Arbor, Mich., 1985); see also for the political significance of temples M. Lichtheim, *Ancient Egyptian Literature* (Berkeley, Los Angeles, and London, 1973–1980), 3.36–41, 45–49. See also several other articles in T. G. Madsen, *The Temple in Antiquity* (Provo, Utah, 1984).

2 See for instance the examples presented by Strabo, especially concerning Asia Minor (cf. n. 6 below).

3 Cf. the Canopus document, Pithom II, Rosetta, and in general H. Sternberg, *Mythische Motive und Mythenbildung in den Ägyptischen Tempeln und Papyri der griechisch-römischen Zeit* (Wiesbaden, 1985); E. Winter, "Der Herrscherkult in den ägyptischen Ptolemäertempeln," in *Das ptolemaische Ägypten*, ed. H. Maehler and V. M. Strocka (Berlin, 1976), pp. 147–158; idem, *Untersuchungen zu den ägyptischen Tempelreliefs der griechisch-römischen Zeit* (Vienna, 1968); M. V. Seton-Williams, *Ptolemaic Temples* (n.p., 1978); D. J. Thompson, *Memphis under the Ptolemies* (Princeton, 1988), pp. 106–114 and passim. For the native cult during Ptolemaic times, see for instance M. Alliot, *Le Culte d'Horus à Edfu au temps des Ptolémées* (Cairo, 1949). Cf. now also in general for the Greco-Roman period

M. Beard and J. North, *Pagan Priests: Religion and Power in the Ancient World* (Ithaca, N.Y., 1990).

[4] For the religious and economic powers of the Babylonian priesthood during the Hellenistic period, see G. J. P. McEwan, *Priest and Temple in Hellenistic Babylonia* (Wiesbaden, 1981). For the traditions of Mesopotamian religious architecture in the Hellenistic period, see S. B. Downey, *Mesopotamian Religious Architecture* (Princeton, 1988). She claims on p. 5 that "the evidence suggests that the traditions of Mesopotamian religious architecture remained strong but that the manifestations of the tradition were different from one city to another." See also in general J. Oelsner, "Kontinuität und Wandel in Gesellschaft und Kultur Babyloniens in hellenistischer Zeit," *Klio* 60 (1978): 101–116. For the indigenous population in Parthian temples of the Hellenistic period, see M. A. R. Colledge, *Parthian Art* (London, 1977), pp. 37–79. And for the continuity of the worship of Bel and other indigenous oriental gods in Palmyra, see H. J. W. Drijvers, *The Religion of Palmyra* (Leiden, 1976). See also J. Teixidor, *The Pantheon of Palmyra* (Leiden, 1979).

[5] McEwan, *Priest and Temple.*

[6] Strabo, for instance, 11, C498(17), C501–503(1f.); 12,C535(3), C537(6), C556(31), C574(9); 14, C676(19), etc. Sternberg, *Mythische Motive;* Winter, *Untersuchungen.*

[7] For the decline of the Greek temple in the Greek world from the fourth century B.C.E. onward, see W. Burkert, "The Meaning and Function of the Temple in Classical Greece," in *Temple in Society,* ed. M. V. Fox (Winona Lake, 1988), pp. 27–47. Cf. in general T. A. Sinclair, *A History of Greek Political Thought* (London, 1951), passim.

[8] Cf. C. Habicht, *Gottmenschentum und griechische Städte,* 2d ed. (Munich, 1970), for deification of kings in the Hellenistic era. See also F. W. Walbank, "Könige als Götter: Überlegungen zum Herrscherkult von Alexander bis Augustus," *Chiron* 17 (1987): 365–382.

[9] For examples see n. 6 above.

[10] For Egyptian history see *CAH,* vols. 1–3. For Amarna (called Aketaten) cf. J. Samson, *Amarna: City of Akhenaten and Nefertiti* (London, 1972), and D. B. Redford, *Akhenaten: The Heretic King* (Princeton, 1984), pp. 137–153 with the older literature.

[11] R. Girshman, *Persian Art 249 B.C.–A.D. 651: The Parthian and Sassanian Dynasties* (New York, 1962), p. 34; and Colledge, *Parthian Art,* pp. 22–23. See in general for Parthian history N. C. Debevoise, *A Political History of Parthia* (Chicago, 1938).

[12] 1 Kings 12. Cf. for the history of Israel J. M. Miller and J. H. Hayes, *A History of Ancient Israel and Judah* (Philadelphia, 1986).

[13] Cf. how Ezekiel 23 makes a parallel between Samaria and Jerusalem. Cf. W. E. Eichrodt, *Ezekiel* (Philadelphia, 1970), pp. 317–334.

14 Cf. D. Mendels, "Hecataeus of Abdera and a Jewish 'Patrios Politeia' of the Persian Period (Diodorus Siculus XL, 3)," *Zeitschrift für alttestamentliche Wissenschaft* 95 (1983): 96–110. For Jerusalem as a religious and political capital, see M. Weinfeld, "Zion and Jerusalem as a Religious and Political Capital: Ideology and Utopia," in *The Poet and the Historian,* ed. R. E. Friedman (Chico, Calif., 1983), pp. 75–115.

15 Cf. Thompson, *Memphis,* p. 106.

16 P. M. Fraser, *Ptolemaic Alexandria* (Oxford, 1972), 2.11–12 n. 28. In a parallel action, Ptolemy Soter founded Ptolemais in Upper Egypt, which became the Greek center competing with the traditional southern religious capital, Thebes.

17 Thompson, *Memphis,* pp. 107–108.

18 Cf. Y. Meshorer, *City Coins of Eretz Israel and the Decapolis in the Roman Period* (Jerusalem, 1985); and cf. A. Biran, "To the God who is in Dan," in *Temples and High Places in Biblical Times,* ed. A. Biran (Jerusalem, 1981), pp. 142–151. I believe it was a local god in Dan. See also J. Geiger, "Local Patriotism in the Hellenistic Cities of Palestine," in *Greece and Rome in Eretz Israel,* ed. A. Kasher et al. (Jerusalem, 1990), pp. 141–150.

19 For instance, H. van Steuben, "Seleukidische Kolossaltempel," *Antike Welt* 12.3 (1981): 3–12. From Egypt the evidence is much more limited, in particular because so little has been preserved of Ptolemaic Alexandria and other Greek settlements; cf. H. von Hesberg, "Zur Entwicklung der griechischen Architektur im ptolemaeischen Reich," in *Das ptolemaische Ägypten,* ed. H. Maehler and V. M. Strocka (Berlin, 1976), pp. 137–145.

20 R. R. R. Smith, *Hellenistic Royal Portraits* (Oxford, 1988), pp. 15–24.

21 Most evidence comes from Ptolemaic Egypt; cf. Seton-Williams, *Ptolemaic Temples,* and A. K. Bowman, *Egypt after the Pharaohs, 332 B.C.–A.D. 642* (London, 1986), pp. 169–190. On p. 169 he says, "From the earliest days of Ptolemaic dominance, preservation of the traditional institutions of Egyptian religion was fundamental. The decree promulgated on March 4, 238 B.C. at Canopus in the Delta provided eloquent testimony." Cf. also G. R. H. Wright, "Ptolemaic Remains from Kalabsha Temple," *Journal of Egyptian Archaeology* 63 (1977): 156–158. For Mesopotamia cf. Downey, *Mesopotamian Religious Architecture.*

22 W. Hornbostel, *Sarapis. Studien zur Überlieferungsgeschichte, den Erscheinungsformen und Wandlungen der Gestalt eines Gottes* (Leiden, 1973).

23 Cf. in general A. H. M. Jones, *The Cities of the Eastern Roman Provinces,* 2d ed. (Oxford, 1971), with C. Preaux, *Le Monde hellénistique* (Paris, 1978). For Palestine in general, see E. Schürer, *The History of the Jewish People in the Age of Jesus Christ,* rev. G. Vermes et al. (Edinburgh, 1973–1987), 2.81–183; and G. Fuks, *Scythopolis—a Greek City in Eretz-Israel* (Jerusalem, 1983) (Hebrew).

24 Cf. for instance C. Bonnet, *Melqart: Cultes et mythes de l'Héraclès Tyrien en Méditerranée* (Louvain, 1988).

25 Most scholars who deal with the Temple in the Second Temple period ignore its political significance; for instance, S. Zeitlin, *Studies in the Early History of Judaism* (New York, 1973), 1.143–175 and D. R. Schwartz, "Priesthood, Temple, Sacrifice: Opposition and Spiritualization in the Late Second Temple Period," diss., Jerusalem, 1979.

26 M. Stern, *The Documents Relating to the Hasmonean War* (Jerusalem, 1973), pp. 28–41 (Hebrew); and idem, *The History of Eretz Israel* (Jerusalem, 1981), 3.142–143 (Hebrew).

27 For a commentary see J. A. Goldstein, *I Maccabees** and *II Maccabees.** For the following in general see K. Bringmann, *Hellenistische Reform und Religionsverfolgung in Judaea* (Göttingen and Zurich, 1983). For the priestly orders see M. Stern, "Aspects of Jewish Society: The Priesthood and Other Classes," in *Compendia rerum iudaicarum,* ed. S. Safrai et al. (Assen, 1976), 2.580–596.

28 E. Bickerman, "Héliodore au temple de Jérusalem," in *Studies in Jewish and Christian History* (Leiden, 1980), 2.159–191.

29 V. Tcherikover, *Hellenistic Civilization and the Jews* (Philadelphia, 1959), pp. 117–174.

30 Cf. M. Stern, "The Death of Onias III," in his *Studies in Jewish History* (Jerusalem, 1991) pp. 35–50 (Hebrew), and V. Keil, "Onias III—Martyrer oder Tempelgründer," *Zeitschrift für die alttestamentliche Wissenschaft* 97 (1985): 221–233.

31 F. Millar, "The Background to the Maccabean Revolution: Reflections on Martin Hengel's *Judaism and Hellenism,*" *Journal of Jewish Studies* 29.1 (1978): 1–21; Tcherikover, *Hellenistic Civilization,* pp. 404–409.

32 Cf. L. H. Feldman, Josephus, *Antiquities* 12 ad loc., in the Loeb Classical Library edition. In general see also H. H. Rowley, "Menelaus and the Abomination of Desolation," in *Studia Orientalia Ioanni Pedersen* (Copenhagen, 1953), pp. 303–315.

33 For Antiochus IV as king of Egypt, see S. M. Burstein, *The Hellenistic Age from the Battle of Ipsos to the Death of Kleopatra VII* (Cambridge, 1985), pp. 52–54.

34 See in general L. Dequeker, "The City of David and the Seleucid Acra in Jerusalem," *Orientalia Lovaniensia Analecta* 19 (1985): 193–210.

35 See also N. Avigad, *Discovering Jerusalem* (Oxford, 1984).

36 For the background of these repressive measures and their result, see E. Bickerman, *The God of the Maccabees: Studies in the Meaning and Origin of the Maccabean Revolt* (Leiden, 1979).

[37] Stern, *History,* p. 163.

[38] And supported by members from the division of Hakkoz. For these divisions, see Stern, "Aspects of Jewish Society," 2.580–596. Cf. in general J. Sievers, *The Hasmoneans and Their Supporters* (Atlanta, 1990), pp. 27–36. The literature abounds regarding the Maccabean upheaval; cf. Bickerman, *God of the Maccabees;* A. Momigliano, *Prime Linee de storia della tradizione Maccabaica* (Torino, 1931); F. Millar, "The Background to the Maccabean Revolution," *Journal of Jewish Studies* 29.1 (1978): 1–21; P. Haas, "The Maccabean Struggle to Define Judaism," in *New Perspectives on Ancient Judaism,* ed. J. Neusner et al. (New York and London, 1987), 1.49–65.

[39] Studies of the tendencies sometimes altogether ignore the rationale behind the historical dynamics. For a good study on the tendencies, see R. Doran, *Temple Propaganda: The Purpose and Character of 2 Maccabees* (Washington, D.C., 1981).

[40] 1 Macc 6:5–16; 2 Maccabees 9, where he vowed to adorn the holy Temple with the finest of votive offerings, v 16; 2 Macc 10:9.

[41] For the Hasidim, see J. Kampen, *The Hasideans and the Origin of Pharisaism: A Study in 1 and 2 Maccabees* (Atlanta, 1988). And for the later scribes see D. R. Schwartz, "Scribes and Pharisees, Hypocrites," *Zion* 51 (1985): 121–132 (Hebrew); and A. J. Saldarini, *Pharisees, Scribes, and Sadducees in Palestinian Society* (Wilmington, Del., 1988).

[42] For this *Tendenz* see Doran, *Temple Propaganda,* and D. J. Harrington, *The Maccabean Revolt: Anatomy of a Biblical Revolution* (Wilmington, Del., 1988), pp. 36–56.

[43] Cf. H. Burgmann, "Das umstrittene Intersacerdotium in Jerusalem 159–152 v. Chr.," *Journal for the Study of Judaism in the Persian, Hellenistic and Roman Period* 11 (1980): 135–176.

[44] Stern, *Documents,* pp. 93–95.

[45] Ibid., pp. 95–106. Demetrius mentions the high priesthood, but according to 1 Maccabees does not offer it to Jonathan. According to Josephus's version he acknowledges him as high priest, but this version (*Antiquities* 13.48–57) is less trustworthy than 1 Maccabees.

[46] F. M. Cross, *The Ancient Library of Qumran and Modern Biblical Studies* (rev. ed. New York, 1961), pp. 127–160; G. Jeremias, *Der Lehrer der Gerechtigkeit* (Göttingen, 1963), and recently see Sievers, *Hasmoneans and Their Supporters,* pp. 88–92.

[47] Cf. J. Sievers, "The High Priesthood of Simon Maccabeus: An Analysis of 1 Macc 14:25–49," *Society of Biblical Literature Seminar Papers* (1981): 309–318.

[48] See in general for this episode G. Alon, *Jews, Judaism and the Classical World* (Jerusalem, 1977), pp. 98–102; M. J. Geller, "Alexander Jannaeus and the Pharisee Rift," *Journal of Jewish Studies* 30 (1979): 202–211.

[49] As for instance the ones in Hellenistic Babylon: Downey, *Mesopotamian Religious Architecture;* and the ones of Hellenistic Egypt: Bowman, *Egypt after the Pharaohs.*

[50] The divisions of the priestly order in the Jerusalem Temple, for instance, are reminiscent of this kind of division in Egyptian temples at the time (cf. Stern, "Aspects of Jewish Society," 2.587), but besides this have nothing else in common.

[51] In general, for the temple in classical Greece, see V. J. Scully, *The Earth, the Temple, and the Gods: Greek Sacred Architecture* (New Haven, 1962). A good summary of the problem is by W. Burkert, "The Meaning and Function of the Temple in Classical Greece," in *Temple in Society,* ed. M. V. Fox (Winona Lake, 1988), pp. 27–47, with bibliography. For the temple and the *polis* see A. M. Snodgrass, *Archaeology and the Rise of the Greek State* (Cambridge, 1977); F. de Polignac, *La Naissance de la cité grecque: Cultes, espace et société VIIIe–VIIe siècle avant J.C.* (Paris, 1984); and Burkert, above.

[52] For Near Eastern descriptions of the situation before Alexander the Great see, for instance, Kramer, "Temple in Sumerian Literature" (an ideal description of a Sumerian holy city and its sanctuary); and Lichtheim, *Ancient Egyptian Literature,* 3.33–36, 46–47 (description of Egyptian temples in architectonic hues).

[53] For this passage, cf. P. W. Skehan and A. A. Di Lella, *The Wisdom of Ben Sira,** ad loc.

[54] Cf. B. G. Wright, *No Small Difference: Sirach's Relationship to Its Hebrew Parent Text* (Atlanta, 1989).

[55] See D. Mendels, *The Land of Israel as a Political Concept in Hasmonean Literature* (Tübingen, 1987), pp. 109–143. Already in the Hebrew Bible an effort was made to link Abraham with the Jerusalem Temple. Thus in Genesis 22, Moriah is not located very clearly, whereas in Chronicles it is located at the very side of Jerusalem, thereby ensuring that the pseudo-sacrifice of Isaac took place where the Temple was later built. The information included in Chronicles (2 Chr 3:1) may well have been written as part of the debate with the Samaritans about which Temple site was more ancient. For the archaeological remains of the Samaritan temple, see Y. Magen, "Mount Gerizim—A Temple-City," *Qadmoniot* 23 (1991–1992): 70–96 (Hebrew).

[56] For Eupolemus, see Mendels, *The Land,* pp. 29–46.

[57] Besides some general references to it, such as "You shall not do within your land as the na[t]ions do" (51:19), or "when you come to the Land which I give you, and you possess it" (56:12, and 64:12–13), the Land is never concretely referred to; it is always spoken of in general terms without mentioning any specific places. Not so Jerusalem, and in particular its Temple, which get an elaborate description.

[58] An ideal picture of a city as an architectural vision can be seen in the Near Eastern art that developed long before Alexander. For this see W. A. P. Childs, *The City-Reliefs of Lycia* (Princeton, 1978), esp. p. 107.

[59] For utopia and Stoa see G. J. D. Aalders, *Political Thought in Hellenistic Times* (Amsterdam, 1975); and J. Ferguson, *Utopias of the Classical World* (London, 1975).

[60] O. R. J. McKelvey, *The New Temple: The Church in the New Testament* (Oxford, 1969), pp. 20–22, and concerning the Damascus Document see P. R. Davies, "The Ideology of the Temple in the Damascus Document," *Journal of Jewish Studies* 33 (1982): 287–301.

[61] Schwartz, "Priesthood, Temple, Sacrifice," pp. 44–90.

[62] For the early Enochic material and the Temple see M. E. Stone, *Scriptures, Sects and Visions* (Oxford, 1980), pp. 27–47, esp. p. 44.

[63] Whether it is a heavenly temple or not is not crucial for this study; cf. the discussion of McKelvey, *New Temple,* pp. 28–31.

[64] The motif of the gods' dwelling place in the temple was common to eastern and Greek sanctuaries (for early eastern temples, see R. D. Barnett, "Bringing the God into the Temple," in *Temples and High Places in Biblical Times,* ed. A. Biran [Jerusalem, 1981], pp. 10–20; for the Greek temples, see Burkert, "Meaning and Function"). In Judaism, however, there is one God and one Temple, as Philo Judaeus phrased it (*De specialibus legibus* 1.67). From the Temple God delivers his judgment; Amos 1:2, Jer 25:30.

[65] One can say, however, that it precedes the first century B.C.E. (cf. C. Newsom, *Songs of the Sabbath Sacrifice* [Atlanta, 1985]).

[66] And see also the heavenly Temple in the *Testament of Levi* 3:4–6; 5:1–2, but the Temple is not described here. Also in compositions subsequent to 70 C.E., when the new (heavenly) Temple is mentioned (as in 2 Bar 4:2–6 and 4 Ezra 10), it is never depicted in architectonic, or clear lines. It always remains very amorphous, even when the new or heavenly Jerusalem is clearly depicted. If one carefully studies the idea of the heavenly Temple in Judaism (Exod 15:17–18; Isaiah 6, and Ezekiel), there is no necessity to bring in Plato's view of the "idea," because there existed a continuity and development within Judaism of the idea of a heavenly or ideal Temple (against McKelvey, *New Temple,* pp. 38–41).

[67] Biran, "To the God," and J. Schwartz, "Jubilees, Bethel and the Temple of Jacob," *Hebrew Union College Annual* 56 (1985): 63–85. See Schwartz's attempts to show that a priestly settlement existed in Jericho during the Hasmonean period: "On Priests and Jericho in the Second Temple Period," *Jewish Quarterly Review* 79 (1988): esp. 23–36.

[68] Cf. M. Stern, *Greek and Latin Authors on Jews and Judaism* (Jerusalem, 1974–1984), vols. 1–2 passim.

[69] For example, a generalization at the end of this period concerning the Hasmonean priests, Psalms of Solomon 8:1–22. In general, for the criticism of priesthood in the literature of the Second Temple period, see Schwartz, "Priesthood, Temple, Sacrifice," pp. 12–35. For the wicked priests in Qumran, see 1QpHab 12.8ff.; CD 5.6–8.

CHAPTER 6

From Militia to Army, 168-63 B.C.E.

This chapter deals with the foundation of the Jewish national army and its importance in the national awareness of the Jews. The decline of this army as a unifying symbol of the Jewish nation from Alexander Jannaeus's reign onward was a severe blow to the concept of statehood, unity, and national existence for the Jewish people. Although it started as a popular voluntary Jewish militia in Judas Maccabeus's time (168 B.C.E.), by the forties of the second century it had become a more organized army, still Jewish in its composition. From John Hyrcanus I's time (135–104/3 B.C.E.) through the reign of Alexander Jannaeus (104/3–76 B.C.E.), the army also included foreign mercenaries. After Queen Salome's death in 67 B.C.E., a civil war ensued between her two sons, Aristobulus and Hyrcanus, who recruited two separate private armies. The Hasmonean army had disappeared. An army of the Jewish state was recreated by Herod the Great, which will be discussed in chapter 11.

Before discussing the history of the Hasmonean army as a symbol of national identity, we should examine the ethnic composition of the armies of the Hellenistic Diadochi. The Hellenistic armies after Alexander the Great were like the armies of the princes in Europe of the fifteenth and sixteenth centuries—they were not "national" armies.[1] Unlike the national armies of the city-states and the federal states in the Greek mainland, the armies in the Hellenistic Near East were not "national" in the sense that their soldiers were of one nation or tribe fighting a war for a common patriotic cause under a national leader. The soldier and the "citizen" were two different entities. Every Diadoch had his "personal" army consisting of troops of mercenaries who were tied to him by the simple fact that he paid their salaries. The Diadochi were also responsible for any promotion of the officers and generals to higher positions. The motivation of such armies to fight was not necessarily the existence of one national purpose; it was, rather, money, as well as the chance of promotion for the officers. As in the fifteenth and sixteenth centuries, many of the Hellenistic armies changed their masters frequently. Even the Jewish army of Jonathan during the fifties and forties of the second century B.C.E. was hired by a Hellenistic Diadoch. But Jonathan's army remained an autonomous military force. Alongside these multinational armies there were, however, some national ones, such as the Nabataean and the Jewish ones. Also, while most of the Hellenistic armies hired mercenary forces, they also had alongside these mercenaries units of *kleruchoi* (settlers), the royal guard, and vassals, as well as *philoi* (friends) of the king.[2] The majority of these units were usually placed within the army according to their original ethnic divisions, and they were kept together during battles because they often served as specialists in certain aspects of warfare. When Polybius described the battlefield at Raphia (217 B.C.E.), he said,

> Antiochus . . . concentrated his forces. These consisted firstly of Daae, Carmanians, and Cilicians, light armed troops about five thousand in number organized and commanded by Byttacus the Macedonian. Under Theodotus the Aetolian, who had played the traitor to Ptolemy, was a force of ten thousand selected from every part of the kingdom and armed in the Macedonian manner. . . . There were Agrianian and Persian bowmen and slingers to the number of two thousand, and with them two thousand Thracians, all under the command of Mendemus of Alabanda. Aspasianus the Mede had under him a force of about five thousand Medes, Cissians, Cadusians, and Carmanians. The Arabs and neighboring tribes numbered about ten thousand and were commanded by Zabdibelus. Hippolochus the Thessalian commanded the mercenaries from Greece, five thousand in number. Antiochus had also fifteen hundred Cretans under Eurylochus and a thousand Neocretans under Zelys of Gortyna. With

these were five hundred Lydian javelineers and a thousand Cardaces under Lysimachus the Gaul. The cavalry numbered six thousand in all, four thousand of them being commanded by Antipater the king's nephew and the rest by Themison. The whole army of Antiochus consisted of sixty-two thousand foot, six thousand horse, and a hundred and two elephants. (5.79)

The composition of the army was similar in 190 B.C.E. (Magnesia) and 165 B.C.E. (the parade at Daphne). Among Thracians, Cretans, Galatians, one can find also Arabs, Lydians, and Misians.[3] As in Europe in the sixteenth century and even more so in the standing armies of the absolute kings (in which there existed a separation of soldier from civilian),[4] the mercenary soldier in the Seleucid army fought for money without necessarily identifying himself with the Seleucid kingdom and its causes. He would easily switch to the side of the enemy if he were paid more. The disadvantages of a mercenary force led Mithridates VI to reform his army, and to dismiss many of his mercenaries (according to Plutarch, *Lucullus* 7). Ptolemaic Egypt also provides a good example of the typical makeup of a Hellenistic army.

The Ptolemies recruited mercenaries from all over the eastern Mediterranean, as is shown by the composition of their army in the famous battle of Raphia against the Seleucids in 217 B.C.E., mentioned above. Polybius stated that

Ptolemy started from Alexandria with an army of seventy thousand foot, five hundred horses, and seventy-three elephants, . . . Ptolemy's two wings were formed as follows: Polycrates with his cavalry held the extreme left wing, and between him and the phalanx stood first the Cretans, next the cavalry, then the royal guard, then the peltasts under Socrates, the latter being next to those Libyans who were armed in the Macedonian manner. On the extreme right wing was Echecrates with his cavalry, and on the left stood Gauls and Thracians, and next to them was Phoxidas with his Greek mercenaries in immediate contact with the Egyptian phalanx. Of the elephants forty were posted on the left, where Ptolemy himself was about to fight. (5.82)

Among all of these foreign mercenaries, Ptolemy IV also recruited—perhaps for the first time on such a grand scale—twenty thousand indigenous Egyptians, who were given the opportunity to fight for a "true" Egyptian cause. Most probably, during the battle at Raphia, their nationalistic feelings were aroused. These feelings suddenly emerged when they so clearly proved that they had contributed to their nation's survival, in a crucial battle between the two great powers of the time. After the battle was over, they felt they had earned more national freedom. The Egyptian Greeks who fought in the Ptolemaic army a century later were convinced that they were fighting for their "noble fatherland," Egypt.[5] The same happened during the eighteenth century when the soldiers were no longer mercenaries, but began to be recruited from the nations themselves. The recruitment of French citizens in 1793 for the war against Austria and the coalition serves as a good illustration of national conscription on a grand scale. This element, along with others, aroused the desire for freedom and the self-awareness of the people as a nation.[6] Marshal Foch said a long time later, "The wars of kings were at an end; the wars of peoples were beginning."[7]

Unlike the armies of most of the Hellenistic princes, but like the ones of the Nabataeans, the "army" created by Judas Maccabeus about 168 B.C.E. was unique in that it was a national army comprised of only Jewish soldiers, who fought for a clear nationalistic purpose with which they identified. In other words, there existed at the time an identity between soldier and "citizen." Not only were its soldiers Jewish but also the officers, and during the first years of its existence even its organizational patterns were in keeping with biblical descriptions of military forces. During the fifties and forties the Jewish army adopted more and more of the Hellenistic methods of warfare, but it remained an army of Jews. Before going to battle, the Maccabean brothers may have addressed the army using many biblical quotations to encourage the soldiers.[8] These addresses were either made up by Jewish historians of the time, or reflect what was really said, but not in a verbatim form. The prebattle speeches of Judas and his brothers always refer to the common national history of the Jewish people.[9] Thus, in contrast to the Hellenistic armies of the time, the Jewish military forces in the first thirty years of their existence were purely nationalistic. A change was brought about by Hyrcanus I, who recruited foreign mercenaries to reinforce the army. We do not know what the relative proportions were at the time of mercenaries and Jews in the Hasmonean army. During Alexander Jannaeus's time the army went for the first time on a grand scale against its Jewish fellow citizens and not merely the Hellenists, who were usually viewed as traitors by religious Jews. Some of the battles of the Jewish state's national army were then fought against Jews, who were themselves imbued with nationalistic feelings (e.g., the Pharisees and their followers). This change reflected a split in the national unity. Unlike the militia of Judas Maccabeus, which was not a state army, Alexander Jannaeus used the army of the Jewish state for operations that were beyond and against the national "consensus," which had already crystallized at the time. Jannaeus abused the raison d'être of the national army. The Pharisees could not help but come into conflict with his policies.

Three factors thus brought about the decline of the Jewish army as a national symbol from Jannaeus's time (about 100 B.C.E.) to 63 B.C.E.: the increase of the use of mercenary forces, the frequent use of this army as a tool for policies that were not popular among many Jews in Palestine (excluding of course the Hellenist group), and the vigorous use of the army on a wide scale against Jews, the fellow countrymen of the soldiers. The army was perhaps not yet "schizophrenic" in terms of its makeup, in the sense that it was to become during Herod the Great's time, but it presented a foretaste of what it was to become later in the century.

Let us view this decline through the history of the Jewish army during the period 160–63 B.C.E., discussing the nationalistic aspects of the Hasmonean army rather than strategic matters or problems of warfare. This survey will show the role the army played in Jewish national awareness; for, after all, the information used here derives from nationalistic sources. Three stages can be discerned in the history of the Jewish military forces: the creation of the Jewish militia or guerrilla forces (168–152 B.C.E.), its development into a Jewish army (i.e., the exclusive recruitment of Jews, 152–ca. 130 B.C.E.), and the supplementation of the Jewish army with mercenaries (ca. 130–67 B.C.E.).

The first Jewish military force was organized by Mattathias and his sons at the end of 167 B.C.E. or during 166 B.C.E.,[10] and the first important decision made was that they would fight on the Sabbath if attacked.[11] We hear that "at that time a company of Hasidim joined them, an exceedingly forceful group of Israel, each one offering himself willingly in defense of the law. All the refugees from misfortune joined them, and came to reinforce them. They mustered an army and smote sinners in their anger, and lawless men in their wrath" (1 Macc 2:42–44). This militia was recruited to tear down the foreign altars, to circumcise the children, and to rescue the Law. On his deathbed Mattathias appointed Judas Maccabeus "strong in might from his youth" to become the leader of the army (*stratia*) "who will fight the peoples' war" (2:66) (between April 20, 166 and April 4, 165). The first steps taken by Judas in his war were against the "sinners" of his own people, the Hellenists. Although the Books of Maccabees want us to believe otherwise, this was a civil war between two parties of Jews.[12]

But Judea was not yet a state, and its military forces were just a loosely organized guerrilla force. From 1 Maccabees we hear that Judas, the son of Mattathias, who was called Maccabeus, arose in his stead. "And all his brothers helped him, as well as those who were adherents of his father, and gladly they fought Israel's war. He spread his people's glory far and wide. . . . He organized battles, protecting his camp with the sword. . . . He sought out and pursued those who broke the Law and exterminated those who troubled his people" (3:1–5). In 2 Macc 8:1 there is a slightly different approach: Judas Maccabeus and his followers "secretly went through the villages, summoned their relatives, and admitted into their army all those who had remained steadfast to Judaism, until they had gathered together about six thousand men."[13] While fighting on the home front with Jews sympathetic to Hellenism (who were driven to pro-Seleucid attitudes by the Maccabees, 2 Macc 8:5–7), Judas was forced to launch an attack against the Seleucids. The fierce war against the "Syrians," as they are called in the sources, started in the spring of 165 B.C.E.

At the beginning of this war against the Seleucids, in 166/165 B.C.E. Judas defeated the Syrian general Apollonius.[14] The Syrian general Seron was then sent to Palestine, and Judas had to encourage his people, who complained that they were so few in number that they could not fight against such a great multitude of Syrians. Such claims were also to be heard in subsequent wars. B. Bar Kochva has ingeniously argued that Jewish historiography of the time made this story up, in order to show the heroism of the few Jews who gained a victory over the giant Seleucid army. In fact, he argues, the Jews may have had a larger army at times than the Seleucids.[15] If this claim, which some scholars doubt,[16] is true, it is of some interest here. The facts should not be taken at face value, but as they were interpreted later. It is important to note that Jewish awareness during the later part of the Hasmonean era (when the books of Maccabees were written) depicted the new Maccabean militia in terms of a David fighting a Goliath, which was most probably true at the beginning of the Maccabean revolt. Be that as it may, the books of Maccabees henceforward emphasized the nationalistic aims of the war and stressed the fact that it was a Jewish army that defended the nation against Seleucid aggression. This remarkable Jewish leader emphasized that no other military force would fight for the Jews: "Victory in battle does not depend on the size of the army, but rather on strength that comes from heaven. They are advancing against us, full of violence and lawlessness, to destroy us, our wives, and our children . . . we are fighting for our lives and our laws. He Himself will shatter them before us; but as for you, be not afraid of them" (1 Macc 3:18–22). This speech may reflect the spirit of Judas's actual words, but even if it does not it shows how, many years later, the Jews reflected on this phase of their history. This motif of the few who fight the many, but who have the approval of God, reappears in later Jewish works.[17]

After Judas crushed Seron,[18] it is said that "the fear and dread of Judas and his brothers began to fall upon the heathen around them." Before the battle of Emmaus in the early summer of 165 B.C.E. we learn again that the army of Judas was completely Jewish; at least slave traders thought so at the time. It is said that "merchants of the country . . . came to the camp to buy the *Israelites* as slaves" (1 Macc 3:41). Its Jewish, probably Hasidic, character was also emphasized in the preparations for the war at Emmaus with Nicanor and Gorgias when the Jewish force was assembled at Mizpah: "They gathered together and went to Mizpah, opposite Jerusalem, because Israel *formerly* had a place of prayer in Mizpah. On that day they fasted, and donned sackcloth, put ashes on their head, and tore their garments. They spread out the scroll of the Law, upon which the heathen had drawn likenesses of their idols. They brought the priestly garments, and the firstfruits and the tithes. They shaved the Nazirites, who had fulfilled their days, and cried to heaven with a loud voice" (3:46–54). Judas organized the army in keeping with biblical descriptions of military forces. In 1 Macc 3:55–57 it is said that Judas appointed officers over the people, colonels, captains, lieutenants, and sergeants (as in the Temple Scroll). He then ordered those who were betrothed to women or planting vineyards, or who were timid or building houses to return to their homes "in accordance with the Law." This passage may again be an afterthought of Jewish historiography, though it is very likely that much of it occurred in reality. A Jewish military force, fighting "biblical" battles, was the complete raison d'être of the Maccabean revolt.[19]

Then the army (*parembole*) moved and encamped to the south of Emmaus. Judas encouraged his army, saying, "Gird yourselves and acquit yourselves like brave men . . . it is better for us to die in battle than to look upon the tragedies of *our nation* and our sanctuary. But whatever be the will in Heaven, thus shall he do" (58–60). Before the battle Judas was seen on the plain with three thousand men, who "had neither such armor nor swords as they would have wished" (4:6; *Antiquities* 12.307). Again, this somewhat guerrilla force, fighting with sticks and stones, stands in contrast to the large, well-organized and experienced Seleucid army. The Jewish character of the army is shown again by the author of 1 Maccabees in Judas's discourses in which he refers to Jewish history. This author, one should emphasize, probably lived in John Hyrcanus I's time and was closer to the events he describes and to the spirit of the time than modern scholars who accuse him of sometimes falsifying the events. According to him Judas said on this occasion, "Remember how our fathers were saved at the Red Sea, when Pharaoh pursued them with a host. Now . . . if He will have mercy upon us, and will be mindful of the testament of the fathers, . . ." (4:8–11). To mercenaries, such a speech would have been a waste of precious time, and it was clear to the writer of 1 Maccabees that Judas had a Jewish army of God-fearing people. But even if this was not the case, his presentation of it adds to the understanding of the army as a national symbol in the second century B.C.E.

Judas's army in Emmaus proved to be very successful. Judas prohibited his soldiers' taking any booty, which was in line with the biblical ordinance against such activity (4:17–18). When Gorgias's army escaped, the Jewishness of the Maccabean army was demonstrated again, in that "on their return they sang a song of thanksgiving and gave thanks to Heaven, for He is good, for His mercy endureth forever. And Israel had a great deliverance on that day" (4:24–25). It is hard to believe that any mercenaries participated in this war, or at least that the author of 1 Maccabees thought they did.

These operations against Nicanor and Gorgias are described in a somewhat different manner in 2 Macc 8:8–29, 34–36. The Seleucids appeared with "not less than twenty thousand heathen of *all nationalities.*" Judas had only six thousand men; again he said to them that they should rely on God, and he recounted the "instances of help they experienced in the time of their forefathers, how in the days of Sennacherib, a hundred and eighty-five thousand had perished; and in the battle that took place in Babylon against the Galatians, only eight thousand went into the fray along with four thousand Macedonians. When the Macedonians were at a loss as to what to do, the eight thousand destroyed the hundred and twenty thousand with heaven's help." After he encouraged them in this manner, he divided his army into four divisions and made each of his brothers commanders, assigning to each of them fifteen hundred men. In addition he appointed his brother Eleazar to read the Torah publicly, "and gave the words God's Help as the watchword." They managed to gain a victory and "slaughtered more than nine thousand of the enemy." On the Sabbath they stopped fighting. The Second Book of Maccabees is even more convinced than First Book of Maccabees of the army's pious attitude, and describes the battles as a victory achieved more by God than by earthly forces.[20]

Some months later (at the end of 165 B.C.E. or beginning of 164 B.C.E.), before the battle with Lysias at Beth-zur, we hear that Judas met the Seleucids with ten thousand men. When he saw how strong the army was, he prayed and said, "Blessed are you, O savior of Israel, who staved off the charge of the mighty man by the hand of Thy servant David, and didst deliver the camp of the Philistines into the hands of Jonathan son of Saul." In encouraging his army, Judas always referred to national battles of the past fought against the oppressors of Israel. Lysias was defeated, and he returned to Antioch where he recruited many mercenaries (4:35). According to 2 Macc 11:1–21, 29 (which is throughout vague and unclear about the battles of the Maccabees, in contrast to 1 Maccabees), in the war against Lysias at Beth-zur there was some divine intervention: "There, while they were still near Jerusalem, a horseman clothed in white and brandishing weapons of gold appeared at their head. All joined together in praising the merciful God."[21]

Some months later Judas and his brothers went to purify and dedicate the sanctuary in Jerusalem. It is said that "the *entire army*" was involved in this act, which took place at the end of the summer of 164 B.C.E. (1 Macc 4:37–60; in 2 Macc 10:1–8 the army is not explicitly mentioned in this context). The army is again depicted as being a purely Jewish group that carried out the assignment, though not a very military one, of purifying the sanctuary ("They tore their garments and made great lamentations and put ashes on their heads"). Meanwhile Judas appointed certain men to fight against the garrison in the citadel (1 Macc 4:41). One gets the impression from the events recounted that the army of Judas was democratic and, like some armies of the Greek world (Aetolians),[22] reflected the will of the people—an identity between army and nation is evident in some instances (e.g., 1 Macc 5:16–17). The Hellenists were, of course, not included. The biblical atmosphere comes again to the fore in 2 Maccabees 12, which relates that when Judas reached the city of Caspin during his fights for the Land, he "invoked the great Sovereign of the world who, without battering rams or war engines, threw down Jericho in the time of Joshua" (12:13–16).

The following incident related in the sources occurred soon after the Feast of Dedication, sometime between December 164 B.C.E. and April 163 B.C.E. Judas left two officers, Joseph and Azariah, "with the rest of the army in Judea to guard it" and ordered them to take command of these people, but not to engage the enemy in battle until he returned (1 Macc 5:18–19). Although one should not take the exact figures appearing in the sources at face value, it seems that the Maccabean army had been increased after it appeared in Beth-zur, because it is said that three thousand men were apportioned to Simeon to undertake the expedition into the Galilee, whereas eight thousand men went along with Judas to the Gilead. Joseph and Azariah brought their army of more than two thousand men into battle against Gorgias at Jamnia. According to 5:55–62 about two thousand men of the army of Israel were slain on that day. This disaster "befell the army because they did not obey Judas and his brothers, imagining that they could perform some heroic deed. They were not of the family of those men into whose keeping was entrusted the power of saving Israel." Today one can say that these commanders had neither the authorized leadership nor the charisma to be the generals of an army. Furthermore, they did not lead an army that was receiving national support at the time. The author of 1 Maccabees emphasizes this incident in order to show that any leader other than the Maccabean brothers was not a legitimate national leader.

The rescue of the Jews at the same time by Judas in the Gilead shows again that the army was preoccupied with "Jewish" assignments. During the wars in the Gilead the Jewish army showed that it had become more advanced in warfare. It was capable of fighting not only in the open field but also against fortified cities.[23] When Judas set out for the next war, in the land of the Philistines, "some priests, wishing to distinguish themselves, fell in battle when they went out to fight ill-advisedly" (5:67; cf. 2 Macc 12:32–45). This verse is probably misplaced in the text; still, it shows again that the Maccabees had a Jewish army. In another incident we hear about some soldiers who were punished because they had idols hidden in their clothes, against the ordinances of the Torah.[24] The purity of the army was an important factor for the Maccabees and their later historians. It should be emphasized that within three years after its foundation as a voluntary militia the army increased in numbers and became more professional.

In the late spring of 163 B.C.E. Judas decided to destroy the people garrisoned in the Akra (1 Macc 6:18–20), so "he called *all the people* together to besiege them," but in the early summer of the same year he had to stop this siege as a result of an invasion by Lysias and Antiochus V, who appeared in Judea with an enormous mercenary army. "The Israelites sallied forth and burned them and fought courageously" (6:31). At Beth-Zechariah Judas and his army killed six hundred of the king's army, and Eleazar, his brother, fell in battle as a consequence of a heroic deed (6:42–47). According to 1 Macc 6:47 the Jews were defeated at Beth-Zechariah. Second Maccabees gives a different version: God assisted the Jews so much that they were victorious (13:1–17).

Many subsequent events occurred, which are recorded in the literature, but they are not of particular interest for the purposes of this chapter. According to 1 Macc 6:49–50 the Seleucids allowed the besieged Jews to leave Beth-zur and garrisoned it with their own troops. The parallel story in 2 Macc 13:20-22 is again different, and in favor of the Jews: "For a second time the king made overtures to the people of Beth-zur. He gave them his right hand, received theirs in turn, and retired."[25]

At the beginning of 162 B.C.E. Antiochus V and Lysias left Palestine after making peace with the Jews. The Seleucid victory at Beth-Zechariah changed the position of the Jewish army vis-à-vis their opponents within the nation itself, the Hellenistic party. The latter, who were not altogether the evildoers and extreme hellenizers the books of Maccabees would wish us to believe, got the upper hand for a while. The Hellenistic party, so it seems, did not recruit an independent standing army. Nevertheless, after the battle of Beth-Zechariah they fought the Jewish army of Judas, in what amounted to a civil war. It was then that the Hellenists called on the Seleucids to rescue them from Judas's forces, which turned to be a tragic mistake.

During the autumn of 162 B.C.E. (1 Macc 7:21-25; 2 Macc 14:5-14) Judas was active on all of the frontiers around Judea, fighting the Hellenistic party lead by Alcimus. The latter called in Demetrius I for help (1 Macc 7:25; in the autumn of 162 B.C.E.). The Hellenists still did not create a counter-army to fight Judas, perhaps because they attempted to be more universalistic than nationalistic— they did not need an independent standing "Israelite" army. This at least is the impression we get from the sources. Also, they apparently did not have sufficient numbers to create an independent army. Be that as it may, Demetrius sent Bacchides with an army, but there is no account of any encounter with Judas's forces on the battlefield. When Judas decided to oppose Alcimus with force, the latter again asked Demetrius for help, which he sent immediately. Then the Seleucid general Nicanor was ordered to take Judas captive, after a skirmish at Dessa and some diplomatic attempts to settle the conflict with the Hasmonean party (2 Macc 14:15-36). When the Seleucid general addressed the priests on Mount Zion he said, "Unless Judas and his army are delivered into my hands right now, it shall come to pass when I return in peace that I will turn down this house" (1 Macc 7:35). The priests, of course, could not fulfill this order. Before the ensuing battle of Adassa (161 B.C.E.) Judas was encamped with three thousand men (*Antiquities* 12.408: two thousand), and he again showed the Jewishness of his army when he prayed: "When the king's men blasphemed, Thine angel went forth and smote one hundred and eighty-five thousand of them. In the same manner shatter this army before us today, that those who remain may know that he spoke wickedly of Thy sanctuary. Judge him as his wickedness deserves" (1 Macc 7:40–42).

The armies met in battle on the thirteenth day of the month of Adar, and Nicanor's army was destroyed (7:43). According to the account of 1 Maccabees, when Nicanor's army escaped, people from all over Judea chased them, though they were not part of the "official" army of Judas (7:46). According to 2 Maccabees the battle was, of course, won more by God's intervention than by the army (15:6–36). It is not accidental that the Second Book of Maccabees ends with the magnificent victory of Judas over Nicanor,[26] which is in line with the whole attitude of 2 Maccabees, namely, to enhance the reputation of the Jewish forces and to show that their great successes were due to God's intervention. The Diaspora Jew who probably wrote this book, or its abridgment, thought more in divine terms and toned down, or even omitted, some of the defeats of the Jews at that time.[27] Both books of Maccabees, however, emphasize that even Rome acknowledged the strength of the new Jewish army.[28]

The final battle of Judas as leader of the Jewish army was fought in Elassa. The Jewish commander encamped at Elassa with three thousand chosen men (1 Macc 9:1–22; *Antiquities* 12.422: one thousand). By now it is clear that the number three thousand is a typological number which was to be repeated later in the sources. At any rate, when the Jewish soldiers saw the size of the army of Bacchides, they were frightened. Many disappeared from the camp and no more than eight hundred of them stayed. When Judas saw that his army was dwindling away and that the battle was imminent, he was troubled. Nevertheless, the army set out from the camp and stood in battle line against Bacchides' army, with the cavalry divided into two parts. Judas fell in battle in the early summer of 160 B.C.E. (9:18), and Jonathan, his brother, was chosen to become the leader.[29] That some remnants of Judas's army remained is alluded to in 1 Maccabees, where it is mentioned that "Jonathan and his men" attacked the Jambrites (9:31–42), but it seems rather as a guerrilla group than as an organized army.

Later Bacchides turned to a new strategy of fortifying the cities around Jerusalem and putting in them troops and stores of food. He also took the sons of the leaders of the country and confined them as hostages in the citadel in Jerusalem (1 Macc 9:50–53). There still does not seem to be any counter-"Hellenistic" army, because after Alcimus's death (early summer 159 B.C.E.) "all the lawbreakers took counsel, saying, Here are Jonathan and his men living confidently in considerable security. Let us bring Bacchides back that he may arrest them all in one night" (1 Macc 9:58). The Jewish army of the Hasmoneans must have shrunk considerably and may even have dispersed, since the defeat at Elassa. As a consequence the relatively organized Jewish army of Judas was replaced by groups of supporters of the Hasmonean brothers. Bacchides, tired of the guerrilla war, left the country; "Thus the sword ceased from the people of Israel. And Jonathan dwelled in Michmash, and began to judge the people" (1 Macc 9:72–73).

The opportunity to gather a new army, both well equipped and almost free of the hindrances of the Hellenistic party, was given to Jonathan by the Seleucid princes, who were fighting each other at the end of the fifties of the second century B.C.E. Here starts a new phase in the history of the Jewish army. It was re-created some time in the fifties, and for approximately twenty years it was ready to serve the warring princes in the region as a Jewish army. When in the autumn of 152 B.C.E. Demetrius I wanted to win the Jews over from his opponent Alexander Balas, he, among other promises, gave Jonathan permission to recruit troops, to equip them with arms, and to be his ally. He also gave orders "to hand over to him the hostages in the citadel" (1 Macc 10:6–14). Jonathan went to Jerusalem and read the letter in the hearing of "all the people" and the men who were in the citadel. When they heard that the king had given him authority to recruit an army, they were frightened. Jonathan then started building and fortifying Jerusalem, during which time the men previously put into the strongholds by Bacchides fled. Some of the Hellenists "who had forsaken the Law and the commandments were left in Beth-zur, for it alone served as a city of refuge" (10:14). When Alexander Balas, competing with Demetrius, offered to make Jonathan high priest and his *philos* (friend), Jonathan agreed and gathered troops, providing them with an abundance of arms (10:17–21).

In the late summer of 150 B.C.E. Alexander Balas, now sole king of the Seleucids, nominated Jonathan as one of his best *philoi* and made him general and civil governor of a province (1 Macc 10:65). In the spring of 145 B.C.E. Apollonius, the general of the pretender Demetrius II, sent a message to Jonathan and inter alia compared his army with Jonathan's, saying that the latter was an army for mountain warfare, and his but a "city army" (10:71). The Jewish army was acknowledged as a powerful force in the region. In spite of this compliment, Jonathan decided to fight for his "friend" Alexander Balas against Apollonius. Thus he "selected ten thousand men, set out from Jerusalem, and his brother Simeon joined him to help him" (1 Macc 10:74). Afterward, we are told, Jonathan fought in the coastal plain against the cities in the service of Alexander; and later, during the quarrels among the various Diadochi of the region, he started to besiege the Akra after a short trip to the Eleutheros River, acting as escort to Ptolemy VI (summer of 145 B.C.E.). When Alexander Balas was murdered, "some men who hated their own nation, men who transgressed the Law, went to the king" (this time Demetrius II, who succeeded Ptolemy VI in Palestine) and asked for help from the new master (1 Macc 11:21). Again, it is remarkable that the opponents of the Hasmoneans never created an army of their own—or at least this is the impression given by the sources. Jonathan's army was a Jewish army, its motivation being to gain favors for the national Jewish cause.

Demetrius II summoned Jonathan to Ptolemais in midsummer 145 B.C.E. and confirmed previous concessions (the high priesthood and the position of *ethnarches* of Judea) and granted him a reduction in taxes and three neighboring districts (1 Macc 11:20–29). Later "Jonathan sent a request to King Demetrius to cast out the garrison from the citadel of Jerusalem and the garrisons from the strongholds, for they were continually fighting against Israel" (11:41). This meant either that the Jewish army was still not strong enough to cope with the Akra, or that Jonathan thought he could still deal with the situation in a diplomatic manner.

Demetrius II was willing to withdraw the forces, provided Jonathan sent him people to fight for him. He indeed "sent three thousand able-bodied men to him to Antioch" (11:44). By now it becomes even more obvious that the recurrent number of three thousand is not exact. This account does show, however, that Jonathan had many more Jews available for recruitment at the time. The

Jewish army then rescued Demetrius from a coup, and "the Jews consequently were held in high esteem before the king and before all the people in his kingdom, and they returned to Jerusalem with great spoil" (1 Macc 11:44–51). It is important to emphasize again that a Jewish military force was highly esteemed by non-Jews at the time, though according to some anti-Jewish accounts the Jews were not considered to be very successful as soldiers. Jonathan and Simeon now served Antiochus VI, the son of the late Alexander Balas, and Trypho, who was an opponent of Demetrius II who had been un-grateful to Jonathan (1 Macc 11:52–12:34). Among other conces-sions Antiochus made, he appointed Simeon the *strategos* of the coastal plain from the Egyptian border to the Ladder of Tyre (11:59). The fact that Jewish blood was shed in wars that were not their own may have had its impact on a morale level. But they gained a great deal of military experience from these wars. The Jew-ish Hasmonean army became more and more a force to be reckoned with in the region, and distinguished the Jews from the armies of their neighbors, which usually employed mercenaries.

At some point during these stormy events, Trypho wished to eliminate Jonathan who, he felt, might hinder him on his way to becoming the "king of Asia" (12:39–40). When Jonathan went out against Trypho, he managed to recruit forty thousand men (12:41) —this is the largest Hasmonean army mentioned so far. Even if the number is exaggerated, it is quite probable that this army was en-tirely Jewish. It is remarkable that a Jewish army of such a size was organized in the forties of the second century. (At Raphia in 217 B.C.E., which was one of the most impressive battles in terms of manpower in the Near East at the time, the Seleucids appeared with seventy thousand footsoldiers, five thousand horses, and seventy-three elephants.) But the Diadochi themselves, it should be remem-bered, gave the Jews both the opportunity and the means to increase their own army. This impressive Jewish army was presumably the trump card of the Hasmoneans when they declared independence from the non-Jewish nations in 143/2 B.C.E. But let us return to the affair of Trypho and Jonathan.

When Trypho learned about this great army he asked Jonathan to send it home, and Jonathan, "believing him, he did just as he said, sending back his troops, who returned to the land of Judah," which strengthens the evidence that it was a Jewish army. He did, however, keep three thousand men, of whom two thousand were left in the Galilee, while one thousand accompanied him (1 Macc 12:46–47). He was then arrested in Acco-Ptolemais by Trypho. When Jonathan's troops found out that he had been arrested and killed along with his men (only later does the reader hear that he was actually killed, 13:23), they returned to Judea (12:50–52). Simeon, his brother, was asked by the people to carry on the war (13:9; summer of 143 B.C.E.). He then gathered all of the fighting men and surrounded Jerusalem with fortifications. When Trypho invaded, Simeon was all ready with the army (1 Macc 13:20), and, as a consequence of a snowstorm, Trypho retreated (winter of 143 B.C.E.). The Jews again acknowledged Demetrius II as king over them. Trypho then killed Antiochus VI and put the diadem of Asia on his head (13:32). Simeon built the fortresses of Judea as quickly as he could (13:33), and when independence was declared in 142 B.C.E. (1 Macc 13:41), Simeon was appointed, among his other functions, as *strategos,* here in the sense of military commander. At that time the Jewish army may have developed considerably in terms of warfare techniques, which it learned from the Hellenistic armies.[30] The Jews thus felt strong enough to take care of the troublesome Akra. We are told that Simeon "fortified the Temple Mount near the citadel more strongly. He and his men dwelled there. Simeon saw that his son John had reached manhood and made him general of all his troops" (1 Macc 13:52–53).

Here we should note, first, that the Temple Mount was not recognized just as a religious and spiritual place. During the years it had become a central military-strategic place. This fact may have had its impact on the notion of holy war that developed in certain circles in Judaism at the time. Second, Simeon's making his son general over the army shows that the Hasmoneans regarded themselves as a dynasty. Like their neighbors, the ruler was also the high commander of the army. In 1 Macc 14:10 Simeon is praised because, among other things, "he provided food for the cities, and furnished them with means for defense." Again, in 14:32–34 it is said that "Simeon stood up and fought for his nation, and spent much of his own money in arming his nation's army and giving them wages. He fortified the cities of Judea and Beth-zur on the borders of Judea, where the arms of the enemy were formerly stored, and placed Jewish men there as a garrison." It is also mentioned that he fortified Gezer near

Ashdod, along with Joppa on the seacoast, "where the enemy formerly lived," and settled Jews there. Simeon's policy, however, was to maintain a purely national army, unlike those of his neighbors, the Diadochi (and cf. 1 Macc 14:35, 42, 47). His military strength was acknowledged again by Antiochus VII, who in 140/139 B.C.E. sent a letter to Simeon stating that "all the arms you have prepared, and the fortifications you have constructed, which you hold, let them remain yours" (1 Macc 15:7). Later, when Antiochus VII invaded Palestine in order to crush his adversary Trypho, Simeon sent him two thousand soldiers, but he "would not accept them" (15:25–27).

The war of the Seleucid Diadochi continued, and against this background the Hasmoneans became stronger. Little is heard of their army until some point between the autumn of 139 B.C.E. and the autumn of 138 B.C.E., when Antiochus VII sent Kendebaios to war against Judea. Simeon, being too old, appointed his sons John and Judas generals of the army. John and Judas received the twenty thousand soldiers that Simeon selected from the country to go against Kendebaios (1 Macc 16:1–4). It is quite probable that a standing Jewish army of some thousands of soldiers was operating all the time, and that on special occasions the reserves were called up from among the Jewish population of Palestine, which would account for the changing numbers of the Jewish army given by the sources. Simeon was murdered by Ptolemy Abubus, and John Hyrcanus, Simeon's son, became the Hasmonean ruler at the beginning of 134 B.C.E. (1 Macc 16:11–24; Josephus, *Antiquities* 13.230).

Between October 135 and October 134 B.C.E. there was a sabbatical year (*Antiquities* 13.234), and all war ceased. Later, in 132 B.C.E., when besieged by Antiochus Sidetes in Jerusalem, John "observed that his great numbers were a disadvantage because of the rapid consumption of provisions by them, and that the work which was being accomplished in no way corresponded to the number of hands, he separated from the rest those who were useless, and drove them out, and retained only those who were in the prime of life and able to fight" (*Antiquities* 13.240). Antiochus did not let them out of the city, and "wandering about the walls between the lines, they were the first to be exhausted by their cruel sufferings." The Hasmoneans had learned something from their neighbors in terms of behavior. But during the festival of Tabernacles these people were admitted back into the city because their "brethren" pitied them, which shows that they were Jews (13.241). Apparently, the siege of Antiochus Sidetes was a frustrating event after the independence that had been declared ten years before in 143/2 B.C.E. Josephus states that "Hyrcanus also opened the tomb of David, who surpassed all other kings in wealth, and took out three thousand talents of silver and, drawing on this sum, became the first Jewish king to support *foreign troops" (Antiquities* 13.249). In 130 B.C.E. Hyrcanus went with Antiochus against the Parthians (13.249; Diodorus Siculus 34.15–17). During this enterprise we hear that Antiochus remained at some spot "for two days at the request of the Jew Hyrcanus because of the festival."[31] It is probable that the Jews in Hyrcanus's army demanded to observe the festival. Antiochus VII was defeated.

When Hyrcanus's conquest of the Land of Israel started at the beginning of the twenties of the second century B.C.E., a new phase began. The Hasmoneans no longer assisted any of the Diadochi with their army, as they had frequently done during the previous twenty years. Josephus says that "for after the death of Antiochus (Sidetes) he (John) too revolted from the Macedonians, and no longer furnished them any aid either as subject or as a friend" (*Antiquities* 13.273). In 109–107 B.C.E., when Samaria was attacked by the Jewish state, we find evidence again of the Hasmoneans' dynastic approach to the state: John Hyrcanus put his two sons, Aristobulus and Antigonus, in charge. After Hyrcanus's death, Aristobulus took over and became the first Hasmonean king (104/3 B.C.E.). At some point, according to Josephus, Antigonus was murdered by his brother Aristobulus (*Antiquities* 13.303–313). Aristobulus died shortly after and Alexander Jannaeus, his brother, became king of Judea (104/3–76 B.C.E.).

During these years a major event occurred that bears directly on the subject of this chapter. Cleopatra III, the Egyptian queen, appointed two Jews as her generals to fight Ptolemy Lathyrus, her rebellious son.[32] The participation of Jews from the Diaspora in foreign armies is interesting because of their national identity. Although they had sympathy for the Jews in the Hasmonean state and belonged to the Jewish nation, they still felt loyalty to the "nation" for which they were fighting. Be that as it may, during the war with Ptolemy Lathyrus (103/2 B.C.E.) Alexander Jannaeus collected an army of about fifty thousand "natives," or eighty thousand, and with this force went out to meet Ptolemy. It is logical to assume that there were non-Jews included among the "natives" of Palestine mentioned by Josephus (*Antiquities* 13.337). Although Josephus calls Alexander's army the "Jewish force" (13.342), he probably only wished to distinguish it from Ptolemy's "Egyptian" force. Even so, from *Antiquities* 13.345–346 it is evident that at least part of Alexander's army was Jewish, because Lathyrus found the villages of Judea empty of men. Jannaeus must therefore have recruited a reserve army to fight Lathyrus. When Alexander conquered territories in Transjordan some years later, his camp was again referred to as the "camp of the Jews" (13.356, 362).

During Alexander Jannaeus's reign, the Hasmonean army was preoccupied more than ever with conquering cities of the gentiles in the Land. It also launched offensive wars against foreign peoples in Palestine, in which the Jewish army behaved outrageously. The Hasmonean army not only had learned better techniques of warfare from their neighbors, but apparently had also learned some of their unpleasant modes of behavior. Moreover, when Alexander turned his attention to eliminating opposition within the nation, he used the nation's army to kill six thousand Pharisees. Josephus says that "he also maintained foreign troops of Pisidians and Cilicians, for he could not use Syrians, being at war with them" (13.373–374), which shows that, although the armies at the time were mercenary forces, "national" considerations were not altogether excluded by the Hellenistic rulers. The majority of Jannaeus's army was Jewish, but Jannaeus could not afford to have more mercenaries than Jews in his army, because the Jews were apparently cheaper to pay than mercenaries, and probably more loyal. Thus in his war against the Pharisees Jannaeus was forced to use an army that had a majority of Jews in it, from a Jewish state, to eliminate another group of Jews who did not agree with the aims and actions of his policy.

In six years, Jannaeus is said to have killed no fewer than fifty thousand Jews. One may say that this is an exaggerated figure, and yet he had been involved in a civil war (anticipating the one that occurred after Salome Alexandra's death in 67 B.C.E.). In contrast to the Maccabean wars against the Hellenists, there was no voluntary militia, but a "standing" army of the Jewish state. Jannaeus's adversaries from among the Jewish population called in Demetrius Akairus (*Antiquities* 13.376). Alexander Jannaeus "took on his side six thousand two hundred mercenaries and about twenty thousand Jews who favored his cause, and went out to meet Demetrius" (13.377). These numbers, though not accurate, may represent the proportions of Jannaeus's army at the time: less than one-third were mercenaries (in *Jewish War* 1.93 Josephus says that Alexander had eight thousand mercenaries, one thousand cavalry, and ten thousand Jews). In these figures one can already see a "schizophrenic" army in terms of its manpower. In this war Jews fought Jews with the assistance of foreign mercenaries: "Now there was much activity in both camps, the one side attempting to cause Alexander's mercenaries to desert because they were Greeks, while the other made the same appeal to the Jews who were with Demetrius. But as neither side could persuade the other, they engaged in a battle" (*Antiquities* 13.378). Demetrius Akairus was victorious, while all of Alexander's mercenaries met with death after giving proof of their loyalty and courage. Many of Demetrius's soldiers also died. This statement may again be exaggerated. At any rate, Alexander Jannaeus went to the mountains where six thousand Jews came to his side, "but later on the Jews fought against Alexander and were defeated, many of them dying in battle" (13.379). As a consequence of Alexander's cruelty toward the Jews, many of his opponents, eight thousand in number, fled, and thereafter he reigned in "complete tranquility."

When Alexander handed over the kingdom to his wife Salome Alexandra in 76 B.C.E. he clearly stated that the Pharisees, together with the army, were a power to be reckoned with (*Antiquities* 13.400–407). And indeed, after his death the Pharisees became the real power in the realm. Salome Alexandra recruited a large force of mercenaries "and also made her own force twice as large, with the result that she struck terror into the local rulers round her and received hostages from them" (13.408–409). She assisted other kings and princes with her army: according to *Antiquities* 13.418 (*Jewish War* 1.115) she sent an army to Damascus in order to keep Ptolemy the son of Mennaeus from seizing the city. But the stability of her realm did not last long. The moment Alexandra became ill, Aristobulus, her son, started a revolution. He first gained the support of his father's "friends," who were given several strongholds by Alexandra (13.417), and within fifteen days he had seized twenty-two strongholds and recruited an army from Lebanon and Trachonitis (13.427). From the places mentioned in Josephus, one can assume that it was in its greater part a mercenary force. The army of the Jewish state remained faithful to Salome at this time (13.429), but later much of this national army, inherited by Hyrcanus II after his mother's death, deserted to Aristobulus II (14.4; *Jewish War* 1.120–121).

It is important to note how fast both sides in the civil war recruited their armies. According to *Antiquities* 14.37–58 (*Jewish War* 1.120–140) the Jews now had two armies, the one of Hyrcanus II and the other of Aristobulus II. The Romans intervened, and in 63 B.C.E. Judea lost its independence. In the famous lament of Josephus in *Antiquities* 14.77–78 he mentions (along with the other symbols of nationalism) the army: "the territory that we have gained by *our arms.*" The division and transformation of the Hasmonean army during Jannaeus's reign, and again during Salome's last years and after her death; the extensive use of mercenaries within the national army; and the use of the army for wars that were not patriotic as such brought about the decline of its meaning as a national unifying symbol.

The books of Maccabees leave an impression of the important role the army played in the consciousness of nationalistic Jews, both before and after the state was created. The concept of the army—as it really was at its start—emerges from these books as a national, political Jewish symbol which was to be entirely Jewish in terms of its manpower. This factor became what distinguished the Jewish army from those of the neighboring nations. The army's leaders were to be Jewish, and its wars, even if in the service of foreign princes, were to be fought for the common national cause, in other words, the conquest of the Promised Land, its purification of non-Jews, and the foundation of a Jewish state in the Land under a Jewish sovereign. The army was to perform tasks that were not necessarily military, such as rescuing Jews from dangerous places, purifying the Temple, and even fighting opponents within the nation itself, namely, the Hellenists. Although the books of Maccabees were not very objective about these opponents, it is quite clear that they thought it was justifiable to try to eliminate the Hellenists because they were "sinners" ("sinners" is, however, open to various interpretations). The use of mercenary forces is not explicitly denigrated by Jewish literature, but this issue does emerge from the literature of the time, where the army is usually only mentioned in passing. Let us give some examples.

In the war of Jacob and his sons against the Amorite coalition, the Book of Jubilees (second century B.C.E.) says that Jacob "and his three sons and all his father's servants and his servants arose from his house and went against them with six thousand men who carried swords and he killed them in the field of Shechem" (34:6–7). If this story in any way reflects a real situation, the servants in this description may represent a mercenary force. But the servants may also denote Jews. A clearer picture is gained from the description in Jubilees of an imaginary war of Jacob against Edom (chapters 37–38). It says that whereas Esau hired mercenaries from Aram, Moab, Ammon, Kittim, and elsewhere who all came to fight Jacob, the latter fought with his sons and all their servants. Here it becomes clear that the Jewish side did not hire mercenaries from other nations (it has already been argued that the Book of Jubilees retrojects many ideas of the present into the past, as does also the Testament of the Twelve Patriarchs). The Book of Judith, which is Hellenistic in its present form, is even more clear in describing the Jewishness of the army. There, after the good news of the murder of Holophernes by Judith, the archenemy of the Jews, is spread in the country, it is said, "Then the *Israelites,* every soldier among them, came after them. And Uzziah sent men to Betomasthiam and Bebai and Chobai and Kola and all the borders of Israel, to tell of what had been accomplished, and to order them all to stream out after their enemies . . . and the Israelites when they returned from the slaughter" (15:3–7).

More direct references to this question are given in two documents usually attributed to Essene authorship. *On Kingship* in the Temple Scroll emphasizes that the nation's army should be Jewish. If this work was written against the background of the kingship of Alexander Jannaeus, it shows that pious Jews at the time resented the mercenaries who fought alongside the Jews in the king's army. The War Scroll, which is a composition of the turn of the second or the first century B.C.E., shows that although Hellenistic and Roman tactics of warfare were adopted by the visionary army that was to lead the war of the *eschaton* (end of the days), it was nevertheless an army of Jews and of the whole nation (meaning the twelve tribes, which by that time no longer existed as separate entities). According to the War Scroll, a holy war of Israel should be performed by a purely Jewish army along with God's angels.

Josephus does not directly state his own views concerning the army when he tells the story of the Hasmonean realm. It seems though that he too preferred to see a purely Jewish army in the nations' wars. He retrojected this view into his interpretation of Jewish history. For instance, it was probably no accident that he completely omitted any mention of David's mercenary troups, the "Pelethi and Kereti," when he recites the history of that period.[33]

The desire to have a "national" or ethnic army can be found in Greek literature as well, but it seems that it had no real influence on Jewish literature. Jewish literature referred to biblical concepts (of the need for a pure Jewish army for the nation) rather than to non-Jewish literature.[34] Plato in his ideal state (the *Republic*) viewed the *Phylakes* (guardians, i.e., the soldiers) as an integral social and economic element of the state. There is a similar trend in Hellenistic literature. Strabo's *Geography* abounds in descriptions of national armies from all over the Hellenistic East, and he emphasized their importance for national perseverance.[35] Diodorus Siculus (from Hecataeus, who retrojected views of the third century B.C.E. into the Egyptian past) mentions that Osiris went on his world conquest with "his army," but he does not describe its nature (1.17–20). In a parallel story (the legend of Sesostris), however, which was reshaped in a utopian manner in keeping with Alexander the Great's myth in the Hellenistic period, the antithesis of the actual Hellenistic army is presented by Hecataeus. The half-historical, half-mythological Sesostris went on his world conquest, unlike Alexander, with a "national" Egyptian army, which again shows that the issue of national versus mercenary forces was alive at the time.

Diodorus Siculus tells us that when Sesostris's father learned that his son would rule over the whole civilized world, "he collected the children of the same age as his son and granted them a royal training, thus preparing them beforehand for an attack on the whole world" (1.53.9–10). Then "in preparation for his undertaking he first of all confirmed the goodwill of all the Egyptians toward himself, feeling it to be necessary, if he were to bring his plan to a successful end, that his soldiers on the campaign should be ready to die for their leaders, and that those left behind in their native lands should not rise in revolt." Diodorus continues to say, "He then chose the strongest of the men and formed an army worthy of the greatness of his undertaking; for he enlisted six hundred thousand footsoldiers" (the size of an army was often exaggerated, and cf. also Ninus's multinational army, depicted by the same author, 2.5.3–7), and "in command of the several divisions of his troops he set his companions, who were by this time inured to warfare, had striven after a reputation for valor from their youth, and cherished with a brotherly love both their king and one another, the number of them being more than seventeen hundred. And upon all these commanders he bestowed allotments of the best land in Egypt, in order that, enjoying sufficient income and lacking nothing, they might sedulously practice the art of war" (Diodorus Siculus 1.54). Part of this passage reflects in an idealized manner the conditions of the *machimoi* (the warrior caste) in Ptolemaic Egypt, but most of it is a Hellenistic view of a utopian national army. Interestingly, when Hecataeus of Abdera describes the ideal Jewish state he refers very clearly to its purely national army whose soldiers were educated in a Spartanlike manner.[36]

Queen Myrina, who also endeavored to conquer the whole Middle East according to the Hellenistic mythograph Dionysius Scytobrachion, seems to have gone on her first conquests with a Libyan national army. She went to war with an army of Libyan Amazons, "being a *race* superior in valor and eager for war" (Diodorus Siculus 3.53.6). When the Amazons wished to invade many parts of the inhabited world (54.1), the "queen of the Amazons, Myrina, collected, it is said, an army of thirty thousand footsoldiers and three thousand cavalry" (54.2). It is not clear whether they were Libyan natives or mercenaries.

In general, the Hellenistic sources took a mercenary force for granted, but apparently viewed an ideal army as being purely national, that is, recruited from the *ethnos* itself. Although the Jews in reality hired mercenaries, they nevertheless emphasized in their own literature the necessity of having a purely Jewish national army, which would be God-fearing and fight the wars of God. We shall see later that, at the moment that certain extreme groups in Judaism held the opinion that they were the sole God-fearing army despite the fact that a state army was already in existence, trouble ensued.

Notes

[1] For mercenaries in Hellenistic armies, see G. T. Griffith, *The Mercenaries of the Hellenistic World* (repr. Groningen, 1968). And for the comparison with armies of the fifteenth and sixteenth centuries of absolutist rulers, see J. F. C. Fuller, *The Conduct of War 1789-1961* (London, 1961), pp. 15-25; T. Ropp, *War in the Modern World* (Durham, N.C., 1959), pp. 3-58.

[2] For the Seleucid army, see B. Bar Kochva, *The Seleucid Army,* 2d ed. (Cambridge, 1979). For Hellenistic warfare, see *CAH* 7.1.353-362 (Y. Garlan). For the Seleucid army in Daphne in 165 B.C.E., see Polybius 30.25: "next came five thousand Mysians, and immediately behind them three thousand Cilicians armed." See Polybius also for the Seleucid army at Magnesia in 190 B.C.E. For the different units and their national identification in the Seleucid army, see Bar Kochva, above, pp. 42-53.

[3] The national differences are seen in the different appearance of the ethnic units in the divisions of the army. See, for Galatians, D. Burr, *Terracottas from Myrina* (Vienna, 1934), p. 12; P. von Bienkowsky, *Die Darstellungen der Gallier in der hellenistischen Zeit* (Vienna, 1908). For Thracian horsemen, see G. Kazarow, "Zur Archäologie Thrakiens (ein Reisebericht)," *Archaeologischer Anzeiger* 33 (1918): 49-51; also S. Casson, *Macedonia, Illyria and Thrace* (Oxford, 1925), pp. 248-254 and elsewhere; G. Danov, *Altthrakien* (Berlin, 1976). For the Bithynian officer, see M. Rostovtzeff, *The Social and Economic History of the Hellenistic World* (Oxford, 1951), 1.288. For the Cretans in Hellenistic armies, see M. Launey, *Recherches sur les armées hellénistiques* (Paris, 1949-1950), 1.248-286; A. F. Willets, in *Armée et fiscale dans le monde antique,* ed. H. van Effenterre (Paris, 1977), pp. 65-77, and Bar Kochva, *Seleucid Army,* pp. 48-53. For the Scythian soldier, see F. Sarre, *Die Kunst des Alten Persien* (Berlin, 1923), pp. 25, 68; G. Sokolov, *Antique Art on the Northern Black Sea Coast* (Leningrad, 1974), nos. 34, 51-54, 57-62, 163, 171; M. I. Artamonov, *The Splendor of Scythian Art* (New York, 1969), nos. 147, 148, 150, 154, 155, 224, 232; and V. F. Gajdukevic, *Das Bosporanische Reich* (Berlin, 1971), no. 30. And for Macedonians, see H. Kaehler, *Der Fries vom Reiterdenkmal des Aemilius Paulus in Delphi* (Berlin, 1965). In general, for the ethnic units in Hellenistic armies, see B. Bar Kochva, *Judas Maccabaeus* (Cambridge, 1989), pp. 90-115 and 573-588.

[4] Cf. Fuller, *Conduct of War,* pp. 15-25.

[5] For the Egyptian army in Raphia, see E. Galili, "Raphia, 217 B.C.E. Revised," *Scripta classica israelica* 3 (1976-1977): 52-126; and F. W. Walbank, *A Historical Commentary on Polybius* (Oxford, 1979), vol. 3 ad loc. For the twenty thousand Egyptians at Raphia and their mutiny for more than thirty years, see Polybius 5.107.1-3, 14.12.4; G. Milne, "Egyptian Nationalism under Greek and Roman Rule," *Journal of Egyptian Archaeology* 14 (1928): 226-234; and C. Preaux, "Esquisse d'une histoire des révolutions égyptiennes sous les Lagides," *Chronique d' Egypte* 11 (1936): 522-552. For the national awareness of an Egyptian Greek a

century later, see E. Van't Dack et al., *The Judean-Syrian-Egyptian Conflict 103–101 B.C.* (Brussels, 1989), pp. 84–88.

[6] Cf. Fuller, *Conduct of War,* pp. 29–41.

[7] F. Foch, *The Principles of War* (Paris, 1903); trans. H. Belloc (1918), p. 29.

[8] For the difference between a speech given at the front and the one given at "home" according to biblical concepts, see A. Rofé, "The Laws of War in Deuteronomy: Their Origin, Intention, and Positivity," *Zion* 39 (1974): 143–156 (Hebrew).

[9] For the nature of speeches before wars in First and Second Maccabees as well as in Josephus's *Jewish War,* see Bar Kochva, *Judas Maccabaeus,* pp. 156–158. For speeches in Hellenistic historiography in general, see F. W. Walbank, *Speeches in Greek Historians* (Oxford, 1965).

[10] For the chronology until 134 B.C.E., see J. A. Goldstein, *I Maccabees,** pp. 161–174.

[11] 1 Macc 2:27–41; M. D. Herr, "The Problems of War on the Sabbath in the Second Temple and Talmudic Periods," *Tarbiz* 30 (1961): 242–256, 341–356 (Hebrew); and Bar Kochva, *Judas Maccabaeus,* pp. 474–493.

[12] For this period see in particular E. Bickerman, *The God of the Maccabees* (Leiden, 1979); M. Hengel, *Judaism and Hellenism* (London and Philadelphia, 1974), chap. 4; and F. Millar, "The Background of the Maccabean Revolution," *Journal of Jewish Studies* 29.1 (1978): 1–21.

[13] It is important here to compare the two different accounts of First and Second Maccabees concerning the wars. For the time of authorship of the two books and their provenance, see Goldstein's introductions to *I Maccabees* and *II Maccabees;* and Bar Kochva, *Judas Maccabaeus,* pp. 151–185, with the older bibliography.

[14] 1 Macc 3:10–12; and Bar Kochva, *Judas Maccabaeus,* pp. 194–206.

[15] For the thesis that the books of Maccabees exaggerated the numbers of the Seleucid army, while they minimized the Maccabean numbers, see Bar Kochva, *Judas Maccabaeus,* pp. 29–67. For the different sources for the Maccabean wars, see ibid., pp. 151–193. In general, 1 Maccabees is much more reliable than 2 Maccabees, which was written by Jason of Cyrene. Josephus for his part paraphrases 1 Maccabees (he did not know the second book).

[16] Cf. D. R. Schwartz, "Review of Bar Kochva, *Judas Maccabaeus"* (forthcoming in *Tarbiz.*) See also I. Shatzman, *The Armies of the Hasmonaeans and Herod* (Tübingen, 1991), chap. 1.

[17] Cf. for instance Pseudo-Philo and D. Mendels, "Pseudo-Philo's *Biblical Antiquities,* the 'Fourth Philosophy' and the Political Messianism of the First Century A.D.," in *The Messiah,* ed. J. H. Charlesworth (Minneapolis, 1992); I. Gafni, "On the Use of 1 Macc by Josephus," *Zion* 45 (1980): 81–95 (Hebrew).

[18] 1 Macc 3:13–26, 2 Macc 8:1–7; Bar Kochva, *Judas Maccabaeus,* pp. 207–218 for the military details.

[19] Cf. now again D. J. Harrington, *The Maccabean Revolt: Anatomy of a Biblical Revolution* (Wilmington, Del., 1988), who follows a standard and traditional view about the Maccabean revolution.

[20] 2 Macc 8:34–36. For the military details, see Bar Kochva, *Judas Maccabaeus,* pp. 219–274.

[21] 2 Macc 11:8–9. This scene is reminiscent of the incident recounted in 2 Macc 10:24ff., not found in 1 Maccabees, about Timotheus; v 29: "when the battle was at its height. . . ." 2 Macc 10:15–38 deals with the Maccabean army's enterprises against the people of the Land. For the military details, see Bar Kochva, *Judas Maccabaeus,* pp. 275–290.

[22] J. A. O. Larsen, *Greek Federal States* (Oxford, 1968), pp. 195–215.

[23] 1 Maccabees 5. This aspect cannot be elaborated here. Cf. I. Shatzman, *The Armies of the Hasmonaeans and Herod* (Tübingen, 1991), pp. 11–35.

[24] 2 Macc 12:39–40. This explains why, in some of the apocrypha and pseudepigrapha, the old views against idolatry still occur (cf. for instance the Letter of Jeremiah with E. Schürer, *The History of the Jewish People in the Age of Jesus Christ,* rev. G. Vermes et al. [Edinburgh, 1973–1987], 3.2.743–745).

[25] For the military details, see Bar Kochva, *Judas Maccabaeus,* pp. 291–346.

[26] J. Geiger, "The History of Judas Maccabaeus: One Aspect of Hellenistic Historiography," *Zion* 49 (1984): 1–8 (Hebrew).

[27] For the military details, see Bar Kochva, *Judas Maccabaeus,* pp. 347–375.

[28] 1 Macc 8:23–32; 2 Macc 4:11. For Rome in the eyes of Jewish literature in general, see D. Flusser, "The Kingdom of Rome in the Eyes of the Hasmoneans, and as Seen by the Essenes," *Zion* 48 (1983): 149—176 (Hebrew); and M. Hadas-Lebel, "L'Évolution de l'image . . . ," *Aufstieg und Niedergang der römischen Welt* 2.20.1 (1987): 715–856.

[29] 1 Macc 9:23–31. For the military details, see Bar Kochva, *Judas Maccabaeus,* pp. 376–402.

[30] Shatzman, *The Armies of the Hasmonaeans and Herod,* pp. 11–97.

[31] *Antiquities* 13.251. See now D. R. Schwartz, "Antiochus VII Sidetes," forthcoming.

[32] *Antiquities* 13.285. For a recent study on this episode from different angles see E. Van't Dack et al., *The Judean-Syrian-Egyptian Conflict, 103–101 B.C.* (Brussels, 1989).

[33] *Antiquities* 7.199–200, 278f, 293 as compared with 2 Sam 15:17ff.

[34] For biblical armies, see "Army," *Encyclopaedia Biblica* 6.650–659 (Hebrew).

[35] See for instance Strabo 15.47 (C707), who describes the Indian "national" army, saying, "The fifth caste is that of the warriors, who, when they are not in service, spend their lives in idleness and at drinking bouts, being maintained at the expense of the royal treasury; so that they make their expeditions quickly when need arises" (probably from Megasthenes' *Indica*).

[36] Diodorus Siculus 40.3.6–7, and Stern, *Greek and Latin Authors,* 1.32–33.

The Jewish Nationalistic Movement— After the Roman Occupation of Palestine

Roman influence was felt in the Near East throughout most of the second century B.C.E., starting in 188 when the treaty of Apamea was signed with the Seleucids after the Roman-Syrian war was over. From then on, Rome interfered extensively in the affairs of the East, and her *imperium* gradually spread toward the region. In 168 B.C.E. it crushed Perseus, the last king of Macedonia, and abolished the Macedonian kingdom. After a long protectorate (200–146 B.C.E.), Rome finally conquered Greece. In 133 B.C.E. the kingdom of Pergamon was bequeathed to the Roman republic by the last Attalid king, Attalus III. By 62 B.C.E., after a fierce campaign led by Pompey, the whole of Asia Minor, Syria, and Palestine came under Roman sway, and in 31/30 B.C.E. Egypt was conquered by Octavianus, who added Cyrene (which had already become a province by 74 B.C.E., but had been granted by Antony to his daughter, Cleopatra Selene). Thus, within 150 years Rome had conquered almost the whole of the eastern Mediterranean basin.[1] In spite of the fact that from Augustus's death we deal with three successive dynasties, the additions made in the Hellenistic Near East between the death of Augustus in 14 C.E. and Trajan (98 C.E.) are minor. Trajan, however, annexed major parts of the East (until 116 C.E.) as well as Dacia, but the areas east of the Euphrates were later abandoned by Hadrian, his successor.

Did nationalism in the ancient Near East change when Rome made it part of her *imperium*? The evidence shows that many of the

ethnic groups and peoples continued to exist undisturbed deep into
the Roman era. We come across Judeo-Edomites and Arabs, as well
as Egyptians, Phoenicians, Armenians, Scythians, Albanians, Iberi-
ans, Galatians, and Cappadocians. Through numerous references,
many of which only appear in passing in the sources (such as the
famous lists in the *Res gestae* of Augustus, Appian's *Mithridaticus
liber* 114.556, various references in Tacitus's *Annals* and *Histories*
as well as Dio Chrysostomus's Fourth Discourse *On Kingship* 30),
one can detect the national frameworks preserved by the conquered
peoples, as well as the national frameworks of those who lived outside the "borders" of the Roman Empire.[2] The basic division of the
three strata of society (Greeks, Hellenists, and the indigenous population) described in the opening pages of this study can also be found
in the two first centuries of the Roman conquest of the Near East,
but with a different emphasis in the various regions. Rome did not
alter the sociocultural order it found in the Near East upon conquering it.

Moreover, during the time under discussion Rome had no intention of uprooting the national identities of the peoples that it found
in the East. Rome let them go on living their daily lives, but exploited them economically and dominated them politically.[3] The
correspondence of Pliny the Younger, the governor of Bithynia, with
Emperor Trajan can serve as an example.[4] Therefore the indigenous
populations continued to hold onto many of their nationalistic traits
such as language, temple, territory, traditions, and history with
practically no hindrance from Rome. The Romans whom the peoples of the ancient Near East encountered were the governor, the tax
collector (unless exempted from tax), and the Roman soldier, but
usually not intellectuals such as Cicero, Sallust, Vergil, and Seneca.[5]
When Rome did not feel threatened it did not interfere in the day-to-
day lives of the peoples under its sway. In many cases the empire
even left their most obvious nationalistic symbols intact, though divested of much of their former significance. Thus some nations in
the empire were acknowledged within the perimeters of their traditional territories, and were left with a native king; their god or gods,
cults, and culture were left untouched. The Greeks all over the East
went on living as they had lived for centuries, with only minor
changes as a consequence of the Roman occupation. The languages

found in the ancient Near East at the time also demonstrate the same continuity.

Although Rome brought along into the East the Latin language —a great many Latin inscriptions from the eastern provinces survive (mostly of legionaries, *coloni,* and other officials)—the peoples continued not only to use Greek as their lingua franca, but also kept on using their native and autochthonous languages.[6] For instance, in Egypt people continued to use Greek alongside the hieroglyphs; Demotic and Coptic are Egyptian languages that were foreign to most Greeks.[7] In Syria, Aramaic, Syriac, and other local dialects are found next to the Greek.[8] In Palestine, Aramaic and Hebrew in particular were used as well as Greek;[9] and in Cilicia, Greek, Aramaic, and Cilician.[10] Languages as expressions of the traditional cultures signified most of all the endurance of the different nations.[11] In addition, during the period under survey, Latin literature did not affect the literature of the East very much. By contrast, Greek literature written in Rome and its provinces had a considerable influence on eastern literature. One need only look at the examples of the influence Polybius had on Jason of Cyrene and Dionysius of Halicarnassus had on Josephus. Thus in the cultural and linguistic aspects a continuity from the Hellenistic era in the East can be detected.

Many of the nations of the East, when conquered by Rome, merely changed masters. Once they had been ruled by Diadochi and Hellenistic monarchs; now Rome became their ruler, but this fact had no major impact on daily life (at least for the first two centuries of Roman rule in the Near East). It was very easy for the non-Jews in the Greek East to adopt the worship of the Roman Pantheon (which had earlier been adapted by the Romans from the Greek world). These gods symbolized in many respects the new "national" Roman superstructure, and thus helped to create a common denominator among the Greeks and hellenized pagans of the eastern empire. But the Roman Empire as a "nationalistic" superstructure was entirely different from the Hellenistic kingdoms. Rome signified a unified ecumene (inhabited world) that was, unlike Alexander the Great's, long-lasting. It was not an Alexandrian one of the eastern ecumene, but a western one containing the whole Mediterranean basin and parts of Europe (cf. map page 407).

Against this background, it is interesting to note that the Jewish "natives" in Palestine remained in their villages without necessarily being influenced by the new conquerors in terms of culture, language, or religion. Even in the mixed cities, where Greeks and Jews as well as other non-Jews were settled together, they apparently lived side by side, but did not necessarily mingle (except for the Hellenists). As one can deduce from Josephus, there were a great many tensions in the mixed cities of Palestine, though they did not always find expression in daily life. The struggle in those cities between non-Jews and Jews was not created in one day (e.g., in the decade before the Great War), but was the result of a long process. The tensions and quarrels in the sixties of the first century in Caesarea, Beth-Shean, and other places in Palestine between Jews and non-Jews can be explained only on the basis of national differences, or rather by the collapse of the delicate status quo between the two national identities living in Palestine. Whereas the Jews in Palestine had the upper hand in the Land during the Hasmonean period, enforcing their own independent nationalistic institutions and symbols, this situation gradually changed after the Roman conquest in 63 B.C.E., and in particular after Herod's takeover in 37 B.C.E. Then the Jews became just one part of a non-Jewish state that was ruled by a king who was of Idumaean descent, that had a pagan capital (Caesarea), and was responsible for the foundation of pagan temples in many places in the Land. The Jews at that time felt the need to differentiate themselves—like the Jews in the Diaspora—from the foreigners in their own land. The situation was an impossible one that finally brought about the Great War against Rome.

What national symbols were retained in the first centuries of Roman rule in the Near East? Each of them will be discussed and elaborated on in the following chapters; here they will only be presented in an introductory manner.

1. *Ecumene versus national territorial concepts.* During Rome's expansion many universalistic ideas received greater attention. Alongside the ideal worlds of Osiris, Dionysus, Semiramis, and Alexander, other concepts of a unified ecumene conquered the world in both idea and practice. One of these concepts was the world of Heracles as described by Matris of Thebes, and later in a more practical way by Polybius. Under Roman rule many peoples of the East became not only part of the Roman Empire, which unified the regions of almost the whole western world, but also became part of a

new conceptual ecumene. It is not accidental then that Aeneas, according to Vergil (writing under Augustus), came from the East (Ilium) and reached Italy, as did Paul, according to Luke in Acts; neither went in the wake of Alexander the Great to their east. Still, even in Roman imperialistic thought we find a recurrence of the wish to go in the footsteps of Alexander the Great, and to broaden the empire beyond the western ecumene. Pompey and Antony wished to become like Alexander. Horace says about Augustus that he will be held to be a god here on earth with the addition to the empire of Britain and Persia (*Odes* 3.5.2–4). And Germanicus in 19 C.E. was impressed by the Sesostris myth of the conquest of the eastern ecumene (Tacitus, *Annals* 2.60–61). Nero made preparations to become like Alexander, and Trajan was the emperor who materialized at least part of Alexander's visions by his conquests in the far eastern end of the empire. He was very much impressed by Alexander (Dio Cassius, 68.29–30). Thus, there existed a tension between the concepts of local boundaries and the universalistic ones. On the one hand, King Mithridates VI of Pontus, driven by some kind of universalistic idea and by great personal ambition, conquered a great part of Asia Minor and Greece in 88 B.C.E. He was crushed by Rome soon after.[12] On the other hand, at the same time Cilicians, Bithynians, Pontians, Cappadocians, and Commagenians wished to maintain some kind of national boundaries,[13] the idea of which they did not want to give up under Roman occupation. One of the severest punishments Rome inflicted on a wayward subject nation was the partition of its traditional territory. Many nations endured this fate, including the Macedonians in 168 B.C.E., Numidia in 104 B.C.E., and several regions of Asia Minor as part of Pompey's final settlement in 64 B.C.E. Palestine was divided into five regions by Gabinius in 57/6 B.C.E.

It was only a natural process that, as a result of the fact that Rome held the idea of a unified ecumene, certain circles in the subjugated nations accepted it. The members of the so-called old "colonial" Greek elites in the Hellenistic cities in the East were the ones who "shared" the governance of the empire with the Romans and who entered, by various means, the Roman Senate and achieved high official rank and status in the empire. The indigenous peoples such as Lycians and Cilicians, however, did not participate, and were thus yearning for their own traditional nationalistic political

pieces of territory. In Judaism at the time under survey both attitudes were to be found, the universalistic as well as the particularistic. The universalistic framework was soon to turn into a spiritual
one in the Jewish Diaspora, and in Paul's thought. The nationalistic,
particularistic attitudes were to become the central ideas of the Palestinian Jews and in particular, of the zealot movement.

2. *Kingship*. Kings and dynasties continued to exist in the East
(and elsewhere in the empire) under Roman domination. Thus in
many places within the Roman Empire, such as Cappadocia, Pontus,
Thrace, Commagene, Numidia, and Palestine, the Romans left in
place the significant nationalistic symbol of kingship, which could be
interpreted by the native populations in the wrong way (as indeed
sometimes happened). Although Rome divested the client kings of
their independence and sovereignty in foreign affairs, many of the
client kings were still regarded as kings by parts of their populations.[14] In fact they kept the outer appearance of Hellenistic kings
and lived in palaces, sometimes in the traditional political capitals.
They usually controlled the priesthoods and even had armies, and
sometimes were granted the right to mint coins. For certain strata in
the societies of the conquered nations such client rulers fulfilled
some of their need for a nationalistic symbol, but others were frustrated by this new kind of ruler. This frustration was expressed in
two ways. The conquered peoples either made complaints to the
Romans that the local rulers were unwelcome, or they rebelled. The
frustration was caused by the fact that these client kings were only
pale imitations of the nationalistic symbol par excellence. In reality
they were—unlike the Hellenistic kings of the time before the Roman conquest—just puppets of Rome, and therefore false symbols,
subordinate to the real king, the emperor.[15]

3. *Army*. In the preceding chapter the meaning of national armies
versus mercenary ones has been discussed. When Rome conquered
the East, it either abolished existing armies or left some limited armies in the hands of its client kings. These armies were very much
like the armies of Hellenistic monarchs inasmuch as they were made
up of mercenaries as well as soldiers from the nations themselves.
For some circles these armies represented the remnants of national
sovereignty. When Herod the Great died in 4 B.C.E. it was part of his
army that attempted to achieve independence. Another trend found
throughout the empire at the time of this survey was that at times of

revolt against Rome, the rebellious peoples created national armies organized in the shape of the Roman legion for tactical reasons (e.g., Germany, Gallia, Numidia).[16] The foundation of the Jewish army in the Galilee by Josephus in 66 C.E. should be seen as part of this trend. These national armies were the first and foremost symbol of national independence from Roman rule. The universalistic trends, however, were also in evidence. The Roman army itself recruited more and more provincials, thus becoming a mirror of the multinational character of the empire.

4. *City-capital and temple.* The new world capital, Rome, coexisted with the ancient capitals of the East. The latter, however, were divested of their political roles as the free centers of one territorial sovereign political entity. The local populations were deeply aware and fully cognizant of the fact that cities such as Jerusalem, Memphis, Thebes, and Babylon were capital cities of great antiquity, but at the same time had ceased to be free political centers. Rome even encouraged the creation of new urban centers in her provinces that competed with the traditional ones. In Palestine Rome supported Caesarea Maritima as a political center, which lowered the status of Jerusalem in the eyes of the non-Jews living in Palestine.

As in the case of the capitals, the temples of the ancient Near East were as a matter of course left intact by the Roman imperial administration. The geographer Strabo, along with some archaeological evidence, provide us many examples of the so-called temple-states of the East.[17] Rome for its part did not touch these temples, provided they did not cause any disturbance in the *pax* (peace) it enforced in the region.[18]

In the indigenous temples in the East the cult of the emperor existed alongside the traditional cults. Rome usually supported the priesthoods that were involved in the emperor cult.[19] It should be emphasized that deep into Roman times there is evidence, literary as well as epigraphic, that many indigenous local "nationalistic" gods were worshiped in the Roman East and coexisted with—and sometimes were even identified with—the Greek and Roman deities.[20] It will be seen that the Jews had a nationalistic God who could not be identified with or worshiped alongside the Greek and Roman gods. The fact that Yahweh was an indigenous nationalistic God who could not tolerate other cults and other gods created most of the friction that occurred in the first century C.E. between the Jews and non-Jews living in the Land, as well as between the Jews and the Roman authorities.

Moreover, the Greeks in the cities all over the ancient Near East used a common mythological language to explain and justify their presence in these cities. This language was also understood by the Romans. A good example can be taken from Tacitus's *Annals* 4.55–56 (cf. 3.60–63), where delegations from eleven cities in Asia Minor to Rome are mentioned. The delegations went in 26 C.E. to receive a decision about the location of a new temple that would be dedicated to the Roman emperor. Every city wished it to be on its own territory. As a result, arguments were brought forward concerning the mythological past of each city and its close association with mythological Rome. The use of the myth for the promotion of local political claims was well known in the ancient Near East long before the Romans conquered it, and continued uninterruptedly during Roman rule there.[21] We have some evidence of this practice from Palestine (Andromeda and Joppa, Semiramis and Ascalon).[22] Some Jews tried to connect their own mythological heroes with those of foreign nations, as we learn from the Judeo-Spartan pact, wherein Abraham is presented as an ancestor of both the Jews and the Spartans. Such attempts were unsuccessful because the Greeks and the Romans were not familiar with Abraham or Isaac.[23] The traditional Jews, in contradistinction to all other peoples, were not willing to equate their own mythological past with any foreign mythology: they were not willing to accept the kind of syncretism that was so common in the ancient Near East at the time. This reluctance contributed to the widening of the cultural gap, which resulted in the seclusion and isolation of traditional Jews in the Land.

In conclusion, in the ancient Near East Rome left nationalistic symbols intact as long as they did not present an obstacle to the *Pax Romana*. The provinces of the East continued their existence unhindered in many respects. Rome did not change much in terms of culture, local law, religion, language, or social organization, as long as these matters did not clash with its interests. Nevertheless, the political significance of the nationalistic symbols was somewhat changed at this time, as compared to the Hellenistic era. Universalistic ideas shifted westward to the western ecumene. Kingship was divested of its independent political significance. Temples gradually became religiosocial and spiritual centers, losing much of their particular political, nationalistic importance. Territories were under the complete sovereignty of the Romans, who exploited them economically and dominated them politically: when they wanted to, they divided them; when not, they left them intact. Even the calendar was changed in certain regions from the Macedonian luni-solar to the Roman-Julian (solar), a change that had a major political significance.[24]

What happened to Judea under Roman rule? In 63 B.C.E. Pompey conquered Jerusalem.[25] The Hasmonean realm was abolished. In 40 B.C.E. the Parthians invaded Palestine and supported Antigonus, the grandson of Jannaeus and Salome, who became king of Judea. After a short reign, he was deposed by Herod the son of Antipatros the Edomite, who was made king of Judea by the Roman triumvirate in 40 B.C.E. With the help of the Romans, Herod conquered Jerusalem in 37 B.C.E. and then ruled Palestine uninterruptedly as a client king until his death in 4 B.C.E. His successors took over after some upheaval (called in the Jewish tradition *Polemus Varus*), which was directed against Herod's house and his allies, the Romans. Palestine was then divided by Augustus into three parts, to be ruled by Archelaus, who was deposed in 6 C.E.; Philip, who died in 33/4 C.E.; and Herod Antipas, who was deposed in 39 C.E. The territory assigned to Archelaus was put under direct Roman rule after 6 C.E. (cf. map page 405). In 41 C.E. Agrippa I, already appointed king of Judea by the Roman emperor Gaius Caligula, reigned over the whole of Palestine as his grandfather Herod the Great had earlier. In 44 C.E. Agrippa I died, and the whole of Palestine was put under Roman governors, most of whom were notorious for their cruel behavior. In 66 C.E. the great upheaval of the Jews of Palestine against Rome started, which was finally suppressed in 70 C.E. Jerusalem and its Temple were destroyed, and in the spring of 73 C.E. Masada fell to the Romans.[26]

During this period, within the Jewish society of Palestine there were essentially three attitudes regarding Jewish nationalism. These three attitudes did not necessarily correspond to the three classes of society mentioned above, namely, Greeks, natives, and Hellenists. The first attitude was more open to Hellenistic influence. This group included the liberal element to be found in the higher classes of Jewish society and some of its intellectuals who favored Rome's rule in the ecumene. The high priestly houses should also be included in this group. This group benefited from the new order Rome brought to the world. The second attitude was held by all those religious Jews who did not interfere in the politics of their day, many of whom were Pharisees and Essenes, and who wished to go on peacefully with their studies. In this group one can include the first Christians (Rom 13:1–7). The third attitude was held by those Jews who were imbued with strong nationalistic feelings and who did not give up the desire for Jewish independence in Palestine. They included some Pharisees and a more extreme group, called by Josephus the "Fourth Philosophy." In fact, the Jewish nationalistic movement had never completely died out after the downfall of the Hasmonean realm. From 63 B.C.E. onward it was often latent or suppressed, but at times it broke out from under the surface. At some junctures it received more support from wider circles of Jews (namely, from among the Pharisees, Sadducees, and Essenes); at others it was supported only by a minority, who carried on the battle for political nationalism. This movement reached its peak in the Great War of 66 C.E.

In this year the Jews went to war against Rome. They fought for four years, until Jerusalem fell and the Temple was destroyed by Titus, the son of the new emperor, Vespasian. Scholars have shown a vast interest in all aspects of this national upheaval. Some have viewed it as just another nationalistic uprising against Rome, of a type to be found elsewhere in the Empire.[27] Others have claimed that the war was mainly motivated by religious considerations specific to the Jews.[28] Some have emphasized the political and social motivations for the rebellion,[29] whereas others have been of the opinion that it was just a revival of the Maccabean upheaval.[30]

There exists a vast literature on the Zealot movement, the group that brought about the Great War. Was it created a short time before the war started, in the fifties and sixties of the first century C.E.,[31] or at the beginning of the century or even earlier?[32] Should it be identified with the Fourth Philosophy group described by Josephus in the context of the beginning of the first century C.E.?[33] Opinions abound. For the present purpose it will suffice to state what Josephus said. He referred to the Fourth Philosophy movement in the context of the census of Quirinius in 6 C.E., and again in the context of the Great War.[34] Stern has convincingly shown that these groups were the two wings of the so-called "Fourth Philosophy," which apparently remained dormant throughout the years 6–65 C.E.[35] In some respects the following survey supports the latter view, though it is not the main purpose here to pursue this argument.

During the decades that followed the crushing defeat of the Jews in 70 C.E., the nationalistic "situation" remained in many respects the same as it had been before the Great War with Rome. Without entering the debate over whether the destruction of the Temple and Jerusalem constituted a dramatic turning point in Judaism,[36] one can observe quite clearly a continuity in Jewish life in Palestine. Although the Sadducees, the Essenes, the Fourth Philosophy, and the priestly order disappeared, the three sociocultural groups mentioned above—pious Jews, Hellenists, and pagans—can be found after 70 C.E. It is true that the capital and the Temple were destroyed, but the Jews believed very strongly, in particular after the destruction, that a third Temple would be built "soon" and "in our own days," in the same manner as people believed in the Second Temple in its time. This implied also the hope for a reestablishment of the priests in the Temple. But the territory of Palestine remained Roman, as it had been before 66 C.E. Jewish rulership was out of question, as it had already been since 44 C.E. (Agrippa II was not regarded as a true Jewish king). No Jewish military forces were recruited until the revolt of Bar Kokhba, and Roman governors were ruling Palestine as in the days prior to the revolt. The Jews were considered by the Romans to be a *gens* and a *natio* (nation), and they kept their religious autonomy. Thus, it would not be too much to say that, in spite of the fact that the destruction of the Temple was a traumatic experience for Jews all over the world, the year 70 C.E. should not be regarded as a crucial date in terms of the *continuity* of the concepts of political nationalism. We shall see later that Bar Kokhba, for a short while in 132 C.E., revived Jewish nationalism in its active form, which means that it must have been latent for many years among the Jews of Palestine.

The following chapters will also tackle early Christianity from an unusual angle. The methodology adopted is one that will examine the different issues or subjects at stake (e.g., Temple, territory) instead of once again comparing one Gospel to another in order to discuss the tendencies to be found in the various books of the New Testament. Within the context of Judaism and its attitude to nationalism, it is quite clear that early Christianity—or its interpreters at

the end of the first century C.E.—was against political nationalism as
understood by certain Jewish circles at the time. For example, the
basileia tou theou (Kingdom of God) must clearly be interpreted as
the antithesis of any real or concrete political order. It is spiritual,
and it is never defined in realistic concrete terms, for instance, as a
new equal society with no slavery and a utopian mode of life. It is
nonetheless significant that this particular term was used instead of
others. From Jesus to Paul one can see a sharpening dissociation
from the political nationalism that led the Jews in 66 C.E. to go to
war against Rome. The raison d'être of early Christianity, starting
with Jesus' movement (as it was perhaps perceived later) and culminating with Paul, was to depart from Jewish nationalism, which
strove for an earthly monarchy with defined territory, an army, a
king, and a religiopolitical temple within a capital. The Kingdom of
God was a more universal religious concept, going back to the Hebrew Bible. Early Christianity emphasized the universalistic character of Israel's God rather than his nationalistic one, in the sense
mentioned above. It is hard to believe, as some scholars have attempted to say,[37] that the Jesus depicted in the Gospels thought of
the Kingdom of God in concrete political and social terms. Its complete vagueness made it attractive to religious circles at the time who
wanted to dissociate themselves from their contemporary politics.

A crucial question for this study is how the Roman occupation
affected the treatment of nationalistic symbols in Jewish literature.
The cultural and ideological background of the ancient Near East
did not undergo dramatic changes after the Roman occupation, as
has already been said.[38] Thus the trends of thought surveyed in the
preceding chapters as a background to the different aspects of political nationalism are still valid in this part of my study. The relevant
changes emerging from the literature will, of course, be mentioned in
the subsequent chapters. Already at this stage, however, it must be
emphasized that some *thematic* changes can be found in the apocrypha and pseudepigrapha of this period. In many respects these
works reflect the same political mood as the New Testament. For
instance, no more is heard of dual rulership (king-high priest), borders of Israel, the Samaritan problem in terms of political nationalism, or the political relations with the foreign nations in Palestine. In
the literature after 63 B.C.E. the themes that appear are of a more
universalistic nature. Also, many documents of this period concen-

trate on the spiritual notion of kingship, sometimes referring to God himself, and sometimes to lesser entities (messianic beings and angels). The literature of the first century c.e. does not show a great interest in the Land or its sites, even when one would expect it to do so. Many Jews in Palestine started to think like Diaspora Jews on national issues. The Law of the first century was individualistic and was in most instances not concerned with statehood and related political matters. The Temple remained a very important institution, but the literature has both laments over it and spiritualizations of it.

Most significant was the fact that the heroes who were most popular in the Hasmonean period were not as popular after the Roman occupation. The most popular biblical heroes were no longer David and Solomon. The story of Dinah and the first ancestors of the world no longer appeared in their Jewish, post-Genesis 11 garb. If these heroes appeared at all in the literature of the second period, they had *different* roles from those they had before 63 B.C.E. For instance, if David or Abraham appeared, the emphasis on their biblical roles was shifted and changed and their roles in history were presented in a totally different way. Abraham in the first century was a universal figure, and his role as a universal leader was emphasized over his more nationalistic role, which is found in the Book of Jubilees. Adam was depicted in the first century c.e. as the first father and as the first king (spiritual king). Melchizedek became more important than in the first period. David (as well as Solomon) was important because of his connection to the messiah, but not for his military conquests. It will also become clear that the summaries of Israel's history changed in emphasis with the changing circumstances. Let us now go into the details.[39]

Notes

¹ For a historical survey, see M. Cary and H. H. Scullard, *A History of Rome* (London, 1975); also E. Gruen, *The Hellenistic World and the Coming of Rome,* 2 vols. (Berkeley, Los Angeles, and London, 1984).

² For the *Res gestae*'s mention of "foreign nations" (3, and the names occur in 26–33; cf. R. K. Sherk, *The Roman Empire* [Cambridge, 1988], pp. 41–52), see in M. Stern, *Greek and Latin Authors on Jews and Judaism* (Jerusalem, 1974–1984), 2.182–184, 187. For nations in the Hellenistic East, see Sherk, above, p. 79, and especially books 12–17 of Strabo. For the latter see in general Germaine Aujac, *Strabon et la science de son temps* (Paris, 1966); and E. C. L. van der Vliet, *Strabo over Landen, Volken en Steden* (Assen and Amsterdam, 1977). Agrippa II says, according to Josephus in 66 C.E., "What strong claims to liberty might be advanced by Bithynia, Cappadocia, the Pamphylian nation, Lycians, and Cilicians? Yet they pay their tribute without resort to arms" (*Jewish War* 2.368).

³ For Egypt, see A. K. Bowman, *Egypt after the Pharaohs, 332 B.C.–A.D. 642* (London, 1986); also E. G. Huzar, "Augustus, Heir of the Ptolemies," *Aufstieg und Niedergang der römischen Welt* 2.10.1 (1988); 343–382, and many other articles in the same volume; for Asia Minor, ibid. 2.7.2 (1980).

⁴ *Letters,* Book 10. For Pliny the Younger in general see A. N. Sherwin-White, *The Letters of Pliny: A Historical and Social Commentary* (Oxford, 1966).

⁵ When they did encounter these intellectuals, they did not encounter them in that role, for example, Cicero. The Cilicians certainly get to encounter him in 51–50 B.C.E., but in the role of conquering soldier (for his brutalities, see B. D. Shaw, "Bandit Highlands and Lowland Peace," *Journal of the Economic and Social History of the Orient* 33 [1990]: 223–226).

⁶ Cf. for instance the languages of Asia Minor as depicted by Strabo, 12.533.1 and elsewhere. See a useful survey by Ruediger Schmitt, "Die Sprachverhältnisse in den östlichen Provinzen des Römischen Reiches," *Aufstieg und Niedergang der römischen Welt* 2.29.2 (1983): 554–586; H. Solin, "Juden und Syrer im westlichen Teil der römischen Welt. Eine ethnisch-demographische Studie mit besonderer Berücksichtigung der sprachlichen Zustände," ibid.: 587–789.

⁷ Cf. H. Sternberg, *Mythische Motive und Mythenbildung in den Ägyptischen Tempeln und Papyri der griechisch-römischen Zeit* (Wiesbaden, 1985); Bowman, *Egypt after the Pharaohs;* and G. Neumann and J. Untermann, eds., *Die Sprachen im römischen Reich der Kaiserzeit* (Bonn, 1980). Cf. also R. MacMullen, "Provincial Languages in the Roman Empire," (1966), repr. in his *Changes in the Roman Empire* [Princeton, 1990], pp. 32–40).

⁸ For Syria see F. Millar, "Empire, Community and Culture in the Roman Near East," *Journal of Jewish Studies* 38 (1987): 143–164.

[9] See J. Barr, "Which Language Did Jesus Speak? Some Remarks of a Semitist," *Bulletin of the John Rylands Library of Manchester* 53 (1970–1971): 9–29; J. N. Sevenster, "Do You Know Greek? How Much Greek Could the First Jewish Christians Have Known?" *Novum Testamentum,* Supplement 19 (Leiden, 1968); J. A. Fitzmyer, "The Languages of Palestine in the First Century A.D.," *Catholic Biblical Quarterly* 32 (1970): 501–531; M. Hengel, *The "Hellenization" of Judaea in the First Century after Christ* (Philadelphia, 1989), pp. 7–18. The recently published Babata archive (from the end of the first and beginning of the second centuries) indicates the use of Greek (alongside Aramaic and Nabataean) by upper-class Jews in Transjordan. See N. Lewis, Y. Yadin, and J. C. Greenfield, *The Documents from the Bar Kokhba Period in the Cave of Letters* (Jerusalem, 1989).

[10] Cf. Shaw, "Bandit Highlands" pp. 201–203 (discussion of Luwian).

[11] See for the Nabataean language and self-identity R. Wenning, *Die Nabatäer-Denkmäler und Geschichte* (Göttingen, 1986); L. Casson, *The Periplus Maris Erythrai* (Princeton, 1989); G. W. Bowersock, *Roman Arabia* (Cambridge, Mass. and London, 1983). For the coinage, see Y. Meshorer, *Nabataean Coins* (Jerusalem, 1975).

[12] Cf. on Mithridates B. C. McGing, *The Foreign Policy of Mithridates VI Eupator, King of Pontus* (Leiden, 1986). In general see A. Schalit, "Roman Policy in the Orient from Nero to Trajan," in *The Revolts of the Jews in the Times of Trajan 115–117 A.D.,* ed. D. Rokeah (Jerusalem, 1978), pp. 1–32 (Hebrew). Tacitus's *Annals* and *Histories* have numerous descriptions of the empire's *nationes,* for example, *Annals* 2.56, where Tacitus mentions the national sentiments and the territory of the Armenians (see now M. Chahin, *The Kingdom of Armenia* [London, New York, and Sydney, 1987], part 2).

[13] Cf. G. W. Bowersock, *Augustus and the Greek World* (Oxford, 1965), chap. 4; and D. Magie, *Roman Rule in Asia Minor* (Princeton, 1950), passim.

[14] In general for these kings see D. Braund, *Rome and the Friendly King* (London, 1984); and R. D. Sullivan, *Near Eastern Royalty and Rome, 100–30 B.C.* (Toronto and London, 1990).

[15] The emperor was worshiped as a god after 29 B.C.E. Still, some later emperors refused divine honors (Tiberius in 15 C.E., and see Sherk, *Roman Empire,* p. 57; and Nero about 55 C.E., and see Sherk, ibid., p. 103), but they were exceptions. For the imperial cult of Tiberius in Galatia in Asia Minor, see ibid., pp. 73–75; and for the cult of Gaius in Asia (40–41 C.E.), see ibid., pp. 81–82.

[16] See for instance the Edui in Gallia in 21 C.E., Tacitus, *Annals* 3.43, and Tacfarinas in Numidia (*Annals* 2.52; 3.20–21, 73–74; 4.13, 23–26; and elsewhere).

[17] Cf. the temple-states described in Strabo 11, C 498(17), C 501–503 (1f.); 12, C 535(3), C 537(6), C 556(31), C 574(9); 14, C 676(19); cf. in Egypt the *Oxyrhynchus Papyri,* vol. 12 no. 1453:

Copy of oath. Thonis (also called Patoiphis), son of Thonis, and Heraclides, son of Totoës, both lamplighters of the temple of Sarapis, the most great god, and of the shrine of Isis in the same place, and Paapis, son of Thonis, and Petosiris, son of the aforementioned Patoiphis, both lamplighters of the temple at Oxyrhynchus of Thoëris, the most great goddess, all four swear by Caesar, god, son of a god, to Heliodorus, son of Heliodorus, and to Heliodorus, son of Ptolemaeus, overseers of the temples of the Oxyrhynchite and Cynopolite nomes, that we will look after the lamplighting of the aforementioned temples as prescribed and will provide the proper oil for the daily lamps burning in the indicated temples from Thoth 1 to Mesore [intercalary] 5 of the present first year of Caesar. . . . If I observe the oath, may it be well with me; if I swear falsely, the opposite. First year of Caesar. . . . (The date is 30–29 B.C.)

[18] For the relations of the emperors with temples and priesthoods, see F. Millar, *The Emperor in the Roman World* (London, 1977), pp. 447–456.

[19] Bowersock, *Augustus and the Greek World,* pp. 116–118.

[20] R. MacMullen, *Paganism in the Roman Empire* (New Haven and London, 1981).

[21] P. Weiss, "Lebendiger Mythos," *Würzburger Jahrbücher für die Altertumswissenschaft* n.s. 10 (1984): 179–208.

[22] Cf. Cleodemus Malchus, in Josephus, *Antiquities* 1.240–241 (translation by H. St.-J. Thackery, Loeb Classical Library ed., 1930):

Cleodemus the prophet, also called Malchus, in his history of the Jews relates, in conformity with the narrative of their lawgiver Moses, that Abraham had several sons by Katura. He moreover gives their names, mentioning three— Apheras, Sures, Japhras—adding that Sures gave his name to Assyria, and the two others, Japhras and Apheras, gave their names to the city of Aphra and the country of Africa. In fact, he adds, these latter joined Heracles in his campaign against Libya and Antaeus; and Heracles, marrying the daughter of Aphranes, had by her a son Didorus, who begat Sophon, from whom the barbarians take their name of Sophakes.

[23] See A. D. Momigliano, *Alien Wisdom: The Limits of Hellenization* (Cambridge, 1975), pp. 74ff.

[24] In 9 B.C.E. in the province of Asia (*Orientis graeci inscriptiones selectae* 2 no. 458):

Now, therefore, with good luck and for our safety, it has been decreed by the Greeks of Asia that the New Year's first month shall begin for all the cities on the ninth day before the Kalends of October [September 23], which is the birthday of Augustus; in order that each time the day might correspond in each city, [the Greeks] shall use the Greek day along with the Roman; they shall make the first month—[called] 'Caesar,' as previously decreed—begin with the ninth day before the Kalends of October, the birthday of Caesar; and the crown decreed for the one who found the greatest honors for Caesar shall be given to Maximus the proconsul, and he shall each time be publicly proclaimed [as having won it], at the gymnastic festival in Pergamum [in honor] of Roma [and] Augustus, [as follows]: "Asia crowns Paulus Fabius Maximus for having most piously devised the honors of Caesar"; there shall be a similar proclamation at the festivals for Caesar in the individual cities.

For the impact of the Julian Roman calendar on the calendars of the Eastern provinces, see A. E. Samuel, *Greek and Roman Chronology: Calendars and Years in Classical Antiquity* (Munich, 1972), pp. 171–188.

[25] For the history see E. Schürer, *The History of the Jewish People in the Age of Jesus Christ*, rev. G. Vermes et al. (Edinburgh, 1973–1987), pp. 243—557.

[26] For the date of the fall of Masada see H. M. Cotton, "The Date of the Fall of Masada: The Evidence of the Masada Papyri," *Zeitschrift für Papyrologie und Epigraphik* 78 (1989): 157–162.

[27] For other revolts cf. S. L. Dyson, "Native Revolts in the Roman Empire," *Historia* 20 (1971): 239–274; idem, "Native Revolt Patterns in the Roman Empire," *Aufstieg und Niedergang der römischen Welt* 2.3 (1975): 138–175; see also P. A. Brunt, *Roman Imperial Themes* (Oxford, 1990), chaps. 2, 3, and 13 with addenda, pp. 517–531.

[28] In particular see M. Hengel, *The Zealots* (Edinburgh, 1989), pp. 76–145; for a somewhat different view cf. M. D. Goodman, *The Ruling Class of Judaea* (Cambridge, 1987).

[29] T. Rajak, *Josephus: The Historian and His Society* (London, 1983), pp. 65–173.

[30] W. R. Farmer, *Maccabees, Zealots, and Josephus* (New York, 1956); and see Hengel, *Zealots*, pp. 171–173 with the older literature.

[31] L. I. Levine, "Megamoth Meshichioth Besof Yemei Habait Hasheni," in *Messianism and Eschatology*, ed. Z. Baras (Jerusalem, 1983), pp. 135–152 (Hebrew); D. S. Rhoads, *Israel in Revolution, 6–74 C.E.* (Philadelphia, 1976); and recently R. A. Horsley, *Jesus and the Spiral of Violence* (San Francisco, 1987), pp. 28–58. See also for these questions in general H. Guevara, "La Resistencia Judía contra Roma en la epoca de Jesus," diss. Rome, 1981.

[32] Hengel, *Zealots*, passim.

[33] Ibid., and M. Stern, "The Suicide of Eleazar ben Jair and His Men at Masada, and the 'Fourth Philosophy,' " in his *Studies in Jewish History* (Jerusalem, 1991), pp. 313–343 (Hebrew).

[34] True, Josephus had fewer sources for the time span between 4 B.C.E. and 66 C.E., but nevertheless he had enough oral material to reflect the main course of events. It should be emphasized that most of the historical sources from Palestine

for that period are written from hindsight, namely, Josephus and the narrative parts of the New Testament as well as most apocrypha and pseudepigrapha. But many of them attempt a restoration of the story and the *Zeitgeist,* if not bringing the authentic traditions.

35 Stern, "Suicide of Eleazar ben Jair."

36 Cf. the excellent survey of M. D. Herr, "From the Destruction of the Temple to the Revolt of Bar Kokhba," in *The History of Eretz Israel,* ed. M. Stern (Jerusalem, 1984), 4.284–287.

37 Horsley, *Jesus and the Spiral of Violence.*

38 See now a useful survey of Palestine in the first through third centuries by F. Millar, *The Roman Near East 31 B.C.-A.D. 337* (Cambridge, Mass., 1993). Millar has a totally different interpretation than my own, but his learned study is important in so far as it views the evidence from Palestine against the broader context of the ancient Near East.

39 Chapters 8-11 contain a great deal about the question of Jesus as a historical figure within the context of Jewish nationalism and his reactions towards it. For the historical Jesus see for instance the more recent works of J. Dominic Crossan, *The Historical Jesus: The Life of a Mediterranean Jewish Peasant* (San Francisco, 1991); J. P. Meier, *A Marginal Jew: Rethinking the Historical Jesus,* 2 vols. (New York, 1992, 1994), and L. T. Johnson, *The Real Jesus* (San Francisco, 1996). My discussion in the following chapters contributes to the understanding of the historical Jesus from a different angle from that taken by scholars thus far.

Colonnades in Sebaste (Samaria). *(Courtesy of David Harris, Jerusalem)*

Roman Theater of Caesarea Maritima. *(Courtesy of David Harris, Jerusalem)*

The "Burnt House" (burnt by the Romans in 70 C.E.), Jerusalem. *(Courtesy of David Harris, Jerusalem)*

The Roman Theater, Sebaste (Samaria). *(Courtesy of David Harris, Jerusalem)*

Official copy of letters and decrees of Antiochus III, Hefzibah, Beth-Shean Valley, c. 195 B.C.E. *(Collection Israel Antiquities Authority. Exhibited and photographed: Israel Museum, Jerusalem)*

Letter of Bar Kokhba to
Yeshua, son of Galgola.
*(Collection Israel Antiquities
Authority. Exhibited and pho-
tographed: Israel Museum,
Jerusalem)*

An Aramaic inscription
that refers to the transfer
of the bones of Uzziah,
King of Judah, to a new
tomb (Jerusalem, Second
Temple Period).*(Collection
and photograph Israel
Museum, Jerusalem)*

Oil press at the Hellenistic site of Marisa (Idumea). *(Courtesy of David Harris, Jerusalem)*

"Place of Trumpeting" inscription in Hebrew, first century B.C.E., Jerusalem. (The approach of the Sabbath and its close were proclaimed by trumpet blasts.) *(Collection Israel Antiquities Authority. Exhibited and photographed: Israel Museum. Jerusalem)*

Excavations of the Southern Wall, Jerusalem, Herodian Period.
(Courtesy of David Harris, Jerusalem)

Columbarium at the Hellenistic site of Marisa (Idumea).
(Courtesy of David Harris, Jerusalem)

Jewish shekel of the first year of the Jewish War against Rome (66 C.E.).
(Collection and photograph Israel Museum, Jerusalem)

Jewish coin of the first year of the Bar Kokhba revolt (132 C.E.).
(Collection and photograph Israel Museum, Jerusalem)

CHAPTER 8

Kingship after the Roman Occupation— From Basileia to Alternative Concepts

I have mentioned previously that the symbols of Jewish nationalism in the Hasmonean period were given different interpretations by various groups in society after 63 B.C.E. In the eyes of some, the symbols were shattered the moment the Romans conquered Palestine. Others believed that they still existed but had been transformed. This chapter will attempt to examine how the concept of kingship underwent a transformation from 63 B.C.E. to 135 C.E., and how this change was reflected in the literature of that period.

It should be noted that as an institution Hellenistic kingship does not seem to have changed during the first two centuries of Roman occupation. Kings who were left on their thrones in the East had the same characteristics as they had before the Roman intervention. But they were now client kings under Rome's strict sway, and this new status changed the authority of their kingship altogether. Thus, alongside the continued worship of the Hellenistic client kings, we also can find worship of the Roman emperor. He was worshiped in the Near East in the same way that the Hellenistic kings had been prior to the Roman occupation. His subjects recognized him as being yet another Hellenistic king, as the titles that were given to him clearly show. For instance, Augustus was thanked by the city of Priene for his "benefactions" (*euergemata*),[1] and Nero was called *soter* (savior) and *euergetes* (benefactor) in Egypt.[2] The regular ties the subjects all over the Empire pursued with the emperor were mainly through the worship of his cult and the cult of Dea Roma.[3]

In practice client kings were restricted as sovereign leaders. They could hardly initiate any independent foreign policy and were not allowed to launch any military actions without Rome's consent. Many restrictions were put on their inner policies, and as a rule they were subject to heavy taxation. Most of the client kings were in fact puppets of Rome. Herod the Great should be viewed against the background of those kings who remained in the East after the Roman occupation, such as the kings of Commagene, Bithynia, Pontus, and Chalcis.[4] The practical changes of the period will be examined first. In what way did Jewish kingship change, and how did any changes affect political and religious thought from 63 B.C.E. to 70 C.E.?

From 67 B.C.E. to 63 B.C.E., the two sons of Salome, the last dynast of the Hasmonean line, had waged a serious civil war. In the spring of 64 B.C.E., while Pompey, the great Roman conqueror, was camping in Damascus, the two warring parties in Judea appeared before the general. Pompey listened to the case presented by the Jews and their leaders, Hyrcanus and Aristobulus, who were fighting each other for the throne. Josephus adds that

> the *nation* was against them both and asked not to be ruled by a king, saying that it was the custom of their country to obey the priests of the God who was venerated by them, but that these two, who were descended from the priests, were seeking to change their form of government in order that they might become a nation of slaves. As for Hyrcanus, he charged that though he was the elder brother, he had been deprived of his rights as firstborn by Aristobulus, and that he had but a small part of the country under his rule, while Aristobulus had the rest, which he had taken by force.

He was supported in making these accusations by more than a thousand of the most reputable Jews (who were sent by the Edomite Antipater). Aristobulus, however, blamed Hyrcanus's fall from power on his own bad character and defended himself by saying that "he had of necessity taken over the royal power for fear that it might pass into the hands of others, and that his title was exactly the same as that of his father, Alexander. He then called, as witnesses to these statements, some young swaggerers, who offensively displayed their purple robes, long hair, and metal ornaments" (*Antiquities* 14.40–47).

Pompey dismissed the parties without making any decision. It should be emphasized that one of the three groups appearing before Pompey represented the "people" who did not want to be ruled by kings any more, and wished to return to theocracy, that is, the rule of the priests.[5] Diodorus Siculus attributes to this period the passage about the Jews in the writings of Hecataeus of Abdera, which claims that the Jews "never had a king" in their past history.[6] There were, however, groups who wished to continue the Hasmonean dynasty, a fact that is important here. Pompey at last ruled in favor of Hyrcanus II (*Antiquities* 14.73–74; *Jewish War* 1.53), but did not give him the royal title. This settlement did not bring peace, as Aristobulus's party continued the war. It is likely that as early as 63 B.C.E. the kingship in Judea was abolished by the Romans and was replaced by aristocratic (priestly) rule. Josephus, however, claims that the abolition of kingship was achieved by Gabinius at 57 B.C.E., after the latter crushed Alexander, the son of Aristobulus (*Antiquities* 14.91): "And so the people were removed from monarchic rule and lived under an aristocracy" (*Jewish War* 1.169–170, meaning priestly rule; cf. *Antiquities* 11.111).

From 57 until 41 B.C.E. the rulers in charge of Palestine possessed the status of *ethnarches* and *epitropos*. This status is reminiscent of that which the early Hasmoneans had held when they were still in the service of the neighboring Diadochi, before their house became a royal dynasty. In spite of the fact that Rome made the settlement in favor of Hyrcanus II, not many agreed to accept him as a "king" of Israel, but reluctantly accepted his rule. At this stage the sources show that nationalism in its most extreme form (e.g., the opposition against Hyrcanus II) was in the process of moving to the lower strata of society, at least in Palestine (according to *Jewish War* 1.153 large numbers from among the rural population were supporters of Aristobulus II as early as 63 B.C.E.). By contrast, in the Diaspora during the fifties and forties of the first century B.C.E., Hyrcanus II appears as the leading figure of world Jewry, in particular in its dealings with the Roman authorities. The sources show that he served as the representative of all social strata of the Diaspora Jews when he appealed to the authorities on behalf of the Jewish soldiers serving in the Roman army. Even after he was deposed by Antigonus, the Jews in Babylonia "honored [him] as their high priest and king, as did all of the Jewish nation occupying the region as far as the Euphrates" (*Antiquities* 15.14–15). This position as the representative of all Jews was later adopted by both Herod the Great and Agrippa I in their dealings with Rome, visits to Alexandria, and other political transactions.[7] This "universal" aspect of Jewish rulership in Palestine, while less apparent in the Hasmonean era, was taken up by the kings and pseudo-kings after 63 B.C.E. They wished to be seen as "king of the Jews," alongside their role as the "king of Judea." This matter shall be taken into consideration later when we discuss the accusation made against Jesus that he was the "king of the Jews" (or "king of Israel") rather than "king of Judea" (i.e., Palestine).

In 40 B.C.E., with the help of the invading Parthians, kingship was restored in Judea, and Antigonus, Jannaeus's grandchild, became the king of Judea (*Antiquities* 14.379); he was apparently very popular among the nationalistic circles.[8] This hegemony only lasted for a short time. Herod, who was forced to flee to Rome during the Parthian occupation of Palestine, was given the kingship of Judea by the Roman triumvirate, who were unanimous on this particular issue.[9] Josephus describes this episode in a dramatic manner:

And when the Senate had been aroused . . . Antony came forward and informed them that it was also an advantage in their war with the Parthians that Herod should be king. And as this proposal was acceptable to all, they voted accordingly. But this was the greatest sign of Antony's devotion to Herod, that not only did he obtain the kingship for him, which he had not hoped for—he had come to the capital not to claim the kingship for himself, for he did not believe that the Romans would offer it to him, as it was their custom to give it to one of the reigning family. (*Antiquities* 14.385–386)

It can be seen that in the case of Antigonus, and even more so in that of Herod, the kingship was granted and strongly supported by an empire. This constitutes one major difference between Hasmonean kingship and the Herodian dynasty: Hasmonean kingship was declared by the Hasmoneans themselves, as in the case of Aristobulus I, rather than by intervention of any external force. The *auctoritas* (higher authority) came from the king himself (with the approval of the majority of Jews), not from an outside power.

It took Herod some time to conquer Judea and to crush King Antigonus;[10] he then sent Antigonus as a prisoner to Antony the triumvir, with a generous bribe attached in order to move Antony to execute the Hasmonean king. In the third year after he was crowned king in Rome (37 B.C.E.), Herod entered Jerusalem as a Roman client king, a judaized Edomite, but one married into the Hasmonean dynasty. Before entering the city he had hastened to marry Miriam, Hyrcanus II's granddaughter. Herod wished to be seen as the successor to the Hasmonean dynasty (at least in the eyes of the Jewish population of Palestine),[11] and thus to become a unifying national symbol, just as the Hasmoneans had been in the past. He failed in this attempt, not only because he was a client king of Rome but also for some other reasons that will be discussed shortly. Herod did not succeed in becoming a symbol of the Jewish political consensus, and this failure turned out to be his greatest tragedy.

Josephus gives an emotional outburst over Herod's accession to the throne, when he says, "and at the same time the rule of the Hasmonean line came to an end after 126 years [this takes us back to 163 or 162 B.C.E.]. Theirs was a splendid and renowned house because of both their lineage and their priestly office, as well as the things that its founders achieved on behalf of the nation" (*Antiquities* 14.490–491). Josephus here states a view opposite to the one arguing for the separation between the secular and the religious authority. "But," he adds, "they lost their royal power through internal strife, and it passed to Herod, the son of Antipater, who came from a house of common people and from a private family that was subjected to the kings." Here is another difference between the Hasmonean dynasty and the one established by Herod the Great: the Hasmoneans came from a secondary, but distinguished priestly house, which was purely Jewish; Herod did not.[12]

Herod then started to eliminate his potential adversaries from the Hasmonean house, the first being the deposed king Antigonus.[13] Many were to suffer this unhappy fate. According to *Antiquities* 15.164,[14] Herod killed Hyrcanus, Miriam's grandfather, whom he believed to be an obstacle in his way.[15] *Antiquities* 15.213–231 (*Jewish War* 1.438–444) describes the tragic death by execution in 29 B.C.E. of his wife, Miriam. Herod's fear of the renewal of the

Hasmonean kingship can be seen in the story of the sons of Baba, who were hidden by Costobar because they were supporters of Antigonus, the last Hasmonean king ("who had a high position and great influence with the masses," 15.263). Josephus says that Herod killed them "so that none was left alive of the family of Hyrcanus and the kingdom was wholly in Herod's power, there being no one of high rank to stand in the way of his unlawful acts" (15.259–266). In this way one can also explain the execution of his mother-in-law and of his two sons by Miriam, Aristobulus and Alexander, and perhaps even of Antipater, who was married to the daughter of Antigonus, the former Hasmonean king of 40–37 B.C.E.[16] In this respect Herod was no different from the Hellenistic kings in the region, who did not hesitate to kill members of their own families (brothers, sisters, and even their own children and parents). By destroying the principal survivors of the Hasmonean royal house, he in reality emphasized his differences with that dynasty instead of becoming its successor. By his frequent murder of members of the Hasmonean family, he caused much damage to kingship as a national symbol for the Jewish population of Palestine. Ironically, he eliminated those who could be, and still were, the symbols of the national identity and unity (in particular Aristobulus, Miriam's brother, and Miriam herself). Herod became thus not only a former Edomite who actually represented the *ethnos* (nation) of the Edomites and the non-Jews of Palestine in the eyes of many Jews,[17] but he also, for a great part of the population, was the king who gradually destroyed the magnificent Hasmonean dynasty that was the symbol of independent Jewish existence in the Land of Israel.

The ambivalent nature of Herod's policies—on the one hand posing as a successor of the Hasmonean dynasty in the eyes of the Jews, while on the other hand destroying its remnants—brings up the question of his political "schizophrenia." Although Alexander Jannaeus may have already had some aspects of this dual nature, he was a Jew and a Hasmonean and still had the approval of much of the Jewish population throughout long periods of his reign. Herod instead had gradually become a "schizophrenic" king of the type already mentioned concerning the Hellenistic kings of the time before the Roman conquest, such as the Ptolemies. This aspect constitutes an important factor in the accelerating decline of Jewish kingship.

Throughout his long reign of thirty-four years Herod tried to appease the native population, the Jews, while playing the Hellenist in the eyes of the non-Jewish population of Palestine, the Greeks in the East, and Rome. In comparing the reigns of Herod and Agrippa I (38–43 c.e.) in Judea, Josephus says that Herod emphasized his Hellenistic aspects while abandoning his Jewish side. This imbalance between his Hellenistic and Jewish sides instigated the strong resistance to him, and to some of his successors, on the part of the Jewish population of Palestine.[18]

How can this imbalance be explained? Josephus is the main source of evidence of Herod's "schizophrenia." He says in a famous passage that

> for this reason Herod went still farther in departing from the native customs, and through foreign practices he gradually corrupted the ancient way of life, which had hitherto been inviolable. As a result of this we suffered considerable harm at a later time as well, because those things were neglected which had formerly induced piety in the masses. For in the first place he established athletic contests every fifth year in honor of Caesar, and built a theater in the plain, both being spectacularly lavish but foreign to Jewish custom. (*Antiquities* 15.267–268)

His schizophrenic, or dualistic, kingship is also emphasized in *Antiquities* 15.326–330 (and elsewhere). This evidence is corroborated by the archaeological material, which shows Herod to have been one of the greatest builders of pagan cities and institutions in Palestine.[19]

Caesarea Maritima was founded by Herod as a city for the non-Jews in Palestine.[20] This project was in keeping with other Hellenistic rulers in the region who needed new capitals to become their "unindigenous" (i.e., Hellenistic) centers. Even if Herod had no such intention when founding the city, his successors, and in particular the Roman governors, used Caesarea Maritima as a new political capital (like the *basileion* Antiochia, which was the capital of the governors in Syria). The policy of Agrippa I concerning the issue of a capital forty years later shows very clearly that the so-called "schizophrenia" was expressed by a two-capitals policy: Jerusalem for the Jews, Caesarea for the non-Jews. Herod emerges as a typical Hellenistic ruler throughout Josephus's account.[21] Among his enterprises one can mention the foundation of a temple for Augustus in Panion (*Antiquities* 15.363–364), the Hellenic festivities at the opening of Caesarea Maritima (16.136–141), and the building of Sebastia (old Samaria) in honor of Augustus, and Herodion and other sites characterized by Hellenistic-style architecture, some of which can still be seen today.[22]

Josephus describes the opposition of the Jews, the natives (*epichorioi*), to Herod's hellenization process: "but to the natives it meant an open break with the customs held in honor by them" (15.274–276); and later he underlines the rift within the population: "most of them were inclined to change their attitude and not to be angry any longer. But some of them persisted in their resentment of these practices as departures from tradition." Thus, Josephus adds, in reality Herod became the "enemy" of the nation.[23] Josephus's words are harsh, but one must take into consideration that his main source for Herod's reign was Nicolaus of Damascus, who was in favor of Herod.[24] As a consequence of these events, there ensued some conspiracies, which were cruelly suppressed by Herod. In *Antiquities* 15.291 Josephus says, "But the steadfastness of the people and their undaunted loyalty to their laws had the effect of making Herod feel uneasy until he had taken measures for greater security." (Also 15.292–298 shows that opposition against Herod was very strong over the issue of breaking the Law of the Torah.) Nevertheless, Josephus's emphasis on the fact that "most" Jews became passive should not be underestimated, and will be treated later.

Although the archaeological and literary evidence alike show that Herod accented his Hellenistic side, he also tried his best to pose as the "king of the Jews." He knew how to appease certain Jewish circles and gained their support, as revealed by the story of Shemaiah and Abtalion and the scattered references about his relations with the Essenes. The story about the Pharisees and the women of the palace also shows that Herod was accepted by certain circles of religious Jews, at certain times during his reign, even though most Jewish circles did not. In other words, in Herod's time there were a great many Jews who preferred peace, even under Roman aegis, to any sort of political unrest.[25] Even so, they did not view Herod as their genuine king, in other words, the king of a Jewish state in Palestine. His alter (Jewish) ego is also expressed in his acts for the indigenous population, the religious Jews, and the Jews in the Diaspora. Herod wanted to be seen by the world as the "king of the Jews" in addition to being the "king of Judea." His coins also point to this Jewish alter ego, and he is called the "king of the Jews" by Italian businessmen on the imported amphoras of wine for his palace.[26] Yet his "schizophrenia" as a ruler was also apparent in his relations with foreigners abroad (*Antiquities* 16.150–159). Even in the magnificent Temple that he built for the Jews, we can trace evidence of his dualistic kingship. He adorned the main entrance of this holy building with a golden eagle, the symbol of the Roman Empire (17.149–154). This Roman eagle was taken down by zealous Jews when rumors were spread about Herod's death. Not long after this incident he died (4 B.C.E.).[27]

On the whole, Herod's Hellenistic side comes much more to the fore than his Jewish one, and the attempts by some scholars to emphasize his Jewish facets have not been very successful. Later Jewish tradition thoroughly denigrated him (except for his initiative in building the Temple), which shows that in the minds of many Jews he never really was the "king of the Jews."[28]

Herod's kingship affected the attitudes about kingship in the first century C.E. Some Jews wished that Herod's dynasty would continue after his death, but there were others who wanted to end rule by a king. They did not like "false" Jewish kingship and found an opportunity to oppose it during the quarrels with Herod's successors (*Antiquities* 17.299–303). They, like the Jewish delegation to Pompey in 63 B.C.E., wanted to abolish the kingship and create an "autonomia" under Roman rule. When this group appeared in Rome at the same time as the various claimants to Herod's throne, they were supported by more than eight thousand members of the Jewish community living in Rome (*Antiquities* 17.300), who probably thought that any Jewish national political symbol or remnant of statehood would be damaging for the Jewish Diaspora. In fact, many groups in the Diaspora were unhappy with Jewish kingship altogether, and even felt embarrassed at certain junctures by the Jewish state. This group spoke of the bad traits of kingship and its "schizophrenia" (17.304–314), and when referring to the kingship of Herod the Great they said to Augustus, "He [Herod] had not ceased to adorn neighboring cities that were inhabited by foreigners although this led to the ruin and disappearance of cities located in his own kingdom . . . and he was wont to kill members of the nobility upon absurd pretexts and then take the property for himself" (17.306–307). These claims were only partially accepted. Augustus ratified Herod's appointments; he named Archelaus as *ethnarches* and Philip and Herod Antipas to be tetrarchs. These titles can be seen on their coins.[29]

While these events were taking place in Rome (4 B.C.E.), we hear of yet another reaction of a violent nature to Herod's death. Claimants to the throne such as Judas, Simeon, Athronges, and Alexander wished to create a new dynasty for Judea. These claimants, as far as can be judged from the scanty sources, were not of royal descent; but of course neither was Herod. They were pretenders of the kind that could be found all over the Hellenistic world at that time.[30] The unrest they caused led to a riot centered in Jerusalem, which the Romans brutally crushed in the same year.

The partition of Palestine, and its division among three successors of Herod the Great, drastically changed the concept of kingship as a unifying national symbol—that is, of one king for the whole of Eretz Israel. Herod's three successors had well-defined borders, they founded their own capitals (Tiberias and Caesarea Philippi), they even minted their own coins and had small armies at their disposal (with an option to recruit larger ones).[31] Although these three rulers did not bear the official title of "king," they were still recognized as such by their subjects (for instance, Matt 14:9). To judge from the scanty evidence we possess for the reign of Herod's three successors, the behavior of two of them, Herod Antipas and Archelaus, showed what kind of kingship they had absorbed in Herod's court.

According to Josephus, Archelaus installed Eleazar the son of Boethus as high priest (*Antiquities* 17.339); in keeping with Herod's policies, this practice became common for both the native rulers and the Roman governors.[32] Archelaus then trespassed the laws of the Torah by marrying Glaphyra, his brother's wife. In the tenth year of Archelaus's rule, the leading men among the Jews and a delegation from the Samaritans brought about his exile by Augustus (6 C.E.; *Antiquities* 17.342–344; *Jewish War* 2.111). As a consequence "the territory subject to Archelaus was added to (the province) Syria, and Quirinius, a man of consular rank, was sent by Caesar to take a census of property in Syria" (17.355). According to *Jewish War* 2.117 the territory of Archelaus was "reduced to a province, and Coponius, a Roman of the equestrian order, was sent out as praefectus, entrusted by Augustus with full powers, including the infliction of capital punishment." Philip, by contrast, was a ruler favored by his subjects and is depicted in a concise manner by Josephus, mainly as a judge. Josephus says that in his conduct of the government he showed a "moderate and easygoing disposition" and that he spent all his time in the territory under his sway. When he went on circuit he had only a few selected companions, and the throne on which he sat when he gave judgment "accompanied him wherever he went." Hence, whenever anyone appealed to him, at once "without a moment's delay" the throne was set up whenever it might be. He then took his seat and gave the case a hearing, and "fixed penalties for those who were convicted and released those who had been unjustly accused. He died in Julias" (18.106–108). After his death in 34 C.E., Tiberius annexed his territory to the province of Syria.

We should point out that the partition of Palestine into three "autonomous" districts in the first century C.E. had its effect on the people of those districts, who in the course of time developed a local patriotism, as can be seen clearly in the Gospels and Acts. In the Trachonitis and Gaulanitis, for instance, they may have identified themselves first and foremost with the new capital, Caesarea Philippi, and with their local "king," Philip.[33] Similarly, Herod Antipas's subjects identified themselves with their capital, Tiberias. Both for them and for the subjects of the other "kingdoms" Jerusalem remained the religious and spiritual center, but it probably waned in its political significance.

Be that as it may, in *Antiquities* 18.127–142 Josephus gives a long excursus on the history of the house of Herod the Great—it is reminiscent of Hellenistic dynasties elsewhere in the region.[34] Later we hear again of direct Roman intervention in the issue of kingship, when a Jewish king was appointed, this time Agrippa I, who was to be the last king of Judea. It was one of the most notorious Roman Caesars of the first century, Gaius Caligula, who in 37 C.E. "put a diadem on Agrippa's head and appointed him king of the tetrarchy of Philip, presenting him also with the tetrarchy of Lysanias."[35] This was too much for Agrippa's sister, Herodias, who wanted a kingship for her husband Herod Antipas as well; she went with him to Rome to see Caligula, who, however, in a fury deposed him from his kingdom. Client kings were worth nothing at the time.[36]

Judea now had a king for the last time, Agrippa I. The concept of kingship in his short reign is important for this study. Unfortunately

Josephus gives very little information about Agrippa's reign, which has recently been treated in an excellent study by D. R. Schwartz.[37] *Antiquities* 19.292–359 covers the kingship of Agrippa I. When he returned to Jerusalem from Rome in 38 C.E., he first went to sacrifice in the Temple, "omitting none of the ritual enjoined by our law" (19.293). He then installed a new high priest, Simeon Cantheras, but according to 19.312–316 he soon thereafter appointed another high priest, Matthias, in place of Simeon. Later in his short reign he named yet another high priest, Elionaeus the son of Cantheras (19.342). This was actually the only quasi-political act he could perform without annoying the Romans. Among his other acts in Judea one should mention his attempt to restore Jerusalem's walls, which Claudius ordered him to stop.[38] He persecuted the Christians (but the scale of the persecution is not mentioned), and therefore was denigrated by Luke in Acts 12.[39] He received almost the whole of Palestine as his territory; hence he, as a king of both Hasmonean and Herodian descent, ruled one of the widest territorial perimeters in Israel's history.[40] According to Josephus he enjoyed residing in Jerusalem, and he scrupulously observed the traditions of his people: he neglected no rite or purification, and no day passed for him without the prescribed sacrifice. This information should be taken with a grain of salt (*Antiquities* 19.331–334).

In short, Agrippa I was an ideal Jewish king for the Jewish population of Palestine, and as such he was disliked not only by the Christians (being a Jewish earthly *basileus*), but also by some non-Jewish communities of Palestine, which caused much tension in years to come. Yet he too became a "schizophrenic" king. It has already been shown that each ruler varied in the degree of Hellenistic or eastern influence he displayed. Herod the Great was more Hellenistic, whereas it seems that Agrippa I emphasized his Jewish side.[41] Josephus says that Agrippa was benevolent to those of other nations and exhibited his generosity to them. For example, he built a theater and an amphitheater for the people of Beirut.[42] Elsewhere Josephus talks of Agrippa's initiation of the assembly of client kings at Tiberias and of the fierce Roman intervention by Marsus, the governor of Syria, which shows that this convention was seen as a threat by the Romans.[43] In contrast to Herod the Great, Agrippa's Jewish side was more "pure" and seems to have overshadowed his Hellenistic one:

It was generally admitted that he [Herod the Great] was on more friendly terms with Greeks than with Jews. For instance, he adorned the cities of foreigners by giving them money, building baths and theaters, erecting temples in some and porticoes in others, whereas there was not a single city of the Jews on which he deigned to bestow even minor restoration. . . . Agrippa, on the contrary, had a gentle disposition and he was a benefactor to all alike. He was benevolent to those of other nations and exhibited his generosity to them also; but to his compatriots he was proportionately more generous and more compassionate. (*Antiquities* 19.328–331)

The story of Agrippa's death is one rare instance in which we find a piece of evidence in Josephus that is corroborated by evidence found in the New Testament. In *Antiquities* 19.343–350 Josephus relates the story of Agrippa's death in an unusual, but positive manner. Unlike Josephus, Acts 12:12–22 has little positive to say about Agrippa (called by the dynastic name, Herod). Yet both accounts agree that the crowd addressed him as a god. This piece of evidence is important. The crowds were apparently mostly pagan. They must have missed the ruler cult of their own local king. It is ironic that the man who is depicted as a king who cared more for the Jewish population than any leading figure since the death of Salome in 67 B.C.E. should die in the non-Jewish capital of Palestine, Caesarea, instead of Jerusalem, the capital of the Jews.

For a short time king Agrippa I created a *fata morgana* of a Jewish national king. But his position should not be exaggerated. The Jews liked him but knew very well that he was but a client king of Gaius Caligula and later of Claudius (as a symbolic act he himself put the golden chain he received from the emperor over the treasure chamber in the Temple, *Antiquities* 19.294). Thus he had very little authority in the political arena. Still, he emerged as a true Jewish king in religious and spiritual matters. In the days of Agrippa I Jewish kingship took on a fresh dimension not found since the Roman occupation of Palestine. He became the symbol of Judaism in Palestine (and attempted as well to become the king and leader of the Jewish world, as his notorious journey to Alexandria shows; Philo, *In Flaccum*). He was, however, divested of all political nationalistic connotations, and in this respect resembled the successors of Herod the Great. His premature death shattered the hopes of many Jews who had wanted to enjoy their religious and spiritual autonomy, as well as their position of priority over the non-Jews living in Palestine in a peaceful manner. Some of this frustrated disappointment nourished the stormy events to come.[44]

Only during the revolt of 66–70 c.e. do we hear again about Jewish kingship. Agrippa II, though he was the son of Agrippa I and was king of Chalcis at the time, was totally ignored by those Jews who wished to renew genuine Jewish kingship as a step toward independence.[45] The extremists among the Zealots (probably the Sicarii) tried to crown Menachem, an important figure from among their own group (not of royal descent), king in Jerusalem. The Zealots wanted a real, pure Jewish king with no divided loyalties (unlike Agrippa II, who was more Greco-Roman than Jewish).[46] The "coronation" seems to have been a purely political act, in keeping with the previous history of kingship in Judea.[47] In these actions one can see the antithesis of a false Jewish kingship; they were instead an attempt to rehabilitate the decaying symbol of Jewish nationalism, which had reached its low point in the character of Agrippa II. The extremists in Jerusalem in 66 c.e. wished to restore the true kingship, which would also be associated with the priesthood, as in the days of old (the Hasmonean rulers). Thus Menachem, with his bodyguard of the Sicarii, "returned like a veritable king to Jerusalem, (and) became the leader of the revolution" (*Jewish War* 2.433–448); he went to the Temple "arrayed in royal robes," but was then murdered by those who "after revolting from the Romans for the love of liberty . . . ought not to sacrifice this liberty to a Jewish hangman and to put up with a master who, even were he to abstain from violence, was anyhow far below themselves" (*Jewish War* 2.443). The leaders of the antikingship movement, which we have met in 64 b.c.e. and 4 b.c.e., were again at work. As far as we know, no further attempt at a renewal of Jewish political national rulership is recorded until Bar Kokhba in 132 c.e. After the Great War Agrippa II remained in control of his northern kingdom until his death at the end of the first century c.e. He was not viewed as a Jewish king who would revive either the Hasmonean or the Herodian dynasties and rule over the whole of Palestine. In the decades after 70 c.e., the rulership of the nation was in the hands of the sages who were the spiritual and religious leaders in the various centers of Palestine. The re-creation of a real Jewish state at present was not one of their main concerns.

It can now be seen that there was a gradual deterioration of genuine Jewish kingship from Herod the Great down to Agrippa II. If this decline is examined against the background of the Hasmonean dynasty, one can clearly say that the successors of Herod the Great were but *epigoni* (pretenders) and weak quasi-kings. They hardly possessed any sovereignty except in limited spheres, such as judging certain matters, collecting taxes for the Romans, and initiating building projects. Thus, although they were titular rulers in the Land of Israel and part of their lineage was Jewish, in the eyes of many Jews they were but false symbols of Jewish political nationalism. Kingship had become very different from the kingship of the Hasmonean era, and this transformation affected Jewish national identity. It is interesting that the shift of emphasis from pure Jewish national rulers in the Land to "schizophrenic" ones, who had a more universalistic approach, brought about the desire in these same rulers to become the leaders of the Jewish world. The Diaspora, however, did not always approve of this kind of leadership, as has been shown in the episode of 4 B.C.E. in Rome.[48] We have also seen that, in their reaction to the kingship of the period, the Jewish population was divided into various groups. There were those who could, reluctantly, live with the Herodian type of kingship; others liked it and identified with it; while many opposed it. Some of these views were expressed in the literature of the period, to be discussed in the next section.

Before entering a discussion of the issue of kingship in Judaism and early Christianity as a political nationalistic symbol, we should again emphasize the fact that the Greeks in the Hellenistic East (group 2) had no difficulty in shifting their loyalty to the Roman emperor because he was seen by them as a Hellenistic monarch. Hence it is not surprising that some of their thinkers picked up the Greek views on kingship and applied them to the emperor, as they did to their "local" Hellenistic monarchs before the Roman occupation. A prominent example are the discourses *On Kingship* composed by Dio Chrysostomus at the beginning of the second century

C.E. He may have addressed them to Trajan directly, or may just have had the latter in mind as a new Alexander the Great when writing these discourses.

Dio Chrysostomus's views of the good king were based on classical Greek political thought (Homer, Plato, Aristotle, and Xenophon). He elaborated the traits of the good king as opposed to a tyrant, but also discussed the hierarchy of kings. On the one hand there is the "king of kings," Zeus (discourse 2.75), who "alone of the gods has the epithets "Father," "King," "Protector of Cities" (1.38–41). Some of the terms mentioned by Dio are the ones that were used by the easterners to describe their own kings as well as the "king of kings," the Roman emperor. In contrast was the ideal earthly king, whose virtues were to exceed all other human beings (discourses 1–4, passim). Against this background, let us examine the views of kingship in Judaism and early Christianity.

Some of the reactions to Jewish kingship are expressed in the literature of the period. Unfortunately, we have little direct evidence from Jewish sources prior to 70 C.E. But the notions of kingship appearing in the New Testament are not unique to early Christianity, inasmuch as they show a continuity with the ideas on kingship found in Judaism before Jesus' ministry. Thus they reflect certain nuances about kingship that were current within pre-70 Judaism, and after this date. As far as we can judge from the Christian sources as well as from the Jewish ones of the period 63 B.C.E.–70 C.E., no real interest is shown in contemporary rulers, and therefore there is no involvement with the so-called *peri basileias* (on kingship) documents. On the contrary, there is a growing interest in the ideas of a heavenly King and messianic kings. The latter were less evident in the literature of the first period (200–63 B.C.E.).[49] The literature of the second period emphasizes the more universal (biblical) concept of godly kingship as opposed to the earthly king, who is usually presented as bad and who symbolizes all the evil done in the world. This view is almost totally absent from the literature of the first period. Although the literature of the second period at times uses terminology referring to actual kingship (such as *euergetes, soter,* king as a judge, etc.), it avoids all of the practical discussions found in the literature of the first period, and is much more amorphous and vague. Many documents of this period escape to a more spiritual and transcendental world. For this reason also the kings of ancient

Israel—except David and Solomon—were not popular in the Jewish documents from before the destruction of the Temple in 70 C.E., or in the New Testament. The frustration with actual kingship, as depicted in the previous section, brought about a reaction, which was expressed in various ways, apparently also after 70 C.E.

As mentioned already, in contrast to the literature of the first period, there was an increasing interest in messianic figures in the second period. Yet the figure of the messiah that emerges from the literature written after the Roman conquest of Palestine takes two different shapes. First, there is the political figure of Messiah the son of David; and, second, there is the transcendental messiah, who is dissociated from any physical kingship. Let us start with the first one, probably the more popular: the Messiah, the son of David. It is found in Jewish sources of the time (Psalms of Solomon 17) and is even more frequently mentioned in the New Testament.[50] There, the son of David seems to appear as the most attractive alternative to earthly Hellenistic kings in general, and the reality of the decaying kingship of the Herodian dynasty in particular. Thus even if these texts were put in writing after 70 C.E., the vicissitudes of the Herodian dynasty constituted their background. The association with the son of David took people's minds back to King David and his son Solomon and their achievements in Israel's remote past.

It is therefore important to examine briefly how the literature of the time copes with the figures of these two kings. David and Solomon were mentioned in great detail in one document of the first period, *The Kings of Judah,* in which Eupolemus depicted both kings in realistic hues and adapted them to the ideas circulating in his own period.[51] But there are no messianic overtones in his description. This work anticipates the increasing interest in these figures found later, as a result of the Roman conquest in 63 B.C.E. In the second period the appearance of a messianic figure who would emanate from the house of David becomes more frequent in the sources, and is presented in a special manner in these sources (the first text being Psalms of Solomon 17). The Aaronic anointed priest is rarely mentioned (cf. 1 QSa 2:11–17). From the various interpretations of David and Solomon a great deal can be learned about what people at the time thought of kingship. Two questions are in order: Why was the messianic figure associated with David? And as the Messiah figure was associated with the present and the future both in Christianity and Judaism, why do both religions look back to the past in their desire to welcome the *eschaton* (end of the days)?

David and Solomon were the most important national figures in Israel's past. They were Jewish kings in their own right and held Jewish sovereignty over the whole Land, subjugating all foreigners in it and even some outside it. David conquered Jerusalem, defeating the Jebusites, and Solomon built the Temple. During their reigns the Israelite kingdom was united; it was in fact the only time in Jewish history that the word "Israelites" referred in real terms to the whole nation settled in the Land.[52] No meaningful Israelite Diaspora existed then. David founded the first legitimate Israelite dynasty, and in retrospect this was the ideal kingship the Jews had always wanted. The Hasmonean dynasty, by contrast, was negatively viewed during the period under discussion (Psalms of Solomon 17:6 and elsewhere, and the Testament of Moses 5). Also, David is depicted by the scriptures as a poet and a musician, and Solomon is shown as a wise man to whom the whole world looked for advice. Josephus in his *Antiquities* expressed his generation's appreciation of these traits.[53] The Jews and early Christians of the first century C.E.—people who knew and daily remembered their past—could not help thinking in a nostalgic manner about David and Solomon. What they had in their daily life they believed to be merely a mockery of a real king. What then were the associations with the Davidic house to be found in the literature of the second period?

First, in some instances David and Solomon were treated as the final part of the historical process of ancient Israel. They were seen as the climax of this process, as if nothing existed after them (needless to say, it is clear from the Old Testament that a great deal happened subsequent to Solomon's reign). This view is readily apparent in the summaries of Jewish history that appear in Acts 7:1–50 and 13:15–23. Stephen and Paul (in Luke) in their discourses reflect what many Jews at the time thought of their history.[54] There is nothing specifically Christian about the historical part of these discourses. Second, the many psalms attributed to David, as well as the wisdom literature attributed to Solomon, show how popular they probably were in the second period.[55] Moreover, if we examine the picture of the ideal king (the son of David) emerging from Psalms of Solomon 17, we cannot help associating it with the actual deeds of

David and his son. The canticle mentions that the son of David shall be ruler over Israel and will "destroy the unrighteous rulers, to purge Jerusalem from gentiles who trampled her to destruction; in wisdom and in righteousness to drive out the sinners from the inheritance . . . to destroy the unlawful nations with the word of his mouth." He will also gather the holy people and "will distribute them upon the land according to their tribes." It is not accidental that this son of David is later associated with God himself as the Messiah (17:21–46). Third, from Josephus's interpretation of this particular period much can be learned about what Jews of Josephus's intellectual circle thought of David and Solomon already before 70 C.E. Josephus never portrayed them in messianic terms, but nevertheless in David's case he slightly polished history to improve his stature. The Bible attempted to depict David's accession to the throne through his war with Saul in a manner favorable to David. But a careful reader finds, when reading this episode in the Hebrew Bible, that it did not succeed, and Josephus was a careful reader. David emerges from between the lines as a rebel (though he receives God's approval), and Saul is depicted as the real villain. Josephus, who came from an environment that was aware of David's new dimension as a figure whose "son" would be the savior of Israel, smoothed over the biblical stories of his accession and minimized the conflict between David and Saul. He enhanced the latter and showed him in a positive manner in order to depict the creation of the first Jewish kingdom in a better light. In contrast to the biblical tradition, he viewed Solomon as a king who practiced exorcism, but he did not see any messianic overtones in either figure. This portrayal might be interpreted in certain Jewish circles as polemics against those who saw messianic overtones in the son of David of the Bible.[56]

It seems that many Jewish groups at the time wanted to return to Jewish kingship as it was in the days of David and Solomon, and Jewish liturgy of later periods shows this desire very clearly. Thus it is no wonder that some of Jesus' followers identified him with a political figure who would restore the political grandeur of Israel's past. They called him "ben-David." Some of the later redactors also interpreted his role as being "ben-David" when they composed the famous genealogies going back to David.[57] The fact that David and Solomon were in the main associated with politics brought about the opposition to them, however, and the adherence to the more tran-scendental king and the spiritual messiah, not connected with the Davidic house.

Thus, the second aspect of messianism was the transcendental one. For this concept we are almost solely dependent on the New Testament. The belief that Jesus was a Messiah of the spiritual type can be traced back to the Gospels themselves, in which we find many of the current Palestinian traditions.[58] For instance, Matt 20:25–28 shows that there was opposition to the notion of a real king. Jesus said to his disciples, "You know that the rulers of the gentiles (*hoi archontes ton ethnon*) lord it over them, and their great men (*hoi megaloi*) exercise authority over them. It shall not be so among you; but whoever would be great among you must be your servant, and whoever would be first among you must be your slave; even as the Son of man came not to be served but to serve, and to give his life as ransom for many."[59] The locus classicus, however, for the wish to be dissociated from any actual kingship that was connected to the house of David remains Matt 22:41–46: "Now while the Pharisees were gathered together, Jesus asked them a question, saying, "What do you think of the Christ [Messiah]? Whose son is he?" They said to him, "The son of David," and he said to them, "How is it then that David, inspired by the Spirit, calls him Lord, saying, 'The Lord said to my Lord, sit at my right hand, till I put thy enemies under thy feet'? If David thus calls him Lord, how is he his son?" And no one was able to answer him (and cf. the earlier version of Mark 12:35–38, which has in addition, "and the great throng heard him gladly"; and Luke 20:41–44). According to this tradition Jesus dissociates himself publicly from David, who was viewed as a political, nation-alistic king.[60] Another example in which kingship is portrayed in a spiritualistic manner is Matt 25:31–34: "When the Son of Man comes in his glory, and all the angels with him, then he will sit on his glorious throne. Before him will be gathered all the nations. . . . Then the king will say to those at his right hand, Come, O be Blessed of my Father, inherit the kingdom prepared for you from the foun-dation of the world."[61] It is not accidental that when the woman at Bethany anoints Jesus, according to Mark 14:3–9, no son of David is mentioned.[62] Also the passage in Luke 22:24–30 shows that, ac-cording to this particular tradition, kingship is not connected to David's house, and *real* kings are in fact implicitly criticized.[63] In the

Gospel of John this trend is very strong; to give only some examples, in 1:49–50 the son of David is not mentioned, and kingship is associated with the son of God. In 6:15 Jesus escapes when his followers want to crown him king.[64] According to 7:40–43, at least part of the people were against the identification of Jesus with "ben-David" because he was not from Bethlehem: "so there was a division among people over him."[65] In 12:12–19 his entry as king into Jerusalem is described, but the name of "ben-David" is not mentioned (as in Luke 19:28–40, but unlike the parallels in Matt 21:9 and Mark 11:10, "Kingdom of David our Father," which may derive from those who associated him with the son of David).[66] The locus classicus in the Gospel of John is 18:33–40: "My kingship is not of this world."[67] It should be emphasized that according to all of the gospel traditions Jesus himself never claims that he is the son of David. In short, a spiritual messiah was to be dissociated from politics altogether (at the end of the days).

It should be added that Jesus himself, when he speaks of the *basileia tou theou* or the *basileia ton ouranon* (in Hebrew *malkut shamayim,* i.e., the Kingdom of God), in fact speaks in all versions *against* the political idea of the kingdom of the son of David. Without going into the problem of whether Jesus thought that the *basileia* (kingdom) would be established in the future or was already there at the present time, one thing is certain, that Jesus thought neither of the Heavenly Kingdom, nor of himself, in terms of a king with an army, servants, conquests, and territory. He wanted to be some kind of spiritual king, not a physical and political one. In fact, many of his parables and discourses allude to those who will be eligible to enter the Kingdom.[68] Yet Jesus never draws a concrete plan, as the Hellenistic utopists have done, of the "Kingdom of God." He wanted it to remain as vague as possible.

The concept of the son of David no doubt was dangerous inasmuch as pretenders could always use it at will. Who could really examine the genealogy of one or another pretender to see if he was trustworthy? Thus the more cautious people and the ones who were antikingship in its Herodian form were opposed to any king who came from a different house than David's. One can find this concept perhaps in Pseudo-Philo. In contrast to the figure of Saul in Josephus's *Antiquities,* in Pseudo-Philo's *Biblical Antiquities* there is a strong bias against Saul, who is portrayed as a king who appeared "before his time," and who did not come from David's house. The message of this book is that local figures rather than a false king-messiah could help greatly in saving the people of Israel during their clashes with their neighbors in the Land, until the son of David would create a new genuine dynasty. The document was written about 70 C.E.[69]

Yet another nuance can be found in the literature of the second period which is less discernible in the literature of the first. It has already been seen in the *Songs of the Sabbath Sacrifice,* namely, the tension between the heavenly king and earthly ones, the notion of which derives from the Hebrew Bible, and therefore can easily have come from Palestine.[70] As has been seen, the Jews, like non-Jews, thought in dualistic terms. On the one hand was their ideal; on the other, reality. This duality is true of their thoughts on kingship, and will be seen to apply also to their ideas of territory, the Temple, and the army as well. In the Jewish mind there existed a heavenly King who was universal, a-political, a-historical (in the sense of phenomenological history), and a-territorial. He was God, who was a universal entity, but who sometimes had nationalistic aspects. On many occasions it was said that the earthly kings were inferior to the "king of kings," as well as to the heavenly figure of a King, and served him. A constant tension existed between the heavenly King, who was universal and national, and the earthly kings, who represented the actual nations, who reigned in particular territories. The heavenly figure of King (i.e., God) was the true alternative to earthly kingship, which had decayed, and which would cease to exist under the imminent new order. Earthly kingship, as the Jews were experiencing it at the time, was soon to be over. 1 Enoch 46:3–8 expresses this view in a blunt and sharp manner, as does Josephus in his re-telling of 1 Samuel (*Antiquities* 6.35–44, 60–61, and elsewhere).[71] This opposition to actual kingship gave rise in certain circles to the concept of the *basileia tou theou,* "the kingship of God."[72] The association of *melek* with God on the one hand, and the notorious reputation of real Jewish kings of the Herodian dynasty and the Hellenistic environment on the other, can now be seen as the cause of Jesus' ambivalence concerning the term "the son of David."

We come now to Philo of Alexandria, who will be mentioned only briefly.[73] Writing in the Egyptian Diaspora in the first half of the first century C.E., Philo held the view that God was the true king, the shepherd of his people and ruler of the world (*De Agricultura* 51–54; 60–66; *De posteritate Caini* 101: "for because God is the first and sole king of the universe, the road leading to Him, being a king's road, is also naturally called royal").[74] In the Diaspora of Asia Minor the same view prevailed among Jews, as we can perhaps deduce from the Book of Revelation, which reflects views current in the first century C.E. (6; 7:9–17; 19; and passim).[75] Both authors had the vicissitudes of the Roman Empire in mind. Whereas the author of Revelation despises all earthly kings and does not mention any alternative earthly king, Philo's ideal earthly (human) alternative to current bad rulers goes back to the remote past of ancient Israel, to the true "kings" Adam, Melchizedek, Abraham, and Moses, as well as to the ideal statesman, Joseph. Their traits as kings and statesmen are depicted by Philo in keeping with classical and Hellenistic descriptions of kings. The human ruler who surpassed all others according to Philo was Moses (*De Vita Mosis* 1.148–154).

Two points can be made about Philo's views of kingship. First of all, although the Alexandrian philosopher wrote in line with classical and Hellenistic views on kingship, he nevertheless remained within Judaism when he discussed the examples for the true earthly king. He picked the most ancient and important founders of Israel to become his ideal kings. In this way he also acted in accordance with the notion of the "ancestral constitution" in Greek political thought, which means that the older the constitution, the better.[76] Second, Philo did not choose David and Solomon as his ideal kings, and this is not accidental. He instead referred to the *universal* figures in Jewish history, three of whom were associated with Philo's home, Egypt. By and large we can say that Philo had universal ideas of kingship (as well as regarding the territory).

In terms of the concept of kingship, the literature of 63 B.C.E. to 70 C.E. is somewhat different from that of the first period. We have not found in the second period all of the topics present in the first period—for instance, the question of priesthood and kingship, the description of the good earthly king, and the particular "schizophrenic" image of the kings expressed in the *peri basileias* documents. Instead there are different motifs and emphases on certain topics that can be interpreted as a reaction to the gradual demise of kingship as a purely nationalistic symbol of Jewish political and spiritual sovereignty in the Land of Israel. In the literature of the second period some look with nostalgia at the past, while others look to the future and wait for the appearance of the Son of David.[77] Still others think he has already come. Some express more transcendental views of a heavenly king or heavenly kingdom. In the national consciousness the actual *basileia* as a nationalistic symbol was shattered, and was transformed into a more pure, spiritual, and holy symbol a long time before the final destruction of the Temple in 70 C.E. This literary dimension of kingship was apparently more promising than any actual earthly kingship.

Notes

[1] *Orientis graeci inscriptiones selectae* 2.458.17. For these benefactions in a more philosophical manner, see P. Veyne, *Bread and Circuses: Historical Sociology and Political Pluralism* (London, 1990), pp. 347–377.

[2] *Orientis graeci inscriptiones selectae* 2.668.5. Cf. A. D. Nock, *Essays in Religion and the Ancient World*, ed. Z. Stewart (Cambridge, Mass., 1972), 2.720–735. In general, for the *apotheosis* (divinity) of the Roman emperors, see L. M. Sweet, *Roman Emperor Worship* (Boston, 1919); L. R. Taylor, *The Divinity of the Roman Emperor* (Middletown, Conn., 1931); and in general some interesting ideas concerning this issue in A. D. Momigliano, "How Roman Emperors Became Gods," in his *On Pagans, Jews, and Christians* (Middletown, Conn., 1987), pp. 92–107; and S. Weinstock, *Divus Julius* (Oxford, 1971); S. R. F. Price, *Rituals and Power: The Roman Imperial Cult in Asia Minor* (Cambridge and Sydney, 1984).

[3] See P. Zanker, *The Power of Images in the Age of Augustus* (Ann Arbor, Mich., 1988), passim; also R. Mellor, *Thea Roma: The Worship of the Goddess Roma in the Greek World* (Göttingen, 1975), for the worship of Roma and Augustus in Judea after the battle of Actium, pp. 94–95.

[4] For client kings see D. Braund, *Rome and the Friendly King* (London, 1984), passim (his description, however, is mostly based on Herod's rule in Judea). The client king was usually called a *philoromaios*. There was no contradiction between his being a "friend of Rome" and his local deification: see, for instance, the client king of Commagene, in S. M. Burstein, *The Hellenistic Age from the Battle of Ipsos to the Death of Kleopatra VII* (Cambridge, 1985), pp. 63–66. In general for these dynasties see R. D. Sullivan, *Near Eastern Royalty and Rome, 100–30 B.C.* (Toronto and London, 1990).

[5] For the relations of the Hasmoneans with the Romans, see in general T. Fischer, "Rom und die Hasmonäer, Ein Überblick zu den politischen Beziehungen 164–37 v. Chr.," *Gymnasium* 88 (1981): 139–150. For this particular episode see A. Schalit, in M. Avi-Yonah and Z. Baras, "The Herodian Period," *The World History of the Jewish People* (New Brunswick, N.J., 1975), 7.30–33.

[6] See A. D. Momigliano, *Alien Wisdom: The Limits of Hellenization* (Cambridge, 1975), pp. 83–84; D. Mendels, "Hecataeus of Abdera and a Jewish 'Patrios Politeia' of the Persian Period (Diodorus Siculus XL,3)," *Zeitschrift für alttestamentliche Wissenschaft* 95 (1983): 96–110. In the first century c.e. we have a nice parallel from Commagene and Cilicia; after the death of their kings, many wanted to be ruled by Rome, while others preferred the rule of kings (Tacitus, *Annals* 2.42).

[7] Cf. M. Hengel, *The "Hellenization" of Judaea in the First Century after Christ* (Philadelphia, 1989), passim for this role. It is very likely that Jews from Palestine did not serve in the Roman army and did not play a significant role in higher Roman civil institutions. Cf. G. W. Bowersock, "Roman Senators from the Near East: Syria, Judaea, Arabia, Mesopotamia," *Tituli* 5 (1982): 651–668; and

H. Devijver, "Equestrian Officers from the East," in *The Defence of the Roman and Byzantine East,* ed. P. Freeman and D. Kennedy (Oxford, 1986), 1.109–225.

[8] For Antigonus's short-lived rule in Judea see E. Schürer, *The History of the Jewish People in the Age of Jesus Christ,* rev. G. Vermes et al. (Edinburgh, 1973–1987), 1.281–286. For Antigonus and Parthia, see U. Rappaport, "The Jews Between Rome and Parthia," in *The Eastern Frontier of the Roman Empire,* ed. D. H. French and C. S. Lightfoot (Oxford, 1989), pp. 376–377.

[9] Cf. W. W. Bühler, "The Pre-Herodian Civil War and Social Debate," Ph.D. diss., Basel, 1974. For the general background, see R. Syme, *The Roman Revolution* (Oxford, 1939), chaps. 14–18.

[10] It is interesting to note that Antigonus was the first Hasmonean to mint coins that had the symbol of the menorah (and table), which may have symbolized the Temple. The reason may be that he was the first Hasmonean to be challenged by a rival king who was not from the Hasmonean house. This non-Hasmonean claimant was supported by Rome. Taking the offensive, Antigonus used the menorah, which was associated with the most obvious of the national symbols for the Jews at the time. In general for Mattathias Antigonus's coins, see Y. Meshorer, *Ancient Jewish Coinage* (New York, 1982), 1.87–97.

[11] This aim is also reflected in his coinage. In the undated coinage that was minted between 37 and 4 B.C.E., some of the Hasmonean coin-symbols appear, such as the anchor, the diadem (used before by Alexander Jannaeus), the double cornucopias (used by Hasmonean kings), and the table (used by Mattathias Antigonus). If Herod had wanted to dissociate himself completely from the Hasmoneans, he could easily have found other symbols that were not reminiscent of this dynasty. Cf. in general Meshorer, *Ancient Jewish Coinage,* 2.12–13, 22–30.

[12] The secondary literature on Herod the Great abounds. A very useful account is A. Schalit, *König Herodes: Der Mann und Sein Werk* (Berlin, 1969); see also Schürer, *History,* 1.287–329, and U. Baumann, *Rom und die Juden. Die römisch-jüdischen Beziehungen von Pompeius bis zum Tode des Herodes (63 v.Chr.–4 v.Chr.)* (Frankfurt am Main, 1983).

[13] He apparently had a great deal of support even after the conquest of Jerusalem by Herod (*Antiquities* 15.8–10).

[14] Cf. already 15.18–22; *Jewish War* 1.434: Hyrcanus "roused Herod's resentment not only by making claims to the throne but because the kingship belonged to him (by right)."

[15] *Antiquities* 15.165–178. See Schürer, *History,* 1.301.

[16] *Antiquities* 17.82. In general, for his family relationships, see K. C. Hanson, "The Herodians and Mediterranean Kinship," *Biblical Theology Bulletin* 19 (1989):75–84, 142–151; 20 (1990):10–21.

[17] For the political history of the Idumaeans at the time, see A. Kasher, *Jews, Idumaeans and Ancient Arabs* (Tübingen, 1988), pp. 126–174.

[18] This dichotomy is also reflected in his coinage. Of the dated coinage, which was apparently minted at the beginning of his reign, five of the seven symbols depicted on them, such as the apex, the tripod, and the winged caduceus, are found on Roman republican coins. The greater bulk of his coinage is undated and was minted after 37 B.C.E. Herod, unlike the Hasmoneans, inscribed his title (*basileus*) as well as his name only in Greek. By contrast, he did not (like the Hasmoneans) have any human features on his coins. Also, some of the symbols that appear on his coins are similar to those used on Hasmonean coins (see note 11 above). Others have symbols that were "harmless" in the eyes of pious Jews (such as the palm branch, the vine, and the galley). The eagle, appearing on one Herodian coin type, may have been problematic, as it may have referred to the eagle put on the Temple gate. For Herod's coinage see Meshorer, *Ancient Jewish Coinage*, 2.5–30. Cf. for a different interpretation D. M. Jacobson, "A New Interpretation of the Reverse of Herod's Largest Coin," *The American Numismatic Society Museum Notes* 31 (1986): 145–165. For various aspects of Herod's Hellenism see Hengel, *Hellenization*, passim, and R. Hachlili, *Ancient Jewish Art and Archaeology in the Land of Israel* (Leiden, 1988), pp. 11–83.

[19] For the archaeology of Herod's time see in particular D. M. Jacobson, "The Design of the Fortress of Herodium," *Zeitschrift des deutschen Palästina-Vereins* 100 (1984): 127–136; A. N. Barghouti, "Urbanization of Palestine and Jordan in Hellenistic and Roman Times," in *Studies in the History and Archaeology of Jordan*, ed. A. Hadidi (Amman, 1982), 1.209–229; and H. P. Kuhnen, *Palästina in Griechisch-Römischer Zeit* (Munich, 1990), chaps. 2–3.

[20] For Caesarea see in particular L. I. Levine, *Caesarea under Roman Rule* (Leiden, 1975), and K. G. Holum et al., *King Herod's Dream: Caesarea on the Sea* (New York and London, 1988).

[21] *Antiquities* 15.365–379, and cf. also 16.12–26.

[22] E. Netzer et al., "Herod's Building Projects: State Necessity or Personal Need?" *The Jerusalem Cathedra* 1 (1981): 48–80; Hengel, *Hellenization*, passim. Cf. also D. M. Jacobson, "King Herod's 'Heroic' Public Image," *Revue biblique* 95 (1988): 386–403; E. Netzer, "Jericho and Herodium . . . ," *Judaica* 45 (1989): 21–44.

[23] *Antiquities* 15.281. This unrest anticipates the Fourth Philosophy movement.

[24] For Nicolaus in general see B. Z. Wacholder, *Nicolaus of Damascus* (Berkeley, 1962).

[25] The strongest support for his rule came from the pagans of Palestine, his army (which was at least half gentile), Idumaeans, his military strongholds, and Diaspora (liberal) Jews: so the real base for his rule was external rather than internal (i.e., not from the Jewish masses at large).

[26] Cf. *Antiquities* 16.30–57—Nicolaus before Agrippa: there is no Jewish history mentioned in the discourses; in 16.62–65, 73 Herod also makes a presentation

before an *ecclesia* of the *hoi polloi*. For the wine amphoras, see H. M. Cotton and J. Geiger, "Wine for Herod," *Cathedra* 53 (1989): 3–12 (Hebrew).

[27] D. J. Ladouceur, "The Death of Herod the Great," *Classical Philology* 76 (1981): 25–34; P. M. Bernegger, "Affirmation of Herod's Death in 4 B.C.," *Journal of Theological Studies* 34 (1983): 526–531.

[28] L. I. Levine, "From the Beginning of Roman Rule until 74 C.E.," in *The History of Eretz Israel,* ed. M. Stern (Jerusalem, 1984), 4.46–63 (esp. p. 63). See also D. R. Schwartz, "Herod in the Jewish Sources," in *King Herod and His Age,* ed. M. Naor (Jerusalem, 1985), pp. 38–42 (Hebrew).

[29] *Jewish War* 2.93–94; *Antiquities* 17.317; Meshorer, *Ancient Jewish Coinage,* 2.31–50.

[30] *Antiquities* 17.269–285, 324–338; *Jewish War* 2.55–65, 101–110; E. Paltiel, "War in Judaea—After Herod's Death," *Revue belge de philologie et d' histoire* 59 (1981): 107–136. For examples of pretenders in the Hellenistic world, see D. Mendels, "Pseudo-Philo's *Biblical Antiquities,* the 'Fourth Philosophy' and the Political Messianism of the First Century A.D.," in *The Messiah,* ed. J. H. Charlesworth (Minneapolis, 1992), n. 28.

[31] In their coinage they kept in line with Herod's principles and, except for Philip, did not depict human images. Philip, however (whose subjects were non-Jews), put his own face and that of Augustus and Tiberius on his coins. Cf. Meshorer, *Ancient Jewish Coinage,* 2.42–50. See also Schürer, *History,* 2.13–14.

[32] See for the high priesthood in general Schürer, *History,* 2.227–313 (and Appendix), and M. D. Goodman, *The Ruling Class of Judaea* (Cambridge, 1987), passim.

[33] And perhaps also with Julias (*Jewish War* 2.168). Recently for his coinage see A. Kindler, "Philippus, Son of Herod I, and the Renaming of Bethsaida/Julias," *Cathedra* 53 (1989): 24–26 (Hebrew).

[34] Cf. Hanson, "The Herodians," and J. Seibert, *Historische Beiträge zu den dynastischen Verbindungen in hellenistischer Zeit* (Wiesbaden, 1967).

[35] *Jewish War* 2.181; *Antiquities* 18.237; for Caligula's rule in general see A. A. Barrett, *Caligula: The Corruption of Power* (New Haven and London, 1989).

[36] *Antiquities* 18.240–256; *Jewish War* 2.182–183; they could be deposed any time. Cf. Braund, *Rome and the Friendly King,* passim. See also Sullivan, *Near Eastern Royalty,* passim.

[37] D. R. Schwartz, *Agrippa I: The Last King of Judaea* (Tübingen, 1990). See also E. M. Smallwood, *The Jews under Roman Rule* (Leiden, 1976), pp. 187–200.

[38] Ibid., pp. 140–144.

[39] We know of only two leaders who were persecuted, James and Peter, who were two of the more extreme ones (ibid., pp. 119–124). Agrippa may have re-

sented the early Christian group because they started to evangelize among non-Jews, which stirred up the delicate status quo between the non-Jews and Jews, the two parts of the population who were normally separate from each other.

[40] Ibid., pp. 111–112.

[41] See for instance how Agrippa makes the distinction between the Greek (or foreign) cities in Palestine and the Jewish ones. The "schizophrenia" is very much evident in his coinage. Many of the coins bear his own portrait together with other features, such as personified Friendship (Philia) and Alliance (Symachia), as well as a temple. By contrast, the coins he struck in Jerusalem (for his Jewish population) had none of these traits. These coins (bronze prutot), which were apparently very popular, are in line with Jewish Law; they bear three ears of grain, and on their other side a canopy and the name of the king (although they bear the date "year 6," which is 42 C.E., they were probably minted over a longer period). All of the coins bear inscriptions in Greek. Only the prutot were minted in Jerusalem, whereas all his other "gentile" series (on which his portrait usually appeared) came from mints all over the country. For his coinage see Meshorer, *Ancient Jewish Coinage*, 2.51–64.

[42] *Antiquities* 19.335–338; and cf. Schwartz, *Agrippa*, pp. 130–132; and Schürer, *History*, 2.311–313.

[43] *Antiquities* 19.338–342; and cf. Schwartz, *Agrippa*, pp. 137–140.

[44] The frustration may have been even greater because Agrippa I may have had the intention of establishing a dynasty. Evidence of this plan can be seen in one series of his coins minted in 38 C.E.: on one side of the coin the young son of the king appears on horseback with the inscription "Agrippa son of the king." For these coins see Meshorer, *Ancient Jewish Coinage*, 2.51–52 and 54–55. S. G. F. Brandon (quoting E. Stapfer, *La Palestine au temps de Jésus Christ* [Paris 1885], p. 85) says, in *Jesus and the Zealots* (Manchester, 1967), p. 99: "In retrospect, it would seem that the brief interlude of Agrippa's reign served only to make the Jews more bitterly conscious of the ignominy of their position as a subject people, and so to render more certain and more fatal their eventual revolt."

[45] For Agrippa II, see D. R. Schwartz, "*Kata touton ton Kairon*: Josephus' Source on Agrippa II," *Jewish Quarterly Review* 72 (1982): 241–268.

[46] Unlike R. A. Horsley's attempt in his "Menahem in Jerusalem: A Brief Messianic Episode among the Sicarii not 'Zealot Messianism,'" *Novum Testamentum* 27 (1985): 334–348.

[47] It should again be emphasized that no Jewish king either in the Hasmonean period or during the first century C.E. had messianic pretensions, or was regarded as a messiah.

[48] It no doubt had to do with the events, shameful in the eyes of the Jews in Rome, that occurred in Palestine in 4 B.C.E. The Diaspora Jews usually were much more proud of their "kingdom" in Palestine when things went along well and the

Palestinian Jews brought grandeur to world Jewry (as in the forties of the first century B.C.E.), than in bad years, when they tried to dissociate themselves from Palestinian Judaism.

[49] The literature of the first period avoids savior figures, though one can find them there. But they have little in common with kings and messianic kings or spiritual messiahs. It is not accidental that the messiah of the house of David is not mentioned at all in First and Second Maccabees, as well as in other literature of the second century B.C.E. Cf. for other views G. W. E. Nickelsburg, "Salvation without and with a Messiah: Developing Beliefs in Writings Ascribed to Enoch," in *Judaisms and Their Messiahs at the Turn of the Christian Era,* ed. J. Neusner et al. (Cambridge, 1987), pp. 49–68; J. A. Goldstein, "How the Authors of 1 and 2 Maccabees Treated the 'Messianic' Promises," ibid., pp. 69–96; J. J. Collins, "Messianism in the Maccabean Period," ibid., pp. 97–119.

[50] If the Gospel of John 7:37–44 really reflects what Jews thought at the time, then there is also evidence about the "Jewish" side. For messianism in this time see two major collections: J. Neusner et al., *Judaisms;* and J. H. Charlesworth, *The Messiah.*

[51] Cf. D. Mendels, *The Land of Israel as a Political Concept in Hasmonean Literature* (Tübingen, 1987), chap. 4.

[52] This is one of the reasons that Paul, in accordance with Jewish sources, defines himself as an Israelite rather than a "Jew" (Rom 11:1, with 2 Cor 11:22 and Gal 1:13–14), a term that came into wide use only in the Second Temple period. For Paul's "nationalism," see W. D. Davies, *Paul and Rabbinic Judaism,* 2d ed. (London, 1965), pp. 58–85. One may say that Paul was an a-nationalist in the sense discussed in this book. This is due in particular to his mission to the gentiles. For this mission see J. Becker, *Paulus Der Apostel der Völker* (Tübingen, 1989).

[53] Cf. his interpretation of these figures as well as L. H. Feldman, "Josephus' Portrait of David," *Hebrew Union College Annual* 60 (1989): 129–174.

[54] For these discourses, see in general H. Conzelmann, *Acts,*† pp. XLIII–XLV. See also Hebrews 11.

[55] Cf. 11QPs^a (ed. J. A. Sanders, *Discoveries in the Judaean Desert,* vol. 4), and J. H. Charlesworth and E. P. Sanders, "More Psalms of David," in *Old Testament Pseudepigrapha,* ed. J. H. Charlesworth (New York, 1983–1985), 2.609–624 (they are probably from the first century C.E.).

[56] Cf. Feldman, "Josephus' Portrait."

[57] Cf. Matt 1:1–17; Luke 3:23–38. Although they differ greatly, they both contain David (among some others) in their genealogy. In Luke he is a son of David but is not of a Davidic descent. For a discussion see J. A. Fitzmyer, *Luke,** 1.488–505.

[58] See in particular W. Wrede, *Jesus als Davidssohn* (Tübingen, 1907) pp. 147–177; G. Hölscher, *Urgemeinde und Spätjudentum* (Oslo, 1928), p. 9; and R. Bultmann, *The History of the Synoptic Tradition* (Oxford, 1963), pp. 136–137.

Cf. also J. Klausner, *Jesus of Nazareth* (New York, 1926), passim; C. Burger, *Jesus als Davidssohn* (Göttingen, 1970); and Mendels, "Pseudo-Philo's *Biblical Antiquities.*" For a general overview of messianism during this period see Schürer, *History,* 2.488–554.

⁵⁹ And cf. Mark 10:35–45. This is Jesus' reaction to the request of the mother of Zebedee's sons that they will be seated on the right and left hands of Jesus in his "Kingdom" (*basileia;* Mark has "Glory"). Cf. in general Albright and Mann, *Matthew,** pp. 241–247.

⁶⁰ Cf. for this question also (in addition to n. 58 above) J. A. Fitzmyer, "The Son of David Tradition and Mt 22:41–46 and Parallels," in *Essays on the Semitic Background of the New Testament* (London, 1971), pp. 113–126; also Mendels, "Pseudo-Philo's *Biblical Antiquities.*"

⁶¹ Cf. also Matt 28:18. First we hear about the Son of Man, and then the same person becomes king. For this whole section, cf. Albright and Mann, *Matthew,** pp. 306–310. For the Son of Man in general, see J. D. Dunn, *Christology in the Making* (Philadelphia, 1980), pp. 65–97.

⁶² Whereas Luke and John describe only an anointing of the feet, Matthew and Mark relate an anointing of the head, which is a sign of royal (and priestly) installation in office (as in 2 Kgs 9:3; 1 Sam 10:1; Ps 133:2). Cf. Mann, *Mark,** p. 555 and cf. his comments on pp. 555–559. It is important to note that none of the four versions of the story mentions this act in association with kingship. Cf. also Luke 7:36–50 with Fitzmyer's very useful remarks in *Luke,** 1.684–694. And Luke 17:20–21: the kingdom of God is meant spiritually here; cf. the commentary of Fitzmyer, *Luke,** 2.1157–1163.

⁶³ Cf. in general Fitzmyer's comments in *Luke,** 2.1411–1420. When Jesus says that "those in authority" (i.e., kings) call themselves "benefactors" (using *euergetes*), he refers to actual Hellenistic kings who were called thus in inscriptions (Fitzmyer, *Luke,** 2.1417 mentions only Roman emperors, but these titles go back to Hellenistic kings).

⁶⁴ And see the comments of Brown, *John I–XII,** pp. 234–235, 249–250. The association in these verses (14–15) between prophet and king is problematic.

⁶⁵ And cf. ibid., pp. 329–330.

⁶⁶ And cf. ibid., pp. 455–464.

⁶⁷ And cf. Brown, *John XIII–XXI,** pp. 843–872. For further bibliography see G. van Belle, *Johannine Bibliography 1966–1985,* Bibliotheca ephemeridum theologicarum lovaniensium 82 (Louvain, 1988), pp. 292–294. Also the Son of Man is dissociated from a political figure. There is no need to claim that the Son of Man traditions in the Gospels are post-Easter (for earlier Jewish traditions concerning the Son of Man see 1 Enoch 45:1–6 and 46:3–7, 51:3–4).

⁶⁸ Cf. for instance Matthew 5–7; 18; 19:23–24; 25 and parallels (there is no description of the "kingdom" to be found). It is not necessary here to enter the

theological speculation about the concept of *basileia tou theou* (or *ton ouranon*), and whether according to Jesus it had already arrived or would arrive in the future. It is sufficient to note that the term is very clearly set against any concept of the real *basileia*. For the more theological discussions on the *basileia tou theou* see for instance D. Hill, "Towards an Understanding of the 'Kingdom of God,' " *Irish Biblical Studies* 3 (1981): 62–76; J. H. Charlesworth, "The Historical Jesus in Light of Writings Contemporaneous with Him," *Aufstieg und Niedergang der römischen Welt* 2.25.1 (1982): 451–476; H. Merklein, *Jesu Botschaft von der Gottesherrschaft. Eine Skizze* (Stuttgart, 1983); H. Schürmann, *Gottes Reich-Jesu Geschick: Jesu ureigener Tod im Licht seiner Basileia-Verkündigung* (Fribourg, Basel, and Vienna, 1983); O. Camponovo, *Königtum, Königsherrschaft und Reich Gottes in den frühjüdischen Schriften* (Göttingen, 1984); B. D. Chilton, *The Kingdom of God in the Teaching of Jesus* (Philadelphia, 1984); D. C. Duling, "Norman Perrin and the Kingdom of God: Review and Response," *Journal of Religion* 64 (1984): 468–483; G. R. Beasley-Murray, *Jesus and the Kingdom of God* (Grand Rapids, Mich., 1986); J. Marcus, *The Mystery of the Kingdom of God* (Atlanta, 1986); H. M. Evans, "Current Exegesis on the Kingdom of God," *Perspectives on Religious Studies* 14 (1987): 67–77; W. W. Willis, ed., *The Kingdom of God in 20th-Century Interpretation* (Peabody, Mass., 1987).

For the question of whether the Kingdom is already present (in time) or will come in the future, see in particular C. H. Dodd, *The Parables of the Kingdom* (London, 1961; orig. 1935); W. G. Kümmel, *Promise and Fulfillment: The Eschatological Message of Jesus*, 2d Eng. ed. (London, 1961); G. Lundström, *The Kingdom of God in the Teaching of Jesus: A History of Interpretation from the Last Decades of the Nineteenth Century to the Present Day* (Edinburgh and London, 1963); N. Perrin, *The Kingdom of God in the Teaching of Jesus* (Philadelphia, 1963); R. H. Hiers, *The Kingdom of God in the Synoptic Tradition* (Gainesville, Fla., 1970); idem, *The Historical Jesus and the Kingdom of God: Present and Future in the Message and Ministry of Jesus* (Gainesville, Fla., 1973); N. Perrin, *Jesus and the Language of the Kingdom: Symbol and Metaphor in New Testament Interpretation* (Philadelphia, 1976); C. Sullivan, *Rethinking Realized Eschatology* (Macon, Ga., 1988).

Recently R. A. Horsley (*Jesus and the Spiral of Violence: Popular Jewish Resistance in Roman Palestine* [San Francisco, 1987], pp. 149–326) revived the theory that *basileia tou theou* is a concrete kind of kingdom. Thus he argues that Jesus, like the Fourth Philosophy people, was a revolutionary and had concrete socioeconomic and political plans (and see also S. Freyne, *Galilee, Jesus, and the Gospels* [Philadelphia, 1988], pp. 244–245). He was even crowned as king, and the claim of the Jews that he was king was indeed justifiable. This position goes, I believe, against the evidence. For a more balanced view, see E. P. Sanders, *Jesus and Judaism* (London, 1985), pp. 228–237. He argues that "Jesus thought of 'the kingdom' in two ways and never brought the two into a systematic relationship." The "Kingdom of God," as Bultmann said many years ago—and this is confirmed by biblical material—is "that eschatological deliverance which ends everything earthly. . . . It is wholly supernatural . . . whoever seeks it must realize that he cuts himself off from the world" (R. Bultmann, *Jesus and the World* [London, 1934], pp. 35–37). This view constituted the difference between Jesus and the Zealots. Utopias of the Hellenistic East always gave a concrete plan of their visions, but Jesus did not, because he did not want to be concrete. It should be noted that the "Kingdom of God" should be examined against the background of Hellenistic Palestine, and not for instance against the background of Babylonian kingship of the era before Alexander the Great. I am grateful to Professor Joel Marcus for the valuable discussions we had on this matter.

[69] Cf. Mendels, "Pseudo-Philo's *Biblical Antiquities.*"

[70] Cf. for instance Psalm 47, and I. L. Seeligmann, "Psalm 47," *Tarbiz* 50 (1981): 25–36 (Hebrew); and in general H. J. Kraus, *Die Königsherrschaft Gottes im Alten Testament: Untersuchungen zu den Liedern von Jahwes Thronbesteigung* (Tübingen, 1951); F. M. Cross, *Canaanite Myth and Hebrew Epic* (Cambridge, Mass., 1973), pp. 91–111; J. Gray, *The Biblical Doctrine of the Reign of God* (Edinburgh, 1979); *The Quest for the Kingdom of God: Studies in Honor of George E. Mendenhall,* ed. H. B. Huffmon et al. (Winona Lake, 1983); J. Jeremias, *Das Königtum Gottes in den Psalmen: Israels Begegnung mit den Kanaannäischen Mythos in den Jahwe-König-Psalmen* (Göttingen, 1987); cf. also M. Weinfeld, "The Day of the Lord: Aspirations for the Kingdom of God in the Bible and Jewish Liturgy," *Scripta Hierosolymitana* 31 (1986): 341–372.

[71] He applies to his history the concept of *metabole* (cf. his "kingship" in *Antiquities* 6.83–85), and D. R. Schwartz, "Josephus on the Jewish Constitutions and Community," *Scripta classica israelica* 7 (1983–1984): 30–52. In *Antiquities* 6.165 he uses terminology reminiscent of the expressions used in the Temple Scroll, in the section dealing with kingship. Cf. also 6.340–350.

[72] For a good survey of the "kingdom of God" in reference to the Fourth Philosophy group, see M. Hengel, *The Zealots* (Edinburgh, 1989), pp. 76–145; however, the rabbinic sources referred to by Hengel may be too late to be considered sources for pre-70 Judaism. For Paul's understanding of the kingdom, see C. E. Hill, "Paul's Understanding of Christ's Kingdom in 1 Cor 15:20–28," *Novum Testamentum* 30.4 (1988): 279–320.

[73] In general for Philo's political thought see E. R. Goodenough, *The Politics of Philo Judaeus: Practice and Theory* (New Haven, 1938; repr. Hildesheim, 1967); S. Sandmel, *Philo of Alexandria: An Introduction* (New York and Oxford, 1979); and in general for Philo, see Schürer, *History,* 3.2.809–889; and Y. Amir, *Die hellenistische Gestalt des Judentums bei Philon von Alexandrien* (Neukirchen, 1983).

[74] For kingship in Philo see R. Barraclough, "Philo's Politics," *Aufstieg und Niedergang der römischen Welt* 2.21.1 (1984): 486–533; S. Sandmel, "Philo: The Man, His Writings, His Significance," ibid., pp. 28–30; G. F. Chesnut, "The Ruler and the Logos in Neopythagorean, Middle Platonic and Late Stoic Political Philosophy," ibid. 2.16.2 (1978): 1310–1332.

[75] For these complex issues, see Ford, *Revelation,** ad loc. For Asia Minor as the book's provenance see, with the older literature, J. P. M. Sweet, *Revelation,* 2d

ed. (London, 1990); M. E. Boring, *Revelation* (Louisville, Ky., 1989), and in particular L. L. Thompson, *The Book of Revelation* (New York and Oxford, 1990), who
dates the book under Domitian. Interestingly, in two of the three instances in which
David is mentioned in Revelation, he is associated with the "root" (*riza*) rather than
with the "son of" (in 5:5; 22:16).

[76] Cf. D. Mendels, "Polybius, Cleomenes III and Sparta's *Patrios Politeia*," *La
Parola del passato* 180 (1978): 161–166; and idem, *The Land of Israel as a Political
Concept in Hasmonean Literature* (Tübingen, 1987), p. 85, for the concept of the
ancestral constitution.

[77] For the "pre-history" of messianism, see now J. J. Collins, *The Scepter and
the Star: The Messiahs of the Dead Sea Scrolls and Other Ancient Literature* (New
York-Auckland, 1995).

CHAPTER 9

From the Territorial to the A-Territorial (after the Roman Occupation)

This chapter addresses the next stage of the territorial dimension, from 63 B.C.E. to the Bar Kokhba rebellion (132–135 C.E.). Two different attitudes about territory after the Roman occupation of Palestine can be traced. The first may be described as a drastic change toward the idea of territory in its political and national dimensions, which occurred as a result of the Roman conquest of 63 B.C.E. Much of the literature of this period reflects a more amorphous idea of the Land. The Land somehow vanished as an important issue, in a reaction to the loss of Jewish independence and to Palestine's gradual transformation into a more pagan territory during the reign of Herod the Great and his successors.

The second attitude was the one that throughout the Roman occupation of Palestine, did not give up the Land as a symbol of political nationalism. The proponents of this view fiercely opposed the Roman concept of a united Roman ecumene (which, of course, included Palestine at the time), and went to war in 66 C.E. in order to free their territory from Roman domination. Let us first look briefly at some of the Roman views concerning the territorial dimension of the empire and how they clashed with the local nationalistic feelings of the Jews.

During the second century B.C.E. the Romans may have already thought that they would become the masters of the world. W. V. Harris has convincingly shown that this wish was expressed both in religious and in secular texts of the time. Indeed, one century later they were the lords of the whole Mediterranean basin. The Romans believed that the empire was given to them by their gods. Thus they turned to them—in particular to Victoria, Mars, Jupiter, and Hercules—when they desired further expansion (or when they achieved it). Inscriptions that were set up by the greatest of Roman generals before 129 B.C.E. read, according to Cicero's evidence in *De republica*, "finis imperii propagavit" (he expanded the borders of the empire). We hear from Plutarch that in the second century B.C.E. many Romans thought that they were "the masters of the whole world" (*Tiberius Gracchus* 9.6). At some point between 86 and 82 B.C.E. the *Rhetorica ad Herennium* was composed, in which is found the saying "imperium orbis terrae" (rule over the whole earth, 4.9.13). Pompey, the great conqueror of the East, says in a famous inscription placed in Rome in 61 B.C.E., "Pompey the Great, son of Gnaeus, Imperator, having liberated the seacoast of the inhabited world and all the islands this side of the Ocean from the war with the pirates [a list of his achievements follows in the inscription] extended the frontiers of the empire to the limits of the earth" (Diodorus Siculus 40.4). Alongside these assertions, there were voices raised in opposition to imperialistic expansion. Sallust in the first century B.C.E. says about Lucullus that he was distinguished in everything, except for his extreme desire to extend the empire (*Histories* 4.70). The latter view was never taken seriously by most of the Roman aristocracy.[1]

To this picture one can add the emphasis in Rome on the worship of Hercules, the Greek Heracles, which can be associated with the myth of Heracles' wanderings around the Mediterranean basin.[2] Matris of Thebes in the third century B.C.E. wrote a book on Heracles' journeys that was still known to Diodorus Siculus in the first century B.C.E. It is perhaps not accidental that the Roman Empire emerging at the beginning of Augustus's reign (30 B.C.E.) corresponded in many of its parts to Heracles' picture of the world according to Diodorus. This myth remained popular throughout the centuries, and was probably adapted during the time of Diodorus Siculus by Greeks, or by the Romans themselves, to the actual conquests of Rome and its imperialistic desires.[3] Heracles as a world conqueror remained popular in the first century C.E., as we learn for instance from Dio Chrysostomus at the beginning of the second century. In his first discourse *On Kingship* he comments that Heracles "was not only king of Greece, but also exercised dominion over every land from the rising of the sun to the setting thereof, aye, over all peoples where are found shrines of Heracles" (1.60–61). Moreover, stoic and cynic ideas about a worldly rule were prevalent from the early Hellenistic period, perhaps Zeno of Citium, to the second century c.e. and later (Dio Chrysostomus, *On Kingship* 1).

Augustus gave an exact limit to the empire. During the reign of his successors in the first century c.e., some additional territories were grafted by conquest onto the "Heraclean" world, as we know it from Diodorus Siculus, book 4.8–39 (cf. map page 407 for the perimeter of the Roman Empire during Augustus's time). Even when Trajan made extensive annexations in the far east of the empire, it is interesting that his successor Hadrian abandoned most of them, for instance, all territories east of the Euphrates.[4] Already in the middle of the first century b.c.e. Vergil presents the idea that Rome's dominion over the world is the will of heaven.[5] It should be stressed that Rome's motivations for conquest and expansion were numerous, and they received varied emphasis during the two centuries of extensive expansion (from the conquest of Sardinia in 238 b.c.e. to the annexation of Egypt in 30 b.c.e.). The motivations include an economic urge, defensive as well as offensive considerations, the private initiatives of Roman generals in the field, and the Roman ethos of "Gloria" and "Virtus."[6] The Romans were very practical in their imperialistic outlook, so it is doubtful whether the Roman Senate or the Roman generals in the field really wished to compete with mythological figures like Heracles, or the eastern wandering gods Osiris, Sesostris, and Semiramis. These myths were in the background, lying quietly behind the historical scene, and probably were known to the great Roman imperialists.[7]

Against the grand scenery of the territorial concepts of the Roman Empire, one may view the ancient Near East and survey the historical development that led to the various concepts of the Land as a nationalistic symbol. But first one should ask: How did people in the East view Rome's might? It depended on one's experience. The author of 1 Maccabees 8, who apparently did not have a bad experience with the Romans in the second century b.c.e., praises them. So does Agrippa II, who was a client king in the middle of the first century c.e. By contrast, Mithridates VI, who was defeated by them, complains according to Sallust that "the Romans have one inveterate motive for making war upon all nations, peoples and kings; namely, a deep-seated desire for dominion and for riches" (*Epistula Mithridatis* 5). Certain views coming from Jewish circles denigrated them; some thought they were the rod of God to punish the Jews for their wayward deeds.[8]

The conquest of the Land by Rome in 63 B.C.E. was a shock to the Jews and resulted in a swift and complete break with previous concepts of territoriality. True, Palestine suffered many times during the Hasmonean period from invasions by foreign armies, but the sovereignty of the Land was always restored. Alexander Jannaeus (103–76 B.C.E.) conquered most of the land on both sides of the Jordan valley. But between 67 and 63 B.C.E., a civil war between his two sons harshly divided the Land of Israel for the first time (*Antiquities* 13.425–428; *Jewish War* 1.117–118). Thus, in less than ten years after Alexander Jannaeus's death, the Land was divided and a foreign people, the Arabs (and Idumaeans), backed Hyrcanus II in the war against his brother, Aristobulus II. This division contributed to the eventual conquest of Palestine by Rome. The latter made territorial arrangements that led Josephus to make an unusually emotional outburst over the loss of the Land: "For we lost our freedom and became subject to the Romans, and the territory (*chora*) that we had gained by our arms and taken from the Syrians we were compelled to give back to them" (*Antiquities* 14.77). From then on the Romans treated the Land as owners would—they divided it, exploited it, and curtailed the freedom of its inhabitants.[9] For religious Jews this behavior was a transgression against their scriptures, because in it the Land was considered to be one holy entity. Viewed from the standpoint of a Jew living during this stormy era, the outrageous treatment of the Land by the Romans at certain points in this period, and in particular its frequent partitions, meant the loss of this Land as an entity and the shattering of it as a national symbol. Domination, however, did not prevent the Jews continuing religious practices related to the Land, such as the tithes and pilgrimages.[10] In the following I shall describe the attitudes to the Land within their historical context.[11]

Pompey was the first to make painful territorial alterations in 63 B.C.E. when he gave the first serious blow to the unity of Palestine by rebuilding "Gadara . . . and the other cities Hippus, Scythopolis, Pella, Dium, Samaria, as well as Marisa, Azotus, Jamnia, and Arethusa he restored to their own inhabitants. And not only these cities in the interior, in addition to those which had been demolished, but also the coast cities of Gaza, Joppa, Dora, and Straton's Tower . . . all of these Pompey set free and annexed them to the province" of Syria (*Jewish War* 1.155–157; *Antiquities* 14.75–76). Pompey's main concern was the rebuilding and favoring of pagan cities in the Land. This offensive act no doubt hurt those Jews who lived in, or remembered, the spiritual climate of a unified Palestine under Jewish sovereignty. Gabinius in 57 B.C.E. was the second to shatter the concept of Palestine as one territorial entity: as a punishment for the recent uprising of Aristobulus II against Roman rule in Palestine, he divided the country into five districts and put them under the governorship of five *synhedria* (councils), instead of a central one in Jerusalem.[12] This act was meant to be symbolic as well as administrative. The Jews remained on their territory no longer as owners and rulers, but as tenants and subjects. The Land of Israel had become a partitioned territory. The Romans carried out such partitions in other parts of their empire as well, and it always had the effect of demonstrating the termination of national existence on a united territory. The same happened in 168 B.C.E. when Macedonia was divided into four republics, and later to Numidia and Thrace.[13] Again, the partition of Palestine was an offensive act in the eyes of many groups within Judaism, who thought of their country as one holy entity that should not be divided, their reasoning based on God's promise of the Land, the settlement of the twelve tribes, and other scriptural precedents. Despite the fact that in 40 B.C.E. Antigonus, the Hasmonean, was crowned king of Judea for a short time with the support of the Parthians, the Land remained torn and exposed to Arabs, Idumaeans, Parthians, and not least to Romans. Palestine was torn by internal strife until Herod seized it and dominated it completely in the thirties of the first century B.C.E. But even after he took over and became king of the whole country, his reign was still viewed as a "false" Jewish sovereignty over the Land. Let us examine this perception of Herod's reign.

During Herod's rule in Palestine, he was granted some of the former territorial acquisitions, which had been conquered mainly by Alexander Jannaeus and then lost during the Roman conquest and occupation. When he visited Octavian, the future Augustus, in Egypt in the autumn of 30 B.C.E., he received from him Jericho, Gadara, Hippos, Samaria, Gaza, Anthedon, Joppa, and Straton's Tower (*An-*

tiquities 15.215–17; *Jewish War* 1.396–397).[14] In 23/2 B.C.E. Augustus presented Herod with the districts of Trachonitis, Batanaea, and Auranitis (*Antiquities* 15.343–348 and *Jewish War* 1.398–400). In 20 B.C.E. Augustus granted Herod the territory of Zenodorus (*Antiquities* 15.360; Cassius Dio, 54.9.3). The Land of Israel had become for the Romans an object that they could use to grant favors to the local rulers. If we examine the perimeter of Herod's kingdom after 20 B.C.E. we may come to the conclusion that from the territorial point of view it almost equaled the kingdoms of David, Solomon, and Alexander Jannaeus.[15] Yet the current situation differed in two major ways from the situation in ancient times. First, although Herod posed as a "king of the Jews" (called thus by Josephus, *Antiquities* 16.311 and elsewhere), he was a client king, and the territory he ruled was under Roman sovereignty, imposed by the Roman governor of Syria at the time. Second, Herod encouraged the increase of the Greco-Roman element in the cities of Palestine, and was himself responsible for the foundation of new pagan cities in the Land, some of which served as his fortresses.[16]

Accordingly, his rule over the Land could not have been seen by the majority of believing Jews as an independent and genuine Jewish sovereignty on the territory of their fathers. At the time there were still people alive who remembered the grandeur of the Hasmonean period, when most of Palestine was under Jewish sway. They may have taught their children about those days, probably mingled with a great deal of nostalgia (cf. Josephus, *Vita* 1.1–6, where the historian traces his descent to the Hasmoneans). Alexander Jannaeus was unpopular within certain circles of Jews, yet he was an independent Jewish king ruling over most of the Promised Land. In contrast, the autonomy Herod enjoyed in domestic affairs sharpened in many instances ethnic divisions between the Jews and their non-Jewish neighbors such as the Arabs, Idumaeans, Greeks, and other foreigners settled in Palestine's network of cities. These divisions had their territorial implications. Some scattered allusions in Josephus point to clashes between Herod, as a Jewish king, and the Arabs.[17] During his war with the Arabs (i.e., Nabataeans) Herod is said to have given a famous discourse to the soldiers of his army (*Antiquities* 15.127–146 and a different version in *Jewish War* 1.373–379). It is evident that, unlike Maccabean discourses on such occasions, in Herod's discourse no Jewish history was intertwined, yet the Holy Land being the goal of the war is mentioned only in passing (*Antiquities* 15.133). Even the Idumaeans, though they had been judaized in 125 B.C.E., had maintained a strong national awareness that could not be ignored in Herod's time, and also became evident during the Great War in 66–70 C.E. (cf. also *Antiquities* 16.285). We even hear of a national Edomite uprising launched from their *own territory* against Herod, the half-Edomite. Herod killed some of his closest friends, among whom was Costobarus, who "was of Idumaean race and was one of those first in rank . . . and his ancestors had been priests of Cos, whom the Idumaeans believed to be a god . . . he did not think that it was proper for him to carry out the orders of Herod, who was his ruler, or for the Idumaeans to adopt the customs of the Jews and be subject to them" (15.253–258).[18] This episode shows that Herod, unlike his predecessors in the Hasmonean dynasty, made neither an effort to judaize the foreigners of the Land nor to purify the territory of foreign influences. On the contrary, he even encouraged the ethnic pluralism within his kingdom. As a result, Herod was acknowledged as sovereign by most of the Idumaeans and other non-Jews in the cities, as well as among the Hellenistic Jews. In fact, he wished to be the king of a multinational Palestine. Thus the more religious Jews refused to acknowledge him as their legitimate sovereign.

After the death of Herod the Great in 4 B.C.E., the territory underwent partition again and again.[19] These partitions were decided upon solely from above, that is, by the Roman emperor. Thus, a local patriotism developed in the different regions of Palestine during subsequent years. This fact, viewed in perspective, is a vital one for an understanding of the Jewish awareness of territory in its search for a reshaped national identity. After the stormy events that followed Herod's death, Augustus decided in 4 B.C.E. that Archelaus would become an ethnarch rather than a king and that he would rule over both Idumaea and Judea as well as the region of Samaria. Some cities were also made subject to Archelaus, namely, Straton's Tower and Sebastia, along with Joppa and Jerusalem. The rest of the territory Augustus divided into two parts and assigned them to Herod's two other sons. Herod Antipas received the revenue of Peraea and Galilee. Batanaea, Trachonitis, Auranitis, and a "certain portion of what was called the domain of Zenodorus he assigned to Philip." As for Gaza, Gadara, and Hippus, they were among the

Greek cities that Augustus added to the province of Syria (*Antiquities* 17.317–320; *Jewish War* 2.93–100). As to Salome, Herod's sister, she received Jamnia, Azotus, and Phasaelis as well as the royal palace at Ascalon. Her estates were, however, subject to Archelaus's rule (*Antiquities* 17.189, 321; *Jewish War* 2.98). In 6 c.e., when Archelaus was deposed by Augustus, his territory was also added to Syria. Hence it is evident that Palestine underwent some major changes in its territorial status within a span of seventy years (63 b.c.e.–6 c.e.), which no doubt had practical as well as emotional effects on the inhabitants, both Jews and non-Jews.

Twenty-eight years later, in 34 c.e., Philip died, who had "ruled over Trachonitis and Gaulanitis, as well as over the tribe called Bataneas."[20] Tiberius took this territory and annexed it to the province of Syria, though the tribute collected from this province was held on deposit (*Antiquities* 18.106–108). Tiberius acted in keeping with Augustus's settlement after he had deposed Archelaus in 6 c.e. (Philip's territory was given later to Agrippa I by Gaius Caligula, *Antiquities* 18.237). In 39 c.e. Herod Antipas was deposed from his province, and Caligula granted his tetrarchy to King Agrippa I (*Antiquities* 18.252).[21] It should be emphasized that the partition of Palestine among Herod's successors had very concrete implications. Not only were borders created between the three parts of Palestine, but every part also had its own ruler, its own capital (Tiberias, Caesarea Philippi, and Jerusalem, as well as Caesarea Maritima), and its own coinage. In the case of Philip we can even detect a special "calendar" which was designed for his tetrarchy: the dates on Philip's coins refer to his regnal years.[22] The localism of the various "kingdoms" into which Palestine was divided is reflected also in the circulation of its coinage. Whereas the coins of the Hasmonean kingdom had circulated all over Palestine and east to the Jordan River, Herod Archelaus's coinage was mostly confined to Judea, and Herod Antipas's and Philip's were mainly found in the north of Palestine.[23]

In 41 c.e. the new emperor, Claudius, issued an edict in which he both confirmed the rule of Agrippa I, "which had been first instituted by Gaius," and added to Agrippa's dominions "all the other lands that had been ruled by King Herod, his grandfather, namely, Judea and Samaria" (according to *Jewish War* 2.215 also Trachonitis and Auranitis; cf. also Cassius Dio, 60.8.2–3). He also added Abila, which had been ruled until then by Lysanias, and all the land

in the mountainous region of Lebanon "as a gift out of his own
territory" (*Antiquities* 19.274–275).[24]

After the death of King Agrippa I in 44 C.E. the whole territory of
Palestine, which until that time had been sporadically ruled by Jewish and half-Jewish princes, was to be ruled directly by a series of
Roman governors, most of whom became notorious for their harsh
treatment of the Jews: "Claudius again reduced the kingdoms to a
province and sent as procurators first Cuspius Fadus" (*Jewish War*
2.220; *Antiquities* 19.363).[25] This year, 44 C.E., was crucial for Jewish nationalism in Palestine. Suddenly the Jews lost what little sovereignty they had over their Land; they lost their last king, and with
him the little Jewish army that he possessed. From then on even their
Temple, as well as their holy city, became subject more than ever to
the caprices of the Roman governors in Palestine. And yet the Temple remained the only surviving physical symbol of nationalism (together with the coins circulating from the reign of Agrippa I until the
beginning of the Great War[26]). This vacuum, into which Jews who
had nationalistic feelings were thrown, was one of the main reasons
for the unrest in Palestine from the mid forties up to the Great
War.[27] We will return to this subject later.

In the time of Felix (52–60 C.E.), who was one of the most notorious Roman governors, Emperor Claudius granted Agrippa II, the
son of Agrippa I, "the tetrarchy of Philip together with Batanea,"
which was added beforehand to Syria, but was still called the "tetrarchy of Philip," "adding thereto Trachonitis and Lysanias's former tetrarchy of Abila (*Jewish War* 2.247 adds, "the tetrarchy of
Varus"); but he deprived him of Chalcis, after he had ruled it four
years" (*Antiquities* 20.137–138). Later Agrippa II received from
Emperor Nero "a certain portion of the Galilee, giving orders to the
cities of Tiberias and Tarichaea to submit to him; he also gave him
Julias, a city in the Peraea, and the fourteen villages that go with it"
(*Antiquities* 20.158–159; *Jewish War* 2.252). Agrippa II had no *locus standi* among the Jews because, among other factors, he had no
meaningful hold on the Jewish territory in Palestine that would have
made him the sovereign of the Jews. During the first stage of the
Great War he received support from all those who felt that the territory was not to be seen at that time as one of the major cornerstones
of Judaism, thinking that to fight for it against the Roman giant
would be suicidal.[28]

Be that as it may, within a time span of 132 years (63 B.C.E.–70 C.E.), Palestine was divided and redivided many times, given to local dynasts, and taken from others by the Roman oppressor. An anomaly already mentioned should now be enlarged upon. Until the forties of the first century C.E. (Agrippa I's death), the territory was partially in the hands of Jewish rulers who sometimes posed as kings. Hence parts of the Jewish nation both in Palestine and in the Diaspora viewed this national symbol as still being a reality. Their limited hopes were shattered when the whole Land came under direct Roman rule in 44 C.E. As time went on, and the Romans did not show any intention of changing the new political situation, frustration grew. This frustration sharpened the two contradictory reactions, which had been under the surface for a long time since the Roman occupation took place.

On the one hand, some circles of Jews thought that the Land could no longer hold the meaning it had had in Hasmonean times, that is, of a solid nationalistic base that signified unity and Jewish sovereignty. Therefore, for these Jews, the Land gradually ceased to be an important factor of Jewish political awareness. Also, those who viewed Palestine as becoming more and more pagan became estranged from their Land as a political national symbol. These Jews, for whom the Land became an unrealistic and vague idea, diverted their energy and interests into other spheres. In fact, they thought about the Land as the Jews of the Diaspora already had for many years. This group reveals itself much more through the literature of the period than through the historical accounts.

On the other hand, the polluted Land aroused, in some Jews, messianic hopes that had many political overtones. The hopes often involved symbolic figures such as David and the son of David, who were strongly associated with Jewish rule over the whole of Palestine. Many from among this nationalistic group wished to fight for the lost Land. This desire brought about a tension that led to unrest, as Josephus's account of the end of the forties shows.

The Great War of 66–70 C.E. was an attempt by many groups of Jews in Palestine to resume political sovereignty over the Land. This goal was particularly apparent in the first stage of the war (66/7 C.E.), when there was still a wide consensus about its aims—it was hoped that the uprising would bring about Jewish independence on its Land. The poorly organized Jewish army led by Jewish generals was to take over the territory; Josephus says that apart from the generals appointed to command Jerusalem, other generals were selected for Idumaea "nor were the other districts neglected; Joseph, son of Simeon, was sent to take command at Jericho, Manasseh to Peraea, John the Essene to the province of Thamna, with Lydda, Joppa, and Emmaus also under his charge. John, son of Ananias, was appointed commanding officer of the provinces of Gophna and Acrabetta; Josephus, son of Matthias, was given the two Galilees, with the addition of Gamala" (*Jewish War* 2.564–568).[29] These appointments reveal not only an organization to be used for strategic purposes, but they also disclose the aim of the Jewish nationalists: to recover Palestine as their sovereign territorial base. Along with the goal of the conversion of the Temple into the main political center (*Jewish War* 2.562) and with the attempt to re-create a native Jewish army and a Jewish kingship, the Jewish rebels considered the reclamation of the territory to be their main target. As is well known, the first phase of the war failed, and the revolt passed over into the hands of the extremists. As the latter lost other pieces of territory in the Land during the war, the territorial base of the rebels moved at last to Jerusalem and its Temple. "Ministates" were established there by the various factions during the revolt. When Jerusalem fell and the Temple was burned down by the Romans in 70 C.E., independent possession of territory in Palestine by the Jews ceased until the revolt of Bar Kokhba in 132–135 C.E.

After 70 C.E., Rome reorganized the province and strengthened its pagan population by founding cities such as Flavia Neapolis and Flavia Ioppe, and in particular by imposing a heavy tax, the so-called *fiscus Iudaicus,* only on the Jews of Palestine and the Diaspora. The Romans also emphasized the Jewish subjugation by issuing coins that were in circulation all over the empire, but also in Palestine, bearing the inscriptions "Iudaea capta" and "Iudaea devicta." Agrippa II received some additional territory in his northern kingdom, which he held until his death at the end of the century, but this grant had no impact on Jewish territorial aspirations after 70 C.E. The groups who still had hopes before 70 of resuming control of the Land, the most important of nationalistic symbols, seem to have given them up for the time being. To judge from the Mishnah and Tosefta, which are much later but may have some early material in them, the rabbis were not interested in statehood and related issues here and now.

The question of how the changes mentioned above affected the spirit of the Jews has been ignored by most historians. They have not asked how Jews and Christians felt about their divided and shattered country during the period under discussion. Does the literature really reveal an emerging localism, estrangement, and despair, along with hopes for a better future for the lost Land? Before attempting to answer these questions three points should be made.

First, although most compositions cannot be dated exactly to a specific decade, we can still place many of them within the two centuries under discussion (first B.C.E. and first C.E.). It should be emphasized that it is not necessary to consider the year 70 C.E. as the upper limit for the textual evidence, because compositions written after that date (until the first decades of the second century C.E.) view the Land in the same manner as the ones written before it. The Land was already shattered and under severe Roman rule many years before 70, as was discussed in the preceding section. The Jews, as well as the Christians, between 70 C.E. and 110 C.E. did not imagine that the Temple would remain in ruins. For them the war was yet another major event in the stormy relationship with the Roman Empire.

Second, it is not always possible to make the distinction, in certain compositions, between what is a Jewish and what is a Christian interpolation—this point in itself shows that Christians in the first century were very close to certain circles of Jews in their thinking about the Land and other topics. This close connection is well reflected in the New Testament.

And finally, in certain instances it is almost impossible to distinguish between compositions that were written in Palestine and those written in the Diaspora. This similarity again shows, in contradistinction to the first period, that after 63 B.C.E. many Jews in Palestine started to think about their Land in ways similar to Diaspora Jews. The issue of a sovereign territory became much more universalized. Thus, taking the literature of the period after 63 B.C.E., the main streams of thought concerning the Land can be detected. These ideas will be seen to correspond to the description already given of the history of the territorial dimension. Four individual streams of thought concerning the Land can be discerned in the literature.

1. Most documents of the apocrypha and pseudepigrapha assigned to this period reveal an indifference about the Land. As far as we can judge from the available texts, some of which are of doubtful date and provenance, they do not show any particular interest in the history of the Land or of any political issues surrounding it. This characteristic applies to the literature that was written in both the Diaspora and Palestine.[30] When observed against the background of the literature of the first period, it is remarkable how interest in the Land disappears in the compositions of the second period (before and after 70 C.E.), say, up to the nineties of the first century C.E. The latter almost totally ignore the process of the biblical conquest of the Land, they do not deal with its settlement by the twelve tribes, and they have very little interest in the heroes of the past who were associated with the conquest and settlement of the Land. Hardly any mention is made of the great kings of the past who were associated with a Jewish state in the Land. There is no systematic discussion about the relationship of Jews and foreigners settled in the Land, and their eventual future. There are only passing remarks that the Land was promised to the first ancestors of Israel. Usually it is emphasized that the first ancestors were universal figures to whom the whole world was promised, rather than just the Land (cf. Genesis Apocryphon; Sibylline Oracles 3.220–264). Also, we can find the repetitive formulas (*topoi*) of the Land as being promised, holy, and fine (1 Enoch 56:5–8; Sibylline Oracles 4.127; 5.281–283, 328–329; Apocalypse of Elijah 5:5–6; Testament of Job 33:3–9; Testament of Abraham 8:1–7; Testament of Isaac 6:32); but in most instances these are amorphous formulas brought forward as lip service, some of which we have already found in the literature of the first stage, and which occur in later literature as well (Testament of Jacob, passim).

The vagueness on the subject of the Land in the literature of the second period, along with the escapes to remote heavens often found in it (perhaps 2 Enoch [J] 8; Apocalypse of Abraham 10:13–15, and chapters 20–21), might be understood as a reaction in some Jewish circles to the disappearance of the Land as a real base for Jewish existence after 63 B.C.E. Hence, in many documents the universal takes the place of the national. The concept of a united world, which resulted most probably from the influence of stoic ideas combined with the fact of the Roman Empire's existence, is mentioned for instance in Sibylline Oracle 2.315–338:[31] "The earth will belong equally to all, undivided by walls or fences. It will then bear more abundant fruits." We can also find a strong interest in the entire earth (2 Enoch [J] 40:12, which may anyhow reflect earlier ideas) and the inhabited world; for example, Testament of Abraham 9–10 (A) states that Abraham's last wish is to see the whole inhabited world in which he traveled according to the Genesis Apocryphon. An interest in the universal is also apparent elsewhere in the literature of this period.[32] Philo of Alexandria, who shows in his two "political" treatises, the *Legatio ad Gaium* and *In Flaccum,* a concrete interest in the Land, reveals in his other works merely an interest in the universal aspects of Judaism, and the spiritualization of the Land.[33]

2. Of all available documents from the first century, apart from Josephus's *Antiquities,* which as a comprehensive history of Israel from the Creation had to mention the Land, Palestine is the most frequently mentioned in the synoptic Gospels, John, and Acts 1–12. In these books there are many inferences concerning the Land that have a direct bearing on this chapter, and which will be elaborated further now. The reader may wonder why this topic appears within the discussion about the literature and not in the survey of events given above. The reason is in the nature of the sources. A great many historical facts and events are recorded in the New Testament, but these facts and events were reshaped and kept alive within various communities in keeping with the particular religious and ideological direction early Christianity had taken before 70 C.E., and afterward.

A great deal has been written about the so-called "political" Jesus, and the political attitudes of his disciples and later followers. The majority of scholars have been against linking either Jesus or his followers with the politics of the first century.[34] Others, however, have propounded the idea that the early Christians up to 70 C.E. were in various degrees connected to the politics of their day.[35] S. G. F. Brandon has been the most prominent proponent of this view in recent scholarship. He vehemently argued that Jesus, and in particular his disciples, were supporters of the Zealot movement, and that the Jewish Christians even fought alongside the Zealots in Jerusalem in 70 C.E. against the Romans. Brandon argues that Mark, and like him the later evangelists, Matthew, Luke, and John, "each for his own particular needs," eliminated the Zealot aspect and drew a picture of a pacifist Jesus "who not only definitively repudiated armed force, but also counseled meek acceptance of injury at the hands of others."[36]

Without going into great detail,[37] it is important to refute this interesting theory. For one thing, it is impossible to deal here with the question of the quest for the historical Jesus, which is still a central issue in scholarship.[38] But attention should be drawn to the fact that the New Testament should be carefully handled when searching for authentic evidence of the events and ideas antedating 70 C.E. While, as we shall see in a moment, earlier traditions can be found in the Gospels and Acts, it seems that Brandon was not cautious enough in this respect. In reaction to Brandon's theory, many scholars have shown convincingly that whatever else they may or may not have been, Jesus and his followers were not liberty fighters.[39]

Another reason to reject this theory is that Josephus, who is our main source for the history of the period, does not indicate that there was any real political unrest against Rome during the twenties and thirties of the first century C.E. There is no reason to believe that he would have wished to tone down such unrest if it had really existed. Tacitus even mentions how quiet it was in Judea during these decades. There was no active Zealot movement at the time in Palestine.[40] Moreover, Josephus, who gives an elaborate account of the events leading up to the Great War and of the war itself—one of the most detailed accounts in antiquity of a single war—does not mention Judeo-Christians, or Christians, in the context of the war in Jerusalem. He would without doubt have mentioned these "strange" Jews in his detailed account of the different parties fighting in Jerusalem at the time if they had in fact been there. So from the twenties through the seventies of the first century there is no evidence concerning any participation of the Christian Jews in the fight against Rome.

Finally, while Jesus may have shared some ideological aspects with the zealotism of the first century C.E., he was closer in nature to the peaceful attitudes of the Pharisees.[41] Jesus was certainly zealous in his teaching,[42] but this does not mean that he became a violent man who fought for the cause of liberty from the yoke of the Romans. What Pontius Pilate may have understood Jesus' intentions to be is irrelevant to what Jesus himself had in mind.[43] The Pharisees were, according to Josephus, a peaceful "sect" in contrast to the Fourth Philosophy, and they held a nonviolent ideology concerning Roman rule in Palestine (*Antiquities* 18.11–25). There exists no reason to disbelieve this description. Jesus, like the Pharisees of his time, thought that Palestine was a Holy Land.[44] But I doubt that he envisioned the idea of the creation of a Jewish state on the Land. Moreover, the concept of holiness, namely, the observance of the ordinances concerning the Land such as the tithe, pilgrimage, sabbatical year, and the political sovereignty of the Jews over the Land were not necessarily one and the same thing. Religious Jews in this period were forced to make a clear distinction between the Holy Land and an Israelite state. The Land—or rather parts of it—could be holy without necessarily having a Jewish sovereign. Also, a Jewish sovereign did not automatically make the Land holy.[45] Thus it is impossible even to imagine that Jesus or his followers were striving for an independent Jewish state similar to the Davidic or Hasmonean one. The four cornerstones of kingship, Land, Temple, and army can be traced in the New Testament, but we will deal here only with the Land (the others are treated in other chapters of this book).

The Land appears in different ways in the various books of the New Testament. The earliest documents of the New Testament, as it now stands, are the genuine Pauline letters. They, along with the later pseudo-Pauline letters of the New Testament and Hebrews, ignore the Land almost totally. Even the famous promise made to Abraham in the Book of Genesis, as W. D. Davies has shown, does not necessarily refer to Palestine; it is understood by Paul in a universalistic manner, not in a nationalistic one.[46] Paul, as is well known, is a universalist in his approach to the territory, as can be seen in Acts 13–28 and elsewhere.[47] Paul wanders into the western inhabited world, the ecumene, and may even have reached Spain. One may recall that the missionary gods Osiris, Sesostris, Semiramis, and Dionysus went to the eastern ecumene and distributed culture there.[48] Against this background the territorial dimension as reflected in Acts 2:9–11 may be mentioned. There we hear about people from different nations who became interested in "Christianity" and assembled in Jerusalem. If the place of origin of these nations is examined, one can discern the perimeter of the eastern ecumene. Acts 13–28 instead depict Paul's wanderings in the western perimeter, somewhat in the fashion of Heracles according to

Matris of Thebes. Paul, as a man of his time, did not go eastward; he shifted the emphasis away from the eastern ecumene to the western one.[49] In terms of Hellenistic thought Paul's mission, like those of Jesus and Peter, was a religiocultural mission, not a political one. In other words, the Land no longer held any political, national significance in Paul's thought. On the one hand Paul's understanding of the Land could be compared with that of a Diaspora Jew, as contrasted to the more local Palestinian ideas of Jesus and Peter. On the other hand, it could have been a spiritual version of the imperialistic idea found for instance in the notion that Pompey would go "to the end of the earth" (Acts 1:8).[50] In general it should be noted that Paul's mission to the gentiles in the larger world makes the Land a very small part of the ecumene rather than its center. The fading away of the Land as a political reality for the Jews had, even before 70 c.e., brought about universalistic concepts of this kind.

Thus those who held the opinion that the Roman ecumene constituted their territorial base were a-political in the sense being used here: that is to say, they were not adhering to a specific national territory. When we read the three synoptic Gospels, Acts 1–12, and the gospel of John, however, the Land emerges in very vivid hues. In fact, it is much clearer than it appears in most of the apocrypha and pseudepigrapha of the first century c.e. The Land, or rather parts of it, provide the background for the dramatic events described in the New Testament. It is unnecessary here to enter into argument with W. D. Davies and others who deal with the theological meaning of the geographical details appearing in the New Testament.[51] Reading the documents as a historian—and there is no reason not to do so, just as others do with the theologically oriented books of Maccabees —one may say that even if some of the sites in Palestine mentioned in the synoptic Gospels, John, and Acts 1–12 are highly symbolic (as some tend to argue), they can still be *real* places in Palestine, and they make sense as being the actual background of the events. Thus healings or encounters in Capernaum, Caesarea Philippi, and Gerasa may be historical reminiscences or purely narrative attempts to sketch a scene with verisimilitude. The historian of this period, as well as the modern reader, would not necessarily associate places in Palestine with symbolism and ideas.[52]

Moreover, if we examine the territorial dimension emerging from the synoptic Gospels, John, and Acts 1–12, we will discover that it may go back to early times, namely, to the twenties and thirties of the first century C.E.[53] One reason is that, as we all know, the evangelists from Mark through Luke and John were tendentious. If so, then they no doubt would have wanted to present the spread of Christianity in geographical terms so as to show that the *whole* of Palestine had become Christian from the very start of the movement, in other words, that Jesus wandered throughout the Land spreading his teaching instead of preaching only in the Galilee, Jerusalem, and some adjacent regions (as we find for instance in Acts 9:31). But they do not present it in such a manner. The only place in which a wish is expressed regarding the spread of Christianity in Palestine as a whole, is at one point very vaguely presented by Jesus' order to his disciples to go only to the Jewish places in Palestine (excluding the gentiles and the Samaritans, Matt 10:5–15; John 3:22; but cf. Matt 28:19).[54] This statement supports what I argue throughout this study, namely, that a dichotomy existed between the two parts of Palestine, the non-Jewish and the Jewish. Besides that, his territory basically remained the Galilee, and people from many other regions in the Land came to see Jesus there. The same is true of John the Baptist, who had a very limited area of "influence" around Jericho, but many from Judea and elsewhere came to him (*Antiquities* 18.116–119). Jesus held the view (which was familiar in Judaism at the time) of the entirety of the nation, expressed in the idea of twelve tribes. For this reason he selected twelve disciples and he said (perhaps Q; but probably attributed to him later) that the twelve apostles would sit on twelve thrones to judge the twelve tribes of Israel (Matt 19:28).[55] If these were his own views, then the limited territory Jesus had "direct" influence on, taken together with the concept of the twelve tribes and the wholeness of the nation, may show that Jesus' actual territorial dimension goes back to the twenties and thirties of the first century C.E. During his ministry Jesus was and remained a local rather than a national figure.

Another piece of evidence for the authenticity of the gospel traditions regarding the Land is the fact that the Gospels were written after Paul's Epistles, which ignore the Land almost completely, but nevertheless depict it as a real background to Jesus' ministry.

Whether the traditions concerning the Land go back to the thirties or were formed later than 70 C.E. makes very little difference.[56] The reason is that the concept of the Land did not undergo any drastic changes in 70 c.e.; Palestine had already been under direct Roman rule since 63 b.c.e., when massive changes in attitude really did take place. After 70 c.e. the Land remained as it had been, under Roman rule. Thus, one may say that the Land in the Gospels indeed corresponds to the picture shown in the historical sources surveyed above. The Land was disintegrated, was disunited, and local patriotism developed because of its political partitions.

Acts 1–12 gives a similar impression. Events no longer take place in the Galilee (and Jerusalem), but in Jerusalem and the coastal plain from Azotus to Caesarea (Acts 8–10).[57] Also, in contradistinction to the three synoptic Gospels, Samaria was added to the Christian "sphere of influence"; in this respect Acts agrees with the Gospel of John, as we can learn from the very problematic chapter 4.[58] This "localism" can be interpreted as a tendentious wish of Luke in Acts to show that "Christianity" (Acts 11:26) had spread to the coastal plain soon after the crucifixion. Yet one can also say that a book, which contains the ideal of the entirety and wholeness of Israel (note the concept of twelve tribes and four corners of the world as well as a typical Lukan summary in Acts 9:31–35) but nevertheless shows its partial regional spread (ignoring even the Galilee, except occasional remarks such as Acts 9:31; 10:37),[59] should be taken seriously for the older traditions it preserves, namely, the local ones of the coastal plain. No political ideology of the Land is even alluded to in Acts 1–12. The Land is depicted as it really was for Jews at the time. They were scattered all over Palestine, which was at the time full of non-Jews, without any awareness of there being a national homeland. Such an awareness was anachronistic. Acts 1–12, as well as certain instances in the Gospels (e.g., Matt 15:21–29), show this, and it was a later development of the tradition that Eretz Israel in its religious dimension was also for non-Jews to live in; but this view was confined to people who accepted Peter's message. This point is clearly illustrated by the story of Peter and Cornelius in Caesarea (Acts 10).[60] In this respect early Christianity was revolutionary, bridging the gap that existed between Jews and non-Jews in Palestine through a religious mission. Although Peter seems to have left the Land for missionary activity, as indicated in Galatians 2:8, 1 Corinthians 9, and traditions such as that of 1 Clement, he recognized the Land as an important base for Christianity.

It should be emphasized that it is not only the casual character of the early Christians' references to places in Palestine that indicates that they did not see the Land as a political issue of sovereignty and freedom.[61] Equally important is the fact that the sayings and discourses in Matthew and Acts, some of which are old traditions, do not refer to the Land as an important factor in the thought of early Christianity. Like many of the Pharisees, the early Christians learned to accommodate themselves to the idea that one can live a perfect religious life on the Land without its being under the sovereignty of a Jewish state. This concept is associated with the idea of the Messiah in the circles of Jesus and his disciples. As we have already seen, the questioning that he was the son of David was a result of the fact that he did not want to be a political figure of any kind. Jesus, according to the New Testament, wished to be seen as a spiritual Messiah.[62] His Kingdom of God was therefore connected to the Holy Land but not in a physical and political way, as was the Hasmonean state.[63] Some of his later followers did not understand this distinction and insisted on his being the son of David. Seen from afar, by authors probably based outside the Land (or in Greek cities in the Land) and already imbued with universalistic ideas, the association with David no longer had any political significance. But at the time of Jesus this was not so. He had no political aspirations concerning the Land of Israel; he was beyond and above such mundane ambitions. The Land in its political aspects was irrelevant to him, and in many ways it went against his mission.[64] Also, the political ideas of statehood which are found in the Hebrew Bible are ignored altogether in the synoptics, Acts 1–12, and John, and so are all the biblical heroes who have any bearing on statehood and politics in the Bible.[65] The whole idea of the conquest of the Land as well as the concept of statehood on it is greatly toned down in the New Testament. It is not simply that the later Evangelists decided not to mention the heroes of the Old Testament who were associated with the conquest and holding of the Land; it is, rather, part of the whole concept of early Christianity, going back to Jesus and his disciples, that the Land as part of an earthly Jewish state had no political importance for the New Israel. Neither had it any importance for many of the Pharisees.

3. The third stream of thought concerning the Land is that of the Zealots. They, and for a short while even other groups, wanted to make territorial acquisitions during the Great War against Rome.

Unfortunately, we have no literature from them that could give us an idea about what they thought regarding the territory. One can guess that they would have expressed views that emphasized past conquests of the Land, the Jewish kingdom, and extensive embellishments on biblical material. These traditions justified the rule of the Jews over the entire Land, excluding the foreigners from it, as well as placing emphasis on heroes such as Joshua, David, Solomon, and the Hasmonean kings.[66] Although the physical concept of territory was of less importance in many circles both in Palestine and in the Diaspora, the Land was still very much alive as a political, nationalistic symbol for those who went to war with Rome in 66 C.E. These people wanted to recreate a Jewish state on the Land. But only the extremists, the so-called Zealots and Sicarii, fought the war to its bitter end. Many Jews gave up the battle when they realized what a giant Rome was, and they justified their defeatist attitude by using a well-known Jewish idea, that God had shifted his support from the Jewish side to the Roman one. It is true that this idea was known well before 70 C.E., but it was easier to apply it after the destruction of the Temple and Jerusalem.

4. Except for a short-lived episode when most Jews were elated by their success in defeating a Roman legion in Palestine in 66 C.E., among the Pharisees there had been strong opposition to any violent acts since the beginning of Roman rule in Palestine. They constitute the fourth stream, which in many respects was close to the Christian group mentioned above. It should be emphasized that the events of the fifties and sixties were generated by the young people within the Jewish society. Some documents of the Pharisees and related groups, who thought that only God would solve a political and military problem, do exist—for instance, the so-called Testament of Moses and Pseudo-Philo's *Biblical Antiquities*. Josephus's *Antiquities* can also serve as evidence for what moderates thought at that time.

Josephus, who had views close to those of the Zealots at the beginning of the Great War, very soon switched over to the other side, which opposed the war.[67] One should emphasize again that the main issue at stake between the so-called Fourth Philosophy group on the one hand (namely, the Zealots and Sicarii) and the Pharisees on the other was the use of violence to regain Jewish independence over the Land. The Land as an ideal within the national awareness was *common* to all groups. Josephus wrote his *Antiquities* in Rome when there was no longer any chance of restoring Israel's independence, as we know from hindsight. Nevertheless he, who knew Israel's history very well, may have had hopes that the future would be more favorable for the Jews in Palestine, as in fact it had been after the destruction of the First Temple. One can learn from his writing a great deal about the moderates' thought about the Land after 70 C.E. His views on the Land of Israel are mingled with ideology, nostalgia, and wishful thinking. To deal with this aspect would require another volume; yet some demonstration will be given in a later chapter. Here it will suffice to mention that, although Josephus changed and embellished the biblical stories, the Land comes very much to the fore in his *Antiquities* 1–11.[68]

In his interpretation of Israel's history, Josephus showed that the Land was promised by God and that the Jews were to live on it and be God-fearing (*Antiquities* 2.269): "They shall inhabit this favored land wherein Abraham dwelt, the forefather of your race, and shall enjoy all the blessings, and it is thou, aye, and thy sagacity that shall conduct them thither." Palestine was seen as part of a universal territorial plan of God, whereby the land was given by him to the Jews along with "liberty" (3.300; 4.1–6). The Land was to be Jewish, but history had proved that non-Jews also lived there. Thus the fight against these non-Jews was God's affair; he was the one who would lead the Jews against the foreigners settled in the Land (3.300–302). The war on the Land was at times seen as a war between local gods (6.1ff.), and the destruction of the foreigners settled on it was frequently toned down by the historian (5.57–61, 115–116).[69] This portrayal was less offensive to Greeks who read the *Antiquities*. But Josephus showed a great concern for the welfare of the Jews on their Land during their long history, hence he viewed many of their wars against foreigners as justifiable (for instance, David's conquests in book 7 and elsewhere). The Land emerges in some passages of the *Antiquities* as a utopian place for the Jews (2.7–8), yet this view did not exclude the legitimacy of a Jewish Diaspora outside Palestine (4.114–117). The biblical interpretation found in the *Antiquities* does not always allow us to believe that the Great War against Rome changed much in Josephus's views of Jewish nationalism that he, and other Jews, held before 70 C.E.

Let us now turn to the other two documents mentioned above,

the so-called Testament of Moses and the *Biblical Antiquities* of Pseudo-Philo. The latter document apparently reflects an anti-Zealot concept of the Land, again through a reinterpretation of the biblical books of Joshua through Judges.[70] The author of this work, probably written around 70 C.E., was of the opinion that the Land as such was not the most important factor at the time that the book was written, because the messiah of the house of David had not yet appeared. It was belief in God and the fight against disruptive foreigners in the Land that really mattered. No conquest of the Land was recorded; the Land emerged as even more disintegrated and shattered than in the biblical books of Joshua through Judges. The dichotomy between Jews and non-Jews is highlighted by the author of this interesting book. The Jews were to rely on God, be pure, and strive for their purity and spiritual existence instead of living in an impure state on their Land.

The other document, probably from the beginning of the first century, is the so-called Testament of Moses. It relates the history of Israel through the mouth of Moses when he hands over the leadership of the Israelite people to Joshua. This document probably contains an earlier layer composed during the Maccabean era, but was finally shaped at the beginning of the first century.[71] Moses says that Joshua was to "lead the people into the land that had been promised to their fathers" (1:7–9; 2:1–2). Then he surveys the history of Israel as directed by God and mentions the Land in several junctures of Israel's history (2:2–3, 5–7; 3:9; 4:5–9; 6:5–6; 11:11). The author, or later editor, of this composition emphasizes what has already been mentioned, namely, that Jewish authority over the Land was never a guarantee of the holy or pure character of this state. Some of the Hasmonean kings were sinners, and they, as well as Herod and his descendants, harmed their own people. All of the atrocities inflicted by Jewish kings occurred on the Land. As R. H. Charles said many years ago, this interesting document expresses the moderate nationalist view of the Pharisees, that everything in Israel's history was directed by God from above. Any initiative taken by the Jews themselves in the past concerning their national existence proved to be disastrous; it brought destruction and despair. The Jews henceforward were to be passive and rely on God. This message is given very clearly in Moses' discourse when he reacted to Joshua's fears regarding the possible attack by the peoples of the Land against Israel after Moses was gone (chaps. 11–12).

These views accord with what Josephus says about the Pharisees and with what little is known about their behavior throughout the period. They were of the opinion that the Land was their physical dwelling, and, like Jesus and Gamaliel II, they taught and learned in it; but the Land could not be at present the political base of the Jewish nation.[72] They believed that God would do something about the Land in due course (e.g., make it a pure place to live in) and that the Messiah would bring this change, provided that the Jews purified themselves.

In conclusion, the conquest of the Land by the Romans in 63 B.C.E., and its becoming more non-Jewish and divided later on, brought about a twofold reaction. On the one hand the Land as a political and national symbol ceased to be the main concern of Jewish thought in certain circles. Frustration, combined with the gradual fading away of this strong symbol of nationalism, brought about the acceptance of other more universal and transcendental ideas. On the other hand, a strong nationalistic feeling produced action rather than poetry. As long as quasi-symbols of nationalism still existed, the equilibrium between the two main segments of Palestinian society stayed intact, and the wish for a violent struggle for liberty was only latent most of the time. The death of Agrippa I in 44 C.E. nourished the frustrated nationalists, who started to act against Roman governors in Palestine; these actions culminated in the Great War of 66–70 C.E. The freedom fighters of antiquity apparently had no time to write books—at least the Zealots and Sicarii. Resistance forces were quiet for years, until they were saturated with frustration. Only then did they resort to physical violence. For that reason some years passed between the death of Agrippa I and the stormy events that led to the Great War. It was unfortunate for their cause that Josephus, their opponent, gave them a negative image in world history.

Notes

[1] Cf. W. V. Harris, *War and Imperialism in Republican Rome* (Oxford, 1979), pp. 117–130; also J. W. Rich, *Declaring War in the Roman Republic* (Brussels, 1976). For a survey of more views concerning the criticism and justification of the empire, see A. Erskine, *The Hellenistic Stoa: Political Thought and Action* (Ithaca, N.Y., 1990), pp. 181–204.

[2] Among other gods, but he seems to have an important role, for instance on coins throughout the republic. Cf. M. H. Crawford, *Roman Republican Coinage* (Cambridge, 1974), 1.450–451, 510–511; 2.714, 719–720, 727, 737–738. Great conquerors like Sulla and Pompey were associated with Hercules. Sulla: Plutarch, *Sulla 35*, and Crawford, above, 1.450; Pompey: Plutarch, *Pompey 1*, Appian, *Mithridateios 478* and Crawford, above, 1.451. Also Marc Antony liked his identification with Heracles: Plutarch, *Antony 4*. It is, then, not accidental that Hercules became popular in the late republic and early empire. Cf. also P. Zanker, *The Power of Images in the Age of Augustus* (Ann Arbor, Mich., 1988), esp. pp. 45–46. H. G. Martin, *Römische Tempelkultbilder* (Rome, 1987), refers to the importance of Hercules in republican Rome (pp. 31–36; 90–98), and in particular highlights the association with Hercules of two of the great imperialists of Rome, namely, Scipio Aemilianus (pp. 35–36) and Pompey (Pliny 34.57 and 34.33; Martin, above, p. 36). Hercules in Vergil's time was a paradigm of Augustus (R.O.A.M. Lyne, *Further Voices in Vergil's Aeneid* [Oxford, 1987], pp. 27–35). Can this association be accidental? Moreover, R. MacMullen shows how, in parts of Italy, Hercules was one of the most popular gods during the empire period, in *Paganism in the Roman Empire* (New Haven and London, 1981), pp. 5–7. On Gaius Caligula and Heracles and Dionysus, see Philo, *Legatio ad Gaium 78–96*. And for Hercules see in general J. Bayet, *Les Origines de l'Hercule romain* (Paris, 1926); M. W. Mackenzie, "Hercules in the Early Roman Empire with Particular Reference to Literature," thesis, (Cornell University, 1967).

[3] Cf. F. Jacoby, *Die Fragmente der griechischen Historiker* (Leiden, 1958) and see on Matris of Thebes, *Pauly-Wissowa Realencyclopädie* (1930) 14.2.2287–2298 (Hobein). Cf. in general for universalism at the time H. Strasburger, "Poseidonios on Problems of the Roman Empire," *Journal of Roman Studies* 55 (1965): 40–53; K. S. Sacks, *Diodorus Siculus and the First Century* (Princeton, 1990), esp. pp. 55–82.

[4] Cf. Tacitus, *Annals* 1.11 and 4.5. See E. Gruen, "The Imperial Policy of Augustus," in *Between Republic and Empire,* ed. K. A. Raaflaub and M. Toher (Berkeley, Los Angeles, and Oxford, 1990), pp. 395–416; P. A. Brunt, *Roman Imperial Themes* (Oxford, 1990), pp. 433–480. The most convenient survey is the one of M. Cary and H. H. Scullard, *A History of Rome* (London, 1975), chaps. 31, 33, and 36.

[5] *Aeneid* 1.279. In general for Vergil's ideas in the *Aeneid,* see J. Griffin, *Virgil* (Oxford, 1986), pp. 58–106; Lyne, *Further Voices;* see also J. M. André, "La Con-

ception de l'État et de l'Empire dans la pensée gréco-romaine des deux premiers siècles de notre ère," *Aufstieg und Niedergang der römischen Welt* 2.30.1 (1982): 3–73.

6 Cf. T. Frank, *Roman Imperialism* (New York, 1914); W. V. Harris, *War and Imperialism in Republican Rome, 327–70 B.C.* (Oxford, 1979); E. Gruen, *The Hellenistic World and the Coming of Rome* (Berkeley, Los Angeles, and London, 1984); E. Badian, *Foreign Clientelae (264–70 B.C.)* (Oxford, 1958); A. M. Eckstein, *Senate and General: Individual Decision-Making and Roman Foreign Relations, 264–194 B.C.* (Berkeley, Los Angeles, and London, 1987); and cf. also J.-L. Ferrary, *Philhellénisme et impérialisme* (Rome, 1988).

7 It is interesting to observe how Germanicus was interested in the mythological hero Sesostris (Rameses, according to Tacitus, *Annals* 2.60–61). For the mythological as background for Rome's conquests in the Caucasus, see D. Braund, "The Caucasian Frontier: Myth, Exploration and the Dynamics of Imperialism," in *The Defence of the Roman and Byzantine East*, ed. P. Freeman and D. Kennedy (Oxford, 1986), 1.31–49.

8 And for the Jewish attitudes see D. Flusser, "The Kingdom of Rome in the Eyes of the Hasmoneans, and as Seen by the Essenes," *Zion* 48 (1983): 149–176 (Hebrew); and M. Hadas-Lebel, "L'Évolution de l'image . . . ," *Aufstieg und Niedergang der römischen Welt* 2.20.2 (1987): 715–856. Cf. also G. Stemberger, *Die römische Herrschaft im Urteil der Juden* (Darmstadt, 1983); N. R. M. de Lange, "Jewish Attitudes to the Roman World," in *Imperialism in the Ancient World*, ed. P. D. A. Garnsey and C. R. Whittaker (Cambridge, 1978), pp. 255–281.

9 For the details and history of the period, see E. Schürer, *The History of the Jewish People in the Age of Jesus Christ,* rev. G. Vermes et al. (Edinburgh, 1973–1987), 1.243–557; and E. M. Smallwood, *The Jews under Roman Rule* (Leiden, 1976).

10 For the Land as a religious "halakhic" concept, see recently S. Freyne, *Galilee, Jesus, and the Gospels* (Philadelphia, 1988), pp. 190–198, 239–247. Freyne, however, along with most other scholars, does not make the necessary distinction between the Land as a halakhic concept and the Land as a nationalistic religiopolitical symbol. The two are not always associated, and the fact that the Jews could live spread out within a vast non-Jewish population for decades and yet still adhere to their customs concerning the Land shows that in practice there was such a distinction.

11 In general for Jewish-Roman relations see U. Baumann, *Rom und die Juden. Die römischen-jüdischen Beziehungen von Pompeius bis zum Tode des Herodes (63 v. Chr.–4 v. Chr.)* (Frankfurt an Main, 1983).

12 For Pompey's settlement see F. M. Abel, "Le Siège de Jérusalem par Pompée," *Revue biblique* 54 (1947): 243–255; E. Bammel, "Die Neuordnung des Pompeius und das Römisch-jüdische Bündnis," *Zeitschrift des deutschen Palästina-Vereins* 75 (1959): 76–82; and V. Burr, "Rom und Judaea im 1 Jahrhundert v.

Chr," *Aufstieg und Niedergang der römischen Welt* 1.1 (1972): 875–886. For Gabinius's settlement see B. Kanael, "The Partition of Judaea by Gabinius," *Israel Exploration Journal* 7 (1957): 98–106; E. Bammel, "The Organization of Palestine by Gabinius," *Journal of Jewish Studies* 12 (1961): 159–162; and E. M. Smallwood, "Gabinius' Organization of Palestine," *Journal of Jewish Studies* 18 (1967): 89–92. Cf. for the Decapolis B. Isaac, *The Limits of Empire* (Oxford, 1990), passim.

[13] For such divisions by Rome, see Cary and Scullard, *History of Rome,* passim.

[14] Josephus demonstrates with this particular incident how Roman generals handled the territories of the provinces (*Jewish War* 1.361–362, and cf. *Antiquities* 15.90–96). Cf. also in his speech during the Jewish-Arab war, that no one should take a piece of Jewish land (*Antiquities* 15.133). For client kings rewarded with territory, see P. C. Sands, *The Client Princes of the Roman Empire under the Republic* (Cambridge, 1908), pp. 112–114, and D. Braund, *Rome and the Friendly King* (London, 1984), passim.

[15] L. I. Levine wished to see its reflection in a famous Baraita (*Caesarea under Roman Rule* [Leiden, 1975], p. 10), but Y. Sussman convincingly showed that this is a "halakhic" map rather than a map that reflects actual political borders of the Hasmonean or Herodian periods; see "The 'Boundaries of Eretz-Israel,' " *Tarbiz* 45 (1976): 213–257 (Hebrew).

[16] For Herod's policies, see A. Schalit, *König Herodes: Der Mann und sein Werk* (Berlin, 1969). For the Greek cities during his rule, see M. Hengel, *The "Hellenization" of Judaea in the First Century after Christ* (Philadelphia, 1989), passim. For Herod as a client king, see also E. M. Smallwood, *The Jews under Roman Rule* (Leiden, 1976), pp. 60–104.

[17] About this aspect see recently A. Kasher, *Jews, Idumaeans and Ancient Arabs* (Tübingen, 1990), pp. 126–174.

[18] Cf. ibid., pp. 214–220.

[19] These events can be compared to the three partitions of modern Poland, and to the partition of Germany after World War II.

[20] The Trachon had, according to *Antiquities* 17.26–28, a special status throughout the period.

[21] Cf. D. R. Schwartz, *Agrippa I: The Last King of Judaea* (Tübingen, 1990), pp. 59–62.

[22] Cf. also the Tiberias coins of Antipas, and Y. Meshorer, *Ancient Jewish Coinage* (New York, 1982), 2.31–50. Bethsaida-Julias in Philip's domain, and the Peraean Julias (in Herod Antipas's) were also local capitals of a sort for the gentiles (*Jewish War* 2.168).

23 Ibid., 1.97–98 and 2.41, 49.

24 Cf. Schwartz, *Agrippa,* pp. 111–112.

25 For the Roman motivations in doing so, see A. Momigliano, *Claudius the Emperor and His Achievement,* 2d ed. (New York, 1961), pp. 39–73; Schwartz, *Agrippa,* pp. 149–153.

26 Meshorer, *Ancient Jewish Coinage,* 2.51–64; Schwartz, *Agrippa,* pp. 84–85.

27 Cf. in general also A. Kasher, ed. *The Great Jewish Revolt: Factors and Circumstances Leading to Its Outbreak* (Jerusalem, 1983), pp. 66–90 [Hebrew], and Schwartz, *Agrippa,* p. 153.

28 For his views, partly Josephus's views too, see his speech in *Jewish War* 2.345–401, and E. Gabba, "L'Impero Romano nel discorso di Agrippa II (Iosepho, B. I., II, 345–401)," *Rivista storica dell 'antichità* 6–7 (1976–1977): 189–194.

29 About this organization, see Avi Yonah, *Carta's Atlas* (Jerusalem, 1966), p. 70, map no. 106 (Hebrew).

30 Of the books from the apocrypha and pseudepigrapha I here use only the ones that can be dated to the period 63 B.C.E.–80/90 C.E., such as the Psalms of Solomon and the Testament of Moses (as well as Philo Judaeus).

31 Cf. Vergil, *Eclogue* 4.18–22. Ideas of this kind were commonplace throughout the ancient Near East as early as Alexander the Great, thus long before the Sibylline Oracle 2 was composed.

32 For instance, the history of the Rechabites, and cf. J. H. Charlesworth, "History of the Rechabites," in *Old Testament Pseudepigrapha,* ed. J. H. Charlesworth (New York, 1983–1985), 2.450–461.

33 Cf. in general S. Sandmel, *Philo of Alexandria: An Indroduction* (New York and Oxford, 1979), pp. 102–110 and passim, with the important article of B. Schaller, "Philon von Alexandreia und das 'Heilige Land,' " in *Das Land Israel,* ed. G. Strecker (Göttingen, 1983), pp. 172–187 with the older bibliography. For the spiritualization of the Land in Philo, see also B. Amaru Halpern, "Land Theology in Philo and Josephus," in *The Land of Israel: Jewish Perspectives,* ed. L. A. Hoffman (Notre Dame, Ind., 1986), pp. 65–93.

34 Some of the scholars who are against the idea of a "political" Jesus in varying degrees are J. Weiss, *Die Predigt Jesu vom Reiche Gottes,* 2d ed. (Göttingen, 1900), now also available in English under the title *Jesus' Proclamation of the Kingdom of God* (Philadelphia, 1971); A. Schweitzer, *Das Messianitäts- und Leidensgeheimnis* (Tübingen, 1901), available in English under the title *The Mystery of the Kingdom of God* (London, 1914); and idem, *Von Reimarus zu Wrede* (Tübingen, 1906), in English *The Quest of the Historical Jesus* (London, 1910). See also E. Bammel, "The Revolution Theory from Reimarus to Brandon," mentioning most of the older literature, and J. P. M. Sweet, "The Zealots and Jesus," both in *Jesus and the Politics of His Day,* ed. E. Bammel and C. F. D. Moule (Cambridge and New York,

1984), pp. 1–68; G. Bornkamm, *Jesus of Nazareth* (New York, 1960), pp. 66–67, 121–123; J. Jeremias, *New Testament Theology* (London, 1971), pp. 71–72, 122–123, 228–229; O. Cullmann, *Jesus and the Revolutionaries* (New York, 1970), pp. 1–10; as well as many others.

[35] Some of the scholars who favor the idea of the political Jesus in varying degrees are H. S. Reimarus, *Von dem Zwecke Jesu und seiner Jünger* (Brunswick, 1778), and the two English editions, one translated by G. W. Buchanan, *The Goal of Jesus and His Disciples* (Leiden, 1970), and one edited by C. H. Talbert and translated by R. S. Fraser, *Reimarus: Fragments* (Philadelphia, 1970); R. Eisler, *The Messiah Jesus and John the Baptist* (London, 1931); J. Carmichael, *The Death of Jesus* (New York, 1962); the most extreme and elaborate in recent times is S. G. F. Brandon, *Jesus and the Zealots* (Manchester, 1967). In recent years scholars broadened the scope of the rather limited problem of Jesus' political stance to sociopolitical and more general sociocultural issues. These ideas are not relevant to this particular study, but see for instance for such works as L. Gaston, *No Stone on Another* (Leiden, 1970); J. H. Yoder, *The Politics of Jesus* (Grand Rapids, Mich. 1972); J. Gager, *Kingdom and Community: The Social World of Early Christianity* (Englewood Cliffs, N.J., 1975); G. Theissen, *Sociology of Early Palestinian Christianity* (Philadelphia, 1978); R. Cassidy, *Jesus, Politics and Society* (New York, 1978); R. Scroggs, "The Sociological Interpretation of the New Testament: The Present State of Research," *New Testament Studies* 26 (1980): 164–179; and H. Kee, *Christian Origins in Sociological Perspective* (Philadelphia, 1980). Cf. the excellent survey of Bammel, "Revolution Theory" (pp. 11–68); and recently R. A. Horsley, *Jesus and the Spiral of Violence* (San Francisco, 1987), esp. pp. 149–326.

[36] Brandon, *Jesus and the Zealots,* p. 323 and passim.

[37] For the reactions on the issue of Jesus as a Zealot after Brandon, see in particular W. Wink, "Jesus and Revolution: Reflections on S. G. F. Brandon's *Jesus and the Zealots,*" *Union Seminary Quarterly Review* 25 (1969): 37–59; Cullmann, *Jesus and the Revolutionaries;* W. Klassen, "Jesus and the Zealot Option," *Canadian Journal of Theology* (1970): 12–21; M. Hengel, *Was Jesus a Revolutionist?* (Philadelphia, 1971); J. Gnilka, "War Jesus Revolutionaer?" *Bibel und Leben* 12 (1971): 67–78; H. Merkel, "War Jesus ein Revolutionär?" *Bibel und Kirche* 26 (1971): 44–47; M. Hengel, *Victory over Violence: Jesus and the Revolutionaries* (Philadelphia, 1973); A. Richardson, *The Political Christ* (Philadelphia, 1973); Sweet, "Zealots and Jesus"; and M. Hengel, *The Zealots* (Edinburgh, 1989). Cf. now also D. R. Schwartz, "On Christian Study of the Zealots," in his *Studies in the Jewish Background of Christianity* (Tübingen, 1992), pp. 128–146.

[38] Recently for the question of the "historical" Jesus see J. Jeremias, "The Present Position in the Controversy Concerning the Problem of the Historical Jesus," *The Expository Times* 69 (1957–1958): 333–339; E. Käsemann, *Essays on New Testament Themes* (London, 1964), pp. 15–47; R. H. Fuller, *A Critical Introduction to the New Testament* (London, 1966), pp. 94–98; H. K. McArthur, *In Search of the Historical Jesus* (New York, 1969), pp. 139–144; M. D. Hooker, "Christology and Methodology," *New Testament Studies* 17 (1970–1971): 480–487; H. K.

McArthur, "The Burden of Proof in Historical Jesus Research," *The Expository Times* 82 (1970–1971): 116–119; D. G. A. Calvert, "An Examination of the Criteria for Distinguishing the Authentic Words of Jesus," *New Testament Studies* 18 (1971–1972): 209–219; N. Perrin, *Rediscovering The Teaching of Jesus* (New York, 1967), pp. 15–53; and recently with the older literature E. P. Sanders, *Jesus and Judaism* (London, 1985); and J. H. Charlesworth, *Jesus Within Judaism* (New York, 1988). A useful bibliographical survey may be found in M. J. Borg, "Portraits of Jesus in Contemporary North American Scholarship" (forthcoming in *Harvard Theological Review*).

[39] See, for instance, Hengel, in his above-mentioned works.

[40] L. I. Levine, D. S. Rhoads, and R. A. Horsley quoted in chapter 7, note 31 (against Hengel).

[41] M. J. Borg, *Conflict, Holiness and Politics in the Teachings of Jesus* (New York and Toronto, 1984). Cf. also M. D. Goodman, *The Ruling Class of Judaea* (Cambridge, 1987), pp. 76–108 (concerning the trends in Judaism at the time); Hengel, *Zealots,* p. 181; cf. also H. Braun, *Spätjüdisch-häretischer und frühchristlicher Radikalismus* (Tübingen, 1957), 2.57ff.

[42] See an elaborate discussion about the term in Hengel, *Zealots,* esp. pp. 59–75, 146–228.

[43] Rome was sensitive to movements that led to unrest in the empire; for examples see the survey of S. L. Dyson, "Native Revolts in the Roman Empire," *Historia* 20 (1971): 239–274.

[44] Cf. Borg, *Conflict, Holiness,* pp. 59–60 and passim.

[45] Cf. chapter 8 above.

[46] W. D. Davies, *The Gospel and the Land* (Berkeley, Los Angeles, and London, 1974), esp. pp. 164–179.

[47] Cf. D. R. Schwartz, "The End of the Line: Paul in the Canonical Book of Acts," in *Paul and the Legacies of Paul,* ed. W. S. Babcock (Dallas, 1990), pp. 3–24. Generally for Paul in Acts see Munck, *Acts,* * and J. Jervell, *Luke and the People of God: A New Look at Luke-Acts* (Minneapolis, 1972), pp. 19–39; P. Borgen, "From Paul to Luke: Observations Toward Clarification of the Theology of Luke-Acts," *Catholic Biblical Quarterly* 31 (1969): 168–182; H. Conzelmann, *Acts of the Apostles,*† p. 186.

[48] Cf. chapter 4 above.

[49] 2:9–11: "Parthians and Medes and Elamites and residents of Mesopotamia, Judea and Cappadocia, Pontus and Asia, Phrygia and Pamphylia, Egypt and the parts of Libya belonging to Cyrene, and visitors from Rome, both Jews and proselytes, Cretans and Arabians. . . ." With the exception of Jews and proselytes, who were "visitors" from Rome (after all, the capital of the empire could not be left out), all other places belong to Alexander the Great's eastern ecumene. I do not

believe that this concoction of places is merely a result of the nature of the sources available to Luke, as Conzelmann (*Acts*,† pp. 14–15) and others have claimed (as for instance J. A. Brinkman, "The Literary Background of the 'Catalogue of the Nations' (Acts 2, 9–11)," *Catholic Biblical Quarterly* 25 [1963]: 418–427). Instead it reflects the dichotomy of the eastern versus western ecumene. Luke, wishing to emphasize that Christianity was also influential in the eastern ecumene (as the western is "covered" by Paul's travels), inserted this list. It is not accidental that the list of Acts 2:9–11 and Paul's itinerary are complementary. Note that Luke distinguishes between the notion of *ethnos* and the geographical region.

[50] "And you shall be my witness in Jerusalem and in all Judea and Samaria and to the end of the earth." For a different interpretation of 1:8 see D. R. Schwartz, "The End of the GH (Acts 1:8): Beginning or End of the Christian Vision?" *Journal of Biblical Literature* 105.4 (1986): 669–676; and W. C. van Unnik, "Der Ausdruck und sein alttestamentlicher Hintergrund," in *Studia Biblica et Semitica, Theodoro Christiano Vriezen* (Wageningen, 1966), pp. 335–349.

[51] Davies, *The Gospel.*

[52] I am not going back to the naïve and romantic views of E. Renan and his followers (*Vie de Jesus*), who accepted most of the topographical elements in the stories at face value. I take a more balanced view (see for instance, E. Trocmé, *Jesus and His Contemporaries* [London, 1973], pp. 15–18).

[53] G. Theissen drew from the localism found in the synoptic tradition the conclusion that many traditions are early and go back to the regions such as the Galilee, Jerusalem, and so on: see *Lokalkolorit und Zeitgeschichte in den Evangelien* (Göttingen, 1989) (see also Freyne, *Galilee, Jesus, and the Gospels*). What follows in many ways supports some of his views, but from a different point of view. Cf. also R. L. Mowery, "Pharisees and Scribes, Galilee and Jerusalem," *Zeitschrift für die neutestamentliche Wissenschaft* 80.3–4 (1989): 266–268.

[54] Mark 6:7–13; Luke 9:1–6. Cf. Mann, *Mark,** pp. 291–293.

[55] Albright and Mann, *Matthew,** p. 234: "As at Qumran, the concern is for the whole assembly of Israel (cf. Rev. VII 4), those to whom the Gospel has been proclaimed." See D. Flusser, "Qumran und die Zwölf," in his *Judaism and the Origins of Christianity* (Jerusalem, 1988), pp. 173–185.

[56] For the various datings of New Testament books, see A. T. Robinson, *Redating the New Testament* (Philadelphia, 1976), chap. 1; and recently Theissen, *Lokalkolorit.*

[57] Cf. Munck, *Acts,** pp. 68–97. Other sites such as Damascus are added as well.

[58] See John 4 and Luke 10:25–37 as well as Acts 8:4–25 with the comments of Brown, *John,** 1.175–185; and E. Haenchen, *The Acts of the Apostles: A Commentary* (Oxford, 1971) pp. 300–308. For John 4 the secondary literature abounds; see

G. van Belle, *Johannine Bibliography 1966–1985,* Bibliotheca ephemeridum theologicarum lovaniensium 82 (Louvain, 1988), pp. 212–220.

[59] And cf. Conzelmann, *Acts,*† p. 75.

[60] See for this story Conzelmann, *Acts,*† pp. 80–84.

[61] There is no reason to argue that Luke or Matthew lived outside Palestine because they are inaccurate concerning the topography of the Land, for even geographers in antiquity who traveled to places they describe make stupid mistakes. For this issue in general see M. Hengel, "Der historiker Lukas und die Geographie Palaestinas in der Apostelgeschichte," *Zeitschrift des deutschen Palästina-Vereins* 99 (1983): 147–183.

[62] For this issue see in particular W. Wrede, *Jesus als Davidssohn, Vorträge und Studien* (Tübingen, 1907), pp. 147–177; G. Hölscher, *Urgemeinde und Spätjudentum* (Oslo, 1928), p. 9; and J. Klausner, *Jesus of Nazareth* (New York, 1926), passim. Cf. also R. Bultmann, *History of the Synoptic Tradition* (Oxford, 1963), pp. 136–137; and C. Burger, *Jesus als Davidssohn* (Göttingen, 1970); and recently for these issues also J. Marcus, "Mark 14:61: 'Are You the Messiah-Son-of-God?' " *Novum Testamentum* 31 (1989): 125–141.

[63] J. Weiss already alluded to this possibility in his classic study, *Jesus' Proclamation,* pp. 93, 102–103, and passim. So also does Borg, *Conflict, Holiness,* passim.

[64] In this respect the late rabbinic literature should also be understood as reflecting the Pharisaic ideas of pre-70 C.E. But these writings are very late, and should be handled cautiously concerning the first century C.E.

[65] The only exceptions are David and Solomon, whose names are associated with many different aspects of biblical and Israelite life besides the territorial. For the statistics of the appearance of biblical figures see N. M. Cohen, *Jewish Bible Personages in the New Testament* (Lanham and London, 1989), pp. 37–41.

[66] It was even ingeniously suggested that they wanted to reinstate the Hasmonean type of state: see W. R. Farmer, *Maccabees, Zealots, and Josephus: An Inquiry into Jewish Nationalism in the Greco-Roman Period* (New York, 1957). Unfortunately there is no evidence in the sources to support this view. Hengel, in his *Zealots* (pp. 146–312 and passim), attempts to show that the aim of the Zealots' ideology was to help bring about the kingdom of God by violent means (in contrast to Jesus' group, who were antiviolence). Whereas he is right about the pacifism of Jesus' group as opposed to the militant spirit of the Zealots, it is hard to find any allusion in the sources of the first century to the type of comprehensive ideology of the Kingdom of God that motivated the Zealot movement. Josephus's statement that they only adhere to God as their master is not sufficient evidence to claim a comprehensive ideology. Even in Christian sources there is no clear outline of the political and socioeconomic dimensions of the Kingdom of God. Hengel emphasized the religious motivations of Zealotism, and somewhat toned down the political motivations (cf. p. 245 and elsewhere).

The emphasis by Hengel (pp. 249–255) on the "wilderness" as a religious and messianic concept (accepted by D. R. Schwartz, "Temple and Desert: On Religion and State in Second Temple Period Judaea," in his *Studies in the Jewish Background of Christianity* [Tübingen, 1992], pp. 29–43) is highly interesting. Yet it was not antithetical to a Jewish national existence on the Land, as Schwartz alleges in his article, because the wilderness in all of the examples brought forward by the two scholars is within the borders of the Land. Thus it was a place of seclusion, hiding, but was not opposed to a political concept of national territory.

[67] Cf. S. J. D. Cohen, *Josephus in Galilee and Rome* (Leiden, 1979), passim.

[68] For his interpretive methods, see H. W. Attridge, *The Interpretation of Biblical History in the Antiquitates Judaicae of Flavius Josephus* (Missoula, Mont., 1976). See also L. H. Feldman, in his collected biblical figures (cf. *Josephus and Modern Scholarship, 1937–1980* [Berlin and New York, 1984]. For Josephus's theological view of the Land, see B. Amaru Halpern, "Land Theology in Josephus' Jewish Antiquities," *Jewish Quarterly Review* 71 (1981): 201–229; also her article "Land Theology in Philo and Josephus." Although Amaru Halpern and others justifiably point to tendentious nuances in Josephus's interpretation of the Land, nevertheless the whole picture is what matters: the Land is very important as a national symbol in Josephus's *Antiquities*.

[69] The magnificent discourse of Joshua before his death (Joshua 23–24) is very much shortened by Josephus (5.115–116), perhaps because the original biblical discourse elaborates upon the destruction of the seven peoples and the prohibition against worshiping idols. Josephus only mentions the goodwill of the people toward God, and God's friendship toward them.

[70] Cf. D. Mendels, "Pseudo-Philo's *Biblical Antiquities,* the 'Fourth Philosophy' and the Political Messianism of the First Century A.D.," in *The Messiah,* ed. J. H. Charlesworth (Minneapolis, 1992), pp. 261–275.

[71] Cf. R. H. Charles, *The Apocrypha and Pseudepigrapha of the Old Testament* (Oxford, 1913), 2.407–424; J. Priest, "The Testament of Moses," in *The Old Testament Pseudepigrapha,* ed. J. H. Charlesworth (New York, 1983–1985), 1.919–934; Schürer, *History,* 3.1.278–288.

[72] See note 64 above for the rabbinic attitudes.

CHAPTER 10

Jerusalem and the Temple, 63 B.C.E.-66 C.E.

The years 67–63 B.C.E. were crucial for Jewish nationalism. The decisive struggle between two Jewish claimants to the throne was centered on Jerusalem and the Temple. From then on nationalistic groups strove to get control of the Temple and Jerusalem at many junctures until 66 C.E. It will be seen that the Roman conquest brought about a gradual change in their status as nationalistic symbols. The picture is complex; Jerusalem remained a religiopolitical and an economic *metropolis* (capital). It was after the foundation of Caesarea by Herod the Great in 10 B.C.E. that Jerusalem lost much of its importance as a political capital in the eyes of the non-Jewish population, as well as in the eyes of Herod and his dynasty. After 63 B.C.E. the Temple remained a religious center for the "indigenous" Jewish population, which resisted Hellenism. It was also viewed as such by the Romans, who by this attitude actually continued the policies of the Ptolemies and Seleucids, tolerating the religious autonomy of their subjects. But the moment there were political aspirations attached to the city and Temple, Rome intervened quickly.

One should bear in mind that in the Roman Empire, as under the Hellenistic monarchies, the local temples were, for the indigenous populations, remnants of past nationalistic grandeur, as can be seen in Egypt, in Asia Minor, and in Palestine itself.[1] But as long as these temples did not create troubles, Rome tolerated them as religious centers. In many instances a cult of the emperor and Roma was added, or intermingled with the existing cult. In Egypt, for instance, the Roman emperors were worshiped as pharaohs in the indigenous temples.[2] In 30/29 B.C.E. Octavian (the later Augustus) granted permission to the Hellenes of Bithynia and the province of Asia to worship the emperor (Suetonius, *Augustus* 52; Tacitus, *Annals* 4.37). After this date we can observe a swift spread of the emperor cult throughout the Roman Near East.[3] In many places altars and temples were erected that were similar to the existing ones, but focused on the cult of the emperor.[4] Some emperors started to believe that they were gods. Domitian (81–96 C.E.) was delighted when he was addressed as *dominus et deus,* and his father Vespasian is said to have proclaimed on his deathbed, "Alas, I think that I am becoming a god." And, indeed, like most emperors since Julius Caesar, he was deified after his death. In some places we know that Rome supported the priesthoods that were involved in the emperor cult.[5]

In Palestine this practice led to the widening of the gap between the Jews and the non-Jews. On the one hand, non-Jews in Palestine (and elsewhere) kept worshiping their local or national gods. A good example is the city of Ascalon, where a coin from Roman times (the rule of Antoninus Pius, 138–161 C.E.) has on its obverse the local god Phanebal.[6] The cult of the local gods was not only a religious matter, but a social and economic one as well—it was the center of life in pagan societies.[7] On the other hand, non-Jews in centers such as Caesarea and Samaria went to the Greek temples so that they could "communicate" with the emperor. Thus, non-Jews all over the ancient Near East had a unifying link in this common awareness of the empire and its leader. By contrast, most Jews could not be part of this shared experience and were limited to the sacrifice on behalf of the emperor, twice a day in their Temple in Jerusalem (Josephus, *Jewish War* 2.197; Philo, *Legatio ad Gaium* 157, 317; and Josephus, *Contra Apionem* 2.77).

Rome strengthened and supported not only the priests of the pagan temples in Palestine but also the aristocracy of the non-Jewish population. Even if Rome created a strong priestly class in Jerusalem, as argued by M. D. Goodman, the Roman emperors were aware of the fact that the Jews were opposed to a temple cult and the cult of Dea Roma (see for instance the letter of Claudius to the Jews of Alexandria).[8] This opposition in itself was not a very serious matter, but the political tensions that were created as a result of it no doubt weakened the status of the Jewish priests when compared to the gentile priesthood in Palestine. Let us see how Jerusalem and the Temple were conceived in reality as religiopolitical centers, after the Roman conquest of Palestine.

There is evidence that in 65 B.C.E., for the first time since the Maccabean independence, Jew fought Jew on the Temple Mount. The Jews, together with Hyrcanus II, the high priest, backed by the Arabs (Nabataeans) and Antipater the Edomite, besieged the priests who were gathered with Aristobulus, the legitimate Hasmonean king, on the Temple Mount during Passover (*Antiquities* 14.20–28). Not only did they fight each other, but Hyrcanus, who had already received money from Aristobulus, jeopardized the cult in the Temple by going back on his promise to deliver animals for the sacrifices. Also, the pact signed in the Temple earlier in the year by the two brothers was nullified (14.6–7; *Jewish War* 1.120–122). It was not a promising start for a new era. But Aristobulus's behavior should be discussed. He knew perfectly well, like many political figures later, that control of the Temple and its priests who practiced the daily cult meant control of the nation. At this juncture of civil war, Josephus tells the famous story of Onias, "a righteous man and dear to God," who was asked by Hyrcanus's supporters to curse Aristobulus and his fellow priests; he then said, "O God, king of the universe, because these men standing beside me are Thy people, and those who are besieged are Thy priests, I beseech Thee not to hearken to them against these men nor to bring to pass what these men ask Thee to do to those others" (*Antiquities* 14.22–25). Onias was probably one of those Jews who wanted to restore the theocracy and wanted to abolish the Hasmonean dynasty altogether.[9]

Hearing these words, some of Hyrcanus's supporters stoned Onias to death.[10] He was unfortunately not the last victim of this civil war. Pompey, who then intervened in the conflict, in keeping with Roman policies elsewhere in the East, realized that he had to get hold of the very heart of the nation, Jerusalem and its Temple. It is interesting to note that while he was on his way with the captured Aristobulus in his camp, the latter's supporters again seized the Temple Mount and even destroyed the bridge leading to the city (*Antiquities* 14.58). They did not seize the Temple for religious motives or for tactical reasons, though the place was very well guarded, according to Josephus (14.60–62). They acted for reasons that are obvious: Aristobulus's followers wanted to have the national symbol of independent sovereignty par excellence in their hands. Josephus shows in great detail that even during the siege of the Temple Mount, when the rest of Jerusalem was already in Pompey's hands, the practice of the cult was carried on without interruption, even though the Romans attacked the Temple daily. They ceased their attack only on the sabbath.

Pompey also understood that in order to conquer the nation he had to capture the Temple, but leave it intact; which he indeed did. Josephus says that "not light was the sin committed against the sanctuary, which before that time had never been entered or seen. For Pompey and not a few of his men went into it and saw what it was unlawful for any but the high priests to see." But they did not touch any of the holy artifacts of the Temple "because of piety, and in this respect also he [Pompey] acted in a manner worthy of his virtuous character" (*Antiquities* 14.71–72). Yet Roman generals were usually not so pious, and it seems that Pompey had a very clear aim. In keeping with Roman policies elsewhere, and in line with many Hellenistic rulers of the period prior to the Roman occupation of the East, he was very clear that from now on the Temple should serve only as a religious center of the Jewish people. He thus "instructed the Temple servants to cleanse the Temple and to offer the customary sacrifices to God, and he restored the high priesthood to Hyrcanus" (14.73; *Jewish War* 1.153). Thus was the issue of the Temple settled in 63 B.C.E.

The Roman approach to the problem of Jerusalem and its Temple—divesting it of its political significance—also came to the fore in the settlement of Gabinius, who crushed the uprising of Aristobulus's son Alexander in 57 B.C.E. The latter, like many Jewish rulers later, tried as a first step to rebuild the walls of Jerusalem. Gabinius, according to Josephus, "brought Hyrcanus to Jerusalem, to have charge of the temple," and made Jerusalem one of the five districts into which he divided the country.[11] By reinstating Hyrcanus II only as a high priest, he clearly divested the Temple of its political significance. The lowering of the political status of the Jerusalem Temple henceforward became one of the reasons for the sporadic clashes with certain strata of Jewish society that culminated in the Great War against Rome in 66–70 C.E. These Jews refused to accept a separation between the two aspects of the Temple. Thus when the opportunity arose they went to war against the Romans. Whereas similar groups of Jews had succeeded in Maccabean times in their aims against the Seleucids, the national movement of the first century C.E. was crushed by the Romans in 70 C.E.

During the years 63–41 B.C.E., many events of a significant nature occurred in the conquered Jewish state, only some of which are of importance here. First and foremost is Crassus's invasion in 53 B.C.E. Josephus refers to it, saying that "Crassus, intending to march against the Parthians, came to Judea and carried off the money in the Temple, amounting to two thousand talents, which Pompey had left." Josephus adds that "Crassus, however, although he took this bar (of solid beaten gold) with the understanding that he would not touch anything else in the Temple, violated his oath and carried off all the gold in the sanctuary."[12] This account shows that, like many other temples, the Jerusalem Temple was known for its riches. Moreover, it strengthens what has already been said concerning the Hasmoneans, that the priestly order had vast economic resources at its disposal and was receiving great amounts of money from the Diaspora (*Antiquities* 14.110–115). This priestly order did not necessarily gain on a personal level, though we know about some notorious cases of stealing from the Temple treasury; but it gave them a great deal of economic as well as political power. Therefore, Crassus's action was not only offensive on the religious level but was also a blow to the economic strength of the priestly order.

An idea of the influence enjoyed by the Temple and its high priest during this period emerges from Josephus. Hyrcanus II, the high priest, was honored not only by the Romans (Julius Caesar, whom he had helped during his fights in Egypt) but also by Athens, and presumably by many other places outside Palestine as well (14.143–155). Hyrcanus was therefore seen as the head of the Jewish state by foreigners, though he was not accepted as such by the nationalistic forces in Palestine (14.156–157). Yet when the chief Jews wished to protest against the Edomite family of Antipater (who was the *epitropos* of Judea) and their wayward deeds, they did approach Hyrcanus. Josephus says that "Hyrcanus was persuaded. And his anger was further kindled by the mothers of the men who had been murdered by Herod, for every day in the Temple they kept begging the king and the people to have Herod (who was then the governor of the Galilee) brought to judgment in the Sanhedrin" (14.168). When Herod was brought to the Sanhedrin and later wanted to take revenge by attacking Jerusalem, his father and brother deterred him from doing so (14.181)—though he was to attack the city some years later. Among the concessions Julius Caesar granted the Jews at this time (48–44 B.C.E.) was the permission to fortify Jerusalem (14.200). During the short period of Caesar's rule the high priesthood of Hyrcanus was invested with a great deal of political power; but this power was soon lost when Herod the Great became king.

When the Parthians conquered Palestine in 40 B.C.E., they naturally headed toward the capital, Jerusalem, and made Mattathias Antigonus, son of Aristobulus II, a real Hasmonean king. Mattathias Antigonus immediately disqualified Hyrcanus II from the high priesthood by cutting off his ear. Josephus emphasizes that the Temple was a sensitive political institution at the time that the Parthians besieged Jerusalem (14.337–338; *Jewish War* 1.253). The rule of Antigonus brought back the political grandeur of the city and its Temple, but only for a short while. When Herod reconquered it in 37 B.C.E. as a client king of the Romans, he knew perfectly well that by holding Jerusalem and its Temple he would control the nation. In fact he had tried to do so in 39 B.C.E., but failed because of the vast support Antigonus had at the time. Josephus says that "he moved his camp and came close to the wall, encamping before the temple, which was the point where the wall could easily be assaulted." The Jews from among the pro-Hasmonean party who were inside the city "fought against Herod and his men; many were the invocations made about the Temple, and many were the things said to encourage the people, to the effect that God would deliver them from danger" (*Antiquities* 14.465–470).

Again Jew fought Jew on the Temple Mount, but this time with the assistance of Romans and mercenaries. Herod soon realized that this was the place he ought to conquer in order to become the central figure of the nation. There was a prophetic atmosphere surrounding Jerusalem at the time, which made Herod even more careful not to cause too much destruction in the city. He had in particular to keep the Romans from doing too much damage. He knew what repercussions any further ruin of the city would have on his future position within the Jewish nation. He had now been king of Judea for three years, and had at last succeeded in seizing the very heart of the nation, the capital and its Temple. As said elsewhere, he wished to become a Hasmonean ruler, a nationalistic unifying figure.[13] Very soon he learned that this aim was impossible. An interesting piece of information is given by Josephus concerning the siege of Jerusalem by Herod. He says in *Antiquities* 15.3 that the sages Shemaiah and Abtalion advised the citizens during the siege to admit Herod. Shemaiah is supposed to be the sage who said, "Love labor and hate mastery and seek not acquaintance with the ruling power" (*m. 'Abot* 1:10). Here one can see the continuing existence of the peace party of the Hasidim, and later of Jesus' group. Many sages did not want to be involved in the stormy and violent politics of the day.[14] They wanted to save Jerusalem and its Temple from destruction and to maintain it only as a spiritual and religious place. This high-minded concern for the Temple and its sanctity persuaded many Jews that the sages were the true spiritual leaders of Israel rather than the priests, whom many regarded as too politicized to serve in that capacity.

Happily, Herod succeeded in tempering the Roman forces fighting with him, the city was saved, and the support of the sages was ensured. At the very start of his reign Herod enacted what so many anti-Hasmonean circles were striving for, and what only Salome, the widow of Alexander Jannaeus, had achieved, namely, the separation between the high priesthood and kingship. Not being of priestly lineage, Herod could not become high priest.[15] That is why he felt free to appoint weak figures from the Jewish Diaspora to be the high priests.[16] But at the very beginning of his reign, after naming Hananel the Babylonian as high priest,[17] he was hard pressed by Alexandra to install her son Aristobulus, grandson of Hyrcanus II, the high priest, and brother of his wife Miriam, to the high priesthood. Herod reluctantly agreed, and learned the hard way a lesson in nationalism. He saw how the high priest became a national symbol, arousing the deepest of nationalistic feelings among the indigenous Jewish population. When he appointed the Hasmonean to be high priest, he suddenly realized that the people were filled with nostalgia for the Hasmonean dynasts, who indeed had been both high priests and kings and symbolized in Herod's time the independence of the nation. In one of the triannual pilgrimages (Tabernacles), when Jerusalem held many times more people than usual,[18] Aristobulus went up to the altar to perform the sacrifices in accordance with the law, wearing the ornamental dress of the high priests and carrying out the rites of the cult, and he was extraordinarily handsome and taller than most youths of his age, and in his appearance, moreover, he displayed to the full the nobility of his descent. And so there arose among the people an impulsive feeling of affection toward him, and there came to them a vivid memory of the deeds performed by his grandfather Aristobulus. Being overcome, they gradually revealed their feelings, showing joyful and painful emotion at the same time, and they called out to him good wishes mingled with prayers, so that the affection of the crowd became evident, and their acknowledgment of their emotions seemed too impulsive in view of their having a king. (*Antiquities* 15.51–52)

This display was of course too much for the real king, Herod, who swiftly corrected his mistake of appointing the youngster. He caused him to be drowned in the pool near Jericho. Remnants of the pool have been found by archaeologists.[19] Herod then reinstated Hananel the Babylonian to the high priesthood, and shortly thereafter got rid of Hyrcanus II. Later he gave the high priesthood to Jesus the son of Phiabi, whom he got rid of after marrying the daughter of Simeon the son of Boethus, whom he made high priest in 23 B.C.E. (*Antiquities* 15.320–322). Both of the latter high priests came from the Egyptian Diaspora.[20] From then until the Great War the house of Boethus was powerful. By separating the high priesthood from kingship, and by appointing weak high priests from the Diaspora,[21] Herod showed very clearly that the high priesthood's role as a political national symbol associated with Palestine and the Jewish state was a thing of the past, and that it had increasingly become a symbol of world Jewry, which may be seen as part of Herod's wish to become the "king of the Jews" as well as the "king of Judea."[22] At any rate, from then on he harshly dominated the high priests. He also watched the Temple Mount carefully from the Antonia, a fortress he built at the beginning of his reign in Jerusalem. It became a sort of an Akra, this time built by a half-Jewish king.

During Herod's reign the position of the Temple underwent an important transformation. In keeping with the change that Herod brought about in the high priesthood, which made the office secondary to his own secular rule, he in fact reduced the political status of the Temple. He did not eliminate its political aspects altogether, as is known from the political statements he issued there from time to time (cf. below); but he also made political announcements in Jericho and Caesarea. Herod in fact decentralized the strong political power of Jerusalem and its Temple by distributing it to his other political centers and palaces. In other words, the moment Jerusalem and the Temple were under his control, he gradually degraded their status through various political tactics. It is also quite clear that the foundation of Caesarea, and in a way that of Sebastia, the former North Israelite capital of Samaria, had its impact on the centrality of Jerusalem. Suddenly Judea had two competitive capitals.

During Herod's reign the Temple became more of a religious and spiritual center for believing Jews. By lowering the profile of the Temple as a political center, Herod was true to his masters, the Romans, who wanted to eliminate any political power from native temples.[23] The effect of Herod's reducing the status and importance of the priesthood was to enhance the status of the sages, who thus occupied a place of leadership. This policy was one of the reasons for the clashes between nationalists, who refused to make the distinction between religious and political, and Herod and his successors, who built their authority in the eyes of Rome on this distinction. The political announcements made at times by Herod in the Temple may have frustrated these nationalists even more, as can already be seen in the attempt by his mother-in-law, Alexandra, to overthrow him in 28 B.C.E. Josephus says of this coup d'état that Alexandra "made an effort to seize control of the fortified places in the city. There were two of these: one (guarded) the city itself, and the other the Temple. Whoever was master of these had the *whole nation* in his power, for sacrifices could not be made without (controlling) these places, and it was impossible for any of the Jews to forego offering these, for they would rather give up their lives than the worship that they are accustomed to offer God" (*Antiquities* 15.247–248). Here we find a reference not only to the important religious role of the Temple, but also to the political role, which was aroused now and again. Alexandra, knowing that Herod was very ill, seized the opportunity. She thought that taking the Temple would be the first and essential step toward national independence. Again, as in the case of Aristobulus II many years earlier, the Temple

Mount was chosen as the first target in a coup not merely for tactical motives. Her coup failed, and Herod was again master of the nation.

Herod the Great made Jerusalem a "dualistic" city. Although Hellenistic influence was noticeable in the city before his rule, the process of hellenization was accelerated by Herod and his successors.[24] He built a theater, amphitheater, palace, and hippodrome there, but refrained from building any pagan temple. The more wealthy of the population followed in his footsteps and hellenized their living quarters. Part of the city thus became a city of Hellenistic type, similar to the ones of Asia Minor, Greece, and Italy. Much of what Herod did to hellenize Jerusalem, for which there is an abundance of archaeological evidence, was offensive to the religious Jews (*Antiquities* 15.267–291). For a man who built pagan temples in the Land (Sebastia, 15.298; Caesarea, 15.339; and Paneion, 15.363) and helped to build more outside the Land (15.328–329; *Jewish War* 1.422–428), these building enterprises in Jerusalem were not exceptional. But Herod made up for all of this hellenization by starting to renovate the Temple in 20/19 B.C.E. When Herod announced this enterprise, the Jews were afraid that he would never accomplish his task and they would remain without a complete Temple. Josephus goes out of his way to describe the Temple built by Herod (15.380–425). It was an enormous building of much grandeur, which could be seen from all over the city and from the hills surrounding it. Much of it was built in the Hellenistic style (15.414), and archaeologists have found some of its remains. The earlier layer of the Testament of Solomon may be an echo of the disputes following its building.[25]

Why did Herod initiate this huge enterprise? He wanted, as he himself said, to elevate his own personal stature. We believe that he wished to be seen as a real Hellenistic monarch who built an indigenous temple (with Hellenic improvements) for the native population. He also wished to associate himself with the great builder of the first Temple, King Solomon. One could even say that he wanted to compete with Solomon. At the same time, he wished to avoid the political associations the Temple had in the days of Solomon. Third, he wanted to be seen more favorably by religious Jews both in Palestine and in the Diaspora, some of whom had no reason to like him. And indeed he may have succeeded in gaining their favor, because many years later even the sages, who hated him altogether, said that his building was magnificent (Babylonian Talmud, *Baba Batra* 4:1, *Ta'anit* 23:1). Like a truly Hellenistic king he celebrated the anniversary of his enthronement on the very same day as the opening of the new Temple (15.421–423). Finally, Herod wished his building to become an international attraction. Many Hellenistic kings, well before the Roman occupation, had built enormous buildings to compete with the great international centers of the region. Important foreign guests, like the Roman official Marcus Agrippa in 15 B.C.E., even sacrificed to Yahweh in honor of Herod (*Antiquities* 16.14). But Herod's non-Jewish side, which was responsible for all other Hellenistic features of his reign, led him to put the Roman eagle on the entrance to the Temple, which was offensive to many Jews. It goes against the ordinance "You shall not make for yourself an idol, whether in the form of anything that is in heaven above, or that is on the earth beneath, or that is in the water under the earth" (Deut 5:8). They had no choice but to accept reluctantly this eagle during Herod's last years, but took it off when the rumor spread that the king was dead (4 B.C.E.).

Jerusalem at the time of Herod became one of many political centers in Palestine, such as Caesarea, Jericho, and Sebastia; yet it remained the most prominent of them all. As mentioned before, he made some of his most important announcements there. For example, when he returned from his journey to Asia Minor in which he had done a great deal for the Diaspora Jews, he went to Jerusalem and called an assembly (*ekklesia*) of all the people of the city. Josephus mentions that "there was a large crowd from the country as well." Herod appeared before the assembly and presented an account of his journey, telling "them about the Jews of Asia, saying that thanks to him they would be unmolested in future. After giving a general picture of his good fortune and his government of the kingdom . . ." (*Antiquities* 16.62–65). At a later date, when he returned from his journey to Augustus, Herod appeared in the Temple and made a speech there concerning his deeds abroad. Josephus says that Herod "gave an account of Caesar's kindness to him and of such of the various things he had done as he thought it was to his interest for the masses to know. At the end of it he directed his words to the admonishing of his sons, and exhorted the countries and the rest of the people to concord, and designated the sons who were to reign after him, first Antipater and next his sons by Miriam, Alexander and Aristobulus." On this occasion Herod promised his officers and soldiers that if they would be faithful to him in the future, they "would lead an untroubled life." Josephus adds, "having said what was acceptable to most but not to some" (16.131–135; *Jewish War* 1.457–466).

For the Jews in the Diaspora, Rome was the political center, whereas Jerusalem was the religiocultural one. In making his announcements in Jerusalem concerning the Jews of the Diaspora, Herod underlined his attempts to universalize Judaism beyond Palestine and to incorporate the Diaspora into it. Within this context we can understand his title "king of the Jews," his appointment of Diaspora Jews to the high priesthood, and the making of Jerusalem and its Temple a religious and spiritual center of world Jewry.[26] Thus one can assume that Jerusalem gained in stature in the eyes of Jews all over the world, as well as in the eyes of non-Jews abroad, as a consequence of Herod's building projects in the capital. Still, Jerusalem could not really become a religiopolitical capital for the non-Jews of Palestine. Although Hellenism influenced the architecture of Jerusalem, it remained very Jewish in character. Archaeologists have not found any Hellenistic pagan temples there, and our sources are silent about such a possibility. Almost no graven images have been found in the ornaments and decorations of the houses of even the most hellenized Jews. The so-called upper city, where these Jews lived, was full of ritual baths and other artifacts that all point to their being God-fearing Jews, for whom hellenization was only skin deep.[27]

Hence, while Jerusalem essentially remained a capital for the Jewish population,[28] there was a need for a capital for the pagan population of Palestine, which had a strong entity of its own.[29] Such a capital had to be dissociated from the old traditional places such as Jerusalem, Samaria (the old capital of the Israelite kingdom),[30] and Shechem, capital of the Samaritans. A place was chosen on the coast that had no significant former associations with the Jewish traditions of the country, like Alexandria in Egypt, which had no former associations with former Egyptian culture.[31] In 10 B.C.E. Herod celebrated the foundation of Caesarea Maritima and dedicated it to Emperor Augustus. This city was from then on to be the capital of the non-Jewish part of Palestine.[32] Even a special coin series was struck on this occasion, with the symbol of a galley on it.[33] Herod introduced the celebration of the games once every five years in honor of the emperor in his gentile capital, Caesarea, which Tacitus called "the capital of Judea."[34]

It is now time to discuss the episode involving the Roman eagle on the entrance to the Temple—this notorious event, which closed Herod's reign. In setting up the golden eagle, the symbol of the Roman Empire, above the great entrance gate of the Temple, Herod had offended most Jews. Some of the Jewish population were offended on the religious level, others because of nationalistic fervor, and some as a result of both. We must remember that the Jews who strove for nationalism saw the Temple as a political institution as well as a religious one. In spite of the fact that Herod toned down this political role, he himself, as we have already seen, at times gave the Temple some political significance. Josephus says that "Judas, the son of Sariphaeus, and Matthias, the son of Margalothus, were most learned of the Jews and unrivaled interpreters of the ancestral laws, and men especially dear to the people because they educated the youth." Apparently they also incited the youth for a long time before Herod's death. Thus when the rumor reached them that the king had died, the youths climbed up to the roof of the Temple, pulled down the eagle, and cut it up with axes. They performed this symbolic act in front of "the many people who were gathered in the Temple."[35] It is not accidental that they took action when the king was thought to be dead. Some Jews were of the opinion that Roman rule in Palestine, symbolized by the eagle, should be terminated with Herod's death. This defiance brought about much commotion. Herod

> summoned the Jewish officials, and when they arrived, he assembled them in the amphitheater (of Jericho), and, lying on couch because of his inability to stand, he recounted all his strenuous efforts on their behalf, and told them at what great expense to himself he had constructed the Temple, whereas the Hasmoneans had been unable to do anything so great for the honor of God in the hundred and twenty-five years of their reign. He had also, he said, adorned (the Temple) with notable dedicatory offerings, and for these reasons he cherished the hope that even after his

death he would leave behind a memorial of himself and an illustrious name. (*Antiquities* 17.161–163)

As a consequence of this sedition Herod deposed the high priest Matthias and burned alive the Matthias "who stirred up the sedition" (17.165–167). Herod died shortly after this incident.

To sum up Herod's reign as far as the Temple and Jerusalem are concerned, one can say that although he initiated the rebuilding of the Temple, he decreased its importance as a national political institution. He also created a competitive capital to Jerusalem in Caesarea Maritima and granted political power to some other cities in Palestine. Some of the more Hellenistic Jews accepted this policy, and some religious circles did not care as long as the Temple remained a pure, religious, and spiritual place. But other pious groups had difficulties with this partial role of their Temple and the degradation of the status of their capital. They associated political freedom with the freedom of the Temple (and Jerusalem) from any foreign rule. These were the circles from which the Zealots and Sicarii were to evolve some decades later.

When Herod died, one of his three successors, Archelaus, went to the Temple after seven days of mourning, and from there started to take over political authority (17.200–205; *Jewish War* 2.1–4). One of the groups that approached him on this occasion included the relatives of Matthias and Judas, executed by Herod because of the Roman eagle affair and since then regarded as martyrs. They insisted that Archelaus remove the high priest appointed by Herod and choose another man who would serve as high priest "more in accordance with the law and ritual purity" (17.207). These adherent Jews were reluctant to accept the appointment of priests not from the legitimate Aaronic or Zadokite lines.

The subsequent upheaval in the Temple and so-called "war of Varus" show that Jerusalem and its Temple became a focus of national political instability. Josephus says emphatically that the Jewish rebels wanted to recover "their country's liberty" (*Antiquities* 17.267). No doubt political freedom is meant, as at the time there was no religious suppression in any form. The first stage of the upheaval started in the Temple during the Passover, a time always ripe for rebellion (because of its association with the Exodus from Egypt). Josephus says that "the fomentors of disorder, who were mourning for Judas and Matthias, the interpreters of the laws, stood together in the Temple and provided the dissidents with plenty of food, for they were not ashamed to beg for it" (17.214–215; but cf. *Jewish War* 2.10: "procuring recruits for their faction"). Archelaus, understanding that it would be a disaster if the Temple were to become a center of upheaval during the annual pilgrimages, sent an army to suppress the instigators in the Temple. By this act, says Josephus, "the rebellious followers of the interpreters (of the laws) and the crowd were infuriated, and uttering cries and exhortations, they rushed upon the soldiers and after surrounding them stoned most of them to death" (*Antiquities* 17.216). This defiance brought a fierce reaction from Archelaus, who sent out his whole army, including the cavalry, "in order that they might prevent the people encamped there from helping those in the Temple. . . . His cavalry killed some three thousand men but the rest got away by making for the neighboring hills" (17.217–218; *Jewish War* 2.11–13). Archelaus ordered the pilgrims to go back to their homes, a radical thing to do during the Passover. Then he sailed to Rome to plead his case for the succession before Emperor Augustus. It is of some significance that when the Temple had almost been seized by the "interpreters of the law" Archelaus, who at the beginning of his reign was eager to court favor with the people, acted in such a drastic manner. He understood that from a political point of view, the Temple was at stake. The instigators seemed to be jeopardizing Archelaus's accession to the throne. So Archelaus had to react harshly, and was blamed later in Rome by another claimant to Herod the Great's throne, Herod Antipas, for "the things that he had done in the Temple" (17.220). Antipater was even more extreme, claiming before Augustus in Rome that "it was especially the slaughter in the Temple and the impiety of Archelaus . . . for this had happened during the festival, and the people had been slaughtered just like sacrificial victims, though some were foreigners and others natives. And the Temple had been filled with corpses, not indeed by an alien but by one who had sought to undertake the act with the lawful title of king in order that he might fulfill his tyrannical nature in an act of injustice abhorrent to all mankind" (17.237, 239). Nicolaus of Damascus defended Archelaus's acts by saying that the instigators in the Temple "though they professed to wage war against Archelaus, it was actually against Caesar, for when they attacked and killed the men sent by Archelaus, who had come to prevent their excesses, they had shown contempt both for God and for the law of the festival" (17.241). By saying that the upheaval in the Temple was against Rome, Nicolaus underlined the possibility that using the Temple for political reasons meant national independence from Rome's yoke. Another group, who wanted to get rid of kingship altogether and be under direct Roman rule, said that Archelaus caused "the slaughter of three thousand of his countrymen in the Temple precinct" (17.313). This group (joined by more than eight thousand of the Jews in Rome) can be associated with those who wished to see the Temple as a purely religious and spiritual place rather than a political one. It was the same group that also complained about Herod's "schizophrenia" concerning Palestine (17.306).

While Archelaus and the other claimants to Herod's throne defended their cases in Rome and emphasized the events in the Temple, there was renewed rebellion in Judea. It can be said that at this delicate juncture of Jewish history, both Herod's successors and various nationalistic groups brought to the fore the question of the nationalistic, political role of the Temple.

The so-called "war of Varus" started during the Pentecost of 4 B.C.E. According to Josephus a rebellion started in Jerusalem, where fighting took place around the main public buildings, such as the palace of Herod, the Temple, and the hippodrome. The rebellion was initially directed against Roman rule in Palestine, as were the riots elsewhere in the country, led by claimants to the throne who acted against royal property. There was no religious motivation behind the uprising, namely, to get autonomy for worship, though it began during the holy pilgrimage of Pentecost. Josephus says that at the festival of Pentecost "many tens of thousands of men gathered (in Jerusalem) who came not only for the religious observances but also because they resented the reckless insolence of Sabinus (the Roman general in Palestine). There were Galileans and Idumaeans and a multitude from Jericho and from those who lived in Transjordan, and there was a multitude from Judea itself who joined all these, and they were much more eager than the others in their desire to punish Sabinus" (*Antiquities* 17.254; *Jewish War* 2.43). Sabinus had apparently not offended their religious feelings up to this point. It was later, during the fighting on the Temple Mount, that Roman soldiers as well as Sabinus himself stole some of the treasury of the Temple.

The insurrection was ended by the decisive intervention of Varus, the governor of Syria. The Temple was damaged and two thousand people were crucified in Jerusalem by Varus.[36]

This episode shows again that Jerusalem and its Temple were the most important goals of nationalistic Jews, who had hoped in 4 B.C.E. to free Judea from the Roman yoke. This uprising, and the acts of Judas and Zadok in 6 C.E. during the census of Quirinius, were the last aggressive acts of these Jews until the sixties of the first century.[37] More spiritual and religious circles led the opposition against Rome when any such opposition was needed. Accordingly, we can infer that the Temple, once a religiopolitical center, had become mainly a religiospiritual one, a change already begun in Herod the Great's time. It was a gradual process, which brought along with it a diminution in the importance of the priestly houses as spiritual and religious leaders, and the rise of the leadership of the sages.[38]

When Archelaus returned to Palestine as ethnarch of Judea in 4 B.C.E.,[39] he removed Joazar the son of Boethus from the high priesthood, blaming him for having supported the rebels in the Varus affair, and in his place appointed his brother Eleazar. Archelaus continued the policy of his father and tried to dominate the Boethians, the high priestly house. Eleazar was deposed shortly afterward and Jesus the son of Shai was nominated instead (*Antiquities* 17.341). The partition of Palestine among the three successors of Herod the Great in 4 B.C.E. was to generate a competition among four capitals: Caesarea Maritima, Tiberias, Jerusalem, and Caesarea Philippi (and perhaps also Bethsaida-Julias). Although the Jews all over the country continued to regard Jerusalem as their religious center, the other local capitals became politically more important, particularly for the gentiles in the three Palestinian "kingdoms." Be that as it may, in 6 C.E. Archelaus was deposed, and the territory under his rule in Palestine went over to direct Roman rule. At this juncture Josephus mentions the census of Quirinius and the Fourth Philosophy movement, but without mentioning Jerusalem and the Temple (the high priesthood was however again changed, 18.26).

The Fourth Philosophy group was a nationalistic group whose aim was to free Israel from the Roman yoke, because according to its ideology God was the only ruler over Israel (*Antiquities* 18.23–25). The center of this ideology was Jerusalem and its Temple, a matter that will become evident in the events of the Great War against Rome (66–70 C.E.). As far as we can learn from Josephus's scanty evidence for the years 6–66 C.E., however, this group did not play a significant role in Palestine during that time.[40] The group that did receive a great deal of popular support was the so-called Pharisaic group. The Pharisees were realists who accepted the Temple in its role as a religious and spiritual center. They could accept the idea that the Temple was divested of its political overtones, at least for the time being. They were, therefore, the ideological successors of the Hasidim of 160 B.C.E., as well as of Shemaiah and Abtalion, mentioned in the episode of 37 B.C.E. when Herod seized Jerusalem. Sages like Shemaiah and Abtalion and their successors Hillel and Shamai were, if one can believe the much later traditions, preoccupied with the Temple as a religious place. Also from Josephus's historical writings one can deduce that the Temple was functioning as a religious and spiritual center until the sixties of the first century. The same picture also emerges from the New Testament and related literature. It should be emphasized that the moment the militant groups of the Fourth Philosophy, apparently Zealots and Sicarii, with their clear-cut political aims, became a powerful movement and attempted to apply their nationalistic interpretation of Temple (priesthood), army, kingship, and territory as independent political entities onto daily life, they led the nation toward the terrible clash with Rome.

Let us now examine briefly how Josephus viewed the Temple and priesthood during the years 6–66 C.E. Two preliminary points can be made: first, until the sixties of the first century C.E. the Temple is mentioned only in religious contexts, but during the Great War with Rome the Temple becomes a major political symbol; and second, the significant priestly houses are divested of their sovereign political power, though not necessarily of their economic power, even more than at the time of Herod the Great and Archelaus.[41] In the sixties of the first century they regained for a short while a great deal of that power.

In his account of the governorship of Coponius (ca. 6–9 C.E.) Josephus relates that during the Passover "the priests were accustomed to throw open the gates of the Temple after midnight. This time when the gates were first opened, some Samaritans, who had secretly entered Jerusalem, began to scatter human bones in the porticoes and throughout the Temple. As a result, the priests, though they had previously observed no such custom, excluded everyone from the Temple, in addition to taking other measures for a greater protection of the Temple" (*Antiquities* 18.30). From this incident one can learn that the clashes with the Samaritans over the priority of Jerusalem and Shechem had continued, but more on a religious than on a national political level (as it used to be in the Hasmonean period).[42] When Gratus arrived to become governor of Judea in 15 C.E., he was given the authority to appoint high priests, as were the Roman governors following him (18.33–35). Thus Rome had taken over the responsibility for the appointment of high priests, which was the last nail in the coffin of a significant Jewish nationalistic symbol, at least for the time being.

Little is heard of the Temple until Pontius Pilate's governorship (26–36 C.E.). Presumably not much of great significance happened involving Jerusalem and the Temple during that time. In *Antiquities* 18.55–59 Josephus tells of the fierce opposition of the Jews to Pontius Pilate's declared intention of bringing the busts of the emperor that were attached to the military standards into Jerusalem "for our law forbids the making of images."[43] When the people discovered that Pilate had carried out his intention, they "went in a throng to Caesarea and for many days entreated him to take away the images. He refused to yield." At last when the Jews, "casting themselves prostrate and baring their throats, declared that they had gladly welcomed death rather than make bold to transgress the wise provisions of the laws," he gave up, "astonished at the strength of their devotion to the laws." He then removed the images from Jerusalem and brought them back to Caesarea (18.59), which became the capital for the Roman governors in Palestine. Later on he extracted money from the sacred treasury to build an aqueduct, and again the Jews protested, the uprising only ending after many were injured and slain.[44] These examples, together with the gathering of the Samaritans on Mount Gerizim (18.85–87), show that the clashes with the Roman authorities between 7 and 36 C.E. were sporadic and initiated from religious motives. There is no reason to believe that Josephus toned down any unrest of a political nature. Moreover, also from the Roman side, we cannot speak of any significant Roman religious persecution. The incidents mentioned in the sources were local and unimportant in the eyes of the Roman authorities (even the census of 6 C.E. was not understood by Rome as a religious transgression of Jewish Law[45]). Tacitus was right when he claimed that "under Tiberius all was quiet" (*Histories* 5.9.2).

We know of only two Roman governors of Syria, Vitellius and Petronius (who were also responsible for Palestine), who acted favorably to the Temple and its cult. They did so largely because during that time the Jews were peaceful, and also because these particular governors were wiser and more tolerant. According to Josephus, Vitellius "went up to Jerusalem, where the Jews were celebrating their traditional feast called Passover. Having been received in magnificent fashion, Vitellius remitted to the inhabitants of the city all taxes on the sale of agricultural produce and agreed that the vestments of the high priest and all his ornaments should be kept in the Temple in custody of the priests, as had been their privilege before." Josephus adds that at the time the vestments were stored in Antonia, and when Herod became king he returned them "there just as he had found them, believing that for this reason the people would never rise in insurrection against him." Herod's successor, his son Archelaus, acted similarly. When the Romans took over the government, they kept the high priest's vestments in a stone building. Seven days before the festival the vestments were delivered to the priests, who had to return them after the first day of the festival. This procedure was followed at the three main festivals each year and on the fast day. Vitellius was, Josephus adds, "guided by our law in dealing with the vestments"; thus he "instructed the warden not to meddle with the question where they were to be stored or when they should be used." Then he removed from the high priesthood Joseph surnamed Caiaphas, and appointed in his stead Jonathan.[46]

In 37 C.E. Vitellius agreed not to offend Jewish laws and diverted his army from marching through Judea, because the insignia of the legions were offensive to the Jews (18.120–122); he and Herod Antipas, as well as some friends, went up to Jerusalem to "sacrifice to God during the traditional festival which the Jews were celebrating there." When Vitellius arrived in the city, he was greeted with special warmth by the Jewish multitude. He spent three days in Jerusalem, during which he deposed Jonathan from the high priesthood and conferred it on Jonathan's brother, Theophilus. It is interesting to note that the Romans insisted on showing their higher political authority over their subjects, namely, in this case appointing the high priests of the Jews even though they had from Herod the Great's time only religious and "spiritual" authority, and not a sovereign political one.[47]

But the good relations between the Romans and the Jews in Palestine did not last long. A serious religious conflict with Emperor Caligula severed these good relations.[48] A delegation from Alexandria to Caligula had already put the Jews in an unfavorable light. One of the non-Jewish delegates, Apion by name, "scurrilously reviled the Jews, asserting among other things that they neglected to pay honors due to the emperor. For while all the subject peoples in the Roman Empire had dedicated altars and temples to Gaius and had given him the same attentions in all other respects as they did the gods, these people alone scorned to honor him with statues and to swear by his name" (*Antiquities* 18.257–258). From Philo we hear of an incident at Jamnia, where Jews acted against an altar for Caligula erected by the foreigners living there.[49] Gaius decided to put a statue of himself in the Temple—and just as in the days of Antiochus IV, the Jews launched an outcry. The man who mediated between them and the emperor was none other than Petronius, the Roman governor of Syria, who understood the religious problem and supported the Jews. This story again shows that the opposition of the Jews throughout this period occurred entirely from religious motives. Scholars who blame Josephus for suppressing the existence of political upheavals underestimate him as a historian. There is no reason why a historian who elaborated upon a great upheaval against Rome in his *Bellum* (in Greek), as well as mentioning the "war of Varus" and the census of Quirinius in his *Antiquities,* would suppress other political conflicts. At any rate, the Jews opposed the presence of a statue of the emperor in the Temple because it was contrary to their religious beliefs. The wording of their petitions to Petronius on this occasion reflects the atmosphere surrounding this whole episode.

Josephus says that many tens of thousands of Jews came to Petronius at Acco-Ptolemais with petitions "not to use force to make them transgress and violate their ancestral code." "If," they said, "you propose at all costs to bring in and set up the image, slay us first before you carry out these resolutions. For it is not possible for us to survive and to behold actions that are forbidden us by the decision both of our Lawgiver and of our forefathers who cast their votes enacting these measures as moral laws" (*Antiquities* 18.264). And later in Tiberias they add, "On no account would we fight, but we will die sooner than violate our laws" (18.271). Petronius himself said to the Jews who came to him in Tiberias, "You are carrying out the precepts of your Law, which as your heritage you see fit to defend, and serving the sovereign of all, almighty God, whose Temple I should not have had the heart to see fall a prey to the insolence of imperial authority" (18.280). There is no political overtone in any of the things said by the Jews, by Petronius, or by Agrippa pleading for the Jews in Rome.[50] Were it a political matter, Petronius certainly would not have helped the Jews. Agrippa I at last succeeded in having the unwise order of the emperor abolished (18.261–309; *Jewish War* 2.184–203).

When Claudius became emperor in 41 C.E., he sent Agrippa I, already appointed by Caligula to be king of Judea, to his kingdom. The Jewish king, as his first political step, entered Jerusalem and offered sacrifices of thanksgiving,[51] "omitting none of the ritual enjoined by our law"; then he hung up, within the sacred precincts, over the treasure chamber, the golden chain that had been presented to him by Caligula "in order that it might serve as a proof both that greatness may sometimes crash and that God uplifts fallen fortunes" (*Antiquities* 19.293–294). Josephus adds that "having thus fully discharged his service to God," Agrippa removed Theophilus son of Ananus from the high priesthood and granted it to Simeon, son of Boethus, surnamed Cantheras.[52] He later offered the high priesthood to Jonathan the son of Hanan and finally gave it to the latter's brother Mathai, all within a period of less than three years (19.312–316). In this regard Agrippa followed his predecessors, but unlike them he emphasized a bit more the religiopolitical function of the Temple, as it was still dominated by the secular authority, namely, the Jewish king.[53] When he endeavored to fortify the walls of Jerusalem and to increase their width and height, he was stopped by Emperor Claudius, because the fortification of the Jewish indigenous capital was interpreted as an independent political move.[54] Not long thereafter Agrippa I died (44 C.E.) in Caesarea, the pagan capital of Palestine[55]—the pious king dying in a place containing a majority of non-Jews in his land.

From then until the sixties, there were several occurrences of unrest in Judea associated with the Temple as a religious place. Let us examine them briefly. During the governorship of Fadus (44–46 C.E.) the vestments of the high priest were again the cause of unrest. Fadus sent "for the chief priests and the leaders of the people of Jerusalem and advised them to deposit the full-length tunic and the sacred robe, which it was the custom for the high priest alone to wear, in Antonia." He further claimed that they were to be entrusted to the authority of the Romans, "as they had been in the past" (*Antiquities* 20.6). Fadus's order made Longinus, then governor of Syria, frightened that it "would force the Jewish people to rebellion." So he traveled to Jerusalem with a large force and allowed the Jews to send a delegation to Claudius. This piece of information is valuable in itself. The event might be regarded as some caprice on behalf of the Jews; but the Roman reaction shows that it was a matter of great importance. Once more, the issue was the religious autonomy of the Jews, not their political autonomy. This distinction also emerges from Claudius's response: "Earnestly and zealously (I have) requested that the holy vestments and the crown might be placed in your hands. I grant this request, in accordance with the precedent set by Vitellius. . . . I have given my consent to this measure, first because I cherish religion myself and wish to see every nation maintain the religious practices that are traditional with it."[56]

Then Herod, brother of the deceased Agrippa I, who was at this time charged with the administration of Chalcis (cf. map page 406), requested that Claudius give him authority over the Temple and the holy vessels as well as over the selection of the high priests. All of these requests were granted. This authority he passed on to his descendants "alone until the end of the war" (20.15–16). In this matter Claudius acted wisely, giving a kind of compensation to the Jews who were frustrated that their land had become a province under direct Roman rule. Herod of Chalcis immediately made use of his new power to remove the high priest and nominated Joseph the son of Camei. Later, while Judea was governed by Tiberius Alexander (46–48 C.E.), the same Herod deposed Joseph and nominated Ananias the son of Nedebaeus. The authority given to the king of the minor kingdom of Chalcis to nominate high priests and to dominate the Temple shows the Roman view of the office of the high priesthood: to them it was an unimportant political position that could only be filled by the Roman authorities or their representatives. Herod the Great, his successors, and the Romans themselves emphasized the fact that the high priesthood was a religious office always subordinate to the secular rule. Occasionally a high priest might acquire political power, but broadly speaking the priests remained subordinate to the royal authority. Josephus, however, never mentions any changes made in the so-called ruling class of Judea other than the appointments of high priests there.[57]

From 48 C.E. onward there was more trouble in Judea, caused by religious clashes with the Romans and Samaritans as well as with other non-Jews in the Land, by socioeconomic problems that aroused the so-called *lestai* (robbers) against Rome and the Jewish wealthy aristocracy, and by the moral corruption of the high-priestly houses.

Trouble started, according to one tradition, when one of the soldiers sent by Governor Cumanus to guard the Temple from insurrection during the Passover (a safeguard also taken by his forerunners, *Antiquities* 20.108) showed his private parts to the pilgrims. Their religious feelings were offended, and in the ensuing fracas they thought they were being chased by the Romans, panicked, and tried to escape; some Jews were killed (20.105–112; *Jewish War* 2.224–227). There were some later incidents that did not involve the Temple or the City, though the clash between the Samaritans and the Jews occurred when pilgrims were going to Jerusalem to sacrifice in the Temple (20.118; *Jewish War* 2.232–233). After the latter incident, in which both Jews and Samaritans were killed, "those who were by rank and birth the leaders of the inhabitants of Jerusalem" changed "their robes for sackcloth and defiled their heads with ashes and went to all lengths entreating the rebels. They urged them to picture to themselves that their country would be razed to the ground, their temple consigned to the flames, and they themselves with their wives and children reduced to slavery" (*Antiquities* 20.123). If we can trust Josephus, his account shows that, as early as the beginning of the fifties, the Jews were aware of the heavy punishment they would incur from the Romans if they were involved in any violent disturbances.

This short survey shows that from 4 B.C.E., after the so-called "war of Varus," Palestine was relatively quiet, and that the few incidents (including the Quirinius affair of 6 C.E.) were of a religious nature; the Jews only argued with the Roman authorities when they thought that their religious autonomy was being threatened or violated. In all of these incidents there seems to have been no attempt by either the Jews or the early Christians to liberate Palestine from the Romans.[58] Rome acted in accordance with the imperial policy of not violating the religious autonomy of a native population provided it did not jeopardize Roman rule. Thus in most instances Rome acted swiftly to solve any issue under question. It is within this context that Jesus' crucifixion in 29/30 C.E. must be viewed. Jesus led a religious movement that was offensive to the leading Pharisees. They accused him of being a political menace to get the authorities to put an end to his movement. This tactic worked very effectively with Pontius Pilate. There is nothing in the New Testament that would indicate that it was a political, anti-Roman movement, which accords with the fact that there is no record of any political movements against Rome in Palestine at this particular time.

The priestly houses became even more notorious than before for their involvement in public life during the fifties under Felix (52–60 C.E.). It started with the murder of Jonathan (not the high priest, but his brother), by the *lestes* (bandit) Doras, who had been bribed by Governor Felix. Josephus argues that "as the murder remained unpunished, from that time forth the brigands with perfect impunity used to go to the city during the festivals and, with their weapons similarly concealed, mingle with the crowds." He adds that these murders were committed not only in certain sections of Jerusalem, but even in some cases inside the Temple itself (*Antiquities* 20.165). Josephus comments that this outrageous behavior was why, in his opinion, "even God himself, for loathing of their impiety, turned away from our city and, because He deemed the Temple to be no longer a clean dwelling place for Him, brought the Romans upon us and purification by fire upon the city, while He inflicted slavery upon us together, with our wives and children; for He wished to chasten us by these calamities. With such pollution did the deeds of the brigands infect the city" (20.166–167; cf. *Jewish War* 2.254–257).

This abuse of the Temple, along with the institution of priesthood serving in the Temple, brought about the decline of the Temple as a religious and spiritual place. Hence, for many Jews, the Temple was in effect destroyed long before its physical destruction in 70 C.E. The priesthood became completely subject to political strife. An illustration of Jerusalem's position at the time is given again by

Josephus, who tells of the prophet from Egypt who came to Jerusalem and "advised the masses of the common people to go out with him to the mountain called the Mount of Olives." He wished to demonstrate from there that at his command "Jerusalem's walls would fall down" (20.169). According to *Jewish War* 2.262 he proposed to "force an entrance into Jerusalem," and "to set himself up as a tyrant of the people." Scholars have not sufficiently recognized the decay of the Temple and its priesthood as a major reason for the Great War against Rome.[59]

The practice of appointing the high priests was carried on throughout these stormy events. This time it was King Agrippa II who in 59 C.E. named Ishmael the son of Phabi (*Antiquities* 20.179; *b. Yoma* 9a), who is praised by the Talmud when it calls him Phineas's disciple (*b. Pesaḥ.* 57a). At the same time, however, we hear that "class warfare between the high priests, on the one hand, and the priests and the leaders of the populace of Jerusalem on the other" was enkindled.

> Each of the factions formed and collected for itself a band of the most reckless revolutionaries and acted as their leader. And when they clashed, they used abusive language and pelted each other with stones. And there was not even one person to rebuke them. No, it was as if there was no one in charge of the city, so that they acted as they did with full license. Such was the shamelessness and effrontery that possessed the high priests that they actually were so brazen as to send slaves to the threshing floors to receive the tithes that were due to the priests, with the result that the poorer priests starved to death. Thus did the violence of the contending factions suppress all justice. (*Antiquities* 20.180–181)

This information, when coupled with Josephus's opinion, speaks for itself. It shows that the priestly orders were basically weak, and had no wide support, if any, from the masses at large. It should be pointed out that at the beginning of the sixties, brigandage, factional strife between priestly houses, and murders by the Sicarii of Jews streaming into Jerusalem to worship in the Temple are to be found (20.186–187), but no political attempts to restore a Jewish state in Palestine.

The Temple is mentioned by Josephus only in a purely religious context throughout the fifties and beginning of the sixties. Not much of a chronological order is preserved for these years. We hear of some scattered incidents such as the one caused by Agrippa II, king of Chalcis, who built a chamber in his palace (the Hasmonean palace) that could overlook everything that went on in the Temple. The Jews found this spying offensive and built a wall that would prevent the king from seeing into the sacred precincts. It was met by opposition from both Agrippa and Festus. They agreed that the Jews should send a delegation to Emperor Nero. The latter consented that the wall be left intact. Nero's wife, however, kept two of the delegates, the high priest and the keeper of the treasury, as hostages. King Agrippa then gave the high priesthood to Joseph, surnamed Kabi, son of the high priest Simeon (20.189–196).

The following four years were crucial, and the events shed some more light on the priesthood. In 62 C.E. Agrippa II removed Joseph from the high priesthood and appointed Ananus. Josephus says that he "was rash in his temper and unusually daring. He followed the school of the Sadducees" (20.199). Ananus, exploiting the fact that Festus was dead and Albinus was still on his way to Palestine, convened the judges of the Sanhedrin and accused James, the brother of Jesus, of having transgressed the law. James and some of his friends were delivered to be stoned to death. For these acts King Agrippa II removed Ananus from the high priesthood, which he had held for three months, and replaced him with Jesus the son of Damnaeus (20.203), once again showing that the high priests were puppets who had no real political power.

From then on there were more conflicts between the high priests on the one hand, and the Roman governor of Judea and the king on the other, in particular over the right of the Sanhedrin to sentence people to death.[60] Also acts of terror against the high priestly houses by the Sicarii were recorded. There were again stories of corruption in the priestly houses. For instance Josephus tells us that "Ananias had servants who were utter rascals and who, combining operations with the most reckless men, would go to the threshing floors and take by force the tithes of the priests; nor did they refrain from beating those who refused to give. The high priests were guilty of the same practices as his slaves, and no one could stop them. So it happened at that time that those of the priests who in olden days were maintained by the tithes now starved to death" (20.206–207). More examples can be given, and a famous Baraita in the Talmud affirms this claim (*b. Pesaḥ.* 57a).

During Albinus's office (62–64 C.E.) Agrippa II deposed Jesus the son of Damnaeus from the high priesthood and appointed as his successor Jesus the son of Gamaliel. According to Josephus "a feud arose between the latter and his predecessor. They each collected a band of the most reckless sort and it frequently happened that after exchanging insults they went farther and hurled stones. Ananias, however, kept the upper hand by using his wealth to attract those who were willing to receive bribes" (*Antiquities* 20.213).

The picture that emerges is that the priestly houses, who had been kept under control until the late fifties, started to engage in destructive power politics. There soon were repercussions. According to Josephus the levitic order also transgressed the law (20.216–218), which gradually lowered even more the religious and spiritual stature of the Temple in the eyes of many Jews and early Christians, a matter that was to get worse during the war against Rome.

The fifteen years from 50 to approximately 65 C.E. were years of growing frustration for many Jews because of the decaying stature of their Temple and the wayward deeds of the priesthood. The growing weakness of the priestly families and the ensuing rift between them and the Jewish population (which was not evident from 4 B.C.E. to 50 C.E.)[61] resulted in the emergence of new Jewish leaders. They rapidly exchanged the former goal of religious autonomy under Roman rule for a more aggressive political one of getting rid of that very rule. During the long period that had passed since the accession of Herod the Great to the throne, until the fifties of the first century, most Jews and Christians accepted the Temple and the priesthood as solely religious and spiritual institutions. There was sporadic criticism of the worship in the Temple and its priesthood, as we learn from the Gospels, but the Temple was basically viewed as an a-political institution. As long as the Romans did not hinder its religious sovereignty the Jews kept quiet.

But when the priesthood extensively abused the Temple as a religious place under the same Roman rule that had once cared for Jewish religious autonomy, many Jews felt that they had little recourse. The Temple had gradually lost its significance as a main political symbol of Jewish nationalism during Herod the Great's rule, and in the fifties and sixties the remnants of its religious and spiritual significance were taken away as well by the priesthood itself. Thus the abuse of Temple and priesthood as religiopolitical and spiritual symbols led some to espouse the more extreme view that total liberation from the Roman yoke was needed (the Zealots), and at the same time led to the emergence of the idea that the Temple and its priesthood should be destroyed altogether (Paul in the fifties). It will be shown later that the emphasis on the political nature of the Temple and priesthood came back for a short while during the Great War fought by the Jews against Rome, and was one of the main causes of that war.

Unfortunately, there is no historical evidence of the period 70–135 C.E. We know, however, that after the Great War was over, the priesthood as a religious and political power disappeared, the high priesthood was abolished, and the Temple was destroyed.[62] The destruction of the Temple was a shock, but the dualistic perception of Jerusalem and its Temple in many ways brought consolation to the Jews. They kept the Heavenly, or spiritual, Temple in their awareness and believed that the earthly Temple would be rebuilt "soon," and "in our own days." Then they did not foresee that it would not be rebuilt at all. When Emperor Hadrian had thoughts of rebuilding the Temple, which did not materialize, the Jews who participated in the Bar Kokhba upheaval made the Temple one of the main issues on their revolutionary agenda (132–135 C.E.). We will return to this matter in chapter 13.

Let us now look at the literature of the period, and see how it corresponds to the historical picture. It is quite clear that both mainstream Judaism and Christianity of the first century C.E. viewed the Temple as a religious and spiritual place, not a political one. Josephus says exactly the same things about the Temple as Jesus is believed to have said some decades before him, namely, that the Temple was abused and therefore deserved to be destroyed. When comparing the literature of this period with that of the period 200–63 B.C.E., in terms of the treatment of the Temple some differences in emphasis can be detected.

First, some of the documents in the earlier period were still preoccupied with the issue of the location of the Temple in Palestine (as in some of the biblical literature). Jubilees, Eupolemus's *The Kings of Judah,* and other works emphasize the fact that the place selected by God was Jerusalem (contrary to other competitive claims, such as by the Samaritans and perhaps the Jews in Tell el-Yahudiah), and that this place was central to Judaism. The literature of the period after 63 B.C.E. no longer tackles this problem[63]—the fact that Jerusalem and its Temple were the only legitimate religious centers was taken for granted, and as far as we can determine there is no meaningful discussion about it.

Second, whereas in many documents of the first period we find various specific descriptions of temples, realistic, ideal, and utopian, the literature of the second period has few such descriptions. There are no concrete descriptions of temples to be found apart from Josephus's descriptions when he recounts the history of the Great War (*Jewish War* 5.184-236, and perhaps the Letter to the Hebrews, which may have very early material[64]). Even in a document like the Testament of Solomon, where the building of the Temple by Solomon is a central theme, no description is given.[65] Perhaps the beauty of the Temple built by Herod the Great lessened the need to describe alternative temples. After its destruction in 70 C.E. certain authors again refer to it in physical terms (as Josephus in *Jewish War* and the Mishnah).

Third, in the literature of the first period both Temple and priesthood (in particular the high priest) play a major political role. Some passages clearly show the high priest's superior position over the secular ruler. The Temple, as Eupolemus and even the Temple Scroll have shown, is presented as a major national political symbol. Less of this element can be found in the literature of the second period. It is presented instead as something that is, or may become in the future, more of a religious and spiritual place. In the literature of the second period, the existing priesthood is either denigrated or ignored. It had lost its position as a religiopolitical entity in Judaism.

Fourth, in the literature of the first period—the period of Jewish national independence—the Land of Israel comes to the fore in many documents and is sometimes even equal in importance to Temple and City. The literature of the second period is less interested in the Land as a solid base for Jerusalem and the Temple.

Fifth, in many documents written during the Roman occupation of Palestine (in the second period), we find prophecies and lamentations concerning the destruction of Jerusalem and its Temple (for instance, *Jewish War* 6.300–309). Some of these texts were composed before the actual destruction in 70 C.E. The literature of the first period has much less of this kind of writing, and what exists is specifically associated with the events of the seventies of the second century B.C.E. In the literature of the first period there are lamentations about the bad condition of the Temple, but no prophecies of the destruction of Jerusalem and the Temple (as a continuation of Psalm 137).

Sixth, there is a shift in the literature of the second period to an alternative spiritual, amorphous Temple not described in concrete terms, as for instance in Paul's Epistles and in Hebrews (9:11; cf. its absence from Rev 21:22: "And I saw no temple in the city," because the Temple is God and the Lamb). The so-called Heavenly Temple of the *Songs of the Sabbath Sacrifice* (which may be post-63 B.C.E. anyway) is heavenly, but is considered to be a duplicate, rather than an alternative, to the earthly temple.

How are Jerusalem, the Temple, and the priesthood depicted in the literature of the second period? One should bear in mind that the theological speculations on Jerusalem and the Temple that usually preoccupy scholars of the New Testament will not concern us here. Also, it should be noted that the literature of the second period contains Christian sources alongside the Jewish ones. As far as can be seen from the available evidence, many of the ideas concerning the state and national existence were common both in early Judaism and in early Christianity. After all, the New Testament is an invaluable source for the study of many aspects of Judaism during this period and should be viewed as a Near Eastern document by historians. Also, whereas we know some of the Pharisaic ideas through their later documents, we do not, unfortunately, possess any document of the Zealots and Sicarii that might reveal their views on the Temple and City. The only conclusions we can draw about their attitudes depend on Josephus's history and on some documents deriving from their opponents.

Like Josephus's writings, the Gospels were almost certainly written after the destruction of Jerusalem and its Temple. But most scholars would agree that beginning with Mark, the first written text, the Gospels reflect traditions emanating from the thirties and forties of the first century C.E.[66] This may be the case with the Gospels' treatment of Jerusalem and its Temple. A substantial difference

in attitude regarding Jerusalem and the Temple can be detected between the Gospels and Acts 1–12 on the one hand, and the remainder of the New Testament on the other. The picture of Jerusalem
and the Temple in the synoptic Gospels and Acts 1–12 (and even in
John) reflects an early layer of tradition.[67] Although the Gospels and
Acts 1–12 were written after 70, the Temple is very much alive in the
minds of their authors, and their descriptions are largely in line with
those of Josephus.[68]

While Paul's ideas, claiming that the Temple should be spiritualized, were influential, the Temple (the physical one of before 70)
nevertheless emerges in the Gospels as a center of worship and
teaching. The complex problem of the many nuances that can be
seen in the various Gospels when compared with one another need
not be addressed here. What is of importance is that the picture of
the Temple and priesthood that one gets from the different Gospels
is more or less similar. There are no clear-cut tendencies that make
one text differ from another in this particular respect. In the Gospels
the Temple is never seen as a national-political center. It never appears as a political place, which is in keeping with what has already
been seen regarding the history of the twenties through the forties of
the first century C.E.

The Mishnah and Tosefta and other related literature also show
that the Temple was recognized as a religious and cultic place by the
rabbis who collected the material of these codexes long after the
destruction of the Temple. After the destruction, there was much
speculation about the lost Temple. The sections of these documents
that deal with the Temple and its priesthood probably reflect earlier
traditions from before the destruction of the Temple, though it is
impossible to prove this assumption. Yet the nationalistic and political aspirations concerning the Temple and its priesthood are toned
down. We frequently find in these sources a continuity with biblical
concepts of worship in the Temple, but adjusted to the new times.
Despite criticism of the priesthood, there is no questioning of the
institution as such.[69] Also, Jerusalem's holiness is emphasized time
and again in the Mishnah and Tosefta, but without any significant
political overtones.

Jerusalem emerges from the Gospels not merely as a background
for Jesus' acts there, but also as a holy city of "the Great King."[70]
The Temple is very important for Jesus and his group, and emerges

—as in wider Jewish circles at the time—as a place of worship and teaching.[71] In Matt 26:55 Jesus says, "Day after day I sat in the Temple teaching"; Mark 12:35 says, "And as Jesus taught in the Temple, he said . . ."; and John 7:28–29, "So Jesus proclaimed, as he taught in the Temple, 'You know me and you know where I come from? . . . I know him, for I come from him, and he sent me!' " In Luke 2:27–28 it says that "inspired by the Spirit he came into the Temple (*eis to hieron*). And when the parents brought in the child Jesus, to do to him according to the custom of the law, he (Simeon) took him up in his arms and blessed God and said. . . ." Luke 2:41 also reports that Jesus' parents "went to Jerusalem every year at the feast of Passover."[72]

After Jesus' ascent into heaven it says about his disciples (Luke 24:52–53), "And they returned to Jerusalem with great joy and were continually in the Temple blessing God."[73] In the gospel tradition, Jesus does not deny the fact that the Temple should be the heart of Judaism, as a cultic and religious place. Like Israel's prophets some centuries before him, however, he opposed the abuse of the Temple by the priests as well as by the people who made it a place of commerce. Here are a few examples: in Matt 5:23–25 Jesus says, "So if you are offering your gift at the altar, and there remember that your brother has something against you, leave your gift there before the altar and go."[74] In Matt 12:5–8 he says, "have you not read in the Law how on the sabbath the priests in the Temple profane the sabbath, and are guiltless?" Matt 21:12–17 says that "Jesus entered the Temple of God and drove out all who sold and bought in the Temple, and he overturned the tables of the money changers and the seats of those who sold pigeons. He said to them: 'It is written, My house shall be called a house of prayer; but you make it a den of robbers.' "[75] In Matt 23:15–22 he says, "Woe to you, scribes and Pharisees, hypocrites! for you traverse sea and land . . . woe to you, blind guides who say, 'If anyone swears by the Temple, it is nothing; but if any one swears by the gold of the Temple, he is bound by his oath . . . you blind men' " (cf. also Matt 27:5; Mark 11:11–19; 12:41–44; Luke 2:41–50; 19:45–48; 21:1–38; John 2:14–22).

His message regarding the Temple was very simple and in keeping with the Judaism of the day: the place should regain its holiness and become once more a place of prayer and teaching. In other words, it was to be a purely religiospiritual place. In Jewish sources, or related ones, there are criticisms that the Temple is being visited by impure people. Thus 2 Enoch (J) 45:3 may preserve the old prophetic view that God did not want sacrifices and burnt offerings, but hearts that were pure: "Does the Lord demand bread or lamps or sheep or oxen or any kind of sacrifices at all? . . . that is nothing, but he demands pure hearts." This passage is not necessarily a Christian addition, because the sentiment can already be found in the prophets of the First Temple period. When Jesus said that the Temple would be destroyed and rebuilt in three days, he could have meant that it should be purified by its rededication:[76] "This fellow said, 'I am able to destroy the temple of God, and to build it in three days' " (Matt 26:61; 27:39–40; Mark 15:29; Acts 6:14; John 2:19). It should be emphasized that Paul does not mention any alternative physical Temple, and, except for some vague allusions, there is no sign of a heavenly Temple in the Gospels (for instance, Matt 12:5–8: "I tell you, something greater than the Temple is here. And if you had known what this means, I desire mercy, and not sacrifice"; and Mark 14:58: "We heard him say, 'I will destroy this Temple that is made with hands, and in three days I will build another, not made with hands' "; perhaps also John 2:19–22: "But he spoke of the temple of his body" [2:21]). It should again be noted that the Gospels were written and edited after the Pauline Epistles were written, which is significant because in Paul's theology the Temple is a spiritual entity.

Josephus, who intertwined his own views about Jerusalem and its Temple in his *Jewish War*, is in some respects close to the views of the Gospels. He too is of the opinion that the Temple was destroyed as a consequence of the abuse of the Holy Place, politically as well as religiously, by the Zealots and priests. God delivered his Temple to the Romans to be demolished as a punishment of his people. In this respect he is close to Israel's prophets, who said similar things about the Assyrians and Babylonians being God's rod for the destruction of Jerusalem.[77] Thus, he could have held such views before 70 C.E. The Gospels as well as Paul offered some alternative to the physical Temple. Josephus did not because he, like many Jews of his day, thought that a new Temple would be built if the existing one was destroyed. This view is also reflected in his interpretation of biblical history. For example, when he describes the Tabernacle (giving it an *interpretatio Graeca*), he writes about it as if the Temple still existed, or would exist very soon again (*Antiquities* 3.179–201). This reading is also supported by his statement in *Antiquities* 3.245, where he perhaps has in mind a third return of the Jews to the Land. The Temple and Jerusalem are very strongly represented in his *Antiquities* (4.200–213; 5.68; 8.61–123; and elsewhere), and so is their centrality.[78]

The Temple is also central in Acts 1–12, as is Jerusalem.[79] In these chapters Peter and his community go (according to Luke) to pray and teach in the Temple as part of their daily routine. There is no sign that they disapproved of the existence of the actual Temple; on the contrary, it is part of their daily life.[80] In Acts 2:46 it is said that "day by day, attending the Temple together and breaking bread in their homes, they partook of food with glad and generous hearts," and in 3:1–4:2, "Now Peter and John were going up to the Temple at the hour of prayer, the ninth hour."[81] In 5:21, when the apostles escape from prison, "they entered the Temple at daybreak and taught" (cf. also 5:12; 5:42; 6:7). In Acts 13–28 the Temple is less central because the story has shifted away from Palestine (and cf. Acts 17:24–25). However, when the converted Paul returned to Jerusalem after his mission in Asia Minor and Greece, he went to the Temple in order to pray there, but was dragged out by angry Jews from Asia, who recognized him.[82] He himself said before the Sanhedrin that he came "to bring to my nation alms and offerings. As I was doing this, they found me purified in the Temple, without any crowd or tumult."[83] Later before Festus, the Roman procurator, Paul said in his defense, "Neither against the Law of the Jews, nor against the Temple, nor against Caesar have I offended at all" (25:8).[84] Note that the order in this sentence is Law of the Jews, Temple, Caesar. Interestingly, apart from one passage, the Temple as an institution is never criticized by Acts. Only in Stephen's speech was it said that "so it was until the days of David, who found favor in the sight of God and asked leave to find habitation for the God of Jacob. But it was Solomon who built the house for him. Yet the Most High does not dwell in houses made with hands; as the prophet says, 'heaven is my throne, and earth my footstool. What house will you build for me, says the Lord, or what is the place of my rest? Did not my hand make all these things?' " (Acts 7:45–50). There was in fact nothing especially Christian in these views, because much of the same picture was to be found in the Jewish sources,[85] and it reflects the reality of the time.

This speech brings us closer to Pauline concepts, an anticipation of which has already been seen in the Gospels.[86] Indeed, Paul in his letters did write about a spiritual and Heavenly Temple, and in this regard he came close to both biblical and later Jewish notions;[87] in this respect he can be seen as a Palestinian Jew.[88] Yet he goes a step farther. In 1 Cor 3:16–17 he said, "Do you not know that you are God's temple and that God's Spirit dwells in you? If any one destroys God's temple, God will destroy him. For God's temple is holy, and that temple you are"; and in 6:19, "Do you not know that your body is a temple of the Holy Spirit within you, which you have from God? You are not your own." In 2 Cor 5:1–5 Paul writes that "we know that if the earthly tent we live in is destroyed, we have a building from God, a house not made with hands, eternal in the heavens, here indeed we groan, and long to put on our heavenly dwelling so that by putting it on we may not be found naked."[89] In other words, there is no elimination of the Temple altogether, but instead an alternative one is presented that is amorphous and, unlike for instance the one in the *Songs of the Sabbath Sacrifice,* not drawn in concrete terms.[90] In Gal 4:26 Paul says that "Jerusalem above is free, and she is our mother."[91] In Eph 2:19–22 we read, "So then you are no longer strangers and sojourners, but you are fellow citizens with the saints and members of the household of God, built upon the foundation of the apostles and prophets, Christ Jesus himself being the cornerstone, in whom the whole structure is joined together and grows into a holy temple in the Lord; in whom you also are built into it for a dwelling place of God in the Spirit."[92]

Elsewhere in the New Testament there is the famous explanation of Heb 8:1–13, which is not Pauline but no doubt preserves many Palestinian traditions. The priests on earth are "a copy and shadow of the heavenly sanctuary; for when Moses was about to erect the tent, he was instructed by God, saying, 'See that you make everything according to the pattern that was shown you on the mountain.' "[93] In 9:11–12, after the author mentions the furniture and artifacts to be found in the earthly sanctuary, he says, "but when Christ appeared as a high priest of the good things that have come, then through the greater and more perfect tent (not made with hands, that is, not of this creation) he entered once for all into the

Holy Place." In 12:22–23 heavenly Jerusalem is mentioned again by him (and cf. Heb 13:10–14; cf. also John 3:10–12; 11:1–19).[94] According to the Roman historian Tacitus the concept of a spiritual temple was also known to Emperor Tiberius (*Annals* 4.38.10: "haec mihi in animis vestris templa").

At the same time in the Diaspora of Alexandria, Philo Judaeus expressed his views concerning Jerusalem and its Temple. Philo refuses to grant both Jerusalem and Temple any political, nationalistic significance associated with a Jewish state. On the contrary, in *De specialibus legibus* 1.66 he says that "The highest, and in the truest sense the holy temple of God is, as we must believe, the whole universe, having for its sanctuary the most sacred part of all existence. . . . There is also the temple made by hands. . . . But he provided that there should not be temples built either in many places or many in the same place, for he judged that since God is one, there should be also only one temple." The Temple is viewed also in religious terms when Philo describes it later, probably having Herod's Temple in mind (1.71–75). Also, he does not associate it—as for instance Eupolemus does—with David and Solomon and the period of the Israelite dynasty when the Temple had a great deal of political meaning.[95]

In his *In Flaccum* 45–46 Philo says, "For so populous are the Jews that no one country can hold them, and therefore they settle in very many of the most prosperous countries in Europe and Asia both in the islands and on the mainland, and while they hold the Holy City where stands the sacred Temple of the most high God to be their mother city, yet those which are theirs by inheritance from their fathers, grandfathers, and ancestors even farther back are in each case accounted by them to be their fatherland." In other words, Jerusalem and the Temple were the religious centers of the Jewish people spread all over the world. Jerusalem and the Temple are perceived by Philo as universal centers, not simply the centers of a Jewish state in Palestine.[96] This view can of course be seen as typical of a Diaspora Jew at the time, one of the more "liberal" groups of Jews. But already Herod the Great, as well as his successors, attempted to promote this universal aspect of Jerusalem and its Temple. This understanding of the Temple and of Jerusalem is more down to earth than the one found in the Book of Revelation, and should be distinguished from it altogether. The author of Revelation, who lived in Asia Minor and was very much at home in the Jewish tradition, says that God dwells in the Heavenly Temple (chaps. 7, 11, 15, etc.). Thus as a result, when the New Jerusalem is reestablished and it has become an earthly city (after the "harlot" Rome is destroyed), the Temple will be absent (in particular chap. 21). In other words, whereas in Philo we can still discern many political aspects in Jerusalem and the Temple, they are all eliminated by the author of Revelation.

Heroes and leaders of the past went in and out of fashion at various periods of history. Solomon, the famous builder of the Temple, is mentioned in the New Testament twelve times, but in connection with the building of the Temple only once, in Acts 7:47 (Stephen's speech). There the project is presented in a negative manner. David, who is mentioned fifty-nine times, is only three times mentioned vaguely in association with the Temple.[97] Solomon was associated with the Temple as a political base for the nation in Jewish literature from Old Testament times; it is therefore significant that he is presented in the New Testament as a wise man, not as the builder of the Temple.

It can therefore be seen from all of these examples that the Temple and capital never appear as political places or as nationalistic *political* symbols in Jewish and Christian literature. In the second period they are hardly associated with any aspect of statehood. On the contrary, the Temple functions as a religious and spiritual place. Therefore if the existing Temple were abused, they believed that either a new purified one should replace the old one, or a spiritual and/or heavenly temple should come to replace the physical one.

The priesthood is also viewed differently by the Gospels and Acts on the one hand, and the remainder of the New Testament on the other. In the Gospels and Acts—and in this respect there is not a great difference between the two parts of Acts (1–12; 13–28)—the present priestly order and especially the high priesthood are described in more moderate terms than in some passages of Josephus or other later Jewish sources (Damascus Rule 16:14f.; Testament of Levi 14:3; 17:11; Testament of Moses 5:6f.; Psalms of Solomon 8:13f.). Examples have already been given of how Josephus describes the high priesthood, and these descriptions are reinforced by documents of the first century B.C.E. from Qumran (Commentary on Habakkuk 9:6; 12:10). Mainstream Judaism of a later period also presents a hostile view, as for instance the famous Baraitas found in later Jewish sources:

> Woe unto me because of the house of Baithos [Boethus]; woe unto me for their lances [or "evil-speaking"]! Woe unto me because of the house of Hanin, woe unto me for their whisperings [or "calumnies"]! Woe unto me because of the house of Qathros [Tosefta: Qadhros, meaning Cantheras], woe unto me because of their reed pens! Woe unto me because of the house of Ishmael ben Phiabi, woe unto me because of their fist! For they are high priests and their sons are treasurers and their sons-in-law are Temple overseers, and their servants smite the people [*Tosefta:* "us"] with sticks. (*b. Pesaḥ. 57*a; *Tosefta Menaḥ.* 13.21.533)

> "The Years of the wicked shall be shortened: refers to the second Sanctuary, which abided for four hundred and twenty years and at which more than three hundred [high] priests served. Take off therefrom the forty years that Simeon the Righteous served, eighty years that Joḥanan the high priest served, ten, that Ishmael ben Fabi served, or, as some say, the eleven years of Rabbi Eleazar ben Ḥarsum. Count [the number of high priests] from then on and you will find that none of them completed his year [in office]. (*b. Yoma* 9a)

Against this background it is interesting to see what the New Testament has to say about the priesthood. One of the most interesting verses concerning the priests in the Gospels and Acts is Matt 12:5–8:[98] "or have you not read in the Law how on the Sabbath the priests in the Temple profane the Sabbath, and are guiltless?" On the occasion that Jesus overturned the tables of the money changers and merchants (Matt 21:12–17 and parallels), the evil deeds of the priests are not mentioned. The most common role the priests play in the Gospels and Acts is that of chasing Jesus and later Peter out of the Temple. In Matt 16:21 Jesus says that "he must go to Jerusalem and suffer many things from the elders and chief priests and scribes, and be killed."[99] Another time, "when he entered the Temple, the chief priests and the elders of the people" asked him who granted him the authority to teach in the Temple (Matt 21:23).[100] In Luke 19:47 it says, "And he was teaching daily in the Temple. The chief priests and the scribes and the principal men of the people sought to destroy him."[101] Caiaphas the high priest plays a major role in the accusation of Jesus, and we hear of priests also when the authors mention them in order to date some events (Luke 3:2).[102] In Acts 4:1–3 it is said that the "priests and the captain of the Temple and the Sadducees came upon" Peter and his followers, and "arrested them." Acts 6:7 says that "the word of God increased; and the number of the disciples multiplied greatly in Jerusalem, and a great many of the priests were obedient to the faith." Later the chief priests and the principal leaders of the Jews inform to Festus against Paul (25:2).[103] Before Paul's conversion, he goes to the high priest and asks him for letters to the synagogues at Damascus (Acts 9:1–2).

It is surprising that, apart from these references, the functions of the priestly order as such were not attacked by either the Gospels or Acts. They are taken for granted as cultic servants of the Temple. In addition, neither Aaron and his priestly line nor any other priestly line is mentioned in the Gospels or Acts (the only exception is the reference to Aaron in Luke 1:5 and in the summary of Israel's history given by Stephen in Acts 7:40; in Hebrews he is mentioned three times: 5:4; 7:11; 9:4). Thus the picture of the priestly order from Jewish literary sources, as early as the first period, showing them as corrupt, exploiting the poorer classes, and unholy, does not appear at all from the Gospels or Acts. This difference may point to the date of the traditions concerning the priesthood preserved in the New Testament. They may derive from the period before the drastic moral decadence of the priesthood, which intensified in the fifties and sixties of the first century C.E.

The letters of Paul contain nothing negative about the priesthood as an order. Only Hebrews, which is not Pauline (and may reflect some notions that circulated in the fifties, though one cannot be sure),[104] presents some original views on the priesthood, and in this regard ironically comes close to certain of the Jewish circles of the day. Hebrews is opposed to the earthly (present) priesthood (8:4), and in particular the high priests. In Heb 7:26–28 there is an allusion to the corruption of the priests in earlier times, but nothing is said explicitly.[105] As a result of this opposition to the high priesthood, the author of Hebrews proposed a new house of the high priesthood to serve in his Heavenly or ideal Temple. According to Hebrews, Jesus was to be seen as a priest; but here there was a problem, because according to Jewish tradition he could not become high priest unless he came from the priestly house of Aaron. Thus, in a sophisticated way, Hebrews offered an alternative priestly line starting from even before the time of Aaron (cf. for instance Heb 2:17–3:6; 4:14–15; 5:1–10; 6:20; 7:11–13; 8:1–13; 9:1–28; 10:21), namely, the line of Melchizedek. This fascinating figure appears in Genesis 14 as king and high priest to "El Elyon."[106] It should be emphasized that Salem in Genesis 14 was interpreted by many documents as Jerusalem, and according to the ambiguous verses of Genesis 14 Abraham was not inferior to Melchizedek.[107] There was a great interest in Melchizedek in the Second Temple period, and a questionable Jewish source (2 Enoch) elaborates his deeds. Hebrews 7 clearly states that Abraham was inferior to Melchizedek.

The interest in an alternative high-priestly line on the part of the author of the Letter to the Hebrews is understandable against the background of the notorious events associated with the high priesthood in the period before 70 C.E. The high priesthood, which had been abused for a long time, was frequently held by people who were thieves such as Jason and Menelaus, and was not given to the legitimate Zadokite house already from Hasmonean times. The position was granted to people as a reward for certain deeds by Herod, his successors, and the Romans. The houses from which the high priests were chosen were minor, unimportant priestly houses, who brought a great deal of embarrassment to Israel. For this reason, when the Zealots wanted to establish a new political order during the Great War, they did not choose a high priest from the existing high priestly houses, but instead elected a minor, unimportant priestly figure.

The Letter to the Hebrews goes a step farther concerning the high priesthood. Hebrews suggests that the new priestly line (within the new covenant[108]) was even more legitimate than the Aaronic one. The Melchizedek line of Hebrews was of earlier origin and derived from Jerusalem because Salem in Genesis 14 was interpreted as Jerusalem as early as the Psalter (unlike the Aaronic line, which derived from the Desert). Melchizedek is associated with a universalistic biblical figure. Still, Hebrews definitely does not abandon the high priesthood as an institution. What kind of high priesthood does the author of Hebrews have in mind? A religious and spiritual leadership with no political nationalistic overtones is clearly indicated.

The "kingship" of Melchizedek is abandoned in most passages, and where it appears the author tones down its political aspect (for instance, Heb 7:2, where he mentions the "king of justice" and the "king of peace," like God's portrayal in the Psalter). The line ends with Jesus, who remains the eternal high priest. Here again the New Testament is in line with certain streams of thought found in the Judaism of the first century C.E. concerning the links among Temple, priesthood, and state,[109] and should be read as a reaction to the politics of the priests.

Josephus was also opposed to the priesthood and in particular the high priests of the first century B.C.E. and first century C.E. He thought that at certain junctures of Israel's history they were corrupt, illegitimate, and unholy. Worst of all, according to Josephus, was their involvement in politics preceding the Great War and in the war itself. Did he offer any alternative to the corrupt high priesthood? We can learn something about his views from his interpretation of Israel's history in the *Antiquities,* which he wrote in Rome in the eighties and nineties. His views are in many cases a result of his audience and of his position after 70 C.E. There, in passages in which he embellished Scripture, he may have revealed some of his own views about national matters. In both the excursus in book 20 (224–251) of the *Antiquities* and his interpretation of the Book of Joshua (as well as elsewhere), he was clear about the fact that it was right that the high priesthood be in the hands of the legitimate Israelite line of Aaron, and that it was equal and even superior to any type of secular authority.[110] He, however, did not rule out altogether the Hasmonean priestly house. Josephus had learned the hard way what foolish priests, not descended from a traditional legitimate line, were up to. Lineage was a very important factor in antiquity.

As a result of Rome's conquest of Palestine, the Temple's loss of political sovereignty in 63 B.C.E., and the religious abuse of it later in the first century C.E., the literature from both Palestine and the Diaspora abounds with lamentations on the still-existing City and its Temple (as early as the Psalms of Solomon, which can be dated almost certainly to just after the Roman occupation of Palestine). There is also the famous lament preserved on parchment from Qumran (4Q179). Josephus intertwines numerous laments within his history of the Great War (*Jewish War* 6.99–102 and passim), as do the pseudepigraphic and apocalyptic literature.

After the destruction of the Temple, as well as before it, a great number of prophecies can be found. For instance in the Sibylline Oracle 1.385–400 it is said that "when the Temple of Solomon falls in the illustrious land cast down by men of barbarian speech with bronze breastplates, the Hebrews will be driven from their land," and in Sibylline Oracle 3.213–217, "Evil will come upon the pious men who live around the great Temple of Solomon, and who are the offspring of righteous men," and later, in 265–290, "and you will surely flee, leaving the very beautiful Temple, since it is your fate to leave the holy plain" (referring to the destruction of the First Temple, which was demolished in 586 B.C.E.). Then "there will be again a terrible judgment . . . because you have utterly destroyed the great house of the immortal" (326–328), and in 657–668: "The Temple of the great God (will be) laden with very beautiful wealth. . . . gold, silver, and purple ornament . . . but again the kings of the peoples will launch an attack together against this land, bringing doom upon themselves, for they will want to destroy the Temple of the great God and most excellent men when they enter the Land" (also 688; and 4.115–129).

In the fifth Sibylline Oracle 150–154 we hear that "he seized the divinely built Temple and burned the citizens, and peoples who went into it, men whom I rightly praised," and in 397–413, "The desired Temple has long ago been extinguished by you, when I saw the Second Temple cast headlong, soaked in fire by an impious hand . . . now a certain insignificant and impious king has gone up, cast it down, and left in ruins." These kinds of "mild" laments are to be found before the destruction, as in the third Sibylline Oracle and elsewhere, and after the destruction in a more dramatic manner, as in the two notable documents 2 Baruch and 4 Ezra. It seems that none of these texts lament the loss of the Temple as a political, nationalistic symbol of a Jewish state. On the contrary, the religious aspect is emphasized. Thus it is not surprising that Mark 13 (and parallels), which predicts the destruction of the Temple, is not necessarily a prophecy composed after the event of the destruction of the Temple in 70 C.E., but could have been uttered in the twenties and thirties of the first century, in keeping with prophecies of that type that are already found in the Old Testament.

After 70 C.E. the literary sources continue to reflect the attitudes concerning Jerusalem and the Temple found in the literature before

70 C.E. (second period). On the one hand they emphasize and continue the laments for the physical City and Temple, while lingering on the heavenly ones. On the other hand, a long time after the Temple was destroyed the rabbis included many *halakhot* concerning its worship in the Mishnah and Tosefta, as if the Temple were still in existence.[111] The rabbis thought that the third Temple would be built, just as the second one had been in the past. In other words, there was little alteration thematically after 70 C.E., but the tone and emphasis indeed changed.

To sum up, the image of Jerusalem, the Temple, and the high priesthood that emerges from the literature of the second period, both Jewish and Christian, is consistent with the historical background. The Temple was divested of most of its political significance, which was accented in the first period. Many Jews learned to live with the Temple as a religiocultural and spiritual symbol instead of a national and political one associated with an independent Jewish state. Some Zealot groups tried to restore the nationalistic, political significance of the Temple by using violence, but these efforts proved to be unsuccessful and were brought to a terrible end. Unfortunately, no document written by this group has yet been found. Such a document might have added another aspect to the overall picture. Nevertheless, it is quite clear that for the main core of Judaism, both in Palestine and the Diaspora, the Temple and Jerusalem lost their nationalistic, political significance a long time before the actual destruction of the Temple took place in 70 C.E. This change was pleasing to the Roman authorities, who wished native temples to be religious and spiritual places rather than political, nationalistic centers.

Notes

[1] Cf. the emphasis Strabo puts on temples of the Roman Near East, chapter 5 above at note 6.

[2] A. K. Bowman, *Egypt after the Pharaohs, 332 B.C.–A.D. 642* (London, 1986), pp. 165–190.

[3] D. Magie, *Roman Rule in Asia Minor* (Princeton, 1950), 2.1293 n. 52. At Gangra in Paphlagonia Augustus is named along with the gods and goddesses (*Inscriptiones latinae selectae* 8781).

[4] Cf. P. Zanker, *The Power of Images in the Age of Augustus* (Ann Arbor, Mich., 1988), pp. 297–302.

[5] Cf. G. W. Bowersock, *Augustus and the Greek World* (Oxford, 1965), pp. 116–117.

[6] Y. Meshorer, *City Coins of Eretz Israel and the Decapolis in the Roman Period* (Jerusalem, 1985), pp. 27–28.

[7] R. MacMullen, *Paganism in the Roman Empire* (New Haven and London, 1981), pp. 1–48.

[8] For this cult, see R. Mellor, *Thea Roma: The Worship of the Goddess Roma in the Greek World* (Göttingen, 1975); and for the claim that Rome created and supported the priesthood of Jerusalem, M. D. Goodman, *The Ruling Class of Judaea* (Cambridge, 1987).

[9] For the idea of the theocracy, see Josephus, *Contra Apionem* 2.164–165. For the idea of theocracy in Josephus see also Y. Amir, "*Theocratia* as a Concept of Political Philosophy: Josephus' Presentation of Moses' *Politeia*," *Scripta classica israelica* 8–9 (1985–1988): 83–105.

[10] Cf. in general O. Betz, "The Death of Choni-Onias in the Light of the Temple Scroll from Qumran (Comments of Ant. 14.22–24)," in *Jerusalem in the Second Temple Period*, ed. A. Oppenheimer et al. (Jerusalem, 1980), pp. 84–97 (Hebrew).

[11] *Antiquities* 14.90. For Gabinius's settlement see E. Schürer, *The History of the Jewish People in the Age of Jesus Christ*, rev. G. Vermes et al. (Edinburgh, 1973–1987), 1.268–269 (with the older bibliography).

[12] *Antiquities* 14.105–109; *Jewish War* 1.179. For Crassus's campaign in general see Schürer, *History*, 1.269–270.

[13] Cf. chapter 8 above.

[14] "Hillel said, Be of the disciples of Aaron, loving peace and pursuing peace, loving mankind and bringing them nigh to the law" (*m. 'Abot* 1:12). For the rise of this group in Herodian times, see M. Stern, "Aspects of Jewish Society: The Priesthood and Other Classes," in *Compendia rerum iudaicarum ad Novum Testamentum*, ed. S. Safrai et al. (Assen, 1974–1976), 2.615–621.

[15] Only Strabo thinks that Herod also tried to become a priest: M. Stern, *Greek and Latin Authors on Jews and Judaism* (Jerusalem, 1974–1984), 1.304.

[16] Except Joseph ben Ellem, who held the office for one day and Mattathias, son of Theophilus; cf. Goodman, *Ruling Class,* pp. 41–42. And cf. Stern, "Aspects of Jewish Society," 2.570–574, who claims that by the installation of Jesus son of Phiabi and Simeon son of Boethus, Herod laid the foundation for "the oligarchy of the high priesthood," which was characteristic of Jewish society until the end of the Second Temple period; and cf. also ibid., 580–612.

[17] ". . . because he wanted to avoid appointing a distinguished person as high priest of God" (*Antiquities* 15.22). He no doubt wanted to appease the estranged Babylonian Diaspora (*Antiquities* 15.16–17, 39–40, 178). By separating the kingship from the high priesthood he may also have had in the back of his mind the foreign examples of Asia Minor, where high priests were secondary in rank only to kings; see examples in Strabo (note 17, chapter 7).

[18] *Antiquities* 15.50–56; *Jewish War* 1.437. Cf. the still invaluable J. Jeremias, *Jerusalem in the Time of Jesus* (London, 1969), and S. Safrai, *Die Wallfahrt im Zeitalter des zweiten Tempels* (Neukirchen-Vluyn, 1981).

[19] Cf. E. Netzer, "Miqvaot (Ritual Baths) of the Second Temple Period at Jericho," in *Qadmoniot* 11 (1978): 54–59 (Hebrew).

[20] For an excellent survey of the problem associated with the high priesthood, see Stern, "Aspects of Jewish Society," 2.600–612. I am referring here to high priests who were officially appointed, not to the oligarchy, that is to say, the group at times called "high priests" in the sources; cf. ibid., p. 603.

[21] They seem weak in the context of Herod's court. For his court see A. Schalit, *König Herodes: Der Mann und sein Werk* (Berlin, 1969), passim.

[22] In some pottery found at Masada we find the inscription "Regi Herodi Iudaic(o)" (i.e., "king of the Jews"): see H. M. Cotton and J. Geiger, "Wine for Herod," *Cathedra* 53 (1989): 3–12 (Hebrew).

[23] This was the case with all of the temples of the ancient Near East (Egypt and Asia Minor) at that time. They were stripped absolutely of those remnants of political national power which they still entertained during the time of Hellenistic monarchies (cf. Strabo's examples, above).

[24] For a good survey see N. Avigad, *Discovering Jerusalem* (Oxford, 1984), chap. 3. For his "hellenization," see M. Hengel, *The "Hellenization" of Judaea in the First Century after Christ* (Philadelphia, 1989).

[25] For the archaeological remains, see Avigad, *Discovering Jerusalem,* pp. 81–83 and passim; for the Testament of Solomon, see D. C. Duling, "Testament of Solomon," in *The Old Testament Pseudepigrapha,* ed. J. H. Charlesworth (New York, 1983–1985), 1.935–987; and idem, "The Testament of Solomon: Retrospect and Prospect," *Journal for the Study of the Pseudepigrapha* 2 (1988): 87–112. Its date of composition is, however, impossible to determine.

[26] By these acts he in fact legitimized the Diaspora. The Hasmoneans have this aspect of "king of the Jews" to a far lesser extent.

[27] Avigad, *Discovering Jerusalem,* pp. 139–150 and passim.

[28] Against D. R. Schwartz, "Temple and Desert: On Religion and State in Second Temple Period Judaea," in his *Studies in the Jewish Background of Christianity* (Tübingen, 1992), pp. 29–43. As is shown in this chapter and elsewhere in the book, the picture of the religiopolitical status of the Temple (and Jerusalem) is much more complex than Schwartz's schematic description.

[29] For the Greek cities in Palestine, their separate organization, and their pagan identity, see Schürer, *History,* 2.85–183; and Hengel, *Hellenization.*

[30] Samaria was rebuilt by Herod and called Sebastia; it did not gain the status of a capital of the state. A distinction should be drawn between a capital (metropolis) of a certain region and the capital of a state. An example of the former is Sidon, which was the "metropolis of Cambe, Hippone, Citium, and Tyre" (A. Houghton, *Coins of the Seleucid Empire from the Collection of Arthur Houghton* [New York, 1983], p. 71). Examples of the latter are Jerusalem, Alexandria, Tiberias (of Antipas), and Petra (the capital of Arabia).

[31] For the question of Alexandria, see M. Rostovtzeff, *The Social and Economic History of the Hellenistic World* (Oxford, 1951), 1.264–265; *Hellenism and the Rise of Rome,* ed. P. Grimal (London, 1968), p. 179; and L. I. Levine, *Caesarea under Roman Rule* (Leiden, 1975), pp. 13–14. For the prehistory of Caesarea see in general G. Foerster, "The Early History of Caesarea," in *The Joint Expedition to Caesarea Maritima,* ed. C. T. Fritsch (Missoula, Mont., 1975), pp. 9–11. For the city in Roman times, see Levine, above, and recently *King Herod's Dream: Caesarea on the Sea,* ed. K. G. Holum et al. (New York and London, 1988), chaps. 2–4.

[32] *Antiquities* 16.136–141. Josephus says clearly about Caesarea that it was "the city Herod dedicated to the Province" (*Jewish War* 1.414). This official founding date does not exclude the possibility that as early as Herod's reign Jews were settling in the city (Levine, *Caesarea,* pp. 16–17)—and their status there was in many respects similar to that of Jews in the Diaspora. In the sixties of the first century we hear of a well-established Jewish community there. Cf. I. M. Levey, "Caesarea and the Jews," in *Joint Expedition,* pp. 43–69. The Jews both within Caesarea and outside it hated its pagan Greek outlook. This attitude can be compared to the hatred of Egyptian natives for Alexandria ("Oracle of the Potter," 33ff.: "The cult images, which had been transported there, will be brought back again to Egypt; and the city by the sea will be a refuge for fishermen because Agathos Daimon and Knephis will have gone to Memphis.").

[33] Y. Meshorer, *Ancient Jewish Coinage* (New York, 1982), 2.28.

[34] *Histories* 2.78. For Caesarea as "little Rome" see A. Rosenzweig, *Jerusalem und Caesarea* (Berlin, 1890); and D. R. Schwartz, *Agrippa I: The Last King of Judaea* (Tübingen, 1990), p. 131.

³⁵ *Antiquities* 17.149–155; *Jewish War* 1.648–651. Cf. M. Hengel, *The Zealots* (Edinburgh, 1989), pp. 302–303, 307.

³⁶ For the so-called "war of Varus" see Hengel, *Zealots,* pp. 325–330, and for crucifixion at the time, idem, *Crucifixion* (Philadelphia, 1977).

³⁷ D. S. Rhoads, *Israel in Revolution, 6–74 C.E.* (Philadelphia, 1976), and others, justifiably.

³⁸ For this change of leadership see Stern, "Aspects of Jewish Society," 2.615.

³⁹ Cf. *Antiquities* 17.339, and Meshorer, *Ancient Jewish Coinage,* 2.31–34.

⁴⁰ This does not mean that the group was not founded already by Judas; cf. Hengel, *Zealots,* passim. Against this claim see Rhoads, *Israel in Revolution,* pp. 52–55; and Goodman, *Ruling Class,* p. 96. Cf. the excellent article of M. Stern concerning this issue, "The Suicide of Eleazar ben Jair and His Men at Masada, and the 'Fourth Philosophy,' " in his *Studies in Jewish History* (Jerusalem, 1991), pp. 313–343 (Hebrew). I do not see any reason to challenge Josephus in his description of the Fourth Philosophy and the time of its foundation.

⁴¹ I am somewhat skeptical about the claim that the priestly houses were made a ruling class by Rome in 6 C.E., as Goodman ingeniously suggests (*Ruling Class,* passim). There is not really much evidence in the sources to support this theory. Appointments of high priests do not result in a formation of a ruling class. Why would the sources throughout be silent about such an event? Also, I think that the reduction in the stature of the high priest and the priestly houses was more of a gradual process, culminating in the fifties and sixties of the first century C.E., instead of at the beginning of that century. The emergence of some powerful priestly houses that coexisted simultaneously (Boethians, Hananians, etc.)—which could not have coexisted during the Hasmonean period—brought about a tension between these houses that weakened them as a political unit. Perhaps it is for this reason that the author of Hebrews, bringing forward traditions from the fifties and sixties, wished to have only one line of priests in Israel.

⁴² For the Samaritans see J. D. Purvis, "The Samaritan Problem: A Case Study in Jewish Sectarianism in the Roman Era," in *Traditions in Transformation,* ed. B. Halpern and J. D. Levenson (Winona Lake, 1981), pp. 323–350; F. M. Cross, "Aspects of Samaritan and Jewish History in Late Persian and Hellenistic Times," *Harvard Theological Review* 59 (1966): 201–211; and H. G. Kippenberg, *Garizim und Synagoge* (Berlin, 1971). Cf. now for their history M. Mor, "The Persian, Hellenistic and Hasmonean Period," B. Hall, "From John Hyrcanus to Baba Rabbah," both in *The Samaritans,* ed. A. D. Crown (Tübingen, 1989), pp. 1–18 and 32–43; and U. Rappaport, "The Samaritans in the Hellenistic Period," *Zion* 55 (1990): 373–396 (Hebrew).

⁴³ *Antiquities* 18.55; *Jewish War* 2.169; and cf. also Philo, *Legatio ad Gaium* 299–305. G. Fuks, "Again on the Episode of the Gilded Roman Shields at Jerusalem," *Harvard Theological Review* 75 (1982): 503–507; D. R. Schwartz, "Josephus and Philo on Pontius Pilate," *The Jerusalem Cathedra* 3 (1983): 26–45; P. R. Da-

vies, "The Meaning of Philo's Text about the Gilded Shields," *Journal of Theological Studies* n.s. 37 (1986): 109–114.

[44] *Antiquities* 18.60–62; *Jewish War* 2.175–177; and cf. the *Suda,* s.v. Korbanas: "Among the Jews (the Korbanas) is the holy treasury. Pilatus spent the holy treasury on an aqueduct and stirred up riot" (R. K. Sherk, *The Roman Empire: Augustus to Hadrian* [Cambridge, 1988], p. 75). In general for Pilatus see J. P. Lémonon, *Pilate et le gouvernment de la Judée* (Paris, 1981).

[45] For the census from the Roman point of view see Schürer, *History,* 1.399–427.

[46] *Antiquities* 18.90–95. Intervention in priestly matters at local temples by the Romans also happened elsewhere: see for instance *Berliner griechische Urkunden* 4.1199 (in Sherk, *Roman Empire,* p. 30, Egypt).

[47] Our sources never say that they built or created a priestly class that supported them (contra Goodman, *Ruling Class*).

[48] In general for Gaius and the Jews from a Roman point of view see A. A. Barrett, *Caligula* (New Haven and London, 1989), pp. 182–191.

[49] *Legatio ad Gaium,* 199ff. Cf. Schwartz, *Agrippa,* pp. 77–89 for Josephus's apologetic tendency in failing to mention the incident at Jamnia. This omission does not mean, however, that he deliberately toned down all other similar events in Palestine.

[50] *Antiquities* 18.296–297. In the *Legatio ad Gaium* 276–329, Agrippa writes to Gaius to consider "the Jewish nation the city of Jerusalem and the Temple"; cf. E. M. Smallwood, *Philonis Alexandrini Legatio ad Gaium,* 2d ed. (Leiden, 1970), ad loc.

[51] There is no reason to put these events in 38 C.E., as Schwartz (*Agrippa,* pp. 55–57, 67–74) does.

[52] *Antiquities* 19.297. By this act he restored the office to the pro-Herodian family of Boethus, "a break with the recent past and a token of his links with the more distant past" (E. M. Smallwood, "High Priests and Politics in Roman Palestine," *Journal of Theological Studies* n.s. 13 [1962]: 16); and cf. Stern, "Aspects of Jewish Society," 2.604–605, and Schwartz, *Agrippa,* pp. 69–70, 185–189, who says it was in 38 C.E.; but there is no particular reason to shift the events of 41 to 38 C.E., because even if Simeon is the high priest mentioned in *b. Sota* 33a, the saying about him may be apocryphal.

[53] It is remarkable that he did not return to the Hasmonean practice of also holding the high priesthood. I would suggest that in this respect not only did he follow in the footsteps of the Herodian dynasty (i.e., separation between the functions), but he also did not want to irritate the emperor by imitating so clearly and bluntly the practice of the Roman emperors themselves. From 12 B.C.E. the Roman emperor was also the high priest of the Roman state (called *Pontifex Maximus;* cf. G. W. Bowersock, "The Pontificate of Augustus," in *Between Republic and Empire:*

Interpretations of Augustus and His Principate, ed. K. A. Raaflaub and M. Toher [Berkeley, Los Angeles, and Oxford, 1990], pp. 380–394). Caligula's early coins show that he took the title early in his reign (Barrett, *Caligula,* p. 58). Claudius took it also (B. Levick, *Claudius* [New Haven and London, 1990], p. 42).

54 *Antiquities* 19.326–327. The story in *Antiquities* 19.332–334, in which Simeon told the people that the king was not pure and thus should not be let into the Temple, is of interest; cf. Schwartz, *Agrippa,* pp. 124–130. Simeon may have had many reasons, according to the code of purity, to think that the king was not pure enough to enter the Temple: see for instance the regulations in the Temple Scroll, col. 46 (Y. Yadin, *Temple Scroll* [Jerusalem, 1983], 2.195–200).

55 For Caesarea at the time see H. K. Beebe, "Caesarea Maritima, Its Strategic and Political Significance to Rome," *Journal of Near Eastern Studies* 49 (1983): 195–207. For Agrippa's death see Schwartz, *Agrippa,* pp. 145–149, 203–207 (dates it to ca. October 43).

56 *Antiquities* 20.12–13; also for this policy see his famous answer to the Jews of Alexandria. In general for Claudius and the Jews see Levick, *Claudius,* pp. 121ff., 179ff.

57 Goodman, *Ruling Class,* part I, chaps. 3 and 5, argues for the political importance Rome granted to the high-priestly order in Judea. But the frequent changes in the holders of the high priesthood from the time of Herod the Great through the Great War weakened the political *locus standi* of the office and lowered its status in the eyes of the Jews, in particular as a religious and spiritual function. Here it should be emphasized that even if they had some political significance as representatives of the people in the eyes of the Roman authorities (as Smallwood and Goodman argue), they were not seen by the Jews themselves as national political figures who would lead the Jews back to independence from Roman yoke, thus to become the new leaders of a newly emerging Jewish state. Also other civil institutions such as the Sanhedrin had no real political power; and cf. correctly Goodman, *Ruling Class,* pp. 113–117.

58 The few cases of such religious demands within fifty years show that Goodman pushes the evidence too far concerning the Jewish population's striving for purity during the first century C.E. (*Ruling Class,* part I, chap. 4). Also, the "sickness" syndrome that Josephus reports seems to be just a common literary *topos,* and an imagery frequently used in Hellenistic historiography (cf. D. Mendels, "Polybius and the Socio-Economic Revolution in Greece [227–146 B.C.]," *L'Antiquité classique* 51 [1982]: 86–110; A. M. Eckstein, "Josephus and Polybius: A Reconsideration," *Classical Antiquity* 9 [1990]: 175–208). For the religious aspect from a theological point of view, see now also H. Schwier, *Tempel und Tempelzerstörung* (Göttingen, 1987), passim. He tones down, however, the political aspect of the Temple altogether.

59 For the role of the priesthood in this decline, see Goodman, *Ruling Class,* part II, chap. 6.

[60] For the Sanhedrin at the time see H. D. Mantel, *Studies in the History of the Sanhedrin* (Cambridge, Mass., 1961), pp. 61–101; Goodman, *Ruling Class,* pp. 113–117.

[61] I would lay the emphasis not on the political aspect of their leadership (as does Goodman, *Ruling Class*), but rather on their religious stature among the wider circles of Jews. In general for the priests in those days see A. Büchler, *Die Priester und der Cultus im letzten Jahrzehnt des jerusalemischen Tempels* (Vienna, 1895). Cf. also H. D. Mantel, "The High Priesthood and the Sanhedrin in the Time of the Second Temple . . ." in *The Herodian Period,* ed. M. Avi-Yona and Z. Baras, pp. 264–281; and R. A. Horsley, "High Priests and the Politics of Roman Palestine: A Contextual Analysis of the Evidence in Josephus," *Journal for the Study of Judaism in the Persian, Hellenistic and Roman Period* 17 (1986): 23–55.

[62] There was an attempt to argue that worship in the Temple continued: see K. W. Clark, "Worship in the Jerusalem Temple after A.D. 70," in idem, *The Gentile Bias and Other Essays* (Leiden, 1980), pp. 9–20.

[63] Not all of it is post-70 C.E.; and cf. rightly also Goodman, *Ruling Class,* pp. 85–87.

[64] It is difficult to date Hebrews exactly (many of its traditions go back to the period prior to 70 C.E.). In Heb 9:1–12 the author mentions the earthly sanctuary, but, apart from some details, purposely avoids a general description of it (he even says in 9:5 "concerning which things [the things of the Temple], this is not the proper time to speak"). Cf. now H. W. Attridge, *Hebrews,*† ad loc. The Mishnah has a picture of a Temple, but this is apparently too late for the discussion here (about 200 C.E.). For Jerusalem and the Temple in rabbinics, see O. R. J. McKelvey), *The New Temple: The Church in the New Testament* (Oxford, 1969), pp. 34–36. Revelation is a good example for the present case: in it there is no Temple in Jerusalem.

[65] But its date of composition and provenance are debated; cf. Duling, "Testament of Solomon." Only in chap. 21 is there a description of some of the artifacts in the Temple.

[66] It is quite clear that the narrative parts of the New Testament can be used for discussing the spirit and ideology of the period antedating 70 C.E. Even if they are not considered by many scholars to depict historical events in the Thucydidean sense, they still reflect ideas of the decades before 70 C.E. preserved by the communities as sacred traditions in an oral or written form. At any rate, the reader should realize that the New Testament is discussed here as literature rather than as history. And regarding historicity see for instance S. G. F. Brandon, *Jesus and the Zealots* (Manchester, 1967), pp. 154–158, and recently G. Theissen, *Lokalkolorit und Zeitgeschichte in den Evangelien* (Göttingen, 1989), passim; C. H. Dodd, *Historical Tradition in the Fourth Gospel* (Cambridge, 1963); F. F. Bruce, "The Acts of the Apostles: Historical Record or Theological Reconstruction?" *Aufstieg und Niedergang der römischen Welt* 2.25.3 (1985): 2569–2603; cf. also G. Vermes, *Jesus and the World of Judaism* (Philadelphia, 1984).

[67] It also reflects Paul's ideas on this issue (2:21: "He spoke of the temple of his body," and cf. 4:21–24 with Brown, *John,** 1.114–125, etc.). Cf. in general the extensive introduction of Haenchen, *John,*† 1.1–97, and ad loc.

[68] The literature about the Temple in the New Testament abounds, and is mostly preoccupied with theological questions: cf. for instance E. Lohmeyer, *Lord of the Temple* (Edinburgh and London, 1961), originally *Kultus und Evangelium* (Göttingen, 1942); B. Gärtner, *The Temple and the Community in Qumran and the New Testament* (Cambridge, 1965); McKelvey, *New Temple;* L. Gaston, *No Stone on Another: Studies in the Significance of the Fall of Jerusalem in the Synoptic Gospels* (Leiden, 1970); G. Klinzing, *Die Umdeutung des Kultus in der Qumrangemeinde und im Neuen Testament* (Göttingen, 1971); D. Juel, *Messiah and Temple: The Trial of Jesus in the Gospel of Mark* (Missoula, Mont., 1977); E. P. Sanders, *Jesus and Judaism* (London, 1985), esp. pp. 61–90; S. Freyne, *Galilee, Jesus, and the Gospels* (Philadelphia, 1988), esp. pp. 178–190, 224–239.

[69] Cf. in particular m. *Maᶜaśer Šeni* 1.5–6; 3.1–5; 5.2–3; *Pesaḥim* 5.5–8; *Šeqalim* 3–8; *Yoma,* passim; *Taᶜanit* 4.2–8; *Nazir* 5.4; etc.

[70] Matt 5:34–36, quoting Ps 47:2. See in general A. Abecassis et al., *Jérusalem dans les traditions juives et chrétiennes* (Louvain, 1982).

[71] It has been asked why, if the Gospels were written after 70 C.E., is there no reference to its destruction (and that of Jerusalem)? The reference to the destruction could have made a good argument for a new beginning of the New Israel (cf. A. T. Robinson, *Redating the New Testament* [Philadelphia, 1976], pp. 13–30 with the older literature). I do not know whether the absence of any explicit mention of the destruction in the Gospels may point to the time of authorship. It may, however, point to the authenticity and early derivation of the traditions incorporated in the various books of the New Testament; cf. in general also M. D. Hooker, "Traditions about the Temple in the Sayings of Jesus," *Bulletin of the John Rylands University Library of Manchester* 70 (1988): 7–19.

[72] Cf. also Mark 14:49; Luke 5:14; 18:10–14; 20:1–8; 22:52–54; John 5:13–14; 7:14; 8:1–2, 20; 10:22–24; 18:13. Cf. Fitzmyer, *Luke,** 1.434–448. In general, for the Temple in Luke from a theological point of view, see M. Bachmann, *Jerusalem und der Tempel* (Stuttgart and Mainz, 1980).

[73] See F. D. Weinert, "The Meaning of the Temple in Luke-Acts," *Biblical Theology Bulletin* 11 (1981): 81–89; cf. Fitzmyer, *Luke,** 2.1591.

[74] Albright and Mann, *Matthew,** p. 62 comment: "If commentators insist on providing a late date for Matthew's material, they must somehow explain this saying, which refers to a sacrificial system which lasted only until A.D. 70."

[75] Cf. in general a tempting explanation by McKelvey, *New Temple,* pp. 61–65; also Sanders, *Jesus and Judaism,* pp. 61–76.

[76] There exists a vast literature on this prophecy: see Sanders, *Jesus and Judaism,* pp. 59–90, mentioning the older literature. See J. Schlosser, "La Parole de Jésus sur la fin du Temple," *New Testament Studies* 36.3 (1990): 398–414.

[77] Cf. justifiably S. J. D. Cohen, *From the Maccabees to the Mishnah* (Philadelphia, 1987), pp. 28–34. Josephus could have thought along these lines long before 70 C.E. When the Temple was destroyed, it "confirmed" his thesis (which was common at the time). See in general O. Michel, "Die Rettung Israels . . . ," *Aufstieg und Niedergang der römischen Welt* 2.21.2 (1984): 945–976; Also C. A. Evans, "Jesus' Action in the Temple: Cleansing or Portent of Destruction?" *Catholic Biblical Quarterly* 51 (1989): 237–270.

[78] For instance, by omitting the story of Micah and his temple (Jud 17–18) from the story of the migration of Dan, Josephus emphasizes the centrality of Jerusalem and its Temple (*Antiquities* 5.175ff). See also 7.60–70 (the conquest of Jerusalem by David).

[79] For a recent theological interpretation see J. B. Chance, *Jerusalem, the Temple, and the New Age in Luke-Acts* (Macon, Ga., 1988); and McKelvey, *New Temple.*

[80] Some New Testament scholars see this positive picture of the Temple as problematic and attempt to solve it in various ways. For instance Acts, like the Gospel of Luke, describes the new order as beginning at the very same place where the old order finishes its existence (H. Conzelmann, *The Theology of St. Luke* [London, 1960], pp. 164ff., 212ff.); or that the early Christian group used the Temple only for prayer, not for sacrifice (F. C. Burkitt, *Christian Beginnings* [London, 1924], pp. 62–63). There is no necessity for such speculation, if we read Acts (as well as other parts of the New Testament) as historians of the ancient Near East rather than as theologians of the twentieth century.

[81] And cf. Conzelmann, *Acts,*† p. 24.

[82] Acts 21:26–30; 22:17; 24:6, 11–12; Conzelmann, *Acts,*† ad loc.

[83] Acts 24:18–19; cf. Munck, *Acts,** p. 230.

[84] Cf. Conzelmann, *Theology of St. Luke,* pp. 142–144.

[85] M. Simon, "Saint Stephen and the Jerusalem Temple," *Journal of Ecclesiastical History* 2 (1951): 127–142; idem, *St. Stephen and the Hellenists in the Primitive Church* (London and Toronto, 1958); and cf. A. F. J. Klijn, "Stephen's Speech—Acts VII:2–53," *New Testament Studies* 4 (1957–1958): 25–31; also discussion in McKelvey, *New Temple,* pp. 86–87; Schwartz, "Temple and Desert," pp. 40–41. In Rev 21:22–23, "But I saw no Temple in the City for its Temple is the Lord God almighty and the lamb . . ." Cf. D. Flusser, "No Temple in the City," in his *Judaism and the Origins of Christianity* (Jerusalem, 1988), pp. 454–465.

[86] The expansion of early Christianity to the Samaritans (as expressed in Acts 8:4–8 and John 4, as opposed to Matt 10:5) and to the gentiles (Acts 10), who did not acknowledge the Jerusalem Temple, should be viewed as one of the causes for

the acceptance by the early Christians of a spiritual Temple that is not necessarily associated with Jerusalem. In general for Paul and the Temple see W. L. Knox, *St. Paul and the Church of Jerusalem* (Cambridge, 1925), pp. 66–93; McKelvey, *New Temple,* pp. 92–124; W. D. Davies, *The Gospel and the Land* (Berkeley and London, 1974), pp. 185–194.

[87] There is no necessity to go as far as the Stoa for these concepts (as H. Wenschkewitz, "Die Spiritualisierung der Kultusbegriffe, Tempel, Priester und Opfer im Neuen Testament," *Angelos* 4 [1932]: 70–230). They can be found in different nuances in Judaism of the time (2 Macc 14:35; Philo, *De Virtutibus* 188, perhaps Isa 28:16; *Rule of the Community* 8.7ff.; etc.). In general for this question see H. Conzelmann, *1 Cor,*† pp. 77–78. See also J. Coppens, *The Spiritual Temple in the Pauline Letters* (Berlin, 1973), pp. 53–66; M. Fraeyman, "La Spiritualisation . . . ." *Ephemerides theologicae lovanienses* 23 (1947): 378–412.

[88] For Paul within Palestinian Judaism, see in particular Davies, *Paul;* E. P. Sanders, *Paul and Palestinian Judaism* (Philadelphia, 1977).

[89] Cf. Furnish, *2 Corinthians,** pp. 295–301.

[90] 2 Cor 6:16, with Furnish's comments, *2 Corinthians,** p. 363. See C. Newsom, *Songs of the Sabbath Sacrifice* (Atlanta, 1985), passim. Because the Temple is spiritualized, in Rev 21:22 there is no Temple in the City "For its Temple is the Lord God almighty and the lamb."

[91] This Jerusalem is an antithesis to the actual political and religious present-day Jerusalem. Thus, it is not surprising that Paul never depicted either the Temple or Jerusalem in concrete terms (even like the vague one in the *Songs*). Any Temple that has architectural features and is earthly would become a political institution (i.e., corrupt) according to the praxis of those days. In general for the heavenly Temple and City, see Betz, *Galatians,*† p. 246. On the concept of "Heavenly City" in Hellenistic literature, see H. D. Betz, *Lukian von Samosata und das Neue Testament* (Berlin, 1961), pp. 92–96.

[92] Cf. M. Barth, *Ephesians,** 1.268–274; also 2 Thess 2:3–4.

[93] Cf. in general Attridge, *Hebrews,*† pp. 216–229.

[94] For a theological discussion see McKelvey, *New Temple,* pp. 147–154.

[95] For his "selection" of heroes in his works, see the list in F. H. Colson, *Philo,* Loeb Classical Library, 10.269–433.

[96] For this issue see Y. Amir, "Philo's Version of the Pilgrimage to Jerusalem," in *Jerusalem in the Second Temple Period,* ed. A. Oppenheimer et al. (Jerusalem, 1980), pp. 154–165. Cf. in general also V. Nikiprowetzky, "La spiritualisation des sacrifices . . . ," *Semitica* 17 (1967): 97–116.

[97] Luke 1:69; Acts 7:45–46; 15:16; cf. N. M. Cohen, *Jewish Biblical Personages in the New Testament* (Lanham and London, 1989), pp. 38, 78–84.

98 Albright and Mann, *Matthew,** pp. 149–150.

99 Some manuscripts add "Messiah." The order "elders, chief priests, and scribes" is to be found in the three synoptic Gospels (Albright and Mann, *Matthew,** pp. 199–200).

100 Cf. also Mark 10:33; Luke 5:14; and Fitzmyer, *Luke,** 1.575.

101 Cf. the comments of Fitzmyer, *Luke,** 2.1269–1276, 1446–1452. Cf. also 20:1–8; 22:52–54.

102 Fitzmyer, *Luke,** 1.458; and cf. John 11:49; 18:13.

103 According to Josephus, *Antiquities* 20.179, Ishmael the son of Phabi was high priest at the time.

104 The date of Hebrews remains a problem. Attridge, *Hebrews,*† pp. 6–9 brings arguments about the dating but concludes, "The most probable range of dates within which Hebrews was composed is thus 60 to 100 C.E. Decisive reasons for a precise dating or a narrower range have not been adduced" (p. 9). Cf. R. M. Wilson, *Hebrews: The New Century Bible Commentary* (Grand Rapids, Mich., 1987); G. W. Buchanan, *Hebrews,** pp. 256–263; and F. F. Bruce, " 'To the Hebrews': A Document of Roman Christianity?" *Aufstieg und Niedergang der römischen Welt* 2.25.4 (1987): 3496–3521.

105 Attridge, *Hebrews,*† pp. 212–214.

106 Cf. an ostracon bearing the inscription "(El) qoneh aretz" ("[God] creator of Earth"), in Avigad, *Discovering Jerusalem,* pp. 41–42.

107 A Melchizedek document was found among the Dead Sea Scrolls. The secondary literature on Melchizedek is vast: see for instance, R. H. Robertson, *After the Order of Malchizedeck* (Los Angeles, 1980); P. J. Kobelski, *Melchizedeck and Melchiresa* (Washington, D.C., 1981); C. Gianotto, *Melchisedek e la sua tipologia* (Brescia, 1984); and Attridge, *Hebrews,*† ad loc.

108 Heb 7:12; this claim is radical, because a new high priesthood requires a new Torah.

109 For more details see Buchanan, *Hebrews,** ad loc, and Attridge, *Hebrews,*† passim.

110 Cf. for instance *Antiquities* 5.15, 43, 55–57, 120, 361–362; 7.72 (David consults the high priest rather than God, according to the Bible). For a stimulating analysis of his complex attitude regarding the priesthood, see S. Schwartz, *Josephus and Judaean Politics* (Leiden and Cologne, 1990), esp. chaps. 3, 6.

111 When the Temple is described in the Mishnah, it is a mixture of reality, biblical descriptions, and an ideal. In fact, one can say that portrayals (i.e., concrete ones of real temples) were available between 200 and 63 B.C.E. Between 63 B.C.E. and 70 C.E. there was nothing of the sort. After 70 C.E., as a result of nostalgia, we again find descriptions, such as the ones in Josephus and the Mishnah.

CHAPTER 11

The Army,
63 B.C.E.-70 C.E.

In this chapter we will examine the question of whether the Roman conquest of Palestine brought about any change in the Jewish army as a nationalistic symbol. The invasion of the Roman legions into Palestine definitely influenced the organizational patterns and the warfare of Herod the Great's army. The Essenes in their important document 1QM (the War Scroll) show that Roman warfare was known to the Jews.[1] When the Jews declared their independence from Rome in 66 C.E., Josephus was the one who organized an army along the lines of the Roman legion. But in this study the armies of Herod the Great and his successors will not be discussed from a military point of view.[2] Instead we shall examine the history of the armies and their development as a national political institution. In chapter 6 we arrived at the Roman conquest of Jerusalem by Pompey in 63 B.C.E. The survey will continue to the year 66 C.E., and then consider the literature relevant to this period. But first some discussion about the armies in the Hellenistic East after the Roman conquest is needed.

Basically everything that has been said about the armies of the Hellenistic monarchs is also true of Hellenistic client kings, namely, that their armies were based on a combination of mercenaries and indigenous peoples recruited from their own territories. Their standing armies, however, could not be as large as they were at the time of their independence.[3] When Marc Antony arrived at Actium in 31 B.C.E. he was accompanied by a huge army. Part of that army was

Roman; another part seems to have been made up of the armies he had assembled from among the client kingdoms of the East. We read in Plutarch, *Antony* 61, "Antony had no fewer than five hundred fighting ships, among which were many vessels . . . he also had one hundred thousand infantry soldiers and twelve thousand horsemen. Of subject kings who fought with him, there were Bocchus the king of Libya, Tarcondemus the king of Upper Cilicia, Archelaus of Cappadocia, Philadelphus of Paphlagonia, Mithridates of Commagene, and Sadalas of Thrace. These were with him, while from Pontus Polemon sent an army, and Malchus from Arabia . . . besides Amyntas the king of Lycaonia and Galatia; the king of the Medes also sent an auxiliary force." This list demonstrates what power these armies had when they were assembled together, and probably after special recruitments were carried out in the various countries. During Rome's conquest of the East, one hears of local armies that attempted to make reforms in their organizational patterns, in keeping with the Roman legion and Roman warfare. For instance, Mithridates reformed his army in this way in order to make it more efficient in his war against Rome (Plutarch, *Lucullus* 7.3–5); such reforms are also later heard of in Numidia and Germany.[4]

But what happened in Judea after 63 B.C.E. in terms of the local army? In 57 B.C.E. Aristobulus's son, Alexander, recruited an army, and "then went around the country and armed many of the *Jews*, and soon collected ten thousand heavy-armed soldiers and fifteen hundred horse, and fortified the strongholds" (*Antiquities* 14.83; *Jewish War* 1.160–161). It is interesting to note that during these years many Jewish soldiers were available in Palestine, presumably the remnants of the dispersed Hasmonean army. Josephus relates that the Romans (assisted by "Antipater's picked troops and the rest of the Jewish contingent," *Jewish War* 1.162) killed three thousand of the Jews who fought for Alexander (*Antiquities* 14.85). After Alexander was defeated by Gabinius, the Roman governor of Syria, Aristobulus himself managed to escape from Rome to Palestine, and many Jews joined him (14.93–94): "Many of those who joined him, however, were unarmed. But Aristobulus, who had decided to retire to Machaerus, dismissed these men, who were without equipment— for they were of no use to him in action—and taking the men who were armed, amounting to some eight thousand, marched away."

Apparently he had more potential soldiers available than means to equip them. The numbers are not very reliable but may give us some idea about the proportions of recruitment. The Romans attacked, five thousand were killed, and the others dispersed. Only Aristobulus went to Machaerus with a thousand or more. He was then caught and sent to Rome (56 B.C.E.). Later Alexander, the son of Aristobulus, reached Palestine again and "had forced many of the Jews to revolt, and was marching over the country with a large army and killing all the Romans he met" (14.100; *Jewish War* 1.176). Gabinius could not restrain Alexander, who with an army of thirty thousand Jews went to meet Gabinius, and was defeated near Mount Tabor, in which ten thousand of his men fell (*Antiquities* 14.102; *Jewish War* 1.177).

A Jewish force is mentioned in accounts of the events of 48 B.C.E., this time helping the Romans. Antipater the Edomite (Herod the Great's father) went with three thousand armed Jews from Palestine in his army to assist Julius Caesar in the so-called *Bellum Alexandrinum*, which was fought against Ptolemy XII.[5] The Jews who were settled at the time in Onias's land in Tell el-Yahudiah also joined (*Antiquities* 14.128–132). As a reward from Caesar, Antipater the Edomite, who already had the title of *epimeletes*, received the title of *epitropos* (guardian) of Judea. Recognizing that Hyrcanus II, the high priest, was a weak figure, Antipater appointed his sons as *strategoi* (military leaders). He also appointed Herod, who was still a young man, as *strategos* in the Galilee, and Phasaelis in Jerusalem. Herod immediately revealed his resolute character by launching a military enterprise against the brigands (*lestai*) with a large troop of soldiers. He was praised by many of the Syrians in the Galilee for his actions (14.159–160). It is difficult to know whether his army at this juncture was Jewish or foreign. Herod's army is also alluded to later when he came to stand trial in Jerusalem before the Sanhedrin. "He arrived with a troop sufficient for the purposes of the journey, and that he might not appear too formidable to Hyrcanus by arriving with a larger body of men" (*Antiquities* 14.169). From this reference we do not get any idea of the size of his army, which was in any case local in nature.[6] When Herod was appointed by Sextus to be the *strategos* of Coele-Syria, he went at one juncture to fight Hyrcanus II with a large army. But his father and brother deterred him from doing so (14.180–181; *Jewish War* 1.214). It is not clear here whether his army was Jewish or not. We have already seen that many veterans from the dispersed Hasmonean army and their children were probably still available at the time, and it is possible that Herod recruited these men. Some further information can be found in the sources about Jewish soldiers at the time.

Josephus says that Hyrcanus II intervened for the Jewish soldiers, asking Dolabella to exempt them from military service for religious reasons, a request that Dolabella granted at Ephesus. This account indicates that some Jewish soldiers were serving in the Roman army as Roman citizens, otherwise Hyrcanus would not have intervened (*Antiquities* 14.223–224).[7] We also hear that after Julius Caesar's murder on the Ides of March in 44 B.C.E., Cassius and Murcus made Herod governor of Coele-Syria, giving him ships and a force of cavalry and infantry. They also promised him that they would appoint him king of Judea (14.280; *Jewish War* 1.225).

In 40 B.C.E. Antigonus, the grandson of Jannaeus and Salome, approached Judea under the aegis of the invading Parthians, "and as some of the Jews near Mount Carmel came to Antigonus and were ready to join him in the invasion, Antigonus expected to take some part of the territory with their help." Being joined by others, he managed to form a large army and rushed to fight over Jerusalem (*Antiquities* 14.334–336; *Jewish War* 1.250–252). During the daily skirmishes that took place between Antigonus and Herod, we hear of many tens of thousands of armed and unarmed men who gathered round the Temple during Pentecost (14.337–338; *Jewish War* 1.253), apparently the former supporters of the Hasmonean realm and their offspring, who formed a good nucleus for nationalistic upheavals. Herod, after spending a short while in Jerusalem, was forced to escape from Palestine as a consequence of the Parthian invasion and the establishment of Antigonus the Hasmonean as king of Judea.

When leaving Jerusalem Herod took with him those soldiers "whom he had there" (*Antiquities* 14.353). It seems that a part of his army had left him when realizing that Antigonus had the upper hand. Most of the soldiers who did not abandon him in his difficult hour were Edomites (more than nine thousand; 14.362). Some months later, in the early spring of 39 B.C.E., Herod returned to Palestine, crowned as the king of Judea by the Triumvirate in Rome. He first landed in Acco-Ptolemais "and had collected a not inconsiderable force of both foreigners and his countrymen, and was marching through Galilee against Antigonus" (14.394). Herod's strength increased day by day as he pressed forward, "and all Galilee, except for a few of its inhabitants, came over to his side" (14.395). The nation was again split in two: those who sided with King Antigonus and those who were against him. Consequently Jews fought each other, with the aid of the many foreigners who were in Palestine. It seems that most of the Jews who joined these rival armies did not have any particular ideological motivations; they merely joined the side that seemed stronger and better off at the time. With the help of the Romans, Herod conquered Jerusalem, a "king of the Jews" taking Jerusalem from a descendant of the Hasmoneans. This picture of a military takeover by a "king of the Jews" was traumatic for many Jews later on.

In descriptions of Herod's takeover more details are given about his army. Before he conquered Jerusalem, he went to Jericho with five Roman and five Jewish cohorts and a mixed mercenary force, to which he added a few mounted men (*Antiquities* 14.410).[8] Finding that there was nothing to achieve there he left a garrison at Jericho, and "dismissed his Roman army to their winter quarters in the districts that had joined his side, namely, Idumaea, Galilee, and Samaria" (14.411). Herod, however, did not wish to remain inactive (it was still before the conquest of Jerusalem); thus he sent off his brother Joseph to Idumaea with two thousand footsoldiers and four hundred mounted men while he himself proceeded to Samaria. He then went to rid the Galilee of the *lestai* and to capture some of Antigonus's strongholds (14.413–417). After doing so he appointed Ptolemy general in the Galilee and departed for Samaria with six hundred mounted men and three thousand footsoldiers "to try the issue of battle with Antigonus" (14.431). On his way to conquer Jerusalem he took on eight hundred men from Mount Lebanon, and arrived in Acco-Ptolemais along with a Roman legion. Later another legion sent by Antonius arrived. He then moved on to Jericho, where six thousand of the army of Antigonus were attacking. Here is more evidence of two mixed Jewish armies fighting each other over the Land of Israel—one with Antigonus, who wanted to continue the Hasmonean dynasty, and the other with Herod, mercenaries and Roman soldiers, wanting to become subject to a Roman client king.

After Herod married Miriam in Sebastia, he and the Roman general Sosius besieged Jerusalem with an enormous army (14.468–469; *Jewish War* 1.342–346). It would be difficult to agree with I. Shatzman's claim that most of Herod's army at that time was Jewish; the evidence about it is not decisive.[9] Following its conquest "Herod, after checking his enemies, took care also to check his foreign allies [e.g., Romans and other gentiles]; for the crowd of strangers was bent on getting a view of the Temple and the holy things in the sanctuary" (*Antiquities* 14.482). It seems from what followed that Herod's army included a large mercenary force, and that the Jews could not restrain it during the attack.

After Herod established himself on the throne in 37 B.C.E., a Roman legion was stationed near Jerusalem to protect his kingdom (15.72). The legion is not mentioned again, but this silence does not mean that it was removed soon afterward. It was most probably removed before the battle of Actium by Antony, who needed Roman soldiers (probably about 32 B.C.E.). Herod may have needed this legion because his army was not strong enough to cope with disruptions in his realm, while the Romans may have wanted the legion to be there so that they could keep an eye on him. Before the famous battle of Actium in 31 B.C.E. in which Octavian (the future emperor Augustus) defeated Antony, Herod, "whose country had been yielding him rich crops for a long time, having procured revenues and resources, enrolled an auxiliary force for Antony and furnished it with the most carefully chosen equipment. Antony, however, said that he had no need of his help and ordered him to march against the Arab king" (15.109–110; *Jewish War* 1.364–365).

Herod, as a client king of the Romans (*amicus*), was not allowed to have a big army of his own, in case he might use it offensively. He was only able to recruit a large army when ordered to do so by the Romans. This fact, along with later inferences, shows that he did not have a big standing army at his disposal. The Romans prohibited most of their client kings' having big national armies, that is, composed of the indigenous population.[10] They had unpleasant memories of national armies in the past. When Herod went to war with the Arabs (Nabataeans) in 32 B.C.E. and equipped a force of cavalry to fight them, "a fierce battle took place, and the Jews were victorious" (*Antiquities* 15.111). But afterward a large army of Arabs defeated Herod.[11] Although in *Antiquities* 15.113, 117, and elsewhere Herod's army is said to be "a multitude of Jews," it may have just been a term used to distinguish it from the "Arabs" whom he was fighting.[12] It is clear from Josephus's account that Herod's army was not strong enough at the very beginning to fight the Arabs, so he started terrorizing them, just as the *lestai* had done to him before (15.119–120). When the Jews lost the battle again, Herod made a speech addressed not only to the commanders but to the "majority" of the army (15.127–146). It is impossible to know exactly what was really said on this occasion, if one compares the two different versions of this speech reported by Josephus himself in *Jewish War* 1.373–379 and *Antiquities* 15.127–146. Both speeches were perhaps addressed to an army that was in its greater part non-Jewish,[13] and it may be for this reason that no Jewish history was incorporated into the speech, as was usually done by Jewish generals or their historiographers. After many maneuvers Herod at last defeated the Arabs and became their "protector" (15.159–160; *Jewish War* 1.380–385). His stature was elevated, and this local war saved him from being defeated with Antony's forces at Actium in September 31 B.C.E. From then on there is much less information about Herod's army, which was especially enlarged for the Arab war. It seems, however, that after Actium most of Herod's army was disbanded.

The sources provide us some further information about his army. Once the battle of Actium was over (*Antiquities* 15.396) Herod came to see Octavian in Egypt in the autumn of 30 B.C.E. and was granted the four hundred Gauls who had served as Cleopatra's bodyguards. Also, according to *Antiquities* 15.247–252 Alexandra, Herod's mother-in-law, attempted to get hold of the two strongholds of Jerusalem while he was ill in Sebastia at a later stage, but in vain. His action against the sons of Baba shows that he used a small army or even an enlarged bodyguard for subduing the country; that is to say, he used it against his own countrymen (15.266). The same is evident in the incident at the theater, when he stopped a group of Jews from murdering him (15.289).

What was his real base of power? His main protection came from the strongholds he built in the country (15.291–298) and his use of a small standing army.[14] It was a small force used to keep the autocrat safe inside his own country. It can be compared to the Praetorian cohorts in Rome during the Julio-Claudian dynasty. Besides its role as a secret police force, there is no clear evidence of any large permanent Herodian army; when he fought the Arabs again he recruited an army ad hoc and ad rem. In 25/4 B.C.E he sent to Augustus five hundred picked men from his bodyguards as an auxiliary force.[15] These men were used by Aelius Gallus, who led them to the Red Sea.[16]

As already mentioned, a *rex cliens* in the last quarter of the first century B.C.E. could not possess a great standing army. The Romans learned their lessons from Mithridates and other rebels who had had large armies not too long before. In *Antiquities* 15.344–348 Josephus relates that Herod was given the Trachonitis of Zenodorus to rid it of the *lestai*. Herod was again said to have a small army with which he enforced a reign of terror (15.366; 16.1). In the course of his long reign, Herod must have had built about forty strongholds in Palestine for guarding the state in times of upheaval, and they replaced a big, permanent mobile army. Some of these strongholds were securely held by small groups of men.[17] His military settlers (*kleruchs*) also assisted him in guarding the country, but they were not a standing army, and most of them were not Jewish.[18] It is not difficult to imagine what a religious Jew at the time must have felt, when he was threatened by strongholds, a police force, and the mob from pagan cities supported by his very own half-Jewish king.

In 14 B.C.E. Herod went to "help" Marcus Agrippa around the Black Sea in his eastern enterprises (16.16–23), but he apparently did not assist him in military matters (16.22). It seems that Herod came just with his bodyguard and a small fleet, without any significant army.[19] While Herod was in Rome with his sons in the year 12 B.C.E., the people of Trachonitis, "a not inconsiderable part of his realm, had revolted, but the *strategoi* whom he had left behind subdued them and compelled them to submit once more" (16.130). Later he went himself with "an army" to Arabia, where he performed a punitive act that could have been carried out by a small army or a police force. Although Silaeus the Arab later called it "a war," it was a local affair and was apparently carried out under the aegis of the local Roman administration, which gave its approval for the recruitment of the police force (16.271–284). Only here, from the time Herod became a king, is some sort of an enlarged army mentioned.[20] When Herod came back from Cilicia and spoke before an assembly in the Temple he claimed among other things that if his generals and soldiers "looked at him alone," they would lead an untroubled life (16.134). After all, they were an important base of power for his rule, and he used them mainly for secret-service actions and terror (16.236, 252).

The effect of an army that, even if Jewish, operated against the Jews themselves, was destructive. Those Jews who were still hoping for an independent sovereign Jewish state could not view this force as their true national army. For them, it was rather a threat and a false symbol of nationalism. Even within the army there is evidence that there was opposition to Herod and support for his "Hasmonean" sons. According to Josephus, an old soldier named Tiro, while attempting to defend Herod's sons, showed great courage. He was supported by the soldiers who were against the killing of Alexander and Aristobulus, Herod's sons from Miriam: "And so when he [Herod] learned who the disaffected soldiers and the indignant commanders (*hegemones*) were, he gave orders that all of those who were designated by name, as well as Tiro himself, should be put in chains and kept under guard" (*Antiquities* 16.386). Later Tiro and three hundred commanders were killed by the "populace." This whole episode seems to have been a plot on a grand scale within the army itself against Herod. There were other instances of opposition to Herod, which were all suppressed by his police forces. Performing many outrageous acts against the Jews themselves, these police forces were seen by many as evil, and as the symbol of action against the Jewish nationalistic cause.[21] In the last decade of Herod's rule it no longer mattered whether the police forces were partly Jewish, entirely Jewish, or non-Jewish. Unlike most of the Hasmonean period, when the army was a state institution used to defend the Jewish state and conquer more of its ancestral land, in Herod's time there were no problems of defense against intruders and no territory to be conquered. Thus the army was entirely preoccupied with the assignment of guarding the autocrat, and it performed its duties in a harsh manner. As we can deduce from the sources, Herod's police forces were seen much more as a threat by the Jews in the Land than as some sort of a national symbol.

From accounts of Herod's funeral in 4 B.C.E. some important details can be extrapolated about his army. Josephus relates that the army was marching "according to the various nationalities and designations. They were arranged in the following order: first came his bodyguards, then the Thracians, and following them, whatever Germans he had, and next came the Gauls. These men were equipped for battle. Tight behind them came the whole army as if marching to war, led by their company commanders and lower officers, and they were followed by five hundred servants carrying spices" (*Antiquities* 17.198–199; *Jewish War* 1.672–673). Clearly, at least part of his army was not Jewish. The strongholds and his army became almost the only base for Herod's authority and the same proved true after his death. As will be seen from the subsequent events, part of the army was indeed Jewish, but it is impossible to determine in what proportions.

The claimant of Herod's throne according to his will, his son Archelaus, was aware of the fact that the army is the only power base of an autocrat (*Antiquities* 17.202). He himself was of the opinion that the army stationed at Jericho wanted him to become king immediately after his father's death, as his father himself had required in his farewell letter to the soldiers (17.193–194). Although some evidence could be taken to imply that not all of the army supported him, we have some information that Herod's army was still effective immediately after his death. When the crowds started to be tumultuous, the *strategos* was sent by Archelaus to the crowds to warn them, but they did not pay attention (17.209–212); and according to 17.215–218 Archelaus used his army both against the ensuing insurrection and as a preventive force (17.237, 240, 313). When the three brothers made their claims in Rome before Augustus, Antipater in the name of Antipas accused Archelaus in Rome of "the changes that he had made among the officers of the army (*hegemones*)" (17.232). The army in itself did not come up as a major issue before the emperor. But the Roman general Varus did not believe that the Jewish army could keep order, hence he left Sabinus with a Roman legion to undertake a peace-keeping mission. When Sabinus made an attempt to seize the treasury of Herod, a Jewish army was not mentioned. Yet in *Antiquities* 17.265–266 there is useful information about Herod's former army: when the Romans were besieged in the Temple with Sabinus we hear that "actually most of the royal troops had deserted to their side [the Jewish side]. But Rufus and Gratus together with three thousand of the best fighters in Herod's army [according to *Jewish War* 2.52, three thousand Sebastians], men who could use their bodies effectively, adhered to the Romans. And there was a cavalry force under

Rufus's command that had also been added to the Roman strength."
Also, in the meantime countless new riots continuously filled Judea,
and in many regions many men rose up in arms against the Romans,
either in hope of personal gain or out of hatred. "For example, two
thousand of the soldiers who had once campaigned with Herod and
had been disbanded, now assembled in Judea itself and fought
against the king's troops" (17.270). It should be noted that from
these passages we also learn how the "schizophrenia" that became a
national symptom in Palestinian society emerged the moment the
king was dead. Many pagans in the Land found in it an opportunity
to fight the Jews.

Be that as it may, the army of Herod was, like many other aspects of his realm, "schizophrenic." This problem became even
clearer during a time of crisis, when the autocrat was dead and the
loyalty of the soldiers was put to trial (4 B.C.E.). Very swiftly one part
of the army of Herod the Great joined the Jewish groups who rebelled against the Roman forces.[22] At that point the Herodian state
seemed to be falling apart, and with the central government gone,
nationalistic feelings developed within many circles, including
among the Jewish soldiers. This situation is similar to many other
revolutions in antiquity and in modern times, when the army, or
usually only part of it, took the role of a revived nationalistic symbol
of a free state. It was the only institution that had the weapons and
equipment at its disposal to facilitate independent political sovereignty. This situation also applied to the various pretenders to the
throne after Herod the Great's death, who recruited local armies to
become a solid base for their new kingship; but they were swiftly
disbanded (*Antiquities* 17.276, 278–284).[23]

The discontent in Judea alerted Varus, the Roman governor of
Syria. As soon as he learned about the events in Judea, he took two
legions (out of three that were stationed in Syria), four troops of
cavalry, and auxiliaries that were furnished by the kings and some of
the tetrarchs. We learn that the people of Berytus gave him fifteen
hundred auxiliary troops "as he passed through their city." Aretas
of Petra, "who in his hatred of Herod had formed a friendship with
the Romans," also sent a considerable force of infantry and cavalry
(17.286–287). Later we hear of ten thousand Jewish rebels (presumably soldiers) who surrendered to the Romans (17.297). When the
rebellion was over, Varus left one legion as a garrison in Jerusalem,

"the legion formerly there" (4 B.C.E.; 17.299). No doubt the remnants of Herod's army were dispersed, and it ceased to exist in its former organized way. Only its non-Jewish part remained as a garrison in Judea.

It is apparent that from then on there was no Jewish army of any sort left in Judea, even to guard the Temple. The Gospels tell us that order was kept in Jerusalem not only by the Roman troops but also by a group of ordinary citizens with swords and stones under the command of the elders and scribes. The presence of Roman soldiers in Jerusalem and in other sensitive locations was to cause a great deal of turmoil in later years because of the barbaric behavior of many of the Roman soldiers[24] and because the Roman garrisons in the provinces became a symbol of suppression and dependence on Rome. After the political settlement of Palestine in 4 B.C.E., Herod Antipas, one of the three rulers, was in the camp of Vitellius in Parthia, but no mention is made of any army with him (*Antiquities* 18.101–105): Another ruler, Philip, moved about with a small number of people, but not with an army (18.107). According to *Antiquities* 18.112–114, however, Aretas the Arab king had an army, which was apparently enlarged for special occasions. We find that client kings sometimes fought over local matters among themselves, and one such battle occurred between Herod Antipas and the Arabs over the issue of the border (18.113–119). The entire army of Herod Antipas, which was probably recruited especially for this occasion, was demolished in this fight. Some interpreted it as a punishment for his murder of John the Baptist. The Romans could not refrain from interfering, and Vitellius went with an army to punish Aretas (18.120–125). From this story it appears again that Herod the Great's successors in Palestine, probably like other client kings elsewhere, could only recruit larger armies on special occasions, usually when they got permission from the Romans to do so. Sometimes they used this right to settle local accounts.

This interpretation is strengthened by further evidence. Herod Antipas did not deny in Rome that he had weapons for seventy thousand soldiers, but apparently he had not actually recruited any at the time (18.251–252). In fact, after 6 C.E. only Herod Antipas had some kind of an army in Palestine. Thus the army as a remnant of a Jewish nationalistic symbol was destroyed almost totally in 4 B.C.E. This situation continued until Agrippa I was made king of

Judea and returned to Palestine, where he appointed Silas "as commander (*hyparchos*)" of the entire army (*Antiquities* 19.299). Also, this army was prohibited to act outside the jurisdiction of Agrippa. When a violent incident occurred in Dor, Agrippa did not intervene with an army, but sent to Publius Petronius, the governor of Syria, to settle the affair. Although Silas was a true friend of Agrippa in Rome, he was removed from the command of the army by the last Jewish king in Judea.[25] After Agrippa's mysterious death Hilkias, who had replaced Silas as the *hyparchos* and *philos* of Agrippa I, killed Silas.[26]

Josephus relates that Agrippa I began to strengthen Jerusalem's walls but was stopped by Emperor Claudius, for this act was interpreted by Rome as hostile.[27] When the story of Agrippa's death was related by Josephus, he did not mention that an army was at the scene of that mysterious death in Caesarea.[28] It should be emphasized that after 39 C.E., when Herod Antipas was deposed and Philip had died, there were no longer any Jewish police forces in the area. Roman soldiers were stationed in Palestine, and when Agrippa became king of Judea, he had no army of any considerable size, but only a small force for guarding himself and the public order.[29] This force was not used against the Jews, as far as one can deduce from the scanty evidence. Thus, however small and mixed this force or army may have been, it no doubt had some meaning as a nationalistic symbol. Among the Jews who adhered to political nationalism it aroused a nostalgia for the good old days of independence. When even this small army was apparently disbanded in 44 C.E., there could have been nothing left except the dream of a Jewish army, in particular by those who started in the fifties to harass the Romans in Palestine. We hear more and more of private "armies," which fought the Romans and then each other.[30]

After the Jews' great success of crushing the legion of Gallus in 66 C.E., generals were appointed for the Jewish army that was being formed to fight against Rome (*Jewish War* 2.562–568). According to *Jewish War* 2.569–584 Josephus organized the defense of the Galilee and, like other nations rebelling against Rome, trained an army in the Roman way.[31] Within a few months this army collapsed and was completely dispersed as a result of the Roman invasion of Palestine. Roman forces during the war were assisted by the local Greeks (*Antiquities* 19.366 and elsewhere), a matter to be mentioned again in chapter 12. It is interesting to note that even while the Jewish army was being formed, some groups returned to the pre-66/7 C.E. situation and organized their own military forces. These groups were the ones that continued the war against Rome when the "formal" army ceased to exist. Of course, they failed completely. The hope to reestablish a Jewish army was shattered, but remained latent until it emerged in the revolt of Bar Kokhba in 132 C.E.

In summary, from 63 B.C.E. Palestine was under Roman rule. Some attempts were made during the years 57–40 B.C.E. to regain Judea for the Hasmonean descendants by using military forces that were partly Jewish and partly mercenary. Antigonus succeeded in regaining power with the help of the Parthians in 40 B.C.E. Herod came with an army to conquer Palestine from Antigonus and liberated it from the *lestai*. He was joined by many Jews, but in fact succeeded because of the help he received from mercenaries and the Romans themselves. When he at last unified the country in 37 B.C.E., he did have some Jewish troops in his army, but most of it was not Jewish; this army was "schizophrenic" in its composition. In this respect it was in line with all other facets of Herodian Judea. Hence some Jewish circles viewed the army as a nationalistic symbol, but most Jews hated it because it was basically non-Jewish, and in fact it was their main enemy. Instead of becoming a unifying symbol it became the symbol of hatred and partition. The army itself, which was in any case not very large, rarely acted against foreign states, and when it did, it was directed against forces to the east of Palestine and never in any other direction. It is interesting to note that many troops from this army joined the Jews who were fighting against the forces of the king (Archelaus) in 4 B.C.E. After this time, there may have been small armies or police forces loyal first to Archelaus and then to Philip and Herod Antipas, but these forces played a very minor role, acting mainly as the keepers of order in Palestine. In 41 C.E. this national symbol, which had been distorted in the eyes of many during Herod the Great's time and shattered during his successor's reigns, became again something of a concrete symbol of a unified Jewish nation. In 44 C.E. even this short-lived, small army vanished. Thus, together with other symbols of political nationalism, the army was dispersed once and for all. This frustration, one can assume, caused the energy of thousands of Jews to be directed into the framework of terrorist groups such as the so-called *lestai*, as well as the Sicarii, Zealots, and later in 66 C.E. the Jewish national army. The Romans did not replace any of the lost symbols of Jewish nationalism after 44 C.E.; this decision was a mistake on their part. Together with the harsher Roman governors sent to Palestine at the time, frustration increased, culminating in the Great War. It was not accidental that when some sort of consensus was achieved and a Jewish state began to emerge after Cestius's defeat in 66 C.E., the army was among the more important institutions of nationalism that was recreated.

Whereas in Hasmonean literature the army emerges as an important facet of national life, as it still does in Greek literature from the eastern Roman Empire (Dio Chrysostom, *On Kingship* 3.66), it is less evident in Jewish and Christian literature after 63 B.C.E. The apocrypha and pseudepigrapha of this period do not mention it at all as an important factor of the real world. Even in Pseudo-Philo's *Biblical Antiquities,* which may reflect some of the real life of the period about 70 C.E., there is no evidence of any state army, but instead groups of God-fearing rebels are mentioned (perhaps this is some expression of life in the fifties and sixties C.E.). In the synoptic Gospels, John, and Acts 1–12, the army does not appear as a factor in Jesus' or his disciples' message. For an a-political group such as they were, it is quite understandable that the army was of no importance, and the heavenly army is not elaborated either. The reality of the time is, however, reflected in certain passages of the New Testament. In the Gospels Jesus' birth is depicted against the background of the attempts to find him and the persecutions by Herod the Great's army. This story may of course be merely a later legend based on the actual reputation of Herod's forces within the Jewish population. The police forces of Herod's successors have no role at all in the narrative parts of the New Testament, except for episodes such as putting John the Baptist and Peter in jail and so on. The Roman forces are mentioned in particular in the episode of the Passion. One Gospel story compares Jesus' authority to that of a centurion (Matt 8:5–13 and parallels).[32] But in general the issue of the army does not worry him at all.

The ones who arrested Jesus were either the crowds (Matt 26:47–57) or "a band of soldiers and some officers from the chief priests and the Pharisees," according to John 18:3. Scholars who

wish to see in his disciples some kind of a private army bring matters
ad absurdum; during those stormy days everyone needed a dagger
for personal safety. Only after standing trial in the Sanhedrin was
Jesus delivered to the Roman force, who mocked him. As in other
respects, the narrative of the New Testament reflects much of what
has been shown here concerning the military aspect in Palestine before 70 C.E. Although Jesus and his disciples knew what an army at
the time was like (Luke 14:31–32),[33] it was not of any major importance for their thought. Even the wars of the end of the days according to the Gospels were to come from heaven, with the elect on earth
remaining passive. This concept goes against the war of the end
(*eschaton*) found in the thought of the Essenes, where the elect were
active and organized as a real army (1QM = *War Scroll*). Jesus is
depicted in the narrative parts of the New Testament as a pacifist
who has nothing to do with politics of his own time. Nevertheless, at
a certain juncture he does become somewhat more aggressive, and
says, "Do not think that I have come to bring peace on earth; I have
not come to bring peace, but a sword" (Matt 10:34, and see also
Luke 12:51 and 22:36–38);[34] but this passage can be seen as being
in keeping with Jewish prophecy, which metaphorically and symbol-
ically used phrases of that kind (compare with Jeremiah, who appears with a sword in Judas Maccabees's dream! 2 Macc 15:15–16).
This statement does not fit the way he was portrayed and is not
repeated anywhere else. Jesus as well as his disciples never mentioned an earthly army when they had the Kingdom of God in mind
(John 18:36). In Paul's teaching the army is even less evident, and
the Book of Acts (chapters 21–28) even views the Roman army in
Palestine in a positive manner. In the Book of Revelation, however,
in keeping with Jewish apocalyptic literature, the army of God has
the major role in crushing the armies of the wayward earthly kings
(6:1–17; 19:11–21; and elsewhere). The author of Revelation shows
how strongly dualism was imbued in the Jewish mind of the day.
The only army that counts for him is transcendental and universal,
rather than earthly and national.[35]

Josephus, who was himself one of the founders of the national
army in 66 C.E., does not comment on it from an ideological point of
view. In his biblical account in the *Antiquities,* he tells us about the
previous armies of Israel with great pride, and nothing would allow
us to conclude that the Great War made him change his mind about

the army as a major political symbol in Israel's history and its *patrios politeia* (ancestral constitution).[36] This matter will be mentioned briefly in the chapter on the reactions to the war.

Thus we can say that in the literature of the second period the real and earthly army has no significance. The only picture that is apparent at the time is of the "army of God," and this concept of a heavenly army was already well rooted in Judaism during the First Temple period and in the first period mentioned above. As said elsewhere, there is no literature extant deriving from the Sicarii and the Zealots. The latter may well have shared the views and expectations of those who wrote the War Scroll and similar documents. From the literature available, one can learn that the symbol of the army, like other aspects of nationalism, underwent a spiritualization and became more transcendental than it had been in Hasmonean literature. It was the actual armies of Herod and his immediate successors that brought about frustration and passivity on the one hand, as reflected in the literature, and on the other activism, as reflected in the actions leading to the Great War.

Notes

[1] Y. Yadin, *The Scroll of the War of the Sons of Light Against the Sons of Darkness* (Oxford, 1962); and J. Duhaime, "The War Scroll from Qumran and the Greco-Roman Tactical Treatises," *Revue de Qumran* 49–52 (1988): 133ff.

[2] For these matters see the excellent survey of I. Shatzman, *The Armies of the Hasmonaeans and Herod* (Tübingen, 1991), pp. 170–276.

[3] For the military value of the client king during the republic, see T. Yoshimura, "Die Auxiliartruppen und die Provinzialklientel in der römischen Republik," *Historia* 10 (1961): 473–495. For the service in war of the client king see P. C. Sands, *The Client Princes of the Roman Empire under the Republic* (Cambridge, 1908), pp. 103–106; and D. Braund, *Rome and the Friendly King* (London, 1984), passim; and in general for client kings at the time, see G. W. Bowersock, *Augustus and the Greek World* (Oxford, 1965), pp. 42–61.

[4] Cf. above, chap. 6.

[5] For the *Bellum Alexandrinum* see E. Schürer, *The History of the Jewish People in the Age of Jesus Christ*, rev. G. Vermes et al. (Edinburgh, 1973–1987), 1.270–271.

[6] Against Shatzman's estimate, *Armies of the Hasmonaeans*, pp. 140–141. For Jews in foreign armies at the time, see the still-useful J. Juster, *Les Juifs dans l'empire romain* (Paris, 1914), 2.265–279.

[7] The same story recurs in Delos and other cities as well. In general for the manpower of the Roman army see P. A. Brunt, *Italian Manpower, 225 B.C.–A.D. 14* (Oxford, 1971), and G. Forni, *Il Reclutamento delle legioni da Augusto a Diocleziano* (Rome, 1953).

[8] Shatzman, *Armies of the Hasmonaeans*, pp. 165–166.

[9] Shatzman, *Armies of the Hasmonaeans*, pp. 157–165 is too optimistic about the Jewishness of Herod's army. Also in this case the size of the army is speculated. Although the Edomites at this stage are Jewish, they still form a different part of the nation (the so-called *homophyloi*). Also, "the people of the Land" (*epichorioi*) are not necessarily Jewish. "The Jews on Herod's side" mentioned during the fighting in Jerusalem may denote deserters who joined Herod after the fighting started (*Antiquities* 14.479). The expression "The Jews of Herod's army" (*Jewish War* 1.351) shows that they only formed part of his army. At any rate, Shatzman's conclusion that the "Jews formed the majority of the Herodian army at the time of the conquest of Jerusalem in 37" (p. 186) is difficult to accept.

[10] As other kings at the time; see Braund, *Rome and the Friendly King.*

[11] For the Arab war, see A. Kasher, *Jews, Idumaeans and Ancient Arabs* (Tübingen, 1988), pp. 130–151; he claims that Herod initiated the war with the Arabs

in order to avoid participating in the battle of Actium. For the Arab "national" army, see J. M. C. Bowsher, "The Nabataean Army," in *The Eastern Frontier of the Roman Empire,* ed. D. H. French and C. S. Lightfoot (Oxford, 1989), pp. 19–30. And for the Nabataean war god Arsu, see G. W. Bowersock, "An Arabian Trinity," in *Christians among Jews and Gentiles,* ed. G. W. E. Nickelsburg and G. W. MacRae (Philadelphia, 1986), pp. 19–20.

[12] When "Macedonians" or "Romans" are mentioned they do not always exclude other nationalities.

[13] Against A. Schalit, *König Herodes: Der Mann und sein Werk* (Berlin, 1969), p. 170 n. 86, who views the episode as a national clash between Arabs and a Jewish army. See also Shatzman, *Armies of the Hasmonaeans,* p. 186. In general for speeches in Josephus, see P. Villalba i Varneda, *The Historical Method of Flavius Josephus* (Leiden, 1986), pp. 89–117.

[14] For Herod's strongholds, see Shatzman, *Armies of the Hasmonaeans,* pp. 217–276.

[15] *Antiquities* 15.317. According to Strabo they were Jews (16.4.23). But from his point of view, every group coming from Judea seemed to be Jewish.

[16] According to *Antiquities* 15.323–327 Herod built Herodion, and it is emphasized that he did so for his own security. In 16.142–143 he built Antipatris and Cypros. Cf. Shatzman, *Armies of the Hasmonaeans,* pp. 217–276, passim.

[17] My interpretation here is against Shatzman, who believes that Herod had a great standing army. See his discussion of Herod's standing army, *Armies of the Hasmonaeans,* pp. 183–216.

[18] Cf. Shatzman for these *coloni, Armies of the Hasmonaeans,* pp. 170–183.

[19] For this mission cf. Shatzman, *Armies of the Hasmonaeans,* p. 187.

[20] And cf. Nicolaus's arguments before Augustus about the incident, Ant. 16.342–350.

[21] In *Antiquities* 17.2, Herod's son Antipater is "troubled about the armed forces, for in their hands rests the entire security of a king whenever his nation is intent upon revolting."

[22] For the mixed nature of Herod's army, see Shatzman, *Armies of the Hasmonaeans,* pp. 186, 193–216. There exists, however, no decisive evidence to ascertain the proportions of its Jewish and gentile elements.

[23] See also for other armies of pretenders, such as "false" Philip, Antiochus in Sicily: n. 28 in D. Mendels, "Pseudo-Philo's *Biblical Antiquities,* the 'Fourth Philosophy' and the Political Messianism of the First Century A.D.," in *The Messiah,* ed. J. H. Charlesworth (Minneapolis, 1992), pp. 261–275.

[24] *Antiquities* 18.55–59, and cf. Tacitus's description of Roman soldiers on the German front in 17 C.E. (*Annals* 1, passim). For the Roman legions see L. J. F.

Keppie, *The Making of the Roman Army: From Republic to Empire* (Totowa, N.J., 1984); R. W. Davies, *Service in the Roman Army* (Edinburgh, 1989).

[25] Cf. *Antiquities* 19.317–325 for the Silas affair; and D. R. Schwartz, *Agrippa I: The Last King of Judaea* (Tübingen, 1990), pp. 13–15, 70–71.

[26] *Antiquities* 18.353. One should note that changes in the high priesthood are recorded, whereas the ones in the leadership of the army are not.

[27] In 19.333 the *strategos* of Jerusalem is mentioned.

[28] *Antiquities* 19.343–352; later his son Agrippa II apparently had an army at his disposal (*Antiquities* 17.30–31).

[29] *Antiquities* 19.357–366. According to Schwartz (*Agrippa*, p. 70), Agrippa had the *coloni* of Babylonians in the Trachonitis at his disposal there. For Agrippa's "army" see also pp. 113–115.

[30] For example, according to *Antiquities* 20.120, the Galileans incited the Jews to start a war, and according to 122, Cumanus recruited Samaritans, alongside the Roman army and the Sebastenians, for the war with the armed Jews (*Jewish War* 2.232–240). In 20.164–165 is the first mention of the Sicarii, who may have been frustrated that the Jews had no independent army. Some of them may have been former soldiers of Herod Antipas's and Agrippa's army. As a group they reappear in *Jewish War* 2.254–257 and *Antiquities* 20.185–188, 204, 208–210. At the time that King Agrippa (II) of Chalcis conferred the high priesthood on Ishmael the son of Phabi (20.179–180; 59 C.E.), we hear of armed groups among the Jews. Then mutual enmity and class warfare occurred between the high priests on the one hand, and the priests and leaders of the Jerusalemite populace on the other. Each of the factions formed and collected for itself a band of the most reckless revolutionaries and acted as their leader. Here we return to the early Maccabean period's notion of militia. Then there was more of a consensus than at this time. These militias eventually led, as they did in Maccabean times, to the creation of a national army. But this "army" was to be dispersed quickly by the Romans.

At the beginning of the dramatic events leading to the Great War, we hear of two armies: the one of Agrippa II and the groups of rebels. According to *Jewish War* 2.421 Agrippa II sends an army to help the moderate Jews who were against the revolt. *Jewish War* 2.422ff. tells of an opposition to the "army" of Sicarii and Zealots; many moderate Jews joined the army of Agrippa II. After all, he was seen by many as a Jewish king (cf. 433–449 for the "army" of the Zealots and Sicarii). In *Jewish War* 2.444 Menachem with some armed groups tried to become king of Judea, but in vain. According to *Jewish War* 2.500 Agrippa II assisted Cestius Gallus in fighting the Jews.

[31] Cf. the next chapter.

[32] Cf. Matt 10:34 (Luke 12:51). Cf. Albright and Mann, *Matthew*,* pp. 91–93 and Mann, *Mark*,* pp. 278–280.

[33] Cf. Fitzmyer, *Luke,** 2.1065–1066.

[34] Ibid., 2.1432 rightly says, "This verse has no zealot tendency." And for the usually pacifist Essenes moving along with swords against the brigands, see *Jewish War* 2.125.

[35] Cf. in general Ford, *Revelation,** pp. 96–113, and elsewhere.

[36] For Josephus's treatment of the wars of the people of Israel, see Villalba i Varneda, *Historical Method,* pp. 19–24, 135–157.

CHAPTER 12

Nationalism in Revolution: The Great War Against Rome (66-70 C.E.)

The main source for the Great War is the *Jewish War* of Josephus as well as his autobiography, the *Vita*.[1] The events of the late fifties and early sixties leading up to the war can be found in the *Antiquities* book 20, which parallels the account of *Jewish War* 2. There is no single war of that duration in antiquity about which such an elaborate account survives. Unlike the Maccabean upheaval, which received "good press" in the first two books of Maccabees, the Great War was not favorably received. The account is of an apologetic nature. In addition, whereas the Maccabean revolt had been successful, the Great War ended in complete disaster for the Jews in Palestine. This concluding chapter will not contain a comprehensive history of the war (which would require another book), but it will view it from the perspective of Jewish nationalism as interpreted in this study.

The Great War against Rome was unique in the ancient Near East in terms of its scale.[2] True, there were revolts against Rome in the western part of the empire and in Africa during the first century C.E., but they should not be compared—as sometimes scholars tend to do—with the war of the Jews starting in 66 C.E.[3] The ancient Near East had a totally different sociopolitical structure as well as a different cultural atmosphere. Hence comparisons between East and West are dangerous. It remains a fact that the Jews were the only ones who launched a revolution on a grand scale against Rome in the ancient Near East. The question is, Why? The answer possibly becomes easier when considered in light of the previous chapters of this book.

Scholars usually attribute the war to an accumulation of causes. Every scholar has his or her own emphasis; but no scholar today would hold the opinion that there was one single cause behind the events of 66–70 c.e.[4] Some of the suggested causes for the war have been socioeconomic reasons (e.g., an uprising of the poor in Palestine—but were only Jews poor? The non-Jews did not participate in the revolt); the polarity between non-Jews and Jews;[5] religious conflicts with the Romans and a striving for purity;[6] alienation from the ruling class that was previously created by Rome;[7] the activity of extremist groups who led the others into the war; Roman interests in the Temple's treasury; and the wayward behavior of her last procurators.[8] In line with what has been shown in the preceding chapters above, yet another cause might be suggested (without negating the other causes, but giving them a different emphasis during the war itself), which may also explain why the Jews were unique in their fight against Rome at the time.

As long as the religious Jews had some sort of authentic nationalistic symbol to cling to, they did not rebel. This situation held during Herod the Great's reign, as well as during the period of his successors, with a few exceptional outbursts, which were mainly on religious grounds. But there was another development. From the time Herod the Great consolidated his throne, the "schizophrenia" in Jewish society became more and more evident. The dichotomy between the non-Jews and Jews as well as between religious Jews and hellenizers within the same Land and their polarized attitudes to the national symbols became more and more problematic. In fact there emerged two totally different "national" identities in Palestine, which shared the same land and had a common king at certain periods. There were tensions all the time (as can be seen from the accounts of Jamnia and Dor during the reign of Agrippa I),[9] but they never caused a total collapse of the delicate status quo that existed between the two different identities. Part of this relative stability can be attributed to the rule of Herod and his successors. Agrippa I's policies in Palestine helped sharpen this dualism or "schizophrenia." The moment Agrippa died in 44 c.e. and the whole of Palestine came under direct Roman rule, there was no longer any local leader who could be a unifying symbol to both strata of society (as the Ptolemies and later the Roman emperors were in Egypt and elsewhere). The result was complete national disintegration in Palestine. The Jews lost even the national symbols that they had managed to retain up to that point. Their Land was overrun and full of non-Jews, their king was gone, their army dispersed, and their Temple in the hands of hated high priestly houses, some of whom the population associated with the Roman authorities. The Temple had thus become very much associated with the oppressor (as it had in the period of the Hellenistic priests Jason, Menelaus, and Alcimus). The non-Jewish population of Palestine could easily adjust to this situation because they had never associated themselves with Jerusalem or its Temple, or with the Land as an entity with a traditional political significance.[10] Moreover, they could easily forget their local king, because they had paid allegiance and even worshiped the emperor well before Agrippa's death in 44 C.E. With disruptive and intolerant Roman governors in Judea matters quickly got out of hand. As far as can be judged from the sources, the non-Jewish population never had any extensive friction with the Roman authorities. Thus they could easily be identified with Rome by the Jews in terms of their common religious and cultural concepts. These tensions had sporadic aggressive outlets, such as the one in Jamnia at the time of Caligula, recorded in Philo's *De Legatio,* and again at the time of Cumanus (48–52 C.E.) between Samaritans and Jews (*Jewish War* 2.232–246), and in Caesarea between Jews and Syrians at the end of Felix's governorship (59–60 C.E., *Jewish War* 2.266–270); but they were intensified and were more politically oriented at the very start of the Great War. Then they became widespread all over Palestine. Thus the gap, or "schizophrenia," between non-Jews and Jews (and within Jewish society itself) in terms of their attitudes about religio-political nationalism in Palestine during and after Herod the Great's reign was a major cause of the Great War.

This state of affairs explains why so many Jews participated at the start, in other words, why people like Josephus and other Jews viewed the war against Rome as the final battle against the split national personality in the Land of Israel. They went to war because they wished to get rid of the disturbing and disruptive "half" that was antagonistic to their own nationalistic aspirations, and which was strongly associated with Rome. By the same token, the non-Jews in the Land became free to act against the Jews at the very

moment that the Jewish or half-Jewish authority, with all of its nationalistic overtones, ceased to exist.[11]

It also becomes easier to explain why, of all the nations of the
ancient Near East, only the Jewish people revolted. The nationalistic
situation described in former chapters cannot be found to such an
extent elsewhere in the region. The indigenous populations could in
most instances adjust to transformed symbols of nationalism (e.g.,
the Roman emperor posed as a pharaoh for the indigenous population in Egypt, and the Egyptian temple was a religiopolitical symbol
that did not contradict the very essence of Roman imperialism). Although scholars at times followed Josephus in attributing the cause
of the war to gentile–Jewish fights,[12] they failed to see it in this wider
perspective, which makes it more plausible. The moment the war
against Rome started, many other contributing factors came to the
surface, such as the socioeconomic polarity and the personal ambition of its leaders.

Let us now very briefly examine the events in keeping with what
has just been said. But first one should remember that Josephus, who
is the main and perhaps the only significant source for the war, has
been accused of being heavily biased in his presentation of it. He
himself was involved in the war at its start as a general in the Galilee
and surrendered to the Romans after the Galilee fell into their
hands. Later he was accused by the Jews of being a traitor. His
Jewish War as well as his *Vita* were designed to refute many of the
accusations made by his opponents. Nevertheless, as in the case of
another famous historian, Polybius (who was accused of the same
thing in a similar situation), Josephus is regarded as a great Hellenistic historian, whose work had a tremendous impact on the historiography of the time.[13] Historians who are trained to read this kind of
historiography are able at times to distinguish between "facts" and
bias. Bearing this in mind, we will examine the emergence of the
four nationalistic symbols of kingship, army, Land, and Temple in
the course of the Great War. Four stages of the war can be depicted.

1. In April and May 66 C.E., after both the emperor and Florus
had shown the Jews that they sided with the non-Jews of Caesarea in
the conflict between them, which already had a long history,[14] the
Roman governor irritated the Jews even more by his confiscation of
seventeen talents from the Temple's treasury. As a result there was a
commotion in Jerusalem, which led to the seizure of the Temple by

the crowds and to clashes between the Jews and the two Roman cohorts brought up to Jerusalem from Caesarea. When these clashes worsened, Florus retreated to Caesarea, leaving the leaders of the city to restore order with the support of one of his cohorts. When Agrippa II, king of the former tetrarchy of Philip (and additional land), heard of the stormy events, he hurried to Jerusalem and made an attempt, together with the "chief priests, the leading citizens, and the council" (*Jewish War* 2.336), to stop the insurrection. His speech is given at length by Josephus (2.345–401) and reflects the opinion of a Jew who suppressed all of his nationalistic political feelings, and in general learned how to live with and to accommodate the Roman Empire.[15] The reaction of the crowds who were listening is described by Josephus: "Having spoken thus, he [Agrippa] burst into tears, as did also his sister; and his emotion much restrained the passion of his hearers. Still they began to cry out that they were not taking up arms against the Romans, but against Florus, because of all the wrong that he had done them" (2.402–403). The people agreed to reaffirm their loyalty to the emperor, but Agrippa also demanded obedience to Florus, whom they resented. Agrippa II was driven back to his own kingdom. Then, while the fortress of Masada was being conquered by the Jews, Eleazar, the son of Ananias the high priest, who was a clerk in the Temple, persuaded "those who officiated in the Temple services to accept no gift or sacrifice from a foreigner. This action laid the foundation of the war with the Romans; for the sacrifices offered on behalf of that nation and the emperor were in consequence rejected" (2.409–410). This action no doubt was the wish of the militant crowds in Jerusalem at this particular juncture, whereas the "principal citizens," the "chief priests" and the "most notable Pharisees," were against this act altogether, but could not oppose the will of the militant majority (*Jewish War* 2.411–417). This act of stopping the sacrifice for the Roman emperor, a small political accommodation that was carried out daily in the Temple, meant that suddenly the Temple became a purely Jewish religiopolitical symbol free of any Roman "nationalistic" connotations. It can be compared to a hypothetical, less serious situation, wherein the worship of the emperor (in the figure of pharaoh) in an Egyptian temple would be provocatively terminated.

In Jerusalem it led to a civil war within the city in the summer of 66 C.E. The leaders of Jerusalem and the high priests called in an army, which was provided by both Florus and Agrippa and fought the rebels who were holding the lower city and the Temple Mount. Within a short time the rebels, along with the Sicarii who had in the meantime joined them, managed to gain the upper hand against Agrippa's soldiers, the Romans, and the moderates who were concentrated in the upper city. While doing so they managed to set the house of Hananiah the high priest, the palaces of Agrippa and Berenice, as well as the public archives on fire, as they were "eager to destroy the money-lenders' bonds and to prevent the recovery of debts" and, Josephus adds, "in order to win over a host of grateful debtors and to cause a rising of the poor against the rich, sure of impunity" (2.427).

This stage ended with a victory by the rebels. The high priest Ananias was murdered, the troops of Agrippa were driven out, and the Roman soldiers, who had made a truce and had been guaranteed a free withdrawal, were killed in spite of the agreement. Then a very interesting thing happened. The moment the rebels got the upper hand and the high priest had died, the leader of the ultraextremist Sicarii, Menachem, who was a grandson of Judah the Galilean,[16] became the leader of the revolution, and as a symbolic act went to pray in the Temple "arrayed in royal robes" (*Jewish War* 2.444). But while doing so (or possibly later on) he was murdered by the people of Eleazar with the support of part of the mob, who wanted to put an end to the rebellion.[17] In fact, Josephus added later that the Zealots under their leader Eleazar wished to continue the revolt, but this murder eliminated any possibility of a takeover of the leadership by the more extreme group of the Sicarii. The latter then retreated to Masada, and henceforward did not participate in the war in Jerusalem. This episode shows that Sicarii and Zealots were two branches of the so-called Fourth Philosophy group, which was mentioned by Josephus in the context of the year 6 C.E., but is not mentioned again in this context.[18]

While these events were taking place at Jerusalem a terrible war flared up all over the country between non-Jews and Jews. In some places it was initiated by Jews and in others by the non-Jews. Some of the places that Josephus mentions are Caesarea, Philadelphia, Heshbon, Gerasa, Pella, Scythopolis, Gadara, Hippos and Gaulanitis as well as Ptolemais, Gaba and Sebastia, Ascalon, Anthedon, and Gaza (2.457–486). This struggle also spread into some Diaspora cities such as Alexandria and various places in the kingdom of Agrippa II, and, after Cestius Gallus's defeat in Judea, also to Damascus (2.559–561). As a result of these events Cestius Gallus, the governor of Syria, went out to quell the fighting between Jews and non-Jews in the cities (*Jewish War* 2.499–516). Among other forces Josephus said that "further auxiliaries in very large numbers were collected from the towns; these, though lacking the experience of the regulars, made good their deficiency in technical training by their ardor and their detestation of the Jews" (2.502). This information is important as it shows that the non-Jews and the very hellenized Jews such as Agrippa II (2.523–526, 556–557) fought alongside the Romans against the Jews. Cestius then advanced with the Twelfth Legion toward Jerusalem (September and October 66 C.E.), causing some damage to Jewish cities (such as Lod, which according to Josephus had no non-Jewish inhabitants, 2.515–516). After some operations around the city of Jerusalem they withdrew unexpectedly. Josephus already says at this juncture, "But God, I suppose, because of those miscreants, had already turned away even from His sanctuary and ordained that that day should not see the end of the war" (2.539). The Jews rejoiced and managed to crush the Twelfth Legion while it tried to retreat. Josephus emphasizes in his account that the clashes with the Roman legion were only with Jews (*Jewish War* 2.545, 547, 549, etc.).[19] As a consequence of Gallus's defeat, the non-Jews of Damascus (who obviously identified themselves with the Romans), though many of their wives were proselytes, massacred the Jews in their town (2.559–561). Here ends the first stage of the war.

Two points should be made. First of all, at this stage a claim for political independence was made by the extremists. The Zealots and Sicarii, together with much of the populace, seized the Temple, eliminated the legitimate high priest, and possibly even made a claim for the foundation of a new dynasty.[20] The rivalry between the two extreme groups of the Zealots and Sicarii, and of the latter with those who were opposed to a revolution against Rome, weakened the extremists. Second, the outbreak of the war between non-Jews and Jews in the Land, along with the complete defeat of Cestius Gallus, resulted in a short-lived unity among the majority of Jews in Palestine, that is to say, between extremists and moderates, a fact that led to the second stage of the conflict.

2. Josephus said in *Jewish War* 2.562 that "The Jews who had pursued Cestius, on their return to Jerusalem, partly by force, partly by persuasion, brought over to their side such pro-Romans as still remained; and, assembling in the Temple, appointed additional generals to conduct the war" and named Eleazar the supreme commander. Then comes a list of the regional military commanders. It is known that coins were also struck as early as 66 C.E., which shows that the rebels were already planning to declare the independence of the nation and a new political calendar.[21] Preparations began for the defense against the coming Roman attack (2.562–654).

The nature of the central government as well as of the commanders chosen for the different regions is interesting. They were from among the moderate section of the aristocracy; no Zealots were included. In addition, some months after the creation of the moderate central government, many of the Pharisees joined under the leadership of Simeon ben Gamliel. Additionally, many of the leaders were from among the priestly order. There may have been a hidden agenda behind the defensive measures taken by the new government, namely, to come to terms with Rome, a policy that was supported by many people in Jerusalem. The defensive organization, as well as the strengthening of the Jerusalem walls and preparation of war equipment, shows that this government was not willing to give in at any price, but was at least more moderate than the Zealots who had shown their aggressiveness at the beginning of the events (2.647–651). Josephus says, "the city before the coming of the Romans wore the appearance of a place doomed to destruction. Ananus (from the leaders of the central government), nevertheless, cherished the thought of gradually abandoning these warlike preparations and bending the malcontents and the infatuated so-called Zealots to a more salutary policy" (2.651). From then on there were differing opinions over what actions were to be taken against Rome. Many groups that were militant became more moderate and vice versa during the war. But at this juncture, many still thought that God had led them into this war, and that they would be successful.[22]

During the winter of 66 C.E. and the first months of 67, the central government in Jerusalem was active but had difficulties imposing its influence on the different regions. Some local leaders acted on their own behalf, as for instance in the area of Ascalon, where the locally organized Jewish army attacked the non-Jewish city of Ascalon and suffered a severe defeat. This act seems to have been initiated by the local governors of the region (*Jewish War* 3.9–28). There was also Simeon bar-Giora who with a private army terrorized and robbed the rich in the region of Akraba in Samaria. The central government even sent forces against him, but in vain, because he found a new base in Masada and for more than a year terrorized the Jews in the region of Idumaea (2.652–654).[23] The tensions between the central government and Josephus, who was the chosen general in the Galilee, and the support this government gave to his rival in the Galilee, John of Gischala, at the beginning of 67 c.e. shows that the central government was very weak. At a certain stage it even ordered Josephus to be deposed from his post, but the order was never carried out.[24] In other words, even when the opportunity arose in the winter of 66–67, and until the Roman invasion in the spring of 67, the Jews did not succeed in creating a firm and clear Jewish state, as the Hasmoneans had done in 143/2 b.c.e. The events at later stages of the war point to the fact that unity against the Roman oppressor was impossible to achieve.[25] The question is, Why?

This is a very complex issue, which has religiopolitical aspects. At this particular juncture (the winter of 66–67 c.e.) the moderates and the extremists united on the issue of fighting the non-Jews and "purifying" the Land from them. There is no doubt that this was already a major issue before Gallus's invasion, and certainly afterward. Also, after the destruction of his legion, there was broad consensus on a defensive policy toward a Roman invasion (the Romans were associated with the non-Jews of the Land and the hellenizers). The moderates might have thought about a peaceful solution, but they organized the defense nevertheless. Independent of what the moderates had in mind, the extremists supported the policy of war against Rome and against the non-Jews of Palestine. For this reason, in spite of the tensions and frictions between the central government and the various districts, for some months there existed a modus vivendi between the moderates and the extremists (mainly the Zealots).

The moderate government wanted to gain time, and perhaps therefore was not very definite about the creation of a Jewish state. Although the government minted coins, it did not officially declare independence (it had been a traditional Jewish habit from biblical times onward to do so), it did not create a central army, and it did not start to conquer the Land (as the three generals in Ascalon wished to do, contrary to the policies of the central government). And if one can judge from Josephus's foundation of a Sanhedrin in Galilee, other places could have had their own "local" governments as well (which is reminiscent of the time of Gabinius's settlement in 57 B.C.E.). The armies were locally organized for defense purposes, in keeping with the Roman model in Josephus's case (*Jewish War* 2.577–582)[26]—as in Numidia and Germany—and even hired mercenaries (2.583). The Hasmoneans, one should remember, were centralistic in every aspect of statehood from the very start of the Maccabean upheaval. Moreover, Josephus's difficulties in achieving some sort of a united front in the Galilee illustrates how much of the Jewish population, after so many generations of being under Roman rule, no longer possessed the will to become independent and create a national, sovereign Jewish state. If some Jews, however, did want to become independent, they were deterred from active participation by many conflicting interests, for instance, socioeconomic fears as well as the fear of the Romans and the non-Jews all over Palestine. As in many revolutionary situations in antiquity, the *neoi* (the young) were more willing to fight than the others (2.576, 595, 649).[27] Yet Josephus's main opponent was John of Gischala, who was more extreme on the subject of the war with Rome (*Vita*). He tried to undermine Josephus's "moderate" defensive cause in the Galilee, but in vain (2.583–594). It should also be emphasized that whereas many aristocrats and wealthy people joined the cause of war, many others either opposed the war or left the country. Many from among the poor and the bandits joined, but others did not. There was also a difference between the big cities in the Galilee and the rural land in terms of participation in the preparations for the war and in the war itself. The rural population was more willing to go to war, while the populations of the big cities were more reluctant (Sepphoris even minted coins in 68 C.E. with the message "the City of Peace"). Still, some of those in the big cities joined the fight, while others did not. In short, the complex Jewish social structure, along with the difficult situation of the presence of Jewish settlements within a strong (and mainly urban) non-Jewish population, determined who participated and who did not.

Thus, when Vespasian landed in Palestine there was no united Jewish front against Rome, though it seems that the majority did support the first stage, which was presented as a defensive war against the Romans and the gentiles of the Land. The central Jewish government in Jerusalem was weak, and most of the non-Jews in Palestine were pro-Roman and anti-Jewish. Nero sent Vespasian with an enormous army to quell the rebellion, and a new stage of the war now started (late spring of 67 C.E.).[28]

3. It is not necessary to give a detailed account of the war here, but some relevant points can be discussed. The Galilee fell quickly to the Romans, as a consequence of the immediate collapse of Josephus's army (*Jewish War* 3.127–131). Vespasian treated the Jews harshly in the Galilee (no non-Jews are mentioned as victims, 3.132–134). Josephus himself fled to Tiberias and then to the fortress of Jotapata, which was soon to be besieged by Vespasian. Josephus himself gives a detailed account of the Roman siege against the Jews in Jotapata (emphasizing that Jotapata contained only Jews, whereas in the Roman army one could find non-Jews such as Arabs, 3.64–69, 168, and Syrians, 3.211). The fortress fell to Roman hands in June or July 67 C.E., after forty-seven days of heroic fighting (3.135–339). Josephus himself managed to escape into a hidden cave, where he found forty of his fellow Jews, but later—after the others committed suicide—by some trick he and another one managed to be the last and thus surrendered to the Roman forces. When he appeared before Vespasian, he prophesied to him that he would become the future emperor of Rome (3.399–408), which later did happen and was very helpful indeed to the career of Josephus. By the end of 67, the Romans managed to pacify the whole of the Galilee. They took Japhia (3.289–306, where again Josephus underlines that the fight happened between the Jews of Japhia and the Roman forces); then Tiberias surrendered (where the older and more wealthy citizens welcomed the Romans, whereas the younger and poorer wanted the war to continue; again only Jews are mentioned, 3.443–461). The Romans also captured Tarichea (3.462–531), Gamala (in the Gaulanitis, 4.1–83), Mount Tabor (4.54–61), and Gischala (where, according to Josephus, the majority of the Jews did not want to fight against Rome, 4.84–120). Thousands of Jews were killed or deported to be sold as slaves (3.539–542). During this time the Roman forces also demolished Joppa, which had been rebuilt by Jewish refugees (3.414–431). Eleven thousand, six hundred Samaritans (probably an exaggerated num-

ber) who were suspected of revolting against Rome (3.307–315) were killed.

Occasionally Josephus gives some allusion to the hostility of the non-Jews to the Jews during this period, and of their joy when hearing about the Jewish defeat. For instance, when Vespasian arrived in Caesarea after his victory in Jotapata, Josephus said, "On the fourth of Panemus, Vespasian led off his troops to Ptolemais and from there to Caesarea Maritima, one of the largest cities of Judea with a population consisting chiefly of Greeks. The inhabitants received the army and its general with blessings and congratulations of every description, prompted partly by goodwill toward the Romans, but mainly by hatred of the vanquished. This feeling showed itself in a loud and universal demand for the punishment of Josephus" (*Jewish War* 3.409–411; cf. also 4.105). The war against Rome was basically a Jewish affair. The campaign of the year 67 ended with some raids on the plain of Judah and the conquest of Jamnia and Ashdod. After a winter break, Vespasian resumed operations, and at the end of the spring of 68 the whole of Transjordan, Judea, and Idumaea were subdued. Only Jerusalem, Machaerus, and Masada were left unconquered. Here started the last stage.

4. The government of the moderates in Jerusalem persisted for more than a year (autumn of 66 to the winter of 67–68 C.E.). Very little is known of what happened in Jerusalem during those days. It is known, however, that the strife between the factions within the city was already going on in the winter of 67–68, among other things because Vespasian told his generals that the inner strife in Jerusalem would weaken the Jews, and it would then be a good opportunity for the Romans to attack the city. It is also known that Vespasian's operations in Palestine in the late spring of 68 resulted in a terrible refugee problem in Jerusalem, because many Jews escaped from the Romans to the capital, which was firmly kept in Jewish hands (Masada was then in the hands of the Sicarii). One famous group that had arrived there in the autumn of 67 was the group led by John of Gischala.[29] The disastrous outcome of the war in the Land and the increase of the population in Jerusalem, which naturally became very diverse in terms of attitudes about the war against Rome, brought about a terrible period of inner conflict within Jerusalem. The Zealots (the extremists) naturally blamed the moderate central government for the defeat in the Land.

In June 68 Nero committed suicide, and a great turmoil ensued in the empire.[30] In the summer of 69 Vespasian was declared the new emperor by the legions and only at a later stage did he leave for Rome. Titus, his son, was left to continue the war in Judea; he did not manage to continue the operation against Jerusalem until the spring of 70. So for about two years Jerusalem was left without any meaningful Roman pressure, but instead of preparing for war, the factions within Jerusalem spent most of the time fighting each other. Beginning in the winter of 67–68 the strife between the moderates and the Zealots, who were joined by John of Gischala, intensified. In fact the Zealots (composed of refugees and priests from the lower strata of the society) only emerged as a strong political group that was to have a major influence on the course of events in Palestine in those crucial months of the winter of 67–68 in Jerusalem. Before 66 they had not been a significant political anti-Roman group. In the winter of 67–68 they seized the inner courts of the Temple, which they held until the end of the war.[31] Against the background of Vespasian's successes in the Land they decided to choose a new high priest who was not a descendant "from high priests" (*Jewish War* 4.155), and then started to terrorize Jerusalem, acting in particular against the still pro-Roman aristocracy and the moderates. The moderates, led by the two priests Hanan and Joshua ben Gamlah, as well as by Simeon ben Gamliel and Joseph ben Gurion, fought back.

The Zealots, first with the support of Judean peasants and later also with the Jews of Idumaea, fought the moderates and massacred a great number of them. Among others, they murdered Hanan the high priest and Joseph ben Gurion. The entire year of 68 C.E. was thus spent in fights between these factions within Jerusalem. In the spring of 69 the remnants of the moderate party, with some of the Idumaeans, besieged the Zealots, who under the leadership of John of Gischala were holding the Temple. The former invited Simeon bar-Giora, who at the time was carrying out raids in Idumaea and in the north of Jerusalem, to help them in their war against John and the Zealots. This war continued for more than a year, and according to later traditions it was then that Rabban Johanan ben Zakkai left Jerusalem.[32] The moderate views that were attributed to him by legend may be afterthoughts concerning this dreadful war.

According to an intriguing story in the rabbinic tradition (preserved in four different versions), it was ben Zakkai who allegedly greeted the emperor with the words "Vive domine imperator" when he met him. Like Josephus two years earlier he thus is said to have predicted Vespasian's becoming the new emperor. And indeed once Vespasian became emperor, his son Titus took over the lead in the war. In the spring of 70 c.e. Titus besieged the city.[33] John of Gischala managed to penetrate into the courts of the Temple and brought the Zealots under his control. Simeon bar-Giora became the high commander of most of the city, while John of Gischala was responsible for the Antonia and the Temple Mount. Nevertheless a great deal of struggle continued within the city during the siege. Josephus describes the last months of Jerusalem very dramatically. He himself was with the Roman forces, and made attempts to encourage the besieged Jews to surrender in peace (*Jewish War* 5.362–419, 541–547; 6.93–110). Among his arguments, some of which were repeated many times (even by Titus himself, 6.34–53) one can find the belief that many Jews held at the time, that God had abandoned the Jews as a consequence of their sins to the mercy of his rod, the Romans.[34]

Josephus's attempts were in vain, and the conditions in the city worsened from day to day. Hunger, murder, stealing of the Temple's treasury, and the like were daily occurrences in the city (books 5–6). The city fell into the hands of the Romans on the tenth of Tammuz (summer 70 c.e.), and the Temple was demolished. According to Josephus it was destroyed by mistake, while according to another historian (Sulpicius Severus) it was Titus's intention to destroy it. The latter may have been correct because the Romans associated the political uprisings of the Jews with the Temple and the capital, and hence decided to put an end to it altogether. Josephus emotionally says, "Deeply as one must mourn for the most marvelous edifice which we have ever seen or heard of . . ." (*Jewish War* 6.267).[35] Later the Romans conquered Herodion and Machaerus; Masada fell in the spring of 73 c.e.[36] The Jewish revolt was over, and the whole of Palestine was again subdued.

This is an important juncture in the history of Jewish political nationalism. During the Great War there were attempts to revive the institutions that symbolized more than others the independent Jewish nation, such as the Land, army, kingship, and Temple. But these symbols were interpreted differently by various groups in Jewish society, and there was no consensus concerning them. Whereas after the elimination of the hellenizers the Maccabees had succeeded in centralizing these national institutions—they had one army, one leader who was also high priest, and one Land—the revolutionaries after 66 C.E. did not even come near to succeeding. When the Sicarii made an attempt to create a dynasty in the summer of 66, their first "king," Menachem, was murdered. When in the winter of 66–67 the central government tried to create some sort of a united Jewish state, they failed because they could not form one united army with a centralized and hierarchical command system. They had no central leader, and their national base, the Land, was divided into two, of which one part belonged to the non-Jews. Unlike in the Hasmonean period, the central government did not (and could not) subdue the non-Jews. When this phase of the war was over, the Land was lost, and the armies were dispersed. In Jerusalem for two years the remnants of the national symbols were still "operating." The Zealots as well as their opponents had a little piece of territory in the Land, as well as small "armies." They held the Temple but had desecrated it so much that it almost ceased to be a religious and spiritual place. It was mainly viewed as a political center, as well as a military stronghold. The leadership of the rebels in Jerusalem was (as during most of the revolt) split and decentralized. Also, there were prophecies made of a king who would rule the entire world; "the oracle, however, in reality signified the sovereignty of Vespasian, who was proclaimed emperor on Jewish soil" (*Jewish War* 6.310–315). But this prophecy was interpreted by the Jews as a prophecy about a Jewish figure. It was a false perception by the fighting Jews of one of the most important symbols of Jewish nationalism. But in any case, it was too late for the Jews to make their dreams of statehood into a reality.[37]

Thus there are three main reasons why the revolt failed. First, there was no chance of becoming independent within the Roman Empire inasmuch as the Romans had enormous military power and economic resources at their disposal to quell the revolt. The Jews, of course, thought that God was on their side and that he would bring them to victory. The more the Roman side succeeded, the less Jews believed in his support. On the contrary, more and more Jews believed that God had left the Jewish people and that the Romans were

God's instrument for punishing the wayward Jews. Josephus held this view, as allegedly did Rabban Johanan ben Zakkai, though it was probably attributed to him many decades after the war was over.[38] The Romans wanted to have a peaceful Judea, and it seems that no other (anti-Jewish) motives were involved on their part when they decided to subdue the Land once and for all.

Second, the Jews could not unite in face of the Roman invasion, and many (for a variety of reasons) did not want to fight the Romans. Many may have been nationalistic in theory, but except for a short while, only a very small group (made up of some extreme Zealots and Sicarii, along with some others from the more moderate group) thought that a Jewish sovereign state could be created. But such a state was in fact never founded, because when a good opportunity did arise, the moderates took over, and they were unable to form a real Jewish state.

Finally, the dualism, or "schizophrenia," in Palestine, which was built up and sharpened from the times of Herod the Great's reign and onward,[39] contributed both to the start of the war and to its tragic outcome. When Vespasian was operating in Palestine, there is no evidence that the non-Jews ever fought seriously against the Roman forces. They were mainly—and they had no reason not to be—pro-Roman. Many Hellenistic Jews followed the same course. Thus not only did a great part of the population living in Palestine avoid participation in the war; it most probably supported the Roman forces who fought the Jews. The gradual destruction of the Jewish population in Palestine by the Roman forces was but a positive matter for the non-Jews. The Romans were in many respects the "saviors" of the non-Jews—and, one might add, the Jews of Hellenistic persuasion—all over Palestine. Thus, with a sporadic revolt that half of the population not only did not support but actually opposed (both non-Jewish and Jewish pro-Romans), this nationalistic upheaval could not succeed.

Eleazar ben Jair—or Josephus himself—in his famous second discourse before the mass suicide on Masada pointed to this problem too, saying, "What Roman weapons, I ask, slew the Jews of Caesarea? Nay, they had not even contemplated revolt from Rome, but were engaged in keeping their Sabbath festival, when the Caesarean rabble rushed upon them and massacred them, unresisting, with their wives and children, without even the slightest respect for the

Romans, who regarded as enemies only us who had revolted. But I shall be told that the Caesareans had a standing quarrel with their Jewish residents and seized that opportunity to satisfy their ancient hate. What then shall we say of the Jews of Scythopolis . . ." (*Jewish War* 7.361–363).

Let us view some of the reactions to this war in the literature of the time. The *Biblical Antiquities* of Pseudo-Philo may still reflect the struggle over the Land in the sixties and seventies of the first century C.E. It takes us back to the period of the Judges, which was according to the Hebrew Bible a transition time before statehood. It also shows some opposition to current messianic concepts.[40] Yet the two major works after 70 C.E. are 4 Ezra and 2 Baruch. They contain the most specific reactions to the events of 70 C.E. Both books, it should be emphasized, hardly lament the Land of Israel, or the loss of Jewish kingship, but show the traumatic experience of the loss of Jerusalem and the Temple. The conquest of the Land by Vespasian was painful, but perhaps not so shocking, because the Land had been under Roman domination for a long time, and had been treated badly by the Romans at many junctures since 63 B.C.E. The most shocking and traumatic event was the destruction of Jerusalem and the Temple, which had survived throughout Roman rule in Palestine. Although the Temple was defiled, and for many Jews was destroyed in a religious sense before 70 C.E., still its physical destruction was shocking. A demolished Temple could not even be cleansed. Whereas the book of 2 Baruch still goes along with the belief (which can be found in the literature concerning the destruction of the First Temple) that Israel's sins brought about the destruction of 70 C.E., the book of 4 Ezra presents it somewhat differently. It asks whether Rome, which was no less sinful than its victim Israel, had been the right force to destroy the Temple, as there were also other nations as sinful as the Jews and nothing had happened to them. In both 4 Ezra and 2 Baruch (which are very much dependent on each other) the destruction of 70 C.E. was described in terms of the devastation of the First Temple by Babylon in 586 B.C.E.[41] These two books will now be examined from the special point of view in this study, to see if they show whether political nationalism was still hoped for in the future.

The answer to this question must be negative. The concrete political nationalism of the sort that was seen prior to 70 C.E. seems to have disappeared from the literature. In 4 Ezra, written about 100 C.E., Zion and its Temple are central. When in his first vision the author summarizes Israel's history in order to show how sinful Israel was in its past (3:4–27), he starts with Adam, mentions Noah, Abraham, Isaac, Jacob, and Esau, as well as the Exodus and the giving of the Law on Mount Sinai, and then immediately leaps to David, and only mentions that "you [God] commanded him to build a city for your name, and in it to offer you oblations from what is yours." The lost City and its Temple are almost unique in the historical awareness of the author. He mourns their loss in laments that are reminiscent of the ones made in earlier literature, when the Temple was still intact but desecrated. It seems, however, that the tone of the laments in both 4 Ezra and 2 Baruch is less highly pitched. But 4 Ezra asks very dramatically, "Are the deeds of those who inhabit Babylon (i.e., Rome) any better? Is that why she has gained dominion over Zion? For when I came here [to Babylon, i.e., the Diaspora] I saw ungodly deeds without number, and my soul has seen many sinners during these thirty years" (since the destruction of the Temple; 3:28–29). He continues by saying that all the other nations are also sinful and "unmindful" of God's commandments. When Uriel, God's angel, answers that Ezra is not capable of comprehending "the way of the Most High," Ezra says that "it would be better for us [the Jews] not to be here [the Diaspora] than to come here and live in ungodliness, and to suffer and not understand why" (4:1–12). The dialogue about sin and reproach continues, and the end of days is mentioned as a world event rather than as a national and local one (in contrast, for instance, to the War Scroll, in which a specific perimeter is mentioned after the war of the end of days). Rome will be "waste and untrodden and men shall see it desolate" (5:3), and the whole world will undergo drastic changes (5:4–13). There is no nationalistic revival of any sort mentioned by the author within this eschatological vision, or within the subsequent one (second vision). The latter, which also deals with the end of the age, is also very universalistic in tone, and Zion is only mentioned occasionally (5:25–26; 6:4–5, 19–20). The fall of the "Fourth Kingdom" (Rome) is also elaborated in the fifth vision (the Eagle Vision, 11–12), where the Messiah will destroy the sinful Romans.[42] Here again—as in the Book of Revelation, which has a similar prediction—there is no particular political, nationalistic message given. Nevertheless, "the Messiah whom the most High has kept until the end of the days, who will arise from posterity of David . . . will deliver in mercy the remnant of my people" (12:32–34). In the third vision the author picks up again the theme of the sinful nations who dominate Israel: "As for the other nations that have descended from Adam, you have said that they are nothing, and that they are like spittle, and you have compared their abundance to a drop from a bucket. And now, O Lord, behold, these nations, which are reputed as nothing, domineer over us and devour us. . . . If the world has indeed been created for us, why do we not possess our world as an inheritance? How long will this be so?" (6:55–59). A very complex theological answer is given, which is not relevant here.

In a main section of this interesting composition the consolation of the Jews after 70 c.e. was shown to be the concept of a Heavenly Jerusalem, which, as has already been seen, was a concept well established in Jewish literature since Ezekiel;[43] but at this time it naturally received a particular emphasis. Most of the fourth vision (9:38–10:59) deals with the "substitute" for the destroyed city. The author again shows that the City and its Temple, as well as certain important strata of society associated with the City and the Temple, were of major concern to him, and not the Land and the other nationalistic symbols. In 10:19–24 he describes the destruction: "For you see that our sanctuary has been laid waste, our altar thrown down, our temple destroyed; our harp has been laid low, our song has been silenced." But the mourning woman whom Ezra views in his vision becomes "an established city, and a place of huge foundations" (10:27). It is interesting that no elaborate description is given either of the Heavenly City or of the Temple (also not in 2 Baruch). Also, no living creatures are mentioned in this city, such as the priests, Levites, and righteous men as well as "the young" who are mentioned by the author when he describes the destruction (10:22). In any case, Jerusalem has been destroyed after many years of prehistory and history,[44] like the son of the woman (who represents the Heavenly Jerusalem in the vision; 10:38–50). The author of 4 Ezra makes it clear that the Heavenly Jerusalem was the mother of the real Jerusalem. The latter died, whereas the mother is still alive:

The woman whom you saw, whom you now behold as an established city, is Zion. And as for her telling you that she was barren for thirty years, it is because there were three thousand years in the world before any offering was offered in it. And after three thousand years Solomon built the city, and offered offerings; then it was that the barren woman bore a son. And as for her telling you that she brought him up with much care, that was the period of residence in Jerusalem. And as for her saying to you 'When my son entered his wedding chamber he died,' and that misfortune had overtaken her, that was the destruction which befell Jerusalem. (10:44–49)

In short, the nationalistic political framework that has been encountered in earlier times is transformed in this document into vague speculations about the end of days and the universe, with a central interest in a messianic figure and in Jerusalem and its Temple. The latter also existed before 70 C.E., but now it receives a special focus. At the same time all the other national symbols are ignored.

Although the Land is mentioned by 4 Ezra (14:31), it is as if it had disappeared from the national awareness after 70 C.E. The same holds true concerning the other major document of the period after 70 C.E., 2 Baruch. Like 4 Ezra its provenance was probably Palestinian, and its original language, Hebrew. It is usually dated by scholars to the first two decades of the second century.[45] In this composition, preserved in Syriac, we find again laments on the destruction of the City and its Temple (chapter 10; 35:1–4; and compare to *Jewish War* 6.267f, and Tacitus, *Histories* 5.13), which has a central role throughout the document. Here there is a reference to the history of the heavenly New Jerusalem. The author says that the Heavenly Jerusalem is not

this building that is in your midst now; it is that which will be revealed, with me, that was already prepared from the moment that I decided to create Paradise. And I showed it to Adam before he sinned. But when he transgressed the commandment, it was taken away from him—as also Paradise. After these things I showed it to my servant Abraham in the night between the portions of the victims. And again I showed it also to Moses on Mount Sinai when I showed him the likeness of the tabernacle and all its vessels. Behold, now it is preserved with me—as also Paradise. Now go away and do as I command you. (4:2–7)

We have already seen that the concept of the Heavenly Temple was well-known in Judaism, but here there is given even a *history* of this Temple. Elsewhere the author says that Zion will be recreated with the new creation of the world (32:1–7), when the "Fourth Empire" (i.e., Rome) will be destroyed (39–40).[46] The author of 2 Baruch is confident that the end of the days will be happier for Zion because Israel's past history proved that there were good times and bad times intermittently (53–76). Thus, days of wrath are to come and terrible things will happen (70:1–10), but the "holy land will have mercy on its own and will protect its inhabitants at that time" (71:1). The Messiah will appear as a warrior and dominate all of the nations that he will spare (72). The *eschaton* is depicted in universal hues, and one can assume (though it is not specifically said) that, as in the bright period after Cyrus's declaration, "Zion will be rebuilt again and the offerings will be restored, and the priests will again return to their ministry, and the nations will again come to honor it" (68:5–8).

In general, these two important documents from the period after 70 c.e. reveal some interesting points concerning political nationalism. There is no longer any mention of statehood as a future option for the Jews. The Land as well as kingship and army are not on the agenda any more. Even the Temple is given a different emphasis and role. Also, the Temple is mentioned as a heavenly entity within a Heavenly City (unlike for instance in Revelation 21, where the Temple is absent from the Heavenly City). It is mentioned as a spiritual and religious institution that stands on its own, whereas its political aspect as the center of the Jewish state is totally gone. It is given, as in some of Israel's prophets, a universalistic form, being the future center of the nations in the world. And the heroes who receive special attention after 70 c.e. are no longer the ones associated with past statehood (except in the epitome of 2 Baruch, but there they appear as part of a historical sketch that is designed to instruct the reader about the imminent future), but are the more universal ones such as Adam, Abraham, and his sons.[47]

But another trend can also be traced. It can be found in Josephus's *Antiquities,* which appeared in 93 or 94 c.e. The first part of this major work (books 1–11) includes his account of Israel's history from the Creation to the Persian era, based mainly on the Bible. The *Antiquities* constitute an interpretation of biblical history made by a Jew, who lived in Rome under the aegis of the emperor himself, and who had experienced the destruction of 70 C.E. Many of his views were retrojected into his interpretation of Israel's history and reflect attitudes current at the time. His own point of view and state of mind, in addition to the nature of his sources (Hebrew and Greek versions of the Bible, as well as many external sources) and the nature of his audience (non-Jews and Jews from the Diaspora), resulted in various omissions, embellishments, additions, and interpretations of the biblical material. It is a very important composition for people who are interested in Jewish apologetics and the general opinions held during the eighties and nineties of the first century C.E. It is a rich source for speeches (which are nonbiblical but attributed to biblical figures), which read like speeches of Greek historians (Thucydides, Polybius) and reflect opinions of the time after 70 C.E. One can find throughout the composition that many details were eliminated, and even whole episodes were omitted (e.g., the Golden Calf) in order to avoid embarrassing the non-Jewish audience. A portrayal of the biblical figures can be traced that is in keeping with common Hellenistic descriptions.[48]

When it comes to Jewish nationalism in the sense used in this book, one should be cautious. It is true, as scholars have shown in a vast secondary literature, that when the details of certain parts of the *Antiquities* are compared with the Hebrew and Greek texts of the Bible, one can discover many discrepancies that point to Josephus's special attitude about Jewish nationalism.[49] It is also true that at certain junctures he presents Israel's history in a more universalistic manner and adjusts it to Greek ideas in order to clarify matters for his Greek-reading audience. Yet when the general picture is viewed, in other words, the picture that emerges from the *Antiquities* in terms of political nationalism as a whole, it becomes quite obvious that the *Antiquities* represent a very nationalistic point of view.

If Josephus's interpretation of biblical history in the first eleven books of the *Antiquities* can be accepted as reflecting his own views in the last quarter of the first century C.E., then one may deduce that Josephus did not give up the idea of a Jewish state altogether. In his account of Israel's history he brings the national symbols and institutions (territory, Temple, army, and kingship) of Israel's past to the fore and on the whole never tones them down. He refers often to the Temple and to the capital, Jerusalem, as a religious and political center. He underscores the role of the legitimate Aaronite high priesthood as a religiopolitical authority in ancient Israel, and elaborately recounts the history of Jewish kingship. He tells the story of Israel's military history and related matters. In spite of his highly interpretive writing, there is nothing in his biblical interpretations to suggest that he thought that Jewish political nationalism was either negative or had come to its end. On the contrary, Josephus probably thought of Israel's history in terms of repetition, and perhaps even as a cyclical process. For this reason he adopts as a framework for his biblical history the Greek cycle of constitutions, the so-called *metabole.*[50] Thus, just as the First Temple and state were destroyed in the past and a Second Temple and even a second state were built instead, so the future of Israel could bring about a third Temple as well as another Jewish state founded on the Land. In this area, Josephus no doubt represented what many other Jews thought of Israel's history. Historians at that time wrote their histories in order to instruct their readers about what they should expect and how they should behave in the future.[51] Josephus's view can therefore be seen as yet another nuance in Judaism after the destruction of 70 C.E., an elaboration of which would require another volume.

Some years after the appearance of the *Antiquities* he published his treatise called *Contra Apionem.* As an aged and experienced man he may have come to the conclusion that the authority of God was what mattered in political life. "Theocracy" was apparently the best form of constitution Josephus could recommend (the so-called *patrios politeia,* 2.152 with 168–296). He says,

> There is endless variety in the details of the customs and laws that prevail in the world at large. To give but a summary enumeration: some peoples have entrusted the supreme political power to monarchies, others to oligarchies, yet others to the masses. Our Lawgiver, however, was attracted by none of these forms of polity, but gave to his constitution the form of what—if a forced expression be permitted—may be termed a "theocracy," placing all sovereignty and authority in the hands of God. (2.164–165).[52]

Josephus then goes on to elaborate on this form of government. It should be noted that in antiquity a Jewish state with a Temple and capital as well as an army or a king was never created again. This does not mean that after 70 C.E., zealous nationalistic ideas were gone.[53] The Bar Kokhba rebellion shows that Jewish political nationalism was not dead between 70 and 135 C.E.

Notes

¹ Cf. in particular H. Lindner, *Die Geschichtsauffassung des Flavius Josephus im Bellum* (Leiden, 1972); S. J. D. Cohen, *Josephus in Galilee and Rome* (Leiden, 1979); and P. Villalba i Varneda, *The Historical Method of Flavius Josephus* (Leiden, 1986).

² For this issue in general see already T. Mommsen, *Römische Geschichte*, 2d ed. (Berlin, 1885), 5.487–542; also idem, *Das römische Imperium der Cäsaren* (Berlin, 1941), chap. 11.

³ M. Hengel, *The Zealots* (Edinburgh, 1989), has rightfully shown the uniqueness of this movement.

⁴ Cf. for instance P. Bilde, "The Causes of the Jewish War According to Josephus," *Journal for the Study of Judaism in the Persian, Hellenistic and Roman Period* 10 (1979): 179–202. Cf. conveniently also W. H. Harter, "The Causes of the Jewish Revolt Against Rome, 66–74 C.E., in Recent Scholarship," Ph.D. diss., Union Theological Seminary in the City of New York, 1982 (*DAIA* 45, no. 5 [1984], 1448).

⁵ In particular U. Rappaport, "Jewish-Pagan Relations and the Revolt Against Rome in 66–70 C.E.," *The Jerusalem Cathedra* 1 (1981): 81–95; A. Kasher, *Jews and Hellenistic Cities in Eretz Israel* (Tübingen, 1990), chap. 5. For the socioeconomic background, see P. A. Brunt, *Roman Imperial Themes* (Oxford, 1990), pp. 282–287.

⁶ For the more religious motives see Hengel, *Zealots;* and H. Schwier, *Tempel und Tempelzerstörung* (Göttingen, 1987). The religious is emphasized by Schwier somewhat to a fault.

⁷ M. D. Goodman, *The Ruling Class of Judaea* (Cambridge, 1987).

⁸ See in general E. M. Smallwood, *The Jews under Roman Rule* (Leiden, 1976), pp. 256–292.

⁹ For a good survey of the "Greek" part of Palestine, see E. Schürer, *The History of the Jewish People in the Age of Jesus Christ*, rev. G. Vermes et al. (Edinburgh, 1973–1987), 2.85–183, as opposed to the Jewish side described at 2.184–226. Cf. also M. Hengel, *The "Hellenization" of Judaea in the First Century after Christ* (Philadelphia, 1989).

¹⁰ They had local loyalties to their cities (cf. Y. Meshorer, *City Coins of Eretz Israel and the Decapolis in the Roman Period* [Jerusalem, 1985], and J. Geiger, "Local Patriotism in the Hellenistic Cities of Palestine," in *Greece and Rome in Eretz Israel*, ed. A. Kasher et al. [Jerusalem, 1990], pp. 141–150), but not to the Land as a whole, as the Jews had.

¹¹ By contrast, a moderate view concerning the relations between non-Jews and Jews is attributed to Johanan ben Zakkai, who allegedly said at the beginning of the

war, when Jews and non-Jews fought each other, "Do not destroy their altars, so that you do not have to rebuild them with your own hands" (*Mekilta,* Deuteronomium 25:14).

[12] As did Rappaport, "Jewish-Pagan Relations."

[13] Cf. Cohen, *Josephus,* and idem, "Josephus, Jeremiah and Polybius," *History and Theory* 21 (1982): 366–381.

[14] Cf. A. Kasher, "The *Isopoliteia* Question in Caesarea Maritima," *Jewish Quarterly Review* 68 (1977): 16–27. For some surveys of the War, see Schürer, *History,* 1.484–513; T. Rajak, *Josephus: The Historian and His Society* (London, 1983), pp. 104–173; Goodman, *Ruling Class,* pp. 152–197.

[15] For Agrippa II see D. Barag, "Studies on the Coinage of Agrippa II," *Israel Numismatic Journal* 5 (1981): 27–32; D. R. Schwartz, "*Kata touton ton kairon:* Josephus' Source on Agrippa II," *Jewish Quarterly Review* 72 (1982): 241–268; A. Stein, "The Undated Coins of Agrippa II under Nero," *Israel Numismatic Journal* 8 (1984–1985): 9–11; and Y. Meshorer, *Ancient Jewish Coinage* (New York, 1982), 2.65–95. For his famous speech, E. Gabba, "L'Impero Romano nel discorso di Agrippa II (Ioseph. B.I.,II, 345–401)," *Rivista storica dell'antichità* 6–7 (1976–1977): 189–194.

[16] Cf. Hengel, *Zealots,* passim.

[17] In general for this episode see R. A. Horsley, "Menahem in Jerusalem: A Brief Messianic Episode among the Sicarii not 'Zealot Messianism,' " *Novum Testamentum* 27 (1985): 334–348.

[18] M. Stern, "The Suicide of Eleazar ben Jair and His Men at Masada, and the 'Fourth Philosophy,' " in his *Studies in Jewish History* (Jerusalem, 1991), pp. 313–343 (Hebrew).

[19] In general for this campaign see M. Gichon, "Cestius Gallus's Campaign in Judaea," *Palestine Exploration Quarterly* 113 (1981): 39–62.

[20] The "dynasty" of Judas the Galilean. For the use of the term "Zealot" outside Palestine in a positive sense, see S. M. Burstein, *The Hellenistic Age from the Battle of Ipsos to the Death of Kleopatra VII* (Cambridge, 1985), pp. 20, 38 (in inscriptions).

[21] Namely, the Jewish Shekels minted in "year 1." Cf. Meshorer, *Ancient Jewish Coinage,* 2.96–131; idem, "A Hoard of Coins from the Time of the Jewish War Against Rome," *Michmanim* 2 (1985): 43–45 (Hebrew); cf. also Goodman, *Ruling Class,* pp. 178–179.

[22] For various aspects of this belief see Schwier, *Tempel und Tempelzerstörung.*

[23] Cf. G. Fuks, "Some Remarks on Simon Bar-Giora," *Scripta classica israelica* 8–9 (1985–1988): 106–119.

²⁴ For more about John, see U. Rappaport, "John of Gischala in Galilee," *The Jerusalem Cathedra* 3 (1983): 46–57.

²⁵ Goodman's picture (*Ruling Class,* pp. 176–197) about an "Independent Jewish State" during the years 67–70 C.E., and a state that "functioned throughout this period quite efficiently" (spring 68 to spring 69) is too optimistic. It is known that many Jews wished for a Jewish state, and in this regard Goodman is right; but the disruptive disunity throughout most of these years prevented any foundation, let alone organization, of a Jewish state in any form. See also the following.

²⁶ Cf. also Josephus's description of Israel's armies in biblical times, when he described them in terms of the Roman army (*Antiquities* 3.289, 7.26, and elsewhere). His famous description of the Roman camp shows that he was aware of the Roman army (*Jewish War* 3.70–109).

²⁷ Plutarch, *Lives of Agis and Cleomenes,* passim; with B. Shimron, *Late Sparta: The Spartan Revolution, 243–146 B.C.* (Buffalo, N.Y., 1972), chap. 2, and in general see P. Cartledge and A. Spawforth, *Hellenistic and Roman Sparta* (London and New York, 1989), pp. 38–58.

²⁸ For the number of Roman legions in the East at the time see L. J. F. Keppie, "Legions in the East from Augustus to Trajan," in *The Defence of the Roman and Byzantine East,* ed. P. Freeman and D. Kennedy (Oxford, 1986), 2.411–429.

²⁹ For more about this, see U. Rappaport, "John of Gischala: From Galilee to Jerusalem," *Journal of Jewish Studies* 33 (1982): 479–493.

³⁰ For Nero see M. Griffin, *Nero: The End of a Dynasty* (New Haven, 1985).

³¹ M. J. Borg (*Conflict, Holiness, and Politics in the Teachings of Jesus* [New York and Toronto, 1984], p. 170) is right in saying that "in the great revolt and in the decades preceding it there was operative an ideology of resistance based on the Temple." For the urban mob in the Zealot group, see T. L. Donaldson, "Rural Bandits, City Mobs and the Zealots," *Journal for the Study of Judaism in the Persian, Hellenistic and Roman Period* 21.1 (1990): 19–40.

³² Cf. J. Neusner, *A Life of Rabban Yohanan ben Zakkai, ca. 1–80 C.E.,* 2d ed. (Leiden, 1970), pp. 152–173. For an interesting approach see also S. A. Cohen, *The Three Crowns: Structure of Communal Politics in Early Rabbinic Jewry* (Cambridge and Sydney, 1990), pp. 133–146.

³³ *Jewish War* 5.39ff. Cf. in general B. W. Jones, "Titus in the East, A.D. 70–71," *Rheinisches Museum für Philologie* 128 (1985): 346–352.

³⁴ For various aspects of this notion see Schwier, *Tempel und Tempelzerstörung,* passim; also D. E. Aune, *Prophecy in Early Christianity and the Ancient Mediterranean World* (Grand Rapids, Mich., 1983), pp. 138–144. This concept is also found in Philostratus, a gentile who wrote at the end of the second and beginning of the third centuries C.E., who claims (M. Stern, *Greek and Latin Authors on Jews and Judaism* [Jerusalem, 1974–1984], 2.343), "After Titus had taken Jerusalem, and when the country all round was filled with corpses, the neighbouring races

offered him a crown; but he disclaimed any such honour to himself, saying that it was not himself that had accomplished this exploit, but that he merely lent his arms to God, who had so manifested his wrath."

[35] There exists a dispute between scholars over whether the act of destruction was an intentional policy of Rome or happened by accident during the end of the war. Cf. in general Schürer, *History,* 1.507–508, and L. I. Levine, "From the Beginning of Roman Rule until 74 C.E.," in *The History of Eretz Israel,* ed. M. Stern (Jerusalem, 1984), 4.276–277.

[36] The secondary literature on the fall of Masada abounds. See for instance Stern, "Suicide of Eleazar ben Jair," pp. 367–398; S. J. D. Cohen, "Masada: Literary Tradition, Archaeological Remains, and the Credibility of Josephus," *Journal of Jewish Studies* 33 (1982): 385–405; M. Luz, "Eleazar's Second Speech on Masada and Its Literary Precedents," *Rheinisches Museum für Philologie* 126 (1983): 25–43. Cf. also H. M. Cotton and J. Geiger, *Masada,* vol. 2: *The Latin and Greek Documents* (Jerusalem, 1989).

[37] Thus Goodman's description of the "Independent State" (pp. 176–197) is implausible.

[38] M. D. Herr, "From the Destruction of the Temple to the Revolt of Bar Kokhba," in *The History of Eretz Israel,* ed. M. Stern (Jerusalem, 1984), 4.320–323.

[39] Cf. also Nicolaus of Damascus (in Stern, *Greek and Latin Authors,* 1.254), who comments that after Herod's death "The Greek cities subject to Herod sent emissaries petitioning Caesar [i.e., Augustus] to grant them freedom." Nicolaus "exhorted Archelaus not to oppose their striving for freedom, as the remaining dominion would be enough for him." This account emphasizes again the dichotomic situation in Palestine.

[40] Cf. in detail its reflection of the time: D. Mendels, "Pseudo-Philo's *Biblical Antiquities,* the 'Fourth Philosophy' and the Political Messianism of the First Century A.D.," in *The Messiah,* ed. J. H. Charlesworth (Minneapolis, 1992), pp. 261–275.

[41] For the reaction to the destruction in these two documents, see in particular M. E. Stone, "Reactions to Destructions of the Second Temple," *Journal for the Study of Judaism in the Persian, Hellenistic and Roman Period* 12 (1982): 195–204; J. J. Collins, *The Apocalyptic Imagination* (New York, 1987), pp. 155–180 (he adds also the Apocalypse of Abraham, in pp. 180–186). In general for these documents see Schürer, *History,* 3.1.294–306 (4 Ezra), and 3.2.750–756 (2 Baruch); also Schwier, *Tempel und Tempelzerstörung,* pp. 338–362. For the rabbinic reaction to the destruction (which is beyond the scope of this book), see R. Goldenberg, "Early Rabbinic Explanations of the Destruction of Jerusalem," *Journal of Jewish Studies* 33 (1982): 517–525; M. Hadas-Lebel, "La Tradition rabbinique sur la première révolte contre Rome à la lumière . . . ," *Sileno* 9 (1983): 157–172; R. Kirschner, "Apocalyptic and Rabbinic Responses to the Destruction of 70,"

Harvard Theological Review 78 (1985): 27–46; and recently also M. Hadas-Lebel, *Jérusalem contre Rome* (Paris, 1990), pp. 423–452.

[42] 4 Ezra 12:31ff.; M. E. Stone, "The Question of the Messiah in 4 Ezra," in *Judaisms and Their Messiahs at the Turn of the Christian Era,* ed. J. Neusner et al. (Cambridge, 1987), pp. 209–224.

[43] Stone, "Reactions."

[44] For the concept of its prehistory see I. M. Gafni, " 'Pre-Histories' of Jerusalem in Hellenistic, Jewish and Christian Literature," *Journal for the Study of the Pseudepigrapha* 1 (1987): 5–22.

[45] For 2 Baruch see in particular A. F. J. Klijn, "2 (Syriac Apocalypse of) Baruch," in *The Old Testament Pseudepigrapha,* ed. J. H. Charlesworth (New York, 1983–1985), 1.615–652.

[46] Cf. in general F. J. Murphy, "*2 Baruch* and the Romans," *Journal of Biblical Literature* 104 (1985): 663–669.

[47] Cf. J. R. Levison, *Portraits of Adam in Early Judaism* (Sheffield, 1988).

[48] H. W. Attridge, *The Interpretation of Biblical History in the Antiquitates Judaicae of Flavius Josephus* (Missoula, Mont., 1976), pp. 109–119 and passim; and P. Villalba i Varneda, *The Historical Method of Flavius Josephus* (Leiden, 1986), passim.

[49] Cf. for example recently L. H. Feldman, "Josephus' Portrait of Jacob," *Jewish Quarterly Review* 79 (1989): 135–137.

[50] D. R. Schwartz, "Josephus on the Jewish Constitutions and Community," *Scripta classica israelica* 7 (1983–1984): 30–52.

[51] Cf. F. W. Walbank, *Polybius* (Berkeley-London, 1972), and Villalba i Varneda, *Historical Method,* pp. 251–256 and passim. Cf. chapter 2 above.

[52] Cf. also Y. Amir, "*Theocratia* as a Concept of Political Philosophy: Josephus' Presentation of Moses' *Politeia,*" *Scripta classica israelica* 8–9 (1985–1988): 83–105.

[53] Perhaps the late rabbinic sources also reveal some of the zealous ideas that were prevalent among some leading sages of the time before 70 c.e.: cf. I. Ben-Shalom, "Events and Ideology of the Yavneh Period as Indirect Causes of the Bar-Kokhva Revolt," in *The Bar Kokhva Revolt,* ed. A. Oppenheimer and U. Rappaport (Jerusalem, 1984), pp. 1–12 (Hebrew).

CHAPTER 13

The "Polemus Quietus" and the Revolt of Bar Kokhba, 132-135 C.E.

In 115-117 C.E. we hear again of a major revolt, this time in the Jewish Diasporas of Cyrene, Cyprus, Mesopotamia (as a part of a general revolt there), and Egypt. It took place at the time that Trajan, the Roman emperor, was busy fighting the Parthians in the East while expanding the empire beyond its traditional borders. Trajan wished to actualize once and for all the grand idea that some Roman political figures had before him, namely, the conquest of the eastern ecumene (in the wake of Alexander the Great), and its incorporation into the Roman Empire.

Unfortunately, we know very little about the circumstances that led to the revolt, or about the revolt itself. From the fragmentary evidence we hear of clashes between the Jews and the Roman authorities as well as between the "Hellenes" (group 2) and the Jews.[1] In Cyrene, while attacking the Greeks there, the Jews even crowned their ringleader king (the "king of the Jews"), and according to one source performed terrible atrocities against their non-Jewish neighbors.[2] When the Roman commanders intervened to quell the riots, the conflict took the shape of real "battles," and thousands of Jews were killed.[3] This revolt is called in the Jewish sources "Polemus Quietus."[4] We do not know whether the Jews of Palestine participated in it at all. We possess, however, some scattered references that may indicate some sort of upheaval also in Palestine.[5] Whether the Jews of Palestine joined the rebel forces or not, it remains a fact that in 117 C.E., after the suppression of the revolts in the Diaspora, the man who was victorious over the Jews in Mesopotamia, Lusius Quietus, was appointed governor of Judea. The latter was upgraded to become henceforward a consular province with two legions stationed in it.

In spite of the fact that we have a significant number of papyri from Egypt that shed some light on the intensity of the tumult and its territorial scope, the evidence concerning its course is so obscure that we can not reach any conclusion about the motives behind this insurrection of the Jewish Diaspora. What can be said, however, is that the Jews of the eastern Diaspora emerge as a worldly *ethnos* that settled an account in a furious manner with the gentiles. To put it bluntly, the revolt of 115–117 C.E. was a war of Judaism against Greco-Roman paganism. We may even conclude that in certain regions the Jews may have formed independent Jewish pockets with a ruler (or even a king, as in Cyrene), some sort of an army, and a separate "constitution." Can this development be seen as a reflection of some of the eschatological universal views that we have already met in Judaism, which are associated with a Jewish domination of the whole eastern ecumene, not just of Palestine? Is it accidental that this sort of insurrection occurred only in the eastern provinces simultaneously with the revival (and even actualization) of the Alexander myth by the emperor himself? These questions cannot be answered until new evidence is found.

It is not accidental that in the seventh decade after the end of the Great War against Rome, another major nationalistic revolt broke out in Palestine (132–135 C.E.). It seems likely that the Jews in Palestine were awaiting the completion of seventy years, as in the days after the destruction of the First Temple (cf. Zech 1:12 and 7:5; Jer 25:11–12; 29:10). The Jews lived in the shadow of their historical precedents. It took seventy years to build the Second Temple (587/6–515 B.C.E.), so after a similar period had elapsed since that Temple's destruction, the circles in Palestine who were active nationalists became restless. Again, it was only the Jewish segment in Palestine, which was more than ever split, who took the initiative. Whereas passive nationalism shows itself in the thought of the rabbis, the revolt of Bar Kokhba shows very clearly that nationalism in its political-activist and zealous form never died out even after 70 C.E. It remained latent, so that any event that could cause its emergence as an aggressive movement had its effect.[6] And indeed the opportunity arose.

The hardships that the Jews endured in Palestine after 70 C.E. at the hands of the Roman authorities were highlighted by the favorable attitude of the same authorities to the non-Jews there. This behavior sharpened even more the dichotomy existing between the two segments of the population. In fact, the non-Jews were the major beneficiaries of the Great War. The fact that Emperor Hadrian removed the hated governor Quietus and perhaps—if one can believe a late Jewish legend—even toyed with the idea of rebuilding the Temple and Jerusalem gave a great deal of hope to the Jews, who regarded the emperor as Cyrus *redivivus*.[7] When the emperor later decided not to go through with his plans (according to this same legend), the frustration was deep, and strengthened the radical Jews who went to war.

In the autumn of 129 C.E. Hadrian arrived in Palestine as part of his visit to the provinces of the East with the aim of promoting Hellenic civilization there. During this visit it became clear that he was the champion of the non-Jews of Palestine. They received him with great enthusiasm; Petra named itself "Adriane Petra," Caesarea and Tiberias had an "Adrianeion," and Gaza had a "panegyris Adriane." Hadrian seems to have decided at this juncture not to exempt the Jews from the Law against castration, which meant for the Jews a ban on circumcision. Also, it became clear that he wished to rebuild Jerusalem as Aelia Capitolina, a non-Jewish city. This provocation was too much for the Jews, because such an act would have terminated any opportunity to rebuild Jerusalem and its Temple as Jewish religiopolitical centers. The circles that were ready for revolt under their leader, Simeon Bar Kokhba, waited until the emperor left the region, then started their rebellion in the spring of 132 C.E.[8]

The war lasted three and a half years, but no historical survey analogous to the ones we possess of the Maccabean revolt and the Great War is available. Also the epigraphical material does not lead us far in our attempts to reconstruct a sequence of events. This material is, however, an invaluable source for the subject matter of this book. The rabbinical sources contain some information about the events, but the question remains whether they are reliable historical sources on the whole. Greek and Latin sources are helpful, but very abrupt.[9] It is interesting to see how the beliefs of certain scholars influence their interpretation of the Bar Kokhba revolt (compare M. D. Herr's account with the one presented in Schürer's *History*, 1.534–557).

Be that as it may, in 132 C.E. the war started after preparations made by the rebels.[10] The Romans were caught by surprise and had to send auxiliary forces to Judea in addition to the two standing legions there. The intensity of the revolt can be deduced by the numbers of troops used by the Romans to quell the rebels (more than fifty thousand soldiers), as well as from Cassius Dio's epitomized history, which claims that during the war the Romans destroyed fifty of the Jewish strongholds and 985 of their villages (69.14.1). From the available sources it is impossible to learn whether Jerusalem was conquered by the rebels before or during the war, whether they renewed the sacrifices on the Temple Mount, or whether the revolt extended beyond Judea proper.

From the little we know, especially from an epitomized version of Cassius Dio, we learn that even the emperor himself came to Palestine during the revolt. On the ninth of Ab 135, according to rabbinic tradition, the last stronghold of the Jewish rebels near Jerusalem fell, called Bethar.[11] Simeon Bar Kokhba was among the victims. According to Dio 580,000 Jews fell in the battles (69.14.1–3). More Jews were killed, and many others were sold as slaves during the aftermath of the war (in the slave market at Hebron at the time a Jew was worth no more than a horse). If we can believe later Jewish traditions, the Romans also enacted restrictive laws on the Jews in Palestine, such as the ban on circumcision and a prohibition against reading the Torah in public. The result was an additional terrible blow for the Jews in Palestine, and the strengthening of the non-Jewish population of the country. The memories of these terrible days emerge in the rabbinic literature in a very vivid manner. The story about the ten martyrs, among whom was Rabbi Akiba, is perhaps the most famous.[12]

Provincia Judaea became Syria Palaestina, and Aelia Capitolina was founded with a pagan temple in its midst.[13] Non-Jews were settled in the new colony instead of the Jews, and no Jew was allowed to enter the city. Moreover, any Jew found there was put to death. Pagan cults of Bacchus, Astarte, and Aphrodite were established in Jerusalem, and on the Temple Mount a pagan temple was built with a statue of Hadrian in it. Viewed from a historical perspective, this was the final victory of the non-Jewish population in Palestine over the Jews in the course of their continuous competition over the Land. Let us now examine the four cornerstones of nationalism as they emerge during this rebellion.

A. *The army*. From the Bar Kokhba letters we learn that Bar Kokhba had a well-organized Jewish army, which was very disciplined. The army apparently was organized in a hierarchical system, having different ranks of commanders (we know of a "head of the camp"), and we even know some of its commanders by their names. Judah bar Manasse was the commander of Kiryath Arabaya, and Jonathan bar Be'ayan and Masabala bar Simeon were the commanders of En Gedi. From the letters it appears that Bar Kokhba's soldiers were God-fearing Jews.

B. *Kingship*. From the documents of the time of the revolt, we learn that the official title of Bar Kokhba was "Nasi," which is already in the Old Testament associated with the king (Ezek 12:10, 12; 34:24; also later in Qumran). In rabbinic literature there is a debate whether Bar Kokhba was the king-messiah (Rabbi Akiba, who interpreted Num 24:17 as the coming of the "star," i.e., the Messiah) or not (because he was not of the Davidic line, Yohanan ben Tortah).[14] Whatever the late rabbinic interpretations were, Bar Kokhba (who was heavily denigrated by Eusebius, who claims that he killed Christians because they refused to join the revolt) was a secular ruler who was also the high military commander of a Jewish army, and who ruled a considerable piece of territory in the Land of Israel.

His authority as the supreme ruler comes to the fore in his letters. In one famous epistle to the "lead of the camp" he writes the following:

> From Simeon ben Kosiba to Joshua
> ben Galgoula and to the men of the fort,
> peace. I take heaven to witness against me
> that unless you mobilize [destroy?] the Galileans who
> are with you
> every man, I will put fetters
> on your feet as I did
> to ben Aphlul.

C. *The Temple*. As has been mentioned already, it is not clear whether the rebels conquered Jerusalem at all, or whether they started to sacrifice on the Temple Mount before the revolt or during it. It is, however, clear that the rebuilding of the Temple and the renewal of the service in the Temple were the main targets of the rebels, as we can learn from their coins. They include, among others, symbols associated with the cult in the Temple as well as the facade of a Temple.[15] Also the foundation of a pagan temple on the Temple Mount after the suppression of the revolt may be seen as a payment in kind made by the Romans in reaction to the rebellious Jews' renewal of the cult on the Temple Mount. From another set of coins we learn about "the Priest Eleazar," who was apparently an important figure in those stormy days, and may have been considered a candidate to the high priesthood in the eventual Third Temple. Eleazar is sometimes identified by scholars with the uncle of Bar Kokhba who fought with him in Bethar, and then was put to death because of accusations that he wished to talk peace with the Romans (Yerushalmi, *Ta'aniyot* 4, 68:4). The Sanhedrin should also be mentioned. It operated in those days as the sovereign high court for the Jewish population of Palestine.

D. *Territory*. From the coinage of the rebels and some legal documents we learn that a new calendar was created for the emerging Jewish state, and that the years were counted according to the "liberation of Israel," the years of Bar Kokhba's rule ("Third year of Simeon the son of Kosba the Nasi of Israel"), and the years of "the liberation of Jerusalem."[16] In spite of the fact that we have information about the daily life of the rebels, and about a few of their symbols of statehood, we know very little about the borders of the territory that came under their sovereignty. There are conflicting pieces of evidence that may indicate that the revolt encompassed, along with Judea, parts of the Galilee and the Golan. But I go along with the "minimalists" who argue only for the region of Judea and vicinity.[17] Be that as it may, a territorial claim on the Land was made by the rebels, and they apparently emphasized it in their "ideology."

Bar Kokhba was the first "nonschizophrenic" leader the Jews had had for many years.[18] His army was composed of religious Jews who fought an army whose manpower reflected the multinational character of the empire.[19] There seems to have been no place for

Jewish Hellenists of whatever kind in his newly created state. In this respect he resembled the Maccabees in the first years of their upheaval against the Seleucids. The revolt of Bar Kokhba, however, failed because from the outset there existed no chance to fight Rome as long as paganism had the upper hand in Palestine itself, and while the Romans were stronger than ever. The rebellious Jews should have learned from their bitter past experiences. But the ardent and continuous wish of some groups among them to create a state made them irrational, emotional, and losers.

In sum, the rift between non-Jews and Jews in the Holy Land brought about a great deal of tension and violent clashes throughout the decades subsequent to the Maccabean upheaval. This rift, along with the complexity of the "schizophrenic" situation in Jewish society itself, caused by the political and social conditions in the Hellenistic world, resulted in disaster. Unlike many hellenized regions outside Palestine, where different ethnic groups lived in harmony with one another, in Palestine coexistence was impossible. The universalistic views of Agrippa II could not in the long run accommodate the extreme views of the Zealots, or even those of much less zealous groups who had a "halakhic" Jewish state in mind. The tensions in Jewish society were not only a result of the contradictory interpretations of nationalism by the different groups of that society, but were also caused by the fact that the nationalistic symbols themselves were "schizophrenic." From the Maccabees until Bar Kokhba, there were hardly any periods in which we could find a real equilibrium existing between the different components of the nationalistic symbols (Hellenistic versus Jewish). After Bar Kokhba was defeated, only passive political nationalism remained, hidden under the surface for hundreds of years in rabbinic Judaism. Some of the rabbis continued to bear this nationalism in the back of their minds for many years to come, but this nationalism never again led to a revolution on a grand scale.

Notes

[1] Eusebius, *Ecclesiastical History* 4.2.2–3; *Chronica,* ed. A. Schoene (Berlin, 1866), 2.164ff. See for the historical reconstruction of the riots A. Fuks, "Aspects of the Jewish Revolt in A.D. 115–117," *Journal of Roman Studies* 51 (1961): 98–104. For an excellent collection, see *The Revolt of the Jews in the Times of Trajan, 115–117 A.D.,* ed. D. Rokeah (Jerusalem, 1978) (Hebrew). Cf. now also T. D. Barnes, "Trajan and the Jews," *Journal of Jewish Studies* 40 (1989): 145–162.

[2] Cassius Dio 68.32, Eusebius, *Ecclesiastical History* 4.2.3, and cf. S. Applebaum, *Jews and Greeks in Ancient Cyrene* (Leiden, 1979), pp. 269–294, which shows that epigraphical and archaeological material supports the destruction there. In Egypt the mother of the *strategos* Apollonios warns him in a letter, "may they not roast you" (*Corpus papyrorum judaicarum* vol. 2, no. 437).

[3] *Corpus papyrorum judaicarum* 435, and Eusebius, *Ecclesiastical History* 4.2.3–4; Orosius, 7.12.6–7.

[4] Referring probably to the revolt in Mesopotamia, *m. Sota* 9:14. A famous statement found in Seder Olam (A. Neubauer *Mediaeval Jewish Chronicles* [Oxford, 1895], 2.66) seems to be mentioning only wars that occurred in the Land of Israel. "From the war of Asverus (Varus) to the war of Vespasian: 80 years whilst the Temple existed. From the war of Vespasian to the war of Quietus: fifty-two years. And from the war of Quietus to the war of Ben Koziba: 16 years. And the war of Ben Koziba: three and a half years" (cf. E. Schürer, *The History of the Jewish People in the Age of Jesus Christ,* rev. G. Vermes et al. [Edinburgh, 1973–1987], 1.534). "Day of Trajan" according to *Meg. Ta'an.* 29.

[5] *Historia Augusta,* Life of Hadrian 5.2, and see E. M. Smallwood, "Palestine c. A.D. 115–118," *Historia* 11 (1962): 500–510.

[6] E. M. Smallwood, *The Jews under Roman Rule* (Leiden, 1976), p. 438 (calls it an "endemic nationalism").

[7] Cf. *Berešit Rabba* 64.10; other non-Jewish and Christian sources are not specific about this matter. For the evaluation of the sources see P. Schäfer, *Der Bar Kokhba-Aufstand* (Tübingen, 1981), pp. 29–38. A passage in the *Sibylline Oracles* (5.46–50) may reflect the expectations in Judaism for the rebuilding of the Temple: "After him another will reign, a silver-headed man. He will have the name of a sea. He will also be a most excellent man and he will consider everything."

[8] For the dating see Schäfer, *Bar Kokhba,* pp. 27–28. For the causes see also L. Mildenberg, *The Coinage of the Bar Kokhba War* (Aarau, 1984), pp. 102–109, and M. D. Herr, "From the Destruction of the Temple to the Revolt of Bar Kokhba," in *The History of Eretz Israel,* ed. M. Stern (Jerusalem, 1984), 4.312–350; Y. Yadin, *Bar-Kokhba* (New York, 1971), pp. 17–27. For a survey of scholarship on the revolt, see B. Isaac and A. Oppenheimer, "The Revolt of Bar Kokhba: Ideology and Modern Scholarship," *Journal of Jewish Studies* 36 (1985): 33–60.

[9] For an excellent evaluation of the sources see Schäfer, *Bar Kokhba;* and for the numismatic evidence see Mildenberg, *Coinage.* For a "history" of the revolt, see Smallwood, *Jews under Roman Rule,* pp. 428–466. For Bar Kokhba's letters, see Yadin, *Bar-Kokhba,* pp. 124–139.

[10] Cf. for instance A. Kloner, "Underground Hiding Complexes from the Bar Kochba War in the Judaean Shephela," *Biblical Archaeologist* 46.4 (1983): 210–221. These were no doubt built some time before the actual fighting started. See now also *The Hiding Complexes in the Judean Shephelah,* ed. A. Kloner and Y. Tepper (Tel-Aviv, 1987) (Hebrew).

[11] For rabbinic sources on Bethar see Schäfer, *Bar Kokhba,* pp. 136–193.

[12] Cf. G. Reeg, *Die Geschichte von den Zehn Märtyren* (Tübingen, 1985).

[13] Cf. now also Y. Meshorer, *The Coinage of Aelia Capitolina* (Jerusalem, 1989).

[14] Cf. an elaborate evaluation of the sources concerning this issue in Schäfer, *Bar Kokhba,* pp. 51–77 (with the older literature). For Bar Kokhba's official title, see also A. Kloner, "Lead Weights of Bar Kokhba's Administration," *Israel Exploration Journal* 40 (1990): 58–67.

[15] Only one document from Murabbaʿat (*Discoveries in the Judaean Desert* [Oxford, 1955–1990], 2.135) has the slogan "For the Freedom of Jerusalem." Appian states that the Romans had to conquer Jerusalem back from the rebels. For the sources on this issue with the older literature, see Schäfer, *Bar Kokhba,* pp. 78–101.

[16] Y. Meshorer, *Ancient Jewish Coinage* (New York, 1982), 2.132–165; and Mildenberg, *Coinage,* pp. 65–68 and passim. D. Goodblatt suggested that priestly circles had much influence on the revolt, "The Title *Nasiʾ* and the Ideological Background of the Second Revolt," in *The Bar Kokhba Revolt,* ed. A. Oppenheimer and U. Rappaport (Jerusalem, 1984), pp. 113–132.

[17] For the problems concerning the perimeter of Bar Kokhba's independent state see Schäfer, *Bar Kokhba,* pp. 102–135 (with the older literature). For a reasonable minimalistic perimeter, cf. ibid., p. 134. See now also the discussion of M. Mor, *The Bar-Kokhba Revolt. Its Extent and Effect* (Jerusalem, 1991), pp. 98–190 (Hebrew).

[18] The evidence for non-Jewish participants in the war is doubtful. For a more optimistic attitude see M. Mor, "The Bar-Kokhba Revolt and Non-Jewish Participants," *Journal of Jewish Studies* 36 (1985): 200–209.

[19] For the nature of the Roman army, see S. Applebaum, *Prolegomena to the Study of the Second Jewish Revolt (A.D. 132–135)* (Oxford, 1976).

What Did Greek and Latin Authors
Think of Jewish Nationalism?

It is not within the scope of this study to deal with Greek and Latin authors and their views about Jews and Judaism in general. Nevertheless, an attempt will be made in this chapter to see what their views were regarding Jewish nationalism. In spite of the fact that the evidence is fragmentary, one can still get a fairly good picture of what Greeks and Romans thought of Jews and Judaism in general and about Jewish nationalism in particular. One should realize that Greek and Roman intellectuals during the period 300 B.C.E.–150 C.E. were interested in Jews and Judaism to the same extent that they were interested in other nations during this period (as can be seen for instance from Strabo's *Geography*).[1] They showed interest in the origin of the Jewish nation (the Greek *ethnos* or *genos,* the Latin *gens*), which many thought was Egyptian (with varying degrees of nuances). Many authors were interested in the "peculiar" customs of the Jewish faith (as for instance circumcision, the adherence to the Sabbath, or the abstention from eating pork). Others were astonished by their "strange" invisible God, and their empty Temple (with no statues of gods put in it, Cassius Dio[2]), as well as by their refusal to worship other gods. Many authors were apparently interested in the geography of Judea (or, as the Latin literature frequently calls it, Palestine) and the so-called Dead Sea. Some merely referred to the Jews in passing within their historical accounts,[3] making casual remarks concerning their unique behavior. There are even references to places in Palestine associated with Greek mythology (Joppa and

Andromeda; cf. Pausanias[4]). A popular motif in Greek and Latin literature was the lawgiver Moses (as part of the interest the Greeks and Romans had in ancient lawgivers).[5] Occasionally one comes across some denigratory remarks such as the one found in Tacitus saying that the Jews were "base and abominable" and that their religion was a "superstition" (along with Christianity, a remark also to be found in the Roman biographer Suetonius),[6] and that they were an "impious nation." Claudius (the emperor who was himself a prolific scholar) expressed a current idea that Jews might attempt to dominate the ecumene.[7] And Philostratus, at the end of the second century C.E. and the beginning of the third, was of the opinion that "the Jews have long been in revolt not only against the Romans but against humanity."[8] Cassius Dio also has terrible things to say about the Jews in relation to their revolt in Cyrene, Cyprus, and Egypt in 115–117 C.E.[9] There is, however, no coherent, systematic anti-Semitic concept to be found in the literature of the gentiles of that particular period. Also, many of the sources from Greco-Roman times drew on one another, and none of the authors really had a profound and exact knowledge concerning the Jews.

When we come to the issue of Jewish political nationalism, it becomes quite clear from the available material that the Greeks and Romans did not have any particular interest in Jewish statehood and political nationalism beyond their interest in other states of the ancient Near East, and perhaps even less. Their interest lay more in Jewish religion and ethnic customs. Some authors refer to their organization in the Diaspora as being a unique *ethnos;* only on a few occasions does one hear about their political organization in Palestine. Whereas the Greek author Hecataeus of Abdera (who wrote a long time before the Hasmonean monarchy was created) described their political organization in Palestine in an idealistic manner, the Roman authors, who were writing after the Hasmonean state fell, denigrated the Jewish state in Palestine altogether.

Hecataeus equated the Jewish political organization of his own time with a Greek *politeia* in a highly positive manner.[10] According to him, Judea was created by Moses, who founded Jerusalem, and

in addition he established the temple that they hold in chief veneration, instituted their forms of worship and ritual, drew up their laws and ordered their political institutions. He also divided them into twelve tribes, since this is regarded as the most perfect number and corresponds to the number of months that make up a year. (4) But he had no images whatsoever of the gods made for them, being of the opinion that God is not in human form; rather the Heaven that surrounds the earth is alone divine, and rules the universe. The sacrifices that he established differ from those of other nations, as does their way of living, for as a result of their own expulsion from Egypt he introduced an unsocial and intolerant mode of life. He picked out the men of most refinement and with the greatest ability to head the entire nation, and appointed them priests; and he ordained that they should occupy themselves with the temple and the honours and sacrifices offered to their God. (5) These same men he appointed to be judges in all major disputes, and entrusted to them the guardianship of the laws and customs. For this reason the Jews never have a king, and authority over the people is regularly vested in whichever priest is regarded as superior to his colleagues in wisdom and virtue. They call this man the high priest, and believe that he acts as a messenger to them of God's commandments. (6) . . . And at the end of their laws there is even appended the statement: "These are the words that Moses heard from God and declares unto the Jews." Their lawgiver was careful also to make provision for warfare, and required the young men to cultivate manliness, steadfastness, and, generally, the endurance of every hardship. (7) He led out military expeditions against the neighbouring tribes, and after annexing much land apportioned it out, assigning equal allotments to private citizens and greater ones to the priests, in order that they, by virtue of receiving more ample revenues, might be undistracted and apply themselves continually to the worship of God. The common citizens were forbidden to sell their individual plots, lest there be some who for their own advantage should buy them up, and by oppressing the poorer classes bring on a scarcity of manpower. (8) He required those who dwelt in the land to rear their children, and since offspring could be cared for at little cost, the Jews were from the start a populous nation. As to marriage and the burial of the dead, he saw to it that their customs should differ widely from those of other men. But later, when they became subject to foreign rule, as a result of their mingling with men of other nation (both under Persian rule and under that of the Macedonians who overthrew the Persians), many of their traditional practices were disturbed.[11]

The motif that was to recur after Hecataeus of Abdera's time in the literature was of Jerusalem being a holy and important *metropolis,* which had a magnificent temple with a rich treasury in it. The Temple is referred to as being the center of world Jewry (as we find later in Philo Judaeus).

Strabo was the first (whose description is available to us) to view the Jewish Hasmonean state in a negative manner, calling its rulers and kings "tyrants." Among other things he says,

> At any rate, when now Judaea was under the rule of tyrants, Alexander was first to declare himself king instead of priest; and both Hyrcanus and Aristobulus were sons of his; and when they were at variance about the empire, Pompey went over and overthrew them and rased their fortifications, and in particular took Jerusalem itself by force; for it was a rocky and well-walled fortress; and though well supplied with water inside, its outside territory was wholly without water; and it had a trench cut in rock, sixty feet in depth and two hundred and fifty feet in breadth; and, from the stone that had been hewn out, the wall of the temple was fenced with towers. Pompey seized the city, it is said, after watching for the day of fasting, when the Judaeans were abstaining from all work; he filled up the trench and threw ladders across it; moreover, he gave orders to rase all the walls and, so far as he could, destroyed the haunts of robbers and the treasure-holds of the tyrants.[12]

This is, of course, a derogatory description of the Jewish state, but it was not an unusual one in terms of Greek (and Latin) political thought. Tyranny was seen as part of the legitimate cycle of constitutions (*metabole*), and many other constitutions of non-Jewish peoples were described by Greek authors in similar terms.[13] Pompeius Trogus, however, is somewhat more positive, saying that the Jews were the "first of all eastern peoples that regained their liberty."[14]

In Tacitus's *Histories* there is an exceptionally long excursus on the Jews, which is intertwined with the account of the Great War against Rome.[15] Among other traits of the Jewish people he said that Jerusalem was "a famous city" and that the Land had exact boundaries—"is bounded by Arabia on the east. . . ." He, like Strabo, describes the Hasmonean kingdom in negative hues, saying,

> Later on, since the power of Macedon had waned, the Parthians were not yet come to their strength, and the Romans were far away, the Jews selected their own kings. These in turn were expelled by the fickle mob; but recovering their throne by force of arms, they banished citizens, destroyed towns, killed brothers, wives, and parents, and dared essay every other kind of royal crime without hesitation; but they fostered the national superstition, for they had assumed the priesthood to support their civil authority.[16]

Interestingly, it is Tacitus who clearly and bluntly blames the wicked procurators of Rome for the outbreak of the Great War. This is how a Roman in a somewhat simplistic manner saw it many years after its occurrence: "Claudius made Judea a province and entrusted it to Roman knights or to freedmen; one of the latter, Antonius Felix, practiced every kind of cruelty and lust, wielding the power of king with all the instincts of a slave" (*Histories* 5.9.3). According to a late tradition it was Tacitus who also claimed that Titus planned to destroy the Jewish Temple in Jerusalem—contrary to Josephus, who claimed that it was an initiative of the undisciplined soldiers—because his purpose was to uproot the religion of both Jews and Christians (Sulpicius Severus, *Chronica* 2.30.7).

Fronto, in the second century C.E., may also have referred to their superstition.[17] Apuleius described the Jews as "superstitious."[18] The revolts of the Jews under Trajan and Hadrian brought about some changes in the views of Greeks and Romans regarding the Jewish nation. Ptolemy, a Greek from Alexandria, draws a detailed map of Palestine and describes the Jews alongside the inhabitants of Coele-Syria and Idumaea as being "bold, godless, and scheming." According to him, astrological as well as geographical conditions influence the character of nations.[19] Fronto refers to the Jewish war under Hadrian, only mentioning the vast numbers of Roman soldiers killed by the Jews.[20] Appian, writing after Bar Kokhba's futile revolt, highlights Jerusalem, saying, "The Jewish nation alone still resisted and

Pompey conquered them, sent their king, Aristobulus, to Rome, and destroyed their greatest, and to them holiest, city, Jerusalem, as Ptolemy, the first king of Egypt had formerly done. It was afterward rebuilt and Vespasian destroyed it again, and Hadrian did the same in our time."[21] Pausanias states that Hadrian "never voluntarily entered upon a war, but he reduced the Hebrews beyond Syria, who had rebelled."[22] According to Cassius Dio during Nerva's reign, "no persons were permitted to accuse anybody of *maiestas* or of adopting the Jewish mode of life."[23]

As far as one can learn from the available evidence, the gentile Greek and Roman authors were interested in the Jews inasmuch as they played a role in the history of the period. Judging from the remaining literary evidence, they certainly had no great interest in them. Jewish political nationalism in the Land of Israel was viewed in keeping with views concerning other states of the Hellenistic Near East before the Roman occupation, in other words, as a (decadent) Hellenistic monarchy. The authors who wrote after the Roman domination of the ancient Near East considered Judea to be a part of the Roman Empire, yet a stormy one. Moreover, the view emerges from most texts that both Judea and other peoples and monarchies were incapable of being independent and sovereign, and therefore ought to be under Roman sway. The Jews of the Diaspora were usually seen by Greek and Latin authors as an *ethnos* that entertained rather strange religious ideas, alien to the gentiles.[24]

Notes

[1] For all of the documents on Jews and Judaism in Greek and Latin literature with the older bibliography, see M. Stern, *Greek and Latin Authors on Jews and Judaism,* 3 vols. (Jerusalem, 1974–1984).

[2] Ibid., 2.351.

[3] It is quite remarkable that someone like Arrian of Nicomedia (ca. 95–175 C.E.) did not mention them throughout his history of Alexander the Great (even when he records Alexander's conquest of Palestine). He did mention them, however, in his lost work the *Parthica* (cf. fragments in Stern, *Greek and Latin Authors,* 2.152).

[4] Ibid., 2.192–194.

[5] For this particular motif see J. G. Gager, *Moses in Greco-Roman Paganism* (Nashville, Tenn., 1972).

[6] Tacitus, *Annals* 15.44.2–5; Suetonius, *Nero* 16.2. And cf. S. Benko, "Pagan Criticism of Christianity During the First Two Centuries A.D.," *Aufstieg und Niedergang der römischen Welt* 2.23.2 (1980): 1055–1118.

[7] His famous letter to the Alexandrians in 41 C.E., lines 100–101: "If they do not obey, in every way I will move against them just as if they were raising up some common plague for the inhabited world." (It may, however, be a reference, as in Tacitus, *Annals* 15.44, to the Christians). Cf. R. K. Sherk, *The Roman Empire: Augustus to Hadrian* (Cambridge, 1988), p. 86.

[8] Stern, *Greek and Latin Authors,* 2.341.

[9] Ibid., 2.385–386.

[10] Cf. D. Mendels, "Hecataeus of Abdera and a Jewish 'Patrios Politeia' of the Persian Period (Diodorus Siculus XL, 3)," *Zeitschrift für alttestamentliche Wissenschaft* 95 (1983): 96–110.

[11] Hecataeus of Abdera, in Diodorus Siculus 40.3.3–8; see Stern, *Greek and Latin Authors,* 1.26–27.

[12] Strabo, 16.2.40; see ibid., 1.307–308.

[13] Cf. Plato, *Republic* books 8–9; and cf. in general T. A. Sinclair, *A History of Greek Political Thought* (London, 1951).

[14] *Libertas* is a very positive political notion in Rome at the time of Pompeius Trogus; cf. C. Wirszubski, *Libertas as a Political Idea at Rome During the Late Republic and Early Principate* (Cambridge, 1950); and Stern, *Greek and Latin Authors,* 1.342.

[15] Stern, *Greek and Latin Authors,* 2.17–63 and F. F. Bruce, "Tacitus on Jewish History," *Journal of Jewish Studies* 29 (1984): 33–44.

[16] Tacitus, *Histories* 5.3; see Stern, *Greek and Latin Authors,* 2.41–43.

[17] Ibid., 2.176.

[18] Ibid., 2.205.

[19] Ibid., 2.165.

[20] Ibid., 2.177.

[21] Appian 11.8.50; see ibid., 2.179–181.

[22] Ibid., 2.192.

[23] Ibid., 2.385.

[24] Ibid., 1–2, passim. See recently I. Shatzman, "The Hasmoneans in Greco-Roman Historiography," *Zion* 57.1 (1992): 5-64 (Hebrew), who claims that some of the denigratory language against Jews in Gentile sources could have had a Jewish origin. He rightly comes to the conclusion that there was no vulgate of "antisemitic" sayings against Jews. I should like to add here that when one views the encounter of Jews with Gentiles during the period my book has surveyed, one can come to the conclusion that clashes with Gentiles were the exception rather than the rule, in particular on the political scene. See recently a stimulating approach to the relations of Jews and Gentiles, L. H. Feldman, *Jew and Gentile in the Ancient World: Attitudes and Interactions from Alexander to Justinian* (Princeton, 1993).

The Maccabean Period

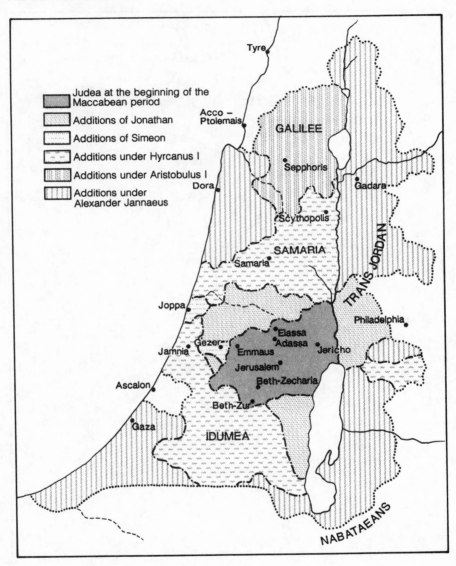

Judea at the beginning of the Maccabean period

Additions of Jonathan

Additions of Simeon

Additions under Hyrcanus I

Additions under Aristobulus I

Additions under Alexander Jannaeus

Tyre

Acco – Ptolemais

GALILEE

Sepphoris

Dora

Gadara

Scythopolis

SAMARIA

Samaria

TRANS-JORDAN

Joppa

Philadelphia

Elassa

Adassa

Gezer

Emmaus

Jericho

Jamnia

Jerusalem

Beth-Zecharia

Ascalon

Beth-Zur

Gaza

IDUMEA

NABATAEANS

Herod's Kingdom

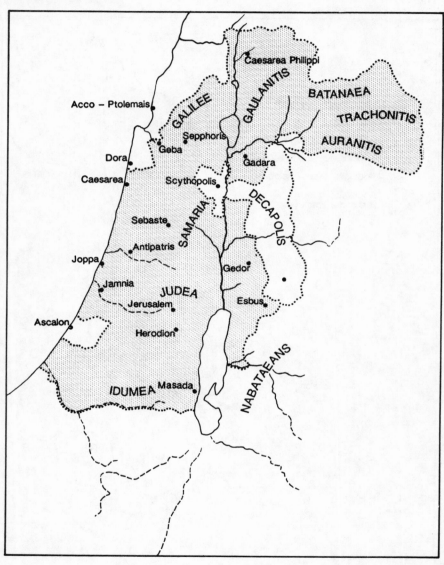

Caesarea Philippi

GALILEE
GAULANITIS
BATANAEA
TRACHONITIS
AURANITIS

Acco – Ptolemais

Sepphoris

Geba

Dora

Gadara

Caesarea

Scythópolis

DECAPOLIS

Sebaste

SAMARIA

Antipatris

Joppa

Gedor

Jamnia

JUDEA

Esbus

Jerusalem

Ascalon

Herodion

IDUMEA Masada

NABATAEANS

The Division of Herod's Kingdom

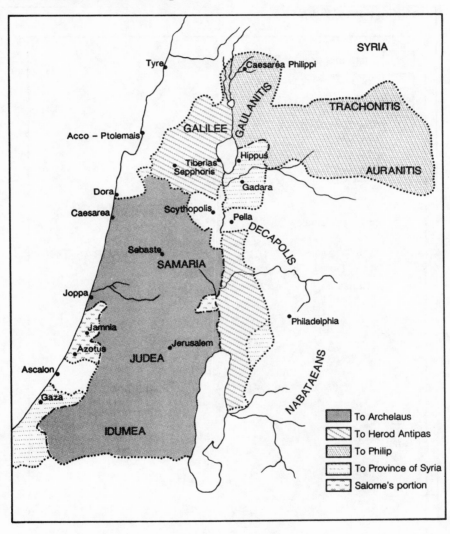

The Kingdom of Agrippa I

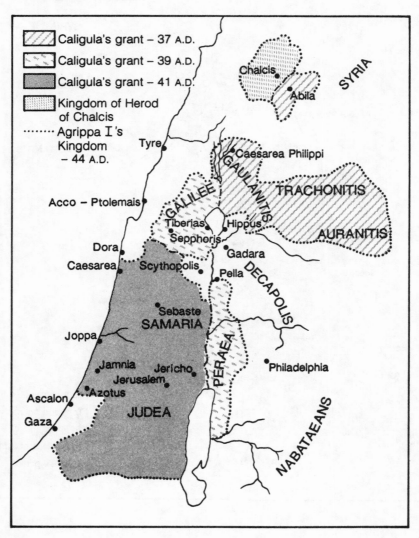

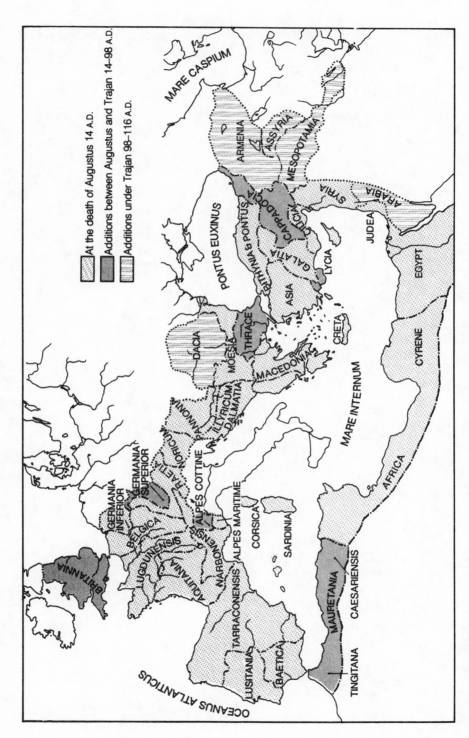

The Roman Empire from Augustus to Trajan and Hadrian

At the death of Augustus 14 A.D.

Additions between Augustus and Trajan 14-98 A.D.

Additions under Trajan 98-116 A.D.

MARE CASPIUM

ARMENIA

ASSYRIA

MESOPOTAMIA

SYRIA

ARABIA

JUDEA

EGYPT

CYRENE

CAPPADOCIA

CILICIA

GALATIA

LYCIA

BITHYNIA & PONTUS

PONTUS EUXINUS

ASIA

CRETA

THRACE

DACIA

MOESIA

MACEDONIA

DALMATIA

ILLYRICUM

PANNONIA

NORICUM

RAETIA

MARE INTERNUM

AFRICA

GERMANIA SUPERIOR

GERMANIA INFERIOR

BELGICA

LUGDUNENSIS

ALPES COTTIE

ALPES MARITIME

ALPES PENNINAE

NARBONE

AQUITANIA

TARRACONENSIS

CORSICA

SARDINIA

LUSITANIA

BAETICA

MAURETANIA CAESARIENSIS

TINGITANA

BRITANNIA

OCEANUS ATLANTICUS

Selected Bibliography

Note: all biblical commentaries used in the notes are *Anchor Bible* (*) and
Hermeneia (†), unless otherwise stated.

Aharoni, Y. and M. Avi-Yonah, *The Macmillan Bible Atlas* (New York, 1968).

Alon, G., *Jews, Judaism and the Classical World* (Jerusalem, 1977).

Amaru Halpern, B., "Land Theology in Josephus' Jewish Antiquities," *Jewish Quarterly Review* 71 (1980–1981): 202–229.

Ancient Israelite Religion, ed. P. D. Miller et al. (Philadelphia, 1987).

Applebaum, S., "The Zealots: The Case for Revaluation," *Journal of Roman Studies* 61 (1971): 156–170.

———, "The Struggle for the Soil and the Revolt of 66–73 C.E.," *Eretz-Israel* 12 (1975): 125–128 (Hebrew).

———, *Judaea in Hellenistic and Roman Times* (Leiden, 1989).

Attridge, H. W., *The Interpretation of Biblical History in the Antiquitates Judaicae of Flavius Josephus* (Missoula, Mont., 1976).

———, *The Epistle to the Hebrews*† (Philadelphia, 1989).

——— and R. A. Oden, Jr., *Philo of Byblos: The Phoenician History* (Washington, D.C., 1981).

Avigad, N., *Discovering Jerusalem* (Oxford, 1984).

Baer, Y., "Jerusalem in the Times of the Great Revolt," *Zion* 36 (1971): 127–190; 37 (1972): 120 (Hebrew).

Bagnall, R. S., *The Administration of the Ptolemaic Possessions Outside Egypt* (Leiden, 1976).

Bar Kochva, B., *Judas Maccabaeus* (Cambridge, 1989).

The Bar Kokhba Revolt: A New Approach, ed. A. Oppenheimer and U. Rappaport (Jerusalem, 1984) (Hebrew).

Barnett, P. W., "Under Tiberius all was Quiet," *New Testament Studies* 21 (1975): 564–571.

Barret, A. A., *Caligula: The Corruption of Power* (New Haven and London, 1989).

Barth, M., *Ephesians (1–3)** (Garden City, N.Y., 1974).

———, *Ephesians (4–6)** (Garden City, N.Y., 1974).

Bartlett, J. R., *Jews in the Hellenistic World* (Cambridge, 1985).

Baumgarten, A. I., *The Phoenician History of Philo of Byblos* (Leiden, 1983).

Ben-Shalom, I., "The Shammai School and Its Place in the Political and Social History of Eretz Israel in the First Century A.D.," Ph.D. diss., Tel-Aviv, 1980 (Hebrew).

———, "Events and Ideology of the Yavneh Period as Indirect Causes of the Bar-Kokhva Revolt," in *The Bar Kokhva Revolt,* ed. A. Oppenheimer and U. Rappaport (Jerusalem, 1984), pp. 1–12 (Hebrew).

Between Republic and Empire: Interpretations of Augustus and His Principate, ed. K. A. Raaflaub and M. Toher (Berkeley, Los Angeles, and Oxford, 1990).

Betz, H. D., *Galatians†* (Philadelphia, 1979).

Bevan, E., *A History of Egypt under the Ptolemaic Dynasty* (London, 1927).

Beyer, K., *Die aramäischen Texte vom Toten Meer* (Göttingen, 1984).

Bickerman(n), E. J., *From Ezra to the Last of the Maccabees* (New York, 1949).

———, *Studies in Jewish and Christian History,* 3 vols. (Leiden, 1976–1986).

———, *The God of the Maccabees: Studies in the Meaning and Origin of the Maccabean Revolt* (Leiden, 1979).

Bilde, P., "The Causes of the Jewish War According to Josephus," *Journal for the Study of Judaism in the Persian, Hellenistic and Roman Period* 10 (1979): 179–202.

Biran, A., "To the God who is in Dan," in *Temples and High Places in Biblical Times,* ed. A. Biran (Jerusalem, 1981), pp. 142–151.

Blenkinsopp, J., "Prophecy and Priesthood in Josephus," *Journal of Jewish Studies* 25 (1974): 239–262.

Borg, M. J., *Conflict, Holiness, and Politics in the Teachings of Jesus* (New York and Toronto, 1984).

Bosworth, A. B., *Conquest and Empire: the Reign of Alexander the Great* (Cambridge, 1988).

Bousset, W., *Die Religion des Judentums im späthellenistischen Zeitalter,* 3d ed. (Tübingen, 1966).

Bowersock, G. W., *Augustus and the Greek World* (Oxford, 1965).

———, *Roman Arabia* (Cambridge, Mass. and London, 1983).

Bowman, A. K., *Egypt after the Pharaohs, 332 B.C.–A.D. 642* (London, 1986).

Brandon, S. G. F., *Jesus and the Zealots* (Manchester, 1967).

Braund, D., *Rome and the Friendly King* (London, 1984).

———, "The Caucasian Frontier: Myth, Exploration and the Dynamics of Imperialism," in *The Defence of the Roman and Byzantine East,* ed. P. Freeman and D. Kennedy (Oxford, 1986), 1.31–49.

Bringmann, K., *Hellenistische Reform und Religionsverfolgung in Judaea* (Göttingen and Zurich, 1983).

Brown, R. E., *The Gospel According to John (I–XII)** (Garden City, N.Y., 1966).

———, *The Gospel According to John (XIII–XXI)** (Garden City, N.Y., 1970).

Bruneau, P., "Les Israélites de Delos et la Juiverie délienne," *Bulletin de correspondance hellénique* 106 (1982): 465ff.

Brunt, P. A., "Charges of Provincial Maladministration under the Early Principate," *Historia* 10 (1961): 189–227.

———, "The Romanization of the Local Ruling Classes in the Roman Empire," in *Assimilation et résistance à la culture greco-romaine dans le monde ancien,* ed. D. M. Pippidi (Paris and Bucharest, 1976), pp. 161–173.

———, "Josephus on Social Conflicts in Roman Judaea," *Klio* 59 (1977): 149–153.

———, *Roman Imperial Themes* (Oxford, 1990).

Buber, M., *Israel and Palestine: The History of an Idea* (London, 1952).

Buchanan, G. W., *To the Hebrews,** 2d. ed. (Garden City, N.Y., 1978).

Bunge, J. G., "Untersuchungen zum zweiten Makkabäerbuch," Ph.D. diss., Bonn, 1971.

Burstein, S. M., *The Babyloniaca of Berossus* (Malibu, Calif., 1978).

———, *The Hellenistic Age from the Battle of Ipsos to the Death of Kleopatra VII* (Cambridge, 1985).

Burton, A., *Diodorus Siculus, Book I: A Commentary* (Leiden, 1972).

Bussink, T. A., *Der Tempel von Jerusalem,* 2 vols. (Leiden, 1970).

The Cambridge Ancient History, ed. F. W. Walbank, A. E. Astin, et al., 2d ed., vols. 7.1–2, 8 (Cambridge, 1984–1989) (= *CAH*).

Camponovo, O., *Königtum, Königsherrschaft und Reich Gottes in den Frühjüdischen Schriften* (Göttingen, 1984).

Cary, M. and H. H. Scullard, *A History of Rome* (London, 1975).

Charles, R. H., *The Apocrypha and Pseudepigrapha of the Old Testament,* 2 vols. (Oxford, 1913).

Charlesworth, J. H., *The Pseudepigrapha and Modern Research with a Supplement* (Chico, Calif., 1981).

———, *Jesus Within Judaism: New Light from Exciting Archaeological Discoveries* (New York, 1988).

Coggins, R. J., *Samaritans and Jews* (Oxford, 1975).

Cohen, N. M., *Jewish Bible Personages in the New Testament* (Lanham and London, 1989).

Cohen, S. A., *The Three Crowns: Structure of Communal Politics in Early Rabbinic Jewry* (Cambridge and Sydney, 1990).

Cohen, S. J. D., *Josephus in Galilee and Rome: His Vita and Development as a Historian* (Leiden, 1979).

———, *From the Maccabees to the Mishnah* (Philadelphia, 1987).

Collins, J. J., *Between Athens and Jerusalem: Jewish Identity in the Hellenistic Diaspora* (New York, 1983).

———, *The Apocalyptic Imagination: An Introduction to the Jewish Matrix of Christianity* (New York, 1987).

Compendia rerum iudaicarum ad Novum Testamentum: The Jewish People in the First Century, 2 vols., ed. S. Safrai et al. (Assen, 1974–1976).

Conzelmann, H., *Acts of the Apostles*† (Philadelphia, 1987).

———, *1 Corinthians*† (Philadelphia, 1975).

Cross, F. M., *The Ancient Library of Qumran and Modern Biblical Studies* (New York, 1958).

———, *Canaanite Myth and Hebrew Epic: Essays in the History of Religion of Israel* (Cambridge, Mass., 1973).

——— and S. Talmon, *Qumran and the History of the Biblical Text* (Cambridge, Mass. and London, 1975).

Cullmann, O., *The State in the New Testament* (London, 1957).

Davies, P. R., "Hasidim in the Maccabean Period," *Journal of Jewish Studies* 28 (1977): 127–140.

———, "The Meaning of Philo's Text about the Gilded Shields," *Journal of Theological Studies* n.s. 37 (1986): 109–114.

Davies, W. D., *The Gospel and the Land* (Berkeley, Los Angeles, and London, 1974).

———, *The Territorial Dimension of Judaism* (Berkeley, Los Angeles, and London, 1982).

The Defence of the Roman and Byzantine East, BAR International Series 297, ed. P. Freeman and D. Kennedy, 2 vols. (Oxford, 1986).

De Lange, N. R. M., "Jewish Attitudes to the Roman Empire," in *Imperialism in the Ancient World*, ed. P. D. A. Garnsey and C. R. Whittaker (Cambridge, 1978), pp. 255–281.

Delcor, M., "Melchizedek from Genesis to the Qumran Texts and the Epistle to the Hebrews," *Journal for the Study of Judaism in the Persian, Hellenistic and Roman Period* 2 (1971): 115–135.

Denis, A. M., *Introduction aux pseudépigraphes grecs d'Ancien Testament* (Leiden, 1970).

De Ste Croix, G. E. M., *The Class Struggle in the Ancient Greek World* (London, 1981).

De Vaux, R., *Archaeology and the Dead Sea Scrolls* (London, 1973).

Discoveries in the Judaean Desert, 8 vols. (Oxford, 1955–1990).

Doran, R., *Temple Propaganda: The Purpose and Character of 2 Maccabees* (Washington, D.C., 1981).

Duhaime, J., "The War Scroll from Qumran and the Greco-Roman Tactical Treatises," *Revue de Qumran* 49–52 (1988): 133–151.

Dyson, S. L., "Native Revolts in the Roman Empire," *Historia* 20 (1971): 239–274.

———, "Native Revolt Patterns in the Roman Empire," *Aufstieg und Niedergang der römischen Welt* 2.3 (1975): 138–175.

Eddy, S. K., *The King is Dead: Studies in the Near Eastern Resistance to Hellenism, 334–31 B.C.E.* (Lincoln, Neb., 1961).

Efron, J., *Studies on the Hasmonean Period* (Leiden and Cologne, 1987).

Egger, R., *Josephus Flavius und die Samaritaner* (Fribourg and Göttingen, 1986).

Eph ʿal, I., *The Ancient Arabs* (Jerusalem, 1982).

Farmer, W. R., *Maccabees, Zealots, and Josephus: An Inquiry into Jewish Nationalism in the Greco-Roman Period* (New York, 1956).

Feldman, L. H., *Josephus and Modern Scholarship, 1937–1980* (Berlin and New York, 1984).

———, "Josephus' Portrait of David," *Hebrew Union College Annual* 60 (1989): 129–174.

Ferguson, J., *Utopias of the Classical World* (London, 1975).

Fischer, T., Hasmoneans and Seleucids: Aspects of War and Policy in the Second and First Centuries B.C.E.," in *Greece and Rome in Eretz Israel*, ed. A. Kasher et al. (Jerusalem, 1990), pp. 3–19.

Fitzmyer, J. A., *The Genesis Apocryphon of Qumran Cave I* (Rome, 1971).

———, *The Gospel According to Luke (I–IX)** (Garden City, N.Y., 1981).

———, *The Gospel According to Luke (X–XXIV)** (Garden City, N.Y., 1985).

Flusser, D., "The Kingdom of Rome in the Eyes of the Hasmoneans, and as Seen by the Essenes," *Zion* 48 (1983): 149–176 (Hebrew).

———, *Judaism and the Origins of Christianity* (Jerusalem, 1988).

Ford, J. M., *Revelation** (Garden City, N.Y., 1975).

Fornara, C. W., *The Nature of History in Ancient Greece and Rome* (Berkeley, Los Angeles, and London, 1983).

Fornaro, P., *Flavio Giuseppe, Tacito e l'Impero* (Turin, 1980).

Frankfort, H., *Kingship and the Gods* (Chicago, 1948).

Fraser, P. M., *Ptolemaic Alexandria*, 3 vols. (Oxford, 1972).

Freudenthal, J., *Hellenistische Studien*, 2 vols. (Breslau, 1875).

Freyne, S., *Galilee from Alexander the Great to Hadrian, 323 B.C.E. to 135 C.E.* (Washington, D.C. and Notre Dame, 1980).

———, *Galilee, Jesus, and the Gospels* (Philadelphia, 1988).

Fuks, A., *The Ancestral Constitution* (London, 1953).

Fuks, G., "Again on the Episode of the Gilded Roman Shields at Jerusalem," *Harvard Theological Review* 75 (1982): 503–507.

Furnish, V. P., *II Corinthians** (Garden City, N.Y., 1984).

Gafni, I., "On the Use of 1 Macc by Josephus," *Zion* 45 (1980): 81–95 (Hebrew).

Geiger, J., "The History of Judas Maccabaeus: One Aspect of Hellenistic Historiography," *Zion* 49 (1984): 1–8 (Hebrew).

———, "Local Patriotism in the Hellenistic Cities of Palestine," in *Greece and Rome in Eretz Israel*, ed. A. Kasher et al. (Jerusalem, 1990), pp. 141–150.

Gichon, M., "Cestius Gallus' Campaign in Judaea," *Palestine Exploration Quarterly* 113 (1981): 39–62.

Ginsberg, L., *The Legends of the Jews*, 6 vols. (Philadelphia, 1910–1938).

Goldstein, J. A., *I Maccabees** (Garden City, N.Y., 1976).

———, *II Maccabees** (Garden City, N.Y., 1983).

Goodman, M. D., *The Ruling Class of Judaea: The Origins of the Jewish Revolt Against Rome, A.D. 66–70* (Cambridge, 1987).

Goudriaan, K., *Ethnicity in Ptolemaic Egypt* (Amsterdam, 1988).

The Great Jewish Revolt: Factors and Circumstances Leading to Its Outbreak, ed. A. Kasher et al. (Jerusalem, 1983) (Hebrew).

Greece and Rome in Eretz Israel, ed. A. Kasher et al. (Jerusalem, 1990).

Green, P., *Alexander to Actium: The Historical Evolution of the Hellenistic Age* (Berkeley, Los Angeles, and Oxford, 1990).

Griffin, M., *Nero: The End of a Dynasty* (New Haven, 1985).

Griffith, G. T., *The Mercenaries of the Hellenistic World* (repr., Groningen, 1968).

Gruen, E., *The Hellenistic World and the Coming of Rome,* 2 vols. (Berkeley, Los Angeles, and London, 1984).

Gutman, Y., *The Beginnings of Jewish-Hellenistic Literature,* 2 vols. (Jerusalem, 1969) (Hebrew).

Hachlili, R., *Ancient Jewish Art and Archaeology in the Land of Israel* (Leiden, 1988).

Hadas, M., *Hellenistic Culture: Fusion and Diffusion* (New York, 1959).

Hadas-Lebel, M., "L'Évolution de l'image . . . ," *Aufstieg und Niedergang der römischen Welt* 2.20.1 (1987): 715–856.

Haenchen, E., *John 1†* (Philadelphia, 1984).

——, *John 2†* (Philadelphia, 1984).

Hamilton, J. R., *Alexander the Great* (London, 1973).

Hanson, K. C., "The Herodians and Mediterranean Kinship," *Biblical Theology Bulletin* 19 (1989): 75–84, 142–151; 20 (1990): 10–21.

Haran, M., *Temple and Temple-Service in Ancient Israel* (Oxford, 1978).

Heinemann, I., "The Relationship Between the Jewish People and Their Land in Hellenistic Jewish Literature," *Zion* 13–14 (1948–1949): 1–9 (Hebrew).

——, *Darke Ha'agada* (Jerusalem, 1952) (Hebrew).

Hellenism and the Rise of Rome, ed. P. Grimal (London, 1968).

Hengel, M., *Judaism and Hellenism,* 2 vols. (London and Philadelphia, 1974).

——, *Jews, Greeks and Barbarians* (Philadelphia, 1980).

——, *The "Hellenization" of Judaea in the First Century after Christ* (Philadelphia, 1989).

——, *The Zealots* (Edinburgh, 1989).

——, J. H. Charlesworth, and D. Mendels, "The Polemical Character of the 'On Kingship' in the Temple Scroll: An Attempt at Dating 11Q Temple," *Journal of Jewish Studies* 37 (1986): 28–38.

Herr, M. D., "The Problems of War on the Sabbath in the Second Temple and Talmudic Periods," *Tarbiz* 30 (1961): 242–256, 341–356 (Hebrew).

——, "From the Destruction of the Temple to the Revolt of Bar Kokhba," in *The History of Eretz Israel: The Roman Byzantine Period,* ed. M. Stern (Jerusalem, 1984), vol. 4, pp. 283–370 (Hebrew).

Holladay, C. R., *Fragments from Hellenistic Jewish Authors,* 2 vols. to date (Chico, Calif. and Atlanta, 1983–1989).

Holum, K. G. et al, *King Herod's Dream: Caesarea on the Sea* (New York and London, 1988).

Horgan, M. P., "A Lament over Jerusalem (4Q 179)," *Journal of Jewish Studies* 18 (1973): 222–234.

——, *Pesharim: Qumran Interpretations of Biblical Books* (Washington, D.C., 1979).

Hornbostel, W., *Sarapis. Studien zur Überlieferungsgeschichte, den Erscheinungsformen und Wandlungen der Gestalt eines Gottes* (Leiden, 1973).

Horsley, R. A., "Josephus and the Bandits," *Journal for the Study of Judaism in the Persian, Hellenistic and Roman Period* 10 (1979): 37–63.

———, "The Sicarii: Ancient Jewish 'Terrorists,' " *Journal of Religion* 52 (1979): 435–458.

———, "Ancient Jewish Banditry and the Revolt Against Rome, A.D. 66–70," *Catholic Biblical Quarterly* 43 (1981): 409–432.

———, "Menahem in Jerusalem: A Brief Messianic Episode among the Sicarii not 'Zealot Messianism,' " *Novum Testamentum* 27 (1985): 334–348.

———, "High Priests and the Politics of Roman Palestine: A Contextual Analysis of the Evidence in Josephus," *Journal for the Study of Judaism in the Persian, Hellenistic and Roman Period* 17 (1986): 23–55.

———, "Popular Prophetic Movements at the Time of Jesus," *Journal for the Study of the New Testament* 26 (1986): 3–27.

———, "The Zealots: Their Origin, Relationships and Importance in the Jewish Revolt," *Novum Testamentum* 28 (1986): 159–192.

———, *Jesus and the Spiral of Violence: Popular Jewish Resistance in Roman Palestine* (San Francisco, 1987).

Horst, P. W. van der, *Essays on the Jewish World of Early Christianity* (Göttingen, 1990).

Hultgård, A., "The Ideal 'Levite,' the Davidic Messiah and the Saviour Priest in the Testament of the Twelve Patriarchs," in *Ideal Figures,* ed. J. J. Collins and G. W. E. Nickelsburg (Chico, Calif., 1980), pp. 93–110.

Ideal Figures in Ancient Judaism: Profiles and Paradigms, ed. J. J. Collins and G. W. E. Nickelsburg (Chico, Calif., 1980).

Isaac, B., "Bandits in Judaea and Arabia," *Harvard Studies in Classical Philology* 88 (1984): 171–203.

———, "Judaea after A.D. 70," *Journal of Jewish Studies* 35 (1984): 44–50.

———, *The Limits of Empire* (Oxford, 1990).

Jacobson, H., *The Exagoge of Ezekiel* (Cambridge, 1983).

Jacoby, F., *Die Fragmente der griechischen Historiker,* 14 vols. (repr. Leiden, 1954–1969).

Japhet, S., *The Ideology of the Book of Chronicles and Its Place in Biblical Thought* (Frankfurt am Main and Paris, 1989).

Jaubert, A., *La Notion d'alliance dans le Judaisme* (Paris, 1963).

Jellinek, A., *Bet ha-Midrash,* 7 vols. (Jerusalem, 1938) (Hebrew).

Jeremias, J., *Jerusalem in the Time of Jesus* (London, 1969).

Jerusalem in the Second Temple Period: Abraham Schalit Memorial Volume, ed. A. Oppenheimer et al. (Jerusalem, 1980) (Hebrew).

Jerusalem Revealed: Archaeology in the Holy City, 1968–1974, ed. Y. Yadin (Jerusalem, 1975).

Jesus and the Politics of His Day, ed. E. Bammel and C. F. D. Moule (Cambridge and New York, 1984).

Jewish Writings of the Second Temple Period, ed. M. E. Stone (Assen and Philadelphia, 1984).

Josephus, the Bible, and History, ed. L. H. Feldman and G. Hata (Detroit, 1989).

Judaisms and Their Messiahs at the Turn of the Christian Era, ed. J. Neusner et al. (Cambridge, 1987).

Kasher, A., *The Jews in Hellenistic and Roman Egypt* (Tübingen, 1985).

———, *Jews, Idumaeans, and Ancient Arabs* (Tübingen, 1988).

———, *Jews and Hellenistic Cities in Eretz Israel* (Tübingen, 1990).

Kloner, A., "Underground Hiding Complexes from the Bar Kochba War in the Judaean Shephela," *Biblical Archaeologist* 46.4 (1983): 210–221.

Knibb, M. A., "The Exile in the Literature of the Intertestamental Period," *The Heythrop Journal* 17 (1976): 253–272.

Kobelski, P. J., *Melchizedek and Melchiresa* (Washington, D.C., 1981).

Koester, H., *Introduction to the New Testament,* 2 vols. (Berlin, 1982).

Kraabel, A. T., "The Roman Diaspora: Six Questionable Assumptions," *Journal of Jewish Studies* 33 (1982): 445–464.

Kraft, R. A., "The Multiform Jewish Heritage of Early Christianity," in *Christianity, Judaism and Other Greco-Roman Cults,* ed. J. Neusner (Leiden, 1975), part 3, pp. 174–199.

Kreissing, H., *Die sozialen Zusammenhänge des judaischen Krieges: Klassen und Klassenkampf in Palästina des I. Jahrhunderts v.u. Z* (Berlin, 1970).

Kuhrt, A., "Berossus' *Babyloniaka* and Seleucid Rule in Babylonia," in *Hellenism in the East,* ed. A. Kuhrt and S. Sherwin-White (Berkeley, Los Angeles, and London, 1987), pp. 32–56.

——— and S. Sherwin-White, eds., *Hellenism in the East: The Interaction of Greek and Non-Greek Civilizations from Syria to Central Asia after Alexander* (Berkeley, Los Angeles, and London, 1987).

Das Land Israel in biblischer Zeit, ed. G. Strecker (Göttingen, 1983).

Levick, B., *Claudius* (New Haven and London, 1990).

Levine, L. I., "On the Political Involvement of the Pharisees under Herod and the Procurators," *Kathedra* 8 (1978): 12–28 (Hebrew).

———, "The Political Struggle Between Pharisees and Sadduccees in the Hasmonean Period," in *A. Schalit Memorial Volume: Jerusalem in the Second Temple Period,* ed. A. Oppenheimer et al. (Jerusalem, 1980), pp. 61–83.

Lewy, J. H., *Studies in Jewish Hellenism* (Jerusalem, 1969) (Hebrew).

Licht, J., "An Ideal Town Plan from Qumran—The Description of the New Jerusalem," *Israel Exploration Journal* 29 (1979): 45–59.

Lichtenberger, H., *Studien zum Menschenbild in Texten der Qumrangemeinde* (Göttingen, 1980).

Lichtheim, M., *Ancient Egyptian Literature: A Book of Readings,* 3 vols. (Berkeley, Los Angeles, and London, 1973–1980).

Liver, J., "The Doctrine of the Two Messiahs in Sectarian Literature in the Time of the Second Commonwealth," *Harvard Theological Review* 52 (1959): 149–185.

Lloyd, A. B., "Nationalist Propaganda in Ptolemaic Egypt," *Historia* 31 (1982): 33–56.

Lloyd-Jones, H. and P. Parsons, *Supplementum hellenisticum* (Berlin and New York, 1983).

MacDonald, J., *The Theology of the Samaritans* (London, 1964).

———, *The Samaritan Chronicle II* (Berlin, 1969).

McEwan, G. J. P., *Priest and Temple in Hellenistic Babylonia* (Wiesbaden, 1981).

McKelvey, R. J., *The New Temple: The Church in the New Testament* (Oxford, 1969).

MacMullen, R., *Roman Social Relations, 50 B.C. to A.D. 284* (New Haven, 1974).

————, *Paganism in the Roman Empire* (New Haven and London, 1981).

Magie, D., *Roman Rule in Asia Minor: To the End of the Third Century after Christ*, 2 vols. (Princeton, 1950).

Mann, C. S., and W. F. Albright, *Mark** (Garden City, N.Y., 1986).

Mendels, D., "Hellenistic Utopia and the Essenes," *Harvard Theological Review* 72 (1979): 207–222.

————, " 'On Kingship' in the 'Temple Scroll' and the Ideological *Vorlage* of the Seven Banquets in the 'Letter of Aristeas to Philocrates,' " *Aegyptus* 59 (1979): 127–136.

————, "The Five Empires: A Note on a Propagandistic *Topos*," *American Journal of Philology* 102 (1981): 330–337 (with an addendum by H. Tadmor).

————, "A Note on the Tradition of Antiochus IV's Death," *Israel Exploration Journal* 31 (1981): 53–56.

————, "Hecataeus of Abdera and a Jewish 'Patrios Politeia' of the Persian Period (Diodorus Siculus XL,3)," *Zeitschrift für alttestamentliche Wissenschaft* 95 (1983): 96–110.

————, *The Land of Israel as a Political Concept in Hasmonean Literature* (Tübingen, 1987).

————, "The Polemical Character of Manetho's *Aegyptiaca*," in *Purposes of History*, ed. H. Verdin et al. (Louvain, 1990), pp. 92–110.

————, "Pseudo-Philo's *Biblical Antiquities*, the 'Fourth Philosophy' and the Political Messianism of the First Century C.E.," in *The Messiah*, ed. J. H. Charlesworth (Minneapolis, 1992), pp. 261–275.

Meshorer, Y., *Ancient Jewish Coinage*, 2 vols. (New York, 1982).

————, *City Coins of Eretz Israel and the Decapolis in the Roman Period* (Jerusalem, 1985).

Meyers, E. M., "The Cultural Setting of Galilee: The Case of Regionalism and Early Judaism," *Aufstieg und Niedergang der römischen Welt* 2.19.1 (1979), pp. 686–702.

Michel, O., "Studien zu Josephus: Simon bar Giora," *New Testament Studies* 14 (1968): 402–408.

Mildenberg, L., *The Coinage of the Bar Kokhba War* (Aarau and Salzburg, 1984).

Milik, J. T., *The Book of Enoch: Aramaic Fragments of Qumran Cave 4* (Oxford, 1976).

Millar, F., *The Emperor in the Roman World (31 B.C.–A.D. 337)* (London, 1977).

————, "The Background to the Maccabean Revolution: Reflections on Martin Hengel's 'Judaism and Hellenism,' " *Journal of Jewish Studies* 29.1 (1978): 1–21.

————, "The Phoenician Cities: A Case Study in Hellenization," *Proceedings of the Cambridge Philological Association* 209 (1983): 55–71.

————, "Empire, Community and Culture in the Roman Near East: Greeks, Syrians, Jews and Arabs," *Journal of Jewish Studies* 38 (1987): 143–164.

Momigliano, A. D., *Prime Linee di storia della tradizione maccabaica* (repr. with a bibliographical appendix, Amsterdam, 1968).

————, *Alien Wisdom: The Limits of Hellenization* (Cambridge, 1975).

————, "The Second Book of Maccabees," *Classical Philology* 70 (1975): 81–88.

————, *On Pagans, Jews, and Christians* (Middletown, Conn., 1987).

Munck, J., *The Acts of the Apostles** (Garden City, N.Y., 1967).

Murray, O., "Hecataeus of Abdera and Pharaonic Kingship," *Journal of Egyptian Archaeology* 56 (1970): 141–171.

Netzer, E., "Miqvaot (Ritual Baths) of the Second Temple Period at Jericho," *Qadmoniot* 11 (1978): 54–59 (Hebrew).

Neusner, J., *A Life of Rabban Yohanan ben Zakkai: Ca. 1-80 C.E.* (Leiden, 1970).

————, *The Rabbinic Traditions about the Pharisees Before 70*, 3 vols. (Leiden, 1971).

Newsom, C., *Songs of the Sabbath Sacrifice: A Critical Edition* (Atlanta, 1985).

Nickelsburg, G. W. E., *Resurrection, Immortality, and Eternal Life in Intertestamental Judaism* (Cambridge, Mass., 1972).

————, *Jewish Literature Between the Bible and the Mishnah* (Philadelphia, 1981).

———— and M. E. Stone, *Faith and Piety in Early Judaism* (Philadelphia, 1983).

The Old Testament Pseudepigrapha, ed. J. H. Charlesworth, 2 vols. (New York, 1983–1985).

Oppenheimer, A., *The ʿAm Ha-aretz: A Study in the Social History of the Jewish People in the Hellenistic-Roman Period* (Leiden, 1977).

Orr, F. W. and J. A. Walther, *I Corinthians** (Garden City, N.Y., 1976).

Peters, F. E., *The Harvest of Hellenism* (London, 1972).

Porten, B., *Archives from Elephantine* (Berkeley and Los Angeles, 1968).

Preaux, C., *Le Monde hellénistique: La Grèce et l'Orient de la mort d'Alexandre à la conquête romaine de la Grèce (323–146 av. J.-C.)*, 2 vols. (Paris, 1978).

Das ptolemaische Ägypten, ed. H. Maehler and V. M. Strocka (Berlin, 1976).

Purposes of History: Studies in Greek Historiography from the 4th to the 2nd Centuries B.C., ed. H. Verdin et al., *Studia Hellenistica* 30 (Louvain, 1990).

Purvis, J. D., *The Samaritan Pentateuch and the Origin of the Samaritan Sect* (Cambridge, Mass., 1968).

Raaflaub, K. A., "Grundzüge, Ziele und Ideen der Opposition gegen die Kaiser im 1 Jh.n. Chr.," in *Entretiens sur l'antiquité classique* 33 (Geneva, 1986), pp. 1–63.

Rajak, T., "Moses in Ethiopia: Legend and Literature," *Journal of Jewish Studies* 29 (1978): 111–122.

————, *Josephus: The Historian and His Society* (London, 1983).

Rappaport, U., "The Hasmonean State," in *The History of Eretz Israel: The Hellenistic Period and the Hasmonean State (331–37 B.C.)*, ed. M. Stern (Jerusalem, 1981), vol. 3, pp. 193–273 (Hebrew).

————, "Jewish-Pagan Relations and the Revolt against Rome in 66–70 C.E.," *The Jerusalem Cathedra* 1 (1981): 81–95.

————, "John of Gischala: From Galilee to Jerusalem," *Journal of Jewish Studies* 33 (1982): 479–493.

Reese, G., "Die Geschichte Israels in der Auffassung des frühen Judentums . . . ," diss., Heidelberg, 1967.

The Revolt of the Jews in the Times of Trajan, 115–117 A.D., ed. D. Rokeah (Jerusalem, 1978) (Hebrew).

Rhoads, D. M., *Israel in Revolution, 6–74 C.E.: A Political History Based on the Writings of Josephus* (Philadelphia, 1976).

Rice, E. E., *The Grand Procession of Ptolemy Philadelphus* (Oxford, 1983).

Robinson, A. T., *Redating the New Testament* (Philadelphia, 1976).

Rofé, A., "Promise and Desertion: Eretz Israel and the Beginning of the Second Commonwealth," *Cathedra* 41 (1986): 3–10 (Hebrew).

Roth, C., "The Constitution of the Jewish Republic of 66–70," *Journal of Semitic Studies* 9 (1964): 304–319.

Rusten, J. S., *Dionysius Scytobrachion* (Cologne, 1980).

Safrai, S., "Jewish Self-Government," *Compendia* 1.1 (Assen, 1974): 377–419.

Saldarini, A. J., *Pharisees, Scribes, and Sadduccees in Palestinian Society* (Wilmington, Del., 1988).

The Samaritans, ed. A. D. Crown (Tübingen, 1989).

Sanders, E. P., *Paul and Palestinian Judaism: A Comparison of Patterns of Religion* (Philadelphia, 1977).

———, *Jesus and Judaism* (London, 1985).

Schäfer, P., "Die Flucht Johanan b. Zakkais aus Jerusalem und die Gründung des 'Lehrhauses' in Jabne," *Aufstieg und Niedergang der römischen Welt* 2.19.2 (1979): 44–101.

———, *Der Bar Kokhba-Aufstand: Studien zum zweiten jüdischen Krieg gegen Rom* (Tübingen, 1981).

Schalit, A., *König Herodes: Der Mann und sein Werk* (Berlin, 1969).

———, "Roman Policy in the Orient from Nero to Trajan," in *The Revolt of the Jews*, ed. D. Rokeah (Jerusalem, 1978), pp. 1–32 (Hebrew).

Schaller, B., "Philon von Alexandreia und das 'Heilige Land,' " in *Das Land Israel*, ed. G. Strecker (Göttingen, 1983), pp. 172–187.

Schalles, H.-J., *Untersuchungen zur Kulturpolitik der Pergamenischen Herrscher im dritten Jahrhundert vor Christus* (Tübingen, 1985).

Schiffman, L. H., *The Eschatological Community of the Dead Sea Scrolls* (Atlanta, 1989).

Schnabel, P., *Berossos und die babylonisch-hellenistische Literatur* (Leipzig, 1923).

Schürer, E., *The History of the Jewish People in the Age of Jesus Christ*, rev. G. Vermes et al., 3 vols. (Edinburgh, 1973–1987).

Schwartz, D. R., "Priesthood, Temple, Sacrifice: Opposition and Spiritualization in the Late Second Temple Period," diss., Jerusalem, 1979.

———, "*Kata touton ton kairon*: Josephus' Source on Agrippa II," *Jewish Quarterly Review* 72 (1982): 241–268.

———, "Ishmael ben Phiabi and the Chronology of Provincia Judea," *Tarbiz* 52 (1983): 177–200 (Hebrew).

———, "Josephus and Nicolaus on the Pharisees," *Journal for the Study of Judaism in the Persian, Hellenistic and Roman Period* 14 (1983): 157–171.

———, "Josephus on the Jewish Constitutions and Community," *Scripta classica israelica* 7 (1983–1984): 30–52.

———, "Scribes and Pharisees, Hypocrites: Who Are 'the Scribes' in the New Testament?" *Zion* 51 (1985): 121–132 (Hebrew).

———, *Agrippa I: The Last King of Judaea* (Tübingen, 1990).

————, *Studies in the Jewish Background of Christianity* (Tübingen, 1992).

————, "Temple and Desert: On Religion and State in Second Temple Period Judaea," in his *Studies* (Tübingen, 1992), pp. 29–43.

Schweid, E., *The Land of Israel* (Rutherford, N.J., 1985).

Schwier, H., *Tempel und Tempelzerstörung: Untersuchungen zu den theologischen und ideologischen Factoren im ersten jüdisch-römischen Krieg (66–74 n. Chr.)* (Göttingen, 1987).

Scully, V. J., *The Earth, the Temple, and the Gods: Greek Sacred Architecture* (New Haven, 1962).

Seibert, J., *Historische Beiträge zu den dynastischen Verbindungen in hellenistischer Zeit* (Wiesbaden, 1967).

Shatzman, I., *The Armies of the Hasmonaeans and Herod* (Tübingen, 1991).

Shaw, B. D., "Bandit Highlands and Lowland Peace: The Mountains of Isauria-Cilicia," *Journal of the Economic and Social History of the Orient* 33 (1990): 199–233, 237–270.

Sherk, R. K., *The Roman Empire: Augustus to Hadrian* (Cambridge and Sydney, 1988).

Sievers, J., *The Hasmoneans and Their Supporters* (Atlanta, 1990).

Sinclair, T. A., *A History of Greek Political Thought* (London, 1951).

Skehan, P. W. and A. A. Di Lella, *The Wisdom of Ben Sira** (New York, 1987).

Smallwood, E. M., "High Priests and Politics in Roman Palestine," *Journal of Theological Studies* n.s. 13 (1962): 14–34.

————, *The Jews under Roman Rule* (Leiden, 1976).

Smith, M., *Palestinian Parties and Politics that Shaped the Old Testament* (New York and London, 1971).

————, "Zealots and Sicarii: Their Origin and Relations," *Harvard Theological Review* 64 (1971): 1–19.

Smith, R. R. R., *Hellenistic Royal Portraits* (Oxford, 1988).

Stern, M., *The Documents Relating to the Hasmonean War* (Jerusalem, 1973) (Hebrew).

————, "Aspects of Jewish Society: The Priesthood and Other Classes," in *Compendia rerum iudaicarum* (Assen, 1976), 2.561–630.

————, *Greek and Latin Authors on Jews and Judaism*, 3 vols. (Jerusalem, 1976–1984).

————, "Sicarii and Zealots," in *The World History of the Jewish People*, ed. M. Avi-Yona and Z. Baras (London, 1977), 1.8.263–301.

———— (ed.), *The History of Eretz Israel*, vol. 3: *The Hellenistic Period and the Hasmonean State (332–37 B.C.E.)* (Jerusalem, 1981) (Hebrew), and vol. 4: *The Roman Byzantine Period* (Jerusalem, 1984) (Hebrew).

————, "Social and Political Realignments in Herodian Judaea," *The Jerusalem Cathedra* 2 (1982): 40–62.

————, *Studies in Jewish History: The Second Temple Period*, ed. M. Amit et al. (Jerusalem, 1991) (Hebrew).

————, "The Suicide of Eleazar ben Jair and His Men at Masada, and the 'Fourth Philosophy,' " in his *Studies in Jewish History* (Jerusalem, 1991), pp. 313–343.

Sternberg, H., *Mythische Motive und Mythenbildung in den Ägyptischen Tempeln und Papyri der griechisch-römischen Zeit* (Wiesbaden, 1985).

Stone, M. E., *Scriptures, Sects and Visions: A Profile of Judaism from Ezra to the Jewish Revolt* (Philadelphia, 1980).

————, "Reactions to Destructions of the Second Temple," *Journal for the Study of Judaism in the Persian, Hellenistic and Roman Period* 12 (1981): 195–204.

Sullivan, R. D., *Near Eastern Royalty and Rome, 100–30 B.C.* (Toronto and London, 1990).

Tarn, W. W. and G. T. Griffith, *Hellenistic Civilisation*, 3d. ed. (London, 1952).

Tcherikover, V., *Hellenistic Civilization and the Jews* (Philadelphia, 1959).

Theissen, G., *Lokalkolorit und Zeitgeschichte in den Evangelien* (Göttingen, 1989).

Thompson, D. J., *Memphis under the Ptolemies* (Princeton, 1988).

Urbach, E. E., *The Halakhah* (Jerusalem, 1986).

VanderKam, J. C., *Enoch and the Growth of an Apocalyptic Tradition* (Washington, D.C., 1984).

Van't Dack, E. et al., *The Judean-Syrian-Egyptian Conflict, 103–101 B.C.* (Brussels, 1989).

Vermes, G., *Jesus the Jew* (London, 1973).

————, *Jesus and the World of Judaism* (Philadelphia, 1984).

Veyne, P., *Bread and Circuses: Historical Sociology and Political Pluralism* (London, 1990).

Villalba i Varneda, P., *The Historical Method of Flavius Josephus* (Leiden, 1986).

Volz, P., *Die Eschatologie der jüdischen Gemeinde* (Tübingen, 1934).

Wacholder, B. Z., *Eupolemus: A Study of Judeo-Greek Literature* (Cincinnati, 1974).

Waddell, W. G., *Manetho* (London and Cambridge, Mass., 1940).

Walbank, F. W., *The Hellenistic World* (Glasgow, 1981).

Weinfeld, M., "Zion and Jerusalem as a Religious and Political Capital: Ideology and Utopia," in *The Poet and the Historian: Essays in Literary and Historical-Biblical Criticism*, ed. R. E. Friedman (Chico, Calif., 1983), pp. 75–115.

————, "Inheritance of the Land—Privilege Versus Obligation: The Concept of the Promise of the Land in the Sources of the First and Second Temple Periods," *Zion* 49 (1984): 115–137 (Hebrew).

————, "The Day of the Lord: Aspirations for the Kingdom of God in the Bible and Jewish Liturgy," *Scripta Hierosolymitana* 31 (1986): 341–372.

Weiss, P., "Lebendiger Mythos," *Würzburger Jahrbücher für die Altertumswissenschaft* n.s. 10 (1984): 179–208.

Welles, C. B., *Royal Correspondence in the Hellenistic Period* (New Haven, 1934).

Will, E. and C. Orrieux, *Ioudaismos-hellenismos: Essai sur le judaisme judéen à l'époque hellenistique* (Nancy, 1986).

Will, W. and J. Heinrichs, *Zu Alexander d.Gr.*, 2 vols. (Amsterdam, 1987–1988).

Yadin, Y., *The Scroll of the War of the Sons of Light Against the Sons of Darkness* (Oxford, 1962).

————, *Bar-Kokhba: The Rediscovery of the Legendary Hero of the Last Jewish Revolt Against Imperial Rome* (London, 1971).

————, *Temple Scroll,* 3 vols. (Jerusalem, 1983).

———— and N. Avigad, *A Genesis Apocryphon* (Jerusalem, 1956) (Hebrew).

Zanker, P., *The Power of Images in the Age of Augustus* (Ann Arbor, Mich., 1988).

Zeitlin, S., *The First Book of Maccabees* (New York, 1950).

————, *The Rise and Fall of the Judaean State,* 3 vols. (Philadelphia, 1962–1978).

Additional Bibliography

Barclay, J. M. G., *Jews in the Mediterranean Diaspora: From Alexander to Trajan (323 B.C.E.-117 C.E.)* (Edinburgh, 1996).

Bar Kochva, B., *Pseudo-Hecataeus "On the Jews": Legitimizing the Jewish Diaspora* (Berkeley, 1996).

Collins, J. J., *The Scepter and the Star: The Messiahs of the Dead Sea Scrolls and Other Ancient Literature* (New York-Auckland, 1995).

Crossan, J. D., *The Historical Jesus: The Life of a Mediterranean Jewish Peasant* (San Francisco, 1991).

Eshel, E., Eshel, H., and Yardeni, A., "A Qumran Composition Containing Part of Ps. 154 and a Prayer for the Welfare of King Jonathan and his Kingdom," *IEJ* 42 (1992): 199-229.

Feldman, L. H., *Jew and Gentile in the Ancient World: Attitudes and Interaction from Alexander to Justinian* (Princeton, 1993).

Goodblatt, D., *The Monarchic Principle: Studies in Jewish Self-Government in Antiquity* (Tübingen, 1994).

Johnson L. T., *The Real Jesus: The Misguided Quest for the Historical Jesus and the Truth of the Traditional Gospels* (San Francisco, 1996).

Lichtenberger, H., "Das Tora-Verstandnis im Judentum zur Zeit des Paulus. Eine Skizze," in *Paul and the Mosaic Law,* ed. J. D. G. Dunn (Tübingen, 1996).

Meier, J. P., *A Marginal Jew: Rethinking the Historical Jesus,* 2 vols. (New York, 1992, 1994).

Mendels, D., *Jewish Identity in the Hellenistic Period* (Tel-Aviv, 1995) (Hebrew).

Millar, F., *The Roman Near East 31 B.C.-A.D. 337* (Cambridge, Mass., 1993).

Shatzman, I., "The Hasmoneans in Greco-Roman Historiography," *Zion* 57.1 (1992): 5-64 (Hebrew).

Wilken, R. L., *The Land Called Holy: Palestine in Christian History and Thought* (New Haven and London, 1992).

Index of Texts

Index of Scholars

Subject Index